The Birds of North Central Texas

Number Nine: The W. L. Moody, Jr., Natural History Series

A. Pulich
1986

The Birds
of North Central Texas

By Warren M. Pulich

FOREWORD BY KEITH A. ARNOLD

ILLUSTRATIONS BY ANNE MARIE PULICH

TEXAS A&M UNIVERSITY PRESS : COLLEGE STATION

The paper used in this book meets the minimum requirements
of the American National Standard for Permanence
of Paper for Printed Library Materials, Z39.48-1984.
Binding materials have been chosen for durability.
(∞)™

Library of Congress Cataloging-in-Publication Data

Pulich, Warren M.
    The birds of north central Texas.

    (The W.L. Moody, Jr., natural history series ;
no. 9)
    Bibliography: p.
    Includes index.
    1. Birds—Texas. I. Pulich, Anne Marie.
II. Title. III. Series.
QL684.T4P83 1988   598.29764   87-9143
ISBN 0-89096-319-3 (alk. paper)
ISBN 0-89096-322-3 (pbk. : alk. paper)

To Anne

Contents

Illustrations

Foreword KEITH A. ARNOLD

With the exception of California, Texas has more species of birds recorded within its borders than any other of the 50 states. This wealth of species reflects, obviously, the large size of the state but also the diverse areas of vegetation and topography, the extensive coastline, and the proximity to the Neotropics. More than 560 species of birds have been recorded in the Lone Star State, albeit some only once. The attractions of birding in Texas are so great that thousands of birders travel to the state each year to look for Neotropical species in the lower Rio Grande valley or to watch spring migrants on the upper Texas Coast. Like many other states, Texas has its own state book, H. C. Oberholser's *The Bird Life of Texas* (1974).

Given the size and diversity of Texas and the wealth and variety of its avifauna, it comes as no surprise that particular regions in the state have received special attention from bird-watchers, producing the need for regional bird guides. Examples are the Big Bend region with its mountain species and the lower Rio Grande valley with its Neotropical species. Other regions receive attention because of their proximity to large population centers. Such is the case with this volume. Although the 32-county area covered here harbors birdlife that is interesting in its own right (being, for example, the northern limit of Texas' only endemic breeding bird, the Golden-cheeked Warbler, and being host to many winter eruptive species), it is the regular use of the area for birding by the populace of the "Metroplex"—the Dallas–Fort Worth complex—that has created a need for this volume.

I can think of no individual better qualified than Warren M. Pulich to write this book. An expert on the Golden-cheeked Warbler, Warren has also been the leading authority on birds in the Metroplex area for more than 25 years. Warren wrote *Birds of Tarrant County* in 1961 and provided an updated revision in 1979. Soon after publication of the second edition he began studying the north central region in earnest. He sought out specimens from the area in museums and spent many hours and days in the field to understand better the current avifauna and how it has changed since the reports of 50 to 75 years past. This work will permit a better understanding of changes in birdlife as they occur in future years and may even help us predict those changes. Such knowledge becomes extremely valuable as we plan for land use around population centers and try to conserve some of the wildlife for future enjoyment.

In this book, as in the two editions of *Birds of Tarrant County*, Warren has called upon the considerable talents of his wife Anne to add portraits of representative birds. Although I am admittedly prejudiced in Anne's favor—a painting by her hangs in my home—I am among many Texas birders who count this remarkable woman one of the finest wildlife artists residing in the state.

This book will serve both the birding and the scientific communities. Warren, always a stickler for accuracy, has carefully checked not only the many specimens but also thousands of sight records before including them in his accounts of the species. I do not believe that any other regional volume has the details of occurrence, migration, peak numbers, breeding status, and change in status that are found in this book. We are fortunate indeed not only for Warren's knowledge and ability but also his persistence in completing this invaluable guide.

Acknowledgments

Anyone who sets out to prepare a book of this kind knows that the final production is not the work of just one person but is the result of many persons assisting in many ways. That is certainly true of this publication. The writing of *The Birds of North Central Texas,* covering 32 Texas counties totaling 25,000 square miles, has been no small task. At times it was frustrating, for I tied myself to a seven-year schedule. Without the help of many cooperators I would have never met the schedule within that time limit.

Although I have visited and worked at least briefly in all the counties covered by this work to get a feel for the study area, I found it impossible to cover them alone in the schedule I set for myself. Thus I sought out interested persons living in the various counties who were fairly knowledgeable about the birds in their areas. With only a few exceptions I met with each person at least once or twice and spent some time with each in the field. This procedure gave me insight into his or her ability as well as an overview of the county. Many of these persons became faithful reporters, sending me monthly accounts or providing me with unusual avian sightings throughout the years of my study. To provide coverage for counties in which I could find no one familiar with birds, some observers from other counties volunteered to visit the areas to obtain data for me.

In a study of this scope it is impossible to thank everyone individually for his or her assistance. If your name does not appear herein, please forgive me. To all, both recognized and unrecognized here, I am grateful for your help.

Among the ornithologists, museum curators, and scientists who provided me with professional assistance were John Aldrich, Keith A. Arnold, Richard Banks, Charles C. Brown, Roger Clapp, Walter Dalquest, John Darling, Karl Haller, John Hubbard, David Lintz, Robert Martin, Terry Maxwell, James Parker, Jr., Amadeo Rea, Chandler Robbins, Steve Runnels, Ray Telfair II, Jack D. Tyler, William Voss, Claudia Wilds, and Jinny and Arthur Wiseman. To my good friend Allan R. Phillips I am especially indebted for the racial identification of many of my specimens as well as for many enlightening discussions and his thorough review of some of the more complex accounts.

I also would like to acknowledge the many courtesies extended to me by the personnel of the U.S. Fish and Wildlife Service and of the Texas Parks and Wildlife Department, especially Ronnie Brooks, William Brownlee, Glenn Collier, and Jim Williams. All took time from their busy schedules to assist me whenever the need presented itself.

Texas landowners play an important role in providing habitat for the birds of north central Texas. In many areas their holdings are the only remaining lands having vegetation typical of the flora that originally occupied much of north central Texas. This is particularly true of the western side of the study area, where there are large holdings of undeveloped land, including the Green Ranch, the Lambshead Ranch, the Hapgood Ranch, and the Waggoner Ranch, owned or managed by Bob Green, Walt Mathews, Randy Hapgood, and Charles Prather, respectively. These persons extended their Texas hospitality to me in many ways, allowing me free access to their ranches to explore and study the fauna and flora and thereby providing me with a clearer understanding of the avian populations of north central Texas.

The following individuals have been especially helpful in providing me with data or reports of their avian sightings: David Arbour, Betty and Joe Bailey, James Beach, Francis Becker, Margaret Brody, Marion Cleveland, Robert Coggeshall, Kenneth Cox, Betty and Charles Crabtree, Sam Crowe, Rebecca and Thomas Dellinger, Terry and Ric Derdeyn, Olin Dillon, Myrna Engle, Angeline and Harold Evans, Joe Gearheart, David Gill, Timothy Gollob, Carol and George Harmon, Carl Haynie, Ron Hill, Helen Hoffman, Wanda Hunter, Dorthea Jackson, Murray James, Irma Kibler, Richard Kinney, Keith Lockhart, Ernie Martin, Arnold Moorhouse, Kenneth Nanney, Julius Nussbaum, Margaret Parker, Mike Perkins, Jerry Schrimpsher, J. W. Seiffert, Ann and Jay Slaugenhop, Larry Sall, June Stacy, Kenneth Steigman, John Tennery, Allen Valentine, Bettye Vernon, Ann Ward, Frances Williams, Florelle and Elgin Wilson, Mike Wolfson, and Sheri and Tom Wood.

My special thanks go to students at the University of Dallas who assisted me in many ways: Laura Felis, Laura Moore, John Pavlov, and Elizabeth Sommerfeldt. Harry Nissen assisted in tedious tasks of library work — condensing of data and development of rough charts for evaluating and organizing data for the project. He also read all of the first and second drafts of species accounts and offered constructive criticism. Kenneth Nanney developed all the distribution maps from the species accounts and prepared the final drafts.

The Arthur Vining Davis Foundation awarded me a small grant to initiate fieldwork in 1980. The Texas Educational Foundation also provided financial support for fieldwork for about two years. The Dallas County Audubon Society and the Fort Worth Audubon Society helped underwrite the cost of producing the distribution maps from the first drafts to camera-ready maps. The University of Dallas granted me a half-year leave of absence to organize the material and write the first draft of the book. The University of Dallas John B. O'Hara Research Program provided funding assistance throughout the summers. I am indebted to its director, Jack Towne, for his support and encouragement. Finally, a special group of friends made possible the reproduction of the frontispiece. To all of these individuals and organizations I am deeply appreciative.

Last, to my wife, Anne, go my heartfelt thanks for her artwork contained herein and her tedious and almost endless task of typing drafts of the species accounts as well as the final copy. The completion of this book would not have been possible without her continuous encouragement and assistance in nearly all phases of the manuscript work.

Introduction

Upon completion of the revised edition of *Birds of Tarrant County* in 1979, I realized that while conducting research for that project I had amassed much unpublished avian material on many nearby counties. Thus I began formulating plans for a systematic study for *The Birds of North Central Texas*. In addition to the data accumulated for Tarrant County, I had conducted many studies (for various purposes) in other parts of north central Texas that have also provided avifaunal background for this book.

The purpose of this book is to assess and evaluate the avifauna of north central Texas. Toward that end a specific study area was established in the summer of 1980. With much care and thought I arbitrarily chose 30 counties, which primarily covered the Blackland Prairies and the Cross Timbers and Prairies. After the fieldwork was under way, two more counties were added on the east side of the study area to include all of Lake Tawakoni, since part of the lake was already in the area. To delineate the study area properly, the boundaries included two small segments of two other ecological vegetative zones, the Post Oak Savannah on the east and the Rolling Plains on the west.

With the publication of H. C. Oberholser's long-awaited two-volume *The Bird Life of Texas* (1974), many birders assumed that answers to most questions on the status and distribution of the birds of Texas would be readily available. That assumption was not borne out. The status and distribution of some birds had not been brought up to date or were completely lacking. In the two large volumes serious avian students discovered how inadequately Texas had been covered, owing to its vast size. The 32 counties that were to become my study area (map 1), covering 25,000 square miles of north central Texas, were treated no differently. Oberholser's work also lacked a clear picture of the avian populations of the area, and some counties lacked records of occurrence of many species, even common species.

North central Texas is extremely important to the birds of Texas, al-

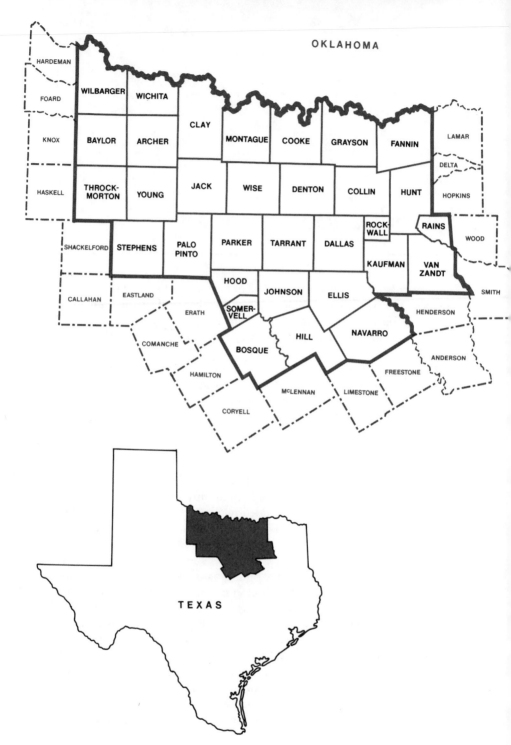

Map 1. Counties in the north central Texas study area

though many persons are not aware of its significance. The area represents a large segment of a major ecosystem and is a vital region for birds in migration, where "eastern" species often mingle with "western" species. Most visitors to the state seeking birds visit the coastal areas, the Rio Grande valley, and the Big Bend. What many fail to realize is that nearly 62 percent of the 555 species recognized in Texas on the Texas Ornithological Society's *Checklist* (TOS, 1984) have been recorded in north central Texas. Finally, the region regularly has winter residents such as longspurs, finches, and other northern species that seldom reach other parts of the state. At appropriate times of the year north central Texas also has its share of migrants, particularly shorebirds, thrushes, vireos, and warblers, as well as an array of sparrows and buntings.

Ecologically, the area of north central Texas covered by this book lies within four vegetational areas (Gould, 1969). From the east side to the west side of the study area, these consist of the Post Oak Savannah, the Blackland Prairies, the Cross Timbers and Prairies, and the Rolling Plains (see map 2). It should be noted that none of the four areas lies completely within the study area. Moreover, to the average observer the areas look very much alike.

The Post Oak Savannah covers a very small portion of the study area. It represents a secondary forest extending from the Piney Woods of east Texas, ending at the Blackland Prairies in Rains and Woods counties, and stretching along the Red River to about Grayson County. Much of the area is still in native or improved pastures of small farms with light-colored acid sandy loam or sands, while the bottomlands are sandy loams and clays. Pines can be found sparingly in parts of the area. Occasionally, birds from the East can be found here. The average annual rainfall is highest in this area, ranging from 35 to almost 45 inches, falling mainly in May or early June.

The Blackland Prairies, gently rolling to nearly level, is a fertile area that was originally covered with little bluestem. Nearly all of the prairie has been cultivated, and very few patches of virgin grasses remain. In the early days agricultural lands were poorly maintained; today, however, proper farming methods are practiced, and most of the lands have recovered from abuse and poor management. In winter this area seems bleak, yet at times it is favored by Horned Larks, pipits, and longspurs. Dallas and many of the surrounding cities lie in this area, and much of the Blackland Prairie farmland is being converted to an urban area. Although there are still open lands on the north, developments are gradually invading the area between Dallas and Sherman, covering the prairies with man-made structures. Someday there will be dwellings on most of the remaining lands between these two cities. Along creeks, streams, and rivers, however, much vegetation may remain. As the prairies were so named, the

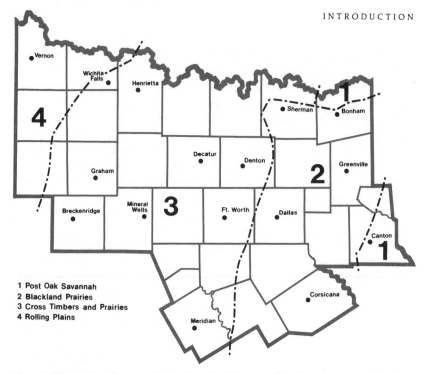

Map 2. Vegetational areas of north central Texas and selected cities and towns

Blacklands are relatively uniform dark-colored calcareous soils interspersed with acid-sandy loams. The average annual rainfall varies from 30 to slightly more than 40 inches, the greatest amount falling in May.

The Cross Timbers and Prairies cover most of the study area. They consist of two strips of timber, the East and West Cross Timbers, varying in width from 10 to 20 miles. They are transected by a prairie known locally as the Grand Prairie, which has a different soil topography that permits changes in vegetation from woody-growth cover to grass and back to woody growth. The region is hilly, cut by creeks and streams that aid in rapid surface drainage. The soils of the Grand Prairie are calcareous clays over limestone, while the timbered lands have acid or slightly acid sandy or sandy-loam soils. The woody growth of the timbered areas consists of blackjack and post oaks, shinnery oak, and live oak, while the tree cover of the drainage consists of cedar, elm, ash, hackberry, pecan, and other oaks, together with cottonwood, willow, and sycamore, especially along permanent water drainages.

Unique on the western edge of the West Cross Timbers is a small, mountainous region of Palo Pinto County called the Palo Pintos. Here the countryside reminds one of the Edwards Plateau extending along the Brazos River from the plateau proper to about Possum Kingdom Lake. Junipers, known to Texans as "cedars," give the mountains quite a different appearance. In early days the cedars were so dense and thick that they were difficult to penetrate on horseback. This area marks the northernmost nesting range of the endemic Golden-cheeked Warbler. Unfortunately, cedars are being cleared at a rapid rate. Visitors still can find a few golden-cheeks at Possum Kingdom State Park, on the west side of the lake.

The climax understory was once rather uniform with grasses; however, where the Cross Timbers have been overgrazed, dense thickets have taken over. Mesquite and cacti have invaded much of the grasslands that have been overgrazed. It is through the prairies of this zone that the earlier cattle drives went north to the railheads of Kansas. Land use today varies from farming on the better soil to large ranches, as well as towns and cities. Fort Worth is the largest city, Denton, Gainesville, Henrietta, and Decatur being a few of the other important cities in the area. The average rainfall is 25 to 40 inches, the greatest amount of rainfall falling in April, May, and June.

The Rolling Plains, in the western part of the study area, range from rolling plains to rather rough topography. Soils vary from coarse sands to tight clays or red-bed clays and shales. Most of the lands are rangelands, but there is farming in some areas. The principal cities of this area are Wichita Falls, Vernon, and Breckenridge. The rainfall is variable, May and September having the most rain, averaging just under 30 inches a year. The summers are long and hot with a high evaporation rate. The original grasses were little and big bluestem, sideoats grama, and three-awn grass with sand sage and shinnery oak. Mesquite and yucca have heavily invaded some of the overgrazed grasslands. Here, typical western avian species are found sparingly but regularly, for example, Golden-fronted Woodpecker, Cactus Wren, Verdin, and House Finch. The bison once roamed here.

Before the construction of dams on the rivers of north central Texas, permanent sources of water were limited. Natural lakes were almost nonexistent except for scattered small bodies of water. The drainage basins in the north central Texas study area consist in part of the Brazos, Red, and Trinity rivers and their tributaries and a very small portion of the Sabine River, arising in Collin and Hunt counties. In their original state the drainages provided extensive river bottoms that served as vast floodplains during periods of heavy runoff from rainstorms, the main source of surface water.

These riparian bottomlands were extremely attractive sites for many species of birds. Part of the Trinity River basin even furnished habitat for the Ivory-billed Woodpecker before the basin was cleared, causing the extirpation of this species in north central Texas. The Brazos and the Red rivers carried large red-soil silt loads from the eroding plains. There were few marshes, and many migrating birds, particularly water birds, shorebirds, and other birds dependent on water, passed right over north central

Texas on their way to and from the coast. With the construction of man-made impoundments, the new, permanent water bodies became important habitats, providing not only stopovers but wintering areas for many water birds. However, with the resulting flood protection woodland habitats below dams were cleared for farmlands, and acreages in the reservoir sites were flooded, destroying important segments of habitat for terrestrial species. Map 3 delineates the drainages and major water bodies in the north central Texas study area today, along with their county locations.

The weather along the counties of the Red River in the north is often quite different from that of the more southern counties of the study area. Storms from the north frequently stall there and occasionally do not reach the southern parts. Thus rain- and snowstorms in the northern counties often do not extend to the southern limits.

Comparisons of average annual rainfalls given in the *Texas Almanac* (Dallas Morning News, 1982–83) show that from east to west along the Red River, 43.62 inches of rain fell in Fannin County, while 26.33 inches fell on the west side, in Wilbarger County. At the southern end of the project area 37.74 inches of rain fell on the east side, in Navarro County, while only 26.33 inches fell on the west, in Stephens County.

Temperatures in the summer are hot and the winters generally mild; the mean temperatures for July in all the counties are above 94°F (mean temperatures for January are below 37°F). Temperatures over 100°F are occasionally recorded in all the counties. The maximum all-time-high temperature officially recorded for the area was 120°F in Baylor County on 12 August 1936 (nearly all the counties in the project area recorded minimum January temperatures below 0°F, and some recorded at −10°F).

Nearly everyone who has studied Texas' weather agrees that the state is drier and warmer today than it was in the past. No doubt the change in climate, coupled with changes in vegetation resulting from land clearing and land abuse by man, has had some adverse effects on the avian populations of north central Texas.

Some readers will be surprised by the records of occurrence of some of the species in various counties and wonder where they can find these species in a particular county. It is beyond the scope of this book to list all the areas where species can be found. Many ranges are on private lands that are not open to the public. This should not discourage anyone who is seriously looking for birds, however. Many counties have public lands that can be entered with permission. The Texas Parks and Wildlife Department oversees a number of parks and wildlife-management areas that welcome bird-watchers. A few of the better natural parks maintained by the state are Dinosaur Valley, Meridian, Lake Mineral Wells, and Lake Arrowhead, in Somervell, Bosque, Parker, and Clay counties, respectively. In the first two parks both Black-capped Vireos and Golden-cheeked War-

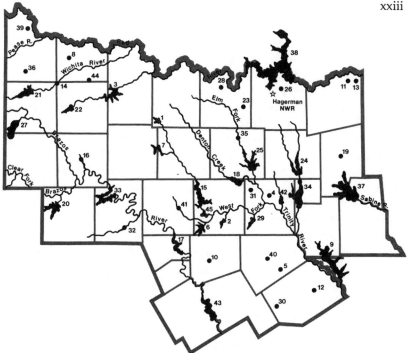

Map 3. Rivers and water bodies of north central Texas

1. Amon Carter Lake, Montague Co.
2. Lake Arlington, Tarrant Co.
3. Lake Arrowhead, Clay Co.
4. Bachman Lake, Dallas Co.
5. Bardwell Reservoir, Ellis Co.
6. Benbrook Lake, Tarrant Co.
7. Lake Bridgeport, Wise-Jack Cos.
8. Buffalo Lake, Wichita Co.
9. Cedar Creek Lake, Henderson-Kaufman Cos.
10. Lake Pat Cleburne, Johnson Co.
11. Coffee Mill Lake, Fannin Co.
12. Corsicana Lake, Navarro Co.
13. Davy Crockett Lake, Fannin Co.
14. Diversion Lake, Archer-Baylor Cos.
15. Eagle Mountain Lake, Tarrant-Wise Cos.
16. Lake Graham, Young Co.
17. Lake Granbury, Hood-Parker Cos.
18. Grapevine Lake, Tarrant-Denton Cos.
19. Greenville City Lake, Hunt Co.
20. Hubbard Creek Lake, Stephens Co.
21. Lake Kemp, Baylor Co.
22. Lake Kickapoo, Archer Co.
23. Lake Kiowa, Cooke Co.
24. Lake Lavon, Collin Co.
25. Lewisville Lake, Denton Co.
26. Loy Lake, Grayson Co.
27. Miller Creek Lake, Throckmorton Co.
28. Moss Lake, Cooke Co.
29. Mountain Creek Lake, Dallas Co.
30. Navarro Mills Reservoir, Navarro-Hill Cos.
31. North Lake, Dallas Co.
32. Lake Palo Pinto, Palo Pinto Co.
33. Possum Kingdom Lake, Palo Pinto-Young–Stephens–Jack Cos.
34. Lake Ray Hubbard, Collin-Dallas-Kaufman-Rockwall Cos.
35. Lake Ray Roberts, Denton Co.
36. Santa Rosa Lake, Wilbarger Co.
37. Lake Tawakoni, Rains–Van Zandt–Hunt Cos.
38. Lake Texoma, Grayson-Cooke Cos.
39. Watt's Lake, Wilbarger Co.
40. Waxahachie Lake, Ellis Co.
41. Lake Weatherford, Parker Co.
42. White Rock Lake, Dallas Co.
43. Lake Whitney, Hill-Bosque-Johnson Cos.
44. Lake Wichita, Wichita Co.
45. Lake Worth, Tarrant Co.

blers have been recorded. Upon request the state parks offices in Austin will provide lists and locations of other parks.

The U.S. Fish and Wildlife Service administers the Hagerman National Wildlife Refuge from Pottsboro, in Grayson County. As of 1984 the refuge had recorded 307 species of birds since its establishment in 1946. This is one of the best places to bird the year round. The U.S. Forest Service administers two national grassland areas, the Caddo National Grassland, in Fannin County, and the Lyndon B. Johnson National Grassland, in Montague and Wise counties. The district offices of both areas are in Decatur, Texas, where interested persons can obtain information on the specific locations of the grasslands.

Some cities and counties maintain parks that favor birds. Although most of the parks are small and have been set aside for special purposes such as environmental education, they may be used by birders. Two such parks are in Plano, in Collin County, and Richardson, in Dallas County. Garland, also in Dallas County, has set aside a woodland basin on Lake Ray Hubbard as a nature area. One of the best urban areas in which to bird is the Fort Worth Nature Center, on upper Lake Worth, in Tarrant County. The center consists of approximately 3,300 acres maintained by the city parks department for natural-history study. A staff of naturalists is on duty at the site to assist visitors. Lucy Park, in Wichita Falls, is attractive to some western species, including Mississippi Kites. Lake Wichita, on the south side of Wichita Falls, is also a favorable birding area, especially attractive for water birds and shorebirds. Dallas likewise has attractive parks, several of which are designated as nature preserves. Although there are few private nature preserves, the Heard Natural Science Museum, in southeastern McKinney, Collin County, is an excellent example of how private funding has advanced the cause of environmental education. In addition to the museum, approximately 300 acres of riparian woodlands have been set aside as a sanctuary where year-round nature walks are provided by guides upon appointment. The area ensures an array of birds common to north central Texas.

In conjunction with water resources the U.S. Army Corps of Engineers has 12 field offices at corps reservoir sites. It is suggested that readers who visit these reservoirs inquire at the field offices for information on natural areas and access to them. The Southwestern Division of the corps, in Dallas, has a complete list of sites and is also able to provide information on other water bodies. Several other important water bodies are Lake Tawakoni, in Hunt, Rains, and Van Zandt counties, under the Sabine River Authority; Hubbard Creek Lake, in Stephens County, under the Central Texas Municipal Water Authority; and Miller Creek Reservoir, in Baylor and Throckmorton counties, under the North Central Texas Municipal Water Authority and the Texas Water Development Board.

Plan of Work

This book is designed to help persons living in north central Texas understand the status of the birds found in their counties. Although the counties of north central Texas have many similarities, the habitat of a particular county as well as the land use in the county may determine the presence or absence of a particular species. Besides data on the occurrence of the birds in the respective counties, information on habitat, breeding, and abundance, as well as other information applicable to a particular avian species, is presented in this book. The book also brings avian records up to date for each of the counties of the study area.

Of the 32 counties in the study area, 15 are included in three metropolitan areas — the Dallas–Fort Worth area, encompassing 11 counties; the Sherman-Denison area, within Grayson County and contiguous with the northern edge of the Dallas–Fort Worth area; and the Wichita Falls–Vernon area, at the far-northwestern corner of the study area, including Wilbarger, Wichita, and Clay counties. As of 1 July 1982, nearly 3.25 million people lived in the study area. It should be apparent to readers that north central Texas is rapidly changing from a rich farm and ranch region to an urban area and will continue to do so in the years to come.

Originally I had planned to use 28 February 1973, the cutoff date of occurrence adopted in *The Bird Life of Texas* (Oberholser, 1974), as the starting point for my study, but as I began to analyze the species, it became apparent that I had to make my own judgments about some of the older records (those between 1882 and 1939) of Douglas Ogilby, George H. Ragsdale, Jerry E. Stillwell, and John K. Strecker, Jr. All of these individuals made important contributions to the early ornithology of north central Texas. Two other men, who may not be very well known to many readers but who contributed to the ornithological records of north central Texas in the early to mid-1900s were William A. Mayer and Robert L. More. Their contributions proved invaluable to my research. Stillwell's *Check List of the Birds of Dallas County, Texas* (1939) contains many references to

Mayer, a Dallas taxidermist and an excellent field collector, from the 1920s through the early 1950s. "Uncle Willie," as he was affectionately known to his friends, had a lifetime interest in birds. After attending schools in Dallas and Austin, he trained with German taxidermists in Europe. When he returned to Dallas, he set up his own taxidermy shop, which became one of the leading facilities of its kind in Texas, and indeed in the United States. Mayer collected and prepared bird specimens for many museums in Texas and other states. His habitat groups can still be seen at the Dallas and Houston museums of natural history. In addition he prepared many trophies for hunters and other private patrons; many of these examples of his work have been lost and cannot be traced. His work was extremely lifelike. Although he prepared mammals as well, his specialty was birds. He did not like for anyone to watch him prepare them, and it was said that even a young relative eager to learn the trade was not permitted to watch him as he formed the bird skins into lifelike poses.

When the Dallas Museum of Natural History was established in the mid-1930s, Mayer was hired to prepare the exhibits. He made numerous trips with museum personnel and artists to various habitats around the state to study the areas in detail and collect material for the habitat groups. Upon completion of the exhibits in the early 1940s, he began collecting local avian specimens, which today are the basis of the Dallas museum's scientific collection. He held the title assistant director of the museum for 20 years. After his death on 22 July 1957, Mayer's widow gave the mounted bird specimens in his taxidermy shop to the museum, where most can still be seen today.

Although Mayer apparently never published any of his findings, he was a keen field collector upon whom Stillwell relied for much of his information about Dallas and adjacent areas. Some of his earlier references to the Ivory-billed Woodpecker and the primitive Trinity River habitat in southeastern Dallas County provided me with important background information on the early days for comparison with the present. Some of his specimens document the early avian records of the Dallas area. In addition to citing the specimens in the Dallas museum, Oberholser (1974) also notes Mayer's early field observations.

When Oberholser was doing fieldwork in Texas, one of the persons who provided him with data was Robert L. More. Oberholser frequently called on him for information on the birds of the northwestern part of the study area and beyond. Since few persons were knowledgeable about the birds in this part of the state in the early 1920s and 1930s, More's records proved "indispensable." However, knowledgeable as he was, More published only three papers, one with J. A. Donald (1894), one with J. K. Strecker (1929), and a third, on the Mississippi Kite that he prepared alone (More, 1927).

Dobie (1941) writes that More was 14 years old when his interest in birds was aroused upon finding two Black Vulture eggs in a brush pile near his home, on the edge of Decatur, in Wise County. Bob More, as his friends called him, never lost his interest in oology. Around the turn of the century he was employed to manage the vast Waggoner estate, and he moved to Vernon, in Wilbarger County. There he continued to add bird eggs to his collection until the day of his death more than 53 years later. His job as estate manager allowed him to travel over the Waggoner ranch holdings not only to check on the cattle and the rangelands but also to look for bird nests and collect eggs. Neither task seemed to interfere with the other. He was a tireless worker in all his undertakings, and he amassed one of the largest egg collections of his time, and the finest ever assembled in Texas.

Unfortunately, More never made a provision to donate his collection to a scientific museum. Today much of the collection is housed over a garage in Vernon and is maintained by his grandson. Although a number of large museums have offered to purchase the collection, the family members will not part with it. It is hoped that the collection will not go the way of many that have been retained by private individuals and lost to science. It contains much valuable historical material that should be saved for ornithologists to study in years to come.

In the course of my work I reevaluated the extensive records in *American Birds* and its predecessor, *Audubon Field Notes*. My research did not stop there; I also examined many other journals containing avian material on north central Texas. The U.S. Fish and Wildlife Service Breeding Bird Surveys conducted nationwide every June were available to me. Ten breeding-bird routes recorded in the study area provided significant records. The surveys, particularly those in the western parts of the study area, were extremely important since little bird-watching is done there.

The Birds of North Central Texas updates the bird populations to the end of 1986, which marks the closing date for most species. However, important dates are given for the early months (through mid-May) of 1987 for some species. No work of this kind is ever complete, and new data will constantly change it, particularly the status and distribution records, which will provide future readers a basis for comparison with the present. Many of the casual and rare species have been treated fully in the accounts to help readers understand their status. For species for which many data are available, readers will find dates of occurrence, usually the extreme arrival and departure dates, for the counties. I have tried to list these data for at least two counties in the northern part of the study area and two counties in the southern part, even though some of the data are very similar. For other species, readers will find even more data. If no data are given for a particular county, dates for an adjacent county that are applicable to that county are substituted (the adjacent county is given in parentheses). Serious birders will find many gaps in the status of local bird populations which they can help fill with new and enlightening information. For example, I have barely touched on Clay, Jack, Montague, and Throckmorton counties owing to the press of time, which prevented me from doing much fieldwork there, and the lack of observers in these counties. Observers visiting these four counties in the future may be able to add data. No doubt avifaunal problems will arise that will require fieldwork for proper assessment of the existing populations. No bird population is ever static, and continued fieldwork in all counties will produce a clearer picture of the avifauna of north central Texas.

This work is not intended to aid in field identification. A number of good field guides are available for that task. Only in a few instances where misidentifications readily occur have I alluded to the pitfalls one may encounter in identifying species. Objective observers are usually careful and diligent in their identifications, giving meticulous details for any unusual species they report, as well as being very familiar with minute details of identification. It is these traits that I hope all persons will develop in reporting birds. Such traits enhance credibility and help keep mistakes to a minimum.

In addition to finding information on the status and distribution of the bird populations in the study area, readers will find at the end of each species account, where applicable, data at the subspecies level. This section is based on specimens. Although many readers may have little or no interest in this subject, they should be aware that all bird guides (e.g., Peterson 1960; National Geographic Society, 1983) are based upon bird collections maintained in large museums. I also point out instances when a particular bird was not collected and thus caused errors to creep into the literature. Occasionally a mistake is made even with the bird in the hand. The misidentified Brewer's Sparrow specimen from Cooke County is one of many errors corrected in this work. If a museum curator can make an error in identification with a bird in the hand, how can we not expect expert birders to do so occasionally in reporting sightings? This comment is not intended to be derogatory but to demonstrate that no one is infallible. If it will help some readers appreciate the value of bird specimens, I will admit that I, too, have made errors in sight identifications.

In the course of writing this book, I studied all the known specimens from north central Texas in the collections held by Texas museums. In addition, I wrote to the large museums in the East for critical specimens (these museums are identified in a list of abbreviations given in the section titled "Accounts of Species"). A number of authorities in the larger museums checked many of the specimens that I sent to them for verification. Specimen data give those interested in taxonomy as well as ornithologists important information about the relationships of birds occurring in north central Texas. They also reveal that the ranges of many subspecies in north central Texas are still poorly known and that much study remains to be done to define the ranges of many species.

I have attempted to evaluate sight records with as much care as I gave to those based on specimens. Some of the records were documented with judiciously selected photographs. I also included records of sightings that were made by at least two persons and records whose validity seemed to be unquestionable. On one occasion I even dismissed a record of my own, a Ruff sighted only by me. In every case the inclusion or exclusion of a species was solely my decision, made with a great deal of care and thought.

Although some authorities have suggested that standards should be developed for categories delineating abundance, frequency, and seasonal occurrence, bird books and checklists vary in their approach to such a system. As I reviewed the literature, it became apparent that much variation exists in the manner in which these designations are used. For *The Birds of North Central Texas* I adopted the categories given below, realizing that another ornithologist might approach the problem differently and yet arrive at a similar status for each species.

Relative abundance is sometimes expressed in numbers, but because of the size of the study area and the diversity of habitats, I decided to use subjective terms. For example, the status of both the Red-winged Blackbird and the Northern Cardinal may be considered abundant, though the latter species will never be as numerous as the former. As another example, 25 Red-tailed Hawks counted on a day's outing might give the species common status, while a sighting of the same number of sandpipers might give that species only fairly common or uncommon status, depending on species, habitat, and season.

In applying terms of relative abundance, an observer may be influenced by the habits, song, and behavior of the species and the ease of access to its habitat. Admittedly, determination is somewhat arbitrary and subject to many variables. The terms for abundance adopted for this work are as follows:

Abundant: Applied to a species that can be found in quantity without any special search in the appropriate habitat during the appropriate season.

Common: Applied to a species noted at least daily with some search in its appropriate habitat. The numbers of birds are as large as those in the preceding category.

Fairly common: Applied to a species that may require some search to be detected regularly in a locality favorable to it.

Uncommon: Applied to a species that occurs infrequently and yet is seen too often to be considered rare.

Rare: Applied to a species that is seldom encountered except by chance in a day's search or by a special search of the locality where it has previously occurred or nested.

Casual: Applied to a species that is out of its normal range but can be expected to occur again.

Accidental: Applied to a species that is far from its normal range and is not expected to appear again (the term *vagrant* is sometimes employed by other authors).

Other terms used in this book are defined below for a better understanding of the status of each species. These terms have to do with seasonal categories. Readers will note that several seasonal categories may be given in the status heading of a species account. Although the species in question may be a resident the year round and may be considered a permanent resident, such a listing does not fully explain that some individuals or populations may not be present throughout the year though the species occurs regularly. For example, both Red-tailed Hawks and Red-winged Blackbirds leave the study area during a particular season, to be replaced at a different season by other members or races of the species.

Permanent residents: Birds that live in an area the year round and never leave. Bobwhites are examples of this category.

Summer residents: Birds that come north in the spring to nest in the area and return to the south in the fall. Some members may be more noticeable in peak numbers during migration, which is sometimes the reason for the second seasonal category in the species account. Usually the more significant status is delineated first.

Of all the birds found in the study area, 35 percent are currently known to nest in the area, while overall (including present and old records) 41 percent have nested there. The difference represents species that are no longer found in the area, species that formerly nested in the area and no longer do so, and species that were on the periphery of their range and now nest to the north owing to changes in habitat or unexplainable one-time nesting records. It may also be possible that misidentifications were made in some of the earlier nesting records. Present records include some species that originally were not found in the north central Texas study area; examples are Olivaceous Cormorants, Cattle Egrets, and western species that are extending their range, such as Inca Doves, Verdins, Cactus Wrens, and Curved-billed Thrashers. Species listed as nesting fall into the category of summer residents or permanent residents.

Winter residents: Birds that spend the winter in the area and are not present during the summer.

Migrants, or transients: Birds that migrate periodically through north central Texas. In many instances these species nest in areas to the north and spend the winter to the south. The terms *migrant* and *transient* are used interchangeably.

Readers should understand that migration dates are not the same for all species. The fall migration of shorebirds, for example, may begin as early as July. At the end of June it is likely that a few may be returning south while others are still passing northward. For many species fall migration is of longer duration than spring migration. Late November dates are not unusual for some species, and some shorebirds may occasionally linger into December if the weather is mild.

Spring migration of the first Purple Martin scouts and most of the waterfowl begins in early February. Some species of waterfowl gradually move back as early as January. The first "push" of the smaller spring migrants generally reaches north central Texas at the end of March. By mid-April migration is well under way, peaking between May 10 and May 15.

Readers are urged to watch and study the weather. Fall migrants usually pass ahead of the arrival of "northers," while spring storms localized in north central Texas may often "put down" species that might pass right on through the region if the weather were mild. It is only during these adverse weather periods that we see the so-called waves of birds, particularly warblers, vireos, thrushes, and other small birds in north central Texas.

Visitors, or visitants: Birds that may visit the area either in summer or in winter. Species that visit the area during the summer either come after the breeding season is over or occur in summer but do not nest in the area. These visitors are also known as *postnuptial wanderers.* Examples of summer visitors are some members of the heron family and Wood Storks. Examples of winter visitors are Evening Grosbeaks, Red Crossbills, and some species of finches that periodically reach north central Texas during severe winters or in years when food is scarce north of the study area.

The Birds of North Central Texas

Accounts of Species

This book gives accounts of a total of 418 species, 385 of which are considered valid for the project area. The remaining 33 species are considered in the section "Species of Uncertain Occurrence." Further information appears at the beginning of that section.

The nomenclature used in the book follows that of the sixth edition of the American Ornithologists' Union *Check-list of North American Birds* (1983). Although not all ornithologists agree with the common names given there and in a few instances with the scientific nomenclature, the *Check-list* provides uniformity and a basis for organization. For species with recent changes in the common names I give the earlier names, which may be more familiar to readers, in addition to the current names. The sixth edition of the AOU *Check-list* does not include names of subspecies, but readers will find these names in the fifth edition (1957) or in the 32nd supplement to the *Check-list* (1973).

In each species account a summary status is given for the 32 counties that constitute the study area. Dates of occurrence and distribution data are included, as well as 109 distribution maps covering more than 200 species. On many of the maps counties outside the study area are marked with stars to indicate new records for the particular counties. Nesting records where pertinent are also given, as well as general information on habitat and bioecology. Specimens and subspecies data, where available, complete the species accounts. Specimens from north central Texas counties are listed, along with their locations in various museums. Abbreviations for museums and frequently used terms are as follows:

ACG	Audubon Center, Greenwich, Conn.
AMNH	American Museum of Natural History, New York
AOU	American Ornithologists' Union
BBS	Breeding Bird Survey
CBC	Christmas Bird Count

CC	Cameron University, Lawton, Okla.
CM	Chicago Museum of Natural History
CMNH	Cincinnati Museum of Natural History
CaM	Carnegie Museum, Pittsburgh, Pa.
DMNH	Dallas Museum of Natural History
ETSU	East Texas State University, Commerce
FWMSH	Fort Worth Museum of Science and History
KH	Karl Haller Collection, Austin College, Sherman, Tex.
KU	University of Kansas Museum of Natural History, Lawrence
MCZ	Museum of Comparative Zoology, Harvard University, Cambridge, Mass.
MVZ	Museum of Vertebrate Zoology, University of California, Berkeley
MWU	Midwestern University, Wichita Falls, Tex.
NTSU	North Texas State University, Denton
NWR	National Wildlife Refuge
OSU	Oklahoma State University, Stillwater
OU	Museum of Zoology, University of Oklahoma, Norman
SE	Southeastern Oklahoma State University, Durant
SFASU	Stephen F. Austin State University, Nacogdoches, Tex.
SM	Strecker Museum, Baylor University, Waco, Tex.
SP	State Park
SUC	Southwestern Union College, Keene, Tex.
TCWC	Texas Cooperative Wildlife Collection, College Station
TNHC	Texas Natural History Collection, Austin
TOS	Texas Ornithological Society
TP-RF	Texas Photo-Record File, TCWC
TTU	Texas Tech University, Lubbock
UCM	University of Connecticut, Storrs
US	United States
USNM	U.S. National Museum, Washington, D.C.
UTA	University of Texas at Arlington
WMP	Warren M. Pulich Collection, University of Dallas, Irving, Tex.

No doubt some of the specimens referred to by Oberholser (1974) that I could not find would be discovered in a search of major museums outside the state. Lack of time and funds precluded a complete search of most of these larger museums. However, an earnest effort was made to find critical specimens whether inside or outside the state.

The reader should be able to find all the localities referred to in this book by checking official county maps issued by the Texas State Highway Department and obtainable from that agency's offices in the respective county seats or in Austin. Rivers and other bodies of water referred to in the book are shown in map 3.

Order Gaviiformes

Family Gaviidae (Loons)

RED-THROATED LOON *Gavia stellata* (Pontoppidan)
Status: Extremely rare winter visitor.
Occurrence: There are only two recent records of the Red-throated Loon for north central Texas. A lone bird was observed on 29 and 30 January 1980 by several competent observers at Burns Run, on the Oklahoma side of Lake Texoma, near Denison Dam, opposite Grayson County. The second observation, of one to three Red-throated Loons, was also made from Lake Texoma on the Texas side by a single observer on 26 and 27 January 1985, and again from 7 February to at least 7 March. It should be watched for on large bodies of water. Its smaller size and slender, slightly upturned bill should set it apart from its larger relative, the Common Loon.
Specimens: There are two mounted specimens in the Dallas Museum of Natural History. One on exhibit but not cataloged is probably the one referred to by Oberholser (1974) and taken on 12 December 1937 in the Trinity River valley, Dallas County. The other (DMNH 3911) was taken at Koon Kreek Klub, Henderson County, by Ted Dealey on 28 November 1948.

COMMON LOON *Gavia immer* (Brünnich)
Status: Uncommon to fairly common migrant; rare to uncommon in winter.
Occurrence: This large loon has been reported in 23 counties in the north central Texas study area, though Oberholser (1974) reported it in only nine counties. The 23 counties are Archer, Baylor, Bosque, Clay, Collin, Cooke, Dallas, Denton, Fannin, Grayson, Hill, Hunt, Johnson, Kaufman, Palo Pinto, Rains, Rockwall, Stephens, Tarrant, Van Zandt, Wichita, Wilbarger, and Wise.

Since this loon is usually found singly or in small numbers as it migrates or winters (when it is less numerous), it goes unnoticed on many bodies of water because of lack of observers regularly checking these areas. The greatest number counted during migration was 58 (although there may have been as many as 70) on 15 and 22 March 1987 at Lake Tawakoni,

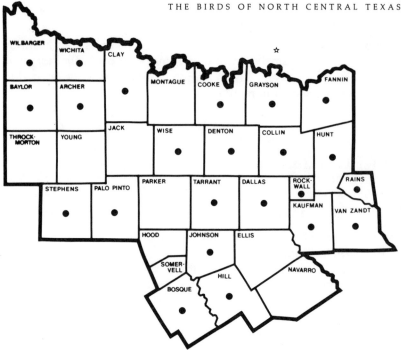

Map 4. Distribution of the Common Loon, *Gavia immer*

Rains–Van Zandt counties. Most loons pass on to the coast, where they spend the winter. However, a few can always be found in winter on suitable lakes and reservoirs if one checks for them in late December and January. For example, at Lake Tawakoni, in Hunt, Rains, and Van Zandt counties, 25 were tallied in a single day on 13 February 1983; 43 were counted on 3 November 1983; and at Burns Run, Lake Texoma, Oklahoma, across from Grayson County, 22 were seen on 12 November 1983. They have occasionally been found on the following CBCs: Caddo National Grasslands, Dallas, Fort Worth, Lake Ray Hubbard, Lake Tawakoni, and Lewisville.

Common Loons are usually found from late October through mid-April. Some extreme fall county dates are: *Collin* – 22 September 1986; *Dallas* – 6 October 1951, 15 October 1962; *Denton* – 22 September 1982, next earliest, 8 through 30 October 1955; *Palo Pinto* –15 October 1978; *Tarrant* – 19 October 1972, 21 October 1980. Some extreme spring county dates are: *Collin* – 24 April 1982; *Dallas* – 22 April 1957, 10 May 1980, 20 May 1963, 23 May 1973, and 31 May 1975; *Denton* – 8 May 1971; *Grayson* –10 April 1967; *Palo Pinto* – 30 April 1980; *Rains–Van Zandt* – normally depart in April, latest 15 April 1984, but lingered until 25 June in 1983 and until 2 July in 1986; *Tarrant* – 7 and 18 April 1985 and 27 April 1967 (specimen).

Specimens: Common Loon specimens have been located for the following counties: Dallas (DMNH), Grayson (MVZ), Hunt (WMP), Kaufman (DMNH), Tarrant (FWMSH), and Wichita (MWU). Those indicated by Oberholser (1974) for Baylor, Cooke, and Wilbarger counties were not located.

Order Podicipediformes

Family Podicipedidae (Grebes)

PIED-BILLED GREBE *Podilymbus podiceps* (Linnaeus)
Status: Abundant to common during migration. Common to fairly common during winter. In summer a few may nest, while scattered numbers of nonbreeding pied-bills have been recorded elsewhere.
Occurrence: The Pied-billed Grebe has been recorded in all of the counties of the study area and the adjacent counties. In many counties — Collin, Cooke, Dallas, Denton, Grayson, Hunt, Palo Pinto, Tarrant, Wichita, and Wilbarger (in the past) — they have been reported every month of the year, although sightings in June are not numerous. They would probably be found during summer in other counties as well if more observers visited appropriate habitats.

Pied-billed Grebes are found on all the annual CBCs of the area. During cold spells many withdraw from the northern part of the area, particularly the Red River drainage. They inhabit an array of water habitats, from large reservoirs to small stock tanks.
Nesting: The Pied-billed Grebe nests locally in north central Texas wherever appropriate aquatic vegetation still exists. Unfortunately, marshes are being lost much too fast; for example, in the Dallas–Fort Worth area low-lying lands are being filled, and many areas where this species formerly nested are now industrial sites. In other areas adverse environmental conditions also have eliminated habitat. Recent county nesting records include: Archer — summer 1981, two adults, three young; Dallas — 19 July 1959, downy chick, first nesting since 1939, 24 July 1966, two half-grown young 5 May 1987, female sitting on nest with young on its back; Denton — Flower Mound area, 5 October 1982, two juveniles; Grayson — Hagerman NWR, June 1979, two pairs, may be the first nesting record of the decade according to refuge manager; Palo Pinto — 24 and 31 July 1976, one young, 25 June 1977, two juveniles; Tarrant — Benbrook Lake area, 1 August 1965, about 20 young, four of eight years (1970–77; Pulich, 1979); Greer Island, 18 April 1982, four young, plus later sightings, and young in 1985.

Specimens: Specimens are available for the following counties: Archer (MWU), Clay (MWU), Dallas (DMNH, UTA, WMP), Denton (DMNH), Ellis (TCWC), Tarrant (FWMSH), and Wichita (MWU).

HORNED GREBE   *Podiceps auritus* (Linnaeus)
Status: Uncommon to rare in migration on larger lakes and impoundments. Rare to casual in winter. May be localized on larger reservoirs in some winters.
Occurrence: Oberholser (1974) lists Horned Grebes only for Dallas, Grayson, Hunt, Tarrant, Palo Pinto, and Wise counties. To these counties can be added Archer, Baylor, Clay, Collin, Denton, Fannin, Hill, Jack, Johnson, Kaufman, Parker, Rains, Van Zandt, and Wichita. Usually they are not abundant, although it is not uncommon to see groups of up to 50. More often they are scattered and are occasionally seen with Eared Grebes. The greatest number reported was 450 on 20 February 1977 at Hagerman NWR on Lake Texoma, Grayson County.

   The Horned Grebe arrives in north central Texas in late October and departs in early April (overall, 14 October to 22 May). Extreme dates for selected counties are: *Dallas*—14 October 1973 to 3 May 1936, next-latest 29 April 1971; *Grayson*—Hagerman NWR, 28 October 1978 to 23 March 1975; *Palo Pinto*—3 November 1979 to 22 May 1977, next-latest 19 April 1976; *Tarrant*—22 October 1977 to 11 April 1978; *Van Zandt* (and Rains County)—16 October 1982 to 28 April 1985; *Wichita*—early May 1975.

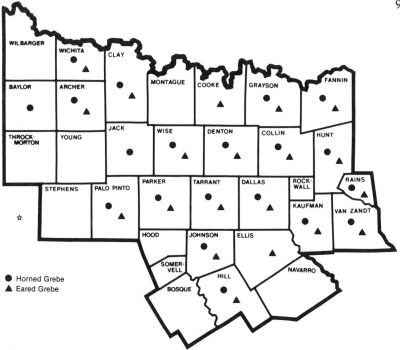

Map 5. Distribution of the Horned Grebe, *Podiceps auritus,* and the Eared Grebe, *P. nigricollis*

All August and September dates have been discounted, since the winter plumage of this species resembles that of the Eared Grebe, which is much more common in the area and tends to arrive earlier. If observers are not careful, they can misidentify the two species.

Specimens: Three specimens are available from Kaufman County: 20 November 1967 (DMNH 5695) and 24 November 1969 (DMNH 6059 and 6060). Two are known from Palo Pinto County: 20 December 1946 (DMNH 3264, mounted) and 25 November 1976 (WMP 2299). Stillwell (1939) indicates that specimens were also taken in Dallas County, but the Dallas Museum of Natural History has no records of any from this county. They may have been taken by Mayer before the museum's inception.

RED-NECKED GREBE *Podiceps grisegena* (Boddaert)

Status: Extremely rare visitor in north central Texas.

Occurrence: Red-necked Grebes can be mistaken for smaller Horned Grebes as well as the larger Western Grebes, and even the Red-throated Loons under certain field conditions, especially since the plumages are rather nondescript at the times the birds are present in north central Texas. Birds of these types are often seen far out over large bodies of water, and it is nearly impossible to identify the species. Unless they are observed under ideal viewing conditions, many grebes may go unidentified. It is a treat to see this grebe near the shore. It is seldom expected and may be considered a vagrant by some authorities.

There are records of this grebe in five counties: *Denton* — 11 October 1952; *Grayson* — Hagerman NWR, 8 November 1973, 19 November 1977, and 8 March 1983; *Palo Pinto* — Possum Kingdom Lake, 25 November 1976; *Tarrant* — Lake Worth Fish Hatchery, 20 October 1961; Benbrook Lake, 5 and 6 December 1978; *Young* — an alleged specimen was taken near Eliasville between 1884 and 1890 by H. Y. Benedict; the whereabouts of this bird are unknown.

Specimens: The only specimen for Texas is the one from Young County.

EARED GREBE   *Podiceps nigricollis* (Brehm)
Status: Common to uncommon during migration. Rare to uncommon in winter; not as numerous in some years as in others.
Occurrence: The Eared Grebe arrives earlier than the Horned Grebe in north central Texas, but the records indicate that it may not be any more widespread. For either species, however, this may be because of lack of observers in many counties. Both would be reported from most of the counties with large bodies of water if proper coverage were possible. This species seems to have a different habitat preference from that of the Horned Grebe, for it is attracted (because of environmental requirements unknown to me) to water-treatment plants in Dallas County and Benbrook Lake, Tarrant County, arriving in flocks of more than 200 birds during migration. It is not surprising to see 100 Eared Grebes even in winter on large impoundments.

Oberholser (1974) gave records for Archer, Cooke, Dallas, Denton, Grayson, Hunt, Tarrant, and Wise counties; this study adds Clay, Collin, Ellis, Fannin, Hill, Johnson, Kaufman, Palo Pinto, Parker, Rains, Van Zandt, and Wichita counties and adjacent Shackelford County.

In north central Texas dates of arrival and departure range from mid-September to mid-May. Some extreme dates for selected counties are: *Dallas* — 1 September 1984 to 31 May 1971, with mean dates of 12 November (1964–71) and 18 April (1965–73, eight of nine years); *Grayson* — 1 October to 18 May; *Palo Pinto* — 16 October 1976 to 22 May 1977; *Rains* — 6 November 1983 to 30 May 1983 (Hunt County); *Tarrant* — 4 September 1969 to 25 May 1966; *Wichita* — 7 November 1982 to 3 May 1975. Most other counties lacked sufficient early-arrival and late-departure dates, but dates given here would be applicable.

Nesting: The only nesting record for north central Texas is one for Wise County before the turn of the century. Donald and More (1894) allegedly found two nests of this species at Herman Station, south of Decatur, near

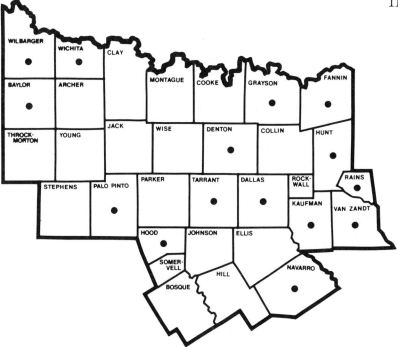

Map 6. Distribution of the Western Grebe, *Aechmophorus occidentalis*

Trinity River, on 5 June 1889 and one nest on 2 July. The garbled date given
by Oberholser (1974) represents dates when the first two nests were checked
and a complete set of eggs was taken. Donald and More were oologists,
and, as far as I can determine, the accounts represent no more than two
pairs of birds nesting. During the summers of 1965 through 1970, Eared
Grebes spent the months of June through August in Dallas County, but
there was no evidence of nesting. Most marshy habitats have disappeared,
and there seems to be little suitable nesting habitat for this species in most
of the counties of north central Texas.

Specimens: Eared Grebe specimens have been located for the following
counties: Archer (MWU), Cooke (TNHC), Dallas (WMP; those indicated
by Stillwell [1939] were not located), Denton (DMNH), Ellis (DMNH),
and Parker (FWMSH).

WESTERN GREBE   *Aechmophorus occidentalis* (Lawrence)
Status: Rare transient. Casual winter visitor.
Occurrence: Western Grebes are not found every year or on every body
of water. Recent records are from large reservoirs and lakes. There are
more records for fall and spring passage, when they may linger for some
time, and very few winter records.

This large grebe of the western United States has been reported in 15 counties in the study area. All recent county records are: *Baylor* — Lake Kemp, 11 January 1976; *Dallas* — 30 September 1972, next-earliest 18 October 1980 through winter months until 7 May 1977, next-latest 19 April 1980; *Denton* — Lewisville Lake, 21, 22, and 27 December 1978, small lake in new reservoir site, Lake Ray Roberts, 5 April 1984; *Fannin* — 12 November 1980; *Grayson* — Hagerman NWR, 9 October to 20 November 1963, 25 and 26 November 1977, 1 and 15 December 1974, 28 and 29 October 1985, 20 December 1986; *Hood* — Lake Granbury, 12 February 1983 (three); *Hunt* — Oberholser (1974), in fall and spring, no recent records; *Kaufman* — Cedar Creek Lake, 22 October 1977, Lake Ray Hubbard, 16 March 1987; *Navarro* — Oberholser (1974), in fall, no recent records; *Palo Pinto* — Possum Kingdom Lake, 10 November 1979; *Rains* — Lake Tawakoni, 1 and 8 April 1984; *Tarrant* — Benbrook Lake, nine reports (including one photograph), 12 October 1972 through 21 March 1967, with an isolated spring date of 9 April 1977 from Lake Worth; *Van Zandt* — Lake Tawakoni, 10 November 1984; *Wichita* — Lake Wichita, 10 October through 22 November 1974; *Wilbarger* — winter of 1975–76 (details lacking; Williams, 1976).

Specimens: The only known specimen for north central Texas is one taken on 10 November 1979 (WMP 2541) from Possum Kingdom Lake, Palo Pinto County.

Order Pelecaniformes

Family Pelecanidae (Pelicans)

AMERICAN WHITE PELICAN   *Pelecanus erythrorhynchos* Gmelin

Status: Fairly common to common migrant, numbers varying from a few to many in nearly all of north central Texas. Occasionally may summer or winter.

Occurrence: American White Pelicans have been recorded in all but one county — Baylor. They should be found in that county, too, as there are large impoundments that would attract them. It is surprising how few persons realize that these huge birds regularly pass over or stop in north central Texas. In fall they may linger for a week or so. They have been observed every month of the year but are more common during migration. Summer sightings represent stragglers or injured birds. In mild winters also it is not uncommon to see a few pelicans.

Large flocks — up to several thousand — make impressive sights as they soar overhead or ride the waters of a large lake. One of the best places to see pelicans in migration is Hagerman NWR, although they can be found elsewhere in many counties of the study area. Examples of large numbers reported are 5,000 at Hagerman NWR, Grayson County, on 28 October 1973 and more than 10,000 on 9 October 1986, and an estimated 20,000 near Grapevine Lake, Tarrant-Denton counties, on 9 October 1983.

In fall they pass regularly through north central Texas from September through early November. The mean arrival date for Grayson County is 19 September, while in Dallas County the mean was 27 September (six years out of ten, 1969–79). Not uncommonly, however, they are reported in several counties on the same date. They peak the first week of October, while the very early fall birds may arrive by mid-July or early August.

Early-spring transients may appear in late January or early February. They are usually found from late March through early May, with the peak of migration about the second week of April. Some may linger into June, and a few stay through July. There are June observations for Clay, Dallas, Denton, Grayson, Hunt, Kaufman, Rains, Tarrant, and Van Zandt counties.

White Pelicans nest mainly in the northwestern part of the United States and western Canada. Being south of the above-delineated range, north central Texas is in direct flight line with the Gulf Coast, where these magnificent birds winter. On 16 October 1982, I saw a color-marked pelican at the Hagerman NWR that had been tagged in North Dakota. It was interesting that another tagged bird (with the same color) was seen the same year at Port Aransas, on the central Texas coast. Five were reported at Hagerman NWR on 12 November 1983, and still another was spotted in the spring of 1984 at Lake Tawakoni, Hunt County. These birds were marked as juveniles, part of an ongoing banding program to understand better the dispersal of nesting pelicans.

Specimens: Specimens of White Pelicans have been collected from the following counties: Archer—specimen not located (Oberholser, 1974), Grayson (OU), Kaufman (TCWC), Tarrant (FWMSH), Wichita (MWU), and Wise (DMNH, mounted specimen).

BROWN PELICAN *Pelecanus occidentalis* Linnaeus
Status: Accidental visitor inland.
Occurrence: Oberholser (1974) indicated sight records for Dallas, Navarro, and Tarrant counties. Since juveniles or dirty American White Pelicans may appear brown, these sightings are questionable. I have never been able to determine the basis of sightings for the latter two counties, and I did not include its presence in Tarrant County (Pulich, 1979).

Reports of this coastal bird for counties under study include: *Dallas—* early fall reports in 1928 and 1937 (Stillwell, 1939). A more recent report was a sighting by two observers of 24 birds on 13 April 1963 (Baumgartner, 1963). This alleged sighting is highly suspect because the number of birds reported is so large. By the late 1950s and early 1960s there was a decided decline in the Brown Pelican population in Texas owing to pesticides. Only a small number remained on the coast, and even there they were seldom observed during this period. The large number reported is extremely doubtful, and the sighting probably represents misidentified White Pelicans. *Denton* — an immature Brown Pelican spent more than two months at Lewisville Lake from 25 August to 31 October 1977. Many observers viewed the bird off and on during that time. *Grayson* — three were reported with 90 White Pelicans on 20 October 1973 at Hagerman NWR. No other details are available.

Family Phalacrocoracidae (Cormorants)

DOUBLE-CRESTED CORMORANT   *Phalacrocorax auritus* (Lesson)
Status: Fairly common to common migrant. Uncommon to fairly common in winter. May be only a transient in some counties, particularly those along the western side of the study area. Although the species formerly bred locally, there is no evidence that it currently does so.
Occurrence: Double-crested Cormorants have been recorded in all of the counties in north central Texas. Many of the large water impoundments attract great numbers during migration. They have been recorded throughout the year in many of the counties where much bird-watching is carried on. They are seldom found in January, February, and June through early August. At these times there is seldom more than a bird or two.

Banding records available to me show that transient cormorants passing through Dallas, Denton, and Hunt counties and adjacent Henderson County originally hatched in the Canadian provinces of Alberta and Saskatchewan as well as in South Dakota.

The birds are most numerous during spring migration from mid-March through mid-May. Some recent peak dates are: 13 March 1982 (400), Lake Ray Hubbard, Dallas-Rockwall counties; 9 through 12 March 1983 (2,000), White Rock Lake, Dallas County; 28 March 1982 (1,400), Lake Lavon, Collin County; 5 April 1975 (500), Dallas County; 12 April 1983 (700), Wise County; 15 April 1978 (300–400), Cedar Creek Lake, Kaufman County; 4 May 1980 (400), Greenville City Lake, Hunt County. During fall migration they pass through north central Texas from mid-September to early November. Some large numbers are as follows: 4 October 1982 (1,500), Lewisville Lake, Denton County; 16 November 1975 (1,000), Dallas County; 14 October 1974 (500), Tarrant County.

In winter they are found scattered throughout the study area. They are not as numerous, but some linger on larger lakes such as Wichita, Texoma, Lewisville, Tawakoni, and Cedar Creek. In more recent mild winters they have been tallied on all of the CBCs (eight) except the count in Palo Pinto County. Although this count area does not have suitable habitat for the species, birds have been observed nearby at Possum Kingdom Lake during the same period. During the relatively mild winter period of 1986–87, flocks of thousands were reported at Lake Ray Hubbard, Dallas-Rockwall counties, and at Lake Tawakoni, Hunt-Rains and Van Zandt counties.

Nesting: Double-crested Cormorants nested in Baylor and Wilbarger counties in the late 1930s, according to Oberholser (1974), but there is no evidence that they do so today. Scattered June and July dates for Archer, Clay, Dallas, Denton, Fannin, Grayson, Rains, and Tarrant counties represent stragglers or extremely early migrants.

Specimens: Specimens are available from Navarro (TCWC), Dallas (DMNH, WMP), Denton (DMNH), and Tarrant (DMNH) counties. Specimens indicated by Oberholser (1974) for Archer, Cooke, and Grayson counties were not located.

OLIVACEOUS CORMORANT *Phalacrocorax olivaceus* (Humboldt)

Status: Uncommon to rare summer visitor locally. Careful scrutiny should produce more records, for they may be overlooked among the hordes of Double-crested Cormorants that pass through north central Texas each year. One nesting site is within the study area proper, and several are just outside.

Occurrence: Olivaceous Cormorants have been recorded in 14 counties of north central Texas. They can usually be expected from late March through the end of November, although they may linger into December. Stillwell (1939) cites one observation for Dallas County from 8 November 1934 to late spring of 1935. Since none have wintered in that county in recent years, this observation may have been of an injured bird or a misidentification.

Dates for all of the counties are: *Archer* — specimen said to have been taken 14 miles south of Electra, 12 October 1920; *Clay* — Lake Arrowhead, first recorded 8 June 1973 and nearly every year since to present (1984); numerous observations, earliest 21 May 1974, latest 23 August 1975; *Collin* — Lake Lavon, 18 June through 18 August 1985; *Dallas* — sightings every month of the year, but in recent years only from 9 April 1978 through 4 October 1975; some of the earlier reports may be misidentifications; *Denton* — one of the few February reports (Rylander, 1959), 21 and 25 October 1979; *Ellis* — 22 May 1986; *Grayson* — observations mainly from Hagerman NWR; many sightings now being recorded nearly every year, earliest 13 March 1979, latest 21 December 1974; Newell and Sutton (1982) gave a number of records for Lake Texoma in Johnston and Marshall counties, Oklahoma, reinforcing occurrence at boundary of the Red River; *Kaufman* — 21 April 1982; other sightings, but not specifically given since species currently (1984) nests just inside Henderson County on Cedar Creek

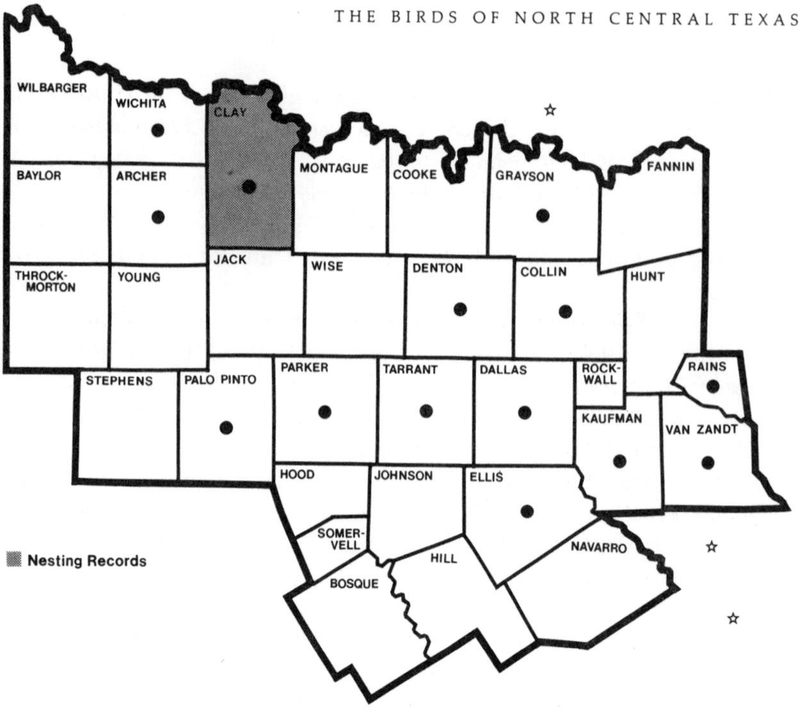

Map 7. Distribution of the Olivaceous Cormorant, *Phalacrocorax olivaceus*, with nesting records

Lake; *Palo Pinto* — Possum Kingdom Lake, 22 May 1977 through 21 August 1977; *Parker* — Lake Weatherford, 26 October 1985; *Rains* — Lake Tawakoni, 23 March 1986 to 1 December 1985 (1983–86); *Tarrant* — first reported 10 August 1978, 9 April 1985 to 27 October 1978, becoming more numerous each year; greatest number 11 in mid-July 1985; *Van Zandt* — 29 August 1986, 1 November 1986, and 14 December 1986. *Wichita* — two sightings, 2 April 1976 and 1 May 1976.

Nesting: The only nesting records of Olivaceous Cormorants in the study area are from Lake Arrowhead, Clay County (Zinn, 1977). From 1975 no nests were found here until 11 June 1984, when five were located in a dead cottonwood along with Great Blue Heron nests. This nesting site may have been just over the county line in Archer County. This species, however, has been reported on Lake Arrowhead every year during the interim nesting period.

There are recent nesting records in the following adjacent counties: Anderson (Telfair, 1980); Henderson, nesting for at least seven years (1978–84) on Cedar Creek Lake (approximately 100 pairs); and Wood, at Lake Fork on 18 August 1981 (no previous record).

Specimens: The specimen said to have been collected on 12 October 1920

in Archer County was not located, nor was the Dallas County bird of February 1939 mounted by Mayer (Oberholser, 1974). The only specimen known to me for north central Texas is one taken on 15 August 1978 for Tarrant County (WMP).

Family Anhingidae (Anhingas)

ANHINGA *Anhinga anhinga* (Linnaeus)

Status: Uncommon to rare visitor in counties in the eastern half of the study area. Occasionally it nests in the study area, currently only in one county; it is nesting regularly in some of the adjacent counties.

Occurrence: The Anhinga has been sighted in Bosque, Cooke, Dallas, Denton, Ellis, Grayson, Hill, Hunt, Kaufman, Navarro, Rains, Tarrant, Van Zandt, and Wise counties and nearby Anderson, Henderson, and Wood counties. The north central Texas study area has gradually lost habitat for this species because marshy areas have dried up and woody lakes have disappeared from the scene. Dates normally range from April through October. However, there are several March dates for nearby Henderson County—7 March 1979, 27 March 1981, 26 March 1982, and 31 March 1984. An early January date and several February dates are discounted as misidentifications of cormorants that frequent large impoundments throughout the winter.

Typical county sightings are: *Cooke*—casual in 1876 (Ragsdale's notes), two recent records, 3 August 1981, 13 August 1980; *Dallas*—numerous sightings owing to many observers, 10 April 1960 through 26 October 1976; *Denton*—20 October 1976, 6 November 1980; *Grayson*—most records are from Hagerman NWR, at least 20 records, 7 April 1983 to 17 May 1981 and 12 July 1967 to 3 October 1978 (85 on the last date, an unusually high number); *Hunt*—8, 20, and 28 August 1982, 27 October 1977; *Kaufman* —21 October 1973, 1979; *Tarrant*—approximately 25 records, 25 March 1949 to 10 May 1975, plus sightings from 23 May through 19 June 1985, 4 July 1986 to 20 October 1982; *Wise*—31 October 1975.

Nesting: Previous nesting has been reported in Dallas (1963) and Wise (1893) counties. The latter may have been in error since the observation (Donald and More, 1894) indicates a nest with nine eggs, and this species normally lays only three to five eggs. The only recent nesting report was from Tarrant County. Four pairs of Anhingas were located at nests at the Fort Worth Nature Center on 23 May 1987. There are currently, however, nesting Anhingas in adjacent Anderson, Henderson, and Wood (not previously recorded) counties.

Specimens: Valid scientific specimens may be lacking for north central Texas. Several specimens collected in the Dallas area between 1920 and 1938 were mounted for private collections and very likely were lost. Ex-

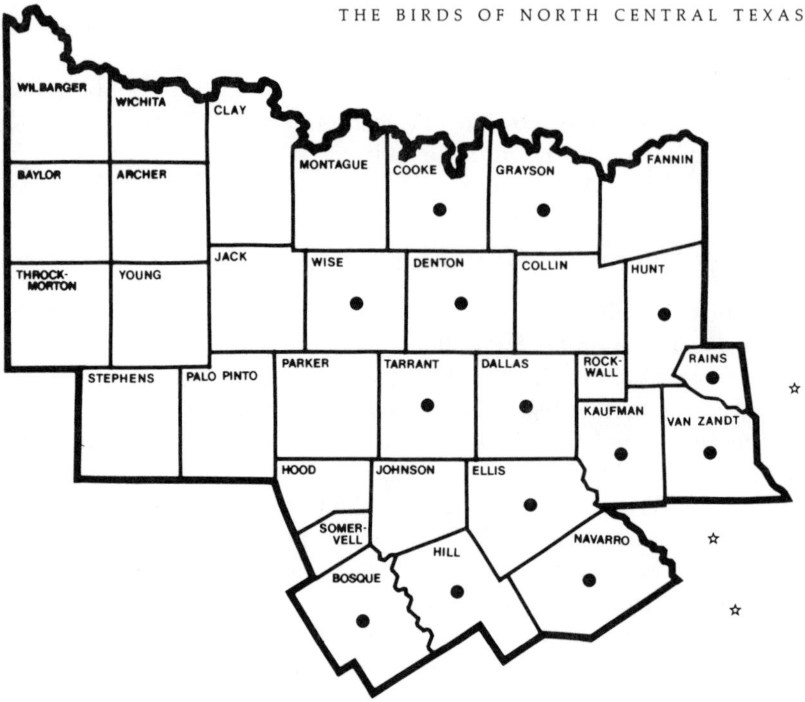

Map 8. Distribution of the Anhinga, *Anhinga anhinga*

cept for mounted birds on display at the Dallas Museum of Natural History there are no specimens in this museum. The mounted birds lack scientific data. Another specimen said to have been taken in Denton County was not examined (originally in NTSU museum). A specimen taken on 2 June 1938 at Midlothian, Ellis County, was one actually taken alive and placed in the Fort Worth zoo (Stillwell, 1939). There are, however, examples (DMNH) from adjacent Henderson County.

Order Ciconiiformes

Family Ardeidae (Bitterns, Herons, and Egrets)

AMERICAN BITTERN *Botaurus lentiginosus* (Rackett)
Status: Common to uncommon migrant. Winter records in some counties. Formerly bred along the Red River.
Occurrence: The American Bittern is widespread in north central Texas, though it is secretive in its habits. It has been recorded in 22 counties —

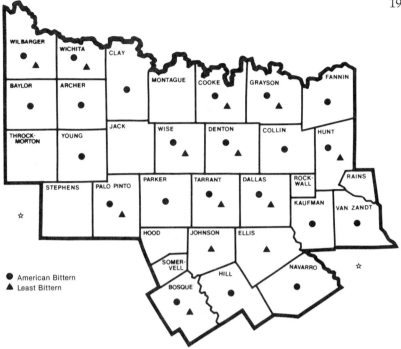

Map 9. Distribution of the American Bittern, *Botaurus lentiginosus,* and the Least Bittern, *Ixobrychus exilis*

Archer, Baylor, Bosque, Clay, Collin, Cooke, Dallas, Denton, Fannin, Grayson, Hill, Hunt, Kaufman, Navarro, Palo Pinto, Parker, Tarrant, Van Zandt, Wichita, Wilbarger, Wise, and Young — and adjacent Henderson and Shackelford counties.

This species is more often observed during spring migration from late March through mid-May and again from late August through November, with peak periods in mid-April and October. Typical extreme county spring and fall dates are: *Dallas* — 6 March 1966 to 26 May 1977, and 5 and 6 September 1962 to 29 October 1959; *Grayson* — 4 March to 22 May 1986, and 19 September 1980 to 16 December, next-latest, 3 December 1977; *Palo Pinto* — 5 September 1976 to 14 November 1976; no spring dates; *Tarrant* — 28 March 1981 to 14 May 1966, and 19 August 1951 to 17 November 1974; *Van Zandt* — 17 March 1984 to 5 May 1983 and 12 November 1983; *Wichita* — 9 April 1977 to 6 May 1978, and 25 August 1975 to 18 November 1976 and an isolated date, 11 December 1958.

The American Bittern is rare to casual throughout the area in winter, having been seen on the Dallas, Fort Worth, and Lewisville CBCs. In addition it has been observed during the winter on 13 December 1980 (Hunt County), 27 December 1980 (Hill County), 7 January 1978 (Palo Pinto

County), 10 January 1975 and 27 February 1973 (Wichita County), 30 January 1983 (Dallas County), and one from 9 February through 17 March 1966 (Tarrant County).

Nesting: In the 1920s the American Bittern was an uncommon summer resident along the Red River, in an area known as Watt's Lake, in Wilbarger County, but this lake has disappeared. Today the only area in which it might still be found nesting along the Red River would be the Hagerman NWR, in Grayson County. Although no actual nests have been seen, it has been reported in that county during June 1955, 1956, 1965, and 1969 and from 24 July to 11 September 1980, 23 July 1981, and 18 July 1984. There is also an isolated date of 21 July 1983 for Denton County.

Specimens: American Bittern specimens have been taken in the following counties: Clay, 10 October 1956 (MWU); Cooke, 24 October 1877 (TNHC); Dallas, 27 October 1970, 11 March 1971 (DMNH), 5 and 6 September 1962 (WMP); Kaufman, 23 April 1978 (DMNH); and Wichita, 11 December 1958 (MWU), 27 February 1973 (MWU). A specimen was also taken on 4 November 1976 (TCWC) from Shackelford County, but specimens indicated for Wise County on 22 June 1891 and April 1892 (Donald and More, 1894) and for Hunt County (Oberholser, 1974) were not located.

LEAST BITTERN   *Ixobrychus exilis* (Gmelin)
Status: Uncommon to rare summer resident where suitable habitat is available. Rare transient elsewhere.

Occurrence: This tiny bittern is seldom seen but will be found where dense freshwater marshes remain. It has been recorded in 13 counties of the study area — Bosque, Cooke, Dallas, Denton, Ellis, Grayson, Hunt, Johnson, Palo Pinto, Tarrant, Wichita, Wilbarger, and Wise — and in nearby Henderson County.

The Least Bittern has been found in north central Texas from mid-April to mid-September. Typical county spring dates are: *Bosque* — 27 April 1974; *Dallas* — 16 April 1969; *Grayson* — 13 May 1972; *Tarrant* — 21 April 1969; *Wichita* — 28 April 1973. Some late fall dates are: *Denton* — 19 September 1983 and 23 September 1972; *Ellis* — 19 September 1982; *Tarrant* — 23 September 1945; *Wichita* — 21 September 1975.

Nesting: Although the Least Bittern nested at Watt's Lake, Wilbarger County, in 1929 (More and Strecker, 1929), it no longer nests there, for the lake was drained in the 1940s for pasturelands. In the Dallas — Fort Worth area the Least Bittern will be found nesting by mid-May. Nests with eggs have been found on 20 May 1978 (Tarrant County) and 22 May 1968 and 26 May 1962 (Dallas County). Adults were noted carrying food many times between 12 June to 13 July 1969 at Hagerman NWR, Grayson County, and in early July 1981 nesting was confirmed when two young were found.

Specimens: Specimens from Dallas (WMP), Denton (DMNH, mounted specimen), and Wichita (MWU) counties have been examined. Those indicated by Oberholser (1974) for Hunt and Wise counties were not located.

GREAT BLUE HERON   *Ardea herodias* Linnaeus
Status: Fairly common to uncommon summer resident. Uncommon to rare transient. More nesting sites seem to be evident in the northwestern and southern parts of the study area than in the eastern parts.
Occurrence: The Great Blue Heron has been recorded in all the counties of the north central Texas study area. It never seems to be as numerous as most of the other members of this family, and except occasionally when foraging with other herons or egrets, it is usually found by itself.

This species can be found throughout the year, but individuals represent two races, a local population and one that moves into the area for the winter. In fall, particularly during October and November, up to 100 birds may gather at favorable foraging habitats.

The average (mean) number of Great Blue Herons reported on each of six CBCs in the area for a 15-year period (1968–82) is as follows: Dallas, 7; Fort Worth (Tarrant County), 29; Hagerman (Grayson County), 43; Lewisville (Denton County), 47; Palo Pinto, 7; and Wichita Falls, 26.
Nesting: Nesting has been recorded in Archer, Baylor, Bosque, Clay, Collin, Grayson (suspected nesting at Hagerman NWR in the 1940s and 1950s but no specific evidence that it did so), Hunt, and Jack counties; in Johnson County (formerly), at Cleburne SP; on the Kaufman–Van Zandt county line; in Palo Pinto County; on the Rains–Van Zandt county line; in Stephens, Tarrant (three heronries), Van Zandt, Young (at Lake Graham; may now be inactive), Wichita, and Wilbarger counties; and in adjacent Anderson, Eastland (formerly), Henderson, Shackelford, and Wood counties. Some of the largest heronries known are those in the following counties: Kaufman (60 pairs), Clay (50 pairs, down from 200 pairs in 1975), Palo Pinto (50 pairs), Bosque (90 pairs), and Rains–Van Zandt (approximately 300 herons) on the Sabine River below Lake Tawakoni in spring 1985. This species does not nest with other members of its family and often nests in small numbers. No doubt the species may be overlooked and may nest in some counties where sites have not been found. Heronries are probably more widespread than indicated by this summary. In Young and Wilbarger counties the herons have been observed nesting at stock tanks singly or on two or three nests.
Specimens: Except for the specimens examined by Oberholser (1974) for Cooke and Navarro counties (whereabouts unknown), none have been examined for subspecific identification. In the *Birds of Tarrant County* (Pulich, 1979), I pointed out that the problem of racial delineation as determined by Oberholser may not be entirely correct, and I recommended that a thorough study of this species be undertaken.

Specimens are known from the following counties: Baylor (MWU), Cooke (TNHC), Dallas (DMNH), Denton (DMNH, WMP), Hood (SM), Tarrant (FWMSH, UTA), and Wichita (MWU). A footnote given by Stillwell (1939) indicated that there was a Hunt County specimen, but it could not be located.

GREAT EGRET   *Casmerodius albus* (Linnaeus)
Status: Common to fairly common summer resident. May occasionally be found wintering in a number of counties of the study area.
Occurrence: The Great Egret has been recorded in all north central Texas counties except Bosque and Young, although they no doubt occur in these counties since they have been reported from the adjacent counties. Persons who have birded in specific locales for a number of years indicate that this egret has increased in recent years.

This species is usually observed by mid-March and departs in early November in the southern part of the study area (Dallas–Fort Worth). They seem to be most numerous in August, dropping off in numbers by early October in nearly all of the counties. Typical extreme arrival and departure dates for several selected counties are: *Dallas* – 2 March 1986 to 19 November 1960; *Grayson* – 25 March 1972 to 30 November 1986; *Tarrant* – 8 March 1986 to 18 November 1978; *Van Zandt* – 23 March 1983 to 14 December 1986, next latest 17 November 1984. There seems to be little difference in the arrival and departure dates in the southern part of the study area and the northern part, especially where many observers concentrate (e.g., Grayson County). In the counties on the west they seem to arrive later and depart earlier.

In winter this egret normally withdraws to the area south of north central Texas, but during the winter of 1982–83 they remained in a number of counties in the study area. It was not uncommon to find 50 or more in Dallas and Denton counties. They have been noted on all of the CBCs at some time except for the Palo Pinto count. They may be changing their winter habits and one might expect them regularly.
Nesting: Great Egrets have been found nesting in Baylor (formerly), Collin, Cooke, Dallas, Denton, Ellis, Fannin, Hunt, Johnson, Parker, Tarrant, Van Zandt, Wichita, and Wilbarger (formerly) counties and on the Kaufman-Henderson county line. They have also been found in nearby Anderson and Wood counties. This egret is well established in inland heronries and is holding its own, if not actually increasing.

Evidence of postnuptial wandering is supported by a Great Egret observed at Possum Kingdom Lake, Palo Pinto County, on 15 July 1974; it had been tagged as a juvenile at a colony in Anderson County in July of the same year.
Specimens: Specimens represent typical race *C. a. egretta* and are known

for Cooke (TNHC), Dallas (DMNH, WMP), Denton (DMNH), and Kaufman (DMNH) counties. An example indicated by Oberholser (1974) for Hunt County was not located.

SNOWY EGRET *Egretta thula* (Molina)
Status: Fairly common summer resident.
Occurrence: The Snowy Egret has been found in 26 counties in north central Texas: Archer, Bosque, Clay, Collin, Cooke, Dallas, Denton, Ellis, Fannin, Grayson, Hill, Hunt, Jack, Johnson, Kaufman, Montague, Palo Pinto, Parker, Rains, Rockwall, Tarrant, Van Zandt, Wichita, Wilbarger, Wise, and Young. It is not as common as other long-legged waders, although occasionally it may be overlooked among immature Little Blue Herons or Cattle Egrets.

This species is usually found from early April until early October. Typical extreme dates for selected counties are: *Dallas* — 5 March 1982 to 13 October 1983; *Denton* —1 April 1976 to 21 October 1979; *Grayson* —18 April 1981 to 23 October 1986; *Hunt* — 28 March 1985 to 31 October 1982; *Kaufman* — 2 March 1983 to 4 November 1979; *Tarrant* —15 March 1986 to 4 November 1986, next latest 18 October 1953; *Wichita* —11 April 1975 to 26 November 1975, next-latest 4 October 1982.

The Snowy Egret is seldom observed in winter. Stillwell (1939) recorded it in Dallas County in all months except January and February. In recent years the only other observations for Dallas County have been 8 January 1971 and 20 December 1980. Besides these sightings there is a Kaufman County report for 31 January 1968 and a report from Van Zandt County for 4 January 1986.
Nesting: Nesting of this egret with other members of its family has been reported in Cooke, Dallas, Denton, Ellis, Fannin, Hunt, Johnson, Parker, Tarrant, and Wichita counties and on the Kaufman-Henderson county line. It has also been found nesting in nearby Anderson, Henderson, and Wood counties.

A nestling banded in Dallas County on 23 May 1963 was recovered in April 1967 in the valley of El Progreso, Guatemala.
Specimens: Specimens are available from Dallas (DMNH), Ellis (TCWC, WMP), Grayson (OU), and Tarrant (FWMSH) counties.

LITTLE BLUE HERON *Egretta caerulea* (Linnaeus)
Status: Common summer resident.
Occurrence: The Little Blue Heron has been found in all of the counties in north central Texas. It is more abundant in the southern and eastern parts of the study area, although it has made its way into the area from the south by way of the Trinity River drainage. Today, however, it is found

in limited numbers around large impoundments and stock tanks in the counties along the western side of the study area.

This species is usually found from mid-March to early November, a few birds lingering into December. Usually they move out during January until late February. In those counties where they do not nest, they are not recorded quite as early. Typical county arrival and departure dates are: *Dallas* — 5 March 1986 to 10 November 1973; *Grayson* — 14 March 1982 to 14 November 1974; *Kaufman* — 20 February 1978 to 4 November 1979; *Tarrant* — 20 February 1984, next-earliest 27 February 1977 (mean 10 March 1973–78) to 20 November 1986; *Wichita* — 25 April 1976 to 4 November 1974.

Winter sightings probably represent stragglers. Most are recorded during CBCs when many observers are in the field. These counties are Dallas — 29 December 1958, 17 December 1977, 6 December 1978, 19 December 1981, 18 December 1982, and 20 December 1986; Denton — 27 December 1973; Palo Pinto — 31 December 1965; Tarrant — 15 December 1973 and 20 December 1986; Wichita — 17 December 1975. The only January dates are 4 and 18 January 1933, Dallas County (Stillwell, 1939).

Nesting: Nesting has been recorded in Collin, Cooke, Dallas, Denton, Ellis, Fannin, Hunt, Johnson, Navarro, Parker, Tarrant, Wichita, and Wise (6 June 1888, none in recent years) counties and on the Kaufman-Henderson county line, as well as in adjacent Anderson and Wood counties. Although reported by Oberholser (1974) as nesting in Grayson County, there is no evidence that it does so today. The basis for this record is unknown.

Some recoveries of Little Blue Herons that I banded at the medical school heronry in Dallas are as follows: banded on 26 May 1963 and recovered in Omaoa, Department of Cores, Honduras, on 15 September 1963; banded on 2 June 1964 and recovered in Duncanville, Dallas County, in February 1966; banded on 15 May 1965 and recovered in Alanje, Panama, in January 1971; banded 20 May 1965 and recovered east of Wichita, Kansas, on 18 March 1967; two banded on 14 May 1969, one recovered nine miles east of Seymour, Baylor County, on 12 July 1969 and the other recovered in Dallas nine years later on 5 April 1978; one banded on 21 May 1969 and recovered in Oklahoma City in April 1971.

I was informed by a bander who lived in Paris, Lamar County, that he had banded Little Blue Herons and received two returns, both less than a year old upon recovery, from Wawa, Nicaragua, and Benito Juárez, Campeche, Mexico.

Specimens: Specimens have been collected for Cooke (Ragsdale's specimen [not located]), Dallas (DMNH, UTA, WMP), Denton (DMNH), Ellis (TCWC), and Grayson (OU) counties.

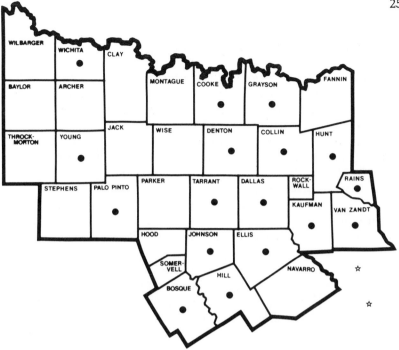

Map 10. Distribution of the Tricolored Heron, *Egretta tricolor*

TRICOLORED HERON *Egretta tricolor* (Müller)
Status: Rare to casual over the area. Principally a postnuptial wanderer.
Nested at the southeastern edge of the study area.
Occurrence: The Tricolored Heron, formerly known as the Louisiana
Heron, tends to wander up the Trinity River drainage, mainly after nest-
ing on the coast. It has been recorded in 17 counties of the study area —
Bosque, Collin, Cooke, Dallas, Denton, Ellis, Grayson, Hill, Hunt, John-
son, Kaufman, Palo Pinto, Rains, Tarrant, Van Zandt, Wichita, and Young
— and adjacent Anderson and Henderson counties.

Extreme overall dates range from April through late October; however, most sightings are from late July through September. A January date
(Stillwell, 1939) was probably a misidentification. Extreme spring county
dates are: *Dallas* — 4 April 1970; *Grayson* — 30 April 1972; *Palo Pinto* —
29 April 1978; *Tarrant* — 25 April 1982; *Henderson* — 18 April 1982. Extreme fall dates are: *Dallas* — 3 October 1966 and 17 November 1966; *Grayson* — 30 September 1982; *Kaufman* — 4 October 1980; *Tarrant* — 24 October 1965.
Nesting: Runnels (1980) reports the northernmost inland Texas nesting of
this species at Cedar Creek Lake, on the Henderson-Kaufman county line,

on 6 June 1979. Although it nested for several years afterward, its status in 1986 was not determined.

Specimens: The only known specimens of the Tricolored Heron from the area are two from Denton County, a study skin and a mounted bird (DMNH), and one taken in Cooke County (DMNH). A specimen said to have been taken in Dallas County in 1937 (Stillwell, 1939), about the time of the inception of the Dallas Museum of Natural History, could not be located. It was probably prepared by Mayer for a patron and is lost.

CATTLE EGRET *Bubulcus ibis* (Linnaeus)

Status: Abundant to common summer resident in many counties. Postnuptial wanderers visit the remaining counties. A few winter casually.

Occurrence: Oberholser (1974) lists the Cattle Egret in seven counties: Dallas (1961*), Denton, Ellis (approximately 1963*), Grayson (1964*), Hunt, Parker, and Tarrant (1963*) (the asterisks indicate the first years known to me in which Cattle Egrets were seen in the respective counties). Since then they have been seen in all but four counties (Bosque, Hood, Somervell, and Wilbarger) of the study area.

The Cattle Egret is a common summer visitor throughout north central Texas. Dates vary depending on the number of observers in a particular locale, but it is reasonable to assume that some of the southern counties may have dates earlier and later than those along the Red River.

Early-arrival and late-departure dates are: *Dallas* — 13 February 1975, next-earliest 29 February 1976 to December 1969; *Grayson* — 27 March 1970 to 21 December 1968, next-latest 18 November 1964; *Palo Pinto* — 15 March 1980 to 16 November 1978; *Rains* — 3 March 1985 to 7 November 1984 (Van Zandt); *Tarrant* — 13 February 1975 to 14 December 1981, next-latest 25 November 1981; *Wichita* — 12 April 1977 to 20 December 1975, next-latest 3 December 1971 (specimen).

Although there are reports for the entire year for a number of counties, records for late November and December may represent stragglers. Winter sightings have been reported in the following counties: Dallas — 14 January 1970; Denton — 26 December 1984 and 27 December 1985; Fannin — 27 December 1971; Hunt — 2 January 1982; Tarrant — 22 December 1985 and 5 and 16 December 1986; Wichita — 3 January 1976.

Nesting: Cattle Egrets nest three or four weeks later than other members of the heron family and usually with other species of egrets and herons. They are common in areas where they nest. They have been reported nesting in 13 counties — Collin, Cooke (about 1979), Dallas (1963), Denton, Ellis (1965, probably as early as 1963), Fannin, Hunt (1975, 1983), Kaufman (late 1960), Johnson, Navarro, Parker (about 1977), Tarrant (1973), and Wichita (about 1977) — and commonly in adjacent Anderson, Henderson, and Wood counties. For example, in Dallas, Denton, Ellis, Kaufman,

Johnson, and Tarrant counties two and three colonies have been utilized simultaneously during one season. For no apparent reason members of this family may not return to a particularly active nesting site the following year. The entire heronry may move to another location. For this reason, and the probable increase of ardeid population, it is impossible to delineate all the heronries in north central Texas. No doubt some have been missed, and new ones will continue to be reported.

Nestling recoveries of Cattle Egrets that I banded from Dallas were as follows: banded 1 June 1963 and recovered at Salvatierra, Guanajuato, Mexico, in November 1964; banded 29 May 1969 and recovered at Tlanchinol, Hidalgo, Mexico, in January 1970; banded 11 June 1970 and recovered four miles north of Rockwall, Rockwall County, on 5 September 1970; banded 11 June 1970 and recovered at Jalisco, Mexico, in January 1971; banded 31 May 1971 and recovered near Torreón, Coahuila, Mexico, on 27 March 1972; banded 31 May 1971 and recovered near Culiacán, Sinaloa, Mexico, in August 1977.

A government scientist who lived in north central Texas in 1971 and 1972 banded Cattle Egrets from a colony at Paris, Lamar County. He later informed me that returns of nestlings banded at Paris were received from the Mexican states Hidalgo, Jalisco, Michoacán, Oaxaca, Sonora, and Sinaloa. One bird was about 12 years old when recovered; all the others were about five years old.

A color-marked Cattle Egret was observed in a small group of eight at a stock tank in Throckmorton County on 17 May 1983. It had been tagged in the nest at least a year before in the Anderson-Henderson counties area, where an ongoing project is under way to explain better the movements of the members of the ardeid family.

Specimens: Cattle Egret specimens have been collected from Dallas (DMNH, WMP), Ellis (TCWC), Parker (FWMSH), Tarrant (FWMSH), and Wichita (MWU) counties.

GREEN-BACKED HERON   Butorides striatus (Linnaeus)
Status: Common to fairly common summer resident. Casual in winter along the southern part of the study area.
Occurrence: The Green-backed Heron, or Green Heron, as it was formerly known, will usually be found from early April to September with an occasional transient bird lingering into October and early November. It has been observed in all of the counties of the north central Texas study area.

Some extreme spring and fall dates for selected counties are: Dallas— 23 March 1936 (Stillwell, 1939); 14 March 1986, mean 12 April—19 years (within 1957–82) to 2 November 1958; next-latest 4 October 1973, mean 22 September—17 years (within 1957–82); Grayson—7 April 1979 to 29 October 1986; Hunt—2 April 1977 to 27 October 1977; Palo Pinto—3 April

1982 to 19 September 1976; *Tarrant* — 27 March 1968, mean 6 April — 9 years (1970–78) to 19 November 1982, next-latest 31 October 1970; *Wichita* — 6 April 1974 to 20 October 1974.

This little heron has been observed only a few times during the winter. The observations in Dallas County on 15 December 1984 and in Hunt County from 16 November 1977 through 5 January 1958 may have been of injured birds. In Tarrant County there were sightings on 15 December 1973, 2 January 1966, 1 and 27 January 1981, and 29 January 1984. It was also seen at Lake Ray Hubbard, Rockwall-Dallas counties, on 19 December 1984. There are no February or early March sightings.

Nesting: Nesting has been observed in Archer, Bosque, Dallas, Denton, Grayson, Hunt, Navarro, Palo Pinto, Tarrant, Wichita, and Wilbarger counties. It is very likely that the Green-backed Heron would be found breeding in all of the counties in the study area if a special effort was made to search for nests. The earliest date for nesting was a bird sitting on a nest on 23 April 1966 (Tarrant County) to a bird possibly attending a nest on 25 August 1979 (Grayson County). Nesting is at its peak in May and June. Although Sutton (1967) indicates that this species is two-brooded, I wonder whether late nests are not due to spring or early summer winds destroying the fragile nests and nesting being attempted again.

Specimens: Specimens representing the race *virescens* are available from Archer (MWU), Cooke (TNHC), Dallas (DMNH, WMP), Denton (DMNH, TCWC), Parker (DMNH), Tarrant (DMNH, FWMSH, UTA), and Wichita (DMNH) counties.

BLACK-CROWNED NIGHT-HERON   *Nycticorax nycticorax* (Linnaeus)
Status: Uncommon to rare summer resident. Uncommon to rare migrant. Casual in winter locally.
Occurrence: Black-crowned Night-Herons have been recorded in 20 counties of north central Texas — Bosque, Clay, Collin, Cooke, Dallas, Denton, Ellis, Grayson, Hunt, Navarro, Palo Pinto, Rockwall, Stephens, Tarrant, Throckmorton, Van Zandt, Wichita, Wilbarger, Wise, and Young — and nearby Shackelford County. Sightings tend to be more numerous where there are more observers, but birds should be found near many suitable bodies of water. This heron may not be as numerous as the Yellow-crowned Night-Heron.

This species is usually found from March through October. Extreme early-spring dates are given for selected counties: *Tarrant* — 3 March 1983; *Wichita* — 3 March 1974, next-latest 24 March 1978. Late-fall dates are: *Dallas* — 16 October 1979; *Denton* — 25 October 1983; *Grayson* — 8 November 1980, next-latest 5 November 1983; *Tarrant* — 23 November 1975, next-latest 2 October 1971; *Wichita* — 20 October 1956, next-latest 29 September 1976.

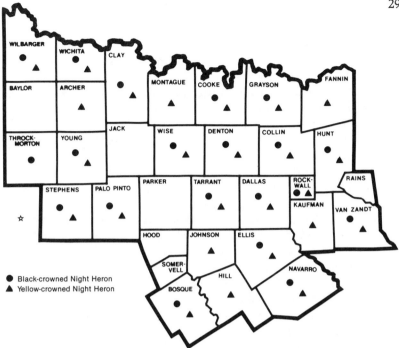

Map 11. Distribution of the Black-crowned Night-Heron, *Nycticorax nycticorax*, and the Yellow-crowned Night-Heron, *N. violaceus*

There are winter sightings for the Dallas–Fort Worth area. Stillwell (1939) gave winter reports for Dallas County for 1935, 1937, and 1939. More recent dates for this county are 31 January 1940, 31 December 1955, 27 December 1958, 31 December 1961, 25 January 1963, 2 January 1965, 20 February 1982, and 27 January 1983; Denton County, 1 January 1959; Tarrant County, 15 January 1983, 19 February 1983, and 18 February 1984.

Nesting: This heron was said to have nested in Wilbarger County (More and Strecker, 1929), but there is no evidence that it nests there today. The only recent nestings in the study area have been in downtown heronries in Dallas County (1963 through 1985) and Tarrant County (1975), both with other species of herons and egrets. A nestling banded in Dallas County on 27 May 1972 was recovered six miles southeast of Decatur, Wise County, on 13 July 1972. This species has also been reported nesting at a heronry in Ellis County. Two nests with large young were found there on 8 May 1985.

Specimens: Specimens have been examined from Dallas County, 25 January 1963 (WMP) and 31 January 1940 (DMNH) and Tarrant County, January 1974 (UTA). The whereabouts of a fall specimen (Oberholser, 1974) for Throckmorton County are unknown.

YELLOW-CROWNED NIGHT-HERON   *Nycticorax violaceus* (Linnaeus)
Status: Fairly common to uncommon summer resident. Uncommon transient. Casual locally in winter.
Occurrence: Because of the nocturnal habits of this species, its status may be obscure, but it has been recorded in 25 of the 32 counties in the north central Texas study area, more often in areas where there are numerous observers. It has yet, however, to be recorded in Baylor, Hood, Jack, Parker, Rains, Somervell, and Throckmorton counties.

This night-heron is usually found from early April until the last of September, with most sightings in April and August (many immatures). Selected county dates for early-spring and latest fall departures are: *Dallas* —11 March 1974 and 27 October 1937, next-latest 19 October 1969; *Denton* — 6 April 1975 and 11 October 1980; *Grayson* —10 April 1975 and 5 October 1975; *Hunt* — 29 April 1985 and 19 to 30 November 1979; *Tarrant* —13 March 1982 and 13 October 1956; *Van Zandt* —1 April 1987.

Winter records include 16 January 1879 (specimen), Cooke County; 2 December 1982, 15 December 1979, 1 January 1966, and 12 January 1976 (specimen), Dallas County; 5 December 1986 and 14 December 1974, Tarrant County. There appear to be no valid February dates for the north central Texas study area.
Nesting: Nesting has been recorded in Dallas, Denton, Ellis, Tarrant, and Van Zandt counties. Oberholser (1974) also gave nesting for Cooke and Rockwall counties, for which there are no recent reports. It is also suspected of nesting in Collin, Kaufman, Navarro, and Wichita counties. In addition there are summer records for Clay, Grayson, Palo Pinto, and Wilbarger counties. Nesting ranges from 4 April 1973 (nests) to 20 July 1980 (young fledged); all dates are from Dallas County.
Specimens: Specimens are known from Cooke (TNHC), Dallas (DMNH, WMP), Denton (DMNH, TCWC), and Tarrant (UTA, WMP) counties and adjacent Eastland County (KU). An August specimen said to have been taken in Wilbarger County (Oberholser, 1974) was not located.

Family Threskiornithidae (Ibises and Spoonbills)

WHITE IBIS   *Eudocimus albus* (Linnaeus)
Status: Casual summer visitor. Known to nest in one county of the study area.
Occurrence: White Ibises are found mainly in the southern part of the north central Texas study area, although they have been reported from the Red River drainage in Cooke and Grayson counties. This species was reported only once in the former county before the turn of the century, on 13 August 1879, when Ragsdale was said to have collected two birds (Oberholser,

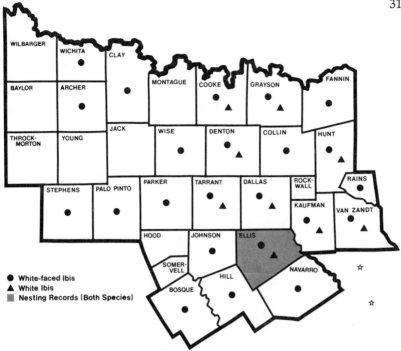

Map 12. Distribution of the White Ibis, *Eudocimus albus,* and the White-faced Ibis, *Plegadis chihi,* with nesting records

1974). In Grayson County there are reports from Hagerman NWR in 1964, 1971, 1977, and 1986, all in August or September.

In addition to the above Cooke and Grayson county reports, there are records of this ibis in Dallas, Denton, Ellis, Hunt, Kaufman, Tarrant, and Van Zandt counties and adjacent Anderson and Henderson counties.

Sightings range from 24 May 1969 (Henderson County) until 4 October 1986 (Tarrant County), with isolated records of 1 May 1977 and 29 June to 13 July 1985 (both from Tarrant County). Most of the observations are of a single bird or two, ranging from mid-July on, and probably represent postnuptial wanderers (immatures) that have moved north from the upper coast. They are not seen every year and may be declining in Texas. On 17 June 1985, 35 were seen flying over Lake Tawakoni, Van Zandt County. However, in the late 1960s several hundred were observed in adjacent Henderson County.

Nesting: The White Ibis has been known to nest sparingly in Ellis and Anderson counties (Telfair, 1980).

Specimens: Specimens from Cooke County referred to above were not located. Apparently there are no valid specimens for north central Texas.

WHITE-FACED IBIS   *Plegadis chihi* (Vieillot)
Status: Uncommon in spring. Fairly common summer visitor in a number of counties, but only one nesting record.
Occurrence: The White-faced Ibis has been found in 23 counties, with sightings in nearly all of the southern counties under study. No doubt it would have been found in some of the other counties if there had been more observers regularly visiting suitable water habitats.

The White-faced Ibis normally ranges in north central Texas from late March through early November. All of the more recent county records known to me are: *Archer* — 5 April 1953, specimen; *Bosque* — 25 April 1982; *Clay* — 25 October 1973; *Collin* — 12 May 1984, 30 August 1983, and 26 September 1984; *Cooke* — 3 August 1981; *Dallas* — numerous records, 29 and 30 March 1975, next-earliest 13 April 1973 to 20 May 1981, 10 July 1983 to 18 October 1981, 1982, with isolated dates 3 November 1963 and 27 January through 10 April 1983; *Denton* — a number of records, 4 April 1981 to 19 May 1981 and 9 August 1976 to 12 October 1983; *Ellis* — 10 September 1980; *Fannin* — 26 September 1984 and 17 August 1983; *Grayson* — number of records, 21 and 24 April 1975 to 28 May 1979, 9 July 1978 to 30 October 1983 and 1986; *Hill* — 11 September 1977; *Hunt* — 4 May 1984 at heronry but not found nesting, 24 August 1980 to 19 September 1982; *Johnson* — 14 April 1984, 19 September 1982, 20 and 25 September 1983; *Kaufman* — 24 September 1979; *Navarro* — 10 September 1980 and 12 September 1984; *Palo Pinto* — four records, 8 May 1977, 17 July 1977, 16 September 1978, and 5 November 1977; *Parker* — 14 September 1972; *Rains* — 5 May 1983, 16 July 1984, 13 September 1983, and 3 and 15 September 1984; *Stephens* — 8 October 1984; *Tarrant* — many records, 27 March 1985, next-earliest 8 April 1986 to 21 May 1985, 14 June 1985 and 1 July 1971, next-earliest 15 July 1983 to 17 December 1983 and 22 December 1984 (the latter dates are of stragglers); *Van Zandt* — 3 September 1984; *Wichita* — 20 April 1973 to 10 June 1975, and 20 August 1976 to 1 October 1975; *Wise* — 8 May 1978.
Nesting: The only county in which the White-faced Ibis was found nesting was Ellis County in 1975 (Telfair, 1980).
Specimens: White-faced Ibis specimens are known from the following counties: Archer (MWU); Dallas, three, one mounted but cataloged, others study skins (DMNH); Kaufman (SFASU); and Tarrant (FWMSH, WMP). Others indicated for Cooke, Tarrant, and Wise counties by Oberholser (1974) were not located.

ROSEATE SPOONBILL   *Ajaia ajaja* (Linnaeus)
Status: Rare to casual postbreeding visitor.
Occurrence: After the nesting season Roseate Spoonbills move into the north central Texas area from the Gulf Coast along the Trinity River drain-

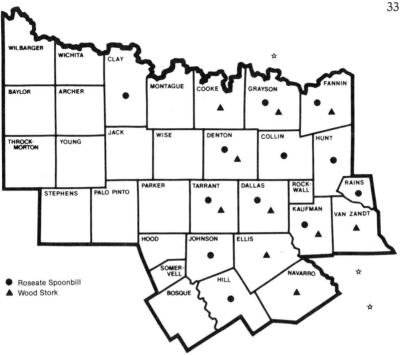

Map 13. Distribution of the Roseate Spoonbill, *Ajaia ajaja,* and the Wood Stork, *Mycteria americana*

age. Although most sightings are from Dallas County, they have been reported north to the Red River in Grayson County, as well as across into Johnson County, Oklahoma. When details of sightings have been given, most have proved to be immature birds.

The species has been recorded in 12 counties of north central Texas. All known records are: *Clay* — Lake Arrowhead on 18 through 20 August 1976; *Collin* — Heard Refuge on 7 August 1976 (TP-RF); *Dallas* — at least 15 times, probably others not recorded (1934–85), 29 May 1984, earliest in north central Texas, next-earliest 15 July 1985 to 6 October 1963, 1971; *Denton* — 12 September 1946, specimen, and 20 September 1959; *Fannin* — 29 September 1986; *Grayson* — all records from Hagerman NWR, 1 August to 23 September 1955, 9 to 16 September 1960, 27 July to 16 August 1971, 21 to 26 July 1983, and again 7 August and 5 September 1985; *Hill* — about 20 miles above Waco on the Brazos River, near Bosque county line, 15 August 1971; *Hunt* — 3 September 1983; *Johnson* — Keene, 12 September 1983; *Kaufman* — Cedar Creek Lake, late summer 1975, 6 and 7 September 1980; *Rains* — 10 October 1986; *Tarrant* — 10 times (1956–85), 13 July 1985 to 2 October 1982.

Specimens: The only spoonbill specimen known to me for north central Texas is the one taken in Denton County on 12 September 1946 (DMNH).

Family Ciconiidae (Storks)

WOOD STORK　*Mycteria americana* (Linnaeus)
Status: Rare to casual postnuptial visitor along the Trinity River drainage, most often seen in the southeastern part of the study area.
Occurrence: Wood Storks have been found in only 10 counties in the study area and adjacent Anderson and Henderson counties. Overall they have been recorded from 8 May 1976 (Ellis County) through 7 October 1973 (Kaufman County), with an isolated date of 2 November 1955 (Denton County). Several alleged March observations for Ellis and Kaufman counties were not included because the dates were too early. Most sightings are for late August and September, mainly representing immature birds.

Pertinent recent county dates are: *Cooke*—12, 27, and 29 September 1879 and 18 and 19 June 1886 (Ragsdale, original notes); *Dallas*—many sightings between 1956 and 1985, extreme dates 11 May 1956 to 6 October 1963; *Denton*—six records, 7 September 1958 through 2 November 1955; *Ellis*—9 September 1938, and 8 and 15 May 1976; *Fannin*—29 September 1986 (30); *Grayson*—4 to 23 August 1963 (eight to 28 birds), 1 to 25 September 1963 (two), 2 to 24 September 1964 (25 to 50), 20 and 21 July 1982 (five), 12 August 1982 (four) and 6 September 1984 (two); *Kaufman*—7 and 23 July 1978, 24 September 1978, 29 September 1972, and 7 October 1973; *Navarro*—24 June 1975; *Tarrant*—4 and 17 July 1954, and 15 through 27 August 1979; *Van Zandt*—8 September 1986, 25 September 1985, and 28 September and 6 October 1986.

Usually only one or two birds, or a few, are observed, but 140 and 150 were tallied at Cedar Creek Lake, Kaufman County, on 29 September 1972 and 7 October 1973, respectively.
Specimens: Specimens referred to by Oberholser (1974) from Cooke and Denton counties were not located. The only Wood Stork specimen located was one taken from Ellis County on 9 September 1938 (DMNH). The September 1935 specimen referred to by Stillwell (1939) for Trinity Valley (Dallas County) could not be found.

Order Anseriformes

Family Anatidae (Swans, Geese, and Ducks)

FULVOUS WHISTLING-DUCK *Dendrocygna bicolor* (Vieillot)
Status: Accidental.
Occurrence: It is assumed that, like the records for the Black-bellied Whistling-Duck, some but not all, of the records for this unique duck are of wild birds. Those birds known to be released, or with other unusual ducks, were discounted. For example, members of this species were noted on 24 October 1982 wtih Red-crested Pochard (*Netta rufina*) and Mandarin Ducks (*Aix galericulata*) within the city limits of Dallas, Dallas County. A former governor received these wildfowl as a gift and released them near his home; they subsequently disappeared. The county records of Fulvous Whistling-Ducks considered to be wild are: *Dallas* — 26 January 1951 (Baumgartner, 1951); *Tarrant* — 5 April 1964, 16 April 1964, 18 May 1967, and 9 November 1979.

BLACK-BELLIED WHISTLING-DUCK *Dendrocygna autumnalis* (Linnaeus)
Status: Recent invader in the Dallas–Fort Worth area. Nesting in the Dallas area.
Occurrence: Oberholser (1974) gave no records of this whistling-duck for north central Texas. It is always possible that this species, like the Fulvous Whistling-Duck, may be the result of introductions or escapees of captive stock, since most of the records are from heavily populated areas. However, recent sightings suggest a movement of this species from the south (see Cain and Arnold, 1974).

Black-bellied Whistling-Ducks have been reported in four counties: *Collin* — near the Fannin County line a pair were carefully observed on 16 May 1984. The local landowner indicated that they had been present earlier in the year. *Dallas* — all in the southeastern part of the county: a single bird on 10 May 1980, 11 birds on 31 July 1980, about a mile from the earlier site, and six again from 2 and 7 August 1980 — this occurrence became a feature story with photographs in a local Dallas paper; two on 11 April 1981, this and the following sightings in the same area as in the previous year; pair, with 16 small young, on 18 July 1981, last seen 29 September 1981; 31 May 1982, 31 July 1982, and 7 August 1982, all adult birds; 3 and 10 July 1983; a lone bird on 21 April 1984 and four birds on 8 July and 5 August; two on 27 April 1985, off and on during summer and 15 on 2 September 1985. *Johnson* — two adults plus 11 immatures on 22 September 1985 (photograph). *Tarrant* — one on 18 and 19 July 1975, an unconfirmed sighting at a city park in Fort Worth, and six birds at Vil-

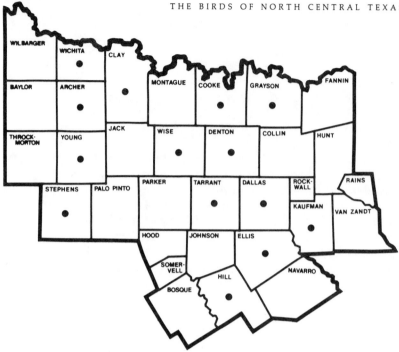

Map 14. Distribution of the Tundra Swan, *Cygnus columbianus*

lage Creek Water Treatment Plant, Arlington, on 4 May 1977, with a lone bird remaining through 17 May. Photographs were taken of the latter group of whistling-ducks.

TUNDRA SWAN   *Cygnus columbianus* (Ord)
Status: Rare winter visitor.
Occurrence: The Tundra Swan, formerly called Whistling Swan, has been reported more often in the northern counties of the study area than in the southern counties. They have been recorded in 14 counties: Archer, Clay, Cooke, Dallas, Denton, Ellis, Grayson, Hill, Kaufman, Stephens, Tarrant, Wichita, Wise, and Young. Most observations are for December and January, yet overall sightings range from 15 November 1959 (Grayson County) to 21 March 1960 (Tarrant County). They apparently fly over north central Texas in migration to the Gulf Coast, and on rare occasions one or two may stop over to rest and to forage at some favorable site. An unlikely number of 15 was reported at White Rock Lake within the city limits of Dallas on 22 December 1971. It is possible these were Mute Swans (*Cygnus olor*), which are frequently kept captive by game-bird fanciers. Members of this species sometimes escape or are released pinioned into city lakes, where they may be misidentified as Tundra Swans. In Texas,

Mute Swans seem to be wholly dependent on man and are seldom, if ever, found in the wild. In recent years Tundra Swans seem to be attracted to stock tanks, where most sightings have been made. They are not reported every year, nor do many actually winter in north central Texas.

Specimens: Tundra Swan specimens are known from three counties: Archer — 3 January 1955 (MWU); Clay — 1 January 1961 (MWU); and Kaufman — December 1969 (DMNH). Specimens mentioned by Oberholser (1974) for Cooke, Dallas, and Grayson counties could not be located.

GREATER WHITE-FRONTED GOOSE   *Anser albifrons* (Scopoli)
Status: Uncommon to rare spring and fall transient. A few may linger in winter.
Occurrence: Greater White-fronted Geese have been observed in 21 counties of the study area: Archer, Bosque, Clay, Collin, Cooke, Dallas, Denton, Fannin, Grayson, Hill, Hunt, Johnson, Kaufman, Palo Pinto, Rains, Somervell, Tarrant, Van Zandt, Wichita, Wilbarger, and Young.

In fall this species usually passes through north central Texas in late September, with its main passage in mid-October. Some typical early-fall arrival dates for selected counties are: *Dallas* — 2 October 1974; *Grayson* — 23 September with an isolated date of 26 August 1982; *Tarrant* — 26 September 1959; *Van Zandt* — 6 October, peaking 15 October 1984 through 10 November; *Wichita* — 3 October 1973.

A few stragglers remain at Hagerman NWR into December, but as soon as it becomes cold they are seldom observed. There is only one January sighting known to me in the Dallas–Fort Worth area — on 2 January 1980 (Tarrant County) — although this may be an oversight, and sightings are not reported. However, these geese can be seen off and on at Hagerman NWR in January.

White-fronted Geese tend to start north early in February and seem to peak in early March. Some typical county early- and late-spring dates are: *Dallas* — 18 February 1967 to 10 April 1982; *Grayson* — 8 February 1981 to 24 April 1981, with an isolated date of 30 May 1950; *Tarrant* — 5 February 1955 to 26 March 1972; *Van Zandt* — 29 January to 30 March 1986; *Wichita* — 11 February 1978.

Hazardous storms occasionally beset flocks of migrating birds. Seventeen white-fronts were killed in such a storm near Terrell, Kaufman County, on 31 October 1977.

Two odd-looking geese were found in a mixed flock of Canada, Snow, and White-fronted Geese at Hagerman NWR on 3 December 1983. They were carefully studied, sketched (drawing in my file), and identified as hybrid Canada and White-fronted Geese.

Specimens: A specimen of this goose from Cooke County, taken by Ragsdale on 15 March (year not given), was considered to be *Anser albifrons*

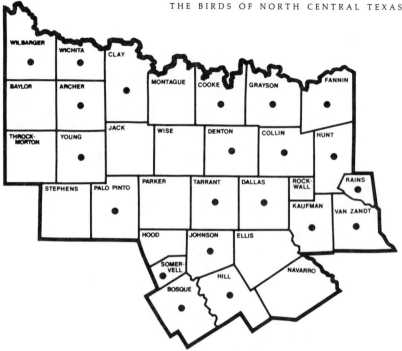

Map 15. Distribution of the Greater White-fronted Goose, *Anser albifrons*

gambelli by Oberholser (1974) but unfortunately was not located. Other specimens were collected at Lake Kickapoo, Archer County, on 2 December 1958 (MWU 16) and in Denton County on 25 February 1947 (DMNH 3360) and 29 November 1949 (DMNH 4327); none of these were identified as to race. Apparently the racial identifications are not clear for north central Texas, and specimens should be reexamined.

SNOW GOOSE *Chen caerulescens* (Linnaeus)
Status: Uncommon to rare migrant. Rare to casual in winter.
Occurrence: Snow Geese have been reported in 26 counties: Archer, Bosque, Clay, Collin, Cooke, Dallas, Denton, Ellis, Fannin, Grayson, Hill, Hunt, Johnson, Kaufman, Montague, Navarro, Palo Pinto, Rains, Rockwall, Somervell, Tarrant, Van Zandt, Wichita, Wilbarger, Wise and Young.

Now that the Blue Goose is considered to be a subspecies of the Snow Goose, distinctions of the two races are not always indicated by observers in their reports. However, the dark race of Snow Geese can usually be found in most north central counties if one searches for it, although it is not as numerous as the white race.

Casual records of "white birds" are clouded by sightings of White Pelicans, which are common throughout north central Texas and are often misidentified. This is particularly true of television weather forecasters reporting early movements in September of "geese," whereas knowledgeable birders have seldom reported Snow Geese before October. For these reasons very few September sightings are included herein, although it is realized that a possible early date or two may have been eliminated that should not have been. The earliest arrival dates of Snow Geese are 22 September (Grayson County) and 2 October 1975 (Dallas County), most arriving in mid-October. Spring passage is early, most moving through in February to mid-March. The latest date is 30 May (Grayson County), and the next-latest dates are 13 May 1972 (Tarrant County) and 25 April 1979 (Dallas County). A 2 June 1977 date at Hagerman NWR may have been a sighting of an injured bird. There are actually fewer observations for spring than for fall. Data on hand do not indicate that north central Texas is on the main flyway of the Snow Geese to and from the coast.

Very few Snow Geese winter in the area, although a few can usually be found at Hagerman NWR (Grayson County). In 15 years (1968–82) of CBCs at this count, there was an average of less than 50 birds, with a minimum count of two (1969) and a maximum count of 300 (1977). In populated areas where there are many birders, a few geese are also reported in winter, but not often on the CBCs. They have been reported on only four of the ten CBCs.

Summer reports of this species are usually of injured birds. This is true of an immature that remained with captive geese in a display pond at Hagerman NWR for two summers (1951 and 1952).

Specimens: Specimens of this species have been collected in Archer (MWU), Clay (MWU), Cooke (TNHC), and Denton (DMNH) counties. Both color races are represented in the latter collection of specimens.

Ross' Goose   *Chen rossii* (Cassin)

Status: Rare winter resident.

Occurrence: Ross' Geese have been reported in Dallas, Grayson, and Wilbarger counties during the winter from mid-November to late March. A few can usually be found on both sides of Lake Texoma at the Tishomingo NWR, Oklahoma, and the Hagerman NWR, Grayson County, if one carefully examines the Snow Geese flocks that normally occur.

This goose was not reported in north central Texas before the 1960s. There is a vague report of one shot in Wilbarger County during the winter of 1956–57 (Oberholser, 1974); however, if one was shot, the location of the specimen is unknown. The only valid record for Wilbarger County was a bird banded in Saskatchewan, Canada, on 24 October 1962 and shot on the Waggoner Ranch on 20 December 1962. This may be the banded bird said to have been shot (1961) in Baylor County (Oberholser, 1974), although the U.S. Fish and Wildlife Service has no other records of Ross'

Geese for north central Texas. One goose spent about a week from 23 to 30 January 1982 near Lake Ray Hubbard, Dallas County, and was seen by many observers.

Haller (1978) reviews the sightings from the Hagerman NWR, Grayson County, from 1965 through 1978. Since that time they have been found every winter, the greatest number being 12 to 40 (winter 1985–86), and most reports are of adult birds. The extreme dates listed were 9 November 1965 to 27 March 1977.

A Ross' Goose took up residence with a local population of ducks and geese (mainly domestic) in the winter of 1983–84. It still remained at a local man-made lake at a light-industrial plant on the outskirts of Sherman, Grayson County (January 1986).

On 3 December 1983 two "blue-phase" Ross' Geese were observed and carefully studied by a group of birders at the Hagerman NWR. Blue- and white-phase Snow Geese were nearby for comparison of the birds.
Specimens: Two Ross' Geese were found dead from pesticides, along with white-fronted and Canada Geese, on 6 January 1981 at Hagerman NWR, Grayson County. The heads and feet of these birds were saved (KH, WMP) for the record.

Brant   *Branta bernicla* (Linnaeus)
Status: Casual winter visitor, may be considered accidental by some authorities since the species normally occurs along the Atlantic and Pacific coasts.
Occurrence: Records of this goose are from two counties — Grayson and Wilbarger — in the study area near or on the Red River and only where there are concentrations of Canada Geese. In addition, they have been reported from adjacent Knox and Lamar counties. They were also observed in Oklahoma (Sutton, 1967), in Johnson County, across Lake Texoma from Grayson County, on 14 November 1955 and from 5 November to 29 December 1964.

Specific records from the study area are: *Grayson* — all from Hagerman NWR, 10 December 1954, 1 through 7 March 1957, 20 through 26 October 1957 (six), 30 November to 28 December 1969, 11 through 14 January 1970, 6 November 1976, and 12 and 18 October 1978; *Wilbarger* — south of Vernon, 28 December 1956 (shot and mounted). A report of two Brants shot during the winter period of 1956 (Baumgartner, 1957, given as Mrs. I. D. Acord) may actually refer to the above record. However, according to Peggy Acord, the reference was only a sight record. Records for adjacent counties are: *Knox* — 15 December 1968; *Lamar* — Gambill Goose Refuge, 9 through 25 January 1969 (may have been present longer).

Formerly Brants (*Branta bernicla*), or "white-bellied" birds, and Black Brants (*B. nigricans*), or "black-bellied" birds, were recognized as two distinct species. Today they are considered two subspecies. In north central Texas only *B. b. nigricans* has been documented by a specimen (Henderson, 1960); however, *B. b. hrota* has been sighted in north central Texas.

A hunter furnished me with a photograph (on file) of a *B. b. hrota* shot at the headwaters of Lake Texoma, Love County, Oklahoma, across the lake from the Cooke-Grayson county line. This example was prepared as a wall mount and is still in the hunter's possession.

The sightings of "black-bellied" and "white-bellied" forms in the field are somewhat artibrary. It is usually the decision of an observer who is unfamiliar with the two forms or who has nothing with which to compare the two in the field. There also are intergrades of the two forms.

CANADA GOOSE *Branta canadensis* (Linnaeus)
Status: Overall fairly common to uncommon migrant. Common to fairly common in the counties along the Red River. In some years, populations winter in some counties.
Occurrence: Canada Geese have been recorded in 27 counties of north central Texas: Archer, Baylor, Bosque, Collin, Cooke, Dallas, Denton, Ellis, Fannin, Grayson, Hill, Hunt, Johnson, Kaufman, Montague, Navarro, Palo Pinto, Rains, Rockwall, Somervell, Stephens, Tarrant, Van Zandt, Wichita, Wilbarger, Wise, and Young. No doubt Canada Geese pass through or occasionally even winter in some of the unrecorded counties; however, lack of observers precludes sightings. Many observations of Canada Geese are no more than sightings of unidentified geese flying over the area.

In migration these stately geese normally pass through north central Texas on their way south to the Gulf Coast, a few going into Mexico, from early October to November and returning north in January through mid-March. Some typical extreme arrival and departure county dates are: *Dallas* – 2 October 1981 and 18 April 1967; *Grayson* – 20 September 1980 and 8 April 1978; *Kaufman* – 2 October 1974 and 9 March 1974; *Tarrant* – 21 September 1973 and 3 April 1954; *Wichita* – 16 October 1976 and 3 March 1974.

The game warden on the Waggoner Ranch, south of Vernon, Wichita County, informed me that in the early 1950s probably 60,000 Canada Geese wintered on the ranch and the nearby prairies. He estimated that by 1982–83 only 7,000 to 8,000 geese wintered in the area. At the time Bellrose wrote his book (1976), he gave a population of 25,000 (undated) for this area.

In some winters when favorable habitat conditions prevail, Canada Geese remain. This is particularly true of the counties along the Red River. At the Hagerman NWR, Grayson County, the annual CBCs (1968–84) have averaged 5,200 Canada Geese, with a maximum of 10,604 (1970) and a minimum of 1,265 (1982). For other counties winter records may be absent. Canada Geese are more likely to winter inland than are other species of geese recorded for north central Texas.

In the late 1940s, 80 to 100 Canada Geese were taken to the Hagerman NWR, pinioned, and released. Some young were produced off and on from this release until about 1969. Since then only an occasional goose has been reported during the summer, and in 1975, four goslings were seen in late May with a pair of Canada Geese. Other nesting records for north central Texas that are known to me likely represent Canada Goose stock introduced into the area by game-bird fanciers. Examples are the geese in Dallas, Denton, Henderson, and Tarrant counties. Some records of summer birds represent sightings of crippled or injured birds lingering in a particular area rather than breeding birds. North central Texas is not the normal nesting range of this species.

The U.S. Fish and Wildlife Service attempts to trap and band Canada Geese at many of its refuges. Records received from Hagerman NWR personnel show that this species was banded from 1962 to the winter period of 1970–71. The records indicate that approximately 495 geese were recovered. Of these, 17 percent were recovered 10 or more years after the banding date. Two of the oldest geese recovered were more than 16 years old, and another was more than eighteen years.

Many Canada Geese were recovered in the vicinity of Hagerman NWR on both sides of the Red River, in Oklahoma and Texas. South of the refuge recoveries were numerous, mainly along the central Gulf Coast and south to the Rio Grande valley of Texas, although there were a few recoveries from southern Louisiana. One was even recovered in Kentucky. A few apparently wintered south of the U.S. border in Mexico (mainly Tampico).

A few geese fanned out to each side of the states directly north. Numerous recoveries were made in Kansas, South Dakota, and North Dakota. To the northwest, in Colorado, and to the northeast, geese were recovered as far as the Horican Marshes in Wisconsin and parts of Iowa and Minnesota.

According to the banding data provided to me by refuge personnel, Canada Geese were recovered in five provinces and the Northwest Territories of Canada: 17 in Manitoba, 15 in Saskatchewan, two in Ontario, one each in Alberta and Quebec, and seven in the Northwest Territories. In general, recovery data at hand were consistent with Bellrose's data (1976). *Specimens:* Unfortunately, the subspecific identification of Canada Geese has been poorly worked out for the area. Some races cannot be distinguished except in the hand. Although a number of birds have been taken during the hunting season, very few examples have found their way into scientific collections. Specimens from the following counties have been located: Archer (MWU), all of December and January; Baylor (MWU), late December; Dallas (DMNH 1658), 28 May 1941 (though I question this date); Denton (DMNH 2321, missing), 27 March 1943, 29 November 1949 (DMNH 4321 and 4329); Wilbarger (CMNH 30421), late December, said to be the race *Branta canadensis moffitti*. The specimens indicated for Cooke and Tarrant counties by Oberholser (1974) were not located.

It appears that three races of Canada Geese occur in north central Texas, a smaller race *hutchinsii* (Richardson's Goose) and the larger races *interior* and *moffitti*, with a possible fourth race, *parvipes*. It is said that *moffitti* was the race brought to the Hagerman NWR in the late 1940s for breeding purposes. More specimens of Canada Geese should be preserved and deposited in museums for study since the subspecies ranging into north central Texas are poorly understood.

WOOD DUCK *Aix sponsa* (Linnaeus)
Status: Uncommon to rare transient. Fairly common to uncommon winter resident. Uncommon to rare nesting species. More apt to be found along the eastern half of the study area than the western half.
Occurrence: Wood Duck sightings are more numerous in north central Texas in recent years due to an increase in man-made impoundments, a possible decrease of hardwood habitat on the east, and better protection.

In north central Texas this beautiful duck has been recorded for Archer, Baylor, Bosque, Clay, Collin, Cooke, Dallas, Denton, Fannin, Grayson, Hill, Hood, Hunt, Jack, Johnson, Kaufman, Montague, Navarro, Palo Pinto, Parker, Rains, Rockwall, Somervell, Stephens, Tarrant, Van Zandt, Wichita, Wilbarger, Wise, and Young counties, as well as adjacent Henderson and Shackelford counties.

Usually only a few Wood Ducks are spotted, but in recent years their numbers have increased. Large groups have been recorded, mainly in the counties on the eastern side of the study area. Some large numbers are: Grayson County—Hagerman NWR, 238 on 22 December 1970 and 140 on 19 December 1981; Hunt County—Greenville City Lake, 150 on 3 January 1978 and more than 100 feeding in a field near Quinlan on 31 August 1982; Tarrant County—about 100 at Greer Island on 5 October 1963 and 300 on Fort Worth CBC on 18 December 1982.
Nesting: Oberholser (1974) gave nesting records for Baylor, Dallas, Denton, Grayson, Tarrant, Wise, and Young counties. To these can be added my own records for Cooke, Hunt, Johnson, Palo Pinto, Parker, Van Zandt, and Wichita counties, as well as Dallas, Denton, Grayson, and Tarrant counties. It is likely that this species nests in many if not all of the north central Texas counties, for there are numerous reports of Wood Ducks from many of the counties during the nesting season.

Recent nesting dates for selected counties are: Cooke — two immature birds, 29 July 1982; Dallas — mainly White Rock Lake and the southeastern parts of the county; numerous reports of young from 20 April 1985, eight small young, to 20 August 1981, four young; Hunt — near Quinlan, at nest boxes in 1983–85; Grayson — Hagerman NWR, summer 1970, 12 young, on 2 August 1982, seven downy young; Johnson — "pair nested," 1983 (Williams, 1983); Parker — Mineral Wells SP, 28 June 1977, four young; Tarrant — Arlington, nesting in chimney of house on 19 April 1973, Fort Worth Nature Center, eight young on 29 June 1979; Van Zandt — Edgewood City Lake, 10 May 1984, eight young; Wichita — Lucy Park, Wichita Falls, 25 May 1975, eggs in a hole of a cottonwood.

Specimens: Numerous specimens are available. Since this beautiful duck is legally hunted, there are a number of mounted specimens from other counties in the possession of duck hunters that I am not aware of. Known examples of Wood Ducks are from Clay (MWU), Dallas (WMP), Denton (DMNH), Grayson (OU, WMP), Hunt (DMNH), Tarrant (DMNH, FWMSH, UTA), Wise (FWMSH), and Henderson (WMP) counties, all taken during winter periods. The one taken in Cooke County (Oberholser, 1974) could not be located.

GREEN-WINGED TEAL   *Anas crecca* Linnaeus

Status: Common migrant, occasionally abundant. Fairly common to uncommon in winter.

Occurrence: These little ducks have been reported from all of the counties in north central Texas. Green-winged Teals are common transients, with some individuals wintering. Overall they have been recorded from 13 August 1980 (Cooke County) to 24 May 1967 (Dallas County). They do not arrive as early as Blue-winged Teals, and few are observed until September. Spring migration seems to end early. There are a few June and July reports, probably representing injured birds, for there is no evidence of nesting in the north central Texas study area.

Except for the Lake Tawakoni CBC, they have been reported on all of the CBCs in the area, and they are much more numerous than Blue-winged Teals. During the ten years (1968–77) of CBCs from Fort Worth, Tarrant County, they averaged 106 birds compared with 27 Blue-winged Teals.

Extreme arrival and departure dates for selected counties are: *Dallas* — 16 August 1977 to 24 May 1967; *Grayson* — 28 August 1986 to 9 May 1977; *Palo Pinto* — 4 September 1976 to 29 April 1978; *Tarrant* — 16 August 1986 to 13 May 1972; *Van Zandt* — Lake Tawakoni, 24 August 1980 to 16 April 1983; *Wichita* — 29 September 1973 to 14 May 1976.

Specimens: Green-winged Teals have been collected in 11 counties: Archer (MWU); Cooke (TNHC); Dallas (WMP); Denton, mount (DMNH); Ellis (DMNH), missing yet cataloged; Fannin (WMP); Grayson (UTA); Hunt

(WMP); Tarrant (WMP); Wichita (MWU, WMP); and Wilbarger. The specimen (Oberholser, 1974) for Wilbarger County was not located.

AMERICAN BLACK DUCK *Anas rubripes* Brewster
Status: Casual winter visitor.
Occurrence: Oberholser (1974) records this species in ten counties—Baylor, Dallas, Denton, Grayson, Fannin, Hunt, Navarro, Wichita, Wise, and Young. This study adds no new counties to the list.

Since 15 January 1976, when one was captured, carefully examined, and banded at Hagerman NWR, in Grayson County, there have been no valid records, although there are occasional reports, especially from Dallas and Grayson counties. Two Hagerman CBC records on 20 December 1976 and 20 December 1980 are questionable. Others are even more unlikely and no doubt in error. There has been a definite decline of this species since the mid-1930s throughout north central Texas.

Sighting of this species should be made with extreme care, since it can be confused with the Mottled Duck, which is extending its range northward from the coast. Any duck hunter who shoots a duck suspected of being a Black Duck should save it for proper identification.
Specimens: The only specimen known to me is an old one collected in the 1930s in Dallas County on 15 April 1936 (DMNH 70). The specimen listed for Wichita County (Oberholser, 1974) has not been located.

MOTTLED DUCK *Anas fulvigula* Ridgway
Status: Rare to casual visitor. Recent nesting records.
Occurrence and Nesting: This coastal duck appears to be spreading its range northward. There are more reports in recent years for north central Texas, with most for spring and summer. The Mottled Ducks have been reported from seven counties: *Collin*—two at Lake Lavon, which may have been this species, on 1 May 1982; *Dallas*—autumn 1926 and 14 April 1936, both by Stillwell (1939); 21 June to 15 August 1970, may have bred (Oberholser, 1974); 17 April to 21 July 1978, young noted on latter date, 28 September 1984, 5 May 1985, and 6 September 1986; *Grayson*—". . . a probable . . . nested at Hagerman NWR"; no specific date, summer 1983 (Williams, 1983); the refuge checklist (1984) does not list the species for Hagerman NWR; *Hunt*—Lake Tawakoni, 6 September (about eight) until 10 October 1982, 28 September 1983; *Kaufman*—Cedar Creek Lake, 10 October 1971; *Palo Pinto*—Possum Kingdom Lake, 27 December 1981; *Rains*—Lake Tawakoni, 16 December 1984, 6 January 1985, and 26 May and 3 June 1985, two seen with five young on 30 June on through July, August to 8 September 1985, 29 December 1985, and again nesting in 1986.
Specimens: Although Stillwell (1939) indicated that there were specimens for Dallas County, they are not at the Dallas Museum of Natural History.

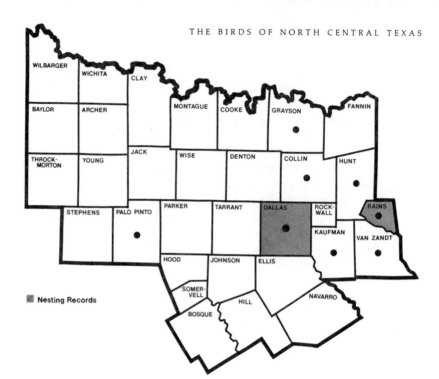

Map 16. Distribution of the Mottled Duck, *Anas fulvigula*, with nesting records

Mayer may have mounted these birds for patrons, or the specimens may have been lost. The records for Kaufman (SFASU) and Palo Pinto (WMP 2733) counties represent the only known specimens for north central Texas.

MALLARD   *Anas platyrhynchos* Linnaeus
Status: Common migrant. Fairly common some winters. Nests sparsely locally.
Occurrence: This popular waterfowl has been reported in all of the counties in north central Texas as well as the adjacent counties.

Data on hand indicate that Mallards have increased over the last 20 years, probably because of a reduction of habitat in east Texas and an increase in permanent impoundments in the study area. They have been reported the year round in many counties, particularly in heavily populated centers. However, it is difficult to evaluate the status in these areas since some Mallards, particularly those in the urban areas of Dallas and Tarrant counties, are the descendants of domestic stock that went wild. In earlier years the Texas Parks and Wildlife Department released in Fannin County brood stock reared from captive birds.

Away from urban centers Mallards are transients from early September to mid-May. Typical arrival and departure dates for selected counties are:

Dallas — 7 August 1976 to 13 June 1970; *Grayson* — Lake Texoma at Cooke county line, 3 August 1981 to 25 March, when most depart; *Palo Pinto* — 18 September 1976 to early April, and an isolated date of 31 July 1976; *Tarrant* — 9 August 1953 to 14 May 1966; *Wichita* — 9 September to 14 June (Zinn, 1974).

This species has been observed on all the CBCs for north central Texas. In some years, depending on habitat and weather conditions, large numbers are seen, and in other years in small numbers. For example, if west Texas playa lakes contain water, Mallards shift to that area. Hagerman CBCs averaged about 4,800 Mallards in 15 years (1968–82). They are not as numerous on other counts, yet it is not uncommon to find more than 1,000 Mallards in various counties.

Nesting: Surprisingly, nesting reports are meager for north central Texas, except in areas where much birding takes place. Most are from the southeastern part of the study area. The counties are: Dallas — many records, if not all, may be Mallards diluted with domestic brood stock. In recent years (since 1975 to 1985) there are a number of reports of this species producing young from White Rock Lake and the southside water-treatment plant area. Denton — eight young on 23 May 1984. Grayson — very few reports, nest with eggs in May or June 1958 (Hagerman NWR), several other suspicious records during the breeding season since, but no nests or young until 5 July 1984, when a female and five small ducklings were observed. Rains — eight young on 9 July 1983, and three young on 2 July 1986. Tarrant — 14 August 1954 (Pulich, 1979). Wilbarger — formerly at Watt's Lake (More and Strecker, 1929), a habitat that no longer exists. Henderson — ". . . breeding near Athens, . . . spring, 1939" (Stillwell, 1939).

Specimens: Specimens have been collected from the following counties: Archer (MWU), Cooke (TNHC), Denton (DMNH), Palo Pinto (WMP), and Tarrant (FWMSH). Those mentioned by Oberholser (1974) for Throckmorton and Wichita counties were not located. There are probably numerous unrecorded trophies from other counties of this popular game bird in the possession of hunters.

NORTHERN PINTAIL   *Anas acuta* Linnaeus
Status: Common migrant. Fairly common some winters. Formerly nested in the northwestern part of the study area.
Occurrence: This beautiful large duck has been reported in all study-area counties except Clay and Jack. It has also been reported in adjacent Comanche, Eastland, and Shackelford counties. Although it is more commonly observed in late September, possibly because early drakes are in eclipse plumage and are easily overlooked among the arriving puddle ducks in mid-August, it seems to be one of the earliest waterfowl to appear.

Early and late departure dates for selected counties are: *Dallas* — 10 August 1976 to 25 May 1967; *Grayson* — 27 July, next-earliest 9 August 1978 to 21 May, with isolated records of 13 June, 18 June, and 30 June; *Tarrant* — 14 August 1955 to 27 May 1976; *Wichita* — 18 September 1975 to 5 May 1974, with an isolated date of 3 June 1974; *Wilbarger* — 10 May 1983.

Nesting: There is no evidence of nesting today, though Oberholser (1974) lists breeding in 1928 (Wilbarger County) and in 1939 (Baylor County). In Wilbarger County it formerly nested at Watt's Lake (More and Strecker, 1929); however, this marsh area no longer exists. It is unlikely that it will nest there again, since all of the suitable marsh habitat has been eliminated. Other summer records (July) for several counties (Dallas, Denton, Grayson, and Palo Pinto) are likely of stragglers or injured birds.

Specimens: Northern Pintail specimens have been taken mainly in the winter (28 November through 13 March) in the following counties: Archer (MWU), Cooke (TNHC), Denton (DMNH), Ellis and Navarro (TCWC), Tarrant (DMNH, WMP), and Wichita (MWU). Oberholser (1974) also indicated that pintails were taken from Baylor, Dallas, Fannin, Johnson, Kaufman, Wilbarger, and Young counties, but none of these specimens were located. These birds may have been shot by hunters and not saved as specimens, since this is a popular game species.

BLUE-WINGED TEAL *Anas discors* Linnaeus

Status: Common to abundant migrant. Uncommon to rare in winter. Rare local summer resident.

Occurrence: The Blue-winged Teal is the most abundant of the three species of teal occurring in north central Texas. It has been reported from all of the counties in the study area and in nearby Comanche, Eastland, and Shackelford counties.

This species has been reported in every month of the year in many locales. The birds arrive very early, even mid-July, although in some instances they may be nonbreeding birds that linger through the summer. Transients are common by the end of August, dropping off in numbers by October. Those that do not winter start to return by March, becoming abundant in late April and early May and a few lingering into early June.

They have been observed on all of the CBCs except in the Caddo National Grasslands, although in some years they may be absent from some CBCs, depending on habitat conditions. They do not seem as abundant in the northern counties during the winter, withdrawing with cold weather. January dates are meager throughout the area.

Nesting: Besides the breeding records noted by Oberholser (1974) for Dallas, Tarrant, Wilbarger, and Young counties, there is a recent record for Hunt County of four young seen on 19 May 1978. Nesting records are scattered, but lack of habitat may preclude more nesting in north central Texas. The last nesting for Dallas County was on 9 April 1985, when young were observed within the city limits of Dallas.

Specimens: Blue-winged Teal specimens are known from the following counties: Bosque (SM), Clay (USNM), Dallas (DMNH), Denton (WMP), Hill (SM), Palo Pinto (WMP), Rockwall (DMNH), Tarrant (DMNH, FWMSH), and Wichita (MWU, WMP). A Wilbarger County specimen (Oberholser, 1974) was not located.

The Clay County specimen (USNM 141426) taken on 19 April 1894 was identified as *A. d. orphna* (misspelled in Oberholser, 1974). Of the other specimens examined not all proved to be *A. discors.*

CINNAMON TEAL   *Anas cyanoptera* Vieillot

Status: Uncommon to rare transient, mainly in the spring. Few valid records in the fall.

Occurrence: The Cinnamon Teal has been observed in 17 north central Texas counties: Archer, Baylor, Clay, Collin, Dallas, Denton, Ellis, Grayson, Hunt, Johnson, Kaufman, Montague, Palo Pinto, Parker, Tarrant, Wichita, and Wilbarger.

The status of the Cinnamon Teal in fall is uncertain and poorly understood, since no fall specimens have been collected from north central Texas, and nearly all reports are unqualified. Any birds that pass through north central Texas in the fall must do so very early in the season, if they pass through the area at all.

Since the male of this species arrives in an eclipse plumage, and females and immature males cannot be distinguished from Blue-winged Teal, many fall observations are likely to be misidentifications. Zinn (1975) assumed birds to be recognizable at Wichita Falls on 25 August 1973 and 24 August 1974. In the local checklist (1976) for this area she has far too many fall records; not all of them can be correct. These are highly unlikely and have been dismissed. There are also a number of unqualified refuge reports from Hagerman NWR, Grayson County, between 2 August 1979 and 21 November 1946. Only one entry of 300 in the refuge files may be valid. One bird that showed cinnamon color was reported on 6 November 1946, but this report, too, can be questioned. Another, observed on 17 and 23 September 1984, in Tarrant County was said to have been a red-eye, a characteristic used to separate this species from Blue-winged Teal.

A hunter brought me an odd-colored teal taken on 30 October 1977 at the headwaters of Lake Texoma, opposite Cooke County in Marshall County, Oklahoma, which looked like a Cinnamon Teal but on careful study proved to be *A. discors.* The specimen in question had been stained with a fine red powdery soil, possibly from the Washita River drainage that empties into Texoma from the Oklahoma side of the lake.

Map 17. Distribution of the Cinnamon Teal, *Anas cyanoptera*

Random samples of teal shot at one of the local Dallas County hunting clubs produced only one Cinnamon Teal in eight years (December 1962). This, however, could have been an early spring migrant.

Taking culmen measurements, I examined about 40 teal collected on 17 September 1978 at Possum Kingdom Lake, Palo Pinto County, and none proved to be Cinnamon Teal. Late dates in October and November are also not very plausible, and, unless details are given, they should be discounted. Ideally, samples of teal should be collected in August and early September. If waterfowl hunters would save heads during the hunting season of teal suspected of being Cinnamon Teal, the species could be easily identified.

Spring migration starts early. It is not unusual to find a drake in full spring color in December. Cinnamon Teals have usually been observed from late January through April; most of the reports for the area are for February. Typical spring dates for selected counties are: *Dallas* — 7 December 1966 through 20 May 1971; *Grayson* — 25 December 1981 through 21 April 1977; *Palo Pinto* — 1 January 1978 through 17 April 1976; *Tarrant* — 16 December 1972 through 16 May 1971.

Specimens: Cinnamon Teal specimens have been reported from the following north central Texas counties: Dallas — 29 March 1942 (DMNH 1871);

Denton—2 March 1939 (DMNH 599), 16 April 1940 (DMNH 1313); Ellis —28 February 1938 (DMNH 286); Palo Pinto—7 January 1978 (WMP 2388); and Wichita—21 March 1956 (MWU 40). The specimen referred to by Oberholser (1974) for Wilbarger County could not be located.

NORTHERN SHOVELER *Anas clypeata* Linnaeus
Status: Common transient. Fairly common winter resident.
Occurrence: This puddle duck has been observed in 28 counties of north central Texas: Archer, Baylor, Bosque, Clay, Collin, Cooke, Dallas, Denton, Fannin, Grayson, Hill, Hunt, Johnson, Kaufman, Navarro, Palo Pinto, Parker, Rains, Rockwall, Somervell, Stephens, Tarrant, Throckmorton, Van Zandt, Wichita, Wilbarger, Wise, and Young. Since it is a common duck of north central Texas, it probably occurs in all of the counties.

Normally, shovelers are found from early September to late May, with more birds observed in migration. Peak of passage is from October through early November and again from mid-February into early April. Late June, July, and early August dates likely represent stragglers or injured birds, for there is no evidence that this species nests in north central Texas. It is not uncommon to see a pair or two of nonbreeding birds lingering into June.

Representative county dates are: *Dallas*—3 August 1982, next-earliest 24 August 1982 to 19 June 1970, next-latest 3 June 1968; *Grayson*—isolated date of one in eclipse plumage on 7 July 1983, next-earliest 26 August 1986 to 7 May 1977; *Tarrant*—4 August 1984, next-earliest 23 August 1983 to 23 June 1956, next-latest 31 May 1980.

Although they have been reported on all but one of the CBCs, they are never as numerous during the winter. They seem to be scarce on the western side of the study area in comparison with the eastern side.
Specimens: Specimens were found in the following counties: Archer (MWU), Cooke (TNHC), Dallas (WMP), Denton (DMNH), and Wichita (MWU). Those indicated by Oberholser (1974) for Clay and Wise counties were not located.

GADWALL *Anas strepera* Linnaeus
Status: Common to fairly common transient. Fairly common to uncommon in winter.
Occurrence: Gadwalls have been reported in all counties of the north central Texas study area except Parker County. Overall, they have been reported from early August to early June, with several isolated records for 1 July 1978 (Grayson County) and 31 July 1971 (Tarrant County). They are more numerous from mid-October to April.

Typical county dates of early arrivals and late departures are: *Dallas*— 2 August 1980, next-earliest 14 August 1977 to 2 June 1935, 1967, and an isolated date of 19 June 1970; *Grayson* — 9 August 1976 to 9 May 1977 (probably later dates); *Palo Pinto* — 3 September 1977 to 15 May 1976; *Rains* — 15 October 1978 to 27 May 1983; *Tarrant* — 14 August 1978 to 2 and 5 June 1964; *Wichita* — 30 September 1974 to 19 May 1976.

They have been reported on all CBCs in north central Texas; however, most probably withdraw to the south during severe weather, though there are always a few in secluded areas.

Nesting: Oberholser (1974) has a record of a Gadwall allegedly nesting in Dallas County (4 July 1961), which may have been in error because Mallards commonly nest in the area where the Gadwall was reported. This and one record for the Panhandle of Texas are the only nesting records for the state of Texas. There are no records from Oklahoma, and in recent years nesting by Gadwalls to the west in New Mexico and Arizona has been said to have declined.

Specimens: Specimens are available from the following counties: Archer (MWU), Cooke (TNHC), Dallas (DMNH), Denton (DMNH), Hood (FWMSH), Johnson (SUC), Tarrant (DMNH), and Wichita (MWU). Specimens indicated by Oberholser (1974) for Baylor and Wilbarger counties were not found.

EURASIAN WIGEON   *Anas penelope* Linnaeus
Status: Accidental visitor.
Occurrence: Males of the Eurasian Wigeon are strikingly different from the males of the American Wigeon and are probably identified correctly, if observers are competent and careful. Females of this species are very similar to female American Wigeons and are usually overlooked. However, all sightings should be qualified with details before being accepted. There are no documented records (photographs or specimens) for north central Texas.

This Old World duck has been reported from three counties in the study area: *Dallas* — Stillwell (1939) reported them for three years, specimen on 24 April 1936 and sight records in 1937 and 1938. Unfortunately, the Dallas Museum of Natural History has no record of the specimen example, though it was said to be at the museum. The latter two years probably represent no more than unqualified, vague sightings. For these reasons the early reports must be questioned. There is, however, a valid sight record of a male that spent time with American Wigeons near Lake Ray Hubbard from 27 February through 9 March 1982. Many observers saw this bird repeatedly on many occasions. *Johnson* — A male Eurasian Wigeon was observed by several persons at a stock tank during the fall of 1982. *Tarrant* — A sighting given for 27 March 1966 by Williams (1966) was dismissed. See Pulich (1979) for details.

AMERICAN WIGEON *Anas americana* Gmelin
Status: Common transient. Fairly common to uncommon winter resident.
Occurrence: In fall migration the American Wigeon is the next waterfowl to appear after the teal and the pintail. Overall this species is normally found from early September to late May, becoming common in October and decreasing in numbers by mid-November. Some winters it has been observed on all CBCs. It moves back north in February, and most have gone through by early April. There is no evidence of nesting. I know of no late June or July occurrences in north central Texas. If there are sightings, they likely are of injured birds or birds unable to migrate.

Wigeons often forage in grassy areas and have been seen grazing with Canada Geese. They prefer fresh waters, particularly the backwaters of lakes and ponds.

This species has been reported from all the counties of the study area. Typical county dates are: *Dallas* – 2 August 1980, next-earliest 22 August 1937 through 2 June 1967, next-latest 24 May 1967; *Grayson* – 3 September 1981 through 26 May; *Palo Pinto* – 4 September 1976 through 9 May 1976; *Tarrant* – 2 September 1972 through 29 May 1955; *Wichita* – 16 September to 2 June 1975, next-latest 31 May.
Specimens: Specimens have been taken from the following counties: Archer (MWU), Cooke (TNHC), Dallas (DMNH), Denton (DMNH), Ellis (TCWC), Hood (FWMSH), Hunt (ETSU, not located), Tarrant (WMP), and Wichita (MWU). Those indicated by Oberholser (1974) for Wilbarger and Wise counties were not located. With the exception of an Ellis County specimen taken 30 March 1970, all were taken during winter hunting seasons.

CANVASBACK *Aythya valisineria* (Wilson)
Status: Common to fairly common migrant. Uncommon in winter. More abundant in some years than others.
Occurrence: This popular waterfowl is found on large bodies of open water and has been recorded in all but two counties – Hood and Jack – of the study area. No doubt it passes through these counties and probably even occasionally winters as well. It has also been recorded in adjacent Shackelford County.

The Canvasback seems to be one of the last regular diving ducks to arrive in and depart from north central Texas. Although there are year-round observations in a few counties, they definitely were of crippled or injured birds. This is true for this species when they were observed in Dallas County during the summers of 1970 through 1972.

Extreme arrival and departure dates for selected counties are: *Dallas* – 5 October 1977 to 22 May 1965; *Grayson* – 7 October to 21 April; *Palo Pinto* – an isolated date of 24 September 1975, next-earliest 16 October

1977 to 22 May 1976; *Tarrant*—10 October 1980 to 27 May 1956; *Wichita*—24 October 1976 to 23 May 1975.

This large duck arrives in mid-October, and a few occur in north central Texas until May. The greatest numbers are found in November, and again in late February and early March during migration periods. The winter population varies, depending on habitat conditions and weather, but they have been found on all of the CBCs except on the Caddo National Grasslands.

Specimens: Canvasback specimens are known from Archer (MWU), Denton (DMNH), Ellis (DMNH), Grayson (DMNH), and Tarrant (DMNH) counties. Those said to have been collected in Cooke and Wilbarger counties (Oberholser, 1974) could not be found.

REDHEAD   *Aythya americana* (Eyton)

Status: Common to fairly common migrant. Uncommon in winter.

Occurrence: Redheads have been recorded in 24 counties of north central Texas: Archer, Baylor, Bosque, Collin, Cooke, Dallas, Denton, Ellis, Fannin, Grayson, Hill, Hunt, Jack, Johnson, Montague, Palo Pinto, Rains, Somervell, Tarrant, Van Zandt, Wichita, Wilbarger, Wise, and Young. Although there are scattered sightings the year round in some counties, this diving duck is usually found on large impoundments from mid-October to May. The greatest numbers are found in late October and early November. Some counts of large numbers are from the following counties: Dallas —2 November 1982 (1,000), 22 March 1959 (600), 19 March 1960 (1,000); Grayson—25 October 1975 (1,500 plus); Palo Pinto—16 October 1977 (large numbers with Canvasbacks); Tarrant—20 February 1982 (1,200).

Typical early-arrival and late-departure dates for selected counties are: *Dallas*—1 October 1978 and 14 June 1967, next-latest 25 May 1967; *Grayson* —an isolated date of 25 August, next 25 September to 2 May, next-latest 17 April; *Hunt*—22 October 1977 and 1 June 1975, next-latest 3 May 1975; *Palo Pinto*—8 October 1977 and 14 June 1970; *Rains*—15 October 1986; *Tarrant*—unprecedented date of 1 August 1965, next-earliest 26 September 1967, and 3 June 1959; *Wichita*—30 September 1974, next-earliest 19 October 1974 and 22 April 1974.

Although many Redheads pass on to the coast, where they winter, they have been reported on all of the CBCs except the Caddo National Grasslands and Lake Tawakoni counts. Their numbers are never very numerous on the CBCs.

Specimens: Redheads have been collected from Archer (MWU), Dallas (DMNH, UTA), Denton (DMNH), Johnson (SUC), and Kaufman (DMNH) counties. Redheads indicated by Oberholser (1974) for Baylor and Cooke counties could not be located.

Ring-necked Duck   *Aythya collaris* (Donovan)
Status: Fairly common migrant and winter resident.
Occurrence: Ring-necked Ducks are usually found from early October to May. The height of migration is in early November and again in February into early March. Records for summer months probably represent stragglers or injured birds unable to migrate. They have been reported in 28 counties: Archer, Baylor, Bosque, Collin, Cooke, Dallas, Denton, Ellis, Fannin, Grayson, Hill, Hood, Hunt, Jack, Kaufman, Montague, Navarro, Palo Pinto, Parker, Rains, Rockwall, Stephens, Tarrant, Throckmorton, Van Zandt, Wichita, Wise, and Young. It is likely that they also occur in the remaining counties but have not been reported. They have also been recorded in adjacent Henderson and Shackelford counties.

Some typical fall arrival dates and spring departure dates for selected counties are: *Dallas* — 2 October 1977 and 25 May 1967; *Grayson* — 3 September 1977, next-earliest 7 September, and 31 May; *Hunt* — 4 October 1979 and 22 May 1985 (nearby Van Zandt); *Palo Pinto* — 24 October 1976 and 14 May 1978; *Tarrant* — 29 September 1956 and 14 May 1966.

A few Ring-necked Ducks are always found in north central Texas during the winter. They have been reported on all of the CBCs. Although usually seen in small flocks, they have been noted in the hundreds, during both migration and winter periods. They often frequent small stock tanks, but they are equally at home on large bodies of water.
Specimens: Ring-neck specimens are available from the following counties: Archer, four specimens (MWU); Cooke, two specimens (TNHC); Dallas (WMP); Denton (DMNH); Henderson, mount (DMNH); and Tarrant (FWMSH). The specimen indicated by Oberholser (1974) for Grayson County could not be located.

Greater Scaup   *Aythya marila* (Linnaeus)
Status: Extremely rare transient. More winter dates than migration dates.
Occurrence: The Greater Scaup has been recorded in the following counties: Archer, Baylor, Bosque, Clay, Collin, Dallas, Denton, Fannin, Grayson, Hunt, Palo Pinto, Tarrant, and Wichita. Very likely because there are more bird-watchers in recent years, they have produced more Greater Scaup records; however, some sightings must be taken with reservation. Pulich (1979) warns birders of sight records because this species is similar to the Lesser Scaup, and, unless all details were given, some records have been excluded.

This species should be looked for from mid-November through early May. Nowhere in north central Texas is the Greater Scaup common, and seldom are more than a few spotted — usually a bird or two — often among

Map 18. Distribution of the Greater Scaup, *Aythya marila*

flocks of Lesser Scaup. The largest number seen at one time that I know of was ten on 22 February 1981 (Dallas County). There are scattered sight records from 6 November 1971 (Grayson County), next-earliest 9 November 1979 (Palo Pinto County) to 10 May 1975, next-latest 9 May 1963 (both for Dallas County). Surprisingly, there appear to be no valid April dates. A June date (Oberholser, 1974) for Denton County very likely represents a misidentification or an injured bird.

Specimens: Specimens of Greater Scaup have been collected from the following counties: Archer—18 December 1955 (MWU 60), Dallas—24 December 1964 (WMP 1454), and Palo Pinto—28 December 1976 (WMP 2307).

LESSER SCAUP *Aythya affinis* (Eyton)

Status: Common to fairly common migrant and winter resident.

Occurrence: Although the Lesser Scaup has been observed in 26 of the 32 counties of the north central Texas study area—Archer, Baylor, Bosque, Clay, Collin, Cooke, Dallas, Denton, Ellis, Fannin, Grayson, Hill, Hood, Hunt, Johnson, Kaufman, Navarro, Palo Pinto, Rains, Rockwall, Somervell, Tarrant, Van Zandt, Wichita, Wise, and Young—it should be found in every county during migration. Unfortunately, some counties lack regular observers, and this species is frequently missed in these counties.

There are sightings of this species throughout the year in many counties, although it does not nest in the study area. Summer records (June through August) are likely of cripples or birds unable to migrate. This scaup is normally found from late October until early April.

Extreme early and late dates for selected counties are: *Dallas* — 6 September 1970 to 25 May 1968; *Denton* — 3 October 1979; *Grayson* — 7 September to 29 May; *Palo Pinto* — 22 September 1978 to 14 May 1978; *Tarrant* — 6 October 1953 to 14 May 1954; *Wichita* —18 October 1975 to 30 March 1976.

They have been seen on all the CBCs of north central Texas, the numbers varying with the season, the availability of food, and weather conditions. They never seem to be quite as numerous in spring migration. During the peak of passage it is not uncommon to see hundreds of scaup, occasionally 1,000 or more. In recent years their numbers seem to be down, although no serious study of the population has been undertaken.

Specimens: There are Lesser Scaup specimens from the following counties: Archer (MWU), Clay (MWU), Dallas (WMP), Denton (DMNH), Hood (FWMSH), and Wichita (MWU). Specimens indicated by Oberholser (1974) for Collin, Ellis, and Kaufman counties were not located.

OLDSQUAW   *Clangula hyemalis* (Linnaeus)

Status: Rare to casual transient, mainly in winter.

Occurrence: This distinctive arctic duck has been observed in seven north central Texas counties, mainly during the winter. Surprisingly, however, it has not been reported in the study area since 1977. Usually this sea duck accompanies other diving ducks, and sightings are of single birds.

Some county dates are: *Archer* — 27 November 1959. *Clay* —1 December 1976 through 28 February 1977. *Dallas* — numerous records from the 1960s to the mid-1970s, none since 1975. Records range from 25 October 1975, next-earliest 1 November 1975, with scattered records to 12 May 1935 (Kelley, 1935), a questionable record of five given without details, next-latest 4 April 1970. *Denton* — 2 December 1940, 14 January 1974. *Grayson* —13 March to 19 March 1969, 1 and 2 March 1970, 6 and 7 November 1971 (five to seven), 21 December 1974 (three); *Kaufman* — 23 December 1967 (two), and 7 January 1977; *Tarrant* — 2 January to 17 April 1960, 11 and 13 February 1971.

Specimens: Specimens have been taken from the following counties: Archer on 27 November 1959 (MWU 69); Dallas on 26 December 1947 (DMNH 3687), 27 January 1950 (DMNH 4438, 4439), and 5 February 1950 (DMNH 4453), others indicated as taken by Mayer (Stillwell, 1939) not located;

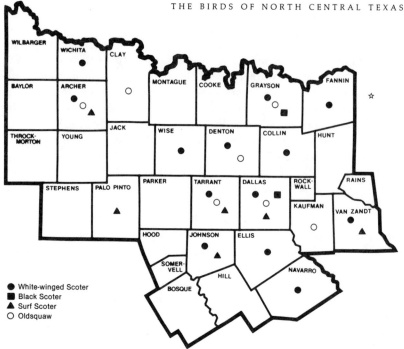

Map 19. Distribution of the Oldsquaw, *Clangula hyemalis;* the Black Scoter, *Melanitta nigra;* the Surf Scoter, *M. perspicillata;* and the White-winged Scoter, *M. fusca*

Denton on 2 December 1940 (DMNH 1438), and another said to be at NTSU (Rylander, 1959) not located; and Kaufman (two females) on 23 December 1967 (DMNH 5699, 5700) and on 7 January 1977 (in private collection, E. Stratton, Dallas).

BLACK SCOTER   *Melanitta nigra* (Linnaeus)
Status: Accidental in north central Texas.
Occurrence: This is the rarest of the three scoters that reach north central Texas and is seldom reported. It has been reported from only two counties: *Dallas* — a lone bird lingered at the west-side water-treatment ponds from 17 November to 23 December 1966; Bachman Lake on 9 February 1967 (two); returned to the 1966 location from 4 November to 30 December 1967; from another part of the county on 6 April 1968 (Williams, 1968); southside water-treatment ponds on 6 May 1973; White Rock Lake on 2 February 1975; southside water treatment ponds on 25 October to 8 November 1975. Some of the isolated dates since 1967 may be questionable, since only one or two persons saw the birds in question. Black Scoters can easily be confused with Surf Scoters and even Ruddy Ducks

in winter plumage. *Grayson* — one reported and carefully observed at Loy Lake by two persons on 28 November 1975.
Specimens: There are no Black Scoter specimens or photographs for north central Texas.

Surf Scoter *Melanitta perspicillata* (Linnaeus)
Status: Rare to casual fall transient. One spring sighting.
Occurrence: There are reports of this rare maritime duck from six counties: *Archer* — 22 December 1965; *Dallas* — single birds from 1964 through 1969 and in 1975 five spotted on 29 October, overall period 25 October 1975 to 12 December 1975, with no sightings since or any spring records; *Johnson* — 30 October to 4 November 1972; *Palo Pinto* — the only spring date for north central Texas is a surprisingly late date of 14 May 1972; *Tarrant* — 9 through 29 November 1973, and 26 January to 15 March 1986; *Van Zandt* — Lake Tawakoni, an immature or female on 10 November 1984.
Specimens: Surf Scoters were collected in Archer County on the same date as that given above (MWU 70) and in Dallas County on 5 December 1965 (WMP 1482).

White-winged Scoter *Melanitta fusca* (Linnaeus)
Status: Rare to casual transient.
Occurrence: White-winged Scoters have been recorded in 13 north central Texas counties and adjacent Lamar County, primarily during migration. The dates for the study area range from 20 October (Grayson County) to 30 April (Wichita County). Most dates are for November; there are none for March. Details for the counties are: *Archer* — 5 November 1955; *Collin* — 27 October 1934, alleged specimen (Oberholser, 1974); *Dallas* — old records in the 1920s (Stillwell, 1939), then none until the 1960s through 1975, with extreme dates from 30 October 1975 to 19 February 1966; *Denton* — 5 January 1977; *Ellis* — winter period 1976–77 (Williams, 1977); *Fannin* — fall sight record (Oberholser, 1974); *Grayson* — 20 October 1980, 3 to 9 November 1960; *Johnson* — 23 to 30 October 1981, 28 April 1968; *Navarro* — 28 November 1984; *Tarrant* — 20 and 21 October 1948; *Van Zandt* — 10 November 1984; *Wichita* — 30 April 1979; an early date of 26 September given in the local checklist (Zinn and Moore, 1976) was not accepted; *Wise* — Stillwell (1939) indicates that a specimen was taken by Mayer on 27 October 1934.
Specimens: Specimens of the White-winged Scoter are known from Archer County (MWU 71), Dallas County (WMP 1749), and adjacent Lamar County — Lake Pat Mayse, no date, mounted specimen (WMP). Early specimens said to have been taken from Collin (Oberholser, 1974), Dallas, and Wise counties (Stillwell, 1939) could not be located.

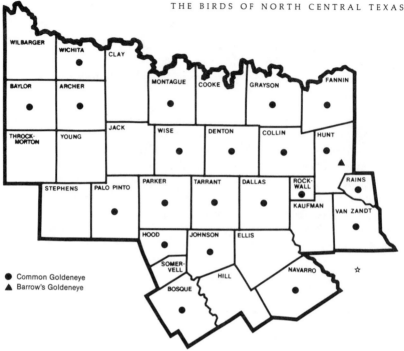

Map 20. Distribution of Common Goldeneye, *Bucephala clangula,* and Barrow's Goldeneye, *B. islandica*

COMMON GOLDENEYE   *Bucephala clangula* (Linnaeus)
Status: Uncommon to rare winter transient.
Occurrence: Common Goldeneyes have been reported from 21 counties of the study area — Archer, Baylor, Bosque, Collin, Dallas, Denton, Fannin, Grayson, Hood, Hunt, Johnson, Montague, Navarro, Palo Pinto, Parker, Rains, Rockwall, Tarrant, Van Zandt, Wichita, and Wise — and nearby Henderson County.

This species arrives late compared to most other diving ducks, and is usually observed from late November to early March. It has been sighted on all the CBCs except the Caddo National Grasslands. Some extreme early or late dates for north central Texas counties are: *Dallas* — 14 October 1934 (Stillwell, 1939), next-earliest 5 November 1968 and 1 May 1971 (exceptionally late), next-latest 13 April 1966; *Denton* — 12 November 1941 and 16 April 1944; *Grayson* — 24 October and 14 April, with an isolated date of 1 May 1980; *Tarrant* — 12 October 1940 and 8 May 1976.

It is not uncommon to find large numbers of Common Goldeneyes wintering on large bodies of water, varying with weather conditions and habitat. Some flocks of 200 to 300 were counted at Possum Kingdom Lake, Palo Pinto County, on 18 and 19 December 1976; an estimated 310 at Lake

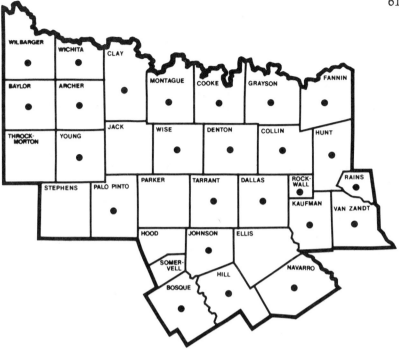

Map 21. Distribution of the Bufflehead, *Bucephala albeola*

Bridgeport, Wise County, on 4 January 1984; and 400 at Lake Texoma, Grayson County, on 5 February 1977.

Specimens: Specimens have been taken from the following counties: Archer (MWU), Dallas (DMNH), Denton (DMNH), Ellis (DMNH), Hunt (DMNH), Kaufman (DMNH) and Wichita (MWU).

BARROW'S GOLDENEYE *Bucephala islandica* (Gmelin)
Status: Accidental in north central Texas.
Occurrence: There is only one record of Barrow's Goldeneye for north central Texas, a male taken by a hunter at Greenville, Hunt County, on 6 November 1958. Oberholser (1974) reports that two females were collected with the male, although the whereabouts of the females are unknown. The male specimen (mount) in question is still in the possession of Tom Cole, of Greenville.

BUFFLEHEAD *Bucephala albeola* (Linnaeus)
Status: Fairly common to uncommon winter resident.
Occurrence: This beautiful little duck, often called "butterball" by hunters, has been recorded in 25 north central Texas counties: Archer, Baylor, Bosque, Clay, Collin, Cooke, Dallas, Denton, Fannin, Grayson, Hill, Hunt,

Johnson, Kaufman, Montague, Navarro, Palo Pinto, Rains, Rockwall, Tarrant, Van Zandt, Wichita, Wilbarger, Wise, and Young. It is very likely that they occur in other counties but have not been recorded. They have been reported on all the CBCs, although not every year.

Buffleheads are usually found from early November to early April. Extreme dates for selected counties are: *Dallas* — 28 October 1968 to 10 May 1967; *Grayson* —1 November 1980 to 6 March 1971; *Palo Pinto* — 29 October 1977 to 9 April 1971; *Tarrant* —13 October 1973 to 11 May 1968; *Rains* — Lake Tawakoni, 11 November 1984 to 11 May 1984; *Wichita* — 2 November 1976 to 17 April 1975.

Specimens: Specimens have been taken in the following counties: Archer (MWU), Cooke (TNHC), Dallas (DMNH), Denton (DMNH), Grayson (WMP), and Kaufman (DMNH). Specimens indicated for Clay and Navarro counties (Oberholser, 1974) were not located.

HOODED MERGANSER   *Lophodytes cucullatus* (Linnaeus)
Status: Uncommon to rare winter visitor. One nesting record.
Occurrence: Hooded Mergansers have been recorded in 23 counties: Archer, Baylor, Clay, Collin, Cooke, Dallas, Denton, Ellis, Fannin, Grayson, Hunt, Johnson, Kaufman, Navarro, Palo Pinto, Rains, Rockwall, Stephens, Tarrant, Van Zandt, Wichita, Wilbarger, and Wise. Of the three species of mergansers, this species is the most abundant, preferring small ponds as well as streams, and the most likely to be encountered. Red-breasted and Common mergansers are more often seen on large bodies of water during migration. Many times the latter two mergansers are so far out on a lake that they are missed or are not identified by bird-watchers.

Hooded Mergansers appear to have a decided preference for the eastern part of the north central Texas study area, where more birding takes place. They are often found with Wood Ducks in similar habitat.

This merganser is usually found from mid-November to early March. Extreme county dates are: *Archer* — 3 November 1965 to 30 April 1976 (Baylor County); *Dallas* — 20 October 1973 to 22 April 1937; *Grayson* — 24 October 1978 to 30 March, and a male seen from 10 April to early July 1986; *Hunt* — 30 October 1983 to 11 March 1981; *Tarrant* —1 November 1980 to 29 March 1986, and a lone male as late as 11 May 1986.

At times it is not uncommon to see more than 100 Hooded Mergansers on some of the CBCs, particularly during the winter period. For example, the mean for 1978–82 on Hagerman NWR CBCs was 121, with the maximum of 237 and a minimum of 52.

Nesting: A female Hooded Merganser accompanied by five nearly full-grown young was observed at the Woodland Basin Nature Preserve at Lake Ray Hubbard, Dallas County, from 30 May to 3 June 1987. The city of

Garland has set aside riparian habitat as a nature study area along Rowlett Creek as it enters the lake. Numerous Wood Duck nesting boxes have been put up, and it is possible that the Hooded Merganser found one of these boxes suitable for its nesting requirements, although the actual nesting site was not located. Numerous persons visited Woodland Basin to see the birds. This record represents the first nesting occurrence of this species for north central Texas.

Specimens: Specimens are available from the following counties: Archer (MWU), Clay (MWU), Dallas (DMNH, WMP), Denton (DMNH), Ellis (DMNH), Grayson (WMP), Hunt (DMNH), Tarrant (FWMSH), Wichita (MWU), and Wilbarger (MWU). The specimen indicated by Oberholser (1974) for Wise County was not located.

COMMON MERGANSER *Mergus merganser* Linnaeus
Status: Rare winter visitor.
Occurrence: Of all the mergansers that visit north central Texas, this species is seen the least often and usually only on large bodies of water. It has been recorded in 17 counties: Archer, Baylor, Bosque, Dallas, Denton, Ellis, Grayson, Hood, Hunt, Johnson, Navarro, Palo Pinto, Tarrant, Van Zandt, Wichita, Wise, and Young. Sightings range from mid-November to early March; most of the observations are for December and January.

Extreme first and last dates for selected counties are: *Dallas* — 7 November 1938 and 4 April 1985; *Grayson* —18 October and 1 April; *Tarrant* — 21 October 1950 and 8 March 1953.

Large numbers of Common Mergansers are not often observed, but on 13 February 1977 a phenomenal number of 2,000 was estimated in a mile-long raft of ducks at Hagerman NWR, Grayson County. An estimated 400 to 600 were found during the severe winter of 1983–84 at Lake Bridgeport, Wise County.

Specimens: There are Common Merganser specimens for Archer (MWU), Palo Pinto (DMNH), and Tarrant (DMNH) counties. A merganser shot from Navarro County (Ogilby, 1882) was not located, nor was a specimen indicated for Dallas County (Stillwell, 1939).

RED-BREASTED MERGANSER *Mergus serrator* Linnaeus
Status: Rare winter visitor.
Occurrence: Red-breasted Mergansers, like Common Mergansers, are not observed every year, and when they are seen, they are mainly on large reservoirs. They have been reported from only 16 counties: Archer, Baylor, Clay, Collin, Cooke, Dallas, Denton, Grayson, Hill, Hunt, Palo Pinto, Rains, Tarrant, Van Zandt, Wichita, and Wise.

This merganser is usually found from mid-November to early May.

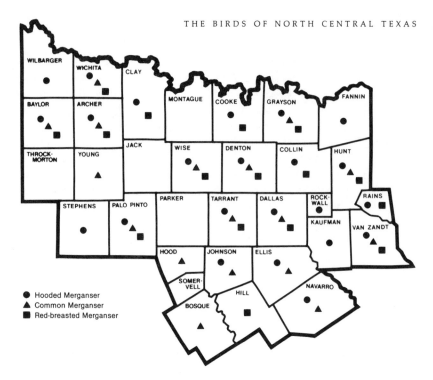

Map 22. Distribution of the Hooded Merganser, *Lophodytes cucullatus;* the Common Merganser, *Mergus merganser;* and the Red-breasted Merganser, *M. serrator*

The earliest arrival record is 27 October 1974 (Wichita County); all other records are for November. The latest spring date, probably a sighting of an injured bird or one unable to migrate, is 9 June 1978 (Dallas County); all other records are for May. Typical county dates are: *Dallas* – 7 November 1971 to 4 May 1958; *Grayson* – 8 November 1979 to 18 April; *Rains* – 3 November 1984 to 28 April 1985; *Tarrant* – 10 November 1973 to 2 May 1966; *Wichita* – 22 November 1976 to 11 May 1974.

Sightings are usually of a single bird or a few birds. The largest number reported was 90, about 60 percent females, on 22 November 1978 at Hagerman NWR, Grayson County, while 100 were observed on 23 December 1984 at Lake Tawakoni, Rains County. They are seldom seen on the annual CBCs, having been reported only twice on the Hagerman CBC and once each on the Lake Ray Hubbard and the Lake Tawakoni CBCS. *Specimens:* Specimens have been taken from Archer County (MWU) and Denton County, (DMNH, mounted), while one said to have been taken from Dallas in 1934 (Stillwell, 1939) by Mayer was not located. It may have been mounted for a waterfowl hunter and not deposited in a scientific collection.

A.P.

RUDDY DUCK   *Oxyura jamaicensis* (Gmelin)
Status: Common to fairly common migrant. Fairly common to uncommon winter resident. Several isolated nesting records.
Occurrence: The Ruddy Duck has been observed in 23 counties of north central Texas — Archer, Baylor, Bosque, Clay, Collin, Cooke, Dallas, Denton, Fannin, Grayson, Hill, Hunt, Johnson, Kaufman, Navarro, Palo Pinto, Rains, Rockwall, Tarrant, Van Zandt, Wichita, Wilbarger, and Wise — and adjacent Henderson County.

Although there are year-round records for some counties, this species is usually found only from early October to late May in most of the area. No doubt scattered June reports represent late transients or ruddies unable to migrate.

Typical county arrival and departure dates are: *Dallas* — 8 September 1972, next-earliest 27 September 1970 to 5 June 1983, next-latest 31 May 1982; *Grayson* — 7 October 1978 to 24 April 1971; *Tarrant* — 26 September 1980, next-earliest 10 October 1983 to 29 May 1955; *Wichita* — 18 October 1974 to 16 May 1974, with an isolated date of 14 June 1974.

It has been reported on most of the CBCs (except McKinney and Lake Tawakoni), although some years it is absent from some of the other counts. At times, apparently depending on habitat conditions, it has gathered in flocks of several hundred in the Dallas area; in the winters of 1970–1972 up to 1,000 Ruddy Ducks were not an uncommon sight. On 27 February 1977 an estimated 3,800 were found at Hagerman NWR.
Nesting: There are two nesting records: 5 and 6 June 1970, Johnson County

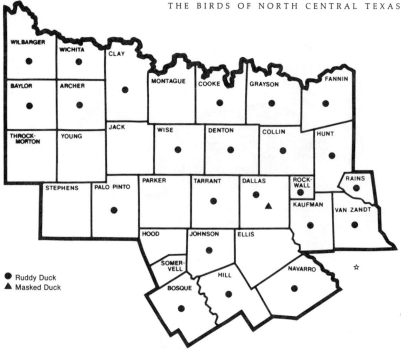

Map 23. Distribution of the Ruddy Duck, *Oxyura jamaicensis,* and the Masked Duck, *O. dominica*

(not Tarrant County as reported by Oberholser [1974]; see Pulich, 1979), and on 8 through 29 August 1981, when an adult and seven immatures were seen by many persons in Dallas County. In two other years (1967 and 1970) it was suspected of breeding in Dallas County, but nesting was never confirmed.

Specimens: Specimens are available from Archer (MWU), Dallas (WMP), Denton (DMNH), Grayson (OU), and Henderson (DMNH) counties. The specimens indicated from Cooke, Navarro, Wilbarger, and Wise counties (Oberholser, 1974) could not be located.

MASKED DUCK   *Oxyura dominica* (Linnaeus)
Status: Accidental.
Occurrence: The Masked Duck is principally a tropical species that formerly reached Texas only as far north as the Rio Grande valley. In the late 1960s it made its way to the upper coast of Texas, and more recently it has been found inland. As in other unusual waterfowl sightings, extreme care should be exercised in identifying this species. It resembles the Ruddy Duck, a near relative.

There are two reports of the Masked Duck from Dallas County. The first includes one on 18 July and two on 22 August 1970 (Oberholser, 1974). Bellrose (1976) apparently researched the *American Birds* (1971) and noted reference to only one Masked Duck on the latter date. The first record for Dallas is questionable, since the two references differ from Oberholser's reference in the number of Masked Ducks and occurrence of the first date (18 July). It is unfortunate that *The Bird Life of Texas* (1974) did not give details to document this rare duck. The second record was on 2 April 1977, when a female Masked Duck was found with Ruddy Ducks at a water-treatment plant in west Dallas and stayed for two days. During this time numerous persons viewed and carefully studied the bird.

Order Falconiformes

Family Cathartidae (New World Vultures)

BLACK VULTURE *Coragyps atratus* (Bechstein)
Status: Resident of all but seven counties of the northwestern and western parts of the study area. Becoming more and more abundant toward the east.
Occurrence: I have no Black Vulture records for Archer, Baylor, Clay, Stephens, and Throckmorton counties, and only one record each for Wichita (undated sight record) and Wilbarger (nesting, see details below) counties. These counties are a part of the high plains, which somehow tend to act as a barrier. This species is a vulture of east Texas — found regularly all year round along the Red River; west to about the eastern edge of Montague County; then south through much of Wise County to the vicinity of Lake Bridgeport, in Jack County; then west to Graham County (rarely), proceeding southwesterly to Possum Kingdom Lake, Palo Pinto–Young counties, and west to the town of Metcalf Gap. It is a bird more of the wooded areas than its congener, the Turkey Vulture. It is absent from the heavily populated urban areas of Dallas–Fort Worth, although it is observed rarely in the southwestern portions of Dallas County. It does, however, regularly reach the northwestern part of Tarrant County (upper Lake Worth). Formerly it must have been more numerous, but in recent years there has been a decided decline of this species throughout north central Texas. Habitat elimination, pesticides, and the reduction of food (carrion) all have had adverse effects on this species and the Turkey Vulture.

There are still a number of roosts in north central Texas, where up to 100 Black Vultures can be found, although no systematic attempts to locate vulture roosts have been undertaken in this study. Some known roosts

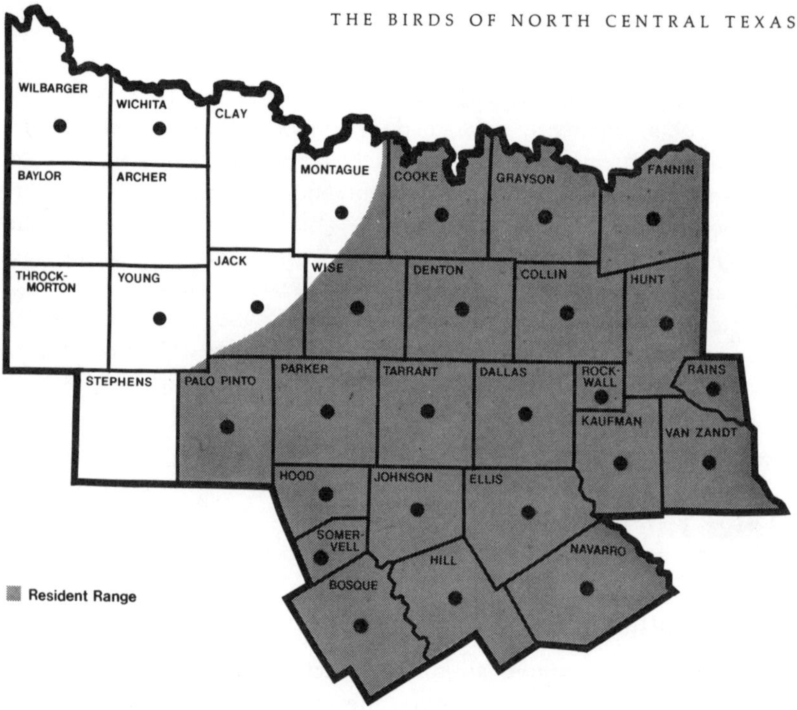

Map 24. Distribution of the Black Vulture, *Coragyps atratus*, with resident range

are: Meridian SP (Bosque County), Moss Lake (Cooke County), Hagerman NWR (Grayson County), Possum Kingdom Lake (Palo Pinto County), the Fort Worth Nature Center (Tarrant County), and Van Zandt County. In all instances they were found in lesser numbers with Turkey Vultures. *Nesting:* Nesting records were given by Oberholser (1974) for six counties, all being old records. Some of the details, as best as can be determined from his data, are presented: Cooke — probably Ragsdale's record, who was particularly active in the Gainesville area before the turn of the century; nesting sites are likely where habitat still remains today. Dallas (Stillwell, 1939) — breeding, no details, and no records since, and today not to be expected. Tarrant (Sutton, 1938) — old record 1915. Urban activities have removed most habitats. Wilbarger (Oberholser, 1974) — the only record of eggs was said to have been taken on 21 April 1930, and no sighting of even a single Black Vulture since this date; this county does not have typical habitat unless some remains along the Red River. Wise (Donald and More, 1894) — egg dates, 3 March 1889 to 24 May 1887. No nesting in present century. Young (Oberholser, 1974) — no details, probably before the turn of the century; habitat has changed in this county, and it is not very likely that this species will be found nesting here.

More recent nesting records are from Bosque County, but details are vague; however, personnel at Meridian SP indicate nesting. There are numerous places in the county where this species could nest, and it is seen there the year round. Denton — nest discovered in greenbrier thicket on 17 April 1971 (young and egg, two young banded on 14 May), and it was found nesting again in the same thicket on 27 February 1974 (two eggs); limited habitat still remains. Fannin — downy young found near Bonham and brought to the Heard Museum, McKinney, on 3 May 1980. Hunt — two eggs laid in barn, 11 April 1985, unsuccessful, eggs destroyed by predators. Tarrant — a recent record in the northwest part of the county when two eggs were discovered on the ground on 25 February 1986. Van Zandt — Black Vultures usually do not build a nest but lay their eggs on the ground in dense thickets or in large hollow tree stumps. They have also been found in old hay barns and deserted buildings. A pair of Black Vultures was suspected to be nesting high above the ground in a heronry on Mill Creek, near Edgewood. On 4 July 1986 a reliable observer noted that a short-tailed vulture remained sitting in a Great Blue Heron's nest when others were startled and flew away.

Unfortunately, records on young vultures brought to the north central Texas bird rehabilitation centers are kept inaccurately and are poorly documented. If these organizations would keep more detailed records, significant data might be acquired today on nesting vultures.

Specimens: The only specimen for north central Texas that I am aware of is one in my collection, taken from Collin County (WMP 1857).

TURKEY VULTURE   *Cathartes aura* (Linnaeus)
Status: Common summer resident throughout the area. Rare to uncommon during the winter, absent from the northwestern part of the study area.
Occurrence: This New World vulture has been reported in all of the counties in the north central Texas study area, as well as the adjoining areas. In summer it is found in all the counties; however, in the winter it is absent from the western side of the study area. There are no winter records for Archer, Baylor, Stephens, Throckmorton, and Wilbarger counties. There are very few sightings at this time of the year for Clay, Jack, Montague, Wichita, and Young counties. Records for Wichita County indicate that most are absent from about 30 September until late March; the earliest is 20 March (nearby Clay County). The abundance in winter elsewhere depends on the severity of weather and the food supply, a conclusion that appears to be confirmed by the annual CBC numbers.

As in the case of the Black Vulture, urban areas hold little interest for this species, and it is rarely seen in Dallas County, and then usually in outlying areas or occasionally over the cities during migration periods. They are found in the southern portion of Tarrant County, where cattle ranching continues, and in the northwestern corner at a roost in the upper

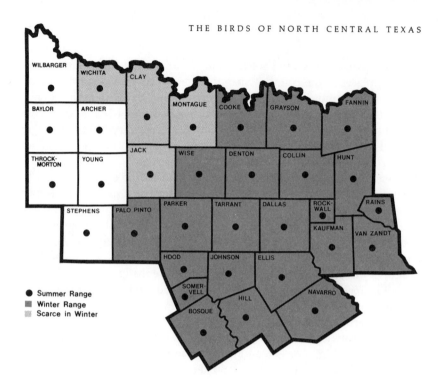

Map 25. Distribution of the Turkey Vulture, *Cathartes aura*, with summer and winter ranges

Lake Worth area. Turkey Vultures are decidedly more numerous than Black Vultures throughout north central Texas.

Except at roosts Turkey Vultures are usually observed singly or in small numbers as they forage, but one observer estimated approximately 1,500 going south in Hood County before the arrival of a cold front on 2 November 1968.

The idea that this species is declining may be questioned since there has been no thorough study of this species. The annual CBC data may be misleading, since participants tend to concentrate on roosts, which are influenced by numerous other factors and may present erroneous data. *Nesting:* Oberholser (1974) cites nesting for Cooke, Dallas, Jack, Tarrant, Wilbarger, Wise, and Young counties and indicates a questionable record for Fannin County. The only county nesting data that can be added are: Bosque—20 May 1979 (two downy young); Dallas—near Coppell, 5 June 1980 (young about three weeks old taken from an old barn); Grayson—no actual nesting data; said to nest at Hagerman NWR, but no details given; Hunt—20 May 1984 (two young, photograph); Palo Pinto—27 April 1974 (one egg). In several other counties—Denton, Collin, Hill, Somervell, and

Wichita — nesting was assumed but not confirmed. It is very likely that, if a study were undertaken, Turkey Vultures would be found nesting in most if not all of the counties except Dallas and Tarrant, which are heavily populated. Unfortunately, searching for nests today to gain a better understanding of many nesting avian species in north central Texas does not interest many persons. If readers find untended Turkey Vulture chicks, they can be readily identified from Black Vulture chicks. Turkey Vulture chicks are downy white compared to the buffy to dirty gray color of Black Vulture chicks.

Specimens: Specimens of Turkey Vultures are available for the following counties: Archer (MWU), Bosque (SM), Cooke (TCWC), Grayson (OU), Johnson (SUC), Tarrant (FWMSH, UTA), Van Zandt (WMP), and Wise (mounted, DMNH).

Oberholser (1974) indicates *C. a. teter* to be the principal subspecies of the area. He cites a specimen taken at Fort Worth on 21 May 1955 as being identified by me as *C. a. septentrionalis* (FWMSH). This, however, may be in error since I originally sent the specimen to Oberholser for subspecific confirmation (see Pulich, 1961); however, the specimen could not be located for reevaluation (Pulich, 1979).

Family Accipitridae (Osprey, Kites, Eagles, and Hawks)

OSPREY *Pandion haliaetus* (Linnaeus)

Status: Fairly uncommon to common migrant. Uncommon to rare in winter locally. No nesting records.

Occurrence: Ospreys have been reported from all the counties in north central Texas. This species is found wherever there are large bodies of water, although I have observed them feeding at stock tanks less than three acres in size in Wilbarger County. They are probably more abundant than many persons realize. Records show that they are more commonly found along the eastern half of the project area, probably because there are more birders in these areas as well as more water impoundments.

Ospreys are regular transients in north central Texas with very few winter records. Those reported in December likely represent stragglers that have not left the area because the weather has remained mild. There are no winter records for the northwestern part of the study area (Wichita County). Along the rest of the Red River there are few December and still fewer January records after the cold weather sets in. Most winter records are from the southern part of the study area.

Ospreys are usually seen singly, but occasionally more are seen: five were observed on 12 April 1950 on the Red River below Denison Dam, Grayson County, and four were reported on Lewisville Lake on 14 April

1985. Most Ospreys are seen in fall from mid-September to late October and in spring from mid-April to early May. Extreme dates for selected counties are: *Dallas* — 7 September 1970 (mean 24 September, ten years) to 27 May 1971 (mean 14 April, nine years). A limited number of sightings for December and January, latest 29 January 1967, and none for February. A 25 June 1960 (Baumgartner, 1960) report of 11 on the ground with a Golden Eagle was dismissed as erroneous. *Denton* — 27 August 1985 to 15 May 1985; none for February. *Grayson* — 7 September 1969 to 4 May 1978, with an isolated date of 14 June 1959 (Marshall County, on the Oklahoma side of Lake Texoma). There are several December and January dates and one on 17 February 1973. *Hunt* — Lake Tawakoni, 17 August 1986 to 20 November 1983 (Rains County), and 13 March 1983 to 26 May 1985 (Rains County). There is one date for December and none for January. *Palo Pinto* — 3 September 1978 to 22 May 1977, and an isolated date of 23 June 1984. Several December and January dates but none for February or March. *Tarrant* — 31 August 1986 to 21 November 1973, and 26 March 1975 to 30 May 1973. Six winter sightings, 14 and 16 December 1986, 15 December 1973, 30 December 1944, 12 January 1980, 22 January 1979, and 14 February 1982. There are no sightings for June or August. *Wichita* — considered rare by local birders, 10 September 1976 to 29 October 1973 (Clay County), and an isolated date of 5 June 1973.

Although it formerly bred in Texas (though never in north central Texas) there is an unexplainable sighting on the Brazos River, Hood County, on 3 July 1966. Several August reports lack details, and, if valid, they represent extremely early fall migrants.

Specimens: Specimens are known only from Denton County (DMNH, seven specimens; WMP, two specimens).

AMERICAN SWALLOW-TAILED KITE   *Elanoides forficatus* (Linnaeus)
Status: Casual transient, formerly many more records. Nested in north central Texas before 1900.
Occurrence: This beautiful subtropical species was never abundant in north central Texas. Early records, however, indicate that they occurred in Cooke, Dallas, Denton, Fannin, Kaufman, Navarro, Tarrant, Wise, and Young counties. According to data at hand, they probably reached their greatest number in Navarro County. In the 1870s they could be found along the cottonwood-lined banks of Richland Creek from April until the end of August (Ogilby, 1882). Some nested there, and in the middle of July they would visit the prairies, where up to 200 birds (young and old) gathered.

Swallowtails were typically kites of wooded areas, and many sightings were undoubtedly of migrants or of birds out of their normal range. Records given by Oberholser (1974) are mainly for spring and fall. Ragsdale's original notes showed that they nested in Cooke County in the mid-1880s.

Mayer (Stillwell, 1939) stated that Swallow-tailed Kites migrated regularly through Dallas in 1915. Preferring low wetlands along heavily wooded rivers and creeks, this species may have declined because of environmental changes that no longer favor it.

Recent county records include: *Cooke* — 4 September 1973; *Dallas* — 29 April 1982, Lorch Park, Duncanville; *Denton* — one on 26 August 1966, with a small flight of Mississippi Kites, at Garza-Little Elm Reservoir (now Lewisville Lake); *Hill* — 31 August 1980, near Aquilla Creek; *Tarrant* — October or November 1964, near Benbrook Lake, not 15 May 1965 but 13 May (Pulich, 1979).

Specimens: The American Swallow-tailed Kite specimen said to have been collected in Cooke County (Oberholser, 1974) has not been located.

BLACK-SHOULDERED KITE   *Elanus caeruleus* (Desfontaines)
Status: Rare visitor.
Occurrence: Oberholser (1974) considered the White-tailed Kite, as it was formerly called, accidental in north central Texas. He gave one observation of a bird seen at Lake Dallas, Denton County, on 2 April 1949, and one adjacent to the study area, a sighting from Freestone County on 4 January 1972. Most of the records in the past and even today are coastal.

The number of sightings for north central Texas has increased considerably since 1980. Although rare, observations are becoming regular, particularly in Navarro County. The mild weather of the 1982–83 winter may account for the almost "explosive" number of reports in six different locations. Although no actual nest was found, kites were seen regularly during the summer of 1980 in the Aquilla Creek watershed, Hill County. On 23 August 1980 three immatures were observed perched in trees where prior courtship activity of adult birds had been noted. It is only a matter of time until nests are discovered in north central Texas. One should watch for pairs of kites in mid-April and May, since this species was found nesting in 1982 in Oklahoma after an absence of more than 100 years (Carter and Fowler, 1983).

County records include: *Bosque* — Kimball Crossing, Lake Whitney, 30 May 1980; *Clay* — northwest of Bellevue, 12 February 1983; ten miles southeast of Henrietta, 1 August 1983; 15 miles northwest of Ringgold, 1 October 1983; *Cooke* — near Era, 21 January 1986; two different observations north of Lake Ray Roberts, 6 March 1987; *Dallas* — 23 May 1973, 26 March 1983; Coppell, 26 May 1981; Richardson, 2 February 1984; Delta, west of Cooper, 6 February 1983; *Denton* — western part of county, September 1982; *Ellis* — Italy, 26 April 1978 (two); *Hill* — vicinity of Aquilla (several locations), 19 April through 23 May 1980 (one to two), and again 15 August through 12 September 1980; *Navarro* — vicinity of Richland, 10 September 1980 and 17 November 1982 (three); near Rice, 5 November 1980;

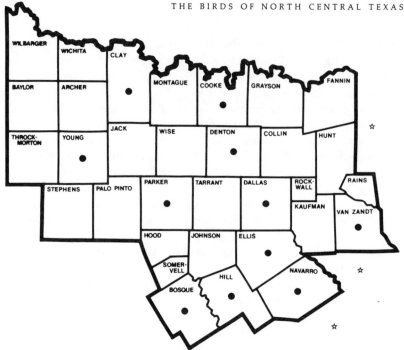

Map 26. Distribution of the Black-shouldered Kite, *Elanus caeruleus*

about eight miles southwest of Corsicana, 24 March 1982; I-45, Navarro-Freestone county line, 1 October 1982; location within county unknown, 12 October 1982; city limits of Corsicana, 28 January 1983; *Parker* — southwestern corner near Tarrant county line, 13 February 1983 (photograph); *Van Zandt* — near Ben Wheeler, 3 March 1983; *Young* — west of Newcastle, near Brazos River, 6 February 1983; *Henderson* — vicinity of Malakoff, 25 January 1983.

Specimen: The only specimen of this beautiful kite is one taken in Clay County on 1 October 1983 (WMP).

Mississippi Kite   *Ictinia mississippiensis* (Wilson)

Status: Uncommon to fairly common transient. Uncommon summer resident locally.

Occurrence: The Mississippi Kite has been recorded in all the counties in the study area except Rains County. There are also records for adjoining Eastland and Shackelford counties, where this species may have been undetected earlier.

This kite was probably once more widespread as a summer resident than it is today. Nesting records were given along the Red River and east to Cooke County before the turn of the century. However, the editor of Oberholser's

The Bird Life of Texas (1974) states that there are recent summer records in the adjoining eastern county of Bowie and nearly to Texarkana, in Red River County, near the Arkansas border. He also implies that a shift in nesting has taken place to the west, giving records from Midland to El Paso. Whether this last statement is completely accurate is debatable since oological pursuits are seldom carried on today, and few persons bird-watch in humid river bottoms after spring migration; therefore, this species may go undetected. One may wonder whether it was ever very abundant in East Texas areas, since there are so few data on early nesting activities.

Surprisingly, in recent years Mississippi Kites have moved into cities and towns in those counties where it formerly nested in prairies and drainages and where originally there was much river bottomland cover. The areas in the cities and towns represent remnants of habitats left as parks and greenbelts. Those to the west may represent man-made habitats where before there was little natural habitat for this species.

There is little doubt in my mind that the increase of mesquite grassland areas brought about an increase in the population of Mississippi Kites and that after World War II there was a noticeable decline of this small, beautiful raptor because of mesquite-eradication programs. One can only guess at the early populations of this species in the north central Texas study area as well as the state as a whole.

Kites in migration from South America usually arrive in north central Texas in late April and early May and return to their winter home in late August and early September. Before and during the 1960s large flocks of Mississippi Kites — 100 or more — were not uncommon, but in recent years sightings are usually fewer than 100 birds. Most counts are of 50 or fewer. Records of more recent large numbers include 138 on 12 September 1974 (Johnson County), 114 on 9 May 1981 (Tarrant County), and approximately 800 in several groups on 28 August 1981 (Denton County). There are some early-March dates, but most have been dismissed as errors since many sightings were given without details. It is possible to mistake this species for Northern Harriers and even falcons. Observers are urged to study carefully any early or late sighting if they suspect that the bird in question is a Mississippi Kite.

Early and late arrival and departure dates for selected counties are: *Collin* — no spring dates, 20 August 1981 to 27 October 1984, next-latest 3 October 1981. *Dallas* — 9 April 1982 to 11 May 1969, and 16 August 1972 to 19 October 1972, next-latest 15 October 1966. There is one unexplainable date of 3 June 1978. *Grayson* — 1 May to 5 June, plus an isolated date of 17 March, 19 and 24 July and 1 August 1984 to 3 September 1984. *Tarrant* — 1 March 1975 (Pulich, 1979) is unacceptable; 3 April 1975 to 29 October 1983, next-latest 17 October 1945. *Wichita* — 3 April 1974, next-earliest 8 April 1978 to 2 October 1974.

Nesting: Oberholser (1974) presented nesting records in the north central Texas study area for Archer, Baylor, Cooke, Stephens, Wichita, Wilbarger, and Young counties, somehow overlooking Throckmorton County, which also had nesting records (Wolfe, 1967). The following nesting reports represent more recent county records: Grayson — Hagerman NWR, nest, 26 June 1984 (pair first seen on 17 May) one young fledged on 1 August; summer 1985; two adults, three young on wing on 21 August 1986, a total of 11 birds on 24 August. Johnson — near Keene, 2 July 1985, nest with two downy young. Palo Pinto — near Santo, summer 1986. Tarrant — 23 April and 18 May 1985 south of Fort Worth in the Burleson area, nest with two young found on 8 June just over the county line in Johnson County. As many as nine kites were also seen on 8 June. Thirteen kites were observed on 25 July, and seven were last seen on 30 August 1985. This species had been seen in the same area in 1983 and 1984. It was also observed in the Roanoke area during June and July 1985. On 12 August 1986 a nesting kite was said to have been rescued below a nest from which it had fallen near Lake Arlington. The bird was taken to the Phoenix Bird Rehabilitation Center, where it was released a month later. This may be the first nesting record for Tarrant County proper. Wichita — pair nesting in Iowa Park 13 July 1974, and ten nests found in the vicinity of Wichita Falls Country Club (Williams, 1977) during the summer of 1977. Wilbarger — bird feeding young at a nest within the city limits of Vernon, 23 May 1974. Young — Graham, bird carrying nesting materials on 21 May 1985.

Specimens: Specimens of this kite are known from the following counties: Archer (MWU), Baylor (one specimen missing, DMNH, KU), Clay (TTU), Cooke (TNHC, USNM), Denton (DMNH), Ellis (DMNH), Navarro (mounted specimen, private collection of Telfair), Throckmorton (TCWC), and Wilbarger (DMNH, some specimens missing, CMNH, KU). A spring specimen indicated by Oberholser (1974) for the Stephens-Young county line was not located.

BALD EAGLE   *Haliaeetus leucocephalus* (Linnaeus)
Status: Rare to uncommon winter resident on large bodies of water. Casual to rare elsewhere; only scattered records. Normally not seen away from water.
Occurrence: The nation's bird has been recorded in 23 counties in the study area — Baylor, Clay, Collin, Cooke, Dallas, Denton, Fannin, Grayson, Hood, Hunt, Kaufman, Navarro, Palo Pinto, Parker, Rains, Rockwall, Stephens, Tarrant, Van Zandt, Wichita, Wilbarger, Wise, and Young — and adjacent Erath, Freestone, Henderson, and Wood counties (not recorded by Oberholser, 1974).

Although this species is considered rare by many persons in north cen-

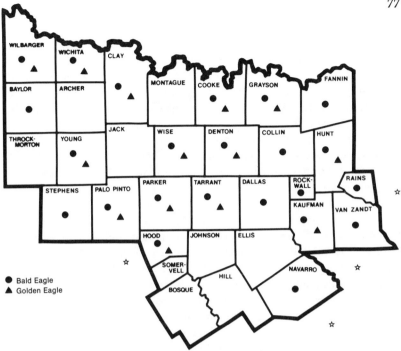

Map 27. Distribution of the Bald Eagle, *Haliaeetus leucocephalus,* and the Golden Eagle, *Aquila chrysaetos*

tral Texas, it has been recorded more frequently in recent years. All the large impoundments—Lake Texoma and Red River below Denison Dam, Lake Tawakoni, Possum Kingdom Lake, and the Brazos River below the dam—attract them regularly, while other bodies of water—Cedar Creek Lake, Lewisville Lake, Lake Granbury, Lake Lavon, Hubbard Creek Lake, Lake Bonham, Benbrook Lake, and Eagle Mountain Lake—may occasionally attract them.

Arrival and departure dates for selected counties are: *Dallas*—recent reports are few since high-density human populations prevent eagles from visiting the few suitable bodies of water. There are only six reports, 18 September 1969 (exceptionally early and questionable), October 1977, 19 November 1973, 19 December 1981, 29 December 1975, and 25 December 1984. *Grayson*—18 October to 11 April; three to six birds can usually be found wintering at Hagerman NWR; six birds (three adult, three immature) were recorded on 18 Mach 1975. The Texas Wildlife Survey (Smith, 1974) estimated that as many as 37 Bald Eagles utilized Lake Texoma in 1972–73. *Hunt*—Lake Tawakoni (including Rains–Van Zandt counties), 15 October 1986, next-earliest 11 November 1984 to 19 March 1983, maximum number eight in 1984. *Palo Pinto*—2 and 7 October 1979, next-earliest 28 October to 28 February 1978, and an isolated date, 4 April 1975 (a bird being harassed by an osprey). As many as 11 were counted along a 20-mile stretch of the Brazos River on 18 December 1977. *Tarrant* — 12 sightings from 21 October 1951 to 15 January 1977, including two isolated dates, 14 April and 10 May 1971. *Wichita* — including nearby counties — 29 September (Clay County) to 23 March 1984. Few sightings are from Wichita County; most are from Baylor and Wilbarger counties, where estimates (1972–73) of 36 and ten, respectively, were made by the Texas Wildlife Survey (Smith, 1974). Since this eagle often forages on waterfowl, its large numbers may be explained by Canada Geese wintering on the Waggoner Ranch, in Wilbarger County.

Nesting: Oberholser (1974) gave a questionable breeding record for Young County (probably before the turn of the century), but to date there is no evidence that the Bald Eagle has ever nested in north central Texas. Several alleged nesting records have proved to be whitewashed cliffs with sightings of transients in the vicinity of the site. In one instance a "nest" proved to be that of a Red-tailed Hawk.

Specimens: Bald Eagle specimens were located from Dallas (DMNH), Palo Pinto (MWU), and Wilbarger (FWMSH) counties. Those indicated by Oberholser (1974) for Clay, Cooke, and Hunt counties could not be located.

Stillwell (1939) listed four specimens taken from the Dallas area in the mid-1920s and 1930s; these are probably the specimens referred to by Oberholser (1974). The files of the Dallas Museum of Natural History reveal that these Bald Eagles were prepared by W. A. Mayer before the permanent collection at the museum came into existence. The specimens in question were mounted for private patrons and probably have gone the way of many specimens in early private collections: they were probably destroyed as they became dirty and tattered. The museum does have a recent cataloged specimen from Dallas County (see paragraph above), as well as mounted Bald Eagles of unknown origin on exhibit.

NORTHERN HARRIER   *Circus cyaneus* (Linnaeus)
Status: Common transient and winter resident. Several nesting records.
Occurrence: The Northern Harrier, formerly known as the Marsh Hawk, has been recorded in all the counties of the north central Texas study area and adjoining Henderson and Shackelford counties, in which it was not previously recorded. This species normally may be looked for from September to April. Extreme arrival and departure dates for counties having sufficient data are: *Dallas* — 9 August 1982, next-earliest 18 August 1986 to 11 May 1975; *Denton* — 30 August 1980 to 30 April 1985; *Grayson* — an isolated date of 19 August 1974, next-earliest 21 August 1980 to 9 May; *Hunt* — 3 September 1981 to 3 May 1981; *Kaufman* — 2 September 1976 to 19 May 1982; *Palo Pinto* — 24 August 1976 to 10 April 1976; *Tarrant* —

9 August 1953, next-earliest 15 August 1974 (Johnson-Tarrant county line) to 11 May 1975; *Wichita*— 8 August 1973 to 7 May 1974.

Harriers are recorded on all of the annual CBCs every year. They are seldom found around cities and towns where urban developments have taken over. Populations are more numerous in open prairie country where native grass prevails and shelters high densities of rodents. In this type of habitat it is often common to see up to a dozen harriers at a time.

Nesting: Nesting was given by Oberholser (1974) for Wise County (20 April 1889; the whereabouts of eggs taken are unknown), and he also gave summer sightings for several counties along the Red River. More and Strecker (1929) noted that the birds were "frequently observed in summer in the vicinity of Watt's Lake," Wilbarger County. This area no longer has any suitable habitat. Nesting, however, was never documented there. The only recent nesting for the north central Texas study area was one for Hill County, where a nest on the ground holding five young was noted on 14 June 1980. A pair was said to have attempted unsuccessfully to nest in Palo Pinto County during the 1972 season. Unfortunately, the details were not given to me; however, the county has much suitable habitat, and this report seems probable. There are June records — the most recent, 16 June 1985, for Young County; however, no nests have been found.

Specimens: Northern Harrier specimens are available for the following counties: Archer (MWU), Baylor (FWMSH), Clay (MWU), Cooke (TNHC), Dallas (DMNH, WMP), Denton (DMNH), Ellis (WMP), Hood (SM), Hunt (DMNH), Palo Pinto (WMP), Tarrant (DMNH, FWMSH), and Wichita (MWU). Specimens indicated for Wilbarger County by Oberholser (1974) were not located.

SHARP-SHINNED HAWK   *Accipiter striatus* Vieillot

Status: Uncommon to fairly common winter resident. Occasionally may visit feeding stations in winter. Evidence that it has ever nested in north central Texas is extremely vague.

Occurrence: Sharp-shinned Hawks have been reported in 25 counties in north central Texas: Bosque, Collin, Cooke, Dallas, Denton, Ellis, Fannin, Grayson, Hill, Hood, Hunt, Johnson, Kaufman, Navarro, Palo Pinto, Parker, Rains, Somervell, Stephens, Tarrant, Van Zandt, Wichita, Wilbarger, Wise, and Young.

This accipiter as well as Cooper's Hawk, below, are sometimes called "blue darters" because of the adults' dark blue-gray backs. Neither is often seen in the open except when they dart out after birds from some thicket or heavier tree cover; they frequently hunt along edges. Occasionally they may be seen soaring overhead, characteristically showing their long tails and short, rounded wings.

Oberholser (1974) gives an extremely early date of 30 April 1888 of eggs for Decatur, Wise County. He also points out that no birds were collected and gives no other data to add substance to this account. The nesting date is so early that it is highly unlikely for this species. He also cites a questionable record for Tarrant County which apparently is based on a footnote by Stillwell (1939). Because both records are vague, I doubt nesting of the Sharp-shinned Hawk in north central Texas. Present-day records do not show this species as nesting in the study area. Several July dates of hawks alleged to be this species are dismissed as errors.

Arrival and departure dates for selected north central Texas counties are: *Collin*—17 September 1983 to 25 April 1982. *Dallas*—3 September 1974 to 12 May 1979. Stillwell (1939) gave extreme dates from 30 August 1936 to 17 May 1933. *Grayson*—1 September to 6 May 1978. *Palo Pinto*—25 September 1976 to 2 April 1977. *Tarrant*—14 September 1980 to 14 May 1977. *Van Zandt*—an isolated date of 28 August 1985, probably in error, next-earliest 1 September 1985 to 8 May 1985. *Wichita*—2 September 1974 to 3 May 1975.

Specimens: Specimens of this small accipiter have been collected from the following counties: Cooke (TNHC), Dallas (DMNH, WMP), Denton (DMNH, WMP), Fannin (WMP), Johnson (FWMSH, SUC), Parker (FWMSH), Tarrant (FWMSH, UTA, WMP), and Wichita (MWU) and nearby Henderson (DMNH). A winter specimen from Wilbarger County (Oberholser, 1974) could not be located.

COOPER'S HAWK   *Accipiter cooperii* (Bonaparte)
Status: Rare to uncommon transient and winter resident. Scattered records the year round in some locales. It is difficult to assess the former nesting status, and there is no evidence to substantiate nesting in recent years.
Occurrence: The assessment of populations of this species and of the Sharp-shinned Hawk, above, is at best extremely difficult. Often we have only fleeting glimpses of these two accipiters, and to try to identify any "hawk" from a brief sighting is folly. The hawks may pass through as transients, especially in fall migration, unrecognized high in the sky. Cooper's Hawks have been reported in all but Ellis, Jack, Montague, and Throckmorton counties. In addition they have been reported on all the annual CBCs conducted in north central Texas.

The Cooper's Hawk is certainly not as numerous as its smaller relative, and it may never have been. It is easily confused with the sharp-shin, for the two are very similar in color. Both are bold and take a heavy toll of birds.

Recent arrival and departure dates for selected counties are: *Dallas*—4 September 1982 to 10 May 1958. There are four dates for the summer proper, an unexplainable date of 5 July 1967, and 8 August 1986, 25 August 1962, and 27 August 1969. Stillwell (1939) considered the Cooper's

Hawk a resident, rare in summer and fairly common in winter. However, no specific nesting data were given to prove conclusively that this species has ever bred in the county. *Grayson* —15 September 1970 to 13 May 1978, with isolated dates of 9 July 1976, 21 July 1983, and 12 August 1978. There is no current evidence that it nests in this county. *Tarrant* — 9 September 1978 to 8 May 1982. Stillwell (1939) reported that this species nested in this county, but it is unlikely. Data are vague and unconvincing, and Sutton (1938) also questioned the validity of earlier reports of nesting. *Wichita* and vicinity— 24 September 1975, with an earlier date of 18 September 1981 for nearby Wilbarger County, to 15 May 1977. The basis of the nesting record given for Wichita County by Oberholser (1974) was undetermined.

Nesting: Oberholser (1974) shows on a map breeding records of the Cooper's Hawk for nine counties of the north central Texas study area. Of these counties only two, Cooke and Wilbarger, are listed as having specimen records. However, neither eggs nor young, if they were collected, could be located. The remaining counties, representing sight records, include Baylor, Dallas, Grayson, Johnson, Tarrant, Wichita, and Wise, some of which are discussed above under the respective county accounts. The Johnson County record is probably based on a footnote given by Stillwell (1939) of three downy young on nest on 7 June 1938. Unfortunately, he gave no other details of this record. I attempted to determine the validity of the records for the remaining counties, Baylor, Grayson, and Wise, but was unsuccessful. It is possible that before the turn of the century the habitat was quite different in some of these counties, and the species nested farther south than it does today.

Specimens: Cooper's Hawk specimens were located for the following counties: Archer (MWU), Cooke (TNHC), Dallas (DMNH), Denton (DMNH, WMP), Grayson (WMP), Hunt (WMP), and nearby Henderson (DMNH), while those cited by Oberholser (1974) for Bosque, Clay, and Wilbarger were not located.

NORTHERN GOSHAWK *Accipiter gentilis* (Linnaeus)
Status: Casual visitor, very rarely reaching north central Texas in winter.
Occurrence: This is the largest and rarest of the accipiters that visit north central Texas. It is said to be extremely secretive yet bold when capturing prey. Adult goshawks are quite distinct in their gray plumage. Size alone, however, is not a reliable characteristic to separate immatures from its near relative the Cooper's Hawk. A light stripe over the eye should be looked for as an aid in distinguishing the two species.

Northern Goshawks are high-mountain birds of prey and are usually thought of as nonmigratory. Some authorities believe that this species is cyclic, periodically moving to lowlands from intermountainous areas of spruce and firs when the food supply diminishes. Its presence in north central Texas is not frequent; its occurrence is casual. Some records may be questionable, since it can be confused with Cooper's Hawk.

All of the county records for the Northern Goshawk that are known to me are presented here with appropriate comments: *Cooke* — Oberholser (1974) cites a specimen allegedly taken before 1889 by G. H. Ragsdale and identified by William Brewster, who does not, however, show its occurrence on the map of records. The specimen in question was not located. *Dallas* — Stillwell (1939) indicated that Mayer mounted three specimens in 1934. Oberholser (1974) points out that actual dates are unknown and follows with a vague phrase: "Birds shot [specimens?]," though it is stated that birds and specimens were identified by Oberholser. The latter report is probably the same one given by Stillwell, who goes on to list a date of 14 February 1937 (a mounted specimen on exhibit at the Dallas Museum of Natural History that is credited to Dallas County by him and Oberholser), but the museum personnel indicate that the specimen was actually taken in Kaufman County. Three recent sightings lacked details and were dismissed as errors in identification. *Denton* — a spring record is indicated on a map by Oberholser (1979) with no details. This was probably taken from the local *Checklist of the Birds of Denton County* (Rylander, 1959), which represents a March date. This record should probably be dismissed. *Grayson* — two birds were listed in the Hagerman NWR reports as being seen on 31 March 1966. No details were presented in the refuge report. On 5 December 1982 nine persons spotted and carefully identified this species at the Tishomingo NWR, Johnson County, Oklahoma (Nanney, 1983). It was seen again at the same location on 12 February 1983. This refuge is across Lake Texoma, north of Grayson County. *Tarrant* — Pulich (1979) lists five sightings for this county, most of which are neither detailed nor convincing. Goshawks were not counted as one of the 324 avian species recorded for this county. *Wichita* — one was said to have visited the backyard of a housing area at the Sheppard Air Force Base, in Wichita Falls, for three days, 17 through 19 January 1973. Unfortunately, only one person saw the bird in question. It was said that an invasion of goshawks to the north at Hays, Kansas, was the largest since the winter of 1916–17 (Williams, 1973), which could have driven them farther south. This record is considered in the hypothetical listing in the checklist of the Wichita area (Zinn and Moore, 1976).

Specimen: The only specimen known for north central Texas is the one collected in Kaufman County on 14 February 1937 (DMNH 6371, on exhibit at the museum).

HARRIS' HAWK *Parabuteo unicinctus* (Temminck)
Status: Probably a casual visitor if records are of wild birds.

Occurrence: Since this hawk can easily be mistaken for the Northern Harrier, and even the dark Swainson's Hawk, the records of this south Texas hawk are difficult to evaluate. Members of the species have occasionally been brought into the north central Texas area by falconers and have escaped from their handlers or failed to return upon release. With the advent of the raptor rehabilitation center in Arlington, Tarrant County, came a series of records (9 October through 18 December 1982) that were actually records of such an escapee. The bird was so tame that it could usually be found perched near the highway, and it seldom flew away from people who stopped to view it.

Not all records can be completely dismissed, since this hawk may wander, and specimens have been collected for Kansas and Oklahoma. County records known to me are: *Dallas* — Stillwell (1939) gives a record for 20 August 1939. It is rather interesting that the year given is also the date of the printing of his checklist as well as of his acknowledgment. Since that time there have been two other observations, 1 May 1960 and 18 February 1963, both of which should be considered hypothetical. *Ellis* — 29 September 1973, an adult reported by a lone observer at Ennis. *Hunt* — listed in local preliminary checklist (Tarter, 1940) for this county as a visitor, but apparently later dismissed since it was omitted from the next checklist. *Jack* — a lone bird on 22 November 1975. A report was published without details in the local North Texas Bird and Wildlife Club newsletter (1975). *Tarrant* — Stillwell (1939) footnotes this species as a possible visitor and indicates its presence in the county. See the paragraph above for recent records. *Wichita* — On 30 September 1973 one hawk believed to be of this species was reported by a lone observer. It was considered hypothetical on the local checklist (1976). One was taken on 14 December 1973 in Jackson County (Tyler, 1979), Oklahoma, north of Wichita County.

Because most of the records are vague and some hawks were released birds, it was impossible to assess the exact status of this hawk for north central Texas.

RED-SHOULDERED HAWK   *Buteo lineatus* (Gmelin)
Status: Rare to fairly common resident in suitable riparian habitat.
Occurrence: Red-shouldered Hawks inhabit wooded river bottomlands along with Barred Owls. Although they have been found in 27 counties in the north central Texas study area, they are localized to the more extensive forest areas and have disappeared from areas that are no longer wooded. This is especially true in parts of the Dallas–Fort Worth area, and in other areas where riparian habitat has been cleared for agricultural and industrial purposes. They are seldom found away from wooded areas. This species is extremely vocal, and its call may be mistaken for Blue Jay notes.

County records include Archer, Bosque, Collin, Cooke, Dallas, Denton, Ellis, Fannin, Grayson, Hill, Hood, Hunt, Jack, Kaufman, Johnson, Montague, Navarro, Palo Pinto, Parker, Rains, Somervell, Tarrant, Van Zandt, Wichita, Wilbarger, Wise, and Young counties and nearby Shackelford County. Where there is considerable birding, Red-shouldered Hawks have been reported every month of the year, and it is likely that they would also be found in many other counties if continuous monthly studies were carried on. In some areas there is little supportive evidence that they are migratory. Where habitat conditions (food and cover) are favorable, this species has been observed regularly.

Nesting: Oberholser (1974) cites nesting records for Cooke, Dallas, Grayson, and Wise counties, and to his data can be added Denton, Hill, Jack, Johnson, Tarrant and Van Zandt counties and nearby Shackelford County. The fact that this bird inhabits low, dense floodplains makes it hard for birders to cover it properly and no doubt precludes the rapid addition of other county nesting records. My data show nesting ranges from 19 March 1981, bird at nest (Tarrant County), to July 1980, and no specific date (Hill County) of fledglings, with a number of April and May records (eggs or young) in other counties. In the upper Lake Worth area (Tarrant County) at least five or six pairs currently nest.

Specimens: Specimens have been located for the following counties: Cooke (TNHC), Dallas (DMNH, WMP), Denton (DMNH), Kaufman (DMNH), Navarro (FWMSH), and nearby Wood (DMNH). The location of a specimen indicated by Oberholser (1974) for Wise County was not determined. Not all specimens were examined, but those that were proved to belong to the nominate race *B. l. lineatus.*

BROAD-WINGED HAWK   *Buteo platypterus* (Vieillot)
Status: Rare to uncommon transient in the eastern half of the project area. Rare in summer, nests found only along the Red River.
Occurrence: Broad-winged Hawks have been recorded in 18 counties, all of them along the eastern side of the study area: Bosque, Collin, Cooke, Dallas, Denton, Fannin, Grayson, Hill, Hood, Hunt, Johnson, Kaufman, Navarro, Palo Pinto, Parker, Rains, Tarrant, and Van Zandt. In addition there are records for adjoining Henderson and Hopkins counties.

This hawk is usually seen only in migration and very rarely in several counties in the summer. Sightings reported in winter are extremely doubtful and are assumed to be misidentified Red-shouldered Hawks. Most members of this species winter south of the United States, mainly in Central and South America. Overall sightings range from late March to the latter part of October, with more reported in late April and again in September. Selected county dates are: *Collin* — 17 April 1981 to 3 October 1981. The hawk has been seen a few times in the vicinity of Lake Lavon

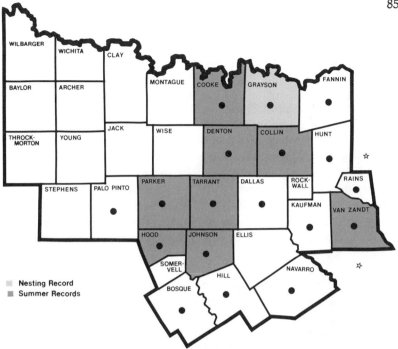

Map 28. Distribution of the Broad-winged Hawk, *Buteo platypterus*, with summer and nesting records

in summer throughout June and July, but there is no evidence of nesting. *Dallas* — an isolated date of 25 March 1975, next-earliest 2 April 1967 to 11 May 1958, and 14 August 1959 to 20 October 1982. Stillwell (1939) says that this species is common in some winters, probably on the basis of a statement by Kelley (1935) which is likely erroneous. *Grayson* — 29 March, next-earliest 3 April 1983 to 28 October 1975, with records through the summer, including sightings of two juveniles on 4 August 1979 in mid-July 1984 and 7 and 21 August 1986. These are the only recent nesting records. Oberholser (1974) indicated that it may have bred there earlier. *Tarrant* — 7 April 1982 to 14 May 1981, an isolated record of 15 June 1985, and again in fall from 13 August 1960 to 8 October 1970.

Nesting: Even though there are nesting records only for Grayson County, other counties in which nesting is inferred from summer dates at hand are Collin, Cooke, Denton, Hood, Johnson, Parker, Tarrant, and Van Zandt. It is very likely that Broad-winged Hawks occasionally nest in some of these counties since this hawk is a woodland species that frequently goes unnoticed. Persons living in these counties or spending much time birding there are urged to search for the nests to document nesting status. They nest in forests and wooded areas, not in open prairies as Red-tailed and

Swainson's Hawks frequently do. Broad-winged Hawks can easily be mistaken for Red-shouldered Hawks, which are more common in north central Texas.

Although Broad-winged Hawks are sometimes seen in vast numbers in the Rio Grande valley of Texas, few flights pass over north central Texas, and if they do so, they are so high in the skies that only a bird or two are identified. However, on 21 April 1985 two kettles (groups) of 75 and 45 Broad-winged Hawks were counted riding the thermals over Rains and Van Zandt counties. On ten different days a total of 658 broad-wings passed over the Edgewood area, Van Zandt County, from 29 August to 9 October 1986, in kettles ranging from two (minimum) to 218 (maximum) birds. *Specimens:* Specimens of this hawk taken from the study area during migration are known only from Cooke (TNHC), Hood (WMP), and Dallas (DMNH) counties.

SWAINSON'S HAWK   *Buteo swainsoni* Bonaparte
Status: Uncommon to fairly common transient and rare summer resident, mainly in the western parts of the study area to about Dallas County.
Occurrence: Swainson's Hawks have been reported in all of the counties under study. These extremely beneficial hawks are often noted resting on the ground as migratory flocks pass through the area, and, since they frequently feed on insects, they often follow farmers plowing fields. They do not winter in Texas but migrate to South America. Sightings in winter are unsatisfactory and, when carefully checked, prove to be misidentified Red-tailed Hawks. All birds reported on the annual CBCs were discounted. There are no winter specimens for north central Texas, and the specimen allegedly taken on 25 January 1878 by Ragsdale at Gainesville, Cooke County (Oberholser, 1974), could not be located. Oberholser's original notes do not list this specimen or even refer to the species. Specimens or photographs should be taken to confirm its occurrence in winter, if it is suspected at this time of the year in north central Texas.

This beautiful buteo has been found in the area from the end of March to early November. However, it is more often observed in late April and early May and again in late August and September. Overall extreme dates for north central Texas range from 3 March 1980 (Hill County) to 3 December 1981 (Grayson County). Extreme dates for selected counties are: *Collin* – 3 April 1982 to 20 October 1982; *Dallas* – 20 March 1982 to 13 November 1964; *Denton* – 3 April 1976 to 4 November 1941 (specimen); *Ellis* – 28 March 1978 to 7 November 1982; *Grayson* – 7 March 1983, next-earliest 18 March 1976 to 23 November 1981, and an isolated date, 3 December 1981; *Palo Pinto* – 11 March 1972, next-earliest 10 April 1983 to 17 September 1978; *Tarrant* – 30 March 1977, mean date 2 April (1969–78) to 30 November 1952, next-latest 20 November 1982; *Wichita* — 21 March 1956 to 9 October 1961 (specimen).

This hawk was formerly more common in north central Texas than it is today. Large concentrations were reported more often in the 1950s. Since they are more common in west Texas, and the area of this study is on the eastern edge of their main migration route to the west, probably more hawks pass through the western counties than through the eastern counties (within the study area); however, a lack of observers precludes conclusive evidence of their abundance in passage. Occasionally large numbers are still reported, although observers may confuse some with Broad-winged Hawks, which also flock during migration, especially since birds of prey ride the thermals high in the sky. Several such reports were of flocks of 30 to 50 hawks totaling 2,500 birds, many of this species, passing on the morning of 8 October 1967 (Dallas County). About 70 hawks (all Swainson's) were observed resting in a field on 23 September 1971 (Hill County), and an estimated 1,000-kettle of hawks, allegedly of this species, were seen on 2 October 1983 (Collin County), but whether or not all of these hawks were members of this species is questionable. A flock of 600 Swainson's Hawks followed the passage of a front on 5 October 1986 (Tarrant County).

Nesting: Oberholser (1974) gave nesting records for Tarrant, Wichita, Wilbarger, Wise, and Young counties. More and Strecker (1929) list Swainson's Hawk as a permanent resident, which is in error, but it was a common nesting bird of the prairies around Vernon, Wilbarger County. They gave egg dates ranging from 9 May to 28 June. Present counties in which it has been reported nesting (nests or young) are the Collin-Dallas county line, Dallas (elsewhere), and Tarrant, and it is suspected of nesting in Baylor, Cooke, Denton, Grayson, Hood, Palo Pinto, and Throckmorton counties. All of the latter records are very likely of nesting birds, yet no actual eggs or young were reported.

Specimens: Specimens of Swainson's Hawks were located from Cooke (TNHC), Dallas (DMNH), Denton (DMNH), Wichita (MWU), and Wilbarger (CMNH) counties and adjoining Eastland (WMP) County. The specimen for Tarrant County may be the one shown for Parker County by Oberholser (1974), since the latter county specimen was not located. The specimens for Clay and Montague counties were not found.

RED-TAILED HAWK   *Buteo jamaicensis* (Gmelin)
Status: Found the year round in all parts of the north central Texas study area. More common in winter than in summer.
Occurrence: Red-tailed Hawks have been reported in all counties of north central Texas and in many the year round. This species is much more abundant during the winter period from early October until early April. At

this time numerous Red-tailed Hawks invade the north central Texas study area. They even come into urban areas if suitable feeding habitat is still available. During migration, particularly in the fall, they can often be seen perched on fence posts and telephone poles along the highways. Unfortunately, many first-year young fail to survive the winter, becoming easy targets for "trigger-happy" hunters who shoot unsuspecting perched hawks. All hawks are protected by law and should not be shot. Though it was once called "chicken hawk," the red-tail takes only an occasional chicken. This buteo is an extremely beneficial hawk, feeding mainly on rodents. Its range normally does not overlap that of the Red-shouldered Hawk, which prefers wet woodlands.

Nesting: Although no systematic effort was made to locate nests, this hawk no doubt nests in all the counties. The counties for which nesting has been recorded are Archer, Baylor, Bosque, Collin, Cooke, Dallas, Denton, Grayson, Hill, Hunt, Jack, Johnson, Kaufman, Montague, Navarro, Palo Pinto (nesting in Great Blue Heron colony), Parker, Rockwall, Somervell, Tarrant, Throckmorton, Wichita, Wilbarger, Wise, and Young. Whether or not the nesting population is sedentary has not been determined, although nesting birds and young disappear after the breeding season. If they are not persecuted by man, Red-tailed Hawks can be found close to human dwellings year after year. They occasionally use steel power-line towers for nest sites in the Dallas–Fort Worth area.

Sutton (1938) gave two nesting dates for Tarrant County from 19 March to 5 May, both nests containing eggs, while most recent dates in this county are 24 March 1956 (active nest) to young in the nest in mid-May 1970. In Dallas County dates range from young on 16 April 1972 to 7 June 1971 (both nestlings banded in nest). These dates are applicable to other counties in north central Texas. Occasionally one can even note a pair of red-tails establishing nesting territories or building and refurnishing nests in late January and early February. Nests are used again if undisturbed or not usurped by Great Horned Owls. Nests are not placed in deep wooded areas but are found on upland prairies or along small creeks, and they can often be noted before trees leaf out in early spring.

Specimens: Red-tailed Hawk specimens have been located from the following counties: Archer (MWU), Bosque (WMP), Cooke (TNHC, USNM), Dallas (DMNH, TCWC, UTA, WMP), Denton (DMNH, WMP), Ellis (DMNH), Grayson (DMNH, SE), Hood (SM), Hunt (FWMSH), Johnson (SUC), Kaufman (DMNH), Navarro (WMP), Palo Pinto (FWMSH), Parker (FWMSH), Rockwall (WMP), Tarrant (DMNH, UTA, WMP), Wichita (MWU), and Wilbarger south (MWU). A specimen (Oberholser, 1974) from Wise County was not located.

Five subspecies of Red-tailed Hawks range into north central Texas, although not all specimens have been studied in detail. As far as can be determined, *Buteo jamaicensis fuertesi* represents the nesting race along the west side of the north central Texas study area, probably to about the vicinity of Tarrant County. Oberholser (1974) points out that this race nests from Wilbarger County east to Cooke County. *B. j. borealis* may represent the subspecies along the eastern edge of the study area. Sutton (1967) points out that no Oklahoma specimen clearly represents *borealis*. There seems to be a lack of specimens known to have been taken at nests; thus the nesting races are far from settled in this part of the Great Plains region and await a thorough study. There are, however, examples of all the races—*borealis, fuertesi, calurus, kriderii,* and *"harlani,"* all taken from the Dallas–Fort Worth area and deposited in local collections. The latter race is not uncommon in winter, although some immature melanistic races of other red-tails are misidentified in the field. Some authorities claim that *"harlani"* is merely a color phase. Unfortunately, the vast array of different races, with many variable plumages, makes this buteo most difficult to identify properly in the field and even in the hand. In the north central Texas area it is often misidentified as to species.

FERRUGINOUS HAWK *Buteo regalis* (Gray)
Status: Rare transient and winter visitor. Not as common in north central Texas as many believe.
Occurrence: Although there are reports of this large buteo from 11 counties in the north central Texas study area, some of the records are questionable. It is an extremely rare species and is seldom seen. Immature Red-tailed Hawks, common in the area, are often misidentified as Ferruginous Hawks by persons unfamiliar with the species. I have seen this species only twice in 30 years in the immediate area of Dallas–Fort Worth. One should give all the details when reporting this species, and all casual observations should be dismissed as misidentifications.

No doubt this species was more common in the earlier days than it is today, for hawk populations in general have dwindled. Data at hand for this species for the 11 counties are given in their entirety: *Baylor*—only spring and fall records were given by Oberholser (1974). It may be found more often in this area if persons watch for it at the appropriate time of the year, in late fall or winter. *Cooke*—said to have been collected in winter (Oberholser, 1974), probably in the 1880s by Ragsdale. The whereabouts of the specimen are unknown. *Dallas*—far more records than in any other county in north central Texas. Winter specimen record and spring sight records are given by Oberholser (1974). Although there is a specimen on display in the Dallas Museum of Natural History, it is not cataloged and its origin is uncertain. Stillwell (1939) lists the species as "winter resident, not common." Some of his records appear to be erroneous and are questionable. Since 1957 there have been fewer than 15 reports. It was

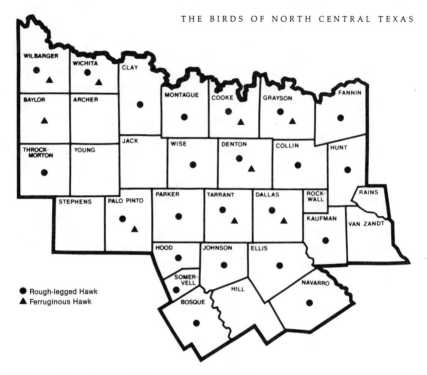

Map 29. Distribution of the Ferruginous Hawk, *Buteo regalis,* and the Rough-legged Hawk, *B. lagopus*

reported on seven annual CBCs. Reports of eight on the 1968 CBC and five on the 1972 CBC were apparently not questioned and certainly were not edited by the compiler. Ferruginous Hawks are seldom seen in these numbers in one day in any place. Dates range from 3 November 1957 through 28 January 1986. *Denton* — spring and winter records are given by Oberholser (1974). The source of the data was not determined. A record of five on 16 January 1966 is highly suspicious. There is an observation of one carefully studied by two competent observers at Lewisville Lake on 2 January 1984. *Grayson* — considered accidental on Hagerman NWR checklist (1984). Oberholser (1974) indicates fall and winter records. The only valid dates known to me are 14 through 23 December 1969, and again on 11 January 1970 (no doubt the same bird). *Hood* and *Hunt* — all reports have been dismissed as highly questionable since the persons making the observations were unfamiliar with the species or did not provide convincing details. *Palo Pinto* — three records provided with convincing evidence, 21 December 1968, 31 December 1977, and 31 January 1977. *Tarrant* — three records, 27 October 1951, 11 February 1958, and 1 January 1968, recent sightings doubtful. *Wichita* — two records, 16 February 1975 and 29 April 1974. The latter date is extremely late and very likely should not be accepted. *Wilbarger*—Oberholser (1974) cites a breeding record, a nest with egg collected from the Vernon area by R. L. More on 29 April 1937. The egg was not located. There seem to be no other records for this county, yet they should occasionally visit the area.

ROUGH-LEGGED HAWK   *Buteo lagopus* (Pontoppidan)
Status: Rare to uncommon winter visitor.
Occurrence: The Rough-legged Hawk has been recorded in the following counties: Bosque, Clay, Collin, Cooke, Dallas, Denton, Ellis, Fannin, Grayson, Hood, Hunt, Johnson, Kaufman, Montague, Navarro, Palo Pinto, Parker, Somervell, Tarrant, Throckmorton, Wichita, Wilbarger, and Wise.

Of the two species of "rough-legged" hawks that reach north central Texas in the wintertime, this hawk is more common and more widespread than the Ferruginous Hawk. Misidentification frequently occurs, and all August and most May dates are unacceptable. Some September dates, especially the earlier ones, were also dismissed, particularly if observers reported small flocks. These were more likely flocks of Swainson's Hawks, a common buteo that passes through the area at this time. Some field guides point out that rough-legs have a habit of hovering in midair; however, it should not be assumed that all hawks behaving in this manner are Rough-legged Hawks. Red-tailed Hawks are also known to hover, particularly on windy days. Dark-phase Rough-legged Hawks reach north central Texas along with an array of other dark buteos, making some identifications nearly impossible.

This species is usually found in the area from late October until March. It has been reported on all of the annual CBCs in north central Texas except the Lake Tawakoni and McKinney counts. On those counts that do not attract many observers, the hawks have been reported only once or twice or at best a few times. On some of the more popular counts, where there are more participants, they are reported more frequently and in greater numbers, though not every year. Some of these reports may be extremely doubtful. Dates on hand for some select counties are: *Dallas*—2 October 1966, next-earliest 17 October 1977 to 2 May 1970. Stillwell (1939) gave extremes as 23 September 1938 to 5 May 1937. *Grayson*—21 October to 29 March, plus isolated dates of 11 and 19 April, and a late sighting of 10 May 1969. *Tarrant*—3 October 1974 to 3 May 1980, next-latest 23 April 1983. *Wichita*—16 October 1977 to 16 April 1974. A number of dates for this county are highly questionable.

Specimens: Specimens are known from only three counties: Cooke (TNHC 1007), Hood (SM 1579), and Throckmorton on the county line next to Haskell (FWMSH 53). A specimen listed for Wichita County (Oberholser, 1974) was not located.

GOLDEN EAGLE   *Aquila chrysaetos* (Linnaeus)
Status: Casual to rare transient and winter resident. Recent records not as numerous as earlier ones.
Occurrence: This stately raptor barely reaches the north central Texas study area. Golden Eagles have been reported in 14 counties of the study area — Clay, Cooke, Denton, Grayson, Hood, Hunt, Kaufman, Palo Pinto, Parker, Tarrant, Wichita, Wilbarger, Wise, and Young — and adjacent Erath County.

Some observers have difficulty distinguishing adult Golden Eagles from mature Bald Eagles, as well as immatures, and even mature Golden Eagles from immature Bald Eagles. Extreme care should be exercised in attempting to identify the two species if they are not seen clearly. Observers should not be hesitant about listing their sightings of eagles as simply "eagle species." The questionable records at hand are very likely the result of observers' efforts to put specific names to eagles without proper study.

Golden Eagles are not as numerous as Bald Eagles anywhere in north central Texas. They have been reported on only four CBCs (1965–83) — once at Lewisville (Denton County), six times at Hagerman NWR (Grayson County), nine times at Palo Pinto (Palo Pinto County), and once at Fort Worth (Tarrant County). Some authorities consider this species to be more of a wanderer than a regular migrant, going south only when lack of food drives it from its home range. Today it is having difficulty coping with environmental intrusions and systematic persecution by man.

Golden Eagles are likely to be found often in and around rough mountainous areas (Palo Pinto County), occasionally around large water impoundments (Hagerman NWR, Lake Texoma, Grayson County), and in the northwestern parts of the study area. Dates are given for all county records known to me: *Clay* — two sightings, 3 and 4 November 1973 and 28 December 1978. *Cooke* — Oberholser (1974) lists one taken on 9 March (the year not given but probably before the 1900s by Ragsdale); the specimen was not located. Winter sightings are indicated, but only one record since — 29 November 1969 (immature). *Dallas* — Stillwell (1939) lists this eagle as a rare visitor and mentions a specimen taken 1 November 1938 in east Dallas by Mayer; its whereabouts are unknown. There are fewer than a dozen sightings between 1958 and 1978, ranging from 8 October 1974 to 5 January 1958. A report of one sighted resting in a field with 11 Ospreys on 25 June 1960 is highly improbable and dismissed as erroneous, along with an August 1974 date. *Denton* — fewer than six records, some considered errors. Golden Eagle dates range from 25 October 1975 to early January (no exact date). *Grayson* — 16 October 1969 to 4 March 1978. *Hood* — one sighting, 3 November 1979. *Hunt* — 1 and 2 October 1979, an eagle feeding on a Red-tailed Hawk, and a vague record of one killed in 1922, not given by Oberholser (1974). *Kaufman* — 27 November 1983, an immature at Cedar Creek Lake. Another doubtful record of an "eagle" said to be this species in migration with other hawks in late September is dismissed. *Palo Pinto* — at least a dozen sightings, 28 October 1978 to 28 February 1978. *Parker* — 31 October 1975. *Tarrant* — nine reports between 1958 and 1978, 21 October 1978 to 23 January 1972 and an isolated older date, 20 April 1958. *Wichita* — two records, 23 October 1975 and 20 January 1974. A recent November date is dismissed as a misidentified Bald Eagle. *Wilbarger, Wise,* and *Young* — sightings given only by Oberholser (1974). A sight record of an alleged nesting was given for the latter county without detail. If it was a nesting record, it was before the present century. *Specimens:* The only specimens located for north central Texas were one from Dallas County on 8 October 1974 (DMNH 6491), and two taken at Roanoke (Denton County) on 25 November 1906 (SM 779, 785).

Family Falconidae (Caracaras and Falcons)

CRESTED CARACARA   *Polyborus plancus* (Miller)
Status: Rare to uncommon local resident in the southern half of the study area. Casual in some of the adjacent counties north and east.
Occurrence: Surprisingly, many persons think of the Crested Caracara as being casual or accidental in this area. However, its range in north central Texas is connected to the middle Gulf Coast prairies by a narrow band of two or three counties of the central prairies. It should be expected throughout the year in suitable cattle grazing areas dotted with brush. It is seldom, if ever, found in the urban areas of Dallas–Fort Worth, though it may reach the southern outskirts of Mountain Creek and Benbrook Lakes.

There are reports of Crested Caracaras for 18 counties in the study area and adjacent Henderson County: *Baylor* — Oberholser (1974), none since. *Bosque* — a local rancher informed me in 1961 that caracaras nested near his ranch east of Cayote, in the southeastern part of the county. It has also been seen in the vicinity of Morgan and Meridian SP in spring and late summer. Last reported on 23 May 1983 and 18 January 1985. *Collin* — five miles north of McKinney (Keating, 1975) on 30 August 1974. *Dallas* — nine sightings, most recent 6 April 1985 (1938–85). *Ellis* — one shot near Ennis on 14 November 1959 (specimen). *Grayson* — Oberholser (1974), source of data unknown. *Hill* — 5 December 1957 (specimen), 6 April 1979, and 10 October 1982. *Hood-Johnson* county line — vicinity of Acton, Cresson, and Joshua, late 1960s. It was common to see them in this area until 1976; nest and young were also seen several times, and very likely are still present but not reported. They were found in Johnson County proper near Alvarado on 3 March 1985. *Hunt* — summer of 1977, in the vicinity of Lake Tawakoni, 22 October 1977, and 9 April 1984, the latter two dates away from Lake Tawakoni, and 21 March 1986. *Kaufman* — frequently seen in the vicinity of Terrell, reports for all months except

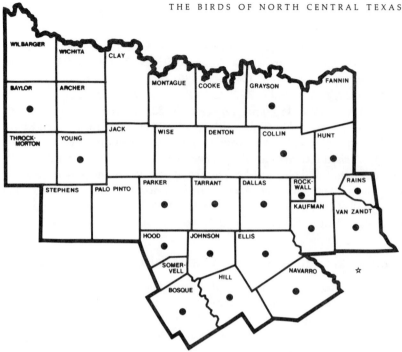

Map 30. Distribution of the Crested Caracara, *Polyborus plancus*

September. Nest with two young on 2 July 1980 and again near the first nest on 9 June 1981. *Navarro* — Ogilby (1882) cites nesting in the vicinity of Rice. The bird continues to nest in the Corsicana-Richland area, for immature birds have been reported several times; reported frequently for all months but August and December. *Parker* — most records are from the junction of the Hood-Johnson county line in the southwestern part of this county, 3 April 1977 to 28 November 1970, said to be nesting but no specific data. *Rains* — two on 18 December 1985. *Rockwall* — 24 November 1984. *Tarrant* — lone bird southeast of Roanoke on the Tarrant-Denton county line on 24 January 1951. Another bird, a possible escapee, near the Fort Worth Zoo on 19 October 1964, one at Benbrook Lake on 5 January 1985, and one in northwestern Tarrant County on 10 May 1986. Two birds of this species were said to have been shot by G. Maxon about the spring of 1907 (Oberholser, 1974), but apparently these specimens could not be located. *Van Zandt* — near Willis Point on 13 May 1978 and Lake Tawakoni and vicinity on 11 March, 11 November, and 23 December 1984; 17 March and 1 July 1985; and 5 May and 4 January 1986. *Young* — Oberholser (1974) gave a summer sighting but with no date. *Henderson* — two winter records at Trinidad, 29 December 1963, and a bird shot on 20 December 1973 (specimen).

Specimens: The only specimens known to me are the ones referred to in the paragraph above for Ellis (mounted caracara, private collection, R. Telfair II), Hill (SM), and Henderson (DMNH) counties.

AMERICAN KESTREL   *Falco sparverius* Linnaeus
Status: Common transient and winter resident. Found the year round in many of the counties, representing a rare summer resident, although not many actual nesting records are available.
Occurrence: This small falcon has been reported in all of the counties of north central Texas as well as the adjacent ones. In many counties there are year-round sightings, although it is much more in evidence during the winter, when populations from the north move into the area, or in the fall, when they pass through the region.

Kestrels are common over open country from about mid-September to mid-April. Extreme dates for selected counties are: *Collin* —13 August 1983 to 24 April 1982; *Dallas* — 4 August 1972 to 8 June 1977, 1983; *Denton* — 20 August 1982 to 30 April 1982; *Grayson* — 3 August to 12 May, and isolated dates 10 July 1974 and 29 July 1982; *Palo Pinto* — 24 August 1976 to 29 April 1978; *Tarrant* — 2 August 1951 to 10 May 1975; *Van Zandt* — 25 August 1983 to 21 April 1985 (19 August 1986, Hunt County).

Kestrels have been reported on all of the annual CBCs of the area and on most counts every year. In general, their numbers have not decreased, though some authorities may not agree with this assessment. In some instances their numbers have increased in recent years; however, this may be due to better coverage and more participants in the CBCs. Their numbers are not as great, however, on the counts along the Red River or to the west in Palo Pinto County.

American Kestrels banded by me resulted in the following encounters: two out-of-state recoveries, both banded in Dallas County, one on 9 January 1971 and recovered on 31 March 1975 in northeast Nebraska and another on 16 January 1971 and recovered in March 1971 in Adrian, Minnesota. One in-state recovery was banded on 12 February 1972 near Commerce, Hunt County, and recovered in December 1972 at Prairie Hill, Limestone County. Another kestrel banded in Minnesota on 9 April 1982 was recovered as a road kill in Van Zandt County on 23 January 1983.

Nesting: Oberholser (1974) gave nesting records from Baylor, Cooke, Dallas, Fannin, Tarrant, Wichita, and Wilbarger counties, with a number of summer observations elsewhere. Present data show that they still nest in Dallas and Tarrant counties and add Grayson and Stephens counties to the overall list having nesting records. The American Kestrel is very secretive around its nest. It would probably still be found if more persons searched for nests. Many of the earlier nesting data represent efforts of oologists who sought the beautiful eggs of this species. In the Dallas–Fort Worth area it has been observed during the nesting season around man-made structures, but no nests have been found. For example, one such structure is Texas Stadium in Irving, which could provide suitable nesting crannies. The meager nesting data at hand are: Duncanville (Dallas County) — three young ready to fledge on 28 May 1975; same site — three young banded on 25 May 1977; North Lake (Dallas County) — pair carrying food to steel high-line structure on 31 May 1984; Fort Worth (Tarrant County) — two young captured on 8 June 1960 and young bird (unable to fly) on 1 June 1978; Hagerman NWR (Grayson County) — two fully-grown young brought on 19 June 1979 from county airport, where they had hatched; they were banded and released; Breckenridge (Stephens County), entering eaves of building, 16 June 1985.

Specimens: Specimens of American Kestrels were taken from the following counties: Baylor (MWU), Cooke (TNHC), Dallas (DMNH, UTA, WMP), Denton (DMNH), Ellis (UTA), Hill (UTA, WMP), Hood (FWMSH), Parker (FWMSH), Tarrant (FWMSH), Wichita (MWU), Wilbarger (TCWC, WMP), and Van Zandt (WMP).

Specimens taken from Tarrant County, as well as others from Dallas County, represent the nominate race *F. s. sparverius.* However, there is one specimen in the Dallas Museum of Natural History (no. 242) that Oberholser (1974) identified as *paulus.*

MERLIN   *Falco columbarius* Linnaeus
Status: Rare transient and winter visitor — casual may be more appropriate for many areas. More records in fall than in spring.

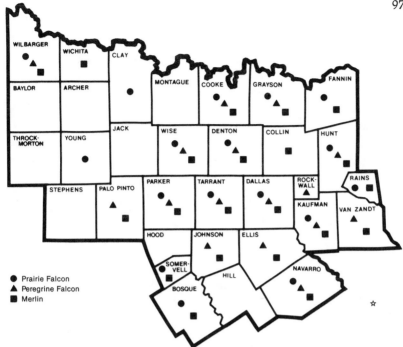

Map 31. Distribution of the Merlin, *Falco columbarius;* the Peregrine Falcon, *F. peregrinus;* and the Prairie Falcon, *F. mexicanus*

Occurrence: Merlins have been recorded in 21 counties of the study area —Bosque, Collin, Cooke, Dallas, Denton, Ellis, Fannin, Grayson, Hunt, Johnson, Kaufman, Navarro, Palo Pinto, Parker, Rains, Somervell, Tarrant, Van Zandt, Wichita, Wilbarger, and Wise—and adjacent Knox County.

This species was formerly known as the Pigeon Hawk, but its small size seldom allows it to take birds as large as pigeons. It is normally found where scattered trees break the open terrain and is rarely found in heavily wooded areas. It comes to north central Texas in early September. Although it is reported in winter and spring, most of the records are for the fall.

Merlins have been reported on seven of the nine CBCs conducted annually in north central Texas but not on the McKinney (Collin County), or Lake Tawakoni (Van Zandt County) counts. Observations are few and scattered, and only once has more than one been reported on any of the counts. Similar species, the little Sharp-shinned Hawk and the American Kestrel, can be easily misidentified as Merlins by inexperienced birdwatchers.

Extreme dates for selected counties are: *Dallas*—11 September 1976 to 14 April 1973 (all months within period); *Grayson*—12 September 1985 to 23 April 1971 (August dates deleted, no sightings for January or March);

Palo Pinto — 28 October 1975 to 3 April 1982 (none for February); *Tarrant* — 3 September 1970, next-earliest 24 September 1984, to 12 May 1952 (all months within period); *Wichita* — 25 September 1975 to an isolated date 30 April 1977, next-latest 13 April 1976.

Specimens: Two subspecies of Merlins are known from Cooke County, one taken on 22 February 1887 (TNHC 1009) and identified as *F. c. richardsoni*, and the other the nominate race *F. c. columbarius* taken on 11 September 1885 (TNHC 1010). A specimen said by Oberholser (1974) to be *F. c. bendirei* was not located. In addition, *F. c. columbarius* was taken from Denton County on 10 September 1944 (DMNH 2266) and from Ellis County on 6 September 1975 (USNM 573671). Other Merlin specimens listed by Oberholser (1974) for Dallas, Hunt, Tarrant (see Pulich, 1979), Wichita, and Wilbarger counties were not located.

PEREGRINE FALCON   *Falco peregrinus* Tunstall
Status: Rare transient and casual winter visitor.
Occurrence: This endangered species has been recorded in 16 counties in the study area — Cooke, Dallas, Denton, Ellis, Grayson, Hunt, Johnson, Kaufman, Navarro, Palo Pinto, Parker, Rockwall, Tarrant, Van Zandt, Wilbarger, and Wise — and adjacent Anderson County. Like the Prairie Falcon, below, the Peregrine Falcon has declined; however, it can be expected around lakes where waterfowl concentrate. The records are more numerous in fall than in spring and casual in winter, being recorded only on the Fort Worth (Tarrant County) and Palo Pinto (Palo Pinto County) CBCs in the last 20-year period. Some of the records are old, some before the turn of the century.

The records are given in their entirety: *Cooke* — spring and winter sightings (Oberholser, 1974), probably representing Ragsdale's records before the 1900s; none since. *Dallas* — Stillwell (1939) recognized this species as a rare winter visitor and gave only three dates. He indicated that a specimen was taken in 1929, but its whereabouts are unknown. More recent reports, approximately 22 records (1951–86), several of which are very likely in error, ranging from 19 September 1964 to 27 May 1954 (seven in fall, seven in winter, and eight in spring). *Denton* — Oberholser (1974) cites summer and fall sight records only (source unknown), probably taken from the local checklist (Rylander, 1959), yet they are not consistent, since the latter reference also gives spring sight records. Three records since, 29 January 1983 and 11 and 20 November 1986. A cataloged specimen (DMNH 3640), allegedly taken on 23 September 1947, is missing from the collection. *Ellis* — one reported at Waxahachie in December 1976, no specific date or details given (Williams, 1977). *Grayson* — Oberholser (1974) lists spring and fall observations. The Hagerman NWR checklist (U.S. Fish and Wildlife Service, 1984) gave it as rare. Eight records are known to me from 19

September 1985 to 26 November 1976 (four in September, two in October, and two in November). *Hunt* — fall 1951 (Baumgartner, 1952), none since. *Johnson* —17 February 1984 (Williams, 1984). *Kaufman* — 29 September 1972, 4 October 1980. *Navarro* — "scarce winter visitor" (Ogilby, 1882). No other sightings. *Palo Pinto* — 23 December 1967, 17 July 1980 (photograph). *Parker* — 28 and 30 January 1972, 28 October 1975. *Rockwall* — 7 April 1979, 22 September 1979. *Tarrant* — 8 September 1982 to 2 May 1985, with two early isolated July records; formerly more abundant than at present (see Pulich, 1979, for other details). *Van Zandt* — 3 October 1982, 29 August and 7 October 1986. *Wilbarger* — Oberholser (1974) indicates that a specimen was taken 1 September (year and whereabouts of specimen are unknown). No other records. *Wise* — winter observation, no details (Oberholser, 1974). *Anderson* —19 June 1973.

PRAIRIE FALCON   *Falco mexicanus* Schlegel
Status: Rare to casual visitor.
Occurrence: This southwestern falcon is rarely reported in north central Texas. The number of records show a decline in recent years in the area, and few birders have observed it in the study area; however, it was never very abundant in north central Texas.

Prairie Falcons are birds of wide-open spaces and are not to be expected in heavily wooded or forested areas. Adults have dark axillaries. They are pale brown in contrast to the much darker Peregrine Falcon, whose bold face pattern and broad black mantle help distinguish the two similar species.

This falcon has been reported in 18 counties of the study area; some of the records are from before the turn of the century and none since. A few records are questionable. The known county records are: *Bosque* —13 April 1985 and 19 November —1986. *Clay* — Lake Arrowhead, 19 January 1985. *Cooke* — Oberholser (1974) gave two summer and winter specimen records, only one located for 5 August 1886 (TNHC 1008). No records since. *Dallas* — Stillwell (1939) listed the species as a rare winter visitor and gave five records, three of which were said to be specimens. None were located. The specimens were taken by Mayer; the dates of collecting precede the establishment of the Dallas Museum of Natural History and apparently were never deposited there. Recent dates, totaling ten dates (1950– 83), range from 24 August 1950 to 17 November 1983, and three isolated reports of 24 January 1959, 9 April 1982, and 21 May 1973. Interestingly, the 17 November 1983 bird spent over a month in downtown Dallas before the given date. *Denton* — four records, 13 September 1986, 13 November 1956, 26 October 1946 (specimen, DMHN 3154), and 5 April 1983. *Fannin* —18 December 1984 and 1986. *Grayson* — two sightings at Hagerman NWR, 6 to 9 March 1955 and 15 December 1984. The local Hagerman NWR checklist (1984) considers this species accidental. *Hunt* — fall observation, no details (Oberholser, 1974) and 27 September 1970. *Kaufman* — 26 October 1984, attacking a Red-tailed Hawk, and 14 and 24 February 1984. *Navarro* — fall and winter sightings, considered "not uncommon" (Ogilby, 1882). No records in present century. *Parker* — 4 March 1969, 15 January 1984, 28 November and 15 December 1985. *Rains* — 25 March 1984. *Somervell* — 1 April 1984. *Tarrant* — six sightings in fall, 30 September 1970 to 25 October 1951, and 16 sightings in late winter and spring from 11 January 1952 to 23 May 1985 (see Pulich, 1979, for specific dates). A date of 11 December 1974 on CBC is questionable. *Wichita* — one record of 26 June (year?) given in local checklist (1976). Whether or not this record is specifically for this county has not been determined; it should be dismissed because of the vagueness of the date and the lack of details. *Wilbarger* — winter specimens given by Oberholser (1974) were not located; one other record for 18 September 1981. *Wise* — two sightings, 15 January 1975 and 1 February 1987. *Young* — winter observation given by Oberholser (1974), but no details, probably before the turn of the century. No other reports.

Specimens: Only two specimens were located for the area under study; see Cooke and Denton counties, above.

Order Galliformes

Family Phasianidae (Turkeys and Quail)

WILD TURKEY *Meleagris gallopavo* Linnaeus

Status: Common to fairly common resident throughout many of the counties of north central Texas, the greatest numbers occurring in the western part of the study area.

Occurrence: Surprisingly, many persons think of the Wild Turkey as a species of the past and believe that it has been extirpated from many counties; however, because of its wiry and secretive nature it is often overlooked by many observers. Although it nearly disappeared, it has made a comeback in recent years and today is frequently observed wherever habitat still exists. Its decline around the turn of the century was due to uncontrolled hunting, especially of toms; habitat destruction; and probably mixing of wild turkeys with domestic stock. The Texas Parks and Wildlife Department has made great strides in restoring this species. Although no efforts have been made to determine all of the reintroductions of Wild Turkeys in the area of study, local hunters and conservation officers were

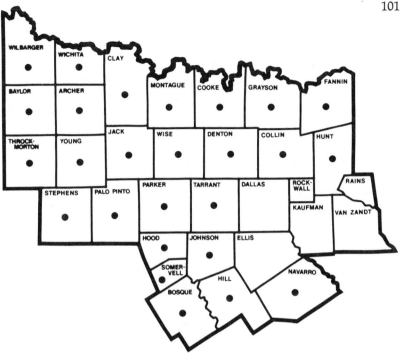

Map 32. Distribution of the Wild Turkey, *Meleagris gallopavo*

quick to mention the efforts to restore this noble bird in north central Texas. For example, on the Waggoner Ranch, in Wilbarger County, local wildlife personnel estimated the Wild Turkey population at 1,500 to 2,000, and the overall county estimate totaled 4,000 in 1983.

Wild Turkeys have been reported in 26 counties in the north central Texas study area. The only counties where they have not been reported are Dallas, Ellis, Kaufman, Rains, Rockwall, and Van Zandt; however, it is very likely that Wild Turkeys historically ranged through these counties too. Nearly all reports except those for Collin and Navarro counties are recent. Ogilby (1882) pointed out that they were common in "wooded districts," yet no sightings have been made in Navarro County since the 1880s.

The Texas Parks and Wildlife Department (pers. comm.) estimated that there were approximately 39,500 turkeys in the north central Texas study area in 1983, the greatest number being found in Palo Pinto (6,000) and Throckmorton (6,500) counties. The counties along the eastern side of the study area have never completely recovered from their near depletion, though small releases have been made off and on. In the eastern part of Texas releases of brood stock apparently of the wrong origin have failed until those acquired from neighboring southeastern states were reintroduced. These now seem to be more successful, according to Texas Parks and Wildlife Department personnel.

Nesting: Nesting has been recorded by Oberholser (1974) from only Clay, Wilbarger, and Wise counties, these being old records. Twelve to 14 young were seen in Tarrant County on 9 July 1986. These were the result of introduced turkeys at the Fort Worth Nature Center. The only other recent nesting record that can be added to this is a nest with 15 eggs found in Eastland County on 13 April 1982. There is little doubt that Wild Turkeys nest in many of the counties in which they occur, but nesting studies have not been undertaken.

Specimens: Oberholser (1974) noted specimens from Collin, Cooke, Grayson, Hunt, and Wilbarger counties. Of these the only specimen located was one taken from Wilbarger County on 27 December 1940 (CMNH 25921).

Originally the subspecies of Wild Turkey in north central Texas was said to represent *Meleagris gallopavo intermedia.* Stocks planted in the area today represent turkeys trapped from the Edwards Plateau, south Texas, and eastern and southeastern United States. Thus bloodlines may come from three races, and the population does not contain the original race that ranged through the area. It is not "true" *intermedia* but a mixture of wild stock.

NORTHERN BOBWHITE   *Colinus virginianus* (Linnaeus)
Status: Common to abundant permanent resident.
Occurrence: This species has been recorded in all the counties of north central Texas, as well as the adjacent counties.

Wherever proper habitat exists — for example, moderate cover where food flourishes — the Northern Bobwhite persists even in cities and towns. Grains and a variety of weed seed, particularly doveweed, *Croton* sp., along with small fruits and seeds from trees and shrubs, are the mainstay food supply. When man destroys its habitat or its food sources dwindle, the population suffers. Prolonged cold and freezing weather also drastically reduces quail. However, it comes back quickly if conditions are present to allow it to recover, and this important wildlife resource will continue to exist in north central Texas as long as some habitats are maintained.

Nesting: The Northern Bobwhite commonly nests throughout the study area but only once a season. Quail will renest several times if they are disturbed or if something happens to the first clutches of eggs. No effort has been made to list all the counties where it has been observed nesting, but if one were to do a nesting survey, it would be readily tallied. It normally breeds from early April to early October.

Specimens: Specimens have been collected from the following counties: Archer (MWU), Baylor (Oberholser, 1974; not located), Clay (MWU),

Cooke (ACG, TNHC), Dallas (DMNH, UTA, WMP), Denton (DMNH, MWU), Grayson (UTA), Hill (SM), Hood (FWMSH), Johnson (SUC, WMP), Kaufman (UTA), Palo Pinto (WMP), Somervell (SM), Tarrant (FWMSH, UTA, WMP), Throckmorton (FWMSH), Wichita (MWU), and Young (FWMSH).

Three subspecies have been recorded in north central Texas, *Colinus virginianus virginianus*, *C. v. taylori*, and *C. v. texanus*, according to the AOU *Check-list* (1957), while Oberholser (1974) describes *mexicanus*, which he split from the nominate race. Unfortunately, the status has not been properly studied. Local sportsmen and the Texas Parks and Wildlife Department have widely introduced hatchery birds whose racial origins are unknown throughout the range. The racial problem is far from settled in the north central Texas counties. Few if any of the specimens listed above have been examined.

SCALED QUAIL   *Callipepla squamata* (Vigors)
Status: Fairly common resident along the western side of the study area.
Occurrence: The Scaled Quail has been recorded in 11 north central counties—Archer, Baylor, Cooke, Grayson, Fannin, Montague, Tarrant, Throckmorton, Wichita, Wilbarger, and Young—and in nearby Haskell, Shackelford, and Stonewall counties.

Scaled Quail formerly ranged along the virgin grasslands of the Red River drainage to Fannin County, but today there is little habitat left there to favor them. The lands are now farms and pastures. The last members of this species collected beyond its present range were four said to have been taken from Montague County on 4 December 1951 (Oberholser, 1974). Records for Cooke and Fannin counties were specimens collected in the mid-1880s. The Grayson County record is unexplainable and, like the Tarrant County record, may represent released birds. The latter county has never had Scaled Quail, and I discounted this record years ago as describing birds that had escaped from a game-bird fancier's aviary.

The present range includes only six counties along the western edge of the study area, all having low rainfall: Archer, Baylor, Throckmorton, Wichita, Wilbarger, and Young. The range is limited to grasslands invaded by cholla and prickly-pear cacti.

Sutton (1963) documents the interbreeding of Northern Bobwhites and Scaled Quail in Stonewall County and adjacent Motley County. In conversations with quail hunters in the counties (all having both species) listed in the paragraph above, they indicated that hybrids would be found in Throckmorton, Wilbarger, and Young counties, yet to date none of the hunters have substantiated their claims with specimens. Examples should be saved and sent to me or other authorities for documentation.
Specimens: Although Scaled Quail specimens are said to have been taken

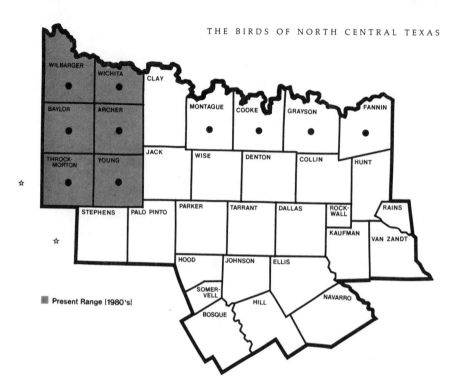

Map 33. Distribution of the Scaled Quail, *Callipepla squamata*, with recent and historic records

in Baylor, Cooke, Fannin, Montague, and Wilbarger counties (Oberholser, 1974), the only specimen that could be found was one taken from Archer County (MWU) on 26 December 1958.

Order Gruiformes

Family Rallidae (Rails, Gallinules, and Coots)

YELLOW RAIL *Coturnicops noveboracensis* (Gmelin)
Status: Casual transient.
Occurrence: Although Oberholser (1974) indicated that this tiny rail has occurred in Dallas, Rockwall, and Tarrant counties, I prefer to accept only the first record. See Pulich (1979) for comments on Tarrant County. Two other vague records for Grayson County in 1975 were also questioned and rejected.

Pulich (1961) provided a detailed account of the Dallas County record at Cedar Hill, which was based on specimens (DMNH, WMP) taken the night of 15–16 October 1960, when 13 Yellow Rails struck a local TV tower. The dates were reported erroneously by Baumgartner (1961). The above Rockwall County record was allegedly based on a winter specimen (Oberholser, 1974), but the whereabouts of this bird are unknown.

BLACK RAIL *Laterallus jamaicensis* (Gmelin)
Status: Casual transient.
Occurrence: Like the records for the Yellow Rail, above, the records for this tiny, elusive rail are questionable. None are recent. Although it has been reported in four north central Texas counties, I have dismissed the records for Dallas (8 October 1957), Grayson (17 June 1958), and Tarrant (Oberholser, 1974) counties. The Black Rail must be listed as hypothetical for these counties until there is more conclusive evidence of its occurrence.
Specimens: Oberholser (1974) lists a specimen taken at Gainesville, Cooke County, on 11 September 1889; however, I have been unable to locate this specimen.

KING RAIL *Rallus elegans* Audubon
Status: Rare to casual transient. Formerly nested.
Occurrence: King Rails have been recorded in 11 counties in the north central Texas study area — Cooke, Dallas, Denton, Grayson, Hunt, Navarro, Palo Pinto, Rains, Tarrant, Wichita, and Wilbarger — and in nearby Henderson County.

Since 1970 there have been fewer than 12 records of this rail for the entire study area. Environmental changes and continued removal of freshwater marshes have eliminated this species from a number of areas where it could formerly be found regularly. This is especially true in the northwestern part; for example, Watt's Lake, in Wilbarger County, was completely drained many years ago.

County records since 1970 include: *Dallas* — common in the 1930s (Stillwell, 1939), 13 September 1970 and 20 April 1984; *Grayson* — 12 May, 11 June, and 18 July, and 13 August record given below, all in 1977; *Palo Pinto* — 5 September 1976; *Rains* — 29 April 1987; *Tarrant* — 21 July and 8 August 1970 (one or two seen daily); *Wichita* — 4 October 1974 (specimen), 6 and 7 November 1982 and 18 December 1982. *Henderson* — 30 August 1980.

Nesting: Few King Rails nest today in the counties of north central Texas: Cooke — records show that they were found nesting before 1900. Dallas — there were nesting sightings in the late 1960s, but there has been no evidence since 1969. Grayson — juvenile noted 13 August 1977. Hunt, Navarro, and Wichita — old records (Oberholser, 1974). Wilbarger — also old records (More and Strecker, 1929). Probably one of the few areas where King Rails can still be found nesting is in nearby Henderson County, especially at Koon Kreek Klub, which provides suitable marshy habitat.

Specimens: King Rail specimens have been taken from the following counties: Cooke (TNHC), two; Dallas (DMNH), five; Denton (DMNH), one; and Wichita (MWU), four. Specimens indicated by Oberholser (1974) from Navarro and Wilbarger counties were not located.

VIRGINIA RAIL   *Rallus limicola* Vieillot

Status: Uncommon to rare transient. Rare to casual in winter. Casual in summer.

Occurrence: This beautiful little rail has been reported in 11 of the north central Texas counties: Archer, Cooke, Dallas, Denton, Ellis, Grayson, Navarro, Rains, Tarrant, Van Zandt, and Wichita.

This seldom-seen, secretive rail may be more widespread than is generally realized. For example, in Tarrant County in recent years observers have been able to readily determine the presence of this rail by using tape recordings and can thereby obtain more records. As many as five Virginia Rails answered tape recordings on 31 March 1985 and seven on 20 December 1986. In other locales the lack of observers is the reason for the small number of records. Limited habitat, along with environmental changes, may also prevent the bird from being more widespread. The available records make it difficult to assess its status accurately.

Spring and fall transient records for selected counties are: *Dallas* —11 April 1983, 19 April 1974, 14 September 1974, 22 September 1957, 16 October 1960, and 26 October 1963; *Grayson* — 3 May 1975, 16 May 1971, 20 May 1968, 9 August 1976 (heard), 23 September 1966, 30 September 1975, 5 October 1969, and 14 November 1985; *Tarrant* —15 and 17 August 1951, 2 and 4 September 1967, 12 September 1958, 20 September 1967, 10 October 1954, 20 and 28 October 1984, 12 March 1984, four times from 12 March to 31 March 1985, 3 and 28 April 1985, 22 April 1984, and 21 May 1983; *Van Zandt* — 4 May 1985; *Wichita* — 2 March 1983, 8 and 9 April 1978, 2 August to 26 August 1974, and 24 October 1978.

The Virginia Rail has been recorded in the following counties in the winter: Dallas — winter period of 1950–51 and 5 November 1956; Denton — 20 December 1952 and 28 December 1982; Grayson —11 and 16 December 1979; Rains — 5 December 1982; Tarrant —1 November 1986 and 20 and 24 November 1984, 21 December 1985 (five), 22 January 1985, and 5 February 1983; Wichita —18 December 1982.

Nesting: The Virginia Rail has been found nesting twice in north central Texas. Adults with two young were carefully observed in Dallas County on 25 July 1937, and in Archer County an adult and five downy chicks were found on 26 July 1973. The latter were viewed by numerous persons

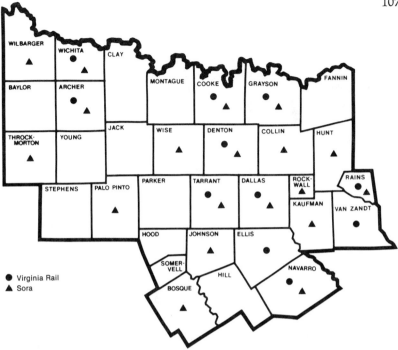

Map 34. Distribution of the Virginia Rail, *Rallus limicola*, and the Sora, *Porzana carolina*

throughout the summer and into September. Oberholser (1974) cites the banding of five young in Navarro County in July 1937, but he questions this record as well as the Dallas record. Since four of the Navarro County young were said to have been banded, I asked the U.S. Fish and Wildlife Service Banding Office to check the band size used, and they proved to be No. 5—too large for Virginia Rails, which require No. 3 bands. No. 5 bands are used for King Rails, which were common in north central Texas in the 1930s. The Virginia Rail is a smaller version of the King Rail. Pulich (1979) discussed a possible nesting record in Tarrant County on 25 July 1972. There is a vague mid-June record (Williams, 1977) for Ellis County. *Specimens:* Specimens have been taken from Dallas (DMNH, WMP), Denton (DMNH, WMP), Grayson (KH), and Tarrant (FWMSH) counties.

SORA *Porzana carolina* (Linnaeus)
Status: Uncommon to common transient. Summer sightings, but nesting has not been confirmed. Rare to uncommon winter resident locally.
Occurrence: The sora has been recorded in 19 north central Texas counties: Archer, Bosque, Collin, Cooke, Dallas, Denton, Grayson, Hunt, John-

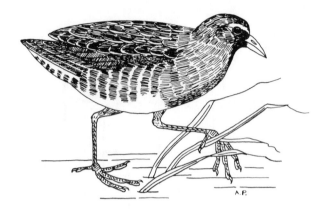

son, Kaufman, Navarro, Palo Pinto, Rains, Rockwall, Tarrant, Throck-morton, Wichita, Wilbarger, and Wise.

This small rail is normally found from late August to early May. Extreme arrival and departure dates for selected counties are: *Dallas* — 23 August 1984 to 15 May 1971; *Grayson* — 7 August to 23 October and 1 April to 26 May (surprisingly, there are no winter dates); *Tarrant* — 25 August 1956 to 27 May 1956; *Wichita* — 23 August 1974 to 10 April 1978.

There are no records for June and only five scattered records for July: 4 July 1935, pair (Dallas County), 10 July 1977 (Grayson County), 18 July 1959 (Denton County), and specimens taken on 28 July 1971, 1985 (Palo Pinto and Henderson counties).

Stillwell (1939) listed this species as a summer resident in Dallas County, and Baumgartner (1959) indicates nesting on 18 July 1959; although he implies that a young was observed, he offers no details. Oberholser (1974) gives this date but then points out that "actual records of nests, eggs, or chicks are lacking" for the state. The local Dallas checklist (Pulich, 1977b) does not consider this species a nesting species. The nearest known southern nesting is Kansas (Johnston, 1964).

The winter records are not as numerous or as widespread. The numbers of sightings for December for various counties are: one for Dallas, six for Denton, one for Kaufman, 15 for Tarrant, and four for Wichita. There are only three sightings for January, 1 January 1955 and 1956 (Tarrant County) and a specimen on 18 January 1960 (Wichita County), and one for February on 22 February 1977 (Wichita County).

Specimens: Sora specimens are available from the following counties: Cooke (TNHC); Dallas (DMNH, WMP); Denton (DMNH, WMP); Hunt and Kaufman (Oberholser, 1974, not located); Palo Pinto (WMP); Tarrant (DMNH, FWMSH, WMP); and Wichita (DMNH, MWU).

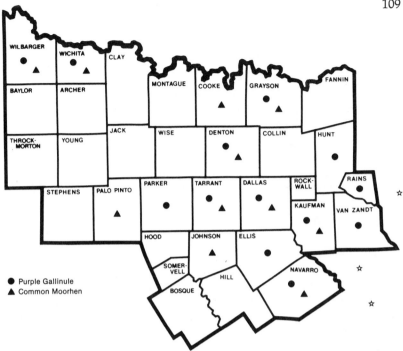

Map 35. Distribution of the Purple Gallinule, *Porphyrula martinica*, and the Common Moorhen, *Gallinula chloropus*

PURPLE GALLINULE *Porphyrula martinica* (Linnaeus)
Status: Rare to casual summer resident.
Occurrence: The Purple Gallinule has been recorded in 13 counties of the study area — Dallas, Denton, Ellis, Grayson, Hunt, Kaufman, Navarro, Parker, Rains, Tarrant, Van Zandt, Wichita, and Wilbarger — and nearby Anderson, Henderson, and Wood counties.

This species is mainly found in the southeastern part of the study area. Like most of the other rallids, it is being eliminated as much of the habitat that favors this rail gradually disappears.

All of the county dates known to me are for spring and summer, except for an unexplainable record of a specimen taken on 25 February 1971 in Wichita County: *Dallas* — 2 May 1962, 5 June 1965, 7 to 16 May 1976, 19 June 1977, 27 May 1978, 31 May 1978 (last two dates at two locations), and 6 May 1987; *Denton* — spring (Oberholser, 1974); *Ellis* — 23 May 1947, 31 May 1984; *Grayson* — 26 May 1977; *Hunt* and *Navarro* — summer and spring records (Oberholser, 1974); *Kaufman* — 19 April 1976; *Parker* — 16 June 1976; *Rains* — 9 June 1983; *Tarrant* — five spring dates, 3 May 1978 to 30 May 1984 (specimen), and three summer dates, 20 July 1946, early

September 1956, and 22 June 1985; *Van Zandt* — 5 June 1974, 9 June 1973; *Wichita* — accidental, see above; *Wilbarger* — old summer record (Oberholser, 1974).

Nesting: Purple Gallinules still breed in Anderson and Henderson counties, just outside the study area. They formerly bred in Dallas County — last report 10 August 1959 (young). Although Sutton (1938) indicated that they formerly bred in Tarrant County, there is no evidence that they do so today. However, they may be overlooked because of their reluctance to leave the few dense marshy habitats that remain.

Specimens: Specimens are from the following counties: Ellis (DMNH); Henderson (DMNH); Hunt (Oberholser, 1974, not located); Tarrant (WMP); and Wichita (MWU).

COMMON MOORHEN   *Gallinula chloropus* (Linnaeus)

Status: Rare to casual summer resident. Scattered winter records, mainly in the Dallas–Fort Worth area. Casual transient in some counties.

Occurrence: The Common Moorhen, formerly called Common Gallinule, has been reported from only 11 counties in the study area — Cooke, Dallas, Denton, Grayson, Johnson, Kaufman, Navarro, Palo Pinto, Tarrant, Wichita, and Wilbarger — and nearby Anderson and Henderson counties.

The secretiveness of this rail, like that of most other members of this family, makes it difficult to assess the population of the Common Moorhen. It was once much more widespread over the area than it is today. Presented herein are county records known to me in the study area: *Cooke* — specimen records only, 15 May 1889 and 20 June 1889. *Dallas* — reported every month except November, seen on every CBC from 1965 to 1970, on only one CBC since. *Denton* — three records, 14 January 1966, May (year?), and 7 September 1958. *Grayson* — 14 October 1946, 13 to 26 September 1960, 1 to 6 June 1967, 9 October 1971, 5 to 8 November 1974, 28 June 1979, 14 August to 4 September 1980, and 22 April 1982, *Johnson* — 2 October 1983. *Kaufman* — 2 September to 4 October 1985. *Navarro* — 23 July 1931 (Stillwell, 1939). *Palo Pinto* — 25 October 1975 and 5 and 6 September 1976. *Tarrant* — reported all months except March, latest reports 7 June 1985, 27 April, 27 September, and 10 through 18 October 1986. *Wichita* — 17 May 1973 to 12 June 1975; *Wilbarger* — no recent records.

Nesting: Like population, nesting appears to be decreasing somewhat in the area. Records for selected counties are: Dallas — commonly nesting up to the 1960s; recent nesting dates: 19 September 1963, adult with four young; 25 July 1965, four family groups; 24 July 1966, two family groups; 19 July 1969, small young; 20 July 1974, adults with four young; 21 July 1982, two adults and five young; 10 July 1983, pair with five young; 28 and 29 July 1984, adults accompanied by seven young and nine young; 7 July 1985, 13 adults, 26 young. Tarrant — no nests have been reported since 30 July

1958. Wichita — Oberholser (1974) notes Common Moorhens "nesting likely," although I have no evidence to support this statement. Wilbarger — More and Strecker (1929) indicated that this species may have "occasionally" bred here, but nests were never found. Anderson — Oberholser (1974) gave nesting records and they can still be found nesting in this county. *Specimens:* Common Moorhen specimens are available from Cooke (TNCH), Dallas (WMP), and Wichita (MWU) counties, and adjacent Henderson County (DMNH).

AMERICAN COOT   *Fulica americana* Gmelin
Status: Abundant to common in migration. Common to fairly common in winter. Rare to irregular summer resident.
Occurrence: American Coots have been reported in all counties of the study area except Montague, and in adjacent Henderson County. No doubt they occur in all of the counties but have been overlooked. They frequently mingle with ducks, and, unlike other rails, they are easily seen and are occasionally mistaken for ducks by persons unfamiliar with them.

This species has been recorded in every month of the year in many counties. They frequent large bodies of water where there are cattails and rushes, and they are usually found in fall from mid-September with numbers peaking in mid-October. Random large numbers for selected counties are: Dallas — 1,500 on 15 October 1972; 3,000 on 19 October 1980; 2,000 on 12 October 1982. Grayson — 4,000 on 2 November 1950; 5,000 on 8 October 1977. Palo Pinto — 10,000 on 16 October 1976; 3,500 on 8 and 9 October 1977. Tarrant — 3,500 from 10 through 18 October 1953. Van Zandt — thousands on 6 October 1985.

Although occasionally several thousand coots can be seen in the spring, they are never as numerous as the large rafts in fall. They peak in the spring, from early March to late April.

Coots have been reported on all the CBCs. Their numbers are never as large as those in migration, but they are usually recorded if the weather is mild and if the participants visit the appropriate habitats. They are more numerous in the southeastern part of the study area than in the northern part along the Red River. The mean count for Hagerman NWR (18 years, Grayson County) count and Wichita Falls (ten years, Wichita County) was 71 and 41 coots, respectively, while in the southern part they averaged the following numbers for 18 years: 370 in Lewisville, Denton County; 345 in Fort Worth, Tarrant County; and 318 in Dallas, Dallas County.
Nesting: Nesting (eggs or young) has been recorded in Baylor (formerly), Dallas, Grayson, Palo Pinto, Tarrant, and Wise (formerly) counties, and nearby Henderson County. Overall nesting ranges from late June to early August.
Specimens: Specimens of American Coot have been taken in the follow-

ing counties: Archer (MWU), Baylor (MWU), Cooke (TNHC), Dallas (DMNH, WMP), Denton (DMNH), Hill (SM), Johnson (SUC), Tarrant (DMNH, FWMSH, SUC, UTA), and Wise (UTA).

Family Gruidae (Cranes)

SANDHILL CRANE   *Grus canadensis* (Linnaeus)
Status: Common to fairly common transient. A few winter in the western portion of the study area.
Occurrence: Sandhill Cranes have been reported in all but three counties of the study area, Jack, Kaufman, and Van Zandt. Since these counties are on the main flyway, it is very likely that they will be recorded there too sooner or later. They have also been reported in nearby Comanche and Erath counties.

This species is primarily a migrant in north central Texas. However, a few winter on the high plains east to about Wichita County down to Palo Pinto County. In the winter of 1982–83 in Wilbarger County about 1,000 wintered on the Waggoner Ranch, and 500 wintered northeast of Vernon on the Red River. They arrived in November, fed on the wheat fields, and departed in early February. Most December dates are records of stragglers that lingered along their way to the Gulf Coast.

Extreme fall and spring dates of passage for counties having numerous observations are: *Dallas* — 3 September 1982 (two), next-earliest 17 October 1980 to 18 December 1976, next-latest 7 December 1973, and 17 February 1939 to 26 April 1971; *Grayson* — 22 October to 20 November 1976 and 2 March to 18 April; *Palo Pinto* — 20 September 1960, next-earliest 16 October 1976 to 26 November 1978, and 14 January 1978 (winter birds?) to 20 March 1977; *Tarrant* — 20 September 1983 to 18 December 1982 and 25 January 1985, next-earliest 23 February 1939 to 26 April 1977; *Wichita* — 7 October 1977 to 16 December 1977, and 4 February 1976 to 8 April 1975.

It is not uncommon to see 1,000 or more Sandhill Cranes on their way north or south in migration. They are seldom seen on the ground but are more frequently observed in passage, calling or bugling in flight. They peak in mid-October and in mid-March. One of the most spectacular flights occurred on 17 and 18 March 1978, when more than 20,000 passed through an area from Dallas County to the west near Palo Pinto County in numerous flocks, some of up to 1,000 cranes each.
Specimens: Sandhill Crane specimens have been collected from the following counties: Archer (MWU), Clay (not located), Cooke (not located), Dallas (DMNH), Grayson (not located), Stephens (MWU), Tarrant (UTA), and Wilbarger (not located).

According to Oberholser (1974), both the nominate race *G. c. canaden-*

sis and the western race *tabida* have been taken in north central Texas. Unfortunately, none of the recent specimens have been identified as to subspecies.

WHOOPING CRANE   *Grus americana* (Linnaeus)
Status: Casual transient, mainly in the northwestern part of the study area. Many more recent observations are due to careful monitoring by federal authorities.
Occurrence: In their annual trek from the Wood Buffalo National Park, in the Northwest Territories of Canada, the Whooping Cranes fly a 5,000-mile round-trip to and from the Aransas NWR on the Texas Gulf Coast. They have been recorded in 13 counties (former and present records) of north central Texas. Oberholser (1974) gives records for Clay, Cooke, Dallas, Fannin, Navarro, Tarrant, and Young counties, where they have been seen or collected in the past. To these counties I have added reports for Baylor, Ellis, Jack, Johnson, Parker, and Wilbarger counties and additional sightings for Clay, Dallas, and Tarrant counties. There are unconfirmed reports from Kaufman and Van Zandt counties that I have dismissed since details are lacking or vague.

Ogilby (1882) indicated that about 100 years ago Whooping Cranes passed through Navarro County "in considerable numbers both at spring and fall migration." The dates coincide with the present "about the last week of March — continue about three weeks," while October was "the season of the return migration." He saw as many as 20 in a flock compared with present-day sightings of only a pair or a family group.

County records known to me but not given by Oberholser include: *Baylor* — three, fall of 1967. *Clay* — family group on Red River near Byers on 27 October to 1 November 1981; pair with young on 29 October 1981; and five (four adults and one immature) on 11 April 1984. *Ellis* — sighted but no details given, 16 April 1976. *Jack* — a film of three passing over Jacksboro area in the spring of 1983 was shown as part of a TV special in 1984. *Johnson* — two over Keene on 27 October 1981. *Parker* — two at Aledo, near the Tarrant county line, on 31 March 1974. *Tarrant* — over the Dallas–Fort Worth Regional Airport in the fall of 1981 (Texas Parks and Wildlife Department, 1983). *Wilbarger* — three north of Vernon in the fall of 1979.

In adjacent Comanche County two landed near Comanche on 25 October 1977 and stayed until 1 November, during which time game wardens guarded the birds from people coming to see them. In October 1982 an immature that had been followed south the previous year by radio transmitter flew into a power line and was killed near Waco, McClennan County.
Specimens: A Whooping Crane collected in Clay County on 14 April 1904 by R. L. More was the only specimen (CMNH 29853) located for north central Texas that bears scientific data. However, one was found in the

Map 36. Distribution of the Whooping Crane, *Grus americana*

More collection that is still held by the family at Vernon, and a mounted juvenile, without any data, was found in the Dallas Museum of Natural History. The dates and locations of these examples are lacking. The other specimens collected for Clay County about 1908 (Oberholser, 1974) were not located.

Order Charadriiformes

Family Charadriidae (Plovers)

BLACK-BELLIED PLOVER   *Pluvialis squatarola* (Linnaeus)
Status: Uncommon transient.
Occurrence: Black-bellied Plovers have been recorded in 18 counties of north central Texas: Archer, Clay, Collin, Cooke, Dallas, Denton, Grayson, Hill, Hunt, Johnson, Kaufman, Palo Pinto, Parker, Rains, Tarrant, Throckmorton, Van Zandt, and Wichita.

This species is usually reported in spring and fall but not in great

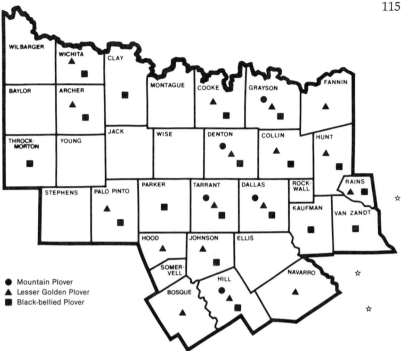

Map 37. Distribution of the Black-bellied Plover, *Pluvialis squatarola; the Lesser Golden-Plover, P. dominica;* and the Mountain Plover, *Charadrius montanus*

numbers. It passes through the area in spring from mid-March to late May, and again in fall from late July to mid-November. There seem to be more observations for fall than for spring and over a longer period of time. Extremes for overall county dates are: 17 March 1959 (Tarrant) to 2 June 1938 (Dallas), and 26 July 1962 (Dallas) to 18 December (Grayson). Peak of movement for fall is from mid-September to mid-October.

Migration dates for selected counties are: *Dallas* — 27 March 1982 to 20 May 1982, and 26 July 1962 to 23 November 1979; *Grayson* — 5 April to 23 May, and 25 July to 18 December; *Tarrant* —17 March 1959 to 21 May 1959, 1985, and 15 August 1953 to 4 December 1954; *Wichita* — 26 March 1974 to 14 May 1975, and 25 August 1974 to 10 November 1973.

There are two winter records: a specimen collected in Archer County on 6 January 1959 and a bird seen on the CBC in Denton County on 29 December 1975. Although the Texas CBC editor questioned this sighting, I have no reason to doubt its validity since it was carefully documented by the persons providing the record. Two other winter records, both for Grayson County, on 20 January and 27 February, neither given with year, were dismissed because the records were vague and the sources of the records were not located.

Specimens: Black-bellied Plovers have been collected in Archer (MWU), Denton (DMNH), and Tarrant (WMP) counties. With the exception of the first record, all are fall specimens.

LESSER GOLDEN-PLOVER   *Pluvialis dominica* (Müller)
Status: Uncommon to rare transient.
Occurrence: Lesser Golden-Plovers have been found in 17 counties of north central Texas: Archer, Bosque, Collin, Cooke, Dallas, Denton, Fannin, Grayson, Hill, Hood, Hunt, Johnson, Navarro, Palo Pinto, Rains, Tarrant, and Wichita.

Overall this species is found in north central Texas from mid-March to mid-May in spring and in fall from mid-August to early November. Early and late spring and fall dates for selected counties are: *Dallas* – 4 March 1973, next-earliest 9 March 1986 to 24 May 1981, and 14 July 1978 to 14 November 1965, 1971; *Grayson* – 1 March to 27 May, and an isolated date, 9 July, and 2 September to 25 November; *Tarrant* – 8 March 1986 to 21 May 1986 and 28 July 1983, next 13 August 1986 to 3 November, next-latest 29 October 1978.

There are two December sightings of this plover: at Hagerman NWR (Grayson County) on 4 December 1980 and a crippled bird in Denton County on 11 December 1965.
Specimens: Only two specimens of this plover, both females, are known from north central Texas: one from Archer County taken on 4 November 1956 (MWU 126) and the other from Denton County taken on 18 September 1948 (DMNH 3635). The whereabouts of a Cooke County specimen (Oberholser, 1974) have not been determined.

SNOWY PLOVER   *Charadrius alexandrinus* Linnaeus
Status: Rare transient in spring and fall. Formerly nested in the north-western part of north central Texas study area.
Occurrence: This little plover has been reported in eight north central Texas counties: Clay, Dallas, Denton, Palo Pinto, Rockwall, Tarrant, Wichita, and Wilbarger.

Some extreme county dates are: *Dallas* – 23 March 1974 to 17 April 1982 and 18 August 1959 to 30 October 1966, next-latest 7 October 1984; *Grayson* – 13 April to 19 May and 7 July 1956 (specimen) to 22 September and a late date, 25 October 1975; *Tarrant* – 28 March 1959 to 29 April 1979 and 10 August 1956 to 26 October 1969; *Wichita* – 3 March 1976 (exceptionally early) to 23 May 1979 and 4 July 1974 to 30 October 1975 and an exceptionally late bird on 18 November 1975.

A record given for Denton County on 29 January 1955 (Baumgartner, 1955) was dismissed. Rylander (1959), who, along with another observer,

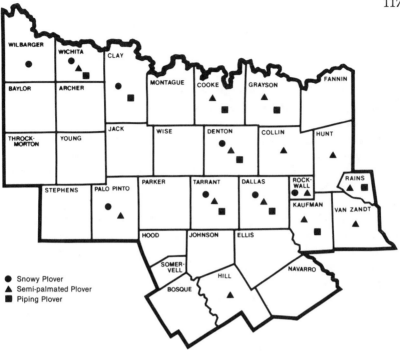

Map 38. Distribution of the one-banded plovers: the Snowy Plover, *Charadrius alexandrinus;* the Semipalmated Plover, *C. semipalmatus;* and the Piping Plover, *C. melodus*

is credited with this sighting, did not include it in his local checklist for the county in question.

Nesting: More and Strecker (1929) found this species nesting not uncommonly with Least Terns on the Pease River, Wilbarger County; however, since that time no nesting birds have been sighted in north central Texas. There is one date from Tarrant County, 13 June 1973, but there were no signs of nesting. This bird was originally misidentified as a Piping Plover (Pulich, 1979). I noted four Snowy Plovers on sandbars on the Red River, Wichita County, on 11 July 1981, but they were so far away that it could not be determined whether they were a migrating group or a family group. It is very likely that this species breeds along the Red River, but there is no evidence to support recent nesting even though it nested during More and Strecker's time. This area of the Red River is virtually unchecked by birders. The Snowy Plover may be declining and becoming as rare as the Piping Plover.

Specimens: Specimens of Snowy Plovers are represented from Grayson County on 7 July 1956, 19 July 1976, and 3 October 1953 (all OU) and from Tarrant County on 25 August 1956 (WMP). These represent the western race *C. a. nivosus.*

SEMIPALMATED PLOVER   *Charadrius semipalmatus* Bonaparte
Status: Fairly common transient in spring and fall.
Occurrence: This little sandpiper has been recorded in 14 counties in the study area: Collin, Cooke, Dallas, Denton, Grayson, Hill, Hunt, Kaufman, Palo Pinto, Rains, Rockwall, Tarrant, Van Zandt, and Wichita.

Semipalmated Plovers are the most common of the small one-ringed plovers that pass through north central Texas. They are never found in flocks; usually only three or four scattered birds are seen at a time, though during peaks of movement ten to 12 have been observed on mud flats or sandbars where shorebirds concentrate. On one occasion, 26 April 1980, 21 were observed in Fort Worth, Tarrant County. The peak of migration in spring ranges from mid-April to mid-May, and in fall from mid-August to mid-September. Extreme overall dates for the study area counties are 27 March 1982 to 23 May 1963 (both Dallas), and 7 July 1985 (also Dallas) to 29 October 1969 (Denton).

Some extreme migration dates where enough county data are available are: *Dallas* — spring (see paragraph above) and fall, 7 July 1985 to 21 October 1976; *Grayson* — 16 April 1978 to 16 May 1975, and 15 July 1973 to 21 October 1978; *Tarrant* — 6 April 1986 to 10 May 1969, and 20 July 1985 to 22 October 1973; *Wichita* — 18 April 1973 to 16 May 1973, and 31 July 1973 to 28 October 1973.

This species was recorded on two Dallas CBCs: 15 December 1973 and 14 December 1974. On these dates two and 26 Semipalmated Plovers, respectively, were tallied by the same compiler. The latter number was not underlined as important. Because of the casual manner in which these reports were given, I have discounted both as misidentifications. There are no other winter reports for north central Texas.
Specimens: Specimens have been taken in Denton (DMNH, WMP), Grayson (OU), and Tarrant (FWMSH, WMP) counties.

PIPING PLOVER   *Charadrius melodus* Ord
Status: Casual to rare transient in both spring and fall.
Occurrence: There are reports of Piping Plovers for nine north central Texas counties: Clay, Cooke, Dallas, Denton, Grayson, Kaufman, Rains, Tarrant, and Wichita. Sightings are most numerous where there is much birdwatching, but in several counties it has been seen only once. There seem to be more sightings for fall than for spring.

Records for the nine counties are: *Clay* — 11 October 1975; *Cooke* — spring and fall "to about Gainesville," no specific dates (Wolfe, Pulich, and Tucker, 1974); *Dallas* — about 12 times, 21 April 1983 to 4 May 1937, and 18 July 1968 to 22 October 1976; *Denton* — May and August (Rylander, 1959); *Grayson* — about 25 times since the early 1970s, all for Hagerman NWR, 13 April to 28 April, and 14 July 1970 to 25 September 1975; *Kaufman* —12 May 1973; *Rains* — 20 August 1984; *Tarrant* — 9 times, 16 April 1985, 12 May 1971, 26 July 1979, 27 July 1986, 31 July 1984, 4 August 1971, 17 August 1985, 26 August 1984, and 30 August through 3 September 1982 (photograph); *Wichita* —14 and 20 April 1975, and 20 July 1975. *Specimens:* No specimens of this little plover for north central Texas are known to me.

KILLDEER   *Charadrius vociferus* Linnaeus
Status: Abundant to common the year round.
Occurrence: This species is the only "true" plover that is found in all north central Texas counties as well as the adjacent counties. The birds are usually found throughout the year, although their numbers may vary. Not only are they found near water, but they are equally at home on short-grass pastures, golf courses, and schoolyards, to give a few examples. Data on hand indicate that they become more numerous during the fall in late August and September into October, when they gather in flocks, possibly family groups, into the hundreds after they have finished nesting. They may also be seen in flocks in spring but never in as great numbers.

Killdeers have been observed on all the CBCs of the area and usually every year. They are less numerous in the northern sectors of the study area than the southern parts. CBCs from Wichita Falls (Wichita County) and Hagerman NWR (Grayson County) show maximum numbers of 35 and 44 over ten and 18 years of counts, respectively, while Lewisville (Denton County), Fort Worth (Tarrant County), and Dallas (Dallas County) show a maximum of 108, 127, and 300 Killdeers, respectively, for 18 years.
Nesting: Young or eggs have been found in 23 counties in north central Texas: Archer, Baylor, Bosque, Clay, Collin, Cooke, Dallas, Denton, Grayson, Hill, Hunt, Kaufman, Navarro, Palo Pinto, Parker, Rains, Rockwall, Tarrant, Throckmorton, Van Zandt, Wichita, Wilbarger, and Wise. No doubt they would be found nesting in all counties if nests were sought during the breeding season. Being ground nesters, they use the shoulders of roads built up with gravel in which to place their nests, which are no more than hollowed-out depressions. In cities graveled rooftops afford nesting sites. Nests are also found on well-drained overgrazed pastures and cultivated fields, especially those containing much gravel and rock.

Extreme nesting dates for Dallas County range from 6 March 1978 (three eggs) to 18 August 1971 (four young banded). Other counties — Collin, Denton, Grayson, Tarrant, and Wichita — show almost identical nesting periods, with peaks of nesting around the middle of April for all counties. *Specimens:* Killdeer specimens are available from the following counties: Dallas (DMNH, UTA); Denton (DMNH); Cooke (Oberholser, 1974), not located; Johnson (SUC, WMP); Kaufman (WMP); Tarrant (FWMSH, UTA, WMP); and Wichita (DMNH).

MOUNTAIN PLOVER   *Charadrius montanus* Townsend
Status: Casual to rare transient.
Occurrence: Mountain Plovers have been recorded in the following north central Texas counties: Dallas, Denton, Grayson, Hill, and Tarrant. They were seldom found in the area in the early days, and today there seem to be even fewer observations.

Dates for the five counties are: *Dallas* — six spring sightings, 25 March 1972 to 26 April 1959, and one for fall on 22 September 1957; *Denton* — spring sighting given by Oberholser (1974) but lacking details, and 16 April 1982; *Grayson* —16 May 1985; *Hill* —10 April 1982; *Tarrant* — nine spring sightings, 9 March 1968 to 25 April 1956, and four for fall, 8 through 10 August 1979, 4 September 1954, 22 September 1984, and an extremely late date, 19 November 1954.

Mountain Plovers mainly range in the Texas Panhandle and in the coastal and western parts of the state, barely reaching north central Texas. They are similar to Lesser Golden-Plovers. In flight the whitish underwings and lighter legs of this species should help distinguish it from the golden-plover's darker grayish underwings and dark legs. In breeding plumage Mountain Plovers have unspotted grayish-brown backs while the Lesser Golden-Plovers are speckled with gold, black, and white.
Specimens: There is only one example of the Mountain Plover known for north central Texas. It was taken by me in Tarrant County on 4 September 1954 (FWMSH 82). Oberholser (1974) recorded a fall specimen from adjacent Haskell County but gave no information on the location of the specimen.

Family Recurvirostridae (Stilts and Avocets)

BLACK-NECKED STILT   *Himantopus mexicanus* (Müller)
Status: Rare to casual transient, mainly in spring.
Occurrence: The Black-necked Stilt is not as common in north central Texas as the American Avocet, below. It is not observed every year, and records are scattered and more likely to be found in west Texas. Except for two nesting records, this species has been reported mainly in spring.

Stilts have been reported in eight counties: *Dallas* — approximately 15 times, 23 March 1985, next-earliest 2 April 1978 through 3 September 1980; *Denton* — five times, 27 April 1961, 5 May 1975 (present for three days),

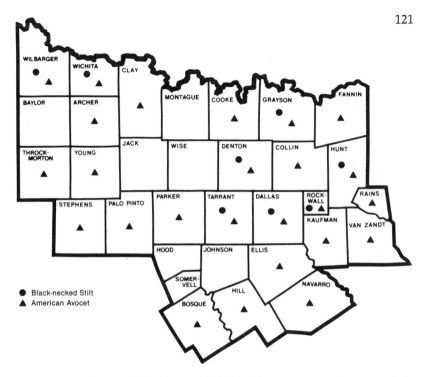

Map 39. Distribution of the Black-necked Stilt, *Himantopus mexicanus,* and the American Avocet, *Recurvirostra americana*

12 June 1947, 16 August 1940, and 10 September 1940 (the last three dates represent specimen records); *Grayson* — four times, 6 May 1982, 7 and 8 May 1964, 12 May 1958, and 14 and 15 May 1980; *Hunt* — Lake Tawakoni, 3 September 1983; *Rockwall* — 24 April 1982; *Tarrant* — six times, 24 and 25 April 1984, 26 April 1985, 2 and 26 May 1986, 23 May 1980 and 1983, and 1 August 1965; *Wichita* — 4 May 1978; *Wilbarger* — "two pairs" during May and June; may have been nesting, but nests were never found (More and Strecker, 1929).

Nesting: Although this species nests in west Texas and along the Gulf Coast, the only known nesting records for north central Texas are from southeast Dallas County, where a pair produced young during the 1981 nesting season (24 May through 16 August), and in Tarrant County, when a pair was seen with two young on 21 July 1986.

Specimens: The only Black-necked Stilt specimens located from north central Texas were a series of five collected in the 1940s from Denton County (DMNH). Those said to have been taken by Mayer in Dallas County in 1909 and 1915 (Stillwell, 1939) are not in the Dallas Museum of Natural History, where many of Mayer's earlier specimens were deposited, and have not been located.

AMERICAN AVOCET   *Recurvirostra americana* Gmelin
Status: Common to fairly common transient in spring and fall.
Occurrence: The American Avocet has been reported in 25 north central Texas counties: Archer, Bosque, Clay, Collin, Cooke, Dallas, Denton, Ellis, Fannin, Grayson, Hill, Hunt, Kaufman, Navarro, Palo Pinto, Parker, Rains, Rockwall, Stephens, Tarrant, Throckmorton, Van Zandt, Wichita, Wilbarger, and Young.

Usually just a few, one to about 12, avocets are observed; however, it is not unusual to see flocks of up to 30 birds in migration. Avocets frequently linger if conditions are favorable, and in fall they are often observed into December.

Some typical county spring and fall dates are: *Dallas* – an isolated date of 14 February 1965, and then 14 April 1974 to 31 May 1979, and 26 June 1986 to 10 November 1971; *Grayson* – 20 April 1983 to 24 June 1984, and 30 June to 31 December; *Tarrant* – 5 April 1987 to 20 May 1971, and 8 July 1980 to 5 November 1986; *Van Zandt* – 21 July 1985 to 27 October 1985 (Rains County); *Wichita* – 30 March 1974 to 19 May 1974, and 26 July 1974 to 15 November 1973.

Specimens: Avocets have been taken from Cooke (TNHC), Denton (DMNH), and Wichita (MWU) counties. Oberholser (1974) refers to specimens from Clay and Wilbarger counties, but these have not been located.

Family Scolopacidae (Sandpipers, Woodcock, and Allies)

GREATER YELLOWLEGS   *Tringa melanoleuca* (Gmelin)
Status: Fairly common to common transient in spring and fall. Rare to uncommon winter visitor in recent years.
Occurrence: Greater Yellowlegs have been recorded in all counties but Baylor, Jack, Throckmorton, and Wise. They will no doubt be recorded in those counties as well when observers learn to distinguish them from the more common Lesser Yellowlegs. Greater Yellowlegs give three to five call notes, while Lesser Yellowlegs usually give only one or two and occasionally three.

This species has been seen in every month of the year, but with only a few observations in June. It is usually found from late February through late May, and again from mid-July through late November.

Typical dates for selected counties are: *Dallas* – 2 February 1966, next-earliest 8 February 1975 to 30 May 1977, and 1 July 1978 to 27 November 1965; *Grayson* – 10 February to 31 May, and 25 June 1981, next-earliest 1 July to 23 December; *Tarrant* – 29 February 1956 to 29 May 1954, and 15 July 1956 to 19 December 1981; *Wichita* – 1 March 1975 to 1 June 1975, and 25 August 1974 to 30 November 1975 (nearby Archer County).

Since the mid-1970s Greater Yellowlegs have been frequently recorded during the winter period throughout the north central Texas areas, including counties along the Red River. They have been reported on six CBCs — seven times on Dallas (Dallas County), seven times on Fort Worth (Tarrant County), three times at Hagerman NWR (Grayson County), eight times on Lewisville, (Denton County), once on Palo Pinto (Palo Pinto County), and eight times on Wichita Falls (Wichita County). Usually only a few were reported, but on 28 December 1982, 95 were tallied on the Lewisville CBC (Denton County). Greater Yellowlegs are reported during the winter more often than its near relative, the Lesser Yellowlegs.

Specimens: The only specimens of this species examined by me were three from Denton County (DMNH). Oberholser (1974) indicates specimens from Clay, Cooke, and Wilbarger counties, but I have been unable to locate them.

Lesser Yellowlegs *Tringa flavipes* (Gmelin)
Status: Common to abundant transient. Casual to rare winter visitor.
Occurrence: Lesser Yellowlegs have been recorded in all counties in the study area but Montague County. They are usually much more abundant than Greater Yellowlegs, and it is not uncommon to count up to 100 Lesser Yellowlegs in migration. Brown (1977) reported more than 575 passing over Sherman, Grayson County, on the night of 28 August 1976. Between 500 and 700 spent about two weeks at a water-treatment plant in southern Dallas County from 5 to 19 April 1986.

In a number of counties they have been seen every month of the year; however, they are more often spotted during spring and fall migration. Peaks of passage are from mid-March to mid-May and again from mid-July to October.

December dates may represent fall stragglers (a few may be misidentifications of Greater Yellowlegs), but since both occur in winter in the area, it is difficult to determine the exact status of many of the records. Somewhat arbitrarily I have included most December observations as wintering birds, along with all January and most February sightings. There are fewer winter records along the Red River than in the Dallas–Fort Worth area, since the weather tends to be more severe along the river and moves them south. Surprisingly, Sutton (1967) gave no winter records for Oklahoma.

Summarized are extreme dates for representative counties with pertinent comments on wintering status: *Dallas* — 7 March 1971 to 7 June 1978 and an isolated date, 20 June 1982, next 23 June 1984 to 25 November 1978, and approximately 12 winter dates for December, three for January, and three for February; *Grayson* —17 February to 5 June and 22 June to 26 November, a late date, 20 December 1976 and 1980, and winter dates 31 January 1971 and 7 February 1972; *Palo Pinto* — 26 February 1978 to 16 May 1976, and 7 July 1977 to 15 November 1978; *Tarrant* — 6 March

1955 to 29 May 1954, and 23 June 1956 to 18 November 1978, with eight December dates, four for January, and none for February; *Wichita* – 31 March 1975 to 17 May 1974, and 7 July 1978 to 19 December 1975 (the only December record).

Specimens: Specimens of this species are available from Cooke (WMP), Dallas (DMNH, WMP), Denton (DMNH), Grayson (OU), and Tarrant (FWMSH) counties. Those mentioned by Oberholser (1974) for Wilbarger and Wise counties were not located.

SOLITARY SANDPIPER   *Tringa solitaria* Wilson

Status: Common to uncommon migrant in spring and fall.

Occurrence: The Solitary Sandpiper has been recorded in all of the north central Texas counties except Jack and Montague. No doubt it passes through these counties as well, but little birding is done there.

This species is seen in a variety of habitats, usually alone and occasionally in twos or threes, but never in flocks. Overall, Solitary Sandpipers are normally found from mid-March to late May and again from late June to late October, with peaks of migration in April and in mid-August. There seems to be little variance throughout the study area, and dates given here apply as well to adjacent counties.

Some extreme county dates are: *Dallas* –17 March 1971 to 22 May 1967, and 30 June 1985 to 24 October 1967; *Grayson* – 26 March to 23 May, and 28 June to 24 October, and isolated dates of 25 and 26 November; *Hunt* – 26 March to 21 May 1984 (Rains) and 29 June 1980, next-earliest 29 July 1980 to 10 October 1939; *Tarrant* – 8 March 1951 to 20 May 1956, and 4 July 1953 to 5 November 1950; *Wichita* – 2 April 1974 to 9 May 1983 (Wilbarger), and 4 July 1974 to 28 October 1982 (Archer).

There are three unexplainable winter records of Solitary Sandpipers for north central Texas. Two were from Dallas CBCs, one on 17 December 1977. This was an ususual count, for several other shorebirds normally not observed so late were also seen on this date. The second observation was on 20 December 1986, which should be questioned as there were no Spotted Sandpipers tallied, although this species is reported some winters in the Dallas area. Spotted Sandpipers were seen on several nearby metropolitan CBCs in 1986. The third Solitary Sandpiper report, verified by a photograph, was of a lone bird from Tarrant County on 30 January 1983.

Specimens: Specimens were found for Dallas (DMNH), Denton (DMNH), Fannin (WMP), Johnson (SUC), and Tarrant (FWMSH) counties. The specimens represent both *T. s. solitaria* and *T. s. cinnamomea*. Oberholser (1974) gives other specimen records for Clay, Cooke, Wichita, Wilbarger, and Young counties, none of which were located. He indicated that *solitaria* was taken in Wichita County while *cinnamomea* was collected in Wilbarger County.

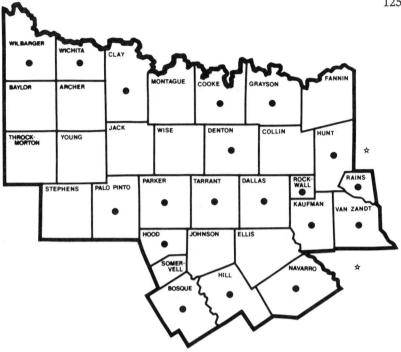

Map 40. Distribution of the Willet, *Catoptrophorus semipalmatus*

WILLET *Catoptrophorus semipalmatus* (Gmelin)
Status: Fairly common to uncommon transient.
Occurrence: This large, striking shorebird has been seen in 19 north central Texas counties — Bosque, Clay, Cooke, Dallas, Denton, Grayson, Hill, Hood, Hunt, Kaufman, Navarro, Palo Pinto, Parker, Rains, Rockwall, Tarrant, Van Zandt, Wichita, and Wilbarger — and in nearby Henderson and Hopkins counties.

Migration dates for selected counties are: *Dallas* — 27 April 1965 to 15 May 1969, and 10 July 1977 to 24 October 1967; *Grayson* — 18 April to 28 May, and 13 June through 30 June (six to 14 birds) to 12 October; *Tarrant* — 14 April 1973 to 28 May 1951, and 22 June 1973 to 27 September 1985, and an isolated date, 5 November 1982; *Wichita* — 26 April 1973 to 7 May 1979, and 17 July 1974 to 6 October 1975.

There are more sightings for fall than for spring. Usually only a few Willets are observed, but occasionally large numbers pass through the area. For example, 200 were counted in Tarrant County on 26 April 1977, and more than 100 were observed in Wichita County on 1 May 1974.
Specimens: Willet specimens have been taken by Mayer from Dallas (Stillwell, 1939, not located), Denton (DMNH), Tarrant (FWMSH, UTA), Wichita, and Wilbarger counties. Specimens referred to by Oberholser

(1974) for the last two counties were not located. Those that have been examined represent the western race *inornatus*.

SPOTTED SANDPIPER   *Actitis macularia* (Linnaeus)
Status: Common to abundant migrant. Rare to uncommon winter resident in southern parts of the study area.
Occurrence: Spotted Sandpipers have been sighted in all but two of the 32 counties of the north central Texas study area. These are Baylor and Jack counties; however, since they have been recorded in nearby counties, they have probably been overlooked in these two counties. There is little doubt that they pass regularly through all the counties.

In a number of counties where bird-watchers frequent favorable areas, Spotted Sandpipers are sometimes seen every month of the year, yet in the counties along the Red River there are no winter records. Once the cold weather sets in, the birds tend to move south. In milder winters they have been recorded in the southern counties along a line from about Palo Pinto County eastward to Tarrant, Denton, and Dallas counties. They are more abundant during the migration periods, the month of June having the least number of records, but there is no evidence that this species nests in north central Texas.

This sandpiper normally migrates in spring from late March until late May, and in fall from mid-July until early October. Typical spring and fall migration dates for representative southern and northern county regions are: *Dallas*—11 February 1967 (may have overwintered), next-earliest 11 March 1982 to 3 June 1968, and 10 July 1983 to 11 November 1982 (isolated date), next-latest 28 October 1973 (where November or October dates extended to December, they were considered winter birds); *Wichita*—9 April 1973 to 29 May 1973 and 25 July 1976 to 28 October 1975.
Specimens: Spotted Sandpipers have been collected from Cooke (TNHC), Dallas (WMP), Denton (DMNH), Grayson (OU), Tarrant (UTA), Wichita (CC), and Wilbarger (Oberholser, 1974) counties; however, I have been unable to locate the last specimen.

UPLAND SANDPIPER   *Bartramia longicauda* (Bechstein)
Status: Common migrant in spring and fall.
Occurrence: The Upland Sandpiper has been recorded in all counties in the study area except Parker County. They should be found in that county as well and have probably been overlooked. They have also been sighted in adjacent Erath, Haskell, and Henderson counties.

Upland Sandpipers frequent open prairies and at times plowed fields. This species can be seen regularly in spring from late March to early June, and in fall from early July to early October, with numbers peaking in April, and from mid-August through early September. Overall extreme county dates for north central Texas range from 3 March 1980 (Tarrant) to 19 June 1974 (Dallas-Ellis county line), and 28 June 1979 (Grayson) to 8 October 1977 (Palo Pinto).

Dates for selected counties are: *Dallas* — 9 March 1984 to 10 June 1968, next-latest 20 May 1969, and 4 July 1986 to 7 October 1972. A bird observed on 23 November 1958 may have been a cripple. *Tarrant* — 3 March 1980, next-earliest 12 March 1981 to 12 May 1947, and an isolated sighting, 15 June 1978, and in fall from 9 July 1971 to 24 September 1978. *Wichita* — 31 March 1976 to 12 May 1939, and 25 July 1976 to 5 October 1974.

Formerly this species was abundant in its movement through north central Texas. It is still common though not as numerous. On 24 April 1984 an estimated 2,000 to 3,000 Upland Sandpipers passed through Denton County. Depending on the amount of rainfall, it may seem more abundant in some years than in others; it does not stop over in dry years. It is often heard giving its high-pitched yet mellow whistle as it flies over in the daytime or at night.

Nesting: Before the turn of the century the Upland Sandpiper was "said to have bred in the northern edge of Texas at Gainesville," Cooke County (Simmons, 1925). There is no evidence that it does so today, although there are observations for June and July in north central Texas. They should not be accepted as evidence of breeding until an actual nest or young are found. The shorebird migration commences early, and these dates may represent migrants. The only recent nesting records are from the Panhandle.

Specimens: Upland Sandpipers have been collected from Cooke (TNHC), Dallas (DMNH, WMP), Denton (DMNH), Kaufman (SFASU), Tarrant (FWMSH, SM), Van Zandt (WMP), and Wichita (DMNH) counties. The specimens indicated by Oberholser (1974) from Clay County have not been located.

WHIMBREL   *Numenius phaeopus* (Linnaeus)
Status: Casual migrant.
Occurrence: Sightings of Whimbrels for north central Texas are not numerous, and, except for three in the fall, all are in spring. Apparently they were seldom seen even in the early days along the Red River, where considerable ornithological work was conducted. Oberholser (1974) showed only spring observations for Cooke, Kaufman, Tarrant, and Wilbarger counties. In addition to Cooke and Wilbarger counties, for which I have no additional data, Whimbrel records include: *Dallas* — 7 May 1973, 18 May 1974, and 13 May 1978 (photograph); *Grayson* — 13 August 1985; *Hill* — one on 28 July 1980 and five on 13 August 1980 (both sightings in the same area); *Kaufman* — 12 May 1973; *Tarrant* — five spring sightings, 31 March 1959 (exceptionally early), 20 in April 1958 and 13 May 1972,

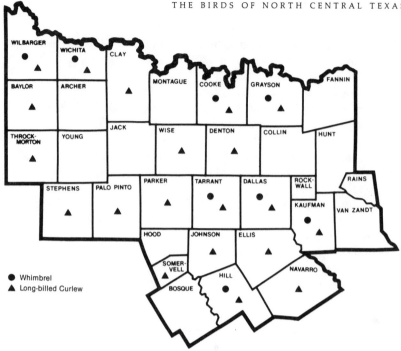

Map 41. Distribution of the Whimbrel, *Numenius phaeopus,* and the Long-billed Curlew, *N. americanus*

36 on 17 May 1953, the latest on 21 May 1983, and 1 in fall on 29 August 1984; *Wichita* — 4 May 1977, 11 May 1978, 19 on 14 May 1975, and 23 May 1975.

Specimens: No specimens of this species have been taken in north central Texas.

LONG-BILLED CURLEW   *Numenius americanus* Bechstein
Status: Uncommon to fairly common transient.
Occurrence: Long-billed Curlews have been reported in 20 north central Texas counties: Baylor, Clay, Cooke, Dallas, Denton, Ellis, Grayson, Hill, Johnson, Kaufman, Navarro, Palo Pinto, Parker, Somervell, Stephens, Tarrant, Throckmorton, Wichita, Wilbarger, and Wise. They are more often observed in prairies and open pasturelands, but in migration they may be observed around bodies of water.

Some spring and fall migration county dates are: *Dallas* — 26 March 1977 to 19 June 1981, next-latest 18 May 1969, and 30 June 1971, next-earliest 20 July 1975 to 25 October 1975; *Grayson* — 29 February to 22 June, and 24 June to 18 September, and 16 October; *Tarrant* — an unusually early date, 17 February 1955, next-earliest 20 March 1969 to 1 June 1965, next-latest

23 May 1954, and 1 July 1945 to 29 September 1984, and an isolated date, 1 November 1964; *Wichita* area — 25 March 1975 to 16 June 1981 (both Wilbarger), and 20 August 1976 to 1 October 1983 (both Clay).

Although More and Strecker (1929) mention this species as a straggler in Wilbarger County "during the summer months," there is no evidence that it has ever nested in north central Texas. Although there are recent dates for June and July from a number of counties, I have considered them all to be records of migrants. In addition to the June and July dates given above, there are a 2 July 1980 date for Kaufman County and a 24 June 1982 date for Wise County.

Oberholser (1974) gives winter sight records for Dallas, Clay, Cooke, Navarro, and Wilbarger counties. The only recent records that can be included are two for Dallas County on 26 December 1959.

Specimens: There is a specimen of a Long-billed Curlew taken in Cooke County on 25 May 1884 (TNHC). Stillwell (1939) lists in a footnote another specimen taken from the same county on 7 April 1935, but it could not be located. Oberholser (1974) also indicates that a specimen was taken in Wise County, but the whereabouts are unknown. He goes on to state that both races of Long-billed Curlews, *N. a. americanus* and *N. a. parvus*, have been taken in Cooke County, although I could not determine the basis for this statement. One cannot properly determine racial origin on the basis of the one specimen, and the race that occurs in north central Texas is uncertain.

HUDSONIAN GODWIT   *Limosa haemastica* (Linnaeus)
Status: Rare spring migrant. Casual in fall.
Occurrence: Hudsonian Godwits have been recorded in eight north central Texas counties: Archer, Dallas, Denton, Grayson, Johnson, Kaufman, Tarrant, and Wichita.

The overall passage of this godwit is in spring, from late March to early June. The spring dates for all of the counties are: *Archer* — 13 and 14 May 1976; *Dallas* — about 15 times, 19 April 1986 to 17 May 1970; *Denton* — 7 April 1956 and 12 May 1947 (specimen); *Grayson* — all from Hagerman NWR, about 20 times, 13 April 1972 to 5 June 1969, next-latest 23 May 1978; *Johnson* — 17 May 1967; *Kaufman* — 12 May 1973 (specimen); *Tarrant* — about 20 sightings, 29 March 1959 to 25 May 1983; *Wichita* — 2 May 1975, 10 May 1978, and 13 and 14 May 1973.

This species has been observed only three times in fall: 14 August 1981 (Dallas County); 7 September 1975 (Grayson County); and 11 October 1978 (Wichita County). In gray plumages this species could be easily overlooked among Willets, if they are not closely examined.

Usually only one or two, or fewer than a dozen Hudsonian Godwits are observed, but a flock of 19 seen on 18 April 1978 increased to 73 birds

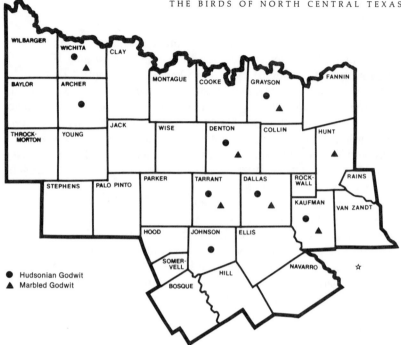

Map 42. Distribution of the Hudsonian Godwit, *Limosa haemastica,* and the Marbled Godwit, *L. fedoa*

on 11 May, and a flock of 32 birds were counted on 8 May 1980, all at Hagerman NWR.

Specimens: Only two Hudsonian Godwits have been taken from north central Texas, one from Denton County (DMNH) and the other from Kaufman County (SFASU).

MARBLED GODWIT   *Limosa fedoa* (Linnaeus)
Status: Rare to uncommon transient.
Occurrence: Marbled Godwits have been reported in only seven counties in the study area — Dallas, Denton, Grayson, Hunt, Kaufman, Tarrant, and Wichita — and nearby Henderson County.

Dates of occurrence for the various counties are: *Dallas* — about nine times, 11 April 1986 and 25 July 1978 to 25 September 1937; *Denton* — spring (Oberholser, 1974), and a specimen taken on 31 October 1949; *Grayson* — about 25 times, all but one from Hagerman NWR, and this is a questionable date of 22 March 1983, next-earliest 19 April 1984 to 12 June 1969, and 24 June 1984 (four other June dates) to 11 October 1979, next-latest 22 September 1985; *Hunt* — Lake Tawakoni, 17 through 24 August 1980, and 3 and 14 September 1980; *Kaufman* — 22 April 1968;

Tarrant—about ten times, 20 April 1956, 24 April 1973, 25 April 1982, 5 May 1985, and 10 July 1955 to 19 September 1981; *Wichita*—23 and 24 April 1973, 26 April 1977, and 1 through 7 May 1973; *Henderson*—28 July 1978.

Usually only one to several are seen, but eight were observed on 11 July 1970 (Grayson County), 13 were reported on 22 April 1968 (Kaufman County), and 36 were counted on 26 April 1977 (Wichita County).
Specimens: The only specimen (DMNH) for north central Texas is the fall bird (mounted) from Denton County.

RUDDY TURNSTONE   *Arenaria interpres* (Linnaeus)
Status: Fairly common fall migrant. Uncommon spring migrant.
Occurrence: The Ruddy Turnstone has been reported in 11 counties in north central Texas: Cooke, Dallas, Denton, Grayson, Hunt, Johnson, Palo Pinto, Parker, Rains, Tarrant, and Wichita.

There tend to be more observations for fall than for spring, except for Tarrant and Wichita counties. They are usually found around large, man-made impoundments that develop mud flats and attract hordes of shore-birds, and where much bird-watching takes place. Usually only one or two individuals are seen, but there are several sightings where numbers were larger. The largest numbers were five on 26 May 1983 at Hagerman NWR (Grayson County), six on 3 September 1972 (Parker County), six on 26 May 1973 (Wichita County), and eight on 27 May 1981 (Tarrant County).

Spring and fall dates for selected counties are: *Dallas*—numerous records, 1 April 1961, next-earliest 17 April 1982 to 24 May 1981, and 2 August 1970 to 13 October 1935 (Stillwell, 1939); *Grayson*—10 May to 28 May, and 4 July to 14 October; *Hunt*—20 August and 28 September 1980; *Rains*—8 August 1985 and 12 September 1982; *Tarrant*—21 April 1985 to 27 May 1964, 1981, and in fall 19 August 1978, 20 August 1983, 2 September 1971, and 20 to 25 September 1986; *Wichita*—14 April 1975 to 28 May 1975, and 8 August 1975 (the only fall record).
Specimens: There is one Ruddy Turnstone specimen (DMNH), taken in Denton County on 20 August 1946.

RED KNOT   *Calidris canutus* (Linnaeus)
Status: Casual fall transient.
Occurrence: The Red Knot has been recorded in only three north central Texas counties: Dallas, Denton, and Grayson. The records are: *Dallas*—four years, 11 September 1971, 28 August 1975, 23 September 1978, and 17 August 1985; *Denton*—a lone bird on 16 May 1987; *Grayson*—eight years, 30 and 31 August, 1 September, and 5 October, all 1969; 4 August and 11 October 1970, 17 October 1971, 10 and 12 August 1972, 9 Septem-

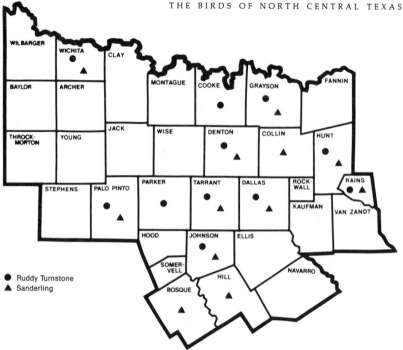

Map 43. Distribution of the Ruddy Turnstone, *Arenaria interpres,* and the Sanderling, *Calidris alba*

ber 1973, 6 through 11 August, 1 September, and 25 and 26 November, all 1977; 6 September 1979; and 14 August and 11 September 1980.

Haller (1976) has carefully documented most of the above dates for Hagerman NWR, Grayson County, where all of the Red Knot sightings have been made to date for that county.

Specimens: There are only two Red Knot specimens (WMP 2137 and 2138), both taken from a flock of eight from Dallas County on 28 August 1975.

SANDERLING   *Calidris alba* (Pallas)
Status: Uncommon to rare transient.
Occurrence: This chunky little shorebird has been recorded in 12 north central Texas counties: Bosque, Collin, Dallas, Denton, Grayson, Hill, Hunt, Johnson, Palo Pinto, Rains, Tarrant, and Wichita.

Any shorebird suspected of being a Sanderling should be carefully examined. Some bird-watchers mistake Dunlins and even Western Sandpipers for Sanderlings. In flight a distinct white wing stripe and a black wrist mark are characteristic. A few of the dates below may be questionable. I have scrutinized all the dates of this species and omitted obvious misidentifications.

Extreme spring and fall dates for selected counties are: *Dallas* — 30 March 1972 to 19 May 1966, and 21 July 1975 to 23 November 1979 (mostly August and September); *Grayson* — 12 April to 24 May 1984, and 16 July 1973 to 25 October; *Tarrant* — 8 March 1959 to 11 June 1955, next-latest 21 May 1959, and 5 August 1978 to 23 November 1954, and two December dates — 8 December 1954 and 16 December 1972 — considered to be stragglers; *Wichita* — 22 March 1975 to 29 May 1976, and 19 July 1976 to 6 October 1976.

Specimens: Sanderling specimens were taken from Denton County on 15 August 1946 (DMNH 3036) and 27 October 1949 (DMNH 4209, 4289 [mount], and 4290), from Grayson County on 3 October 1953 (OU 797 and 801), and from Tarrant County on 11 June 1955 (FWMSH 72).

SEMIPALMATED SANDPIPER   *Calidris pusilla* (Linnaeus)
Status: Fairly common to rare transient in migration only.
Occurrence: Semipalmated Sandpipers have been reported in 21 counties of the study area: Bosque, Clay, Collin, Cooke, Dallas, Denton, Fannin, Grayson, Hill, Hunt, Johnson, Kaufman, Navarro, Palo Pinto, Parker, Rains, Tarrant, Van Zandt, Wichita, Wilbarger, and Young.

This *Calidris* is easily misidentified as a Western Sandpiper. However, after careful scrutiny, limited collecting, and free editing, I feel confident that the dates below represent Semipalmated Sandpipers. These birds do not winter in the north central study area, or anywhere in Texas. I have deleted all winter observations since none is based on a specimen. Readers are urged to review Phillips's paper on Semipalmated Sandpipers (1975) and to become aware that this species often cannot be identified unless it is in the hand. In the field there is nothing wrong with calling small sandpipers "peeps" and letting it go at that.

Overall spring and fall dates for north central Texas counties range from an unusually early date of 26 February 1976 (Grayson) to 2 June 1968 (Dallas), and from 28 June (Grayson) to 30 October 1954 (Tarrant). Extreme dates for counties that have sufficient data are: *Dallas* — 16 March 1969 to 2 June 1968, next-latest 24 May 1970, and 12 July 1974 to 19 October 1968 and 1969; *Grayson* — 13 March to 27 May, and 28 June to 12 October; *Tarrant* — 6 March 1959 to 25 May 1952, and 13 July 1951 to 30 October 1954, next-latest 15 October 1953; *Wichita* — 9 March 1973 to 29 May 1975, and 4 July 1982 to 1 September 1973 (there are probably later dates, but none are available).

Specimens: Specimens have been taken from Denton (DMNH, WMP), Grayson (OU), Kaufman (SFASU), and Tarrant (UTA, WMP) counties. According to Allan Phillips, a specimen (TNHC 1569) taken by Ragsdale on 16 May 1878 in Cooke County is probably *C. mauri*, and not this species.

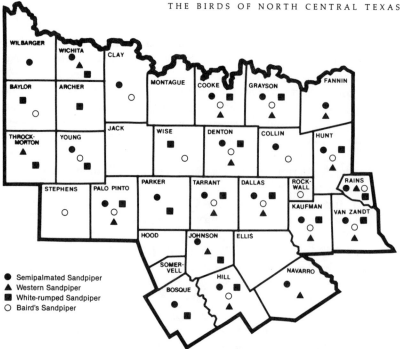

Map 44. Distribution of the "peeps": the Semipalmated Sandpiper, *Calidris pusilla;* the Western Sandpiper, *C. mauri;* the White-rumped Sandpiper, *C. fuscicollis;* and Baird's Sandpiper, *C. bairdii*

WESTERN SANDPIPER   *Calidris mauri* (Cabanis)
Status: Fairly common to common transient. Rare to casual in winter.
Occurrence: Western Sandpipers have been recorded in 16 north central Texas counties: Cooke, Dallas, Denton, Fannin, Grayson, Hill, Hunt, Johnson, Kaufman, Navarro, Palo Pinto, Rains, Tarrant, Throckmorton, Van Zandt, and Wichita.

Like the Semipalmated Sandpiper, the Western Sandpiper may be misidentified by bird-watchers who are not careful in their observations. This species has been reported every month of the year, twice in January for Dallas and Tarrant counties, both questionable and dismissed since no details of observations were given. It has also been recorded three times in February, twice from Denton County and once on 17 February 1983 from Grayson County. The Denton County records have been deleted as misidentifications. Most December records, of which there are a number — that is, where much bird-watching takes place (Dallas, Denton, Grayson, Rains, and Tarrant counties) — are valid. Some of these may represent injured birds or late stragglers, since they are not usually found in the area after cold weather sets in.

Extreme spring and fall migration dates for counties for which there are sufficient records are: *Dallas* — 8 March 1966, next-earliest 13 March 1971, 1977 to 2 June 1968, next-latest 25 May 1967, and 8 July 1984 to 7 November 1982, next-latest (specimen) on 29 October 1945 (Denton County); *Grayson* — an isolated date of 17 February 1983, next-earliest 20 March to 26 May, and 28 June 1979, next-earliest 1 July 1978 to 3 December 1977, next-latest 30 November; *Tarrant* — 3 March 1943, next-earliest 2 April 1956 to 28 May 1951, and 12 July 1953 to 10 November 1954, next-latest 1 November 1980; *Wichita* — 3 March 1973 to 28 May 1973, and 4 July 1974 to 5 October 1956.

Specimens: Western Sandpiper specimens have been collected from Cooke (TNHC), Denton (DMNH), Grayson (OU), Kaufman (SFASU), and Tarrant (WMP) counties. To my knowledge no specimens have been collected in winter from north central Texas.

LEAST SANDPIPER   *Calidris minutilla* (Vieillot)
Status: Abundant transient. Common to fairly common in winter.
Occurrence: This common "peep" has been recorded in all but Jack, Montague, and Stephens counties in the study area, although there is no doubt that it occurs in those counties as well.

There are only three or four dates for June (Dallas, Grayson, and Tarrant counties) all at the first of the month, which represent late-spring migrants. In fall migration, a few always return in July.

This species has been reported on all of the CBCs and seldom goes unreported at that time. Their numbers are greater in the southern and eastern parts of the study area than along the Red River. The CBC averages (means) for 18 years are: 125 in Dallas (Dallas County), 52 in Fort Worth (Tarrant County), 28 in Lewisville (Denton County), ten at Hagerman NWR (Grayson County), six in Wichita Falls (Wichita County), and four in Palo Pinto (Palo Pinto County). They have also wintered in Rains and Van Zandt counties.

During migration it is not uncommon to see thousands of Least Sandpipers frequenting a variety of habitats alone or with other sandpipers, particularly where there are mud flats.

Specimens: Specimens have been located for Dallas (DMNH, WMP), Denton (DMNH, WMP), Grayson (OU), Palo Pinto (WMP), and Tarrant (FWMSH, UTA, WMP) counties. Oberholser (1974) indicated that they were also taken in Clay, Collin, Cooke, Jack and Navarro counties, but they were not located.

WHITE-RUMPED SANDPIPER   *Calidris fuscicollis* (Vieillot)
Status: Fairly common to uncommon spring migrant.
Occurrence: The White-rumped Sandpiper has been recorded in 20 north

central Texas counties: Archer, Baylor, Bosque, Cooke, Dallas, Denton, Grayson, Hill, Hunt, Johnson, Kaufman, Palo Pinto, Parker, Rains, Tarrant, Throckmorton, Van Zandt, Wichita, Wise, and Young.

Since this shorebird has an elliptical migration, passing north through the interior of the United States in the spring on its way to the high Arctic tundra and returning to the east in the fall along part of the Atlantic Coast to its winter home in the southern part of South America, the fall records in north central Texas seem to be clouded with misidentifications. Therefore, sight records for 18 September 1957 (Grayson County), 12 October 1973, and 15 November 1974 (both Wise County) were dismissed. Since most reports are vague or are given without any details, I have not accepted them. Possibly in doing so I have discounted one or two good sightings, but it is better to omit them altogether than to compound existing errors. Until valid photographs or specimens are taken, I cannot accept this bird as a fall migrant.

Overall movement through the north central Texas study area ranges from 9 April 1964 (Tarrant County) and 9 April 1983 (Rains County) to 26 June 1974 (Grayson County). There are two unexplainable dates for July, one recorded by Hagerman NWR personnel (Grayson County on 1 July 1976 and the other at Possum Kingdom Lake on 17 July 1977 (Palo Pinto County). Although I cannot vouch for the correctness of the first date, the second was made by a competent observer. They could have been late-spring stragglers or injured birds. They peak in mid-May, and at that time it is not uncommon to see hundreds; the largest number was 300 on 9 May 1977 (Tarrant County).

Extreme dates for selected counties are: *Dallas* – 25 April 1976 to 8 June 1979; *Grayson* –19 April to 31 May, and 2 June through 26 June 1974; *Tarrant* – 9 April 1964 to 11 June 1978; *Wichita* – 21 April 1974 to 22 June 1974, next-latest 28 May 1974.

Specimens: White-rumped Sandpiper specimens have been taken in Cooke (TNHC), Dallas (WMP), Denton (DMNH), Grayson (OU), Kaufman (DMNH), and Tarrant (FWMSH, UTA) counties. All were collected during May, with the exception of a 11 June 1955 specimen (FWMSH) from Tarrant County.

BAIRD'S SANDPIPER   *Calidris bairdii* (Coues)
Status: Fairly common to uncommon migrant. Most winter records questionable.
Occurrence: Baird's Sandpiper has been recorded in 18 north central Texas counties: Baylor, Clay, Collin, Cooke, Dallas, Denton, Grayson, Hill, Hunt, Kaufman, Palo Pinto, Rains, Rockwall, Stephens, Tarrant, Van Zandt, Wise, and Young.

There are reports of this peep for every month of the year, including two for January and four for February. A report of 25 for 1 January 1966 (Dallas County) has been discounted as an error, since no details were given for this most unusual number. A report for 20 January 1960 from Hagerman NWR (Grayson County) is dubious and also dismissed. Unfortunately, many persons have difficulty distinguishing these peeps from other small sandpipers, such as Sanderlings. The dates given for February (late) very likely represent early migrants. Valid December sightings represent stragglers lingering because of mild weather or possibly injury.

There is little reason to believe Baird's Sandpipers winter in north central Texas or elsewhere in Texas, since this species normally goes to the temperate zone of South America for the winter. There are December records made on CBCs from Dallas, Grayson, and Wichita counties. Most undoubtedly are misidentifications, since the persons making the identifications did not know that the bird was unusual and failed to qualify their reports. In another instance large numbers were reported with no mention of Least Sandpipers, which are the common winter sandpipers of north central Texas and are nearly always reported. I have, however, carefully studied a Baird's Sandpiper on 21 and 22 December 1977 in Dallas County. Numerous other persons also saw this bird. There are five December observations for Grayson County ranging from 7 December to 27 December, most of these questionable and very likely misidentifications, though the early dates could represent stragglers. Two December reports for the Wichita Falls CBCs of 1976 and 1977 were dismissed as errors.

Baird's Sandpipers are usually observed in the north central Texas study area from March to the end of May, and again from early July to early November, with peaks of passage from mid-April to early May, and from early August through September. The largest number reported on one day was 500 on 15 April 1984 (Tarrant County). Extreme spring and fall dates for selected counties are: *Dallas* — 8 March 1980 to 27 May 1979, one seen on 13 and 20 June 1982, and 10 July 1977 to 18 November 1970; *Grayson* —11 February 1974, next-earliest 26 February 1981 to 31 May, and 3 July to 25 November, next-latest 6 November 1986; *Tarrant* — 22 and 28 February 1986 to 29 May 1954, and 22 July 1978 to 9 November 1947; *Wichita* — 23 March 1975 to 1 June 1975, and 31 July 1975 to 10 November 1973.

Specimens: Baird's Sandpipers have been taken from Denton (DMNH), Kaufman (SFASU), Tarrant (FWMSH, UTA, WMP), and Wichita counties. The last specimen (Oberholser, 1974) was not located.

PECTORAL SANDPIPER   *Calidris melanotos* (Vieillot)
Status: Common transient. Accidental in winter.
Occurrence: Pectoral Sandpipers have been reported in 26 north central Texas counties: Archer, Baylor, Bosque, Clay, Collin, Cooke, Dallas, Den-

ton, Fannin, Grayson, Hill, Hunt, Johnson, Kaufman, Navarro, Palo Pinto, Parker, Rains, Rockwall, Stephens, Tarrant, Van Zandt, Wichita, Wilbarger, Wise, and Young.

This species is a common migrant in the study area and is frequently observed with other shorebirds. It is found in the study area from March to early June and July to November. The overall extreme spring and fall dates range from 22 February 1955 (Tarrant County), next-earliest 26 February 1978 (Palo Pinto County) to 11 June (Grayson County), exceptionally late 13 and 20 June 1982 (Dallas County), and in the fall from 7 July 1985 (Dallas County) to 26 November 1977 (Grayson County). Pectoral Sandpipers peak in spring from mid-April to early May, and in fall from August through early September. During these periods several hundred may be observed. An estimated 500 were seen in Dallas County on 9 August 1982, and 300 were seen at Hagerman NWR, Grayson County, on 9 August 1984. The dates for various counties do not seem to vary much from one county to another and are applicable for most of the other counties in north central Texas.

Surprisingly, there are six records for December from four counties (Dallas, Grayson, Parker, and Tarrant), which very likely represent stragglers. There is only one winter date: one bird (photographed) that was observed in Tarrant County from 29 January to 4 February 1983. Since this species winters in South America, it is difficult to assess the winter dates. Other February dates are at the end of the month and represent early-spring migrants. The bird's status as a winter visitor is extremely rare, and at best accidental.

Specimens: Pectoral Sandpiper specimens have been examined from Cooke (TNHC), Dallas (DMNH, WMP), Denton (DMNH), Navarro (TCWC), Stephens (WMP), and Tarrant (FWMSH) counties. Those from Wilbarger and Wise counties (Oberholser, 1974) could not be located.

DUNLIN   *Calidris alpina* (Linnaeus)
Status: Uncommon to rare transient during migration. Rare to casual winter resident.
Occurrence: Dunlins have been recorded in 13 north central Texas counties: Clay, Collin, Cooke, Dallas, Denton, Grayson, Hunt, Johnson, Kaufman, Navarro, Rains, Tarrant, and Wichita. The records show that they are more common along the eastern side of the study area than along the western side; however, the paucity of records may be due to lack of observers.

Dunlins have been reported in every month of the year except June. Overall migration dates for this species range from 4 March (Grayson County) to 27 May 1983 (Tarrant County), and 10 July 1975 (Dallas County) to 30 November (Grayson County). Most of the records are for May and

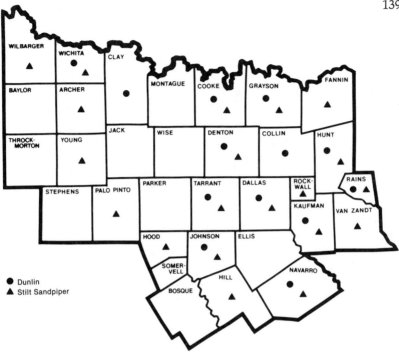

Map 45. Distribution of the Dunlin, *Calidris alpina,* and the Stilt Sandpiper, *C. himantopus*

from mid-October to early November. These dates are applicable to most other counties in the study area.

Some of the Dunlin records are difficult to evaluate, especially the number of winter records. However, not all are in error. There are reports from two CBCs, four times (1956–86) for Lewisville (Denton County) and three times for Hagerman NWR (Grayson County). In the latter county the numbers given in two of the reports seem exceedingly high. The other counties for which there are winter records are Dallas, Johnson, Tarrant, and Wichita, as well as other records for Grayson County besides the CBCs. It is possible that some observers misidentify this species, since its gray upperparts and white underneath parts are similar in some of the peeps. The drooped bill tip and the size of this species should be noted.
Specimens: Dunlin specimens are known from Dallas (WMP), Denton (DMNH), and Tarrant (UTA) counties. Specimens said to have been taken in Cooke (Oberholser, 1974) and Navarro counties (Ogilby, 1882) were not located.

STILT SANDPIPER *Calidris himantopus* (Bonaparte)
Status: Fairly common to common transient.

Occurrence: Stilt Sandpipers have been recorded in 20 counties of the study area: Archer, Cooke, Dallas, Denton, Fannin, Grayson, Hill, Hood, Hunt, Johnson, Kaufman, Navarro, Palo Pinto, Rains, Rockwall, Tarrant, Van Zandt, Wichita, Wilbarger, and Young.

This shorebird is probably more common than most observers realize. It is often overlooked among yellowlegs, unless the observer is careful. The birds are frequently seen among the hordes of shorebirds that pass through north central Texas, and flocks of 100 or so are often tallied in the fall, especially during mid-September, when they peak. An estimated 400 were observed on 10 September 1970, and about 500 were counted on 6 September 1980 (both in Grayson County).

Extreme spring and fall arrival and departure dates for selected counties are: *Dallas* — 26 March 1983, next-earliest 4 April 1976 to 27 May 1979, and 4 July 1985 to 24 October 1968; *Grayson* — 5 April 1980 to 31 May, and 7 July to 27 October; *Tarrant* — 2 April 1982 to 4 June 1955, and 12 July 1953 to 7 November 1983, next-latest 21 October 1951; *Wichita* — 4 May 1973 to 8 June 1975, next-latest 28 May 1973, and 4 July 1974 to 28 October 1973.

Specimens: Stilt Sandpiper specimens are available from Cooke (TNHC), Dallas (WMP), Denton (DMNH, TCWC), Grayson (OU), Kaufman (SFASU), Tarrant (FWMSH, UTA), and Wilbarger (CMNH) counties. A specimen said to have been taken by Mayer (Stillwell, 1939) for Dallas County in 1927 was not located. This date precedes the establishment of the Dallas Museum of Natural History, and the specimen was probably mounted for a patron and subsequently lost.

BUFF-BREASTED SANDPIPER   *Tryngites subruficollis* (Vieillot)
Status: Fairly common to uncommon transient.
Occurrence: Buff-breasted Sandpipers have been reported in 16 counties of the north central Texas study area: Collin, Cooke, Dallas, Denton, Grayson, Hill, Hunt, Johnson, Kaufman, Navarro, Palo Pinto, Rains, Rockwall, Tarrant, Wichita, and Wise.

This beautiful shorebird forages in shortgrass prairies and plowed fields. Although it is also found at the open margins of lakes and reservoirs, it may often be overlooked in passage. It tends to peak in spring in early May and in fall through August to early September.

Overall sightings for selected counties are: *Dallas* — 17 April 1982 to 19 May 1973, and 25 July 1971 to 18 October 1982; *Grayson* — 17 April 1985 to 20 May 1971, an asolated date, 9 June 1974, and 26 July 1977 to 27 September 1984; *Hunt* — 20 April 1951, and 4 August 1953 to 11 October 1980; *Palo Pinto* — 17 July 1977, earliest fall date; *Tarrant* — 12 April 1969 to 20 May 1981, and 29 July 1978 to 30 September 1978.

Specimens: Buff-breasted Sandpiper specimens have been taken from

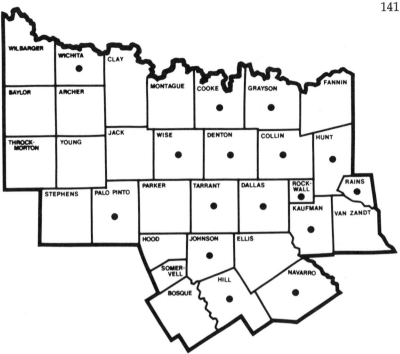

Map 46. Distribution of the Buff-breasted Sandpiper, *Tryngites subruficollis*

Cooke (TNHC), Dallas (WMP), Denton (DMNH), Kaufman (SFASU), Tarrant (FWMSH, UTA), and Wise counties. The specimen reported by Oberholser (1974) for Wise County could not be located.

SHORT-BILLED DOWITCHER   *Limnodromus griseus* (Gmelin)
Status: Rare to casual transient, mainly in fall.
Occurrence: The status of this species of dowitcher, and that of the Long-billed Dowitcher, for north central Texas is not well understood, and care should be exercised in identifying these two species in the field. Bill length should not be used as a means of identifying them. Short-bill calls are distinct and described as *tu-tu-tu* compared with the high *keek* of the Long-billed Dowitcher; however, sometimes not all three *tus* are given.

Short-billed Dowitchers have been reported in only six counties: Cooke, Dallas, Denton, Grayson, Tarrant, and Wichita. The identifications here are based on calls or specimens for the following counties: *Dallas* — 2 August 1978 (identified by voice and plumage). *Denton* — 20 August 1946, two specimens. *Cooke* — 3 August 1981 (voice and plumage). *Grayson* — all records except the specimen, are from Hagerman NWR. Reported in 13 years in the 1968–84 period, with two May sightings, 20 May 1968 and 21 May 1981, and 19 fall sightings, July (six), August (eight), and Septem-

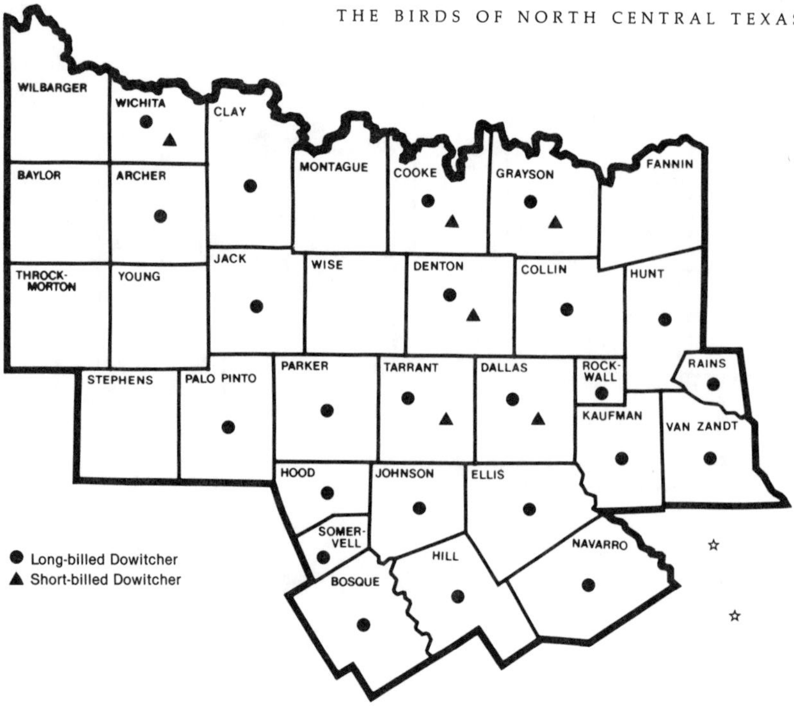

Map 47. Distribution of the Short-billed Dowitcher, *Limnodromus griseus,* and the Long-billed Dowitcher, *L. scolopaceus*

ber (five) from 4 July 1974 to 23 September 1972. *Tarrant* — 9 and 10 August 1986 carefully studied and photographed. *Wichita* — 14 May 1973 (voice, also compared with Long-billed Dowitchers). Two other spring dates were deleted for lack of details.

Specimens: Specimens of two Short-billed Dowitchers, both juveniles, were collected from Denton County on 20 August 1946 (DMNH 3044 and 3045), and one in alternate plumage was taken from Grayson County on 28 July 1976 (OU 11020). All of these were assigned to the race *hendersoni.* A specimen (USNM) taken in nearby McLennan County on 26 July 1934 is also said to represent that race.

LONG-BILLED DOWITCHER *Limnodromus scolopaceus* (Say)
Status: Common to fairly common transient. Casual in winter.
Occurrence: Long-billed Dowitchers have been reported in 24 counties of the study area — Archer, Bosque, Clay, Collin, Cooke, Dallas, Denton, Ellis, Grayson, Hill, Hood, Hunt, Jack, Johnson, Kaufman, Navarro, Palo Pinto, Parker, Rains, Rockwall, Somervell, Tarrant, Van Zandt, and Wichita — and adjacent Anderson and Henderson counties.

Dates of migratory passage of Long-billed Dowitchers for selected counties are: *Dallas*—13 March 1966 to 18 May 1981, and 1 July 1978 to 18 November 1973; *Grayson*—2 March to 1 June 1956 (12 birds), and 1 July to 4 December 1982 and scattered later dates until 31 December; *Tarrant*—1 March 1956 to 13 May 1972, and 9 July 1959 to 2 December 1955; *Wichita*—3 March 1975 to 30 May 1980, and 20 July 1975 to 15 December 1973; a date of 20 December 1976 on CBC of 47 dowitchers was deleted because no snipe were reported. I believe that this unusual number of dowitchers should have been qualified and that it probably represents a misidentification of Common Snipe, which regularly winters in north central Texas.

There are a number of December records (Dallas, Grayson, Kaufman, Rains, Tarrant, and Wichita counties), most of which represent stragglers. There are a few records for January and February. Some of the January sightings (Anderson, Dallas, Grayson, Tarrant, and Wichita counties), particularly early dates, may also represent lingering dowitchers. The February records include one for Dallas County on 20 February 1982, which was seen again on 8 March, and others for Grayson County on 1, 15, and 24 February 1966, 28 February 1974, and 24 and 26 February 1976. During the winter of 1981–82 Long-billed Dowitchers stayed over in Dallas, Tarrant, and Wichita counties. Although the actual winter status in north central Texas is not clearly understood, small numbers very likely overwinter if the weather is mild and the dowitchers are able to find food. During migration they are often found with other shorebirds in small groups and in flocks of up to 100 (26 April 1980, Tarrant County), yet they seldom seem to intermingle with other members of this group.

Specimens: Long-billed Dowitcher specimens have been collected from the following counties: Clay and Cooke (Oberholser, 1974, not located), Dallas (DMNH), Denton (DMNH), Kaufman (SFASU), Navarro (WMP), and Tarrant (FWMSH).

COMMON SNIPE *Gallinago gallinago* (Linnaeus)
Status: Common transient and winter resident.
Occurrence: The Common Snipe is found regularly in 27 counties of north central Texas—Archer, Bosque, Clay, Collin, Cooke, Dallas, Denton, Ellis, Fannin, Grayson, Hill, Hood, Hunt, Johnson, Kaufman, Navarro, Palo Pinto, Parker, Rains, Rockwall, Somervell, Tarrant, Van Zandt, Wichita, Wilbarger, Wise, and Young—and nearby Eastland and Shackelford counties.

Snipes should be found in all of the counties if watched for, and can usually be observed from early September to early May. In some counties they have been observed every month of the year but June. They have been recorded on all of the annual CBCs conducted in the study area, but they are more common in migration than in the winter season.

The dates at hand indicate that they arrive and depart on about the

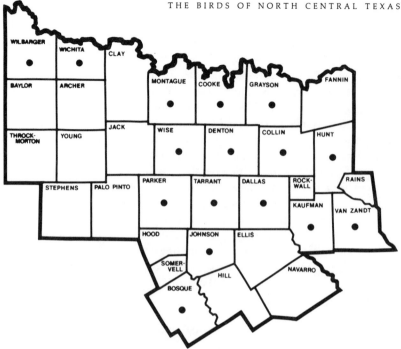

Map 48. Distribution of the American Woodcock, *Scolopax minor*

same dates in all parts of north central Texas. The following county dates are typical: *Dallas* — 24 August 1973, isolated dates of 28 July 1935 and 9 August 1938, next 4 September 1984 to 18 May 1986; *Grayson* —15 July to 11 May (every month except June); *Palo Pinto* —14 September 1974 to 7 May 1977; *Tarrant* — isolated date of 7 August 1976, next 29 August 1971 to 13 May 1972; *Wichita* — 31 August to 3 May 1974 (nearby Archer County).

Specimens: Specimens have been taken from Archer (MWU), Clay (MWU), Dallas (WMP), Denton (DMNH, OU, WMP), Navarro (WMP), Parker (FWMSH), and Wichita (MWU) counties, as well as adjacent Eastland County (MWU). Oberholser (1974) cites specimens for Cooke, Fannin, Wilbarger, and Wise counties, none of which were located.

AMERICAN WOODCOCK   *Scolopax minor* Gmelin
Status: Rare winter visitor.
Occurrence: This elusive bird has been reported in 16 counties in the study area, mainly along the eastern side to about Grayson County and south through Denton, Johnson, and Bosque counties to Tarrant County. On the west there are scattered records along the Red River. It is mainly found in wooded areas along the river drainages but is seldom seen.

A.P.

Most sightings are from the Dallas–Fort Worth area and Grayson County, where much bird-watching occurs. All of the county records known to me are: *Bosque* — one shot, but not saved, on 10 January 1981. *Collin* — listed in the preliminary checklist (1978) from the Heard Museum. A more recent sighting in the northern part of the county was recorded on 20 November 1985. *Cooke* — Oberholser (1974) questioned the occurrence of this species but gave no details. *Dallas* — approximately 30 records (1920 through 1984), because there are more observers, 6 October 1984, next-earliest 24 October 1978 to 1 March 1975; Stillwell (1939) gave the earliest date as 25 August 1934 and the latest as 16 March 1930. *Denton* — about a dozen reports, 19 November 1982 to 8 March 1978. *Grayson* — at least 12 reports, 29 August through 11 September 1980, and 25 and 26 November 1977 to 17 February 1973. *Hunt* — Oberholser (1974) refers to summer and winter records, probably taken from the local checklist of this region. Four recent records, two from Greenville, 24 October 1978 and 11 November 1979, and two from the Quinlan area, winter period (December) 1984, 19 November 1986. *Johnson* — 23 November 1974. *Kaufman* — fall of 1947, 2 January 1971, and 20 November 1982. *Montague* — 18 January 1981. *Parker* — 16 November 1966. *Tarrant* — about 20 reports, isolated date of 7 August 1984, said to have been present about two weeks before, next 16 October 1939 to 16 February 1986. *Van Zandt* — one shot during December 1974, 10 February 1977 (16 birds), 27 February 1977, 28 February 1982, 19 November 1986 to 17 February 1985, and 17 April 1985. *Wichita* — fall of 1971 and 1972 (Zinn and Moore, 1976). *Wilbarger* — 12 November 1982. *Wise* — spring of 1964 and 4 December 1976 (Pulich, 1979). *Young* — questionable records for spring and fall (Oberholser, 1974).

Nesting: Oberholser (1974) pointed out that nesting has occurred in east Texas. I documented the nesting of American Woodcock in Smith County east of Van on the Van Zandt county line (Pulich, 1977a). On 27 February 1977 two nests were found by members of the Dallas County Audubon Society while they were being conducted by a local guide to see the species.

A female American Woodcock, at least two years old when it was banded on 24 August 1971 near Butternut, Wisconsin, was recovered about five miles south of Van, Van Zandt County, during December 1974 (no specific date given).

Specimens: Woodcock specimens are known from Dallas (DMNH, WMP), Grayson (WMP), and Tarrant (FWMSH) counties. According to Stillwell (1939), some were shot in Dallas County in the 1920s before the inception of the Dallas Museum of Natural History, but there are no records that these birds were saved as scientific specimens.

WILSON'S PHALAROPE   *Phalaropus tricolor* (Vieillot)
Status: Fairly common to common in spring. They do not seem as numerous in fall.
Occurrence: This phalarope is much more common and widespread in north central Texas than the Red-necked Phalarope or the Red Phalarope. It has been recorded in 19 counties — Archer, Collin, Cooke, Dallas, Denton, Grayson, Hill, Hunt, Jack, Johnson, Kaufman, Palo Pinto, Parker, Rains, Tarrant, Throckmorton, Wichita, Wilbarger, and Young — and nearby Shackelford County. Phalaropes sometimes travel in good-sized flocks of several hundred (the largest 400) in spring migration. They peak from late April to early May. In summer they may be overlooked, or they may pass through so early that they are seldom recorded, since birdwatching activities frequently subside during hot weather.

Extreme spring and fall dates for selected counties having sufficient data are: *Dallas* — 6 March 1982, next-earliest 21 March 1970 through 6 June 1970, next-latest 27 May 1979 and 3 July 1982, next-earliest 20 July 1975 to 5 November 1978, next-latest 22 October 1968; *Grayson* — 27 February to 3 June, and 26 June and 17 July to 20 November 1982; *Tarrant* — 13 March 1985 to 9 and 10 June 1964, next-latest 21 May 1955, and 21 July 1974 to 27 October 1983; *Wichita* — 20 April 1978 to 1 June 1975, and 20 and 23 August 1975 (the only fall record; however, there must be other sightings).

Specimens: Wilson's Phalarope specimens are recorded from Cooke (TNMC, USNM), Denton (DMNH), Kaufman (SFASU), Tarrant (FWMSH, UTA, WMP), Wichita (MWU), and Wilbarger counties (Oberholser, 1974). The specimen for Wilbarger County was not located.

RED-NECKED PHALAROPE   *Phalaropus lobatus* (Linnaeus)
Status: Rare fall migrant. Casual in spring.
Occurrence: The Red-necked Phalarope, formerly called Northern Phala-

A.P.

rope, is not often seen. Usually only one, rarely two, are seen and then frequently with other species of phalaropes, or wherever hordes of shorebirds concentrate. Except for three spring observations all county records are for fall. These are: *Dallas*—11 sightings, 26 September 1959, 26 and 27 September 1965, 2 through 7 October 1965, 22 October 1968, 17 September 1969, 6 June 1970 (two females, carefully identified by two competent observers), 8 August 1977, 31 August and 3 September 1978, 20 and 21 September 1978, 30 September 1984 (photograph), and 28 September 1985; *Grayson*—eight sightings, all but one record from Hagerman NWR, 3 October 1953, 11 September to 2 October 1963, 5 and 7 October 1973, 2 through 30 September 1975, 5 October 1978, 2 to 23 September 1980, 1 October 1981, and 19 through 23 August 1984; *Tarrant*—25 August 1956, 16 October 1964, and 20 May 1976; *Wichita*—5 June 1973 (Zinn, 1975). *Specimens:* Specimens of this species are available from three counties: Dallas—22 October 1968 (WMP 1678); Grayson—Lake Texoma, 3 October 1953 (OU 829); Tarrant—25 August 1956 (WMP 532), and 20 May 1976 (DMNH 6595, mount on exhibit).

RED PHALAROPE *Phalaropus fulicaria* (Linnaeus)
Status: Rare to casual fall migrant.
Occurrence: This pelagic phalarope is the rarest of the three phalaropes that occur in north central Texas. It has been recorded in four counties, all representing fall migrants: *Dallas*—6 to 20 September 1972, 8 October 1977, 23 October 1979, and 20 to 25 September 1980; *Grayson*—7 to 20 October 1973 (slides), 21 July to 13 August and again on 10 September

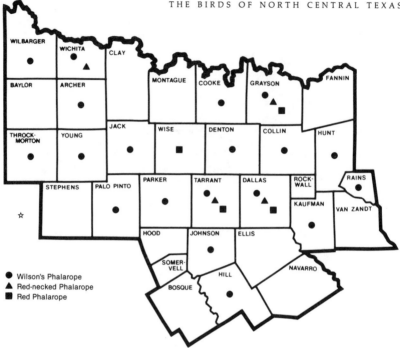

Map 49. Distribution of the Wilson's Phalarope, *Phalaropus tricolor;* Red-necked Phalarope, *P. lobatus;* and the Red Phalarope, *P. fulicaria*

1977, and 20 September 1980 (photographs); *Tarrant* — 7 November 1949; *Wise* — 26 September 1893.

Specimens: A specimen (WMP 1929) taken in Dallas County on 8 September 1972 is probably the only one in existence for north central Texas. I have searched in vain for the second specimen, said to have been taken in Wise County on 26 September 1893. Note comments under Lewis' Woodpecker.

Family Laridae (Gulls, Terns and Allies)

POMARINE JAEGER   *Stercorarius pomarinus* (Temminck)
Status: Accidental. One fall specimen record.
Occurrence: There is only one record of this rare arctic bird in the north central Texas study area (Dalquest, 1958). It was collected at Lake Kickapoo, Archer County, on 8 October 1957 (MWU 134).

Although this falconlike seabird is seen in both fall and spring on pelagic trips off the coast of Texas in the Gulf of Mexico, there are no valid inland spring records. A sight record of 5 May 1975 (Williams, 1975) from nearby Wichita County was dismissed. It was apparently seen by one observer, and in the local checklist for that area the date is given as 29 May. Because this oceanic bird rarely comes inland and the record is garbled, the sighting is highly unlikely.

LAUGHING GULL   *Larus atricilla* Linnaeus
Status: Accidental after southerly storms or at best casual.
Occurrence: The acceptable Laughing Gull county reports are: *Cooke* — 10 April 1886, which seems exceptionally early. Two were said to have been collected on this date (Oberholser, 1974), but unfortunately the specimens were not located. *Grayson* — one was sighted and compared with eight Ring-billed Gulls on 26 July 1977; an immature was taken on 13 August 1980 at the headwaters of Lake Texoma, probably resulting from the passage of Hurricane Allen on the Texas coast; one was carefully studied for two days on 16 and 17 June 1983, and another was reported on 17 May 1984. All of the sight records were made at Hagerman NWR.

This species is a bird of coastal waters, and its occurrence inland is due to strong southerly winds or hurricane disturbances. It is easily confused with Franklin's Gull, a migrant in north central Texas, especially if the wing tips of the latter are worn. Unless observers were known to be extremely cautious and presented details, many sight records for north central Texas were not accepted; therefore, all records for Dallas, Tarrant, and Wichita counties were dismissed awaiting the collection of a specimen, photographs, or carefully documented notes. The current records for these three counties were presented too casually and lacked convincing details, but with careful scrutiny they should be found in these counties.
Specimens: Except for the one Laughing Gull taken in Grayson County (above) on 13 August 1977 (WMP 2569), there are no other specimens for the north central Texas study area.

Reference (Williams, 1976) to Sutton's collecting of this species on 21 July 1976 in Marshall County, Oklahoma, is likely in error.

FRANKLIN'S GULL   *Larus pipixcan* Wagler
Status: Common to abundant transient. A late straggler in passage.
Occurrence: Franklin's Gulls have been reported in all the north central Texas study area counties except Montague, Navarro, and Throckmorton.

Although there are reports of this gull for every month in counties where much birding takes place, it is principally a transient. Most of the population winters along the western coast of South America. Many Franklin's Gull records for December are birds that linger en route because weather and feeding conditions are favorable. There are a few late December, January, and early February records, but usually the numbers sighted are not numerous, and no doubt some are misidentifications. Extreme care is urged in identifying late gulls such as Franklin's Gull, and details should be given along with any extenuating circumstances such as atypical or ragged appearance.

Franklin's Gulls are usually found in north central Texas from mid-April to mid-May, and from early October into early November. Extreme spring and fall arrival and departure dates for selected counties are: *Dallas* — 21 February 1976 to 31 May 1982, and 24 September 1974 to 2 December 1978 and at least ten other December dates through 31 December. They are reported every month. Stillwell (1939) reports extreme dates of 10 June 1938 in spring and 2 August 1935 in fall. *Grayson* — reported every month, usually 4 March through 31 May, with scattered dates for June, July (specimen, 19 July 1976), and August, and again 3 September through 18 December. There are at least 12 December dates; a lone January date, 8 January 1983; and a record of three birds on 23 February 1974. Some winter records are questionable. *Rains* — 17 February 1985 to 30 May 1984, and 6 October 1985 to 2 December 1984. *Tarrant* — 1 March 1975, next 3 March 1981 to 11 June 1955, an isolated date, 23 June 1978, and 11 October 1946 to 20 November 1954. There are 12 reports for December in 25 annual CBCs (1952–77), some of which are questionable. Not reported in January and February, or August and September. *Wichita* — 24 March 1973 to 29 May 1974, an isolated date, 31 July 1974, and 13 September 1975 to 16 November 1974. It was reported several times in December. Not reported every month.

Franklin's Gulls are more numerous in fall than in spring, and up to 10,000 of the birds, mixed with Ring-billed Gulls, are often reported on man-made lakes. Some dates for large numbers, all for Lake Texoma, Grayson County, are: 20 October 1968 (estimated 10,000), 4 November 1971 (estimated 750,000), and 17 October 1976 (estimated 20,000). In spring they can often be seen following tractors plowing fields, and farmers welcome their presence, as the gulls glean for insects. The striking black heads and the pink blush on many of the breasts present a beautiful sight. In fall they apparently take hordes of grasshoppers as well as other insects. Fishermen often find schools of fish (especially sand bass) by watching gulls foraging over lakes.

Specimens: Specimens are known for Archer (MWU), Cooke (USNM), Dallas (TCWC, WMP), Denton (DMNH; WMP, winter specimen), Grayson (OU), Kaufman (SFASU), Tarrant (DMNH, FWMSH, UTA), and Wichita (MWU) counties. Those indicated by Oberholser (1974) for Clay and Wilbarger counties were not located.

LITTLE GULL   *Larus minutus* Pallas
Status: Accidental.
Occurrence: There are two valid records of this small gull for north cen-

tral Texas. A specimen was collected in Dallas County on 5 April 1965 (Pulich, 1966).

The second gull was seen from 22 December 1986 until 21 February 1987 at Lake Ray Hubbard, near the dam on the Dallas-Kaufman county line, attracting bird-watchers from far and near to view it.

There are only two other valid Little Gull records for Texas. One was seen at Austin, Travis County, from 20 through 27 December 1969, and was documented by photographs during that time. More recently another was seen on 21 January 1987 at Granger Lake, Williamson County, by two competent observers who provided a detailed report of its occurrence and an accurate drawing of it.

One was cited in the list of Species of Uncertain Occurrence for Tarrant County (Pulich, 1979). It was said to have been seen for two days on 2 and 3 February 1967, but no details were given. Bonaparte's Gulls often winter on Benbrook Lake, where the Little Gull was allegedly seen, and it is very possible that an immature was mistaken for a Little Gull.

BONAPARTE'S GULL   *Larus philadelphia* (Ord)
Status: Uncommon to fairly common winter visitor. More common in recent years than formerly.
Occurrence: There appear to be few records of Bonaparte's Gull before the 1960s. Oberholser (1974) reported it from only four counties of the north central Texas study area: Cooke, Dallas, Denton, and Wise. To these can be added Archer, Clay, Collin, Fannin, Grayson, Hill, Hunt, Kaufman, Palo Pinto, Rains, Rockwall, Stephens, Tarrant, Van Zandt, and Wichita counties.

Extreme arrival and departure dates for selected counties are: *Dallas* — 26 October 1975, next-earliest 8 November 1967 to 18 May 1976; early August and September records have been dismissed as misidentifications, since this species usually does not arrive until November; *Denton* — 3 November 1973 to 14 April 1985; *Collin* — 21 November 1981 to 24 April 1982; *Grayson* — 14 October, next-earliest 30 October 1976, and 11 November 1978 to 4 May; *Palo Pinto* — 7 November 1978 to 9 April 1983; *Rains* — 5 November 1983 to 2 May 1987 (adjacent Hunt County); *Tarrant* — 31 October 1976 to 26 April 1976 and an unexplained isolated date, 23 June 1978; *Wise* — 21 November 1981 to 12 April 1983.

In recent years this dainty little gull has occurred regularly on all of the large reservoirs, sometimes reaching large numbers. The largest numbers were 1,925 at Lewisville Lake, Denton County, on 1 January 1977; 250 at Hagerman NWR, at Lake Texoma, Grayson County, on 11 March 1976; and the same number at Possum Kingdom Lake, Palo Pinto County, on 4 and 5 February 1984. A report of 700 Bonaparte's Gulls at Mountain

Map 50. Distribution of Bonaparte's Gull, *Larus philadelphia*

Creek Lake, Dallas County, on 26 October 1975 (see above paragraph) may be misidentified Franklin's Gulls. This latter species arrives and migrates through the area earlier, and by this date it is not uncommon to see large numbers.

Specimen: The only specimen of this small gull for north central Texas was one found dead in Dallas County on 4 December 1966 (WMP 1533).

Ring-billed Gull   *Larus delawarensis* Ord
Status: Common to abundant transient and winter visitor. Limited summer records for a few counties.
Occurrence: Ring-billed Gulls have been reported in all of the north central Texas study area counties except Ellis, Hood, Navarro, and Somervell. There is little doubt that they have occurred in those counties as well, but not reported.

This gull is a common transient in migration, especially in fall, around large impoundments. At times it becomes abundant at Lake Texoma, Grayson County, and Lake Tawakoni, Hunt, Rains, and Van Zandt counties. It seems to be more abundant on the eastern side of the study area than on the western side, although this may be due to the larger number of observers in the eastern part.

The gull has been reported on all of the annual CBCs but was missed some years on the Palo Pinto count. On the CBCs at Hagerman NWR, Grayson County, between 1965 and 1982 its numbers varied from 730 to 35,000. The gulls concentrate at open landfills, especially in winter. They are opportunists, feeding on whatever they can find—on insect eruptions; at fish kills; in plowed fields, like Franklin's Gulls; formerly in open peanut fields; and in cities in early mornings, even at drive-in movie theaters. Their numbers often reflect shifts of populations to sources of food.

There are only scattered midsummer records of Ring-billed Gulls. One usually finds them in north central Texas from mid-September to early May. Extreme early and late dates of arrival and departure for selected counties are: *Dallas*—12 August 1971 (mean arrival date 8 September, 1959–75) to 24 May 1981. Stillwell (1939) gave dates of 27 September 1936 to 21 April 1935. *Grayson*—an isolated date of 19 July 1976 (specimen) and 26 July 1983, then 2 August 1982 to mid-May. *Rains*—an isolated date of 30 July 1984, next-earliest 10 August 1986 to 7 May 1983. *Tarrant*—4 August 1970 to 21 May 1959. *Wichita*—16 August 1975 to 24 May 1973.

Two Ring-billed Gulls banded as nestlings, one in central Saskatchewan, Canada, and the other in the northwestern part of the province, were recovered from Dallas County and just north of the Red River in Oklahoma above Cooke County, respectively.

Specimens: Ring-billed Gull specimens are known from Dallas (WMP), Denton (DMNH, WMP), Grayson (OU), Tarrant (FWMSH, UTA), and Wichita (MWU) counties. One allegedly taken in Wilbarger County (Oberholser, 1974) was not located.

HERRING GULL *Larus argentatus* Pontoppidan
Status: Rare to uncommon winter visitor.
Occurrence: Herring Gulls have been recorded in 18 north central Texas counties: Bosque, Clay, Collin, Cooke, Dallas, Denton, Ellis, Grayson, Hill,

Map 51. Distribution of the Herring Gull, *Larus argentatus*

Hunt, Johnson, Palo Pinto, Rains, Tarrant, Van Zandt, Wichita, Wilbarger, and Young.

This large gull from the far north is occasionally found in passage, and now and then a few birds may winter, especially where Ring-billed Gulls winter. They have not been reported on every annual CBC of the area. Several high counts for Dallas and Fort Worth CBCs, more than 100 in each case, seem unlikely, but small counts are not unreasonable. The high counts probably came about when inexperienced bird-watchers saw one or two Herring Gulls in a large flock of Ring-billed Gulls, above, and assumed that all of them were Herring Gulls. The highest counts recorded at Hagerman NWR, Grayson County, were 32 on 8 January 1972, 46 on 23 February 1974, and 30 on 13 February 1977.

This species usually arrives in the area later than the Ring-billed Gull and tends to leave earlier. Most of the sightings are during the winter months November through March.

Extreme dates for counties for which there are sufficient data are: *Dallas* — 7 September 1975 to 27 March 1982. An 8 August 1953 date without details is questioned. Stillwell's (1939) earlier records seemed to be even more doubtful and cloud the extent of occurrence in Dallas County. Certainly his source of some data (Kelley, 1935) was in error. The author of the latter reference stated that Herring Gull was a "common summer resident." *Grayson* — an isolated date of 12 August 1974 (no details given), next-earliest 5 September 1975 to 5 April 1975. Dates given in Hagerman NWR reports cite a period from 11 October to 20 April, with isolated dates of 27 September and 3 and 4 May. *Palo Pinto* — 17 September 1978 to 8 February 1974. *Rains* — 28 October 1984 to 22 April 1984. *Tarrant* — 17 September 1944 to 16 April 1974. *Wichita* — 9 October 1974 to 4 April 1978. *Specimens:* Specimens indicated for Dallas and Wilbarger counties (Oberholser, 1974) could not be found, while another cataloged from Denton County (DMNH) was missing from the collection. A mounted gull (DMNH 6656) is labeled Thayer's Gull (*Larus thayeri*). It was not examined since it was behind glass in the exhibit case and could not be measured and compared with known specimens of Thayer's Gull. It may be a Herring Gull. The only known Herring Gull specimen located from north central Texas was one from Hill County (SM).

LESSER BLACK-BACKED GULL   *Larus fuscus* Linnaeus
Status: Casual.
Occurrence: On 20 December 1985 a Lesser Black-backed Gull was seen at the Eagle Mountain Fish Hatchery, Tarrant County, with a flock of Ring-billed Gulls by a lone observer who carefully studied the bird for ten to 15 minutes. Since that time it has been viewed on 22 December 1985 and 11 and 30 January 1986 by a number of persons. It disappeared after 23 February. Photographs have been taken of this gull, and they have been submitted to the TOS Bird Records Committee for acceptance and inclusion in the north central Texas region.

The occurrence of this species is not unexpected, for a number of reports, including photographs (TP-RF), are available from the Texas coast. This would be the first inland record for the state.
Specimens: At present there are no Lesser Black-backed Gull specimens available from Texas.

GLAUCOUS GULL   *Larus hyperboreus* Gunnerus
Status: Casual winter visitor.
Occurrence: Glaucous Gulls have been reported in three north central Texas study area counties: Clay, Denton, and Grayson.

County dates are: *Clay* — 17 December 1880, A. Hall (MCZ 33036), representing *L. h. hyperboreus* intergrading with *barrovianus*. The location is given as "in Red River." Sutton (1967) points out that Oklahoma extends to the south bank of the Red River, and thus the specimen in question is in reality the first record from Oklahoma, not Texas. Since there is no way of knowing what Ragsdale (1881) meant when he documented this example, the exact location remains in doubt. Many birds forage along the Red

River, passing freely back and forth. To this day the record is claimed by both Oklahoma and Texas. A second specimen (MCZ 32371), representing *L. h. hyperboreus*, lacks both date and the exact location and bears the label "Texas, G. H. Ragsdale." Whether or not the specimen is from this state will never be known, nor will the exact date be known; a newspaper used to stuff the specimen was dated 22 November 1879. Ragsdale lived in Gainesville, Cooke County, and did most of his collecting in that area. Oberholser (1974) apparently gave this as a questionable record for Cooke County. *Denton* – 8 November 1973, a single Glaucous Gull fed with Franklin's and Ring-billed Gulls and an immature Herring Gull at the Lewisville State Fish Hatchery (photographs). *Grayson* –18 December 1982 to 18 January 1983, below Denison Dam, on both sides of the Red River, in Oklahoma and Texas. On 24 January 1983 a specimen (KH 3361) of a male was picked up at Hagerman NWR, less than 15 miles from Denison Dam. Haller and Beach (1984) present the details of its discovery and subsequent subspecific determination by Richard Banks, of the U.S. National Museum of Natural History.

In attempting to determine to which race the Grayson County specimen belongs, Banks became convinced that there were four subspecies of Glaucous Gulls rather than the three currently recognized. Thus three, rather than two, occur in North America, and one occurs in Europe. He believes that the Glaucous Gull from Grayson County represents the population of eastern Canada yet unnamed at this time, rather than the Alaskan race *L. h. barrovianus.*

BLACK-LEGGED KITTIWAKE　*Rissa tridactyla* (Linnaeus)
Status: Casual winter visitor.
Occurrence: This arctic gull has been observed three times in north central Texas in the following counties: *Johnson* – Lake Pat Cleburne on 27 December 1965 through 2 March 1966 (seen by many observers); *Tarrant* – Benbrook Reservoir on 21 through 25 November 1976; *Wichita* – Lake Wichita on 29 December 1975 through 5 January 1976.

SABINE'S GULL　*Xema sabini* (Sabine)
Status: Casual fall transient.
Occurrence: There are records of this species for only five counties in north central Texas: *Dallas* – briefly spotted at oxidation ponds in west Dallas on 26 September 1965. *Grayson* – one at Sandy Point, Lake Texoma, Hagerman NWR, on 11 November 1978, and another near refuge observation tower on 24 September 1985. There also is a record of a juvenile male collected on the Oklahoma side of Lake Texoma on 24 October 1954 (Sutton, 1967). The specimen was taken on a sandbar in the lake in Marshall County. *Kaufman* – at Cedar Creek Lake on 22 September 1973. *Tarrant* – at Ben-

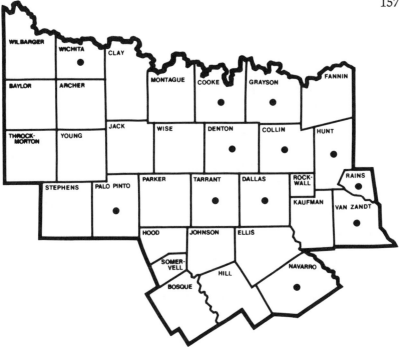

Map 52. Distribution of the Caspian Tern, *Sterna caspia*

brook Lake on 8 and 9 October and again on 20 October 1986. *Wichita* —
at Buffalo Lake, about three miles west of Iowa Park, on 26 September
1976. Each sighting was of a lone bird in passage, was carefully documented, and was observed by more than one person.

CASPIAN TERN *Sterna caspia* Pallas
Status: Uncommon to rare transient, more in fall than in spring. Summer
records represent early transients.
Occurrence: The Caspian Tern has been reported in 12 north central Texas
counties: Collin, Cooke, Dallas, Denton, Grayson, Hunt, Navarro, Palo
Pinto, Rains, Tarrant, Van Zandt, and Wichita.

This large tern is more common in fall than in spring and is seen mainly
around the large water impoundments, particularly Lake Tawakoni
(Hunt–Rains–Van Zandt counties) and Lake Texoma (Grayson County).
Usually only one or two are observed at a time, but 18 were counted in
Grayson County on 5 May 1979, and 15 were counted in Dallas County
on 26 September 1973. Caspian Tern records are more numerous on the
east side of the study area. Along the western side there are records from
only Palo Pinto and Wichita counties.

The largest numbers of reports are in mid-May and again in September. Records for selected counties are: *Dallas* — five times in spring, 15 April 1977, 7 May 1977, 15 May 1971, 18 May 1958, and 22 May 1982, and a number in fall from 13 August 1966 to 8 October 1976; *Denton* — 15 May 1953 to 28 May 1955, twice in midsummer — 4 July 1957 and 26 July 1975, and the remainder for September — 1 September 1977 to 19 September 1958; *Grayson* — 28 April 1983 to 2 June, isolated dates, 22 and 23 June, and 19 and 30 July to 29 October 1973; *Rains* — at least a dozen times in spring, 26 April 1987 to 30 May 1984, an isolated date of 24 June 1985, and 9 July 1953 to 3 November 1984; *Tarrant* — five times, 8 May 1976, 19 May 1983, 3 August 1983, 14 October 1945, and 14 through 27 October 1984; *Wichita* — two times, 22 May 1973 and 13 through 20 September 1975. *Specimens:* No Caspian Tern specimens have been collected from north central Texas as far as I can determine.

COMMON TERN   *Sterna hirundo* Linnaeus
Status: Casual; at best a rare transient.
Occurrence: The status of the Common Tern in north central Texas is extremely vague. Since this species can easily be confused with Forster's Tern, and because many of the published records are given without details, it has proved difficult to assess its status accurately. One can only guess at the validity of many of the reports of Common Terns.

Oberholser (1974) indicated records of this species, some of which are no doubt in error. These records include Cooke, Dallas, Denton, Hunt, and Tarrant counties. To these records can be added Archer, Clay, Ellis, Grayson, and Wichita counties.

County dates are: *Archer* — two records, specimen MWU 619, 18 October 1971 (not given by Oberholser, 1974) and fall of 1974 (Williams, 1975). *Clay* — 7 and 8 May 1978, one said to have been seen with Forster's Tern. *Cooke* — Oberholser (1974) gives a summer record without any details, no other records since. *Dallas* — Stillwell (1939) gives a number of records, some by inexperienced observers. An alleged specimen, DMNH 3563, said to have been taken on 19 May 1947, was missing from the collection. Many sightings in the mid-1950s and the 1960s were dismissed since it was impossible to assess them. There are few records since. One tern was carefully studied at North Lake on 25 July 1984. An immature was seen at a south-side water-treatment plant on 6 September 1986. The local checklist includes the species as hypothetical. *Denton* — one specimen (TCWC 1984), 11 July 1939, was not cited by Oberholser (1974). Other records were dismissed as misidentifications. *Ellis* — 18 May 1976 (Williams, 1976); no details given. *Grayson* — given as accidental on local Hagerman NWR checklist (U.S. Fish and Wildlife Service, 1984). One was identified by bill color on 15 and 18 April 1975. *Hunt* — Oberholser (1974) indicated a summer record but gave no details. The record was dismissed. *Tarrant* —

an alleged specimen (Oberholser, 1974) was not located. The records are not acceptable; it was listed as species of uncertain occurrence (Pulich, 1979). *Wichita*—15 April 1973 (Williams, 1973); details lacking.

FORSTER'S TERN   *Sterna forsteri* Nuttall
Status: Fairly common to common transient. Rare to uncommon winter visitor.
Occurrence: Forster's Terns have been recorded in 20 counties in the north central Texas project area: Bosque, Clay, Collin, Cooke, Dallas, Denton, Fannin, Grayson, Hill, Hunt, Johnson, Kaufman, Palo Pinto, Rains, Rockwall, Tarrant, Van Zandt, Wichita, Wise, and Young. There seem to be more records of this species along the east side of the study area, west to about Grayson, and south through Denton, Tarrant, and Bosque counties; however, there are scattered records at large reservoirs on the west side.

Forster's Tern is primarily a migrant through north central Texas, although there are records for every month for some of the counties, especially where much bird-watching occurs regularly. They tend to linger in fall passage and have wintered in Collin, Dallas, Denton, Grayson, Hunt, Kaufman, Rains, Tarrant, and Van Zandt counties, their numbers dropping off in January, February, and early March. Wintering is due to mild weather and an abundant supply of fish at suitable man-made reservoirs.

Peaks of migration dates in spring are from April through mid-May and again in fall from early August through early October. Some select extreme county dates of spring and fall passage are: *Dallas*—observed every month, an isolated date, 2 March 1983, next-earliest 1 April 1978 (mean 16 April) through 12 June 1958 and 13 July 1934, next 29 July 1978 through 28 November 1980; *Grayson*—seen every month but February, 21 March 1974, next-earliest 5 April 1980 to 10 June 1975, an isolated date, 28 June, and 17 July 1982 through 30 November 1986; *Hunt*—includes Rains and Van Zandt counties, reported every month, 3 March 1985, next 1 April 1984 through 30 June 1985, an isolated date, 27 June 1981, and 2 July 1986 through 23 November 1986; *Palo Pinto*—isolated dates, 29 and 30 April 1978, 26 June 1977, and 24 July 1977, and 25 September 1978 to 8 October 1977, and an isolated date, 5 November 1977; *Tarrant*—seen every month but June: five in January; one on 2 February 1986; 13 March 1981, 14 March 1964 and 1979, and 26 March 1975; 13 April 1974 to 12 May 1978; and 22 July 1981 and 1983 to 14 December 1986; *Wichita*—5 April 1976 to 8 June 1975, an isolated date, 2 July 1976, and 14 and 16 September 1975 through 5 October 1976.

Specimens: Forster's Tern specimens have been taken from Denton (DMNH, mounted), Grayson (OU), Kaufman (SFASU), and Tarrant (FWMSH, WMP) counties.

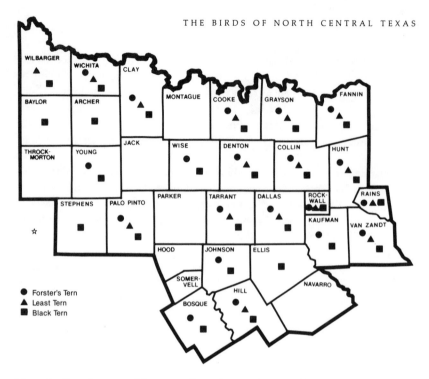

Map 53. Distribution of Forster's Tern, *Sterna forsteri*; the Least Tern, *S. antillarum*; and the Black Tern, *Chlidonias niger*

LEAST TERN *Sterna antillarum* (Lesson)
Status: Rare to common transient. Formerly bred in Denton County and along most of the Red River, but current nesting records may be limited to Grayson County.
Occurrence: Least Terns have been recorded in 16 counties of the study area: Clay, Collin, Cooke, Dallas, Denton, Fannin, Grayson, Hill, Hunt, Palo Pinto, Rains, Rockwall, Tarrant, Van Zandt, Wichita, and Wilbarger.
　　Some arrival and departure dates of Least Terns for select counties are: *Dallas* — 3 May 1985 to 13 June 1982, an isolated date, 30 June 1953, and 21 July 1985, next-earliest 27 July 1969 to 14 September 1980. Stillwell (1939) gave records for 6 May 1935 through 22 September 1937 and indicated that there were numerous summer sightings, which is not true today. *Denton* — 14 April 1941 (specimen), formerly through summer months, and 27 August 1977 to 25 September 1985. *Grayson* — 21 April through summer months to an extremely late date, 20 October. *Tarrant* — 23 April 1971 to 19 May 1983, an isolated date, 11 June 1955, and from 3 August 1971, 1983, to 1 October 1955. *Wichita* — observations not numerous, ranging from 15 April 1973 to 28 May 1975, an isolated date, 23 June 1973, and

23 August 1975 to 15 September 1975, and an isolated date, 4 October 1975.

Nesting: Formerly this little tern was considered to be a nesting species in north central Texas, mainly along the Red River, but today the only area where it may still nest is the Hagerman NWR and upper Lake Texoma, Grayson County. Actual nesting records include Denton County, probably in the late 1950s (1959), but since then only transients have been recorded. In Grayson County the latest actual sighting was in early July 1976, when ten nests were found (Williams, 1976), and a suspected nesting as late as 1980 that was based on an immature that was able to fly and was still being fed. In Wilbarger County (More and Strecker, 1929) a small colony nested on the sand bars of Pease River near Vernon. The colony was destroyed by high water on 6 June 1929. There are no recent records. It is becoming rare, and in 1984 the inland race of Least Tern was placed on the federal roster of endangered species.

Specimens: Specimens of Least Terns are available from Denton (DMNH) and Grayson (OU) counties. Oberholser (1974) gave specimen records for Collin, Dallas, and Palo Pinto counties, but these could not be located.

BLACK TERN   *Chlidonias niger* (Linnaeus)
Status: Common to abundant transient.
Occurrence: Black Terns have been recorded in the following counties of the north central Texas study area—Archer, Baylor, Bosque, Clay, Collin, Cooke, Dallas, Denton, Ellis, Fannin, Grayson, Hill, Hunt, Johnson, Kaufman, Palo Pinto, Rains, Rockwall, Stephens, Tarrant, Van Zandt, Wichita, Wilbarger, Wise, and Young—and in nearby Shackelford County.

Along with the Forster's Tern this is one of the common terns of north central Texas, appearing rather late and departing fairly early. The peak of migration is in May, with numerous sightings for June and July and again from early August through mid-September. Black Terns, in a variety of plumages, are not uncommon in summer on many large bodies of water; however, there is no indication that this species nests anywhere in north central Texas.

Extreme arrival and departure dates from selected counties are: *Dallas* — 9 April 1978 (mean 6 May) to 6 June 1970 (mean 20 May), and 16 July 1983 to 10 October 1965. Stillwell (1939) gives extreme dates 15 June 1935 to 1 November 1934. *Grayson*—15 April 1976 to 8 June, an isolated date, 15 June, and 27 June 1976 to 28 October 1986. *Tarrant*—28 April 1985 to 20 June 1955, and 1 July 1951 to 19 October 1952 and an isolated date, 1 November 1955. *Wichita*—5 May 1976 to 10 June 1975 and an isolated date, 13 July 1975, next 2 August 1973 to 19 September 1973.

The Black Tern varies in abundance from single individuals to several hundred during the peak of migration, particularly in the spring (mid-May). They are often seen feeding singly or in loose flocks over prairies, capturing winged insects. Unusually large flocks of about 1,500 were reported on 13 May 1954 and of 1,000 on 17 May 1955 and 1976 from Tarrant County; 500 on 13 May 1969 and 22 May 1967 from Dallas County; and 350 on 16 May 1976 from Grayson County. Their numbers in the fall never seem to be as large since their period of passage is longer.

Specimens: Black Tern specimens are known from Denton (DMNH), Grayson (OU), and Tarrant (FWMSH, UTA) counties. Those said to have been collected from Cooke (Oberholser, 1974) could not be located.

BLACK SKIMMER   *Rynchops niger* Linnaeus
Status: Casual in fall, to be watched for after storms.
Occurrence: There are five records of the Black Skimmer for north central Texas: *Dallas* — on 15 August 1954 (Miller, 1955) and on 20 and 21 August 1983 after Hurricane Alicia; *Grayson* — at Hagerman NWR on 22 September 1957 and 9 through 19 August 1984; *Tarrant* — at Lake Arlington on 25 August through 3 September 1980 (photographs) after Hurricane Allen on the Texas Gulf Coast. It is likely that this species occurs inland only after weather disturbances, especially after the passage of hurricanes, and at these times large bodies of water in north central Texas would bear checking.

Order Columbiformes

Family Columbidae (Pigeons and Doves)

ROCK DOVE   *Columba livia* Gmelin
Status: Common to abundant resident.
Occurrence: The Rock Dove is found throughout north central Texas. It is more common in urban areas than in rural areas. In counties with small cities and towns they are not as numerous, although it is not uncommon to see flocks of common pigeons, or "wild pigeons," feeding by the hundreds in plowed grain fields. They frequent ledges of buildings and under bridges and are seldom if ever seen perched elsewhere. In some cities their nests produce so much litter that the pigeons are trapped and eliminated. This species is often ignored by many bird-watchers because it is not considered a wild bird, although it is officially counted on CBCs. The actual population figures given on CBCs for this introduced species nowhere rep-

resent its actual numbers. In recent years they are becoming abundant, and they are reported coming to feeders, competing with native birds. The species has been developed from pigeons kept in captivity and is found in an array of colors. The natural color of the parent stock was blue-gray, much like that of the Homing Pigeon used for racing. Rock Doves are prolific nesters, and if a particular population was carefully studied, it would probably be found nesting throughout the year except during molt and some winter periods.

BAND-TAILED PIGEON   *Columba fasciata* Say
Status: Accidental.
Occurrence: There is only one record of this species for the north central Texas study area: a Band-tailed Pigeon observed on 18 August 1969 in a scrub-oak woodland of Stephens County (Williams, 1970). This species usually occurs in the southwestern mountains of the Chisos-Guadalupe area of west Texas and is not to be expected so far east.

WHITE-WINGED DOVE   *Zenaida asiatica* (Linnaeus)
Status: Casual.
Occurrence: This southwestern species of dove is not often reported in north central Texas. It seldom ranges beyond San Antonio and rarely to Austin and the upper Gulf Coast.

It has been reported for four north central Texas counties: *Archer* — one shot during dove season a mile south of Holliday on 21 September 1986 (MWV 1073). The specimen is represented by only the left wing. *Dallas* — nothing is given by Oberholser (1974) or Stillwell (1939). There are five records from 1964 to 1982, some without details. Whether or not persons actually saw White-winged Doves, or whether the birds were wild stock, was difficult to ascertain since they are often kept in captivity by game-bird fanciers. Those for which details were given are as follows: One that was seen and photographed on 25 and 26 April 1979 at Richardson appeared wild, according to the observer who photographed the bird. A second dove was briefly seen in north Dallas on 6 October 1980, and careful details were presented in the report. Another visited a bird feeder in Dallas on 18 April 1982 for several hours but did not return. *Navarro* — one was listed as a fall sighting by Oberholser (1974); no details were given. *Stephens* — one said to have been shot by a hunter on 1 September 1969, but it was not saved as a specimen.

MOURNING DOVE   *Zenaida macroura* (Linnaeus)
Status: Common to abundant summer visitor and transient. Found the year round.

Occurrence: Mourning Doves are widespread and found the year round in a variety of habitats in all of the north central Texas counties. They are migratory. Local birds banded (young in nests) show a definite movement in a southwesterly or southerly direction from Dallas County. Migrants arrive from the south in early February and remain until mid-September, although fall birds may leave the area even earlier during the hunting season. Available food supply from wheat fields and favorite weed patches, as well as the weather, often influence population numbers.

My limited banding shows that a few doves live to be four and five years old. Numerous doves returning to the same feeding stations and retrapped in late winter and early spring were one and two years old.

Nesting: Although they have been observed in every county, Mourning Doves have not been found nesting in every county. There is little doubt, however, that if efforts were made to find nests, Mourning Doves would be found nesting in all counties. Nesting dates in Dallas County extend from 18 February 1976 (gathering nesting material), 5 March 1984 (sitting on nest), 9 March 1984 (eggs), and the latest, 26 September 1971 (young banded). Although October nesting is implied for north central Texas, no specific dates could be located. It is likely that these dates represent dates for south Texas, since Mourning Doves have been reported nesting the year round in the Rio Grande valley. Doves are two-brooded, occasionally three-brooded, and rarely nest four times. Although they usually build a flimsy nest, or on rare occasions nest on the ground where there are no trees, they also lay their eggs in old nests of other birds. Sightings of more than two eggs in a nest indicate that two doves are using the same nest.

Specimens: Specimens have been located from Cooke (TCWC), Dallas (DMNH, WMP), Denton (DMNH), Hood (FWMSH), Tarrant (FWMSH), and Wichita (DMNH) counties. Those indicated from Clay County (Oberholser, 1974) were not located.

Studies by Aldrich and Duvall (1958) showed that breeding Mourning Doves secured in late May, June, and July in Tarrant County were nearest to *Z. m. marginella.*

INCA DOVE   *Columbina inca* (Lesson)
Status: Irregular to uncommon visitor in most counties, probably becoming more common in recent years. Small local populations with nesting reported in several counties.

Occurrence: Oberholser (1974) gave records from Navarro, Palo Pinto, Tarrant, and Wilbarger counties and adjacent Eastland County. To these counties can be added Bosque, Dallas, Denton, Ellis, Grayson, Hill, Hood, Johnson, Parker, Somervell, Stephens, Wichita, and Young, as well as nearby Comanche and Erath counties.

There has been a definite northward movement of this little dove in re-

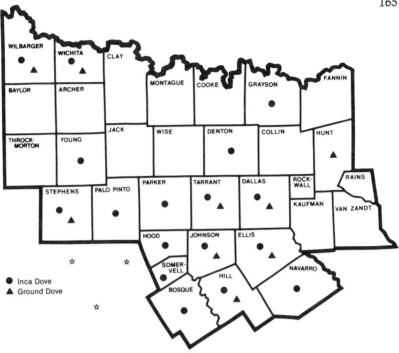

Map 54. Distribution of the small doves: Inca Dove, *Columbina inca,* and the Common Ground-Dove, *C. passerina*

cent years. The earliest records known for north central Texas are those for the 1920s in Wilbarger County (More and Strecker, 1929).

Except where Inca Doves have been reported nesting, dates of sightings are not numerous and are scattered. Populations may be attempting to establish themselves and then die off awaiting another northward push of colonization. Observers in counties not listed as having Inca Doves are urged to record dates so that dates of colonization can be documented. It has been suggested that the Inca Dove showing up for the first time in a new area appears in the winter.

Nesting: Oberholser (1974) showed the Inca Dove nesting only in Navarro County. Today a small population can be found nesting regularly in southwest Fort Worth, Tarrant County, and in Wichita County. In Fort Worth it was first discovered nesting on 23 March 1979; the earliest nesting date is of one sitting on a nest on 22 February 1983. It was found nesting in Wichita County in the spring of 1976. In addition, nesting has been suspected in Dallas, Palo Pinto, Parker, Somervell, and Wilbarger counties, and adjacent Erath County.

Specimens: Specimens in my collection (WMP) are from Tarrant and Wichita counties.

COMMON GROUND-DOVE *Columbina passerina* (Linnaeus)
Status: Casual, if not accidental.
Occurrence: The Common Ground-Dove has been reported in nine north central Texas counties: Dallas, Ellis, Hill, Hunt, Johnson, Stephens, Tarrant, Wichita, and Wilbarger. Some of the records are old and questionable, and it is possible that the casual birder mistook the Inca Dove for this species. It is normally found in the south Texas brushlands and is seldom reported north of its normal range. It does not associate with man as readily as does the Inca Dove.

County dates are: *Dallas* — Stillwell (1939) listed two dates, both of which have been questioned and until recently considered hypothetical (Pulich, 1977). One was substantiated by a photograph on 17 December 1977. *Ellis* — two visited a yard in a small community of Bristol on 29 March 1982. *Hill* — one was seen near Aquilla on 18 April 1980. *Hunt* — a fall record given by Oberholser (1974) was based on two reports (O'Neil, 1957). It is interesting that no Inca Doves have been reported in this county since the 1950s. *Johnson* — a local bird-watcher at Keene indicated that ground-doves had been seen but gave no date of occurrence. *Stephens* — one was carefully observed on a ranch on 7 September 1984. *Tarrant* — until recently early records from this county were questioned (Pulich, 1979). One was reported near Grapevine Lake on the Dallas-Tarrant county line on 24 October 1981. *Wichita* — two were allegedly sighted near Sheppard Air Force Base, on the edge of Wichita Falls, on 9 May 1974; none since. *Wilbarger* — sightings are given for spring and summer (Oberholser, 1974), probably in the 1930s during R. L. More's time.
Specimens: No specimens of this species occur from north central Texas.

Order Psittaciformes

Family Psittacidae (Parrots)

MONK PARAKEET *Myiopsitta monachus* (Boddaert)
Status: Accidental
Occurrence: This South American species has been reported in three north central Texas counties: Collin, Dallas, and Johnson. In addition there is a report of one from Cass County, in east Texas.

Whether these exotic birds are escaped caged birds, or whether the species has established itself from wild populations spreading from the eastern United States, has not been determined. It is very possible that parakeets from the Dallas area were escapees since members of the parrot family (in general) that have eluded their owners are often observed flying around neighborhood yards.

Records of Monk Parakeet sightings that could not be traced to human intervention are given for the following counties: *Collin* — 11 July 1980, two flying overhead, calling noisily, were reported as this species, but no other details were given. *Dallas* — a pair was reported in Oak Cliff, in south Dallas, from May 1973 and remained until spring 1976. They attempted nesting two years, once on a telephone pole and once in a martin house. Although they never successfully reared young, the eggs hatched, for I have a mummified downy-young specimen that was found beneath the nest in the spring of 1974. The Dallas zoo, about three miles away, indicated that it had had no Monk Parakeets before the first observation, and the origin of this nesting pair remains a mystery. On 8 and 9 December 1981 a Monk Parakeet visited a bird feeder in Coppell, and one was seen on 10, 18, and 22 December 1984 on the campus of the University of Texas at Dallas in Richardson. On 14 September 1986, Monk Parakeets were reported at a nest in a telephone pole a short distance west of Love Field in Dallas. Many observers viewed the birds, and at times as many as four parakeets were reported. One of the local residents claimed the birds have nested two years and that they like to have the birds around and often feed them. *Johnson* — on 17 October 1982 one was reported at Alvarado, a small rural community; no other details were given. *Cass* — one observed off and on during the summer until early November 1979 at McLeod, in the southeastern part of the county. A single bird fed at a feeder and in late fall on fruits of a pear tree.

Order Cuculiformes

Family Cuculidae (Cuckoos, Roadrunners, and Anis)

BLACK-BILLED CUCKOO   *Coccyzus erythropthalmus* (Wilson)
Status: Rare transient. More records for spring than for fall. Nesting allegedly documented for Wise County in 1888 has been discounted. Does not nest in north central Texas.
Occurrence: Oberholser (1974) gave records of occurrence of Black-billed Cuckoos for Dallas, Denton, Hunt, Tarrant, and Wise counties. To these can be added Clay, Collin, Grayson, and Van Zandt counties, making a total of nine counties in which this rare cuckoo has been recorded.

If careful examination is made under favorable conditions, this species can be separated from the Yellow-billed Cuckoo, the common cuckoo of north central Texas. The names of the two species may imply that the bills are distinctive, but this is not always a foolproof means of identification. All of the characteristics should be noted, including the lack of rufous on the black-bill's wing, the narrow white tips of the tail, and an inconspicuous red eye-ring.

Records at hand for all of the counties are: *Clay* — sightings by competent observers from 3 through 21 May 1973. *Collin* — 3 times, 1 May 1976, 10 May 1983 (one banded), and 13 May 1982. *Dallas* — although not seen every year, there are a number of spring records, 13 April 1929 (Stillwell, 1939), next-earliest 15 April 1978 to 30 May 1978, more common from early May to mid-May. An isolated observation, one carefully studied 13 June 1987. Five fall sightings — allegedly seen 8 August 1953 and 1983, 6 September 1982, 10 September 1960, and 29 September 1959 (TV-tower kill examined but not saved). A 22 July 1978 record is unacceptable since only one person saw the bird in question and did not provide all of the characteristic markings. Another, said to be an immature (Oberholser, 1974), seen in July 1940 is also discounted as an error. The original field notes of C. T. Gill in my possession show only Yellow-billed Cuckoos observed in Dallas County on his July field trips. *Denton* — listed by Oberholser (1974) as occurring in spring and fall, probably based on a sighting given in *Audubon Field Notes* for spring on 23 May 1953 and for fall on 30 July to August 1951, and 21 September 1958. Some of the summer records seem highly unlikely. No records since. *Grayson* — six spring records, 12 and 18 May 1968 (Hagerman NWR); 20, 25, and 29 May 1976; 11 and 22 May 1977; 18 and 25 May 1978; 9 and 13 May 1982; and 13 May 1984 (all from Sherman). Two fall records, 26 August 1968 and 11 August 1975 (both from Hagerman NWR). *Hunt* — spring and fall records (Oberholser, 1974); none since. *Tarrant* — 12 spring records, 5 May 1963 through 27 May 1983. One allegedly seen on 17 July 1960 seems highly unlikely and should probably be dismissed. Extremely late dates of 7 October 1986 and 9 October 1956 are questioned as being misidentified Yellow-billed Cuckoos. *Van Zandt* — second week in September 1981, carefully checked. *Wise* — three sets of eggs were said to have been collected from this county in 1888 (Oberholser, 1974). One set was taken near Decatur by R. L. More on 2 May 1888 (three eggs) and another on 4 May (four eggs); the third set was collected at Decatur by J. A. Donald on 21 May. According to Dobie (1941), More was only 14 years old and had not begun collecting eggs. It was not until June 1888 that More took his first set of eggs, two eggs of a Turkey Vulture. If Dobie is correct, the records are highly suspicious, since Donald and More (1894) gave no records of any cuckoos in Wise County. Admittedly, they may not have published all their notes. In Oberholser's original notes (copy on microfilm at the University of Dallas library, Irving) there is a discrepancy in the year of the second set of eggs taken by More. In the microfilm the date is given as 4 May 1892, not 4 May 1888. Since the Yellow-billed Cuckoo is the common nesting bird of north central Texas and the Black-billed Cuckoo nesting records are without details and rather vague, the nesting records for the Black-billed Cuckoo are rejected.

Specimens: The only specimens known to me of the Black-billed Cuckoo are from Dallas (DMNH, WMP) and Tarrant (FWMSH) counties.

YELLOW-BILLED CUCKOO *Coccyzus americanus* (Linnaeus)
Status: Common summer resident.
Occurrence: Yellow-billed Cuckoos have been reported in all of the counties in the north central Texas study area. "Rain crows," as many call them, are among the most common summer birds, particularly in open woodlands as well as in dense areas.

This species normally arrives in north central Texas in late April and departs in mid-October. Extreme arrival and departure dates for selected counties are: *Dallas* — 31 March 1977, next-earliest 4 April 1976 to 16 November 1984, next-latest 30 October 1968; *Grayson* —17 April to 21 November 1986, next-latest 16 November 1976 (bird that hit a window); *Kaufman* — 23 April 1979 to 18 October 1973; *Palo Pinto* — 3 April 1982 to 2 September 1974; *Tarrant* — 5 April 1979 to 4 November 1972, next-latest 30 October 1970; *Van Zandt* — 3 April 1982 to 17 October 1983; *Wichita* — 2 April 1976 to 22 October 1975.

There are two December records, representing late stragglers. One, collected in Hunt County on 14 December 1977 (WMP 2384), may have been unable to migrate since its left wing seemed abnormal, even though it could fly. Another was banded in Collin County on 9 December 1982.

Nesting: Nesting (young or eggs) has been recorded in 17 counties of the study area — Archer, Cooke, Dallas, Denton, Grayson, Hood, Hunt, Kaufman, Navarro, Palo Pinto, Tarrant, Throckmorton, Van Zandt, Wichita, Wilbarger, Wise, and Young — and nearby Henderson County. Cuckoos may be two-brooded, since nesting ranges from May until September, with peak of nesting in June. Dates for Dallas County, which would also be applicable to other counties, range from 31 May (one egg) to 6 September (young banded still in nest). Just across the Red River from Grayson County in Mead, Bryan County, Oklahoma, on 2 October 1971 a dead young Yellow-billed Cuckoo was found that had probably left the nest a day or so previously. It was saved as a specimen (OU; Haller, 1972).

Specimens: Yellow-billed Cuckoos have been collected in the following counties: Clay (MWU), Cooke (TNHC), Dallas (DMNH, UTA, WMP), Denton (DMNH), Ellis (DMNH), Henderson (DMNH), Hill (SM 1415, specimen dated 13 March 1967), Hood (FWMSH), Hunt (FWMSH, WMP), Jack (MWU), Palo Pinto (WMP), Parker (FWMSH, WMP), Tarrant (DMNH, FWMSH, UTA), Van Zandt (DMNH), Wichita (DMNH), and Young (TCWC).

GREATER ROADRUNNER   *Geococcyx californianus* (Lesson)
Status: Common resident where habitat still prevails.
Occurrence: The Greater Roadrunner has been recorded in all but one county — Rockwall — in north central Texas, not because there is no habitat for the species but because it has been overlooked. It should be found in that county as well as in the unrecorded adjacent counties.

This species may be more common and widespread over the counties in the western parts of the study area than in the eastern parts. It shuns deep forests. It has disappeared from areas where population pressures, housing developments, and land developments have cleared its natural habitat. However, where habitat is left, this species persists. For example, less than a half mile from Texas Stadium in Irving, at least two pairs remain today and will do so until the remaining habitat is destroyed.

Roadrunners are more or less sedentary and move little unless they are forced to. In counties where much birding takes place, they have been recorded the year round, but only occasionally in seldom-birded areas.

Much has been written about this interesting ground cuckoo, and readers are urged to read other accounts. It feeds on a wide variety of foods, which it must capture and kill. It is an opportunist, feeding on insects, amphibians, reptiles, birds, and mammals as it comes upon them. On 14 August 1974 it was observed in Wichita County killing a rattlesnake.
Nesting: Nesting (eggs or young) has been recorded in Bosque, Cooke, Dallas, Jack, Tarrant, Wichita, Wilbarger, Wise, and Young counties, and nearby Shackelford County. Although I have few nesting dates, the earliest is 8 April 1967 (Bosque County) — four eggs — and the latest is 9 August 1972 (Dallas County) — young banded still in the nest. These dates are more typical of nesting populations in north central Texas than the breeding dates (5 March to 10 October) given by Oberholser (1974), which represent overall nesting dates for Texas.

"Winter nesting or roosting" has been noted twice from 11 through 25 January 1983, the bird utilizing an old nest in Denton County, and on 5 March 1983 one was said to have been coming to roost for about six months in the observer's yard in Wichita Falls, Wichita County.
Specimens: Greater Roadrunner specimens have been located for the following counties: Archer (MWU), Baylor (MWU), Bosque (SM), Dallas (DMNH, OU, UTA, WMP), Denton (WMP), Ellis (DMNH), Johnson (SUC), Palo Pinto (MWU), Tarrant (FWMSH, UTA, WMP), and Wilbarger (CMNH). Those indicated by Oberholser (1974) for Cooke and Hood counties were not located.

GROOVE-BILLED ANI   *Crotophaga sulcirostris* (Swainson)
Status: Casual visitor.
Occurrence: This strange-looking bird has been reported in four north central Texas counties. Except for a May observation and three June reports the records represent wandering fall or early winter birds. The county records are: *Dallas* — 30 November 1966, 15 and 17 December 1973, 30 September 1976, 10 September 1977, and 21 May 1987; *Palo Pinto* — June 1960; *Tarrant* — 21 October 1973, 25 October 1979, and 9 June 1985; *Wichita* — 1 June 1978. The Groove-billed Ani should be searched for among flocks of Great-tailed Grackles, which it resembles.
Specimens: The Palo Pinto County record represents a collected specimen that was mounted and is still in the possession of the collector (Telfair).

Order Strigiformes

Family Tytonidae (Barn-Owls)

COMMON BARN-OWL   *Tyto alba* (Scopoli)
Status: Uncommon to fairly common permanent resident.
Occurrence: The Common Barn-Owl is more common than many birders realize. It has been recorded in 24 counties in the study area — Archer, Bosque, Collin, Cooke, Dallas, Denton, Ellis, Fannin, Grayson, Hill, Hunt, Johnson, Kaufman, Navarro, Palo Pinto, Rains, Somervell, Stephens, Tarrant, Throckmorton, Van Zandt, Wichita, Wilbarger, and Wise — and nearby Shackelford County.

This species is strictly nocturnal and is seldom observed during the day unless disturbed from an old abandoned building or dense tree cover (especially evergreens). It is more often heard at night flying about. One who is familiar with its long, drawn-out cry realizes that it is not uncommon even around towns and cities. In recent years probably as many are seen when it is brought to a bird-rehabilitation center or is found dead along a highway. The bird is infrequently reported on most of the CBCs but not every year. It may use caves and burrows along creeks and rivers. It is a highly beneficial owl; where roosts are discovered, barn-owl pellets are found to consist solely of the remains of rodents.
Nesting: Nesting (young or eggs) has been reported from Cooke, Collin, Dallas, Denton, Fannin, Grayson, Hill, Kaufman, Tarrant, Throckmorton, Wichita, and Wilbarger counties. Nesting dates range from 8 March 1959, five eggs (Dallas County); through spring until 17 July 1977, five young

fledged (Kaufman County); and again from 6 September 1980, five young (Hill County); 7 October 1986, five young banded (Collin County); and young through December (Dallas, Denton, Fannin, Grayson, and Tarrant counties). Five pairs were reported nesting in man-made duck blinds at a private gun club in south Dallas County on 11 May 1972. The largest number of young reported was ten, ranging from tiny young to owls ready to fledge, on 30 November 1976 (Denton County).

Specimens: Common Barn-Owl specimens are available from Archer (DMNH, MWU), Cooke (TNHC), Dallas (DMNH, WMP), Denton (DMNH), Grayson (KH), Hunt (DMNH, WMP), Johnson (UTA), Kaufman (DMNH, WMP), Navarro (UTA, WMP), Stephens (MWU), Tarrant (DMNH, FWMSH, TCWC, WMP), Wichita (MWU), and Wilbarger (TCWC) counties and nearby Henderson (DMNH) County.

Family Strigidae (Typical Owls)

EASTERN SCREECH-OWL *Otus asio* (Linnaeus)
Status: Common permanent resident.
Occurrence: Although the Eastern Screech-Owl is the most common of all the owls that occur in north central Texas, it has not been reported from all of the counties. There are no records for Baylor, Clay, Jack, Montague, Rains, or Rockwall counties. No doubt it occurs in these counties and could be found if a special effort were made to do so. It has been seen in nearby Eastland County, where it was not previously recorded.

Eastern Screech-Owls are found in many places, even spending the day in cities and towns where there are some hollow tree limbs or secluded thickets. For example, they come to my yard regularly at night to bathe in my birdbath. In wooded areas, both riparian and upland, they are frequently routed from their daytime roosts by Blue Jays and other small birds. In winter they occasionally take over a martin house.

Birders often try to imitate this little owl or play tape recordings of its call to attract other birds, especially chickadees and titmice. These birds in turn may bring an array of other small birds seeking the "calling owl."

In north central Texas this species occurs in two color phases, gray and red, the former color predominating. Both color phases may be found in one family group. It is usually recorded on all of the annual CBCs of north central Texas, becoming more evident in recent years owing to the use of tape recordings.

Eastern Screech-Owls eat a wide variety of foods, chiefly insects (large moths and beetles attracted to lights) and small mammals. Birds are also taken. One screech-owl killed a Harris' Sparrow in a mist net that had been set just before sunrise.

Nesting: This species has been found nesting in Bosque, Collin, Cooke,

Dallas, Ellis, Grayson, Navarro, Stephens, Tarrant, Van Zandt, Wichita, Wilbarger, Wise, and Young counties. Nesting ranges from mid-March to mid-June. Typical county dates are: Dallas — 23 April 1967 (young out of nest). Tarrant — 30 March 1919 (eggs collected), 2 June 1914 (one small young in nest; Sutton, 1938). Van Zandt — 5 July through 1 August 1984 (two adults with four young out of nest). Wilbarger — "breeds from middle of March until first of May." Most of the nests recorded "between 19 and March 26" (More and Strecker, 1929). Young — 18 June 1981 (large young out of nest). *Specimens:* Specimens of Eastern Screech-Owls were located for the following counties: Archer (MWU), Collin (WMP), Dallas (CaM, DMNH, USNM, UTA, WMP), Denton (DMNH, WMP), Ellis (DMNH), Grayson (DMNH), Henderson (WMP), Johnson (SUC), Somervell (WMP), Tarrant (DMNH, FWMSH, UTA, WMP), Van Zandt (WMP), Wichita (MWU, WMP), and Wilbarger (MWU).

All specimens except one examined from the north central Texas study area proved to be *O. a. hasbroucki* (FWMSH, UTA, WMP). The specimen from Van Zandt County (WMP 2693) is possibly *O. a. mccallii/floridanus.*

GREAT HORNED OWL   *Bubo virginianus* (Gmelin)
Status: Common resident throughout the area.
Occurrence: Great Horned Owls have been reported in all the counties

of the north central Texas study area and adjacent Henderson, Hopkins, and Shackelford counties.

This large owl is found the year round if searched for and is well adapted to a human environment, although many birders seldom if ever see it. It is more frequently heard than actually seen in the wild. However, road kills and injured birds brought to bird-rehabilitation centers are not uncommon. Between 1 January and 25 July 1983, 25 Great Horned Owls were brought to the Phoenix Center, Tarrant County.

This large owl feeds on a variety of foods, sometimes animals larger than itself. One such animal is the skunk, which it apparently captures readily. Not only does it take mammals, but it also feeds on birds as well as other members of the owl family, such as screech-owls. Like many other birds it is an opportunist, which likely has given it a bad name, since it takes domesticated animals — chickens, cats, and in one instance even a small dog. A pair of Great Horned Owls on 19 November 1986 fed upon a deer head and hide left from a deer hunt (Bosque County).

Most authorities agree that this species is nonmigratory. The few Great Horned Owls banded in the area tend to support this assumption, although some shifting of populations probably takes place in the winter. The few recoveries of local banded owls were not far from their banding sites. This may account for the fact that the exact range of eastern and western Great Horned Owls is poorly understood.

Nesting: Oberholser (1974) gives nesting records for ten counties: Baylor, Cooke, Dallas, Denton, Fannin, Tarrant, Wichita, Wilbarger, Wise, and Young. To these can be added Bosque, Collin, Grayson, Hopkins, Hunt, Jack, Johnson, Palo Pinto, Parker, Throckmorton, and Van Zandt counties. There is little doubt that the Great Horned Owl would be found nesting in all of the counties of the study area if efforts were made to look for them. It would not be hard to locate them, since they use old hawk and crow nests and begin nesting early, before the trees leaf out. Oologists and others searching for nests to band nestlings frequently spot this species at nests in leafless trees in January and early February. It was seen nesting at a Great Blue Heron heronry in Wichita County on 27 March 1976. Other sites include caves, hollow trees, and man-made structures: the oddest site was on the walkway of a water tower on the edge of Fort Worth (Tarrant County), where a pair attempted to nest on 13 February 1975.

Nesting dates for north central Texas range from 29 January (Wilbarger County; More and Strecker, 1929), next-earliest 7 February 1960 (Dallas County), sitting on nest, to one banded in nest on 20 July 1979 (Denton County). The peak of banding young in nest is from early April to early May.

Specimens: Great Horned Owl specimens are known from the following counties: Archer (MWU, UTA), Dallas (DMNH, TCWC, WMP), Denton (DMNH), Ellis (DMNH), Grayson (DMNH, TCWC), Hood (SM), Hunt (WMP), Johnson (FWMSH, SUC, UTA), Kaufman (UTA, WMP), Montague (MWU), Palo Pinto (FWMSH), Parker (OC), Tarrant (DMNH, FWMSH, UTA), Throckmorton (TCWC), Van Zandt (TCWC), Wichita (MWU), Wilbarger (MWU), and Wise (OU, WMP).

Only a few of these specimens were examined. The race *B. v. virginianus* has been collected as far west as Tarrant County, while Oberholser (1974) indicates that nesting birds of Wichita and Wilbarger counties are *B. v. pallescens*. He does not, however, indicate whether or not he examined specimens for these counties. Some appear to be intergrades between eastern and western races, and a thorough study should be undertaken.

SNOWY OWL *Nyctea scandiaca* (Linnaeus)
Status: Casual winter straggler, irregularly.
Occurrence: Snowy Owls rarely reach north central Texas. Sight records of this beautiful owl are questionable, and most should be dismissed. Several reports proved to be Barn Owls. County records are: *Archer* — one taken on the shores of Lake Wichita, three miles south of Wichita Falls on 16 February 1955 (MWU 165). *Dallas* — there is a mounted specimen in the Dallas Museum of Natural History, probably the one taken by W. A. Mayer in 1934. Some of Mayer's specimens were not given to the museum by his widow until after his death. For this reason the museum personnel did not catalog this owl. However, Mayer was dependable, and if he had taken one elsewhere he would have indicated this fact before his death. Stillwell (1939) lists this species as a "rare winter resident." There are no other records for this county. *Grayson* — the records at Hagerman NWR list a sighting for 30 December 1957. It is now included as accidental in the Hagerman checklist (U.S. Fish and Wildlife Service, 1984). *Hunt* — one report given without details as "winter 1921" in *Check-list of the Birds of East Texas* (1940). This has been discounted since the person making the observation was apparently alone, and many of his records are unreliable. Oberholser (1974) makes no reference to this sighting. *Tarrant* — a sighting on 26 January 1975 was discounted even though a number of these owls invaded Oklahoma, and one even traveled as far south as Waco (McLennan County) during the winter of 1974–75 (see Pulich, 1979, for other details). *Wichita* — there is a mounted specimen in the possession of Hal Mosley, of Dallas, that was taken in the winter of 1900 from Waco, McLennan County, not Wichita County. This is very likely the specimen referred to by Oberholser (1974) as "Wichita Co (?), vicinity of Wichita Falls."

BURROWING OWL *Athene cunicularia* (Molina)
Status: Uncommon to rare transient throughout most of the area. Casual

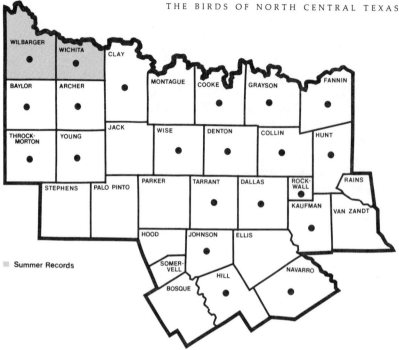

Map 55. Distribution of the Burrowing Owl, *Athene cunicularia*, with summer records

in winter, very few records. Nesting in the northwestern corner of the study area.

Occurrence: The Burrowing Owl has been recorded in 21 counties of the north central Texas study area. Oberholser published (1974) Archer, Clay, Cooke, Dallas, Denton, Fannin, Grayson, Hunt, Kaufman, Navarro, Tarrant, Wichita, Wilbarger, Wise, and Young counties. Six new counties added by this study are: *Baylor*—at Lake Kemp on 9 May 1983; *Collin*—at a housing development in Plano on 2 and 9 March 1983, east of Allen on 13 March 1983, at the Dallas-Collin county line between 8 and 27 March 1984, and at the same location from 29 October 1984 until 20 February 1985; *Hill*—in the vicinity of Vaughan on 7 and 9 March 1980; *Johnson* —18 October 1974 and near Lake Pat Cleburne on 15 December 1979; *Rockwall*—in the Lake Ray Hubbard area on 9 March 1980; *Throck-morton*—two capturing insects in the northwestern part of the county on 7 June 1987.

Data on hand show that this owl can be found in the fall, mainly in October, and again in the spring, in March. The earliest fall dates are 16 September 1975 (Wichita County), and 28 September 1974 (Tarrant County), the latest dates being 8 November 1979 (Grayson County) and

30 November 1986 (Dallas County), next-latest 26 November 1938 (Denton County). The earliest spring date is 2 March 1983 (Collin County), and the latest is 9 May 1983 (Baylor County).

Although Burrowing Owls are mainly migratory, a few may winter if food conditions are favorable. Winter dates include data reports from the following counties: Collin—12 December 1984; Cooke—11 January 1887, specimen, no recent dates; Dallas—16 December 1936, specimen (Stillwell, 1939), 26 December 1959, and 28 February 1939, specimen; Grayson— 7 January 1932; Johnson—15 December 1979; Tarrant—4 December 1957 and 28 January 1942; Wichita—20 December 1980.

Nesting: Zinn (1975) indicated that the Burrowing Owl nested on the campus of Midwestern University in Wichita Falls, Wichita County, in the early sixties. This is not true today as the city surrounds the campus. Oberholser (1974) recorded nesting for Tarrant County and gave questionable records for Navarro and Young counties, but I found no recent data to support his statement. Surprisingly, many persons consider this species to be a summer resident in other counties, although records are lacking. Reduction of prairie-dog colonies, as well as removal of prairies by cultivation and urbanization, has no doubt reduced this species in many areas of north central Texas where they may have formerly nested.

More and Strecker (1929) considered the Burrowing Owl "very abundant, nesting during the months of May and June" in Wilbarger County. They still nest among prairie-dog colonies on the Waggoner Ranch (10 May 1983). One was also observed perched near a nest burrow on 17 June 1987 in the southeastern part of this county. The pair of Burrowing Owls reported for Throckmorton County on 7 June 1987 were suspected of nesting because of their behavior.

Specimens: Burrowing Owl specimens have been located from the following counties: Archer (MWU), Cooke (TNHC), Dallas (DMNH), Denton (TCWC), Grayson (KH), Tarrant (DMNH, UTA), and Wilbarger (TNHC). Those indicated for Wichita and Wise counties (Oberholser, 1974) could not be located.

BARRED OWL   *Strix varia* Barton
Status: Uncommon to common resident.
Occurrence: Barred Owls have been recorded in 27 north central Texas counties—Archer, Bosque, Clay, Collin, Cooke, Dallas, Denton, Ellis, Fannin, Grayson, Hill, Hood, Hunt, Jack, Johnson, Navarro, Palo Pinto, Rains, Rockwall, Stephens, Tarrant, Throckmorton, Van Zandt, Wichita, Wilbarger, Wise, and Young—and adjacent Shackelford County, where it was not previously recorded.

This species inhabits dense bottomland woods and is probably more abundant in the eastern part of the study area, where there is more ap-

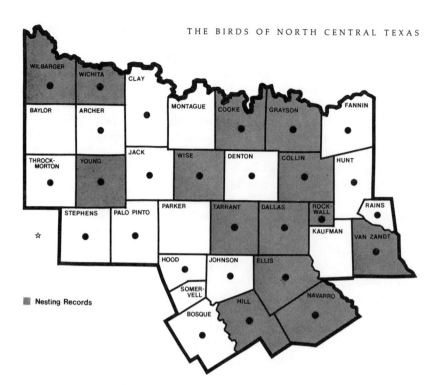

Map 56. Distribution of the Barred Owl, *Strix varia*, with nesting records

propriate habitat. It does not appear to occur in upland or cottonwood areas, which seem to be more typical of Great Horned Owl habitat.

In areas where there is much bird-watching, this species has been recorded the year round, but it is not likely to be seen as often as its larger counterpart, the Great Horned Owl. During the day the Barred Owl often seeks hollowed tree shelters, where it is not come upon as easily by crows or human beings. During the day, however, I have attracted Barred Owls by squeaking, and on two occasions in the daytime during the heat of summer I have found them bathing in secluded bodies of water. They have been recorded on all of the CBCs of the north central Texas area, although they are occasionally missed. In recent years the use of taped calls of this species has produced higher numbers on the CBCs. The bird's weird call is readily recognized, if one is familiar with it. The typical call, "who cooks for me? who cooks for you?" is distinctive.

Nesting: Oberholser (1974) indicated nesting for Cooke, Dallas, Grayson, Tarrant, Wichita, Wilbarger, Wise, and Young counties. He questions the last two counties, though he gives no explanation for doing so, and I see no reason for questioning these records. Even today there is still habitat in these two counties, and there have been recent sightings of the species. Oberholser apparently overlooked Navarro County, where Ogilby (1882) saw young out of the nest in June. The only recent nesting records that I have are from Collin, Dallas, Ellis, Grayson, Hill, Rockwall, Tarrant, and Van Zandt counties. Dates range from 24 February 1980 (Ellis County), probable nesting since it had been seen for several years at the same tree hollow; 27 February 1971 (Rockwall County), adult at nest hollow and seen regularly after that date; young out of nest but too small to fly well were seen on 27 April 1984 (Van Zandt County); downy young in nest on 12 May 1977 (Tarrant County); young fledged on 2 June 1980 (Hill County); young fledged on 21 June 1980 (Dallas County); and a downy young specimen (DMNH 6661), dated 17 July 1977 (Dallas County).

Specimens: Barred Owl specimens are available from Archer (MWU), Clay (CC), Collin (DMNH), Cooke (TNHC), Dallas (DMNH, WMP), Denton (DMNH), Ellis (WMP), Grayson (WMP), Hill (TCWC), Johnson (UTA), Navarro (WMP), Tarrant (DMNH, FWMSH, UTA), Van Zandt (WMP), and Wichita (MWU) counties, and nearby Henderson County (DMNH).

All the specimens of this species examined by me from Dallas and Tarrant counties represent the southern race *S. v. georgica.* There are two specimens taken from Cooke County (TNHC 1019 and 1020), said by Oberholser (1974) to be the nominate race *S. v. varia.*

LONG-EARED OWL   *Asio otus* (Linnaeus)

Status: Very rare winter visitor. Formerly said to have nested in north central Texas; some records are very likely erroneous. No evidence of recent nesting.

Occurrence: Long-eared Owls have been recorded in only 12 north central Texas study area counties: Clay, Collin, Cooke, Dallas, Denton, Fannin, Kaufman, Palo Pinto, Tarrant, Wichita, Wilbarger, and Wise.

This species inhabits thickets of live oaks, elms, and salt cedars. Although Long-eared Owls are said to gather sometimes in a winter roost, most observations are of a single bird or two. They are not reported every year in north central Texas. For example, the last reports in Dallas and Tarrant counties, where much birding takes place, were 1976 and 1979, respectively. Many of the records are extremely old. Those for Clay, Cooke, and Wise counties were made in the 1870s and 1880s and those for Wilbarger in the early 1920s.

Records for all the counties are: *Clay* — Oberholser (1974) gave indications of a spring specimen, but its whereabouts are unknown; no other records are known. *Collin* — one brought to the Heard Museum on 17 January 1980 was banded and released. *Cooke* — see paragraph above. The whereabouts of an alleged specimen (Oberholser, 1974) were not determined; no recent records. *Dallas* — Stillwell (1939) gave sightings, all by one observer, for 20 March 1930 and 29 January, and 19 and 21 November 1933; fewer than ten since 1959 through 1976, from 31 October 1976 (photo-

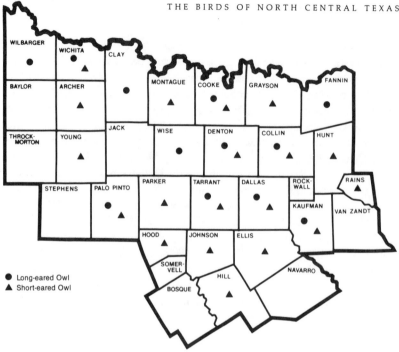

Map 57. Distribution of the Long-eared Owl, *Asio otus,* and the Short-eared Owl, *A. flammeus*

graph) to 28 March 1959. *Denton* — three records, 25 November 1977 (specimen), 20 December 1952, and 23 December 1973. *Fannin* — 21 December 1982 on CBC, carefully described. *Kaufman* — one sighting on 27 January 1979. *Palo Pinto* —1 February 1971 (specimen). *Tarrant* — see paragraph on nesting. Six recent records, 1 November 1954 to 30 April 1964 (specimen); no records for January and February. *Wichita* — three times, 20 November 1973 (MWU, photograph), 23 February 1974, and 12 April 1978. *Wilbarger* — sight records for spring and winter by Oberholser (1974); source of these was not determined. *Wise* — see nesting record below; no recent records. *Nesting:* Oberholser (1974) cites nesting for Cooke, Dallas, Tarrant, and Wise counties. In recent years there have been no records of Long-eared Owls nesting anywhere in north central Texas. As far as I can determine, the early records for Dallas and Tarrant counties are in error, while the other two county records were made in the 1880s. Those for Dallas County are apparently based on Stillwell's checklist (1939), and except for 20 March 1930, the dates are not in the nesting period. A footnote in the same reference also mentions a breeding record for this species in Tarrant County, which, upon checking Sutton's work (1938), I found to be misleading. Sutton's reference is only "hearsay" and highly suspicious, since the reference states that the nest was "in a hole in a washed-out sand bank." This certainly is not a typical nesting site for the Long-eared Owl. To me it represents a misidentified Great Horned Owl, for Long-eared Owls appropriate old nests of crows and other large tree nesters in dense woods for their nesting sites. Even in the early days the Long-eared Owl rarely bred in north central Texas, and present environmental conditions make it highly unlikely that the species will be found nesting today.

Specimens: Known Long-eared Owl specimens are available from Dallas (DMNH, WMP), Denton (WMP), Palo Pinto (MWU), and Tarrant (FWMSH, UTA) counties. My specimens and those from Tarrant County represent *A. o. wilsonianus.*

Short-eared Owl   *Asio flammeus* (Pontoppidan)

Status: Rare to uncommon winter resident.

Occurrence: Short-eared Owls have been reported in 19 counties of the study area: Archer, Collin, Cooke, Dallas, Denton, Ellis, Grayson, Hill, Hood, Hunt, Johnson, Kaufman, Montague, Palo Pinto, Parker, Rains, Tarrant, Wichita, and Young.

This owl often shares open grassland areas with the Northern Harrier, although it never seems as widespread. It is not reported every year, but when it is reported, its numbers are sometimes rather large. Populations of Short-eared Owls tend to gather where there is an explosion in the rodent population. Concentrations of 25 or more owls are not unusual. Some records of such instances are: 20 or more on 3 to 26 March 1959 (Tarrant County); 25 to 30 on 16 February 1964 (Dallas County); and 40 said to have been shot, according to a local game warden, on 1 January 1981 (nearby Lamar County). Many observations are of single birds, however, and in some years the species may be missed over the study area because the more favorable grasslands are remote or inaccessible to birders.

Most reports of Short-eared Owls are for the months of December through early March, possibly when the severe weather to the north pushes them farther south. Some extreme county dates are: *Dallas* —19 October 1967 to 20 March 1970. Stillwell (1939) gives dates for 8 September 1934 (exceptionally early), next 14 November 1937 to 28 March 1937. The specimen record given for Trinity Valley by Stillwell as 21 October 1937 is actually a Kaufman County record, according to personnel at the Dallas Museum. In the 1930s the habitat of Dallas County was much more favorable than it is at present. Most of it has been eliminated by urban sprawl. *Grayson* —17 and 21 October 1977 to 10 and 22 March 1971. *Tarrant* — 23 October 1939 to 14 May 1944, next-latest 11 April 1973 (specimen). *Wichita* —2 October 1973 to 7 April 1974.

Specimens: Specimens of Short-eared Owls are available from the following counties: Cooke (TNHC), Dallas (DMNH, WMP), Denton (DMNH,

FWMSH), Hood (SM), Kaufman (DMNH), Tarrant (DMNH, FWMSH), and Wichita (MWU) and adjacent Lamar County (DMNH).

NORTHERN SAW-WHET OWL   *Aegolius acadicus* (Gmelin)
Status: Accidental.
Occurrence: This tiny, secretive owl has been collected once in north central Texas. There is a specimen of one found dead in Somervell County on 15 March 1964 (TCWC 11130). The location was near the Rainbow community, on the Brazos River where cedars (*Juniperus* sp.) are found. Northern Saw-whet Owls, even as transients, have a decided preference for evergreens.

A small owl brought to the Heard Museum in Collin County in the 1970s proved to be a Northern Saw-whet Owl that had been brought into the area from Colorado and had been confiscated by a game warden at a local pet store.

Three reports for Dallas County have been dismissed as misidentifications. In each instance observations were made either by only one person or by persons who had never seen this species before or were unfamiliar with owls.

A Northern Saw-whet Owl was heard on the Caddo CBC in Fannin County on 18 December 1984 after a taped call of the Eastern Screech-Owl was played before daybreak. One of the observers claimed to be familiar with this species, having heard it in the northeastern United States. The owl in question called from a dense stand of Eastern Red Cedars, *J. virginiana.*

The local checklist for the Hagerman NWR (U.S. Fish and Wildlife Service, 1984) lists the presence of this species as accidental; however, I can find no other details regarding the record of this owl for Grayson County and have dismissed its occurrence.

Order Caprimulgiformes

Family Caprimulgidae (Goatsuckers)

COMMON NIGHTHAWK   *Chordeiles minor* (Forster)
Status: Fairly common to common transient and summer resident.
Occurrence: Common Nighthawks have been reported in all of the counties in north central Texas except Montague, and this is probably an over-

sight since they have been reported a number of times in all of the nearby counties.

Common Nighthawks winter in South America. The species normally occurs in north central Texas from early April to early October, representing both transient and summer-resident nighthawks. Early dates of February and March and late dates after mid-October and in December are exceptional records, if the species was correctly identified. Two February dates and one March date have been dismissed, since they were documented poorly or not at all. One record of this species for mid-December was carefully observed by two persons on 18 December 1982 (Fort Worth CBC) in Tarrant County. This record cannot be completely dismissed, yet it is unbelievably late. It may have been a straggler or an injured bird, though the observers indicated that it appeared normal in flight. It is possible that this sighting may have been a Lesser Nighthawk, though there are no documented records of this species for north central Texas. Lesser Nighthawks winter in other parts of the United States. Efforts should be made to collect any early or late nighthawks for correct identification.

Extreme arrival and departure dates for selected counties are: *Dallas* — 1 April 1982, next-earliest 4 April 1981 to 24 October 1978; *Grayson* — 7 April to 16 October; *Kaufman* — 1 April 1978 to 26 October 1985 (nearby Van Zandt County); *Palo Pinto* — 29 April 1978 to 1 October 1983; *Tarrant* — 4 April 1978 to 23 October 1984; *Wichita* — 23 April 1975 to 16 October 1974.

Of all the members of this family, Common Nighthawks are the most frequently observed. They can be observed during the day hawking over a wide variety of habitats. Commonly called "bull bats," they forage in summer evenings around lighted baseball diamonds and other sports fields. Hundreds can be viewed in both spring and fall migration. In reference to Navarro County, Ogilby (1882) said that he watched them pass by "for an hour at a time" in the fall. They fly high in contrast to Lesser Nighthawks, which fly low.

Nesting: The Common Nighthawk does not make a nest but lays two eggs in a little hollowed-out depression in a barren open area. The hollow is well camouflaged and easily missed if one does not look carefully for it. Except for one such "nest" containing eggs seen on a graveled rooftop on 11 July 1968 (Tarrant County), I have seen none in north central Texas. These nighthawks have become well adapted to gravel rooftops and nest in the midst of cities. Farmers inform me that they find them nesting in cotton and grain-sorghum fields. I saw young brought to the bird rehabilitation center in Fort Worth on 21 June, and judging from their size, I estimated that they hatched at the end of May or the first of June.

Although I have few nesting records of Common Nighthawks, Oberholser (1974) lists this species nesting in Cooke, Denton, Grayson, Tarrant, Wichita, Wilbarger, Wise, and Young counties. There is little doubt that it would be found nesting in all of the counties in north central Texas if the nesting habits of this species were studied extensively.

Specimens: Specimens of Common Nighthawks were located for the following counties: Clay (MWU), Cooke (TNHC), Dallas (DMNH, USNM, WMP), Denton (DMNH), Ellis (WMP), Hill (UTA), Hood (FWMSH), Johnson (SUC), Tarrant (FWMSH, UTA, WMP), Throckmorton (WMP), and Wichita (MWU). Those listed by Oberholser (1974) for Baylor, Kaufman, Wilbarger, and Young counties were not located.

Specimens (FWMSH, UTA, WMP) of the races *minor, howelli,* and *sennetti* were identified from Tarrant County, while a nighthawk taken on 15 June 1964 (UTA) was identified as *minor,* the colors of the back being much like those of *hesperis.* Specimens (WMP) in my collection from Dallas County represent races of *minor, howelli,* and *aserriensis,* while Stillwell (1939) indicated examples (DMNH) of *hesperis,* along with *minor, howelli,* and *sennetti,* taken in the late 1930s. Specimens (MWU) from Wichita County were identified as *howelli, sennetti,* and *hesperis,* tending toward *minor,* while a single specimen from Throckmorton County (WMP) was identified as *minor.* The remaining examples listed above from other counties were not identified racially.

COMMON POORWILL   *Phalaenoptilus nuttallii* (Audubon)

Status: Uncommon to fairly common summer resident in the western half of the study area.

Occurrence: The Common Poorwill has been recorded in 20 counties of the north central Texas study area: Archer, Baylor, Bosque, Clay, Cooke, Dallas, Grayson, Hill, Hood, Johnson, Navarro, Palo Pinto, Parker, Somervell, Stephens, Tarrant, Throckmorton, Wichita, Wise, and Young. They have also been recorded in nearby Comanche and Shackelford counties, where they were not previously reported.

This caprimulgid is recorded mainly during its nesting period, although it may be found from March through September. Overall extreme dates range from 10 February 1953 (Wichita County) to 2 November 1982 (Dallas County), both dates representing examples of specimens. Many of the county records represent single occurrences. Records are given for counties for which there are sufficient data: *Dallas* — three times, 4 April 1961, 22 April 1937 (Stillwell, 1939), and November specimen above; *Hood* — many times, 29 March 1980 to 7 September 1980; *Palo Pinto* — a number of records, 11 March 1986 to 11 September 1976; *Parker* — 23 March 1975 through July 1974; *Somervell* — 23 February 1985 to 15 September 1984; *Tarrant* — 12 times in the spring, 10 February 1985 to 31 May 1985, and

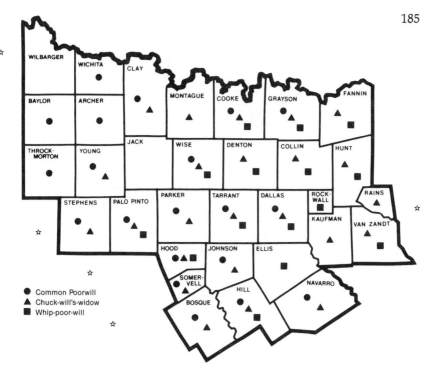

Map 58. Distribution of the goatsuckers: Common Poorwill, *Phalaenoptilus nuttallii;* Chuck-will's widow, *Caprimulgus carolinensis;* and Whip-poor-will, *C. vociferus*

three times in the fall, 17 September 1954, 25 September 1981, and 15 October 1970.

Many readers are aware that a Common Poorwill was found in a torpid state on the same rock ledge in a southern California desert during four winter periods. The only winter record in north central Texas is the February specimen in Wichita County mentioned above. It was said to have been hibernating at the time of collection, but no other details were given of this phenomenon. Other February records appear to be migrants.

Ogilby (1882) lists the poorwill in Navarro County as a "scarce summer visitor frequenting the very densest thickets of the river bottom" and as a fall migrant during September and October. He apparently never collected this species, and I question whether he was mistaken about the identity of this species, since the habitat does not seem typical for Common Poorwills in the summer. This habitat is more typical of that of the Whip-poor-will. There has been no report of poorwills in Navarro County since Ogilby's time.

Nesting: Oberholser (1974) indicated that nests were found in Baylor,

Stephens, and Young counties and listed suspected or probably nesting for Bosque and Wichita counties. The only nesting reported since Oberholser's time was a nest with two eggs discovered on 7 and 8 April 1981 in nearby Eastland County. It should, however, be found nesting east to about Clay County and south through Wise, Parker, Somervell, Hood, and Bosque counties, since there is proper habitat in these counties.

Specimens: Specimens were found from Dallas (WMP), Grayson (KH), Palo Pinto (WMP), Parker (WMP), and Wichita (MWU) counties and nearby Hardeman County (MWU). Those said to have been collected from Bosque, Cooke, and Wise counties (Oberholser (1974) were not located.

CHUCK-WILL'S-WIDOW   *Caprimulgus carolinensis* Gmelin

Status: Fairly common summer resident as well as transient.

Occurrence: Chuck-will's-widows have been reported in 24 north central Texas counties — Bosque, Clay, Collin, Cooke, Dallas, Denton, Fannin, Grayson, Hill, Hood, Hunt, Johnson, Kaufman, Montague, Navarro, Palo Pinto, Parker, Rains, Somervell, Stephens, Tarrant, Van Zandt, Wise, and Young counties — and adjacent Eastland, Hardeman, and Wood counties.

This is the largest of the caprimulgids found in north central Texas and is more widespread than the Common Poorwill or the Whip-poor-will, all of which are found in the same or similar habitat, especially in migration. Like the other members of this family, Chuck-will's-widows are usually seen singly, except at a nest, which is no more than a depression in the ground. They are more often heard than seen and are frequently misidentified as Whip-poor-wills, especially if one identifies them by voice and is not familiar with their call.

This species is most often reported from mid-April throughout the summer and appears to be gone by late September. Some extreme county dates are: *Dallas* — 29 March 1961, next-earliest 5 April 1982 to 24 September 1960. Stillwell (1939) gives an isolated fall departure date of 17 October 1934. *Grayson* — 8 April to 14 September and isolated dates of 2 and 14 October. *Hood* — 7 April 1985 to 13 September 1982 (nearby Johnson County). *Tarrant* — 31 March 1982, next-earliest 7 April 1959 to 28 September 1951. *Van Zandt* — 3 April 1985 to 5 October 1986.

Nesting: Oberholser (1974) gives nesting records for Cooke, Dallas, Grayson, Stephens, Tarrant, and Wise counties. To these can be added Bosque, Hood, Hunt, Kaufman, and Van Zandt counties, and nearby Hardeman County. In addition there are summer records for Clay, Denton, Fannin, Hill, Navarro, Parker, Somervell, and Young counties, all of which have typical nesting habitat. Nesting dates ranged from eggs on 30 April 1960 (Dallas County), eggs on 31 May 1984 (Van Zandt County), to large young on the wing on 30 June 1982 (Kaufman County).

Specimens: Specimens of Chuck-will's-widow have been collected in Cooke

(TNHC), Dallas (DMNH, WMP), Parker (FWMSH), and Tarrant (DMNH, FWMSH, UTA) counties.

WHIP-POOR-WILL *Caprimulgus vociferus* Wilson
Status: Rare to uncommon transient. Although there are old nesting records, some of which are questionable, there are no recent records for the study area.
Occurrence: Whip-poor-wills have been reported in 15 counties in north central Texas — Collin, Cooke, Dallas, Denton, Ellis, Fannin, Grayson, Hill, Hood, Hunt, Palo Pinto, Rockwall, Tarrant, Van Zandt, and Wise — and nearby Eastland County.

It is likely that a few sightings of this caprimulgid are in error. Some records are based only on calls, and since Chuck-will's-widows are more common in the area and are often called Whip-poor-wills by persons unfamiliar with the two species, some confusion may exist among birders about the status of these two species. An example may be an earlier sighting given by Oberholser (1974) for Young County, which would be highly unusual even in the early days. A nesting record given by Oberholser (1974) for 20 May 1891 for Wise County (without habitat details) is also very suspicious. The whereabouts of the eggs are unknown. Moreover, no reports were given for nesting Common Poor-wills for Wise County. I have dismissed the occurrence of this species in Young County. Admittedly, Whip-poor-wills are very elusive, and much needs to be learned about the status of the caprimulgids in north central Texas. At one location along the Brazos River in Hood County during spring migration, I heard all three species calling on the night of 28 April 1973.

All of the recent Whip-poor-will records are: Collin — 1 September 1984, 4 and 18 September 1982, 15 September 1985, 11 October 1982. *Cooke* — early record of species collected on 20 April 1885 (TNHC 1421); no records since. *Dallas* — numerous recent records, 27 March 1981 (WMP 2670) to 5 May 1954, and 4 September 1971 (specimen) to an unusually late date of 6 November 1961, next-latest 23 October 1963. There is no evidence of this species in the summer, though Stillwell (1939) indicated that it was possible. *Denton* — given for spring (Oberholser, 1974); no other records. *Ellis* — given for summer and nesting indicated (Oberholser, 1974), though no evidence to support this statement could be located. *Fannin* — no recent data, only one record for spring (Oberholser, 1974). It is likely that the species would be found there if more observers worked the county. *Grayson* — reported six times in recent years, 25 April 1982, 28 April 1968, 11 July 1975, 19 August 1971, 9 and 30 September 1979, and 7 October 1982. Although the Whip-poor-will is listed as breeding in this county (Oberholser, 1974), the basis for this listing could not be determined. It may be based on the assumption that nesting takes place along the Red River in the northeastern part of the county. To my knowledge no nests or eggs have been found to date. *Hill* — the Texas Parks and Wildlife Department checklist for Lake Whitney (1976) cites the species as a rare migrant. The basis for this listing is unknown and is questionable. *Hood* — heard by two competent observers on 28 April 1973. *Hunt* — Oberholser (1974) lists a spring sight record. A specimen was taken on 16 October 1938 (FWMSH 1142). *Palo Pinto* — one record, 17 April 1976, identification based on voice only. *Rockwall* — reported on 22 September 1979 by a number of observers. *Tarrant* — seven spring records, 22 March 1986, 14 April 1954 and 1975, 15 and 17 April 1967, 29 April 1987, and 8 May 1976. *Van Zandt* — 29 March 1986, 4 and 20 April 1986, 9 April 1985, 2 September 1986, 4 September 1985, and 27 September 1982. *Wise* and *Young* — see paragraph above for comments; no records for the twentieth century.

Specimens: Specimens listed for Cooke (TNHC), Dallas (one DMNH, seven WMP), and Hunt (FWMSH) counties represent the eastern race *C. v. vociferus.*

Order Apodiformes

Family Apodidae (Swifts)

CHIMNEY SWIFT   *Chaetura pelagica* (Linnaeus)
Status: Common to abundant summer resident and transient.
Occurrence: Chimney Swifts have been reported in all of the counties of north central Texas as well as those adjacent to the study area. Man-made structures, particularly chimneys, have provided more nesting sites, which have helped spread this species throughout the area and increase the population. They are more noticeable around cities and towns because of the availability of nesting sites; however, during migration, especially in the fall, they are frequently observed feeding near bodies of water away from urban areas. In spring and especially in fall passage they gather for the night in large flocks in chimneys and industrial stacks. It is not uncommon to see thousands preceding a cold front in late September and early October.

Swifts usually occur from early April to early October throughout the study area. Extreme dates of arrival and departure for selected counties are: *Dallas* — 2 March 1981, next-earliest 10 March 1984 to 31 October, next-latest 26 October, both in 1984, with mean dates of 3 April and 15 October for 27 years (1957–84); *Grayson* — 28 March 1973 to 21 October

1979; *Tarrant* – 15 March 1974 to 26 October 1984; *Van Zandt* – 18 March 1984 to 20 October 1983; *Wichita* – 4 April 1982 to 14 October 1973.

A report of 350 swifts at Cleburne, Johnson County, on 3 November 1983 (Williams, 1984) is the only date available for November. This is an exceptionally late sighting.

Nesting: Although nesting has been recorded only in Collin, Dallas, Denton, Fannin, Grayson, Hood, Navarro, Tarrant, Wichita, and Wilbarger counties, nearly all of the remaining counties in north central Texas have summer dates. If one were to check specifically for swifts' nests, all the counties would have nesting records. Dates of nesting for Dallas County range from 15 May 1974 (eggs) to 2 August 1960 (two barely feathered young; one survived and was banded and released on 9 August). Most nest sites known to me are in chimneys, but swifts have been observed nesting in abandoned wells and even in upright concrete structure. There is also one report of the use of a hollow tree as a nest site in Van Zandt County.

Specimens: Chimney Swift specimens are available from Dallas (DMNH, WMP), Denton (WMP), Grayson (WMP), Hunt (FWMSH), Tarrant (FWMSH, UTA, WMP), Wichita (MWU), and Young (WMP) counties.

Family Trochilidae (Hummingbirds)

Ruby-throated Hummingbird *Archilochus colubris* (Linnaeus)

Status: Uncommon to fairly common transient, particularly on the east side of the study area. Rare to uncommon summer resident.

Occurrence: Ruby-throated Hummingbirds have been reported in 25 north central Texas counties: Bosque, Collin, Cooke, Dallas, Denton, Ellis, Fannin, Grayson, Hill, Hood, Hunt, Johnson, Kaufman, Navarro, Palo Pinto, Parker, Rains, Rockwall, Somervell, Tarrant, Van Zandt, Wichita, Wilbarger, Wise, and Young.

This species is fairly common to common as a transient in the eastern part of the study area, west to about Cooke County, and southward through Denton, Tarrant, Hood, and Bosque counties. Farther west, they become increasingly uncommon, probably owing to habitat limitations; however, in Palo Pinto County, where a considerable amount of birding takes place, one observer has seen ruby-throats only in the fall, on 4 September 1976 and 17 September 1978, and never in the spring.

Arrival and departure dates for selected counties are: *Dallas* – 27 March 1980 to 16 November 1970 (adult male). Stillwell (1939) quotes an early date of 10 February 1929 without details. There is one winter record of 19 December 1981 on the local CBC of an adult male still feeding at a feeder. *Ellis* – 14 March 1975 (specimen) to 27 October 1979. *Grayson* – 24 March 1983 to 5 October 1975. *Hood* – 27 March 1976 to 14 September

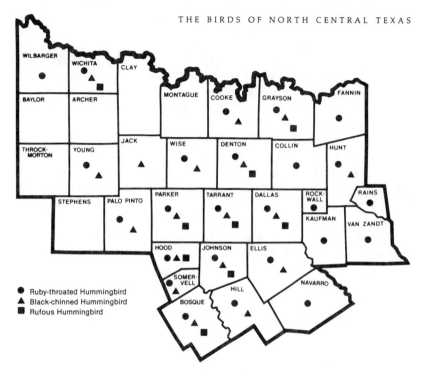

Map 59. Distribution of the Ruby-throated Hummingbird, *Archilochus colubris;* the Black-chinned Hummingbird, *A. alexandri;* and the Rufous Hummingbird, *Selasphorus rufus*

1982 (both this species and the Black-chinned Hummingbird occur during migration, with ruby-throats in the minority). *Hunt* — 29 March 1984 to 31 October 1983. *Tarrant* — 22 March 1975 to 30 October 1974. There were two late stragglers on 27 to 30 November 1972 and 7 and 8 December 1973, both of which were reported as unidentified females or immature birds, and another bird reported from 9 through 29 February 1980. *Wichita* — 31 March 1973 to 16 October 1975, and a late unidentified hummingbird on 20 November 1975.

On 16 October 1973 (Denton County) a hummingbird thought to be of this species was captured by a praying mantis. The observer was able to retrieve the bird from its captor and release it.

Nesting: Nesting ruby-throats have been recorded from Cooke, Dallas, Denton, Grayson, Tarrant, and Wichita counties, and a possible nesting was reported in Hood County on 24 June 1982. Nesting dates range from 2 May 1970 (Tarrant County) to 27 June 1975 (Wichita County). Sutton (1938) questioned the nesting records of the western Black-chinned Hummingbird, below, for Tarrant County in the early 1900s, since no specimens were collected at nests, and identified them as ruby-throats, while

Oberholser informed Sutton that the black-chins ranged eastward "occasionally as far as east central Texas." I find that today both species nest in Tarrant County and that they tend to separate into distinct niches. The Ruby-throated Hummingbird prefers shaded woods along riparian areas, while the Black-chinned Hummingbird prefers the drier habitats — areas of post oak and blackjack oak.

Specimens: Ruby-throated Hummingbirds have been collected from the following counties: Cooke (TNHC), Dallas (DMNH, MWU, WMP), Denton (DMNH, WMP), Ellis (TCWC), Grayson (WMP), Johnson (SUC), Parker (skeleton; OU), Tarrant (FWMSH), Wichita (MWU), and Wilbarger (WMP), and nearby Henderson County (DMNH).

An adult male hummingbird found dead at Austin College, Grayson County, on 2 May 1975 (KH) was said to be a hybrid between a Ruby-throated Hummingbird and a Black-chinned Hummingbird (confirmed by Lester S. Short).

BLACK-CHINNED HUMMINGBIRD *Archilochus alexandri* (Bourcier and Mulsant)
Status: Rare to uncommon transient and uncommon summer resident.
Occurrence: Reports of the Black-chinned Hummingbird are not as numerous as those of the Ruby-throated Hummingbird. Oberholser (1974) listed them for only Dallas, Denton, and Parker counties. Since then they have been reported in Bosque, Cooke, Dallas, Denton, Ellis, Grayson, Hill, Hood, Hunt, Jack, Johnson, Palo Pinto, Parker, Somervell, Tarrant, Wichita, Wise, and Young counties.

They are much more common in Texas in the Trans-Pecos and the Edwards Plateau than in most of north central Texas. Records indicate that they can be found along the Brazos River, where they are attracted to sugarwater feeders put out for hummingbirds. One observer in Hood County estimated that about 40 pairs summered in this area, and on 22 September 1974 the same observer had at least 100 birds, mainly females or immatures of this species and Ruby-throated Hummingbirds, at his feeders after a cold front had blown in.

Extreme dates for selected counties are: *Dallas* — 25 March 1985 to 18 August 1982; Stillwell (1939) gave a date of 13 September 1935. There is a questionable sighting of 16 October 1981. *Grayson* — 30 March 1975 to 30 August 1978. *Hood* — 19 March 1972 (mean 8 April, 17 sightings, 1965–85) to 23 September 1968. *Palo Pinto* — 20 March 1982 to 24 September 1975. *Tarrant* — 13 March 1972 to 1 October 1948, next-latest 30 September 1974. *Wichita* — 25 March 1975 to 12 October 1974 (unconfirmed), next-latest 13 September 1935.

An albino spent some time from 11 to 30 July 1981 at a feeder in Hood County. At this time of the year only Black-chinned Hummingbirds occur in this part of north central Texas.

Nesting: Nests or young in May have been confirmed in Bosque, Dallas, Hood, Tarrant, and Wichita counties. The only actual dates for nesting are 21 April 1984 (two eggs), Meridian SP, Bosque County; 24 April 1977 (one egg), Hood County; and 27 May 1977 (active nest), Iowa Park, Wichita County. Early-summer records include Denton, Ellis, Hill, Parker, Palo Pinto, Somervell, and Young counties.

Specimens: Black-chinned Hummingbird specimens are said to have been taken from the following counties: Dallas (DMNH, WMP), Denton (DMNH, missing from collection), Ellis (SM), Parker (FWMSH), Somervell (TCWC), and Tarrant (FWMSH, UTA).

ANNA'S HUMMINGBIRD   *Calypte anna* (Lesson)
Status: Accidental.
Occurrence: There are two records of this western hummingbird for north central Texas, both from Tarrant County. They represent recent records of adult males. The first Anna's Hummingbird spent over a month at an observer's feeder in Fort Worth from 3 December 1973 until 5 January 1974, a report that was documented by photographs. The second visited a feeder in Crowley on 26 September 1977 and presented the lone observer a good view of its bright, rosy-red crown. It is said to have increased in abundance in Texas as a winter resident in the mid-1970s, particularly along the coast.

CALLIOPE HUMMINGBIRD   *Stellula calliope* (Gould)
Status: Accidental.
Occurrence: There is only one record of this tiny hummingbird for north central Texas. In 1976 a fully adult male spent two and a half days, from 11 August to the morning of the thirteenth, at a residence in Fort Worth, Tarrant County. Numerous persons viewed the bird, which displayed its long, purple gorget feathers on a white throat. It was photographed, and a photograph documenting its occurrence is deposited in TP-RF (no. 107) at Texas A&M University. Usually only a few of these western hummingbirds reach even the western edge of Texas.

RUFOUS HUMMINGBIRD   *Selasphorus rufus* (Gmelin)
Status: Uncommon to rare transient in late summer and early fall. One winter record. No authentic spring records.
Occurrence: Rufous Hummingbirds have been recorded in nine north central Texas counties: Bosque, Dallas, Denton, Grayson, Hood, Johnson, Parker, Tarrant, and Wichita. Surprisingly, there were few records of this hummingbird before the early 1970s. Either it was missed in the early days, or there has been a change in movement of the species since the 1970s. Admittedly, there are more bird-watchers scrutinizing hummingbirds today. Adult males are unmistakable, except for Allen's, whose status is far

from satisfactorily documented in Texas. Sightings of birds in immature plumages and nondescript females are open to question.

County records include: *Bosque* — 17 August 1980 (specimen). *Dallas* — first county sighting, 21 July 1971 (also earliest fall date for this county). Most records are in August, tapering off in September. Some October sightings are not satisfactory; the latest is 24 October 1982. One wintered in Garland with the aid of several feeders and an electric light from 23 October 1978 to 14 February 1979. One unexplainable spring record of 16 June 1979 is highly doubtful. *Denton* — 12 September 1983. *Grayson* — four records in fall, 19 July to 31 July 1977, 21 and 22 July 1975, 8 to 16 August 1975, and in September (no specific date). *Hood* — two records, 1 August 1971 and 24 and 25 August 1974. *Johnson* — 10 through 15 August 1985. *Parker* — one record, 15 and 16 August 1975. *Tarrant* — first county sighting, 29 August 1964. Fall records extend from 25 and 26 July 1981 through 24 November (the last an adult male). An alleged 27 November 1974 date of an immature is questionable. Two spring sightings, 25 and 26 May 1981 and 17 June 1971, were deleted for lack of details. *Wichita* — seven records ranging from 22 July 1972 through 26 September 1976. A spring date of 13 April 1978 without details is unacceptable. *Specimens:* Two Rufous Hummingbird specimens have been taken in north central Texas — one on 17 August 1980 (SM) in Bosque County and the second on 21 August 1981 (WMP) in Dallas County.

Order Coraciiformes

Family Alcedinidae (Kingfishers)

BELTED KINGFISHER   *Ceryle alcyon* (Linnaeus)
Status: Common to fairly common year-round resident.
Occurrence: The Belted Kingfisher has been reported in all the north central Texas counties as well as in the counties adjacent to the study area.

Wherever there are streams, lakes, and large impoundments one can usually find this interesting fish-eating bird. It may even be found at water-filled borrow pits and roadside ditches, if there are small fish present. Although it has been found the year round and on all of the CBCs of the area, it is difficult to ascertain whether there is much movement in the study area, though no doubt there is some movement. If large numbers could be banded, this point would bear further study, but the solitary nature of the kingfisher does not lend itself to this kind of investigation. In Tarrant County, where there are annual Spring County as well as CBCs, the numbers reported over a 14-year period (1965–78) showed that there were twice as many Belted Kingfishers in winter as in spring. Yet it may simply be that nesting kingfishers are not as evident as winter kingfishers. *Nesting:* Nesting (eggs, young, or pairs at nest holes) has been recorded for Cooke, Dallas, Ellis, Grayson, Palo Pinto, Parker, Tarrant, Van Zandt, Wichita, and Wilbarger counties, while there are summer records, including the month of May, for Baylor, Bosque, Clay, Collin, Denton, Fannin, Hill, Hood, Hunt, Johnson, Kaufman, Rains, Somervell, and Throckmorton counties.

Nesting activities range from late March, pair at nest on 24 March 1985 in Van Zandt County, to 11 May, five young out of nest in Ellis County. More and Strecker (1929) did not find nests but observed eight birds together along a small creek on 6 June. A pair became a meal for a seven-foot kingsnake at a burrow in Palo Pinto County on 8 July 1977. The nest burrow was some distance from water.

Specimens: Specimens belonging to the nominate race have been collected for the following counties: Cooke (TNHC), Dallas (DMNH, WMP), Denton (DMNH, WMP), Grayson (SE), Henderson (DMNH), Kaufman (WMP), Palo Pinto (MWU), Parker (FWMSH), Tarrant (DMNH, UTA), and Wichita (MWU). A winter specimen said to have been taken from Wise County (Oberholser, 1974) could not be located.

GREEN KINGFISHER *Chloroceryle americana* (Gmelin)
Status: Accidental. Can be expected casually.
Occurrence: There is but one record of this little kingfisher for the north central Texas study area. One was collected at Decatur, Wise County, on 3 January 1889 by J. A. Donald, but, unfortunately, the whereabouts of this specimen are unknown. It has probably been lost to science.

There are only two recent sightings: one just outside the study area from nearby Comanche County on 3 August 1971, when a female was spotted on the south Copperas Creek, about seven and a half miles northwest of Sidney, and one seen by two observers on 9 June 1982 in Coryell County, just south of Bosque County.

Order Piciformes

Family Picidae (Woodpeckers)

LEWIS' WOODPECKER *Melanerpes lewis* (Gray)
Status: Casual visitor. One specimen.

Occurrence: There are four winter reports of this western woodpecker for the north central Texas counties: *Dallas* — one Lewis' Woodpecker on exhibit at the Dallas Museum of Natural History was collected in the Trinity Valley in the southeastern part of the county on 23 December 1935 (DMNH 6782); *Collin* — one was sighted by two observers at Lake Lavon on 23 December 1970; *Grayson* — one was seen by two observers at Eisenhower SP on 26 December 1975; *Wise* — Oberholser (1974) gives a winter sighting without details.

Specimens: While I was trying to trace the whereabouts of the J. A. Donald specimens cited for Wise County (Donald and More, 1894), I found a small collection of mounted birds at the Trading Post and Old Western Museum, at Sunset, about eight miles northwest of Alvord. The owner of the museum reported that he bought the collection, which had been stored in a shed or barn at Alvord, about 1956. Most of the small bird specimens were so deteriorated that they were discarded at the time of purchase, but among the specimens saved was a badly damaged Lewis' Woodpecker, which is still at the Sunset Museum. Since I could not locate the Wise County specimen, it is possible that this specimen is the one referred to by Oberholser (1974).

RED-HEADED WOODPECKER   *Melanerpes erythrocephalus* (Linnaeus)
Status: Uncommon to rare transient and summer resident over most of the area. Casual and local in the western part of the range. Not found every year in winter, but to be expected.

Occurrence: Red-headed Woodpeckers have been recorded in all of the counties in the north central Texas study area except Baylor, Hood, Somervell, and Stephens. They have also been found in adjacent Shackelford County, where they had not previously been reported.

In many areas this species may be seen the year round, but it is by no means common. Its distribution, especially in the nesting season, is very local. Although many persons remark about its decline, and certainly some of its habitat has been destroyed, it may never have been abundant as a nesting species in north central Texas. For example, Ogilby (1882) remarked that he never observed it in Navarro County during the breeding season, and More and Strecker (1929) also remarked that it was by no means common in summer in Wilbarger County.

They have been recorded on the CBCs, but not every year. The largest number reported was 36 at the Hagerman NWR, Grayson County, in 1979, when there was an influx of Red-headed Woodpeckers — many immatures — into north central Texas, probably from the north.

The decline of Red-headed Woodpeckers in urban areas is due to removal of dead trees by man and competition for nest sites with European Starlings, which usually win.

Nesting: Nesting has been recorded in Cooke, Dallas, Denton, Ellis, Fannin, Grayson, Hunt, Tarrant, Wichita, Wilbarger, and Wise counties. No nests have been reported in Tarrant County since Sutton's (1938) report, and the last nesting for Dallas County was on 13 July 1970, when a pair was observed carrying food into a nest hole at Irving. A pair was also seen on 29 March 1980 at a nest hole in Shackelford County. In addition, an immature was seen with two adults in Fannin County on 10 July 1983. *Specimens:* Specimens have been located from Dallas (DMNH, WMP), Denton (DMNH), Ellis (DMNH), Hunt (FWMSH), Kaufman (DMNH), and Tarrant (UTA) counties, and nearby Henderson County (DMNH). Those that were examined represented typical *M. e. erythrocephalus.* Oberholser (1974) mentions specimens collected from Clay, Cooke, Wilbarger, and Wise counties, none of which could be located. He also indicates that *M. e. caurinus* was taken from Wilbarger County.

GOLDEN-FRONTED WOODPECKER   *Melanerpes aurifrons* (Wagler)
Status: Uncommon to fairly common the year round east to about Clay, Jack, and Palo Pinto counties; east of these counties they are considered stragglers.
Occurrence: Golden-fronted Woodpeckers have been reported in 18 counties along the western portions of the study area—Archer, Baylor, Bosque, Clay, Hill, Jack, Johnson, Montague, Palo Pinto, Parker, Somervell, Stephens, Tarrant, Throckmorton, Wichita, Wilbarger, Wise, and Young—and adjacent Shackelford County. In most of these counties they are considered permanent residents, although they may be stragglers in Bosque, Hill, Johnson, Parker, and Tarrant counties.

Although Oberholser (1974) indicated records for Dallas County, this is extremely doubtful, since most of the records are in periods when immature Red-bellied Woodpeckers would be present. An alleged specimen said to have been collected in Dallas on 31 July 1897 (Stillwell, 1939) could not be located. I prefer to await a specimen to document the occurrence of golden-fronts in Dallas County. Although Oberholser (1974) showed fall and winter records for Tarrant County, the species was only recently documented for the county when two were seen and photographed on 22 January 1984. The remains of a male were found three days later; the tail feathers, which were saved, clearly show that it is all black.

While both this woodpecker and the Red-bellied Woodpecker are found in some counties during the breeding season, there seems to be a decided separation of the two species in nesting sites. Golden-fronts seldom frequent cities and towns where red-bellies were noted. This is particularly true of the northwestern part of the study area where this separation is noted in the Red River drainage. In fall and early winter, however, they come together to feed in pecan groves along the Clear Fork of the Brazos

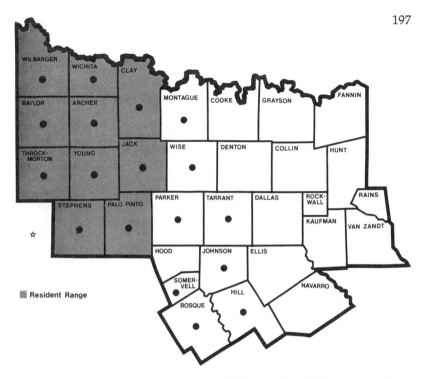

Map 60. Distribution of the Golden-fronted Woodpecker, *Melanerpes aurifrons*, with resident range

River in the southwestern part of Throckmorton County, both species being fairly numerous.

Golden-fronts are closely associated with mesquite, and in areas where brush-eradication programs have been undertaken, this woodpecker has no doubt declined. One such county is Palo Pinto, where CBCs clearly show a decline in its population since 1971.

Nesting: Oberholser (1974) showed that these woodpeckers nested in Archer, Baylor, Wilbarger, and Young counties. To these counties can be added Clay, Palo Pinto, Throckmorton, Wichita, and nearby Shackelford. *Specimens:* Golden-fronted Woodpecker specimens have been collected from Palo Pinto (TCWC), Throckmorton (WMP), and Wichita (MWU) counties. The specimen in my collection represents *M. a. incanescens*.

RED-BELLIED WOODPECKER *Melanerpes carolinus* (Linnaeus)
Status: Abundant to common resident in the eastern parts of the study area. Fairly common locally in counties to the west.
Occurrence: Red-bellied Woodpeckers have been recorded in all of the counties within the study area. They have also been reported in nearby Erath and Shackelford counties, where they had not previously been recorded.

This species is common over most of the eastern area to about Cooke, Denton, Tarrant, Johnson, and Hill counties. They are found along the Red River and scattered along main drainages where cottonwoods prevail. They are frequently found in cities and towns, often coming to bird feeders in winter for suet, corn, nutmeats, and even table scraps. In their normal habitat they feed on hackberries and other wild fruits, acorns, and pecans, as well as insects. They seem to be better adapted to man than are the Golden-fronted Woodpeckers.

Nesting: Nesting records have been established for the following counties: Baylor, Bosque, Collin, Cooke, Dallas, Denton, Ellis, Grayson, Hill, Hunt, Johnson, Kaufman, Navarro, Tarrant, Van Zandt, Wichita, Wilbarger, and Wise. It has also been suspected of nesting in nearby Henderson County.

Nesting data, adults or young at nest, are limited, but recent dates are 8 April 1972 (Kaufman County) to 11 May 1957, latest 28 June 1970, young banded and female seen entering nest on 10 July 1984 (the last two dates for Dallas County). Birds digging nest holes have been noted in late March. More and Strecker (1929) established nesting in Wilbarger County from mid-May to mid-June. Starlings frequently take over their nest cavities, although a woodpecker was noted nesting next to a pair of starlings in Dallas County on 26 April 1961. One apparently nested no more than a foot above the ground at Sherman, Grayson County, in 1967 or 1968.

Specimens: Specimens have been taken from the following counties: Cooke (ACG, TCWC), Dallas (DMNH, WMP), Denton (DMNH), Ellis (DMNH), Grayson (SE, WMP), Hill (KU), Hood (FWMSH), Hunt (FWMSH), Johnson (SUC), Kaufman (DMNH), Navarro (USNM), Tarrant (DMNH, FWMSH, UTA, WMP), Wichita (MWU), Wise (DMNH), and nearby Henderson County (DMNH). Those indicated for Clay County (Oberholser, 1974) were not located.

Most specimens have not been examined, but those for Tarrant County proved to be *M. c. zebra*. One specimen (DMNH) collected on the Tarrant-Wise county line on 6 December 1949 was identified as intermediate between *harpaceus* (from south Texas) and *zebra*. This specimen should be checked again.

YELLOW-BELLIED SAPSUCKER   *Sphyrapicus varius* (Linnaeus)
Status: Fairly common to common winter resident.
Occurrence: Yellow-bellied Sapsuckers have been reported in all counties of the study area but Baylor, Throckmorton, and Wilbarger.

This woodpecker inhabits mature woods as well as scattered trees in cities and towns, where it drills evenly spaced holes in trees in parallel rows, causing sap to exude, the practice for which the species receives its name. It feeds not only on the sap but also on small insects trapped in it. In winter the bird is sometimes observed feeding on small berries or other winter fruit, as portrayed by Audubon in his paintings of this species. I believe that, except for old, dying trees or extremely young trees not yet well established, few trees are actually killed by this species.

Although this species is considered a winter resident, some members are transients. They are usually observed from mid-October to early April. Extreme dates for counties for which sufficient data are available are: *Dallas* — 21 September 1976 to 23 May 1959, next-latest 10 May 1932 (Stillwell, 1939); *Grayson* — 4 October to 29 March; *Tarrant* — 12 September 1968 (mean arrival date, 10 years, 11 October) to 10 May 1969; *Wichita* — 14 October 1978 to 2 April 1978.

Yellow-bellied Sapsuckers are usually reported every year on all of the CBCs, although they are not as numerous toward the western part of the study area. The greater number are found in the Dallas–Fort Worth area, probably owing in part to the larger numbers of people participating in the annual counts there. No more than one or two birds are observed at a time.
Specimens: Specimens have been taken from the following counties: Cooke (OSU, TNHC), Clay (TCWC), Dallas (DMNH, WMP), Denton (CC, DMNH, WMP), Ellis (DMNH, OSU), Grayson (WMP), Hunt (FWMSH), Jack (DMNH), Kaufman (DMNH), Parker (FWMSH), Tarrant (DMNH, FWMSH, UTA), and Wise (Oberholser, 1974) and nearby Hopkins (FWMSH). The specimen from Wise County was not located. Although not all specimens were examined, some of those from Dallas and all of those from Tarrant County represented the northeastern race *varius*.

LADDER-BACKED WOODPECKER *Picoides scalaris* (Wagler)
Status: Uncommon to fairly common permanent resident.
Occurrence: Ladder-backed Woodpeckers are found in mesquite prairies the year round. In some of the eastern counties of the study area their distribution is very local, while they can be expected throughout the western portion. Along the larger creeks and rivers, for example, on the Red River bordering the north, they are seldom observed except in the adjacent prairie areas. They have been recorded in all of the north central Texas study area except Collin, Kaufman, Rains, Rockwall, and Van Zandt counties.

Ladder-backs have been reported on all of the CBCs except those for Caddo National Grasslands in Fannin County; Lake Tawakoni, in Van Zandt County; and McKinney, in Collin County. Their numbers are usually largest on the Palo Pinto count, although even there the numbers have decreased in recent years because of the extensive mesquite eradication. In winter they can be seen in similar overlapping habitats, normally associating with Downy Woodpeckers, although the nesting and summer ranges of the two species are distinct.
Nesting: Nesting has been reported for Baylor, Bosque, Dallas, Denton, Ellis, Tarrant, Wichita, Wilbarger, and Young counties, while late-spring and early-summer records include Archer, Clay, Grayson, Hill, Jack, Navarro, Palo Pinto, Parker, Somervell, Throckmorton, and Wise counties. They have been reported nesting in north central Texas counties from mid-April to early June, usually in low trees, principally mesquite, and along roads in fence and telephone poles. The last sites often provide nest holes for Eastern Bluebirds, and occasionally for Carolina Chickadees and Ash-throated Flycatchers.
Specimens: Specimens of Ladder-backed Woodpeckers have been located from Baylor (FWMSH), Hill (UTA), Tarrant (DMNH, FWMSH), Wichita (MWU), Wilbarger (DMNH), Wise (DMNH) counties, while those mentioned for Cooke, Dallas, and Somervell by Oberholser (1974) could not be located. Those examined represent *P. s. symplectus*.

DOWNY WOODPECKER *Picoides pubescens* (Linnaeus)
Status: Fairly common to common in the eastern part of the study area. Uncommon to rare in parts of the western area.
Occurrence: The Downy Woodpecker has been seen in all of the counties except Baylor, Stephens, Throckmorton, along the western side of the study area. It is likely that it would be found there also, at least in the proper habitat favoring this species, if more observers bird-watched regularly in those counties. This species is readily found in the eastern part of the study area the year round and very locally as one proceeds toward the west. It is replaced in much of the latter area by the Ladder-backed

Woodpecker. It seems to be more numerous in fall and winter. Its habitat is the same as that of the Hairy Woodpecker, but it is more common than its larger relative.

Nesting: Nesting has been recorded in the following counties: Archer, Bosque, Dallas, Denton, Fannin, Grayson, Hunt, Navarro, Tarrant, Van Zandt, Wichita, and Wise, while summer sightings have been tallied in Clay, Collin, Cooke, Ellis, Hill, Hood, Jack, Kaufman, Parker, Rains, and Young. Although Ogilby (1882) indicated that this species was two-brooded in Navarro County, there is little evidence to support this statement. Dates of nesting range from late March to May, most records being for April.

Specimens: Downy Woodpecker specimens are known for the following counties: Collin (DMNH), Cooke (TCWC, TNHC), Dallas (DMNH, WMP), Denton (DMNH), Fannin (WMP), Grayson (OU), Hunt (FWMSH), Tarrant (DMNH, FWMSH, UTA, WMP), and Wise (DMNH), and nearby Henderson County (DMNH). Those indicated from Clay and Ellis counties (Oberholser, 1974) could not be located.

Five specimens examined for Tarrant County by Allan R. Phillips were identified as *P. p. medianus,* while Oberholser (1974) identified downies collected in the 1930s as the nominate race. Sutton (1967) pointed out that most examples collected in Oklahoma represented intermediates between *pubescens* and *medianus.*

HAIRY WOODPECKER *Picoides villosus* (Linnaeus)

Status: Rare to uncommon transient and winter resident. Formerly considered a nesting bird in a few counties; however, recent nesting records are limited.

Occurrence: Hairy Woodpeckers have been reported from 19 counties in north central Texas: Collin, Cooke, Dallas, Denton, Ellis, Fannin, Grayson, Hill, Hunt, Johnson, Navarro, Palo Pinto, Parker, Rains, Tarrant, Van Zandt, Wichita, Wilbarger, and Wise.

This species has been reported on all of the CBCs within the study area, though the numbers decrease as one moves from east to west, and only on the counts in the eastern parts has it been reported regularly. Since it is more secretive than the Downy Woodpecker, and requires much more forested areas, this decrease is normal though alarming. The maximum numbers seen have been 26 (1968) at Hagerman NWR, Grayson County, and 22 (1981) in Dallas County.

Nesting: The Hairy Woodpecker was never a common nesting bird of north central Texas. Only four counties were listed by Oberholser (1974) as having breeding records: Cooke County, probably before the turn of the century; Dallas County, on the basis of Stillwell's work (1939) and a record of a pair carrying food to young on 9 April 1959; Fannin County, a questionable record; and Grayson County with no details, though the Hager-

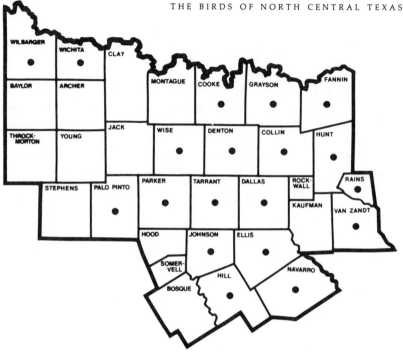

Map 61. Distribution of the Hairy Woodpecker, *Picoides villosus*

man NWR checklist (U.S. Fish and Wildlife Service, 1984) indicates that it still nests in this county. In recent years there is a nesting record for this woodpecker from Tarrant County on 16 April 1985, when a pair was seen going in and out of a nest hole in Arlington; and from Van Zandt County, where two young were observed following their parents around on 20 June 1984. Adverse environmental conditions, as well as present climatic changes, seem not to favor nesting of Hairy Woodpeckers in north central Texas, and only occasionally will nests be found.

Specimens: Specimens of Hairy Woodpecker have been taken for Cooke (TNHC), Dallas (DMNH, WMP), Denton (DMNH), Ellis (DMNH), Fannin (WMP), and Wilbarger (CMNH) counties. Examples indicated from Tarrant County by Oberholser (1974) were not located. Specimens in the Dallas Museum of Natural History from Dallas and Denton counties represent the nominate race *P. v. villosus.* Oberholser (1974) indicates that the specimen for Cooke County (TNHC 1887) is the southern race *auduboni,* which is highly unlikely; the specimen should be reexamined.

NORTHERN FLICKER   *Colaptes auratus* (Linnaeus)
Status: Common winter resident. No evidence of breeding today in the

study area, although it is seen on rare occasions in the counties along the Red River in the summer.

Occurrence: Northern Flickers, formerly called Common Flickers, include Yellow-shafted Flickers and Red-shafted Flickers, which are now treated as subspecies. Both races winter in north central Texas. Yellow-shafted Flickers have been reported in all of the counties of the study area, while the red-shafted have been reported in all counties but Archer, Bosque, Fannin, Hill, Parker, and Rockwall. They no doubt occur in these counties as well but have not been reported. The yellow-shafted complex is much more abundant than the red-shafted group. Examples of hybridization are evident from Cooke, Dallas, Denton, Johnson, Kaufman, Tarrant, and Young counties.

Extreme arrival and departure dates for selected counties are: *Dallas* —14 September 1974 to 11 May 1975 (YSF), and 26 September 1976 to 2 April 1969 (RSF); *Denton* — 3 September to 12 May 1969 (YSF), 21 September 1982 to 7 April 1976 (RSF); *Grayson* — 6 September 1975 to 9 May 1972, and isolated summer dates 6 June 1977, 26 June 1981, 27 July 1976, 29 July 1982, 11 August 1977, and 23 August 1975 (YSF), and 24 September to 29 March (RSF); *Palo Pinto* —15 October 1977 to 3 April 1977; *Tarrant* — 8 September 1973 to 9 May 1969 (YSF), 19 September 1968 to 28 March 1948 (RSF); *Wichita* — 2 September 1974 to 11 May 1976, and isolated summer dates 17 June 1981 (RSF) (Wilbarger County), 26 June 1975 (Wilbarger County), 27 July 1976, 9 August 1976, and 19 August 1975 (the last three dates for Wichita County).

Nesting: Although Oberholser (1974) indicates nesting for Cooke, Denton, Fannin, Grayson, Hunt, Kaufman, Tarrant, Wichita, Wilbarger, and Wise counties, there have been no nesting records for any of these counties in recent years. The last nesting record in the study area that I have been able to determine was one given by More and Strecker (1929) on 2 May (year not given) for Wilbarger County, where it was considered a very rare summer resident. Sutton (1938) reported this species as a breeding bird in Tarrant County, but there are no recent records to support this today. Except for an occasional June and July sighting in Cooke, Grayson, and Wilbarger counties along the Red River, there is little evidence to support any nesting today in north central Texas. The only recent nesting record is one for nearby Henderson County on 11 June 1984, when a bird was observed carrying food to a nest hole.

Specimens: Thirteen specimens (FWMSH, UTA) for Tarrant County represent 11 examples of the Yellow-shafted Flicker complex as follows: *auratus* (one), *borealis* (four), and *luteus* (six). Specimens in my collection (WMP) from Dallas County also show examples of all three subspecies, *luteus* being the most abundant.

Two other specimens examined from Tarrant County represent a spring 1964 female *collaris* (FWMSH) and a bird taken on 24 October 1972 (FWMSH) that was interpreted as an example of *luteus* tending toward *collaris*. Two winter specimens (WMP) from Denton County also represent pure *collaris*, while a winter bird from Johnson County represents a hybrid *collaris* with *luteus*. Other specimens, not examined for race, are from the following counties: Baylor (MWU), Collin (WMP), Cooke (Oberholser, 1974; not located), Dallas (DMNH, SUC, UTA), Denton (DMNH, WMP), Ellis (DMNH, TCWC), Hood (FWMSH), Hunt (FWMSH), Jack (MWU), Kaufman (DMNH), Navarro (FWMSH), Parker (FWMSH), Van Zandt (WMP), Wichita (MWU), Wise (DMNH, FWMSH), and Young (DMNH).

PILEATED WOODPECKER   *Dryocopus pileatus* (Linnaeus)
Status: Extremely rare resident locally in the southeastern part of the study area and along the Red River to about the Cooke-Grayson county line. Casual straggler beyond its present range.
Occurrence: The records for this large woodpecker include the following counties: Cooke, Dallas, Denton, Ellis, Fannin, Grayson, Hunt, Johnson, Kaufman, Navarro, Rains, Tarrant, Van Zandt, Wise, and Young. To these can be added adjacent Freestone and Wood counties (not shown by Oberholser, 1974).

The Pileated Woodpecker requires forests with tall trees along river bottoms. Thus in north central Texas it ranged mainly along the Trinity River and Red River drainages; sightings in these areas account for most of the county listings above. The habitat was formerly much more extensive than it is today. Land clearing, developments, and dams have reduced its habitat.

Since 1972 there are records for only Cooke, Fannin, and Grayson counties, along the Red River drainage and for Dallas, Denton, Ellis, Freestone, Johnson, Kaufman, and Tarrant counties, along the Trinity River drainage. The records for Hunt, Rains, Van Zandt, and Wood counties represent remaining forested areas influenced by the east Texas Piney Woods. There are no present-day records for Navarro, Wise, and Young counties. It is unlikely that this woodpecker will ever again be reported in the two last-named counties, for even in its original state in the 1880s the habitat was limited and represented the marginal perimeter of the species' range. Today the habitat is gone from these two counties. It is very likely, however, that if one worked along the deep wooded river bottoms of the Trinity River in Navarro County one might still find a pair or two of Pileated Woodpeckers.

This majestic woodpecker can still be found by bird-watchers who know where to search for it. This is particularly true of the southeastern corner of Dallas County, or on the Hagerman NWR, Grayson County, or the

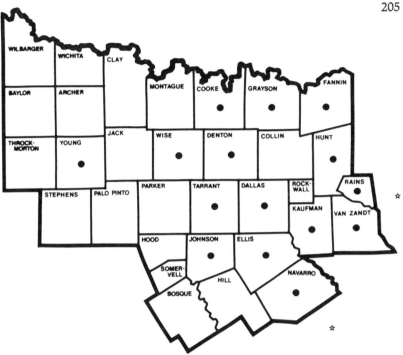

Map 62. Distribution of the Pileated Woodpecker, *Dryocopus pileatus*

Caddo National Grasslands areas of Fannin County, where it is sometimes sighted on the annual CBCs.

A 2 February 1975 sighting for Vernon, Wilbarger County, was dismissed since the county is so far out of range, and the bird was seen by only one person. It seems unlikely that this species would reach that county even along the Red River because there is little habitat for the woodpecker, and it is more than 125 miles from the nearest known area of occurrence in Grayson County. Nesting has, however, been reported in Stephens County, Oklahoma, about 60 to 75 miles northeast of Vernon.

Nesting: Oberholser (1974) showed the bird's nesting range for Cooke, Tarrant, and Wise counties and a questionable range for Fannin County. These are old reports, all before the 1900s, except the report for Tarrant County. The only recent nesting records were a pair seen at a nest hole on 8 and 18 April 1972 in Kaufman County and another pair at a nest hole from 31 March through 6 May 1985 in Van Zandt County. The Hagerman NWR checklist (U.S. Fish and Wildlife Service, 1984) indicates that it nests in Grayson County, but I can find no data to support this, although some habitat for nest sites is still available.

Specimens: Three specimens of Pileated Woodpeckers taken in 1938 and 1939 are known for Dallas and Ellis counties (all DMNH). It has been indicated that W. A. Mayer took other specimens in Dallas County before 1900, but these have apparently been lost. Specimens and eggs said to have been taken in Cooke and Wise counties (Oberholser, 1974) were not located.

Order Passeriformes

Family Tyrannidae (Tyrant Flycatchers)

OLIVE-SIDED FLYCATCHER   *Contopus borealis* (Swainson)
Status: Uncommon to fairly common transient during migration.
Occurrence: Olive-sided Flycatchers have been reported passing through the following counties of north central Texas in spring and fall migration: Archer, Bosque, Clay, Collin, Cooke, Dallas, Denton, Ellis, Fannin, Grayson, Hill, Hunt, Jack, Johnson, Kaufman, Navarro, Palo Pinto, Rockwall, Somervell, Tarrant, Van Zandt, Wichita, and Wise.

Most Olive-sided Flycatchers pass through north central Texas in spring in late April and early May and in late August to mid-October. Extreme overall spring and fall dates for selected counties are: *Denton* — 28 April 1979 to 23 May 1956, and 7 September to 25 September 1985; *Dallas* — an extremely early date of 8 March 1975 (Williams, 1975), the earliest for north central Texas given without any details, next-earliest 5 April 1986 to 2 June 1968, and 7 August 1952 to 27 November 1936 (Stillwell, 1939), an extremely questionable record which I have discounted, next-latest 18 October 1969; *Collin* — 2 May 1982 to 20 May 1984, and 8 August 1984 to 29 August 1982; *Grayson* — 7 May to 30 May, and 17 August 1986 to 21 October; *Tarrant* — 15 April 1982 to 24 May 1952, and 10 August 1964 to 28 October 1954; *Wichita* — 27 April 1974 to 27 May 1974, and no fall records.

Some early June dates may represent migrants, but late ones present problems: Grayson County — the observation "two birds vigorously chasing a female cowbird" east of Sherman on 27 June 1976 (Williams, 1976) suggests possible nesting, but the area is not typical nesting habitat for this species. The report is extremely doubtful since Eastern Wood-Pewees nest in the Red River drainage and may be misidentified as Olive-sided Flycatchers. Palo Pinto County — a date of 24 June 1974 is unexplainable, though the observer, a competent birder, had no doubts about the sighting. He was alone at the time of observation but presented a full description of the species in question. Wichita County — a "late June" report for 1974 (Williams, 1974) is questionable because of the casual manner in which the report was given and the absence of a reference to this observa-

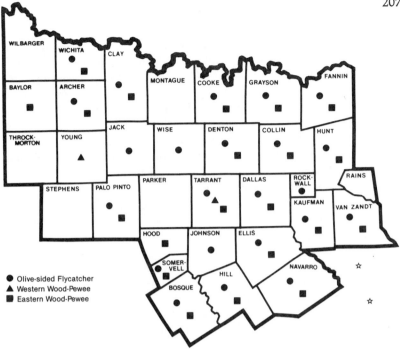

Map 63. Distribution of the Olive-sided Flycatcher, *Contopus borealis*, the Western Wood-Pewee, *C. sordidulus*, and the Eastern Wood-Pewee, *C. virens*

tion in the newsletter or checklist of the local bird society; therefore, I have dismissed this citation.

Specimens: Olive-sided Flycatchers have been collected from Cooke (TNHC), Denton (DMNH), Ellis (DMNH), Kaufman (SFASU), and Navarro (USNM) counties. Specimens listed by Oberholser (1974) for Collin, Tarrant, and Wise counties could not be located.

WESTERN WOOD-PEWEE   *Contopus sordidulus* Sclater

Status: Casual visitor. Two records.

Occurrence: The inclusion of the Western Wood-Pewee in north central Texas is based on two specimens that I found in the collection of Eastern Wood-Pewees in the Dallas Museum of Natural History. These two specimens have been checked by authorities at the U.S. National Museum and identified as the race *C. s. veliei.* One specimen, taken on 7 August 1954, is from Tarrant County (DMNH 4866), and the other, taken on 28 August 1956, is from Young County (DMNH 5035). Surprisingly, no specimens have been taken since then.

Nesting: Oberholser (1974) indicates that the Western Wood-Pewee bred in Bosque County in 1967. This species normally breeds in the Trans-Pecos mountains of Texas. Upon checking the reference (Williams, 1967) that was probably the basis for Oberholser's inclusion of the Western Wood-Pewee in Bosque County, I dismissed the nesting of this species in north central Texas. It hardly seems possible that both Eastern and Western Wood-Pewees were found in both Bosque and nearby McLennan counties – and all in one season. Oberholser does not include the latter species for Mc-Lennan County, though it is mentioned in the original reference. The reference gave no specific date or details of nest or young, nor did it comment on how the Eastern Wood-Pewee was distinguished from the Western Wood-Pewee. I have searched for pewees in Bosque County during the breeding season and have not even located the eastern species. The reference is too vague to assume that the Western Wood-Pewee nests so far from its normal range.

EASTERN WOOD-PEWEE *Contopus virens* (Linnaeus)
Status: Fairly common transient. Summer resident locally.
Occurrence: Eastern Wood-Pewees have been recorded in 21 counties of the study area – Archer, Baylor, Bosque, Clay, Collin, Cooke, Dallas, Denton, Ellis, Fannin, Grayson, Hill, Hood, Hunt, Kaufman, Navarro, Palo Pinto, Somervell, Tarrant, Van Zandt, and Wichita counties – and adjacent Anderson and Henderson counties. They do not quite reach the western edge of the study area; at least they have not been recorded there.

Although few wood-pewees are reported before early May, the following county dates represent some early-spring arrivals and late-fall departures: *Collin* – 12 April 1980, and 9 October 1982; *Cooke* – 18 April 1885, and 5 September 1940 (both specimens); *Dallas* – 1 April 1937 (Stillwell, 1939), next-earliest 21 April 1973 to 29 October 1972, next-latest 13 October 1976; *Grayson* – 25 and 26 March 1972, and 1 October; *Hunt* – 24 April 1985 (Van Zandt County), and 4 October 1978; *Tarrant* – 20 April 1971 to 24 October 1952.
Nesting: There are June and July dates from many counties, a number of which represent breeding birds. However, actual nesting has been recorded in only the following counties: Cooke – (Oberholser, 1974); Dallas – feeding young on 29 June 1974 and 28 June 1982; Grayson – nest on 9 June 1973, bird carrying nesting material on 26 May 1974; Kaufman – two fledglings out of nest on 30 June 1982; Van Zandt – bird carrying nesting material in spring 1984. It has been suspected of nesting in Bosque, Hunt, Tarrant, and Wichita counties, but no actual nests or young have been found.
Specimens: Eastern Wood-Pewee specimens have been collected from Cooke (TCWC, TNHC), Dallas (WMP), Denton (DMNH), Ellis (DMNH), and Kaufman (WMP) counties.

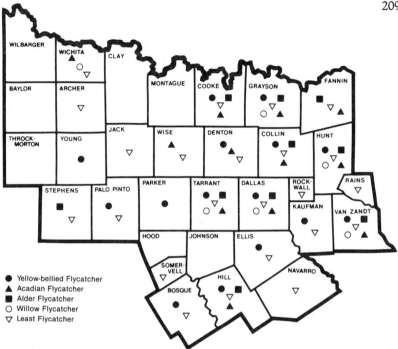

Map 64. Distribution of the Yellow-bellied Flycatcher, *Empidonax flaviventris;* the Acadian Flycatcher, *E. virescens;* the Alder Flycatcher, *E. alnorum;* the Willow Flycatcher, *E. traillii;* and Least Flycatcher, *E. minimus*

YELLOW-BELLIED FLYCATCHER   *Empidonax flaviventris* (Baird and Baird)
Status: Fairly common to uncommon transient.
Occurrence: Yellow-bellied Flycatchers have been recorded in 15 counties of north central Texas: Bosque, Collin, Cooke, Dallas, Denton, Ellis, Grayson, Hill, Hunt, Kaufman, Palo Pinto, Parker, Tarrant, Van Zandt, and Young. It should be noted that sightings tend to be concentrated in areas where there are qualified observers.

Spring and fall migration dates for selected counties are: *Collin* — 12 May 1983, 15 and 18 May 1980, 24 May 1984, and 25 August 1984 to 5 October 1982, all birds banded. *Dallas* — a series of March dates given by Stillwell (1939) have been discounted as possible errors because the dates lack qualification. More typical dates are 25 April 1937 to 2 June 1968, and 22 July 1972 to 11 October 1958. *Grayson* — 14 May to 29 May 1986 and 16 September 1982. *Palo Pinto* — 7 May 1977 to 23 May 1976, and 21 August 1977 to 17 September 1978. *Tarrant* — 30 April 1972 to 28 May 1982, and 26 August 1978 to 9 October 1986.
Specimens: Specimens of this *Empidonax* have been taken in the follow-

ing counties: Cooke – 21 May 1884 (TNHC 1469); Dallas – 12 May 1948 (DMNH 3799, 3855, 3856), 2 June 1968 (WMP 1655), 3 September 1960 (WMP 1024), 5 September 1964 (WMP 1430), 5–6 September 1962 (WMP 1313), 18 September 1958 (WMP 605), 28–29 September 1959 (WMP 796), and 11 October 1958 (WMP 629); Denton – 16 May 1949 (DMNH 4207) and 19 May 1947 (DMNH 3561); Ellis – 23 September 1948 (DMNH 3889); Kaufman – 9 September 1981 (WMP 2718); Parker – 15 August 1963 (FWMSH 589); Tarrant – 21 September 1950 (DMNH 4806) and 25 September 1954 (DMNH 4874); Young – 28 August 1956 (DMNH 5034).

ACADIAN FLYCATCHER   *Empidonax virescens* (Vieillot)
Status: Casual to rare transient. Status clouded with misidentifications. Suspected nesting on the eastern edge of the study area.
Occurrence: Acadian Flycatchers have been recorded in 12 counties of the study area: Collin, Cooke, Dallas, Denton, Fannin, Grayson, Hill, Hunt, Tarrant, Van Zandt, Wichita, and Wise.

Although Acadian Flycatchers are identified in north central Texas, and may even nest along the eastern edge of the study area, this species does not occur as regularly as many believe it does. As many conservative birders know, the identification of members of the genus *Empidonax* is exasperating. This species is easily confused with all the other members of the genus, but especially with Alder and Willow Flycatchers, below, and, unfortunately, few specimens have been taken to help us clarify its status in north central Texas. Some authorities claim that only its nesting habits and voice help distinguish it in the field. To my knowledge, no nests have been discovered in north central Texas, and few if any flycatchers sing in passage through the area. Thus confusion of records reigns among members of this genus, especially in fall, when the species look even more alike. It should also be pointed out that, unless one has an extremely good ear, identification of the songs of the various species with certainty is hopeless.

County records are: *Collin* – A local bander claimed to have captured a number of these birds (more than 30) in spring, ranging from 7 May 1981 to 26 May 1981, an unbelievably early bird on 26 March 1981, and one each on 10 and 15 September 1981. However, no specimens were collected for confirmation. It is interesting that in the southern part of this county, less than 20 miles from the first bander's station, another bander in similar habitat and during the same periods netted only members of Traill's complex (see Alder Flycatcher). A specimen suspected of being an Acadian Flycatcher collected at the latter site on 3 September 1983 (WMP) proved to be an Alder Flycatcher. *Cooke* – specimens were taken by G. H. Ragsdale on 13 June 1878 (USNM 84041), 18 May 1880 (TNHC 1471), and 22 June 1883 (TNHC 1689). There have been no records since, although there is still some habitat along the Red River. *Dallas* – Stillwell

(1939) listed this species as a rare transient and gave only two dates, 9 May 1931 and 10 May 1936, both by Kelley, whose identifications are far from satisfactory. Oberholser (1974) indicates a spring specimen, which has not been located and is probably an old Mayer record. Since then there are six records—four for May and two for September. The Dallas County checklist (1977) gives the species an uncertain status. *Denton*—Oberholser (1974) lists a spring record based on Rylander's checklist (1959). There have been no records since. *Fannin*—Oberholser (1974) lists summer and fall sight records, but details are lacking. These are likely early records, before the turn of the century, and there have been no records since. *Grayson*— nine spring records ranging from 20 April 1984 to 29 May 1978 and an isolated date, 29 June 1974. All identifications were based on call. *Hill*— study of a proposed reservoir site near Aquilla indicated that this species might be regularly present. However, with the exception of a bird collected on 16 May 1980 that proved to be this species (TCWC), all other identi- fications were based on calls, and most of the sightings (May, June, July, and August) are extremely doubtful. *Hunt*—listed as a summer resident (Oberholser, 1974). There have been no records since, though there are typical riparian habitats in the county that could maintain a few members of this species. *Tarrant*—I listed this species as a rare summer resident on the basis of a sighting of an alleged young on 23 June 1964 (Pulich, 1979). The details of nesting are questionable. There are, however, two speci- mens of Acadian Flycatchers for this county: 19 May 1963 (FWMSH) and 6 September 1977 (WMP). *Van Zandt*—an observer tentatively identified an *Empidonax* as this species and noted it feeding two young on 15 Au- gust 1982 on Mill Creek, east of Edgewood. The habitat is typical of the east Texas area where the species is known to nest. The bird was said to have been present since 24 July. Another bird was identified by call on 22 July 1984. *Wichita*—one record on 31 May 1973; the observer admitted that identification of the *Empidonax* group is difficult and only because the bird in question called was it identified as this species. *Wise*—Oberhol- ser (1974) shows a spring sight record but gives no details. It probably represents an early record.

ALDER FLYCATCHER   *Empidonax alnorum* Brewster
Status: Rare to uncommon transient.
Occurrence: The Alder Flycatcher has been recorded in ten counties of the study area: Collin, Cooke, Dallas, Fannin, Grayson, Hill, Hunt, Stephens, Tarrant, and Van Zandt.

This species and the Willow Flycatcher were formerly considered one species, known as Traill's Flycatcher. Although they are now recognized as two species, they are extremely difficult to distinguish in the field and are often misidentified as other members of the genus *Empidonax*. The members of Traill's complex are said to be distinguishable by their behavior and differences in song. Since both are migrants in north central Texas and not all sing in passage, or the songs are seldom correctly recognized, these two species are not often easily identified. The song of the Alder Flycatcher is described as a *fee-bee-o*, while that of the Willow Flycatcher is described as *fitz-bew*. On the breeding ranges they separate into distinct niches, while in migration through north central Texas they occupy the same habitats and are not always separable. If members of this complex are identified in the field, they should be listed as Traill's Flycatchers even though they are now two separate species.

Specimens at hand suggest that more Alder Flycatchers than Willow Flycatchers pass through north central Texas. More collecting should be undertaken, especially along the eastern and western edges of the study area, to clarify the status of these two species.

The separation of the two species is recent. Earlier Oberholser (1974) listed all the records as Traill's Flycatchers. Records were given for Cooke, Dallas, Denton, Grayson, Hunt, and Tarrant counties.

Most of the records for north central Texas are based on specimens, although some comments are offered on sight records: *Collin* — bird banders have identified and banded a number of members of the Traill's complex in spring from 23 April 1983 to 23 May 1980, and in fall from 8 August 1984 to 18 October 1980. However, there is only one specimen of the Traill's complex, collected from this county on 3 September 1983 (WMP 2861), that belongs to this species. *Cooke* — two old specimens, 16 May 1885 (TNHC 1467) and 27 May 1884 (TNHC 1472). *Dallas* — four spring specimen records, 11 May 1948 (DMNH 3775), 12 May 1948 (DMNH 3805), 12 May 1968 (WMP 1648), 13 May 1947 (DMNH 3602), and one sight record based on song on 18 May 1983. Three fall specimen records, 5 and 6 September 1962 (WMP 1384), 12 and 13 September 1975 (WMP 2181), and 14 and 15 September 1974 (WMP 2050). *Fannin* — one specimen, which hit a window about 15 August 1986 (WMP 3033). *Grayson* — no specimens. Records based on song or call notes. Spring, 9 May to 29 May. Five fall records, 13 August to 3 September 1976. *Hill* — alleged spring records are vague. Fall records are unacceptable. Some are no doubt Traill's complex. *Hunt* — five birds identified as Traill's complex were banded on 12 May 1981, 21 May 1981, and 11 September 1981 (three), and probably represent this species. *Stephens* — one fall specimen, 7 September 1984 (WMP 2907). *Tarrant* — 18 May 1986, 23 May 1983, both sight records; 6 September 1977 (WMP 2376); sight records on 15 September 1985. *Van Zandt* — three sight records, 19 April 1984, 9 May 1986, and 26 August 1984, tentatively identified on the basis of calls. The April date is questionable.

WILLOW FLYCATCHER   *Empidonax traillii* (Audubon)
Status: Rare to uncommon transient.
Occurrence: The Willow Flycatcher has been recorded in eight counties
of the study area.

Like the previous species, Willow Flycatchers are often misidentified (see
Alder Flycatcher).

The county records are: *Cooke*—a fall sight record of 11 October 1967,
allegedly this species, has been dismissed as a member of Traill's complex.
Dallas—eight specimens, all for fall, ranging from 5 to 16 September (TV-
tower kills, six in WMP collection and two in USNM, 479654, 479655).
Sight records for spring and a 6 October 1980 date said to be of this species
should be considered members of Traill's complex, not Willow Flycatchers.
Denton—listed as a summer record (Traill's) by Oberholser (1974) and probably based on Rylander's checklist (1959), questionable and not accepted,
since no details were given. *Grayson*—like the records for the Alder Flycatcher, sight records are based on call, and some of them are questionable. Spring, 18 April to 13 May, and one fall sighting on 3 September
1976. *Hunt*—a sight record identified as this species by call on 23 April
1984. *Tarrant*—four specimen records, 11 May 1887 (CM), 23 May 1950
(DMNH 4717), spring 1968 (WMP 1674), and 2 July 1963 (FWMSH 612).
Only the last two specimens were critically examined. A 8 September 1985
sight record and other fall sight records are questionable. *Van Zandt*—ten
sight records, 8 May 1985, 14 May through 23 May 1984, 15 May 1985,
18 through 26 May 1986, 27 May 1983 (*fitz-bew* call), 26 and 27 August
1984, 1 October 1984, and 18 October 1983, the last three thought to be
this species. *Wichita*—one spring specimen of this species, 9 May 1962
(MWU 197), and one fall record, 7 and 9 September 1977, of Traill's complex.

LEAST FLYCATCHER   *Empidonax minimus* (Baird and Baird)
Status: Fairly common to common migrant in spring and fall.
Occurrence: Least Flycatchers have been recorded in 23 counties of the study
area: Archer, Bosque, Collin, Cooke, Dallas, Denton, Ellis, Fannin, Gray-
son, Hill, Hunt, Jack, Kaufman, Navarro, Palo Pinto, Rains, Rockwall,
Somervell, Stephens, Tarrant, Van Zandt, Wichita, and Wise.

Although many members of this genus are simply recorded as *Empidonax*, this species is the most common of the group that passes through
north central Texas. More than 110 birds of this genus were recorded on
a spring count in Tarrant County on 5 May 1979.

Dates usually range from late April to early June, and again from August to early October. Several alleged sightings of *Empidonax* in December have been dismissed.

Extreme dates for counties for which sufficient data are available are:

Collin — 27 April 1983 to 23 May 1980, and 11 August 1984 to 9 October 1982 (all banded birds); *Dallas* — an isolated date, 23 March 1970, next 19 April 1975 to 20 May 1972, and 21 July 1979 to 27 November 1930 (Stillwell, 1939) — the last date extremely doubtful — next-latest 11 October 1936; *Tarrant* — 27 April 1976 to 6 June 1961, and 10 July 1977, next-latest 26 July 1976 to 11 October 1974.

Specimens: Numerous Least Flycatchers have been collected from the following counties: Bosque (WMP), Cooke (TNHC, USNM), Dallas (DMNH, WMP), Denton (DMNH), Ellis (DMNH), Fannin (WMP), Hunt (DMNH), Kaufman (DMNH), Palo Pinto (WMP), Stephens (WMP), and Tarrant (DMNH, FWMSH, UTA, WMP). All specimens have been confirmed as *minimus*. The specimens indicated for Collin and Wise counties, as well as one said to have been taken on 26 July (year unknown) from Hunt County, were not located (Oberholser, 1974).

BLACK PHOEBE *Sayornis nigricans* (Swainson)
Status: Accidental.
Occurrence: Black Phoebes have been recorded only in four counties: Bosque, Dallas, Grayson, and Tarrant.

County records are: *Bosque* — 7 May 1978; *Dallas* — 18 and 31 August 1963; *Grayson* — 11 November 1977; *Tarrant* — 28 February 1953 and 28 October 1954. There are two other sightings, both for nearby Shackelford County, one at Fort Griffin on 21 October 1967 and the other just over the Stephens County line on the Clear Fork of the Brazos River on 2 August 1982.

The 31 August date for Dallas County represents the only specimen (WMP 1410) for north central Texas.

EASTERN PHOEBE *Sayornis phoebe* (Latham)
Status: Fairly common migrant. Uncommon in winter locally. Fairly common to uncommon summer resident.
Occurrence: The Eastern Phoebe has been recorded in all of the counties of north central Texas except Baylor and Stephens, and in many the year round. No doubt it also occurs in these counties, too, but not enough birding takes place there to record it.

Migration in the Dallas–Fort Worth area is from early March to early May, and again from mid-September to early October. However, the actual status and dates are difficult to evaluate without a detailed study, since some birds may be nesting in a particular area while others are passing through in the same period of time. For example, in an area where birds may winter the species may nest later, and whether or not the birds are the same cannot be determined without color-banded birds for individual recognition.

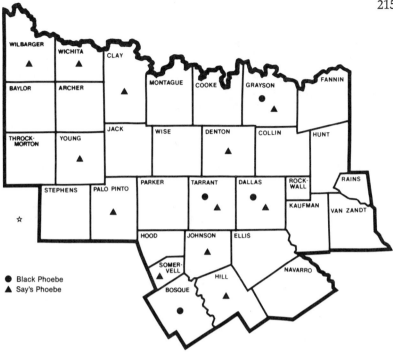

Map 65. Distribution of the Black Phoebe, *Sayornis nigricans,* and Say's Phoebe, *S. saya*

This species has been recorded on all of the CBCs of the area. Its numbers are reduced, especially in the western and northern parts of the study area, when compared with the southern portions, where it appears to be more common during the winter.

Nesting: Nesting records have been established for Archer, Bosque, Clay, Collin, Cooke, Dallas, Denton, Fannin, Grayson, Hill, Hunt, Jack, Kaufman, Montague, Palo Pinto, Parker, Rains, Somervell, Tarrant, Van Zandt, Wichita, and Wise counties, as well as nearby Eastland County. Since this species seems to have adapted well to man-made structures, it may actually have increased. In Palo Pinto County, for example, in early March Eastern Phoebes frequent many of the concrete culverts and bridges where there is fresh water, often raising two broods of young in a wet season. As a rule, the species is two-brooded throughout north central Texas. Some overall early nesting data range from 11 February 1967 (Palo Pinto County), building nest; next-earliest is 25 March 1972 (Grayson County), building nest; 30 March 1971 (Kaufman and Van Zandt counties); eggs and young in nests in a number of counties in April and May, while some late dates include 24 June 1976, nesting (Clay County); 25 June 1967, nest (Denton County); 28 June 1977, nest (Parker County).

Eastern Phoebe young in the nest have been banded in the following counties: Collin — earliest 24 April 1985 (four), latest June 21 1984 (five); Dallas — earliest 20 April 1978 (five), latest 17 June 1967 (three); Hunt — 15 June 1984 (four); Jack — 23 April 1978 (five); Kaufman — earliest 15 April 1974 (one), latest 2 July 1972 (three); Palo Pinto — earliest 8 April 1981 (five), latest 20 June 1970 (nests of four and five young); and Eastland — 10 April 1985 (four).

Specimens: Specimens of this phoebe have been taken from the following counties: Cooke (TNHC), Dallas (DMNH), Denton (DMNH), Ellis (DMNH), Hunt (FWMSH), Kaufman (DMNH), Navarro (USNM), Palo Pinto (DMNH), Parker (DMNH), Tarrant (DMNH), and Henderson (DMNH). The whereabouts of the Collin County specimen indicated by Oberholser (1974) is unknown.

Say's Phoebe   *Sayornis saya* (Bonaparte)

Status: Rare visitor in fall and winter.

Occurrence: This western phoebe has been recorded in 12 counties of the north central Texas study area — Clay, Dallas, Denton, Grayson, Hill, Johnson, Palo Pinto, Somervell, Tarrant, Wichita, Wilbarger, and Young — and adjacent Shackelford County. It has been recorded in all months except June through September, with more observations in winter.

County records are: *Clay* — spring record (Oberholser, 1974); no recent records known to me. *Dallas* — once, 12 January 1980. A date of 5 March 1939 given by Stillwell (1939) is actually a Johnson County record, according to a footnote in his book. *Denton* — three times, 12 January 1978, 22 and 23 March 1981, and 17 through 28 December 1982. *Grayson* — once, 17 April 1983. *Hill* — 22 March 1980; *Johnson* — twice, 5 March 1939 and 8 December 1979. *Palo Pinto* — twice, 28 October 1975 and 31 December 1979 (photographed). *Somervell* — February record, no specific date (Guthery, 1974). *Tarrant* — six times, 8 February record, 21 February 1955, 4 April 1954, 25 April 1952, 21 November 1958, and 14 December 1966 through 7 January 1967. *Wichita* — four times, 25 January to March 1980 (specific date not given), 13 March 1974, 28 March 1979, and 5 April 1979. *Wilbarger* — Oberholser (1974) gives a spring record and a nesting record. The last is the only nesting record that I know of for north central Texas. Although it was indicated that R. L. More took a nest and five eggs at Vernon on 29 May 1932, the whereabouts of this set of eggs are unknown. It is possible that the eggs are in the More collection, still housed in Vernon. *Young* — a winter record (Oberholser, 1974), probably from before the turn of the century. *Shackelford* — once at Lake McCarty, southwest of Albany, on 13 March 1983.

Specimens: To my knowledge there are no specimens of Say's Phoebe for north central Texas. Oberholser (1974) stated that a specimen was taken

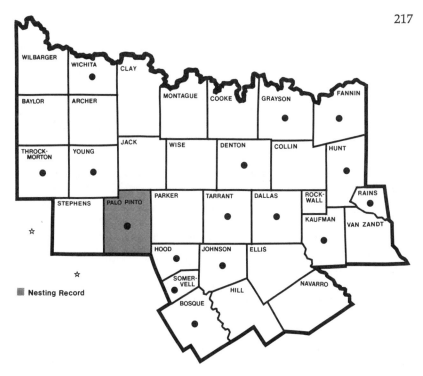

Map 66. Distribution of the Vermilion Flycatcher, *Pyrocephalus rubinus*, with nesting record

at Dallas on 13 November. Research on this date indicated that this specimen was taken in 1898 by W. A. Mayer. Unfortunately, most of Mayer's earlier specimen records could not be traced and are assumed to be lost.

VERMILION FLYCATCHER *Pyrocephalus rubinus* (Boddaert)
Status: Uncommon to rare visitor, becoming more numerous in recent years. Only one record of nesting in north central Texas.
Occurrence: Oberholser (1974) shows records of the Vermilion Flycatcher for only Dallas, Hunt, and Tarrant counties. To these study-area counties 13 more can be added—Bosque, Denton, Fannin, Grayson, Hood, Johnson, Kaufman, Palo Pinto, Rains, Somervell, Throckmorton, Wichita, and Young—as well as nearby Eastland and Shackelford counties.

Sightings range through every month except February. A complete list of counties follows: *Bosque*—a pair was seen repeatedly from 12 through 22 April 1961 near a farmhouse; the farmer claimed that they had nested in previous years, but I have been unable to confirm nesting. *Dallas*—no records given by Stillwell (1939); six times since then, 3 March 1965, 10 March 1955, 31 March 1968, 30 June and 4 July 1973, 25 October 1979, and 29 October through November to 1 December 1965. *Denton*—13 June

1984. *Fannin* — once, 10 October 1979. *Grayson* — four times (all sightings at Hagerman NWR, except the first, at Sherman), 25 March 1982, 28 March 1976, 1 April 1982, and 20 September 1957. *Hood* — Lake Granbury, 23 October 1974. *Hunt* — Oberholser (1974) lists fall and winter sightings, no observation since. *Johnson* — 9 March 1975. *Kaufman* — Terrell, 25 January 1980. *Palo Pinto* — five times, 1 January 1970, 2 January 1971, 2 May 1966, 20 May 1971 (nest with three tiny young found by me), 27 September 1981. *Rains* — once, 20 November 1983. *Somervell* — March, April, and May, details and specific dates not given (Guthery, 1974). *Tarrant* — 13 times, 27 March 1974 and 1981, 28 March 1965, 2 April 1941 and 1957, 4 April 1983 (photograph), 8 April 1978, 6 May 1958, 13 September 1951, 25 September 1955, 9 October 1951, 15 October 1978, and 12 December 1959. *Throckmorton* — once 1 April 1979. *Wichita* — pair noted repeatedly near a farmhouse from 12 April to 11 May 1974; nesting suspected but never confirmed. *Young* — Lake Graham, 19 November 1966. Records from adjacent counties are: *Eastland* — once, 22 April 1987; and *Shackelford* — twice, 24 August 1974 and 17 September 1966.

Specimens: The only specimen of this beautiful flycatcher for north central Texas is one taken from Throckmorton County on 1 April 1979 (TCWC 1978).

ASH-THROATED FLYCATCHER   *Myiarchus cinerascens* (Lawrence)

Status: Uncommon summer resident along the western part of the project area. Casual winter transient.

Occurrence: This pale flycatcher has been reported from ten counties in the study area — Archer, Bosque, Clay, Hood, Palo Pinto, Tarrant, Throckmorton, Wichita, Wilbarger, and Young — and adjacent Shackelford County. The records for Dallas and Fannin counties (Oberholser, 1974) have not been accepted. An early May date for the former county by a lone observer who gave no details seems highly unlikely. A second is given as a questionable breeding observation which is out of range and lacks substantiation. Special care should be exercised to identify this species in the western portion of the study area, where the Ash-throated Flycatcher and the Great Crested Flycatcher range together. It is likely that this species is overlooked or that many observers do not distinguish the species but call all of them crested flycatchers.

Except for two winter observations all sightings are in spring and early summer, normally ranging from April through mid-July. Some county dates are: *Archer* — 4 and 5 May 1974; *Bosque* — 23 April 1961; *Clay* — 3 April 1975, and 8 June 1986; *Hood* — 18 May 1985; *Palo Pinto* — 22 May through 17 July 1977; *Tarrant* — see below; *Throckmorton* — 2 May 1978, 20 May 1979, 24 April 1983, 10 May 1983, 4 June 1983, 21 and 22 June 1984, and 16 June 1985; *Wichita* — 15 March (extremely early) to 10 August (no year

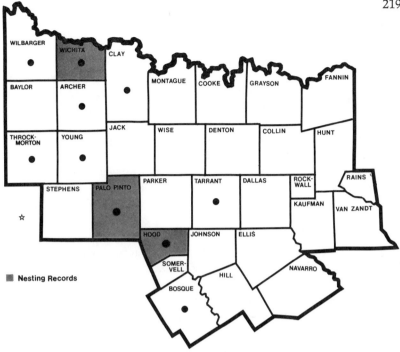

Map 67. Distribution of the Ash-throated Flycatcher, *Myiarchus cinerascens*, with nesting records

available); *Wilbarger* — 17 May 1937 and 16 June 1982; *Young* — 28 April 1983 through 17 June 1983, also seen on 16 June 1985.

There are two winter reports of the Ash-throated Flycatcher for north central Texas. One was seen by numerous observers in Palo Pinto County from 31 December 1965 through 8 January 1966; the second was photographed at Benbrook Lake, in Tarrant County, on 23 January 1980 and remained for several more days.

Nesting: Nesting was recorded for four counties: Hood — on 18 May 1985, five eggs were hatched before 7 June, but whether the fledging was successful is unknown; only old birds were seen on 15 June; Palo Pinto — five young fledged on 22 May 1977; Wichita — two young and eggs on 5 May 1975; Wilbarger — Oberholser (1974) gives a breeding record.

Specimens: Specimens of this species were taken from Wilbarger County on 17 May 1937 (CMNH 24232) and 25 May 1948 (DMNH 3789).

GREAT CRESTED FLYCATCHER *Myiarchus crinitus* (Linnaeus)
Status: Common summer resident over all of north central Texas.
Occurrence: The Great Crested Flycatcher has been reported in all the counties of the study area except Baylor County. The lack of observers in that

county probably accounts for the absence of records. The species becomes less abundant toward the western side of the study area.

This species can usually be found from mid-April until late September. Overall extreme dates range from 20 March 1986 (Kaufman County) to 19 October 1983 (Collin County). Some typical county dates are: *Dallas* — 23 March 1965, next-earliest 2 April 1975 (mean date, 16 years, 16 April, 1957–76) through 16 October 1960 (TV-tower kill, specimen not saved), next-latest 9 October 1981 (mean date, nine years, 19 September, 1970–80); *Grayson* — 3 April 1981 to 30 September; *Tarrant* — 29 March 1941 (mean date, eight years, 13 April, 1970–77) through 9 October 1983; *Wichita* — 8 April 1974 through 23 September 1978.

Nesting: Nesting records were shown by Oberholser (1974) for Cooke, Dallas, Grayson, Tarrant, Wilbarger, and Wise counties, with a questionable record for Fannin County. To these county records can be added the following data: Clay — nest, 13 July 1975; Dallas — nest, 2 June 1969, eggs hatching on 24 June 1970; Hood — four eggs in a bluebird house on 6 June 1981; Hunt — adults building a nest on 22 May 1982; Palo Pinto — adults carrying food on 4 and 12 June 1977; Van Zandt — two young on 17 July 1982; Wichita — adults carrying nesting material on 4 May 1974; Wise — adults carrying nesting material on 17 May 1984.

Specimens: Specimens are available for the following counties: Cooke (TNHC), Dallas (DMNH, WMP), Denton (DMNH), Ellis (DMNH), Fannin (WMP), Johnson (SUC), Kaufman (DMNH, WMP), Parker (FWMSH), Stephens (WMP), Tarrant (DMNH, FWMSH, UTA), and Wise (DMNH). All examples represent *M. c. boreus.*

WESTERN KINGBIRD   *Tyrannus verticalis* Say

Status: Fairly common to common transient and summer resident.

Occurrence: Western Kingbirds and Eastern Kingbirds are reversed in their distribution in north central Texas. Western Kingbirds are more common in the western parts of the study area, while the opposite is true for the Eastern Kingbirds. However, both species are found throughout the area. They have been recorded in all counties except Fannin and Rains, though there is no doubt that if there were more bird-watchers they would be observed in these counties as well. They have also been seen in adjacent Eastland, Erath, and Henderson counties.

Western Kingbirds usually arrive in mid-April and stay until the third week in September, although there are a few October sightings. Overall extreme dates are 7 April 1986 to 22 October 1979, both for Dallas County. An unconfirmed date of 17 March 1975, given for Tarrant County without any details (Williams, 1975), is unacceptable. They seem to disappear from their nesting sites once the young leave the nests and are able to forage for themselves. In August they are difficult to find and are not as abundant as their counterparts, the Eastern Kingbirds.

Typical arrival and departure dates for selected counties are: *Dallas* — 7 April 1986 to 22 October 1979, next-latest 4 October 1959; *Grayson* — 10 April to 24 September; *Hunt* — 23 April 1983 to 5 September 1980; *Palo Pinto* — 30 April 1978 to 2 September 1974; *Tarrant* — 16 April 1979 to 20 October 1964; *Wichita* — 14 April 1982 to 20 September 1974.

Nesting: Breeding Western Kingbirds have a decided preference for drier habitats, while Eastern Kingbirds prefer water habitats and often nest in dead trees extending over bodies of water. This species is common in summer to about Cooke County and south through Dallas and Tarrant counties. There are nesting records for Clay, Collin, Dallas, Denton, Grayson, Hunt, Kaufman, Navarro, Tarrant, Van Zandt, Wichita, and Wilbarger counties. Nesting ranges from mid-May until late July, latest 3 August 1984 (probably second nesting), next-latest 26 July 1970. The last two dates represent young banded in the nest in Dallas County.

Specimens: Western Kingbird specimens are available for Cooke (TCWC), Dallas (DMNH, WMP), Denton (DMNH), Ellis (DMNH), Hood (FWMSH), Tarrant (UTA), and Wichita (MWU) counties.

EASTERN KINGBIRD   *Tyrannus tyrannus* (Linnaeus)

Status: Fairly common to common transient. Uncommon to fairly common summer resident.

Occurrence: The Eastern Kingbird has been found in all the counties of the north central Texas study area. The eastern portions of the area have more typical habitat for this species than do the western parts, where the Western Kingbird is more often found.

This species is usually found in north central Texas from mid-April through September. The peak of movement occurs in early May and the first week of September. It is not unusual to observe hundreds of birds. The species is principally a diurnal migrant. For example, in Collin County on 9 May 1981, 50 to 100 were conservatively counted, and in Ellis County on the following day hundreds passed through the area. Ogilby (1882) indicates seeing "at least 1,000 individuals in last week of September" in Navarro County. The latter number would be unusual today in north central Texas.

Early arrival and departure dates for selected counties are: *Dallas* — 4 April 1974 to 17 October 1981, next-latest 3 October 1970; *Denton* — 3 March 1981, next-earliest 14 April 1982 to 28 September 1984; *Grayson* — 8 April to 20 September; *Tarrant* — 10 April 1983 to 1 October 1946; *Van Zandt* — 4 April 1983 to 6 October 1986; *Wichita* — 9 April 1974 to 20 October 1982, next-latest 18 September 1975.

Nesting: The Eastern Kingbird has been recorded nesting in Archer, Clay, Collin, Cooke, Dallas, Denton, Fannin, Grayson, Hunt, Johnson, Kaufman, Tarrant, Wichita, Wilbarger, and Wise counties. Recent nesting dates for north central Texas range from 17 May through 11 August, some of the late dates representing second broods.

The "defiant" nature of the Eastern Kingbird seldom tolerates friend or foe. Many persons have observed it attacking crows and hawks and even driving off small birds. This is also true of its near relative, the Western Kingbird. However, on 7 June 1983 at Fair Park, Dallas County, a pair of Eastern Kingbirds was seen sharing with a pair of Western Kingbirds a crape myrtle about 20 feet tall as a common nesting site. The two nests were about six feet apart and about 14 and 15 feet above the ground. At that time neither nest was inspected, but on 16 June the Western nest had four eggs and the Eastern nest had two young. They seemed to be tolerant of each other, but both chased away House Sparrows and grackles. On 20 July one juvenile Eastern still in the nest was banded; the other had apparently fledged. On 26 June the Western Kingbirds had young, and on 2 July only one young remained in the nest and was banded, with no evidence of the missing juveniles or the Eastern Kingbirds.

Specimens: Specimens of Eastern Kingbirds have been collected from the following counties: Dallas (DMNH, OU, WMP), Denton (DMNH), Ellis (DMNH), Grayson (UTA), Kaufman (DMNH), Tarrant (DMNH, UTA, WMP), Van Zandt (WMP), and Wilbarger (Oberholser, 1974). The specimens from Wilbarger County were not located.

Scissor-tailed Flycatcher   *Tyrannus forficatus* (Gmelin)
Status: Common to abundant summer resident. One winter record.
Occurrence: The Scissor-tailed Flycatcher has been recorded in all north central Texas counties and the adjacent counties. This flycatcher is well known and to many persons marks the coming of spring in Texas.

Scissor-tails are usually found from mid-March to late October, with stragglers lingering into mid-November. Some extreme county dates are: *Dallas*—10 March 1968 to 19 November 1982, (mean dates, 18 years, 25 March to 27 October); *Denton*—20 March 1975 to 2 December 1986, next-latest 27 November 1984; *Grayson*—14 March 1977 to 1 December 1982, next-latest 30 November 1982; *Johnson*—23 March 1975 to 15 November 1982; *Kaufman*—6 March 1979 (earliest for study area), next 15 March 1972 to 8 November 1978; *Palo Pinto*—28 March 1980 to 26 October 1979; *Tarrant*—13 March 1986 to 2 December 1980, next-latest 22 November 1985 (mean dates, 18 years, 1 April to 18 October); *Van Zandt*—18 March 1982 to an isolated date, 18 December 1970 (latest for study area), next-latest 16 November 1986; *Wichita*—25 March to 23 November 1974.

There is one winter record, a single bird observed at Arlington, Tarrant

County, on 24 January 1967. The four December records above are considered to be stragglers.

Nesting: Although there has been no systematic search for Scissor-tailed Flycatcher nests in every county, nesting has been observed in all the counties except Baylor and Montague. There is little doubt that they also nest there since there are summer records for these counties. Scissor-tails seem to prefer semiopen rather than forested areas. They have a decided preference for mesquite, though they readily use newly developed industrial areas, especially those that are landscaped with newly planted trees, such as live oaks and other ornamentals 12 to 20 feet tall. In the late 1960s and early 1970s it was not uncommon to find more than 20 nests at the peak of nesting (late June and early July) at North Lake, Dallas County. In 1983 this population dwindled to fewer than ten pairs. However, on 1 June 1983, along two miles of a main street in Irving, Dallas County, 17 nests were found, 12 of which were active. The nests were 300 to 600 feet apart in a median strip planted with thick crape myrtle and other ornamentals, where hundreds of cars pass daily. Nesting records range from

15 May 1961, four eggs (Dallas County), earliest banded 22 May 1985 (Stephens County), to 20 August 1977 (Dallas County). Most scissor-tails nest only once, although second nestings can be expected on rare occasions. One such record was two young banded on 22 July 1970 in a nest where four young had been banded on 7 June. Many second nestings occur after the first nests are destroyed. Only one instance of social parasitism is known for the study area, on 29 June 1959, when a Scissor-tailed Flycatcher was observed feeding a fledgling Brown-headed Cowbird (Tarrant County).

Banding of hundreds of Scissor-tailed Flycatchers (young in nest) in north central Texas has produced no significant recovery data. Only once has a banded young been recovered the following spring in a nearby area.
Specimens: Specimens of Scissor-tailed Flycatchers have been located for the following counties: Cooke (CMHH, OSU, TNHC, USNM), Dallas (DMNH, OU, WMP), Denton (DMNH, FWMSH, WMP), Ellis (DMNH), Grayson (UTA), Johnson (FWMSH), Kaufman (WMP), Somervell (FWMSH), Tarrant (DMNH, FWMSH, UTA), Wichita (MWU), and Wilbarger (FWMSH, TCWC). Specimens indicated for Clay County (Oberholser, 1974) could not be located.

Family Alaudidae (Larks)

HORNED LARK *Eremophila alpestris* (Linnaeus)
Status: Common to abundant transient and winter resident. Rare to uncommon summer resident locally with more records from the northwestern part of the study area.
Occurrence: Horned Larks have been reported from all the counties of the north central Texas study area, except Hood and Wise counties. They have been reported in many of the counties the year round; however, they are more often reported during the winter. In summer they are very local and are more often seen in the northwestern part of the study area, in Wichita and Wilbarger counties. Their numbers increase to thousands during some winters, especially in barren areas of the blackland prairies or in plowed fields. In the last ten years it has been noted that in the Dallas–Fort Worth area they are not as numerous because of urban sprawl extending into open areas that formerly favored this species. They can still be found, however, in the adjacent counties in proper habitats.

They have been reported on all of the CBCs held in north central Texas, but never on all of the counts in the same year. Their numbers range from one or two to more than 1,500 (Lewisville, Dallas, and Denton counties). The largest number, possibly more than 7,000, was at Hagerman NWR during a severe cold spell on 22 through 24 December 1983. Horned Larks are often found with Lapland Longspurs. Whether or not the winter populations today are less than those of earlier years is difficult to ascertain. They seem unpredictable in their occurrence, though this may be a species that is missed by many birders.

Arrival and departure dates of this species can be only generalized since detailed data are lacking. Most of the population in the Dallas–Fort Worth area do not show up in any numbers until mid-November, and they have left by mid-March.

Nesting: Oberholser (1974) shows Horned Larks nesting in eight counties of the study area — Baylor, Collin, Dallas, Grayson, Navarro, Tarrant, Wichita, and Wilbarger — to which I can add little information. The following county data are offered to show how few recent nesting records there are of this species for north central Texas: Dallas — last reported 29 April 1934, a bird carrying food (Stillwell, 1939). Seldom seen from May to August, 1952–76, none since. Grayson — most from Hagerman NWR, a pair feeding a juvenile on 21 May 1968, and one on 24 and 31 May and again on 7 June 1984. Two to four all summer, 1972–75, but no nests or young being fed were seen; juveniles were found dead on a road west of Pottsboro on 18 June 1981 (specimen not saved) and 14 July 1974 (specimen saved). Tarrant — a stub-tailed young banded 27 May 1956, young being fed on 27 March 1974, and juvenile road-kill on 27 April 1986. Wichita — immature Horned Lark in June 1974. There are no further data on other counties mentioned by Oberholser (1974).

Specimens: Specimens are said to have been taken from the following counties: Collin (DMNH, UTA), Cooke (USNM, 12 specimens), Dallas (DMNH, OU), Denton (DMNH), Ellis (DMNH), Grayson (KH), Hunt (DMNH, FWMSH), Navarro (USNM), Tarrant (DMNH, FWMSH, UTA, WMP), and Wichita (FWMSH, MWU). Specimens said to have been collected from Clay and Montague counties (Oberholser, 1974) could not be located.

The subspecies of Horned Larks, at least those from Tarrant County, are mainly *praticola* and *leucolaema*. However, not all specimens (those from other counties) have been examined. One specimen taken on 20 January 1966 (MWU 198) has been identified as *leucolaema*. A series of twelve Horned Larks taken in Dallas County on 8 January 1940 (DMNH), as well as two taken 10 January 1940 (DMNH) from Ellis County, were identified by Oberholser as *praticola*. A specimen dated 6 November (year not given) said to have been taken from Cooke County was identified by Oberholser as *enthymia*, but this one was not located.

Family Hirundinidae (Swallows)

PURPLE MARTIN   *Progne subis* (Linnaeus)
Status: Common to abundant transient. Widespread resident over north

central Texas during the summer, more common in the eastern half of the study area than in the western half.

Occurrence: This well-known species had been recorded in all the counties of the north central Texas study area, as well as adjacent Shackelford County, in which it had not been previously reported.

Extreme arrival and departure dates for selected counties are: *Dallas* — an extremely early date of 17 January 1979, next-earliest 3 February 1986 to 21 September 1968, and a report by Stillwell (1939) for 14 October 1934 that may be questionable but cannot be completely dismissed: *Denton* — 16 February 1984 to 15 September 1985; *Grayson* — 7 February 1976 to 25 September 1976, and another extremely late date, 11 October 1975 (observed by Brown); *Kaufman* — 22 February 1977 to 22 September 1977; *Palo Pinto* — 5 March 1983 to 1 October 1977; *Tarrant* — 21 January 1974, next-earliest 4 February 1973 (mean arrival for 1939-60: 28 February; for 1968-78: 8 February) to 18 September 1945; *Wichita* —11 February 1975 to 6 September 1975.

As soon as Purple Martins have finished nesting, they gather in premigratory flocks at some favorable site, often as far as 30 or 40 miles from their earlier nesting sites (birds nesting in Sherman later moved north to Tishomingo NWR, Oklahoma). A roost, estimated at 15,000 birds, was established at Tishomingo NWR in the late 1970s. On 6 July 1982 in Dallas County more than 2,000 gathered together and departed ten days later. The largest roosts reported for Tarrant County were one with about 3,000 martins, on 31 July 1956, and one of 8,000, in 1983. On 3 August 1985 at Wichita Falls, Wichita County, at least 50,000 Purple Martins gathered before departure. Their number dwindled to about 200 by 23 August, and two days later none was observed at this roost.

In late January 1985, the U.S. Fish and Wildlife Service engaged in "microtagging" Purple Martins from five cities in São Paolo, Brazil. From 21 to 23 January a Brazilian team marked 250,000 martins with five distinct colors representing the five cities. Martin fanciers in the United States were urged to salvage dead martins or to pull out several wing feathers from live birds suspected of having been sprayed with ultraviolet sensitive paint. The paint could be detected only with the use of a special lamp. To date four Purple Martins have been recovered in Duncanville, Dallas County, and one in Denton, Denton County. Except for one bird sprayed at Araraquara, all the birds were from Barretos. The bird sprayed at Araraquara was a lone bird from Duncanville. Most martins discovered in the United States had their origin in Barretos, and recoveries ranged from Texas to Missouri, Kansas, and two Middle Atlantic states (data as of 25 July 1985).

There are no valid winter records of Purple Martins for the north central Texas area, though one was said to have been seen in early December. Purple Martins normally winter in South America.

A Purple Martin was reported trying to catch a Ruby-throated Hummingbird on 3 April 1979 (Grayson County).

Nesting: Nesting Purple Martins (young or eggs) have been recorded in Archer, Bosque, Clay, Collin, Cooke, Dallas, Denton, Ellis, Fannin, Grayson, Hill, Hunt, Jack, Johnson, Kaufman, Navarro, Palo Pinto, Rains, Rockwall, Tarrant, Van Zandt, Wichita, Wilbarger, and Wise counties. There is no doubt that this large swallow nests in all the counties, since martin houses are present throughout the area. Nesting ranges from 15 April 1978 (six eggs) to 9 August 1978 (young fledged), all in Dallas County, compared with 7 April 1974 (first egg) to 4 August 1979 (second brood fledged) in Grayson County. In Ellis County seven martins fledged from a clutch of nine eggs (1984). Whether or not this clutch involved two females was not determined.

No doubt man's interest in putting up birdhouses has helped increase the martin population. It is one of the most common birds in man's environment in the study area during the nesting season. Martins have been noted using traffic light signals suspended at intersections in Dallas, Jack, and Palo Pinto counties. Before man's intervention the Purple Martin had to depend on natural nesting sites, mainly woodpecker holes. I have only one record of martins nesting in such sites; in this record they were nesting in a large post oak harboring old woodpecker holes, before 1982 (Van Zandt County).

Usually the Purple Martin nests only once a season, although Brown (1973, 1980, pers. comm.) found that 1.9 percent of a Sherman (Grayson County) population of 209 pairs nested a second time. (I have drawn freely on Brown's data [1978] for Grayson County). Clutches of eggs normally ranged from three to seven, though the latter number is unusual (three times in about 700 nests from 1972 to 1979). About 8 percent of more than 2,000 martins banded as nestlings returned to their natal colony or surrounding colonies in the Sherman area in subsequent years. Banded nestlings dispersed widely both north and south the following year, being recorded in Topeka, Kansas, and Arlington, Tarrant County. Another bander at Duncanville, who banded thousands of Purple Martins in and around Dallas County for seven years (1978–85), suggested that martins returning in spring from their winter home in South America may stop over at martin houses to spend the night. One such bird, an adult female at least two years old when captured in Dallas County on 15 April 1983, was found dead on 27 May 1984 in Kansas near Leon, Butler County. A Purple Martin banded as a nestling by the same person at Duncanville on 17 June 1979 was captured alive in Manaus, state of Amazonas, Brazil, during the Brazilian summer (our winter) of 1982.

Interactions of this species with European Starlings and House Sparrows for nesting sites are often reported. Brown (1981) concluded that starlings are a serious threat to Purple Martins when people fail to clean and maintain their martin houses. Starlings readily take over neglected martin houses and may eliminate martins from some locations. In many areas people must remove starlings and their nests if martins are to persist in residential martin houses. The same words of caution apply to House Sparrows. There is one report of Blue Jays killing young martins (see account of Blue Jay), while screech-owls are suspected of taking young martins from nest boxes.

Specimens: Specimens of Purple Martins are available from Dallas (DMNH, UTA, WMP), Denton (DMNH), Ellis (WMP), Grayson (WMP), Tarrant (FWMSH, UTA, WMP), Wichita (MWU), and Wilbarger (DMNH) counties and nearby Henderson County (DMNH). Not all specimens have been examined. Those that have been studied represent the race *P. s. subis.*

Albinos are not uncommon in this species. I have received reports of at least three "white" martins in 20 years (1962–82). One was found and saved as a specimen (UTA).

TREE SWALLOW   *Tachycineta bicolor* (Vieillot)
Status: Common to fairly common transient.
Occurrence: Tree Swallows have been recorded in 21 counties of the study area: Archer, Bosque, Clay, Cooke, Dallas, Denton, Fannin, Grayson, Hill, Hunt, Johnson, Navarro, Palo Pinto, Rains, Rockwall, Somervell, Tarrant, Throckmorton, Van Zandt, Wichita, and Wilbarger.

This species, along with the Northern Rough-winged Swallow, is one of the first members of the swallow family to arrive in north central Texas in the spring. It is strictly a transient. Its numbers vary from hundreds to a single bird, depending on the time of passage. There appear to be more sightings in fall than in spring.

Some extreme county dates for spring and fall passage are: *Dallas* – 3 March 1965 to 18 May 1981, and 2 August 1980 to 27 November 1974, next-latest 24 November 1964; *Denton* – 2 March 1939 (specimen) to 30 May 1956, and 29 August 1985 to 19 October 1978; *Grayson* – two early dates of 16 February 1979 and 17 February 1976, all others in March to 20 May and 14 July, next-earliest 29 July to 28 October; *Tarrant* – 2 March 1972 to 4 May 1974, and 15 August 1964 to 11 October 1978; *Wichita* – 16 March 1975 to 11 May 1975, and 31 July 1974 to 7 November 1982, next-latest 28 October 1973.

This species is usually observed around bodies of water. Unless one clearly sees its field marks, it is difficult to identify, especially among the hordes of swallows that migrate through north central Texas.

Oberholser (1974) indicates summer records for Cooke, Dallas, Navarro, and Tarrant counties, though I have no data to support them. These sight-

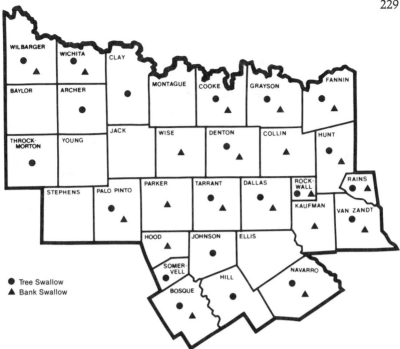

Map 68. Distribution of the Tree Swallow, *Tachycineta bicolor,* and the Bank Swallow, *Riparia riparia*

ings may have been observations of early-fall migrants or late-spring stragglers. Two such unexplainable sightings were a lone bird seen by two observers on 8 June 1983 in Fannin County, and another carefully studied on 6 July 1977 in Palo Pinto County.

Specimens: Tree Swallows have been collected from three counties: Cooke (TNHC), Dallas (DMNH, WMP), and Denton (DMNH).

NORTHERN ROUGH-WINGED SWALLOW   *Stelgidopteryx serripennis* (Audubon)
Status: Fairly common to common transient and summer resident.
Occurrence: Northern Rough-winged Swallows have been reported in 27 counties of north central Texas: Archer, Bosque, Clay, Collin, Cooke, Dallas, Denton, Fannin, Grayson, Hill, Hood, Hunt, Johnson, Kaufman, Palo Pinto, Parker, Rains, Rockwall, Somervell, Stephens, Tarrant, Throckmorton, Van Zandt, Wichita, Wilbarger, Wise, and Young.

Extreme arrival and departure dates for selected counties are: *Dallas —* 8 March 1975 (Stillwell, 1939, gave 7 March 1930) to 7 November 1970; *Grayson —* 10 March 1979 to 8 November 1975, next-latest 29 October 1973; *Palo Pinto —* 27 February 1977, next-earliest 14 March 1976 to 29 September 1979; *Rains* — 10 March 1985 to 22 October 1984; *Tarrant* — 26 February 1985, next-earliest 28 February 1986 to 25 October 1941; *Wichita* — 29 March 1978 to 22 October 1975.

Nesting: Nesting has been observed in the Bosque, Clay, Cooke, Dallas, Grayson, Palo Pinto, Tarrant, Wichita, and Wilbarger counties, and suspected nesting (summer records) in Hunt, Kaufman, and Van Zandt counties. Rough-winged Swallows have been observed going to nest burrows in sandy cutbanks from late March to late June in Bosque, Dallas, Grayson, and Tarrant counties. This period falls within the period of other nesting observations for north central Texas, although most activities were in the month of May. The latest date was 30 June 1973 (Wichita County), when a pair was seen entering a hole. Three young still in the nest were banded on 24 June 1971 (Dallas County). Nesting seldom occurs in large numbers; usually this species nests alone or with no more than one other pair. However, several semicolonial sites of about 20 pairs and one of about ten pairs have been observed along the Red River and Lake Texoma, Grayson County. A pair was observed using a drainpipe as a nesting site on 4 June 1955 (Tarrant County).

Specimens: Specimens have been collected for Dallas (DMNH, WMP), Denton (DMNH), Somervell (TCWC), Wilbarger (Oberholser, 1974, not located), and Wise (DMNH) counties. Not all specimens have been examined; those from Dallas County (WMP) represent *S. s. serripennis*.

BANK SWALLOW   *Riparia riparia* (Linnaeus)
Status: Uncommon to fairly common transient.
Occurrence: Bank Swallows have been recorded in 20 counties in the study area: Bosque, Collin, Cooke, Dallas, Denton, Fannin, Grayson, Hood, Hunt, Kaufman, Navarro, Palo Pinto, Parker, Rains, Rockwall, Tarrant, Van Zandt, Wichita, Wilbarger, and Wise.

This species does not seem as abundant as the Tree or the Northern Rough-winged Swallows; however, it might be recorded more often if flocks of swallows passing through the area were more carefully scrutinized. Bank Swallows may be confused with immature Tree Swallows and resident Northern Rough-winged Swallows. The Tree Swallow appears to have a faint wash of dusty gray across its breast, often giving an impression of a breastband, leading to misidentifications if an observer is not careful.

Extreme arrival and departure dates for spring and fall for selected counties are: *Dallas* — 20 March 1982, next-earliest 5 April 1938 (Stillwell, 1939) to 18 May 1981, and 2 August 1980 to 23 October 1982; *Grayson* — 7 April to 16 May, and 29 July 1982 to 29 October 1983, peaking in August and September; *Tarrant* — 17 March 1969, next-earliest 1 April 1951 to 20 May 1967, an isolated date, 7 June 1951, and 25 August 1956 to 25 October 1942; *Wichita* — 3 April 1977 to 13 May 1976, and 31 July 1974 to 19 October 1973.

Nesting: Oberholser (1974) indicated that Bank Swallows nested in Dallas, Tarrant, and Wilbarger counties and questioned nesting in Fannin County. I believe that the records for Dallas and Tarrant counties are in error; inquiries of persons who claimed to have recorded this species nesting convinced me that they had mistaken Northern Rough-winged Swallows for Bank Swallows. More and Strecker (1929) recorded the Bank Swallow as a "very rare summer resident" in Wilbarger County but presented no explanation for this comment or any breeding dates. Whether nesting represented large numbers of swallows or only a pair or two is not clear. A Bank Swallow colony consists of large numbers of nests placed at the end of burrows near the top of a vertical bank of sand or gravel. The banks are honeycombed with nesting holes. Both the male and the female work at excavating the nest. Observers familiar with the species indicate that the burrow entrances are smaller and neater than those of the Northern Rough-winged Swallow. If the numbers nesting had been given in the records they would have provided a clue to the species. Although this swallow has disappeared as a breeding bird from some parts of the United States, I wonder whether it ever nested in north central Texas. The only Texas nesting records are for south Texas, along the Rio Grande. The southernmost breeding record in the Great Plains is from Ottawa County, in northeastern Oklahoma (Wilson, 1981). Alleged summer records may be late and early migrants through the area (note extreme dates listed), not nesting birds.

Specimens: Specimens are available from Clay (TNHC), Cooke (WMP), Dallas (DMNH, WMP), and Denton (DMNH) counties.

CLIFF SWALLOW   *Hirundo pyrrhonota* Vieillot

Status: Common to abundant transient. Summer resident westerly from western parts of Grayson County, south through Tarrant and Hill counties, with isolated colonies in the eastern parts of the study area.

Occurrence: Cliff Swallows have been reported in all the counties of the study area. They are commonly seen as transients in spring from mid-March through May, and again in fall from late August through early October.

Extreme arrival and departure dates for selected counties are: *Dallas* — 10 March 1983 to 22 October 1932 (Stillwell, 1939); *Grayson* — 18 March 1982 and 1983 to 14 October; *Palo Pinto* — 27 March 1976 to 22 September 1978; *Tarrant* — 11 March 1978 to 17 October 1973; *Wichita* — 29 March 1975 to 19 October 1973.

Nesting: This species has been reported nesting regularly on the western side of the study area in all of the counties except Archer, to about the west side of Grayson County, south midway into Denton and Tarrant counties, and mainly along the Brazos River in Hill and Bosque counties. There are isolated established colonies at Cedar Creek Lake, Henderson County;

at Lake Ray Hubbard, Dallas County; and at the spillway bridge below Lake Tawakoni Dam, Rains and Van Zandt counties.

Cliff Swallows build completely enclosed gourd-shaped nests of mud pellets and place them under overhangs. They are usually found nesting apart from Barn Swallows, but occasionally they share a concrete bridge. Three isolated instances have been recorded: two nests (later destroyed) in Ellis County on 27 May 1981 and one nest among Barn Swallows and four young banded on 19 July 1968 in Van Zandt County. There is a mixed colony of approximately 250 nests just across the Red River from Grayson County, at the U.S. 377 bridge in Marshall County, Oklahoma. Nesting, depending on the availability of a mud supply, ranges from 20 April 1981 (small young in the nest) in adjacent Eastland County to 27 July 1968 (young banded) in Cooke County. Nesting tends to peak in late May and early June. Spring rains have been known to destroy nests under bridges, causing swallows to move elsewhere to renest. Cliff Swallows along the Brazos River drainage tend to utilize rocky cliffs adjacent to lakes, and man-made structures may have encouraged the increase or spread of the population in the more northerly counties of north Texas. In Bosque County several colonies utilize open limestone caves. House Sparrows frequently occupy Cliff Swallow nests. In a small colony—fewer than ten pairs—in Cooke County the sparrows had taken over all the swallows' nests. Cliff Swallows are the most colonial of all swallows, with colonies of up to 3,000 nests in the western Great Plains. These birds probably live in colonies to socially hunt for ephemeral patches of small insects, such as midges. Cliff Swallows alternate using colony sites and nests from year to year, probably in response to buildups of ectoparasites such as fleas, ticks, and bedbugs in the nests (Brown, pers. comm.).

Specimens: Cliff Swallow specimens are available for the following counties: Clay (DMNH, MWU), Cooke (TNHC), Denton (DMNH), Hill (WMP), Hood (DMNH), Kaufman (SFASU), Palo Pinto (FWMSH, UTA, WMP), Parker (DMNH), Tarrant (DMNH, FWMSH), and Young (FWMSH).

Specimens examined from Tarrant County taken in the summer of 1963 (FWMSH) and from Palo Pinto County on 27 May 1965 (WMP) were identified as *H. p. tachina,* while one collected from Hill County on 10 May 1969 (WMP) and two from Wichita County on 24 May 1953 (MWU) were identified as *H. p. pyrrhonota.*

Barn Swallow *Hirundo rustica* Linnaeus
Status: Fairly common to common summer resident over most of north central Texas. Abundant transient, much more noticeable in large flocks in fall than in spring.

Occurrence: Barn Swallows have been recorded in all of the counties in the study area and nearby Eastland, Henderson, and Shackelford counties.

Barn Swallows are found from early March to early November, although most of them are found in spring passage in mid-April, and again in fall from mid-September to mid-October. They are much more common in the fall, thousands sometimes being noted ahead of a cold front. The greatest number was 10,000 on 10 October 1983 (Tarrant County).

Extreme dates for selected counties are: *Dallas*—10 March 1983 to 25 November 1984, next-latest 19 November 1981; *Grayson*—16 March to 30 November 1974, next-latest 11 November 1978; *Hunt*—10 March 1986 (Van Zandt County), 19 March 1976, and 1980 to 13 November 1977; *Palo Pinto*—11 March 1986 to 15 October 1977; *Tarrant*—2 March 1974 to 17 November 1982; *Wichita*—5 March 1974 (nearby Clay County), 9 March 1974 to 13 November 1977.

Winter sightings include a very late fall straggler on 3 December 1977 and a very early date of 5 January 1985 (both for Grayson County) and an extremely early arrival on 17 February 1974 (Wichita County). These sightings were made by competent observers, who presented all the identifying features of Barn Swallows.

Nesting: Surprisingly, nesting records from the first half of this century are meager. Oberholser (1974) lists only Cooke, Grayson, Tarrant, and Wise counties as having breeding birds, although he presents a number of summer occurrences. Ogilby (1882) attributes their absence from Navarro County to "want of suitable breeding places," and More and Strecker (1929) and Sutton (1938) list them as nesting in Wilbarger and Tarrant counties, respectively. There was a surge of nesting reports in the early 1960s, and today they are widespread, especially in the eastern half of the study area. Nests have been reported from the following counties: Archer, Bosque, Clay, Collin, Cooke, Dallas, Denton, Ellis, Fannin, Grayson, Henderson, Hill, Hunt, Johnson, Kaufman, Navarro, Palo Pinto, Parker, Rains, Rockwall, Tarrant, Van Zandt, Wichita, and Wise. It would not be surprising to find them nesting in all of the counties of north central Texas if one visited suitable nesting sites during the breeding season.

Barn Swallows nest twice in a season in north central Texas and occasionally three times. They readily build their open mud nests under concrete bridges along highways; some nest on buildings. At times they are as numerous as Cliff Swallows. They begin nesting almost immediately upon their arrival from the south and continue to do so into July. Extreme dates for banded young are 30 April 1979 (Henderson County) to 16 August 1972 (Van Zandt County).

A Texas rat snake (*Elaphe obsoleta*) was found feeding on young Barn Swallows on 7 June 1969 in Van Zandt County.

The only banding recovery known to me of a Barn Swallow from north central Texas was in Asunción, Paraguay. This nestling, banded on 21 May 1972 near Paris, Lamar County, was recovered on 22 October 1972. *Specimens:* Specimens are available from Clay (DMNH), Cooke (WMP), Dallas (WMP), Denton (DMNH), Ellis (DMNH), Fannin (WMP), Kaufman (WMP), and Wichita (MWU) counties.

Family Corvidae (Crows and Jays)

BLUE JAY *Cyanocitta cristata* (Linnaeus)
Status: Year round in most north central Texas counties. Abundant to common in eastern portions. Fairly common to uncommon in western parts.
Occurrence: Blue Jays have been reported in all counties of north central Texas except Baylor. Their numbers tend to decrease from east to west, and they may be absent during the nesting season toward the west (beyond Clay, Wise, and Parker counties), except for very local areas along creeks or some towns. They do, however, range west along the Red River to Wilbarger County the year round. Thus the Blue Jay will usually be found in forested areas, as well as gardens and yards.

Blue Jays have been reported on all of the annual CBCs of the area. A comparison of average number of jays on 14 years (1965–78) of the annual Spring Bird Counts in Tarrant County with those of annual CBCs shows an approximate increase of 67 percent during the winter period.

In late September and early October movements of Blue Jays are noted throughout most of north central Texas; most of these observations represent transient birds. In Comanche County, south of the study area, an observer indicated that he never found Blue Jays in late spring and summer, but Oberholser (1974) gave nesting sightings in two adjacent counties to the north and west. In fall and winter Blue Jays are fairly common in Comanche County. This is also true of Stephens County, where they were observed feeding on live-oak acorns on 8 October 1984. In spring (12 and 26 April 1975) large flocks in loose formation were seen moving across Lake Texoma, Grayson County, into Oklahoma. Efforts to band large numbers of Blue Jays might help clarify the status (movements) of local populations thought by many to be permanent residents.

Much has been written about the bold habits of Blue Jays attacking other birds. Several observations are worth mentioning: three instances of jays attacking Great Horned Owls, an observation of a jay robbing a House Sparrow's nest on 25 May 1975 in Irving (Dallas County), and in Dallas a report of jays taking at least three young Purple Martins (about a week old) from a martin house on 13 May 1982 and eating them.
Nesting: Many Blue Jays nest twice a year in north central Texas. Nesting (most dates here are from the Dallas–Fort Worth area) extends from 28

February, beginning nest; 3 March, gathering nesting material; 28 March, four eggs; 13 April, young banded; 20 May, second brood; 29 June, feeding young in nest; 11 July, stub-tailed young out of the nest banded; 2 August, young banded in nest. At Coppell, Dallas County, on 13 April 1975 a pair of Blue Jays alternated with a Northern Cardinal in an attempt to build a nest, but after several days both species quit working on the nest.

Within the study area Blue Jays have been found nesting in the following counties: Bosque, Collin, Cooke, Dallas, Denton, Fannin, Grayson, Hill, Hunt, Johnson, Kaufman, Navarro, Parker, Somervell, Tarrant, Van Zandt, Wichita, Wilbarger, and Wise.

Specimens: Blue Jays have been collected in Clay (Oberholser, 1974, not located), Cooke (TNHC), Dallas (DMNH, MWU, WMP), Denton (DMNH, WMP), Ellis (DMNH), Grayson (UTA, WMP), Hood (FWMSH), Johnson (SUC), Kaufman (DMNH), Parker (FWMSH), Tarrant (DMNH, FWMSH, UTA, WMP), Wichita (DMNH, MWU), and Wilbarger (CMNH) counties and nearby Henderson (DMNH) County.

Although not all of the specimens have been checked, both the nominate race *cristata* and the race *cyanotephra* have been identified from Dallas and Tarrant counties. There are three old specimens, two from Dallas County (DMNH 181 and 294), taken on 28 January 1937 and 14 February 1938, and one from Denton County, taken on 28 October 1939 (DMNH 994), which were identified as *bromia* but have not been reexamined or compared with material taken from the north. These were identified by Oberholser, but there is no reference to them in *The Bird Life of Texas* (1974).

GREEN JAY   *Cyanocorax yncas* (Boddaert)
Status: Accidental in the north central Texas study area; one record for Johnson County.
Occurrence: This south Texas jay has been reported in the small community of Keene, Johnson County, from 23 October 1980 until 27 March 1983. As many as three Green Jays were reported, and some of the local birders claimed that the birds nested during the observation period. This species was substantiated by photographs (Williams, 1982). They were last reported on 2 April 1984. The Green Jay had not been reported north of San Antonio before these observations. Although it is not known how this species reached Johnson County, it is suggested that the bird may have moved north with Hurricane Allen, which struck the Texas coast in the fall of 1980.

CLARK'S NUTCRACKER   *Nucifraga columbiana* (Wilson)
Status: Accidental in north central Texas.
Occurrence: Clark's Nutcracker invaded Texas in the winter of 1972–73, mainly in the Panhandle and Trans-Pecos areas. It is normally reported only from the mountainous areas of southwest Texas. One, however, reached the north central Texas town of Burkburnett, Wichita County, where two observers sighted it in a backyard on 7 January 1973.

BLACK-BILLED MAGPIE   *Pica pica* (Linnaeus)
Status: Accidental; records may represent escapees.
Occurrence: This striking black-and-white bird with a long tail has been reported from two north central Texas counties.

Pulich (1979) gave records for Tarrant County. There is one report of a magpie said to have wintered and possibly even nested, though the details are somewhat vague. Two other reports are sightings from near the Fort Worth zoo area, which may or may not have been an escaped caged bird. The other record was a magpie seen in a field south of Fort Worth. The species was last reported for Tarrant County in 1966.

The second report is for Wichita County. It represents a specimen which was caught just north of Wichita Falls, in October 1973 and was kept in captivity until it died in December 1974. It is very likely that this bird was a captive magpie that was brought into the area, escaped, and was recaptured.

Since in the past persons have frequently taken young magpies from nests and transported them elsewhere, the occurrence of the Black-billed Magpie as a native species in north central Texas is questionable. The nearest area in which Black-billed Magpies occur in Texas is the upper Panhandle, to which winter stragglers drift only rarely from the Oklahoma Panhandle.

AMERICAN CROW *Corvus brachyrhynchos* Brehm

Status: Common to abundant resident. Records indicate that the species is more abundant in the eastern parts of the study area and along the Red River.

Occurrence: Crows have been reported in all of the counties of north central Texas except Stephens County. There is little doubt that it occurs in that county as well, since it has been found in all of the surrounding counties.

Crow populations vary from year to year and season to season. There is a definite increase in the winter populations, reflecting birds from the north. Their numbers tend to swell in early October, and in winter they are numerous in some locations. Their numbers are largest in the eastern parts of the study area, which provide more favorable habitat. They have become more abundant in northwest Texas in recent years. Crows were formerly considered rare residents in Wichita and Wilbarger counties, where they were confined to creek bottoms (More and Strecker, 1929). Farmlands, replacing open prairies and scrub areas in these counties, have favored crows at the expense of ravens. In Tarrant County a comparison of the annual CBCs (1965-78) with the formal Spring Bird Counts held each year shows an increase of more than 40 percent of the winter crow populations. They are not often observed in cities except those with large parks and pecan crops.

Nesting: The crows' wariness, especially around their nests, precludes much gathering of data on nesting, since only a few persons ferret out nests and eggs today. In the Dallas–Fort Worth area nesting begins early; crows have been noted carrying nesting material in late February, and a nest containing eggs was found on 5 March 1972. Another nest with five eggs was found on 17 March 1985 in Hunt County. Young have been noted out of the nest by 4 May 1959. In Wilbarger County crows were found with a brood of young ready to leave the nest on 5 June 1929 (More and Strecker, 1929). The dates are typical for all of the north central Texas area.

Actual nests or young have been noted in Clay, Collin, Cooke, Dallas, Denton, Ellis, Grayson, Hill, Hunt, Johnson, Kaufman, Navarro, Rockwall, Tarrant, Van Zandt, Wichita, Wilbarger, Wise, and Young counties.

Specimens: Crow specimens have been taken from Cooke (TNHC), Dallas (DMNH, UTA, WMP), Denton (DMNH, mounted), Hill (SM), Johnson (SUC), Tarrant (FWMSH, SUC, UTA), and Wichita (MWU) counties.

The nesting race in Tarrant County is said to be the nominate race *brachyrhynchos* (Sutton, 1938); however, few of the specimens have been examined to determine race. Oberholser (1974) mentioned that the resident crow in Cooke County was also this race and that *hesperis* was collected in the winter (1 November) from Tarrant County (neither of these specimens was examined).

CHIHUAHUAN RAVEN   *Corvus cryptoleucus* Couch

Status: Uncommon to rare summer resident in the northwest corner of the study area. More widespread and abundant in former days than in the present. Data at hand do not support evidence that it was formerly a winter resident.

Occurrence: This species was formerly called the White-necked Raven; however, AOU changed it (1983) because there is an African species so named (it is difficult to conceive a confusion of the two names since the species occur on different continents).

This raven is not as abundant today as it was formerly. American Crows have replaced this species over much of the area. A few ravens will probably be found regularly in Baylor, Throckmorton, Wichita, and Wilbarger counties.

There are accounts of this raven occurring in seven counties within the study area. Oberholser (1974) gives most of the data for these counties in his work, from which many of my data are taken. A summary of the earlier records and a few recent records are presented to help clarify the status of the species: *Archer* — said to have nested and wintered (Oberholser, 1974). *Baylor* — nested and summered (Oberholser, 1974), two to six ravens at a garbage dump near Lake Kemp on 9 and 10 May 1983, and also seen west of Seymour on 1 April 1984. *Throckmorton* — nested and summered (Oberholser, 1974). I observed them near Elbert on 31 May 1965 and on 22 May 1984. I found a nest with seven eggs south of Millers Creek Lake on 21 May 1984. *Wichita* — previously nested and viewed in the fall, according to Oberholser, (1974). The local checklist for birds of north central Texas area indicates that it is rare "but to be expected at certain times of year, at least locally." There are no current reports, however, and the assumption is probably based on specimens (DMNH 1162; 1163, missing; 1171) taken on 12 May 1939 and on specimen records in adjacent counties. None are reported on local Wichita Falls CBCs. Specimens (MWU 214, 215) taken on 19 March 1955. *Wilbarger* — this county has more records than any other county because of R. L. More's early oological activities in the vicinity of Vernon. More and Strecker (1929) indicated that the raven was an abundant resident in the winter and could be found nesting from 5 May to 10 June. Most ravens nested in mesquite. Nice (1931) indicated that More reported to her that he saw as many as "a thousand," figuratively speaking, in the city limits of Vernon during the winter of 1922, yet today they have virtually disappeared. There are few present-day records. I saw several on the Waggoner Ranch, south of Vernon, on 9 and 10 May 1983. One was observed in the southeast corner of the county on 17 June 1987. Specimens were taken on 11 May 1937 (DMNH 23821) and 17 May 1937 (DMNH 23820).

Stillwell (1939) wrote in a footnote that "in previous years this species was reported breeding in Tarrant and Wise counties." In 1938, however, he had reported that it was "not closer than 175 miles west of Dallas." There is no positive evidence that this species ever occurred in these two counties. Oberholser (1974) also refers to these counties but does not say where he obtained his information. His data were likely taken from Stillwell's book, and not much credence should be given to nesting reports in these two counties. Oberholser (1974) indicates that nesting in Wise County is questionable.

Many persons assume that the Chihuahuan Raven is a winter resident in north central Texas. Except for an alleged specimen (not located) shown by Oberholser (1974) on his species status map for Archer County and Nice's account (see above) from More for Wilbarger County, there is no evidence that this species wintered in the study area. I can find no January dates of occurrence, and until a January specimen is collected, the species cannot be considered a winter resident. This is one of many unanswered questions awaiting research by a serious student of ornithology.

Family Paridae (Titmice and Chickadees)

CAROLINA CHICKADEE   *Parus carolinensis* Audubon
Status: Common to fairly common resident in all of north central Texas. May not be as numerous in the western portions owing to the absence of woodlands except for those in bottomlands along creeks and rivers.
Occurrence: Carolina Chickadees have been reported throughout the year in all of the north central Texas study area. They inhabit wooded areas, though in winter they may visit nearby fields of ragweed and brushy edges containing seed plants. These interesting little birds are always active, moving from tree to tree, and readily come to feeders supplied with sunflower seeds, peanut butter, and suet. They seldom go to the ground and often glean the terminal parts of tree branches, hanging upside down in search of insects. The young are identical in plumage and usually cannot be distinguished from old birds except when they are first fledged. They are said to be nonmigratory. In winter they accompany titmice, kinglets, and other small birds.
Nesting: Carolina Chickadees may begin singing early in January, if weather permits, establishing their territories for the forthcoming nesting season. They may compete with Tufted Titmice for nesting sites, and they are said to produce only one brood of young a year. In addition to utilizing natural cavities and many that they dig themselves, they may use many types of bird boxes and are often found in bluebird houses. They begin nesting early (4 March 1984, working on nest hole), and young are fre-

quently out of the nest in April, May, and early June. In Tarrant County one observer reported that the chickadees in her yard fledged from 17 April to 30 April (1971–78).

Nesting (birds at nests or stub-tailed young) has been recorded in Bosque, Collin, Cooke, Dallas, Denton, Fannin, Grayson, Hill, Hunt, Kaufman, Navarro, Palo Pinto, Rains, Tarrant, Van Zandt, Wichita, and Wilbarger counties. They would probably be found nesting in the remaining counties of north central Texas if efforts were made to find their nests.

Specimens: Specimens of Carolina Chickadees from north central Texas belong to the race *P. c. atricapilloides*. Examples have been found from Archer (MWU), Bosque (SM), Clay (MWU), Cooke (TCWC, USNM), Dallas (DMNH, WMP), Denton (DMNH), Hill (UTA), Hunt (DMNH), Kaufman (DMNH), Navarro (USNM), Palo Pinto (DMNH), Parker (FWMSH), and Tarrant (DMNH, FWMSH, UTA) counties.

Tufted Titmouse *Parus bicolor* Linnaeus

Status: Fairly common to common resident the year round.

Occurrence: The Tufted Titmouse has been reported in all of the counties in the north central Texas study area, as well as the adjacent counties. Until recently the Tufted Titmouse (*Parus bicolor*) and the Black-crested Titmouse (*P. atricristatus*) were considered separate species. However, the two interbreed freely west of Tarrant County, in Parker County, and thence north to the Red River, probably along a line through the western edge of Denton and Cooke counties. Those ranging toward the east are now considered as subspecies *P. b. bicolor*, while those ranging to the west are considered *P. b. atricristatus*.

This noisy and comical little bird is widespread in wooded areas and along creek and river bottoms. It and its near relative, the chickadee, are readily attracted to feeders in cities, especially near forested areas. It is restless and will come to squeaking and screech-owl calls, fussing rather aggressively, often bringing other little birds. Its well-known *peter-peter-peter* call gives it away even when it is unseen.

In several counties, for example, Wichita and Palo Pinto counties, both race *bicolor* and race *atricristatus* are often reported. If possible observers should identify titmice by race in making their reports. If the titmouse in question has a distinct black cap, that should be noted and the bird listed as the black-crested race; otherwise it should be listed as Tufted Titmouse. Observers who are not aware of this distinction in subspecies add confusion to the reports. Examination of titmouse specimens from areas of overlap is the only certain way to properly distinguish the races inhabiting the areas of overlap.

Nesting: The titmouse uses old woodpecker holes, natural cavities, and birdhouses. Nests have been recorded only in Bosque, Collin, Cooke, Dallas,

Denton, Fannin, Grayson, Hill, Hunt, Kaufman, Navarro, Palo Pinto, Rains, Tarrant, Throckmorton, Van Zandt, Wichita, Wilbarger, and Wise counties. There is no doubt in my mind that they also nest in the other counties. They begin nesting rather early. Specific dates are 23 March 1984, adults at nest box, Van Zandt County, to 14 June 1970 and 1981, young still in the nest banded, Dallas and Hunt counties, respectively. These dates would be similar in the other north central Texas counties.

In Hunt County (April 1982) this species took over the nest of a Carolina Chickadee that had two eggs and proceeded to lay three of its own. It is said that all the eggs hatched successfully.

Specimens: Specimens are available from the following counties: Archer (MWU), Cooke (TCWC, TNHC), Dallas (DMNH, WMP), Denton (DMNH), Ellis (Oberholser, 1974, not located), Fannin (WMP), Grayson, (OU), Hill (KU), Hood (DMNH, FWMSH), Hunt (DMNH, FWMSH), Jack (DMNH), Johnson (DMNH), Kaufman (DMNH, WMP), Navarro (USNM), Palo Pinto (DMNH), Parker (DMNH, FWMSH), Somervell (DMNH, TCWC), Stephens (DMNH), Tarrant (DMNH, FWMSH, WMP), Wise (DMNH), Young (DMNH).

Family Remizidae (Verdin)

VERDIN *Auriparus flaviceps* (Sundevall)
Status: Uncommon to rare summer resident. Although it is not widespread, it can be found the year round in some localities in the western part of the study area.

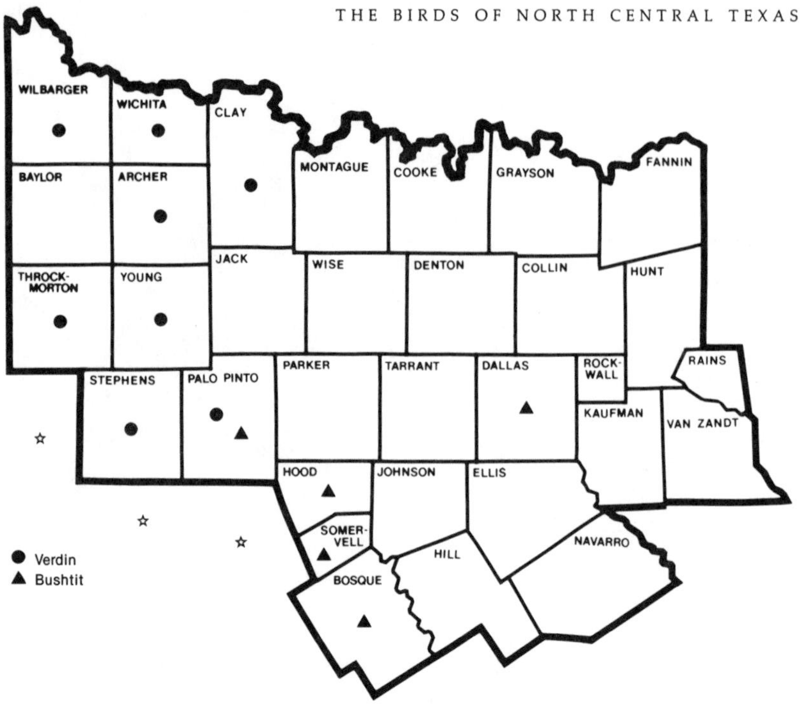

Map 69. Distribution of the Verdin, *Auriparus flaviceps,* and the Bushtit, *Psaltriparus minimus*

Occurrence: Oberholser (1974) records the presence of the Verdin in Palo Pinto, Stephens, Wilbarger, and Young counties, and I have since then recorded it in all of these counties as well as in Archer, Clay, Throckmorton, and Wichita counties and nearby Erath and Shackelford counties. While most of the Verdin reports come from Palo Pinto and Wichita counties because there is more birding here, one could find this species in the proper habitat if one searched for it in the cluster of eight counties in the northwestern and western parts of the study area.

Verdins inhabit rough, brushy areas, particularly washes covered with mesquite and thickets of acacia, condalia, and agarita. Often one hears the bird before seeing it, and if one searches for it in spring, its large (for the size of the bird), ball-like nest can easily be found adorning one of the above-mentioned plants. It also builds roost nests for winter occupancy.

Although there is an earlier questionable record given by Oberholser (1974) in Wilbarger County (probably in the 1920s or 1930s), it was not until 21 April 1974 that the Verdin was first found nesting in north central Texas, in Wichita County. Later the same year (26 May 1974) Verdins were also found nesting about 15 miles away. They continued to nest in the area until the spring of 1976; however, no nests have been found since then.

They were still present in Wichita County on the Wichita Falls CBC of 1982. More recently Verdin nests have been discovered in Palo Pinto, Shackelford, Stephens, and Throckmorton counties.

Specimens: A verdin was said to have been collected south and east of Harrold, Wilbarger County, "in a smilax tangle" along Beaver Creek on 5 December 1967 (Seyffert, 1971); however, the whereabouts of this specimen are unknown.

Family Aegithalidae (Bushtit)

Bushtit   *Psaltriparus minimus* (Townsend)
Status: Very rare local resident. Nearly all of the populations are found along the Brazos River drainage.
Occurrence: This tiny bird is not widespread but has been reported in five counties in the study area — Bosque, Dallas, Hood, Palo Pinto, and Somervell — and adjacent Eastland County.

Bushtits, members of the Edwards Plateau avifauna, have apparently moved along the cedar-lined Brazos River as far north as Palo Pinto County, where most of the records have been reported. They are not often seen and may even be considered erratic wanderers, yet they seem to be permanent residents wherever they have been seen.

All of the county records known to me are: *Bosque* — Oberholser (1974) indicates a breeding record, but I have been unable to confirm this vague record. No other reports. *Dallas* — I have seen this species twice in cedar brakes in the southwestern part of the county, on 29 July and 2 August 1962. Since no habitat is left in the county it is not to be expected again. *Hood* — 21 March 1965 and 24 April 1977. *Palo Pinto* — numerous records. Seen on six CBCs. No records for February, August, or September; reported 11 March 1972 to 28 June 1974 and an isolated date of 4 July 1974, and 16 October 1976 to 2 January 1970. One was reported building a nest at Possum Kingdom Lake on 24 March 1963, but the report was not confirmed. *Somervell* — 4 May 1974. *Eastland* — 24 April 1974.
Specimens: The only specimen known to me for north central Texas is one collected on 9 December 1986 (WMP) for Palo Pinto County.

Family Sittidae (Nuthatches)

Red-breasted Nuthatch   *Sitta canadensis* Linnaeus
Status: Fairly common to rare transient and winter visitor; irregular; may be absent some winters.
Occurrence: Red-breasted Nuthatches have been recorded in 20 counties in the study area — Archer, Bosque, Collin, Cooke, Dallas, Denton, Fannin, Grayson, Hill, Hood, Hunt, Johnson, Kaufman, Navarro, Palo Pinto,

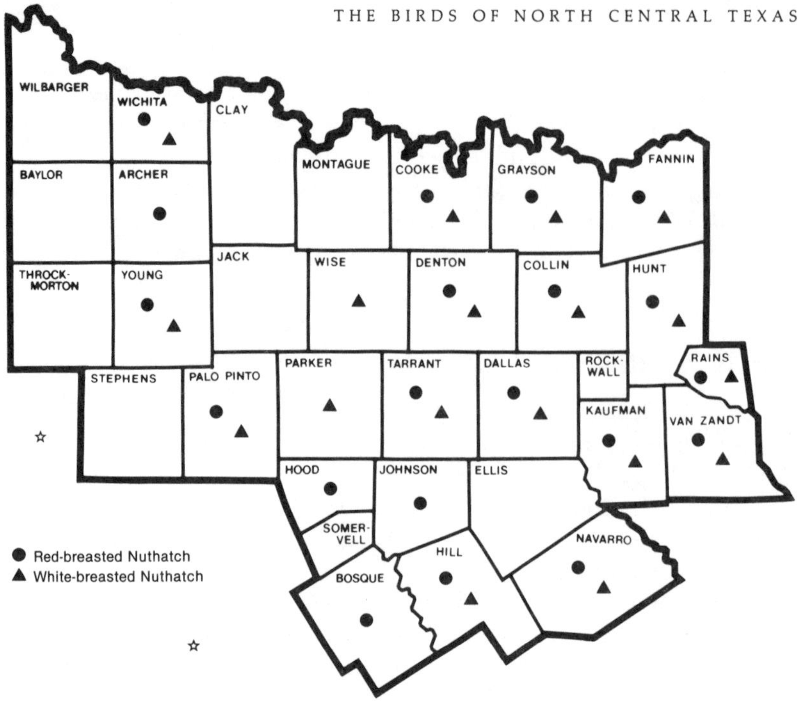

Map 70. Distribution of the Red-breasted Nuthatch, *Sitta canadensis*, and the White-breasted Nuthatch, *S. carolinensis*

Rains, Tarrant, Van Zandt, Wichita, and Young — and nearby Comanche and Shackelford counties.

This northern species does not visit north central Texas every year. In some years when they do arrive, they are very rare, and in other years there seem to be massive invasions of these little birds.

This species is usually found in the winter, but extreme dates for several counties where there are many sightings show that it can be expected from late September to April. Dates are given for three counties that are applicable to adjacent counties: *Dallas* — 2 September 1959, next-earliest 25 September 1963 and 1965, to 29 April 1961; *Tarrant* — 21 September 1977 to 9 May 1971; *Wichita* — 20 September 1975 (nearby Archer County) to 18 April 1976.

Many sightings of Red-breasted Nuthatches are observations of visitors at feeders, where they tend to take up temporary residence for handouts of nutmeats, sunflower seeds, and peanut butter. Usually only one or two can be found at a feeder, but in the winter of 1975–76, five to eight nuthatches visited a feeder daily in Fort Worth, Tarrant County. The largest number counted on any CBC for the area was 15 in Fort Worth on 2 January 1966. They are much more difficult to locate in forests because food is not as plentiful at any one place or as dependable as food supplied by humans. A forest may have only one or two nuthatches that have wandered in to search for food and may easily be missed by birders. If one has a keen ear and knows their distinctive call notes, however, one can readily locate them.

Specimens: Only four specimens are known from north central Texas, from Cooke (CC), Dallas (DMNH, WMP), and Denton (DMNH) counties.

WHITE-BREASTED NUTHATCH   *Sitta carolinensis* Latham

Status: Formerly considered an uncommon permanent resident; now an extremely rare winter visitor. Nesting limited to the Red River and the southeastern part of the study area.

Occurrence: White-breasted Nuthatches have been recorded in 18 counties in north central Texas: Collin, Cooke, Dallas, Denton, Fannin, Grayson, Hill, Hunt, Kaufman, Navarro, Palo Pinto, Parker, Rains, Tarrant, Van Zandt, Wichita, Wise and Young.

Today this species is rare throughout the study area, being seen mainly in winter periods in locales where mature oak woods fulfill their requisites. Oberholser (1974) records the species in ten counties, and I have recorded it in 13 counties, duplicating some of his counties. Many of the present-day records represent wandering transients, and there may be only one sighting for some of the counties.

White-breasted Nuthatches have been recorded on all of the CBCs in north central Texas from 1976 to 1986. They have not been recorded on every count, and seldom were there more than two or three reports on any particular count. However, Grayson and Fannin counties had five reports each. The largest numbers recorded were seven in 1976 for Tarrant County and six in 1980 for Dallas County.

Nesting: Although the earlier records indicated that this nuthatch was a permanent resident and that it bred in Cooke and Dallas counties (Oberholser, 1974), there have been no recent nesting records in these areas. It may have been more abundant at that time than it is today, but even then probably only locally. Today much of the limited habitat in these areas, especially in the Dallas–Fort Worth area, has been destroyed by urban progress, eliminating a regular occurrence of the species as a nesting bird and reducing it to the status of a winter transient or visitor that does not appear every year.

The species is still commonly found along the Red River and in the southeastern part of the study area. On the Red River in Wichita County the only place where it is found regularly is the Perkins Boy Scout Camp. In the spring and early summer of 1985 it was found in Tarrant County. Other counties in which it was sighted during nesting periods (May) in 1973–87 are Grayson, Kaufman, Hunt, and Van Zandt counties. These

A.P.

sightings actually represented young being fed out of the nest or at the nest hole by the parents.

Specimens: The only specimens of this nuthatch that could be located were from Dallas (DMNH), Denton (DMNH), and Grayson (KH) counties. Oberholser (1974) indicated that specimens were collected from Collin, Cooke, and Navarro counties, but they could not be located. Oberholser lists two subspecies for north central Texas, *S. c. carolinensis* and *S. c. cookei.* The latter is said to be the subspecies breeding in Cooke County. Two specimens (DMNH) from Denton County have also been identified as *cookei.* Sutton (1967) discusses the occurrence of these two races in Oklahoma and implies that most of the specimens there are intermediates between these two races. It is possible that more specimens and a thorough study of the White-breasted Nuthatch would produce results similar to the findings reported by Sutton.

Pygmy Nuthatch   *Sitta pygmaea* Vigors
Status: Accidental.
Occurrence: This little nuthatch has been found only once in north central Texas: one was collected in a typical post-oak–blackjack-oak habitat at Irving, Dallas County, on 31 December 1966 (WMP 1537). This western species resembles the Brown-headed Nuthatch (*Sitta pusilla*), which

ranges in the pine forests of east Texas. The latter species has never been properly documented for the north central Texas area, although it is more likely to occur along the eastern side of the study area than is the Pygmy Nuthatch.

Pygmy Nuthatches are similar to Brown-headed Nuthatches except for their black caps, which set them apart from the latter species. Some authorities consider the two species conspecific and thus simply two races.

Family Certhiidae (Creeper)

BROWN CREEPER *Certhia americana* Bonaparte
Status: Fairly common winter visitor.
Occurrence: The Brown Creeper has been reported in all but three counties of the study area: Baylor, Clay, and Throckmorton. No doubt it will be recorded in those counties as well, when more birding is done there.

This rather wary, secretive, tree-climbing little bird is usually found in north central Texas from late October through early April. Extreme dates for selected counties are: *Collin* — 18 October 1980 through 10 April 1983; *Dallas* — 25 September 1980 through 23 April 1956; *Grayson* — an extremely early date, 12 September 1986, next 16 September through 19 April; *Tarrant* — 4 October 1975 through 25 April 1983, and an exceptionally late isolated date, 5 May 1979; *Wichita* — 1 October 1975 through 6 April 1977.

This species has been observed on all of the CBCs and usually every year, though it may occasionally be missed. On these counts it seems to be more numerous toward the southeastern part of the study area, in the Dallas–Fort Worth area. If one tramps the woods, only one or two will be found, and an observer who cannot hear high notes will miss this rather inconspicuous brown bird. The largest number reported on any one count was 108 on 15 December 1979 for Dallas County. On 20 CBCs (1958–77) from Tarrant County the average number was 34, with a minimum of nine (1971) and a maximum of 92 (1963). Occasionally transients may be seen in loose flocks. On 6 March 1880, Ogilby (1882) recorded in Navarro County more than 20 Brown Creepers unaccompanied by any species with which it normally associates. On 16 February 1974, ten creepers were tallied in Collin County.

The characteristic feeding habits of this bird are worth mentioning, even though they are well known to most people. It usually starts low on the trunk of a tree, spiraling upward, foraging as it proceeds. When it reaches an appropriate level, usually fairly high, it drops off downward much like a falling leaf. Only when it swoops to another nearby low tree trunk does the observer realize that it is a creeper.
Specimens: Brown Creeper specimens are known from Collin (DMNH), Dallas (DMNH, WMP), Denton (DMNH), Ellis (DMNH), Hunt (FWMSH),

Jack (DMNH), Johnson (DMNH), Kaufman (DMNH), Tarrant (FWMSH, WMP), and Wichita (MWU) counties. Those indicated by Oberholser (1974) for Cooke and Wise counties could not be located.

Specimens in my collection for Dallas and Tarrant counties represent the nominate race *C. a. americana*. A specimen taken on 19 February 1981 (WMP 2714) in Tarrant County represents *C. a. interior,* a race from Alaska not recognized by the AOU (1957).

Family Troglodytidae (Wrens)

CACTUS WREN   *Campylorhynchus brunneicapillus* (Lafresnaye)
Status: Rare summer resident. Recent invader to the western part of the study area.
Occurrence: This southwestern wren is normally found to the south (Austin) and west (around Lubbock) of the study area. Oberholser (1974) cited this species as a "casual visitor (non-breeder)" in Young County, but on his map he questions its occurrence there. The Cactus Wren is a recent invader of the area, and except for this one reference by Oberholser, all of the records of this species are from the late 1970s on. Its loud, harsh call is very distinctive and can often be heard before the bird is seen. It sings, or at least calls, the year round. It appears to be moving northward in the study area, where it has been recorded in seven counties, as well as in four adjacent counties.

Records from the study area and adjacent counties are: *Dallas* — Duncanville, 27 July 1977, brief sighting by a competent observer; *Palo Pinto* — nest that appeared to be of this species found near Graford on 29 May 1983 (no birds observed); 4 December 1983, first bird recorded for the county; *Stephens* — I noted an old nest on 6 September 1984, and heard what was possibly a wren on 8 October 1984; *Tarrant* — first seen at Crowley on 28 March 1982 by lone observer; may have been seen there previously but not reported; *Throckmorton* — 10 May 1983, north of Throckmorton, nest only, and again on 17 May 1983 in the southwestern part of the county on the Clear Fork of the Brazos River; four birds were seen on 25 August 1983 at the 10 May location, and old nests were seen on 22 and 23 May 1984 at the Clear Fork location; *Wichita* — southwest of Iowa Park on 11 and 23 April 1973, at nest seen by numerous observers; *Young* — see above for questionable record, probably in late 1880s; 27 June 1981 on BBS, one reported; southwest of Newcastle on 28 April 1983, two nests with five eggs each; 5 June 1983 on BBS, four reported; *Eastland* — two seen by two observers on 10 August 1983; *Erath* — 1 November 1986; *Haskell* — 8 and 9 September 1979; *Shackelford* — near Albany on 29 April 1983; on BBSs 11 birds tallied on 4 June 1983, 12 on 17 June 1984, and four on 16 June 1985.

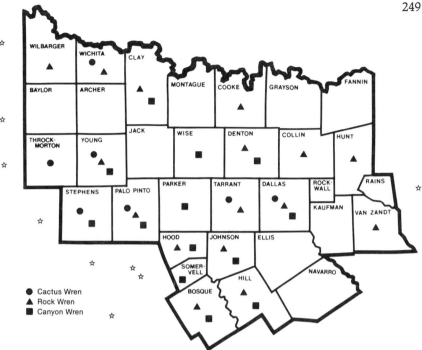

Map 71. Distribution of the Cactus Wren, *Campylorynchus brunneicapillus;* the Rock Wren, *Salpinctes obsoletus;* and the Canyon Wren, *Catherpes mexicanus*

Specimens: A young bird was collected on 25 August 1983 (WMP 2866) from the group of four birds reported in Throckmorton County.

ROCK WREN   *Salpinctes obsoletus* (Say)

Status: Rare winter visitor scattered throughout the study area. Said to have nested at one time.

Occurrence: Oberholser (1974) reported Rock Wrens from Dallas, Denton, Wichita, Wilbarger, and Young counties and adjacent Eastland, Hardeman, and Knox counties. This study adds Bosque, Clay, Collin, Cooke, Hill, Hood, Hunt, Johnson, Palo Pinto, Tarrant, and Van Zandt counties and nearby Comanche and Wood counties. As its name implies this species inhabits rocky outcrops and desolate cliffs. However, in the eastern parts of the study area, the rock riprap of dams now provides suitable winter habitat for Rock Wrens.

Recent county records are: *Bosque* — 15 November 1983; *Clay* — near Lake Arrowhead dam, 27 October 1974 and 23 March and 3 April 1975; *Collin* — 8 February 1976; *Cooke* — extremely late date, unconfirmed but said to have been seen by two persons on 18 May 1970; *Dallas* — 21 October 1938 (Stillwell, 1939); the 16 June 1972 date (Williams, 1972) is unusual, and no details are available; considered hypothetical in the Dallas checklist (1979), it is deleted here as a misidentification; *Denton* — 21 October 1956 through 1 January 1957; *Hill* — irregular visitor, Lake Whitney State Recreation Area (1976), no other details given (area has numerous rocky outcroppings); *Hood* — during snowstorm, 8 February 1980; *Hunt* — City Lake Dam, near Greenville, 8 February 1976 and 16 November 1977; *Johnson* — Cleburne, 17 December 1978; *Palo Pinto* — other records besides the nesting records in the paragraph above, 29 December 1973, 29 December 1978, 7 and 31 December 1979, 28 March 1980, 4 December 1983, and 23 November 1984; *Tarrant* —Trinity River riprap, Fort Worth, 24 October 1982 through 30 March 1983; *Van Zandt* — 24 October 1975, 6 and 7 October 1985, 19 October and 14 November 1986, and 3 January 1987. There are no records for Wichita, Wilbarger, and Young counties other than those indicated by Oberholser (1974).

Nesting: Oberholser (1974) cites nesting for Wilbarger, Wichita, and Eastland counties and a summer sighting for Young County. Today the only suspected records of nesting have been from Palo Pinto County. Four birds were noted below Possum Kingdom Dam in rocky riprap on 3 April 1982. The birds were catching insects and carrying food up the slope. The following year they were noted again on 9 April 1983, having been seen there before that date on nearly every visit to the area. As far as can be determined, however, nest, eggs, and young were never observed.

Specimens: There are no known specimens of Rock Wrens for north central Texas. The specimen catalog at the Dallas Museum of Natural History lists one (DMNH 140) collected in Dallas County on 2 February 1936 and adds the notation that the specimen was "destroyed."

CANYON WREN *Catherpes mexicanus* (Swainson)
Status: Uncommon local resident along the western part of the study area. Also occasional fall visitor farther east.

Occurrence: Canyon Wrens have been found in 13 counties of north central Texas — Bosque, Clay, Dallas, Denton, Hill, Hood, Johnson, Palo Pinto, Parker, Somervell, Stephens, Wise, and Young — and adjacent Comanche, Eastland, and Erath counties. They are very localized, being found where rocky canyons provide secluded habitats. They are often found along canyon bluffs and outcrops of the Brazos River drainage that extends from the Edwards Plateau proper. Occasionally they take up residency in outlying ranch buildings. They are permanent residents in most of the counties and can usually be found the year round, although I have no June records. However, other than during the breeding season, when they sing, they may be difficult to find because of their secretive habits. The records for Dallas County on 13 August 1962 and for Denton County in October (Rylander, 1959) are of wandering fall birds. However, unlike the records for the Rock Wren, the records for the Canyon Wren are not scattered throughout the study area but are mainly confined to the western part of the north central Texas study area.

Nesting: Breeding activities were observed on 7 May 1977 (Palo Pinto County), when adult birds were seen carrying food into a rock crevice, and on 20 May 1979 (Bosque County), when a nest was found with at least three young. In comparing the current range of this species with old records, it is evident that today the Canyon Wren occupies about the same range that it has in the past.

Specimens: The only reference to specimens from the study area is one said to have been taken in Stephens County (Oberholser, 1974); it could not be located, however.

CAROLINA WREN   *Thryothorus ludovicianus* (Latham)

Status: Fairly common to uncommon over much of north central Texas, though rare in the western and northwestern parts of the study area, where it is limited to localized riparian habitat.

Occurrence: Carolina Wrens have been reported in all but two counties — Baylor and Stephens — in the study area. This species is considered a permanent resident throughout the area, although it is not as widespread since its habitat requirements limit it to dense wooded areas along creeks and rivers. It is more common along the Red River and in the eastern and southeastern parts of the study area.

In some locales one finds both this species and Bewick's Wren, yet there apparently is not direct competition since the two species have different niche requirements. They have not been observed competing for nest sites. In several areas in Wise and Parker counties I have found this wren with Canyon Wrens, but again I do not believe that there is direct competition.

In the 1980s there are indications over much of the north central Texas study area that the Carolina Wren population is down from that of former years. A thorough study should be undertaken to determine whether or not this is true.

Nesting: Although Oberholser (1974) shows the Carolina Wren nesting as far west as Wise County, it is assumed to nest in all of the counties in which it has been reported. Most nesting data come from the Dallas–Fort Worth area. Nesting dates for Dallas County range from 10 February 1983 (building nest) to 2 August 1974 (second brood fledged). There is an extremely late date of three Carolina Wrens fledging on 14 September 1986 in south Dallas. In Tarrant County nesting extends from late March to 1 June, when young still in the nest were banded on the latter date in 1955. In the same county a Carolina Wren was observed feeding a fledgling cowbird on 11 July 1951. This wren appears to be persistent in its nesting habits. An observer reported that a pair near Quinlan, Hunt County, had their fourth nest on 20 May 1985, after their earlier nests had fallen down or been destroyed.

Specimens: Carolina Wren specimens are available from the following counties: Cooke (TNHC), Dallas (DMNH, OU, WMP), Denton (DMNH), Ellis (DMNH), Hill (KU), Hood (FWMSH), Hunt (FWMSH), Kaufman (DMNH), Navarro (USNM), Tarrant (DMNH), and adjacent Henderson County (DMNH). Specimens indicated by Oberholser (1974) for Collin County could not be located.

BEWICK'S WREN   *Thryomanes bewickii* (Audubon)
Status: Fairly common to common throughout north central Texas.
Occurrence: Bewick's Wrens have been reported in all of the study area counties and many adjacent ones. Although they are seen year round in many counties, there are few or no records in the eastern counties from late May through July.

This wren's numbers appear to be the same throughout the year, yet at times there seem to be a few more in the spring than in the winter. This may be due to its active song period, from late February through July, which may make it more conspicuous. It has, however, been recorded on all of the CBCs and is seldom missed on any counts.

Like all other members of this family, the Bewick's Wren is busy and constantly moving over its territory. It comes readily to investigate squeaking sounds, fussing and calling at observers. In spring it can very often be found perched in full view at the top of a tree, singing from some conspicuous perch.

Nesting: During the course of this study Bewick's Wrens were found nesting in 19 north central Texas counties — Bosque, Clay, Cooke, Dallas, Denton, Grayson, Hill, Hood, Johnson, Navarro, Palo Pinto, Parker, Somervell, Tarrant, Throckmorton, Wichita, Wilbarger, Wise, and Young — and adjacent Eastland County. It is likely that they nest in all the other counties of the study area. Although Oberholser (1974) gives summer records for Hunt County, I have no evidence to support nesting there. It is possible that the local checklist (Tarter, 1940) was the basis for this record. It states without qualification that the Bewick's Wren was a "resident" of the county. There is no reference to actual nests or young. Unfortunately, there are a number of errors in this local county list.

Nesting starts in February (Dallas County, 17 February 1981), and although it usually is complete by the end of June, an occasional pair may still be carrying on nesting activities in July (Tarrant County, 20 July 1974, fledglings). Many are two-brooded. The placement of this wren's nests seems more widespread than those of the Carolina Wren.

Specimens: Bewick's Wrens have been taken in the following counties: Bosque (DMNH, WMP), Cooke (TNHC, USNM), Dallas (DMNH, UTA,

A.P.

WMP), Denton (DMNH, USNM), Ellis (DMNH), Jack (DMNH), Johnson (DMNH), Kaufman (DMNH), Navarro (WMP), Parker (FWMSH), Tarrant (DMNH, FWMSH, UTA, WMP), Wichita (MWU), and Young (DMNH). Oberholser (1974) indicated that there was a specimen for Palo Pinto County, but it was not located.

According to Oberholser (1974), examples of both the nominate race *T. b. bewickii* and *T. b. cryptus* have been taken in north central Texas. He also indicates that *cryptus* is the breeding race of the area. After studying recent Bewick's Wren material in my collection, however, I am convinced that more specimens must be collected and examined from north central Texas and the specimens studied by Oberholser scrutinized again before subspecific lines can be delineated accurately.

HOUSE WREN   *Troglodytes aedon* Vieillot
Status: Fairly common to common transient. Rare to fairly common winter resident.
Occurrence: House Wrens have been recorded in 24 counties of the study area — Bosque, Collin, Cooke, Dallas, Denton, Ellis, Fannin, Grayson, Hill, Hunt, Kaufman, Montague, Navarro, Palo Pinto, Parker, Rains, Rockwall, Somervell, Stephens, Tarrant, Van Zandt, Wichita, Wise, and Young — and nearby Shackelford County.

This wren is a fairly common transient; however, the casual bird-watcher may mistake the Bewick's Wren for it if care is not exercised in distinguishing the two species. Since the Bewick's Wren sometimes nests in bird boxes and some persons call it the "House Wren," the reports of nesting House Wrens given by Stillwell (1939) and Oberholser (1974) are suspected of being in error. Until young or eggs of the House Wren are actually re-

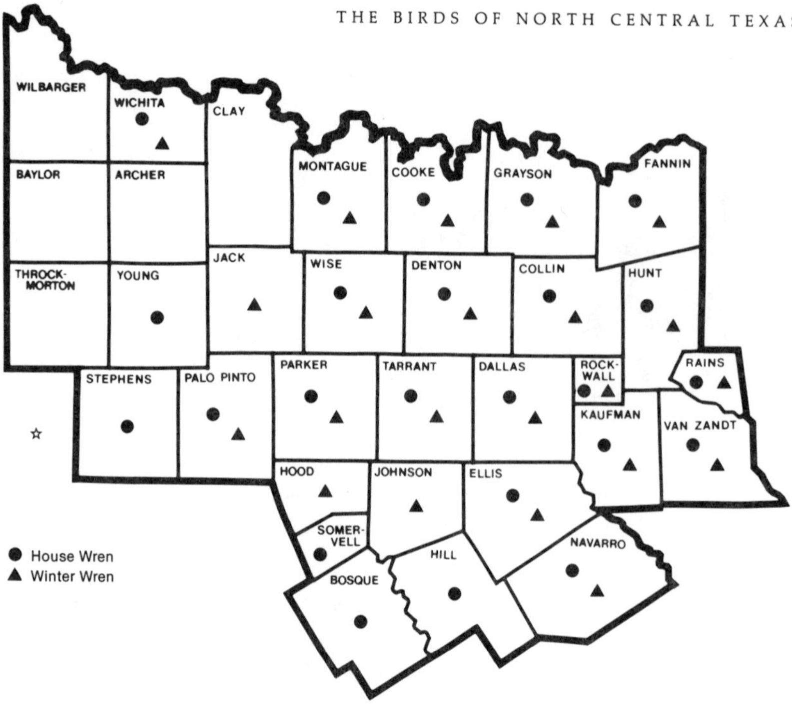

Map 72. Distribution of the House Wren, *Troglodytes aedon,* and the Winter Wren, *T. troglodytes*

corded, it should not be considered a nesting species in north central Texas. This is also true of Wichita County, where it is said to have been seen in June and mid-July, and of Collin County, where it was reported in early July. None of these records was confirmed, and no nests, eggs, or young have been reported. Brown (1985) points out that the southernmost record of successful nesting House Wrens for Oklahoma was in Duncan, Stephens County (less than 50 miles northeast of Wichita Falls, Wichita County), where nestlings were observed on 9 June 1985.

This species has been reported on all of the CBCs in the study area, but not regularly and never in large numbers. It is much more abundant during migration than during the winter period. In winter it is absent from many areas of north central Texas. Its passage through the area ranges from September through mid-May. Extreme county dates are: *Collin* — 7 September 1982 (banded) to 15 May 1983; *Dallas* — 9 September 1974 to an isolated date, 31 May 1980, next-latest 20 May 1981; *Grayson* — 8 September to 5 November, and 29 November, 11 and 15 December, and 3 April to 16 May; *Tarrant* — 1 September 1976 to 17 May 1953; *Van Zandt* — 16 September 1984 to 7 May 1983 (Hunt County); *Wichita* — 16 September 1975 to 15 May 1976.

Specimens: House Wren specimens have been collected from the following counties: Cooke (TNHC), Dallas (DMNH, OU, WMP), Denton (DMNH, WMP), Ellis (DMNH), Kaufman (DMNH), Navarro (USNM), Tarrant (DMNH, FWMSH, UTA, WMP), and Wichita (MWU). The specimens examined from Tarrant County represent all three races — *aedon, baldwini,* and *parkmanii.* Most of the specimens are *parkmanii,* taken in September and October.

WINTER WREN   *Troglodytes troglodytes* (Linnaeus)
Status: Rare to uncommon winter resident.
Occurrence: Winter Wrens have been reported in 22 counties in the study area — Collin, Cooke, Dallas, Denton, Ellis, Fannin, Grayson, Hood, Hunt, Jack, Johnson, Kaufman, Montague, Navarro, Palo Pinto, Parker, Rains, Rockwall, Tarrant, Van Zandt, Wichita, and Wise — and nearby Shackelford County.

This tiny wren is seen only seldom, and then for no more than a minute or two in thick tangles and brush near the ground. Usually no more than one or, rarely, two are glimpsed; it is extremely nervous as it moves through the undergrowth.

Most dates at hand are primarily for winter, but Winter Wrens have been reported from early October to early May. Extreme dates for the three following counties, where much birding takes place, are typical of the other counties as well: *Dallas* — 1 October 1934 (Stillwell, 1939) to 2 May 1977, 1984; *Grayson* — extremely early 22 September 1979, next-earliest 14 October to 22 April; *Tarrant* — 8 October 1950 to 1 May 1977.
Specimens: Winter Wren specimens have been collected from the following counties: Cooke (USNM), Dallas (DMNH, WMP), Denton (DMNH), Hunt (FWMSH), Jack (DMNH), Johnson (DMNH), Kaufman (DMNH), Tarrant (FWMSH, WMP), and Wichita (WMP). Specimens of *T. t. hiemalis* have been taken in Dallas, Tarrant, and Wichita counties, while *T. t. pullus* is represented from Dallas and Kaufman counties. Unfortunately, the sample size of specimens was small, and since the species may have more distinct taxonomic populations than many persons are aware of, more study should be given to this species (*fide* Amadeo Rea).

SEDGE WREN   *Cistothorus platensis* (Latham)
Status: Rare to uncommon transient. Localized in winter in a few counties.
Occurrence: Sedge Wrens are not as widespread or abundant as Marsh Wrens. Although they are found in marshes, their niche requirements are typically sedges and water-loving grasses, which may explain why they are less common than Marsh Wrens, since this type of marsh is rather scarce in north central Texas. Oberholser (1974) recorded this species in only six counties: Dallas, Ellis, Grayson, Hunt, Navarro, and Tarrant. To these counties I have added Collin, Denton, Kaufman, Palo Pinto, and Van Zandt.

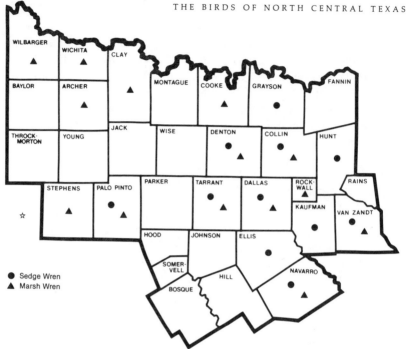

Map 73. Distribution of the Sedge Wren, *Cistothorus platensis,* and the Marsh Wren, *C. palustris*

Thus Sedge Wrens have been recorded in only 11 counties of north central Texas. Their secretive nature makes them difficult to find. They are much more retiring than Marsh Wrens.

Like Marsh Wrens, Sedge Wrens are more often seen in migration than during the winter, but in several counties, particularly Denton, they are usually seen in the winter. Counties and dates for which there are suffi-cient data are: *Dallas* — surprisingly, not reported by Stillwell (1939), prob-ably overlooked. The first date for the county is 7 October 1978, 1982, to 7 May 1961 (specimen). *Grayson* — 24 September 1981 to 15 December, and 24 April to 3 May. *Palo Pinto* — 7 October 1979 to 19 March 1978 (not seen every month). *Tarrant* — 24 September 1964 to 10 May 1986. *Van Zandt* — 22 September 1982 to 3 May 1984; May winter in the county. *Specimens:* Sedge Wren specimens are available from Dallas (WMP) and Ellis (DMNH) counties.

Marsh Wren   *Cistothorus palustris* (Wilson)
Status: Rare to uncommon transient and local winter resident. No posi-tive nesting records for north central Texas.
Occurrence: Oberholser (1974) records the Marsh Wren in Collin, Dallas,

Denton, Tarrant, Van Zandt, and Wilbarger counties. Marsh Wrens are still reported in all of the counties listed above except Wilbarger and also in Archer, Clay, Grayson, Navarro, Palo Pinto, Rockwall, Stephens, and Wichita counties and adjacent Shackelford County.

Although Oberholser (1974) indicated that the Marsh Wren bred in north central Texas, there is little evidence to support this claim. Except for one reference by More and Strecker (1929) to "a completed nest but no eggs" on 20 May, no young or eggs have been found in Wilbarger County. In the 1920s the only area that might have supported nesting Marsh Wrens was Watt's Lake, a 40-acre marsh north of Vernon. It was drained many years ago, and today the area is a shortgrass pasture. It is highly improbable that Marsh Wrens ever nested in Wilbarger County or any other part of north central Texas. Sutton (1974) listed no breeding records of Marsh Wrens for Oklahoma.

The Marsh Wren prefers marshy areas with dense stands of cattails and bulrushes, though in migration it may be found in weedy areas atypical of marshes. It has been recorded from late September to early May in a number of the counties listed above, though in some counties the records are not numerous. Counties for which there are sufficient data are: *Dallas* — 29 September 1959 to 3 May 1980. In recent years they are more often reported as transients than as winter residents. Much of their winter habitat has been lost. *Grayson* — 21 September 1979 to 4 May 1975. *Palo Pinto* — 22 September 1978 to 2 April 1977. *Tarrant* — 24 September 1964 to 11 May 1968. *Wichita* — 29 September 1976 to 8 April 1978. Although the local checklist indicates that the species is present in proper habitat the year round, there are no data to support this assumption. It was probably on the old report of alleged nesting in nearby Wilbarger County (More and Strecker, 1929).

Specimens: Marsh Wren specimens are available for Dallas (DMNH, WMP), Denton (DMNH), and Tarrant (FWMSH) counties. An example for Collin County (Oberholser, 1974) was not located.

Races of Marsh Wrens in my collection, all from Dallas County, represent *C. p. dissaeptus* (WMP 630), *C. p. iliacus/laingi* (WMP 813), *C. p. laingi* × *plesius* (WMP 1937), and *C. p. pulverius* (WMP 2170); a species from Tarrant County (FWMSH 211) was also identified as *pulverius*. The last race is not recognized and would be included in *plesius*. The specimens from Dallas and Denton counties (DMNH) were said by Oberholser to be *C. p. iliacus;* they have not been reexamined for race.

Family Muscicapidae (Thrushes and Allies)

GOLDEN-CROWNED KINGLET   *Regulus satrapa* Lichtenstein
Status: Uncommon to fairly common winter resident.

Occurrence: Golden-crowned Kinglets have been reported in all counties of north central Texas except Baylor, Clay, Jack, Stephens, and Throckmorton. They would probably be reported in those counties as well if more observers birded throughout the study area. They have also been reported in adjacent Shackelford County.

The Golden-crowned Kinglet forages in forests or edges in small numbers of its own kind or with "troops" of other small birds. Seldom is it alone. Like its near relative, the Ruby-crowned Kinglet, below, it is constantly moving and nervously flicking its wings. Its head marking, a white eye stripe sharply bordering a black stripe above, distinguishes this species from the ruby-crown, which has an eye-ring.

This species usually arrives later and leaves earlier than the Ruby-crowned Kinglet, and in some years it is very difficult to find. It has been found on all the annual CBCs of the area, although during years when it is scarce it may not be tallied. It is not usually as abundant as the Ruby-crowned Kinglet, but at times during fall migration it may outnumber the ruby-crown as a transient.

Golden-crowns usually arrive near the end of October and depart by early April. Extreme arrival and departure dates for selected counties are: *Collin* — 18 October 1980 to 1 April 1982. *Dallas* — Stillwell (1939) gave sightings from 4 October to 19 April, while more recent data give 12 October 1980 to 2 April 1960, 1975. *Grayson* — 10 October to 24 April. *Tarrant* — 14 September 1946, and two isolated dates, 1 May 1965 and 4 and 5 May 1974 (Pulich, 1979), were rechecked and reevaluated. These are now considered unacceptable and have been deleted. Earliest and latest dates are 16 October 1943 and 4 April 1956. *Wichita* — 19 October 1980 (TV-tower-kill specimen) to 17 April 1975.

Specimens: Specimens have been located for Dallas (DMNH, WMP), Denton (DMNH), Johnson (DMNH), Parker (FWMSH), Tarrant (FWMSH), Wichita (WMP), and Wilbarger (TCWC) counties. Specimens indicated by Oberholser (1974) for Cooke and Wise counties could not be located. Those examined from Dallas, Tarrant, and Wichita counties represent the nominate race *R. s. satrapa.*

RUBY-CROWNED KINGLET   *Regulus calendula* (Linnaeus)
Status: Common winter resident. Common to abundant transient.
Occurrence: The Ruby-crowned Kinglet has been reported in all of the counties of north central Texas except Baylor and Jack, and there is little doubt that it also occurs in those counties as well. It has also been recorded in nearby Delta, Eastland, Lamar, and Shackelford counties.

This species occurs in a variety of habitats. It is an extremely active little bird, spending its time in constant motion catching tiny insects, alone or in the company of other small birds. It is often mistaken for a warbler by observers unfamiliar with the species. It usually arrives before its near relative, the Golden-crowned Kinglet, and stays longer. It has been reported on all of the CBCs in north central Texas in most years. It is more abundant along the eastern parts of the study area than in the western parts in the winter, at times becoming extremely common. In late April or May it is often heard singing quite a beautiful song for such a tiny bird.

Extreme arrival and departure dates for selected counties are: *Collin* — 18 September 1982 to 7 May 1980 (all banded birds); *Dallas* — an isolated date, 24 August 1980, next-earliest 3 September 1974 (mean 12 September, 15 years) to 26 May 1971 (mean 8 May, 17 years); *Grayson* — 3 September to 27 May 1972 and an isolated date, 30 May 1971; *Hood* — 7 September 1979 to 29 April 1973; *Palo Pinto* — 10 October 1976 to 3 May 1956; *Tarrant* — an isolated date, 28 August 1978, next-earliest 2 September 1981 (mean 13 September, ten years) to 2 June 1963; *Van Zandt* — 2 September 1985 (Rains County) to 7 May 1986; *Wichita* — 9 September to 11 May. *Specimens:* Specimens have been found from the following counties: Dallas (DMNH, WMP), Denton (DMNH), Ellis (DMNH), Fannin (WMP), Hunt (FWMSH), Johnson (DMNH, SUC), Kaufman (DMNH), Palo Pinto (DMNH, FWMSH), Parker (FWMSH), Somervell (FWMSH), Tarrant (DMNH, FWMSH, UTA), and Wichita (WMP). Specimens indicated by Oberholser (1974) for Cooke and Wise counties could not be located. Although not all have been racially examined, those for Dallas, Tarrant, and Wichita counties represent the eastern race *R. c. calendula*.

BLUE-GRAY GNATCATCHER   *Polioptila caerulea* (Linnaeus)
Status: Fairly common to common migrant. Uncommon during summer and irregular in winter.
Occurrence: Blue-gray Gnatcatchers have been reported in all counties of the study area except Throckmorton County. They are usually found from mid-March to early October. A few stragglers linger in the area in winter, though not every year. Where there is much birding they have been reported every month, though there are few reports for January and February. They often accompany kinglets, vireos, particularly Solitary Vireos, and several species of the commoner warblers. Occasionally as many as 20 birds have been observed in early May and October migration.

Extreme arrival and departure dates for selected counties are: *Dallas* — 13 March 1971 to 23 November 1978 (seen irregularly every month), and winter records for 27 December 1958, 25 January 1959, 31 December 1966, 12 December 1970, 4 December 1984 (one), and 20 December 1984 (six); *Grayson* — 8 March 1977 to 10 November 1979, and one winter or early-spring date, 14 February 1976; *Palo Pinto* — 20 March 1972 to 26 September 1978, and isolated dates 2 January 1971 and 1986; *Rains* — 18 March 1984 to 25 November 1984, and 16 December 1984; *Tarrant* — 14 March

1959 (mean 23 March, seven years, 1972–78) to 16 November 1974, next 1 November 1981, and winter records for 2 December 1981, 15 December 1973, 25 January 1980, 2 February 1965, and 27 February 1983; *Wichita* — 28 March 1970 to 8 November 1976 (observed several times every month but not every year).

Nesting: From mid-April through August, Blue-gray Gnatcatchers can be found in suitable nesting habitat, preferably in drier areas. Nests or young have been reported in Archer, Bosque, Collin, Cooke, Dallas, Denton, Grayson, Hood, Hunt, Jack, Navarro, Palo Pinto, Rockwall, Tarrant, Wichita, Wilbarger, Wise, and Young counties. Most nesting activity is in April with extreme dates from 28 March 1977 (building nest, Hood County) to the latest, 29 July 1982 (feeding young in nest, Grayson County).

Specimens: Blue-gray Gnatcatchers have been collected from Cooke (TNHC), Dallas (DMNH), Denton (DMNH), Ellis (DMNH), Hood (DMNH), Kaufman (DMNH), Palo Pinto (DMNH), and Tarrant (DMNH, FWMSH) counties. Specimens said to have been taken from Wilbarger County (Oberholser, 1974) were not located. Although not all specimens were examined for race, those from Tarrant and Dallas counties represent examples of the nominate race *P. c. caerulea*.

EASTERN BLUEBIRD   *Sialia sialis* (Linnaeus)
Status: Fairly common to common resident the year round in wooded areas. Localized in many areas, especially in the western counties of the study area.

Occurrence: The Eastern Bluebird has been recorded in all of the counties of north central Texas as well as the nearby counties. Wherever woodlands exist, one can find this species. It is widespread in fall and winter. In winter it is fairly common to see flocks of 20 to 30. Although the species is not wholly sedentary, it is found in more or less the same area throughout the year. It has disappeared from large cities and towns, but it can still be found in adjacent areas where there are open woods and forests.

Removal of old trees and clearing of the woodland habitat that favored bluebirds have reduced many natural nest sites. Readers who live in the country are urged to erect bird boxes to help this species. Eastern Bluebird populations have been restored by man where bluebird houses have been put up and maintained. For example, in Hunt County more than 100 bluebirds were banded in 1982 at birdhouses erected for them on a farm of fewer than 300 acres.

The European Starling and the House Sparrow compete with the bluebird in north central Texas. Winter weather may also have harmful effects on this species, even though bluebirds rear two and occasionally three broods of young. Severe spells of bad weather probably kill off some bluebirds, since populations do not move far from their summer residence.

Nesting: Like many other common species, specific data on nesting Eastern Bluebirds are lacking for many of the counties. Nesting has been recorded in only 23 counties in north central Texas: Bosque, Collin, Cooke, Dallas, Denton, Fannin, Grayson, Hill, Hunt, Jack, Johnson, Kaufman, Navarro, Palo Pinto, Parker, Rockwall, Somervell, Tarrant, Throckmorton, Van Zandt, Wichita, Wilbarger, and Wise. There is little doubt that they also nest in the remaining counties of the study area.

Extreme nesting dates taken from a five-year (1980–84) study of Eastern Bluebirds south of Quinlan, Hunt County, showed that the earliest egg was laid on 13 March 1984, with earliest hatching on 25 March 1983, while the latest young was fledged on 20 August 1983. Spot-breasted young have often been observed from late August into September in the Dallas–Fort Worth area and were reported on 21 September 1983 in nearby Van Zandt County. Although these data are applicable to the southeastern part of the study area, they would apply to all the counties in the area.

Specimens: Specimens of Eastern Bluebirds are available from Clay (MWU), Cooke (TNHC), Dallas (DMNH, WMP), Denton (DMNH), Ellis (DMNH), Fannin (WMP), Hill (UTA), Hunt (UTA, WMP), Johnson (SUC), Kaufman (DMNH), Tarrant (DMNH, WMP) counties and adjacent Henderson County (DMNH).

WESTERN BLUEBIRD *Sialia mexicana* Swainson
Status: Casual; observations only in winter.
Occurrence: Some sight records of the Western Bluebird for north central Texas are questionable. It is a bird of west Texas and can easily be confused with the Eastern Bluebird. Although Western Bluebirds were allegedly taken in fall and winter in Dallas County (Oberholser, 1974), there are no records of this species in the Dallas Museum of Natural History, where many earlier specimens were deposited. This is also true of a report of a July sighting in Denton County, which has been discounted. The only record, a February sighting, for Hunt County (Baumgartner, 1957) has also been deleted, since no details were given.

The remaining records indicate that the species has occurred in only three counties: *Cooke* — January 1876; *Palo Pinto* — five times in December CBCs, 1966 through 1973; *Tarrant* — four sight records, all for December, some of which are questionable.

Specimens: Specimens document the above Cooke County record (TNHC 1526) and the Palo Pinto County December record on 29 December 1973 (WMP 2029).

MOUNTAIN BLUEBIRD *Sialia currucoides* (Bechstein)
Status: Rare winter visitor.
Occurrence: Mountain Bluebirds have been reported in 14 counties in the

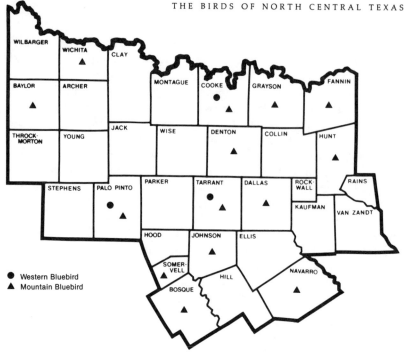

Map 74. Distribution of the Western Bluebird, *Sialia mexicana*, and the Mountain Bluebird, *S. currucoides*

study area—Baylor, Bosque, Cooke, Dallas, Denton, Fannin, Grayson, Hunt, Johnson, Navarro, Palo Pinto, Somervell, Tarrant, and Wichita—and adjacent Hardeman County.

This bluebird normally migrates south into west Texas from the Rocky Mountains. However, during severe winters it may move onto the Edwards Plateau south of the study area. From here it makes its way north to the study area as the food supply becomes depleted on the Edwards Plateau. It has been recorded from 4 November 1978 (Wichita County) to 18 March 1960 (Tarrant County).

Selected county dates are: *Dallas*—about ten times (1934–64), 4 November 1951 to 5 March 1939; *Grayson*—twice, 27 January 1977 and 14 February 1979; *Palo Pinto*—four times, 31 December 1965, 29 December 1971, 27 November 1976, and 28 December 1980; *Tarrant*—about 12 times (1951–77), 12 November 1977 to 18 March 1960.

Specimens: Mountain Bluebird specimens have been taken from the following counties: Cooke—22 November 1886 (TNHC 1529); Dallas—30 December 1934 and 10 January 1935 (Stillwell, 1939, on exhibit at DMNH) and 28 February 1960 (WMP 978); Johnson—22 February 1956 (DMNH 4950); and Somervell—22 February 1956 (DMNH 4946).

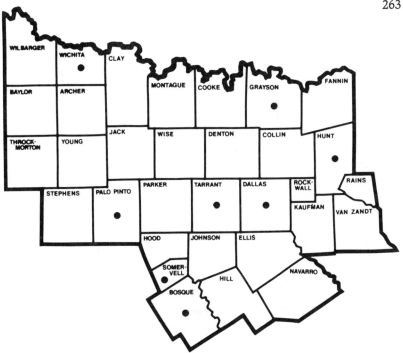

Map 75. Distribution of Townsend's Solitaire, *Myadestes townsendi*

Townsend's Solitaire *Myadestes townsendi* (Audubon)
Status: Rare winter visitor.
Occurrence: This Rocky Mountain species rarely reaches north central Texas. It has, however, been recorded in eight counties—Bosque, Dallas, Grayson, Hunt, Palo Pinto, Somervell, Tarrant, and Wichita—during the winter from 19 October to 30 March (extreme overall dates for Dallas County).

Specific dates known to me for various counties are: *Bosque*—30 March 1962; *Dallas*—seven times, 24 November 1898, 5 January 1958, 14 January through 30 March 1962, 5 January 1964, 19 October 1969, and winter period, 1972–73, and 21 February 1987; *Grayson*—7 through 16 March 1979 and 24 March 1985; *Hunt*—a spring record indicated by Oberholser (1974), but no details given, probably based on a record for 14 March 1948 given in a local checklist of the Commerce area (O'Neil, 1957); *Palo Pinto* —three times, 2 January 1971, 29 December 1972, and 2 January 1987; *Somervell*—March (Guthery, 1974); *Tarrant*—seven times, 26 December 1955, 16 January 1956, 28 December 1963, 4 through 7 March 1972, 17 November 1972, 20 January 1979, and 17 February 1982; *Wichita*—twice, 17 February 1974 and 10 March 1979.
Specimens: Townsend's Solitaires were collected from Bosque County on

30 March 1962 (WMP 1297) and Dallas County on 24 November 1898 (Stillwell, 1939); however, there is no record of the latter specimen in the Dallas Museum of Natural History. This date precedes the establishment of the museum in the mid-1930s and may represent a specimen taken by Mayer that has since been lost.

VEERY   *Catharus fuscescens* (Stephens)
Status: Rare to casual transient in spring.
Occurrence: All Veery records in the study area are for spring, except for a fall record for Dallas, which is questionable. This species is never very abundant, although it is noted on rare occasions when it lands during bad weather. Data also indicate that it is found in the north central Texas study area from late April to mid-May but that it does not appear every year. It has been reported in only nine counties in the study area: *Bosque* — listed for spring (Pulich, 1980). *Collin* — seven times, 1 May 1976 to 17 May 1980, four of which represent banded birds. *Cooke* — specimen only, 12 May 1885. *Dallas* — earlier records by Stillwell (1939), many of which are questionable, especially those for February and March; recent records, fewer than 20 times since spring 1950, 22 April 1970 to 30 May 1964, the latter date representing a mounted specimen. There is one fall record, 15 September 1975. A winter sighting is questioned by Oberholser (1974) and should be dismissed as an error since the species winters in South America. Only specimen records for winter should be accepted, and even coastal winter records are dubious. *Grayson* — 2 May 1983. *Hunt* — twice, 6 May 1956 and 29 May 1977. *Navarro* — Oberholser (1974) indicates spring records for which I have no details. *Tarrant* — about 25 spring records since 1940, 24 April 1940 to 18 May 1968. Some of the earlier records are in error. *Van Zandt* — 10 May 1979.
Specimens: Veery specimens are available from Cooke (TNHC 1540), Dallas (DMNH 5369), (WMP 1233), and Tarrant (WMP 1891) counties. All of these represent the race *C. f. salicicola*.

GRAY-CHEEKED THRUSH   *Catharus minimus* (Lafresnaye)
Status: Rare to casual transient in spring.
Occurrence: Gray-cheeked Thrushes have been reported in 11 north central Texas counties: Bosque, Collin, Cooke, Dallas, Denton, Grayson, Hunt, Johnson, Kaufman, Somervell, and Tarrant.

   Extreme care should be taken in identifying this species. Although Gray-cheeked Thrushes pass through the area, their retiring habits in thickets, both in river bottoms and in upland woods, make identification difficult. They are far from common, and in some years none are reported from north central Texas. They are the most difficult of all thrushes to identify, and in fall it is nearly impossible to distinguish them from Swainson's

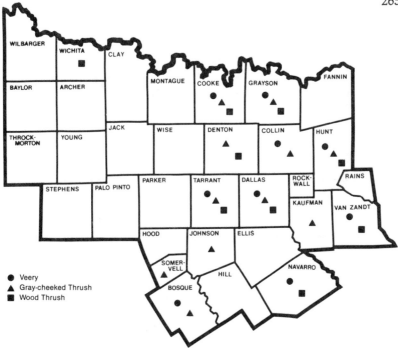

Map 76. Distribution of the Veery, *Catharus fuscescens;* the Gray-cheeked Thrush, *C. minimus;* and the Wood Thrush, *Hylocichla mustelina*

Thrushes. For this reason I have dismissed all fall reports as being unauthentic, lacking sufficient details. Until a specimen is obtained, fall records cannot be accepted.

Movements of the Gray-cheeked Thrush through the area in spring are mainly in early May. Extreme dates for selected counties are: *Collin* – 27 April 1985 to 19 May 1981, all the latter banded birds; *Dallas* – 22 April 1974 to 24 May 1977; *Grayson* – 26 April 1986 to 20 May 1978; *Tarrant* – 29 April 1956 to 15 May 1957.

Specimens: Specimens of Gray-cheeked Thrushes have been collected from two counties: Cooke on 9 May 1885 (TNHC 1535) and Dallas on 25 April 1941 (DMNH 1559) and 10 May 1948 (DMNH 3784 mount). One (DMNH 4365) taken on 28 December 1949 proved to be a misidentified Hermit Thrush (*Catharus guttatus*).

SWAINSON'S THRUSH *Catharus ustulatus* (Nuttall)
Status: Fairly common to common transient.
Occurrence: Swainson's Thrushes pass through north central Texas in both spring and fall migration, though there seem to be more records for spring than for fall. They prefer river bottoms and shaded woods, but when they

Map 77. Distribution of Swainson's Thrush, *Catharus ustulatus,* and the Hermit Thrush, *C. guttatus*

are numerous, they may visit fruited mulberries in residential areas as well as many other types of woods.

Oberholser (1974) reported this species in eight counties of the study area, to which I have added 12 more counties: Bosque, Collin, Cooke, Dallas, Denton, Ellis, Grayson, Hill, Hood, Hunt, Jack, Johnson, Kaufman, Montague, Somervell, Tarrant, Van Zandt, Wichita, Wise, and Young counties — and nearby Shackelford County.

Swainson's Thrushes are usually seen in the spring from mid-April through late May, and again in the fall from mid-September through the latter part of October. Extreme sight records for north central Texas for spring range from 21 March 1965 (Hood County), next-earliest 29 March 1981 (Dallas County), to 16 and 17 June 1980 (Hill County), next-latest 9 June 1983 (Collin County), and for fall from 7 September 1983 (Tarrant County) to as late as 7 November 1982 (Dallas County). Extreme specimen dates range from 8 April 1958 (Dallas County, DMNH 5115) to 6 June 1966 (Tarrant County, FWMSH 942) to 15 and 16 September 1966 (Dallas County, WMP 1508) to 13 October 1982 (Dallas County, DMNH 6809). The lateness of the spring records may be explained by the attraction of thrushes to mulberries. In years when there is a good berry crop, it is not unusual to see this species and other frugivorous species lingering at this food supply. One should not expect to see many Swainson's Thrushes in March or November and should make sure that observations are not Hermit Thrushes.

Extreme dates for selected counties are: *Collin* — 25 April 1981 to 29 May 1980 (all banded birds) and 10 April 1983 to 9 June 1983 (sight records); no fall records; *Dallas* — an unexplainable early date, 29 March 1981, next-earliest 7 April 1985 to 3 June 1984, and 10 September 1970 to late 7 November 1982 (sighting), next-latest 30 October 1966; *Grayson* — 8 April to 31 May, and 8 September to 16 October 1986 (rare in fall); *Tarrant* — 10 April 1976 to 6 June 1966 (mean 14 May, 1968–78), and 7 September 1983 to 18 October 1973; *Wichita* — 12 April 1977 to 4 June 1976, and two fall sightings, 29 September 1975 and 30 September 1976.

All reports of Swainson's Thrush for winter are extremely doubtful and have not been accepted because details are unconvincing or absent. They very likely represent misidentified Hermit Thrushes. Winter records need substantiation by a specimen.

There is an interesting banding recovery of a Swainson's Thrush, recovered in Dallas County on 1 May 1981. It had been banded the previous fall on 26 September 1980, near Julietta, Indiana, just east of Indianapolis. *Specimens:* Specimens of Swainson's Thrush are available from Cooke (TNHC), Dallas (DMNH, WMP), Denton (DMNH, WMP), Ellis (DMNH), Kaufman (SFASU, TNHC), and Tarrant (DMNH, FWMSH, UTA, WMP) counties. All specimens from Dallas and Tarrant counties and some from Denton County represent examples of the race *swainsoni*, except for one taken on 21 May 1966 from Tarrant County. This was identified as *incanus* (FWMSH). Some of the specimens, although identified as *swainsoni*, possibly represent an undescribed race from the Appalachian Mountains (*fide* Mario A. Ramos).

HERMIT THRUSH   *Catharus guttatus* (Pallas)
Status: Uncommon to fairly common transient and winter resident.
Occurence: Hermit Thrushes have been reported in 27 counties of the study area: Archer, Bosque, Clay, Collin, Cooke, Dallas, Denton, Ellis, Fannin, Grayson, Hill, Hood, Hunt, Jack, Johnson, Kaufman, Montague, Navarro, Palo Pinto, Rains, Rockwall, Somervell, Tarrant, Van Zandt, Wichita, Wilbarger, and Wise. There is little doubt that Hermit Thrushes also occur in the remaining counties of the study area.

This is the only thrush species that winters in north central Texas. It has been recorded on all of the CBCs in the study area, usually every year, but not in great numbers. It is the only member of the thrush group that flicks its wings and moves its tail upward and then slowly lowers it. In good light its reddish tail contrasts with its olive-brown back.

No doubt a few Hermit Thrushes linger or pass through north central Texas in early May, but birders should take extra care to distinguish them from Swainson's Thrushes, which are commonly found in the study area in May. The latest spring specimen record of a Hermit Thrush is one taken in Dallas County on 19 April 1939 (DMNH 657). One said to have been taken in Clay County on 21 April 1894 (Oberholser, 1974) could not be located.

Hermit Thrushes are usually found in north central Texas from mid-October to mid-April. Extreme dates for selected counties are: *Collin* – 13 October 1982 (banded) to 9 April 1982. *Dallas* – 7 October 1979 to 5 May 1950 (Stillwell, 1939, gives a 7 May 1937 sighting). May specimens (DMNH) identified as this species proved to be Swainson's Thrushes (*C. ustulatus*). *Grayson* – 28 October 1972 to 26 April 1976. *Tarrant* – 4 October 1956 to 20 May 1942 (five times in 17 May Spring Counts, 1965–82); most of these sightings are questionable. *Wichita* – 4 October 1979 to 26 April 1975. *Specimens:* Hermit Thrush specimens have been taken from 12 counties – Bosque (DMNH), Clay (see above paragraph), Collin (DMNH), Cooke (AMNM, MCZ, TNHC, USNM), Dallas (DMNH, WMP), Denton (DMNH, OU), Ellis (DMNH), Hunt (FWMSH, WMP), Johnson (DMNH), Kaufman (DMNH), Navarro (WMP), and Tarrant (DMNH, FWMSH, WMP) – and adjacent Anderson (KU) County.

Among recent specimens examined from Tarrant County (mainly from DMNH, FWMSH, WMP) the *euborius*, *faxoni*, and *munroi* races have been identified, while in Dallas County these three races plus *auduboni* and *guttatus* (WMP) have been collected and identified. An example from Cooke County (AMNH) taken on 7 February 1887, probably the reference specimen referred to in Oberholser's work (1974) as *sequoiensis*, does not belong to this race, according to Allan R. Phillips (pers. comm.); it may represent *munroi*. Most if not all *sequoiensis* records for north central Texas are very likely invalid. Clearly the taxonomic status of the various races of Hermit Thrushes occurring in north central Texas, as well as in the plains states, needs further study. It would be an excellent project for a graduate student, who could assemble all the known specimens and collect fresh seasonal material from which to assess the racial status of this complex group. Anyone interested in the taxonomic problems of the Hermit Thrush is urged to read and study the comments of Phillips, Marshall, and Monson (1964).

WOOD THRUSH *Hylocichla mustelina* (Gmelin)
Status: Transient. Uncommon to rare in spring; rare to casual in fall. Occurs mainly in the southeastern part of the study area and along some parts of the Red River.
Occurrence: The Wood Thrush has been reported in only ten north cen-

tral Texas counties: Cooke, Dallas, Denton, Grayson, Hunt, Navarro, Tarrant, Van Zandt, Wichita, and Young. It is not as common as many persons believe and is usually reported only in spring. There are not as many fall records, and a few are highly suspicious. It is very possible that the more common Hermit Thrushes, are sometimes misidentified and reported as Wood Thrushes. This is true of an old winter date of 24 December 1925 reported for Tarrant County (Iseley et al., 1926); see Pulich (1979) for details. All winter records are unacceptable, and any future winter record should be substantiated with a specimen.

All of the Wood Thrush records for the ten counties are: *Cooke* — three records, 16 April 1972, 29 September 1965, and 10 October 1969. *Dallas* — 15 April 1929 to 25 May 1930 (Stillwell, 1939), 22 April 1974 to 28 May 1984, present in June and July 1974, 1975, and 1976, but not found nesting. Six times in fall (1955–77), 24 September 1968 to 25 October 1955. A specimen said to have been collected in this county (Oberholser, 1974) was not found. *Denton* — 4 October 1974. *Grayson* — 19 April 1981 to 30 May 1971, with dates in June and July as late as the 26th, and an isolated date, 16 August 1979, suspected of nesting but not located. The first definite nest was discovered at Denison on 20 June 1986, but it produced only a Brown-headed Cowbird. *Hunt* — spring, date unknown (Oberholser, 1974), and an extremely late report by two observers for 11 November 1974 that may be questionable. *Navarro* — November 1879 (Ogilby, 1882), no date since. *Tarrant* — 7 April 1959 to 25 May 1981, an isolated date, 13 June 1975, and seven times in fall (1938–86), 22 September 1974 to 13 November 1938. *Van Zandt* — twice, 10 May 1982 and 21 and 28 July 1985. *Wichita* — twice in fall only, 3 October 1974 and 15 November 1974, the latter date questionable. *Young* — Oberholser (1974) refers to a specimen collected about 1890 but on the species map gives the record as questionable. No data were given on the whereabouts of the specimen. Unless the specimen is found, this reference should be deleted to await future confirmation.

AMERICAN ROBIN   *Turdus migratorius* Linnaeus
Status: Fairly common to common transient. Common to abundant winter visitor irregularly. Uncommon to fairly common summer resident locally.
Occurrence: This well-known species has been recorded in all of the counties of the study area in north central Texas. There have been recent observations for nearby Shackelford County which were not indicated by Oberholser (1974).

In many counties robins have been reported every month of the year, making it difficult to determine the exact movement of the species in and out of the area. They may be unnoticed in many areas until fall migration (mainly October), when they become more numerous and remain so until early spring (late March and early April).

Robins have been reported regularly on all the CBCs within the area, seldom being missed. It is not uncommon to tally 1,000 or more. The greatest number was on the 1975 CBC for Grayson County, when one-half million were estimated. Palo Pinto also has high counts because of the county's supply of juniper berries, which attract the species. At least 28,639 were present on the 1967 Palo Pinto CBC. Numbers vary according to food supply and weather conditions. In the Dallas–Fort Worth area, as well as other urban areas, increases are usually noted after the first of the year when robins invade yards with berry-bearing plants, often competing with Cedar Waxwings. They frequently roost in cedar brakes (*Juniperus* sp.); in the Cedar Hill area of Dallas County they roosted with blackbirds in late January and early February 1985. On their return passage north it is not unusual to see robins feeding in open pastures if rain has provided ground moisture. As a sidenote, among the large flocks albinos or partial albinos may be seen. Robins seem to be more susceptible to this aberration than many other species.

Nesting: Robins have only recently become rather common as a nesting species in north central Texas. Formerly they were very local and were probably found only where there were nesting requisites, such as forested areas, mainly in the eastern part of the study area. For example, More and Strecker (1929) did not report them as nesting in Wilbarger County, yet today it is not uncommon to find them nesting in Wichita and Wilbarger and probably other northwestern counties. Sutton (1938) pointed out that he did not find them breeding in Tarrant County during 1911–14 but gave a reference to nesting in 1925. Stillwell (1939) did not actually point out that they nested in Dallas County, but Kelley (1935) reported that a few pairs nested. It is very likely that they nested earlier than the 1930s in Dallas County. As cities and towns developed and landscaping increased, the robin became more widespread as a nesting species. Unfortunately, there are no complete records of when the species was first reported nesting in the respective counties. At present, however, robins have been reported nesting (actual nests, spot-breasted young, late spring or summer dates) in 22 counties of the study area in north central Texas — Archer, Baylor, Clay, Cooke, Collin, Dallas, Denton, Ellis, Fannin, Grayson, Hill, Hunt, Kaufman, Navarro, Palo Pinto, Somervell, Tarrant, Throckmorton, Van Zandt, Wichita, Wilbarger, Wise — and nearby Shackelford County.

Nesting has been noted for Tarrant County from 20 March (building nest) to 19 May (young in nest). One still in the nest at Flower Mound, Denton County, on 29 June 1985 represented a second nesting. These dates are applicable to overall nesting periods in north central Texas. Juveniles have been reported in July and early August; the latest is 5 September (Navarro County). There are many examples of robins rearing two broods in a number of counties in the study area.

Specimens: Robin specimens are known from the following counties: Bosque (SM, WMP), Cooke (TCWC, TNHC), Dallas (DMNH, UTA, WMP), Denton (DMNH, FWMSH, WMP), Ellis (DMNH), Grayson (UTA), Hood (FWMSH), Hunt (FWMSH), Johnson (SCU), Parker (FWMSH), Tarrant (DMNH, FWMSH, UTA, WMP), Wichita (MWU), and Wilbarger (WMP).

All species examined by me for Dallas, Denton, and Tarrant counties proved to be the nominate race *migratorius,* and the breeding species of the area was *achrusterus.* Oberholser (1974) indicates that the western race *propinquus* was taken in Cooke and Navarro counties, but the whereabouts of these specimens are unknown.

Family Mimidae (Mockingbirds and Thrashers)

GRAY CATBIRD   *Dumetella carolinensis* (Linnaeus)
Status: Uncommon to fairly common migrant. Rare to fairly common summer resident locally. Casual over winters locally.
Occurrence: Gray Catbirds have been recorded in 20 counties of the study area — Bosque, Clay, Collin, Cooke, Dallas, Denton, Ellis, Fannin, Grayson, Hill, Hunt, Johnson, Kaufman, Navarro, Rains, Somervell, Tarrant, Van Zandt, Wichita, and Wilbarger — and nearby Shackelford County.

This species is principally a transient in the western half of the study area, being absent except in the counties through which the Red River passes. Along this corridor it occasionally reaches Wilbarger County. Throughout most counties it is mainly observed in migration, although in some counties it has been reported every month of the year, mainly toward the eastern part, where it breeds locally.

Normally the Gray Catbird passes through north central Texas from late April through May, and again in September and early October. Ex-

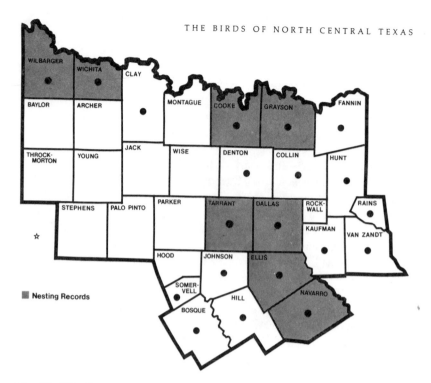

Map 78. Distribution of the Gray Catbird, *Dumetella carolinensis*, with nesting records

treme transient dates for selected counties are: *Dallas* — two isolated dates, 16 March 1976 and 30 March 1980, next 19 April 1958 to 31 May 1969 and 1981, and 7 August 1974 through 27 October 1973 and 1968, and isolated dates, 6 and 7 November 1970; *Grayson* — 22 April to 29 May and 13 August 1981, next-earliest 3 September 1981 to 21 October 1981 and an isolated date of 20 November 1986; *Tarrant* — an isolated date, 3 April 1987, next 22 April 1977 to 2 June 1967, and 20 August 1976 to 21 October 1980, and fall isolated dates, 30 October 1983 and 25 November 1979; *Wichita* — 28 April 1976 to 23 May 1976, and 6 September 1973 to 11 October 1978, and an isolated date, 9 November 1980.

Gray Catbirds have been reported in winter from the following counties: Collin — 2 January 1982; Dallas — twice, 1 January 1966 and 3 through 14 January 1969; Denton — twice, 1 March 1986 and 29 December 1986; Fannin — specimen record (Oberholser, 1974); Grayson — 18 February 1978; Tarrant — four times, 26 December 1963 to 20 March 1974, 21 January to 5 February 1978, 25 January 1980, and 19 December 1985.

Nesting: Oberholser (1974) cites old nesting records for Cooke, Dallas, Ellis, Navarro, and Wilbarger counties. Since today few oologists or birdwatchers hunt for nests in the tangles and dense shrubbery of riparian habitats, there are not many current nesting records of this species. The late-spring and early-summer dates for Collin, Denton, Hill, Hunt, Kaufman, and Van Zandt counties indicate that one might find the species nesting in these counties if careful searches were made for nests or young. It is also likely that most if not all counties listed by Oberholser (1974) still harbor one or two pairs of nesting Gray Catbirds.

Counties in which recent nesting has been recorded are: Dallas — off and on in the Dallas area from 1938 to 1985, more records in recent years, young noted sparingly from late May through 14 July 1984, and 18 August 1985 (fledgling); Grayson — June and July records, two young found at Denison on 11 July 1979; Tarrant — prior nesting suspected, first nesting record on 20 July 1980, when young were observed near Crowley; Wichita — nest under observation from 25 June 1984 (two eggs) to 9 July (young sitting on the edge of a nest) at Iowa Park; also suspected breeding along the Red River near the Perkins Boy Scout Camp on 11 July 1981.

Specimens: Specimens have been collected in the following counties: Cooke (TNHC), Dallas (DMNH, WMP), Denton (DMNH), Ellis (DMNH), Fannin (alleged specimen indicated above, not located), Kaufman (WMP), Tarrant (CM, DMNH, UTA), and Wilbarger (WMP).

Although the AOU (1957) does not recognize any races of Gray Catbirds, Oberholser (1974) lists three subspecies — the nominate race *carolinensis*, the western race *ruficrissa*, and the southeastern race *meridianus* — all of which he claims have been found in north central Texas. He indicates that all three races are found in Tarrant County, but I have examples of only the first two. He also states that *meridianus* breeds north to Cooke County. Some authorities (e.g., Ramos and Warner, 1980) conclude that only two races should be recognized, *D. c. carolinensis* and *D. c. ruficrissa*. *D. c. meridianus* is not distinguishable from *D. c. carolinensis*. Further examination of all the specimens for north central Texas should be undertaken.

NORTHERN MOCKINGBIRD *Mimus polyglottos* (Linnaeus)
Status: Common the year around throughout the study area.
Occurrence: The Northern Mockingbird is found in all of the north central Texas counties as well as the adjacent counties. Its conspicuous presence and the fact that it is the state bird of Texas make it well known to everyone. In Texas only the Purple Martin and the Northern Cardinal may be more popular. Its singing and mimicking, or its ability to imitate other birds, are known to nearly everyone. This trait has been spelled out even in its scientific name, which means "mimic with many tongues." It may sing both in daytime and throughout moonlit nights. The mockingbird can imitate some of the songs of birds frequently seen in its area or songs it picked up in traversing other birds' territories. True mimicry makes up

no more than 10 to 15 percent of its song. To me its song is a combination of both its own song and those of other birds, and research on this point might reveal some interesting song behavior.

Northern Mockingbirds are found in a variety of habitats and are very partial to man's dwellings, especially in suburban areas. In fact, they may be more abundant around human habitations than in the countryside. They are highly territorial: some banded mockingbirds have remained in my yard the year round. They guard ornamental berry bushes and ward off robins and waxwings in late winter. They are not gregarious — usually only one or two are seen; however, in August during extremely hot weather it is not unusual to see seven or more mockers at a time, bathing together when lawns are being watered. Their aggressive behavior is well known, for they attack pets, people, and even snakes, particularly when they have nests nearby.

Nesting: No special effort was made to list all the counties of the study area in which nesting has occurred, but the Northern Mockingbird would no doubt be found nesting in all of the counties if searches for nests were undertaken. Some mockers begin nesting early: a bird was seen carrying twigs on 2 March 1985 in Dallas County. In Denton County fledglings have been recorded out of the nest as early as 3 April 1981, and in Dallas County young ready to leave the nest have been seen on 4 April 1974, while young still in the nest were found in the latter county as late as 21 August 1982. Numerous nests have been found in May and early June. These dates are applicable to the entire study area. The species is often two-brooded and places its nests in a variety of trees and shrubs. I have never found an active nest containing Brown-headed Cowbird eggs, though I have two records of cowbird eggs in abandoned mockingbird nests.

I formerly banded as many local nestling mockingbirds as possible, but the returns produced so little significant data that I ceased banding this species. Some local mockers stay in my yard the year round and seem to be permanent residents, but seasonal movements, especially in the countryside, no doubt take place. It is puzzling to me what happens to the young and excess members of this species. A few more birds appear to be counted in the annual CBCs, especially in the southern part of the study area, perhaps because more observers participate in the CBCs. It is possible that climatic conditions of north central Texas make it difficult to understand local shifts in populations as clearly as those in areas to the north, where winter weather drives them from their summer homes. We often know more about rare or unusual birds than we do about common species.

In addition to studies of the species' movements in north central Texas, further attention should be given to various other behavioral activities of this species that are poorly understood. An example is the bird's wing flashing, a wing and tail display that has been observed by many persons.

Specimens: Mockingbird specimens are available from the following counties: Bosque (SM), Cooke (TNHC), Dallas (DMNH, OU, UTA, WMP), Denton (DMNH), Hood (FWMSH), Kaufman (DMNH), Somervell (FWMSH), Tarrant (DMNH, FWMSH, SUC, UTA, WMP), Wichita (DMNH, MWU), Van Zandt (WMP), Wilbarger (WMP), and Wise (DMNH). The specimens examined from Dallas and Tarrant counties represent the nominate race *polyglottos*.

The *Checklist of the Birds of Texas* (TOS, 1984) points out that two races, *polyglottos* and *leucopterus*, intergrade in north central Texas. Most authorities studying races of this species emphasize the need for fresh fall material, since faded, dusty study skins cannot be used to identify the races of mockingbirds more accurately.

SAGE THRASHER   *Oreoscoptes montanus* (Townsend)
Status: Casual winter visitor.
Occurrence: This species normally occurs west of the study area, but some winters it invades parts of north central Texas. It resembles the Northern Mockingbird except that it has a shorter tail and a heavily streaked breast. It does not have the mockingbird's striking white wing patches, and the white of the tail is confined to the outer tips. Care should be exercised in identifying these two species.

Sage Thrashers have been recorded in 12 north central Texas study-area counties and nearby Comanche County. It can be expected from November through March. All of the county records and extreme dates known to me are: *Clay* and *Cooke* — early records (Oberholser, 1974) not located, no records since; *Dallas* — 3 December 1956 to 14 March 1957; *Denton* — 11 November 1956 and 26 December 1968; *Grayson* — 4 November 1972; *Hill* — 10 through 14 November 1984; *Hood* — 8 March 1975; *Hunt* — 2 December to 10 February 1957; *Johnson* — 21 November 1950; *Palo Pinto* — 6 March 1977, probably wintered; *Tarrant* — nine times, 21 February 1950, 4 March 1956, 16 October 1956 through 2 March 1957, 11 January 1964, 4 October 1966, 25 January 1967, 29 November 1969, 6 and 12 November 1972, and 4 April 1975; *Wichita* — early record by Oberholser (1974); three times since, 16 December 1973 to 4 January 1974, 24 January and 11 April 1975, and 11 November 1978; *Comanche* — winter 1974–75.
Specimens: Sage Thrashers have been located for Denton (WMP 1633), Hood (FWMSH 1236), and Johnson (DMNH 4816) counties. A specimen said to have been taken on 11 April (year not given) for Clay County (Oberholser, 1974) was not located.

BROWN THRASHER   *Toxostoma rufum* (Linnaeus)
Status: Fairly common to common transient and summer resident. Found the year round in many locales.

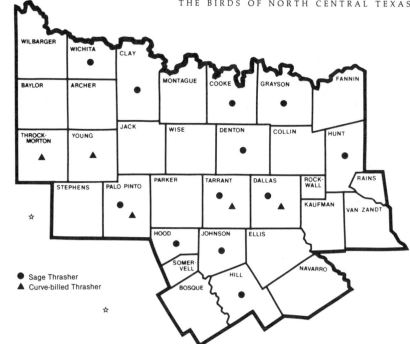

Map 79. Distribution of the Sage Thrasher, *Oreoscoptes montanus,* and the Curve-billed Thrasher, *Toxostoma curvirostre*

Occurrence: Brown Thrashers have been observed in all but four counties of the study area: Baylor, Montague, Stephens, and Throckmorton. They have also been reported from nearby Shackelford County.

This retiring species is more often reported along brushy edges and wooded thickets in the eastern counties than toward the western counties. It is often overlooked because of its secretive habits, but near man's habitations it may become quite tame and frequent feeders with other birds.

Like the dates of a number of other rather common species found the year round, the exact dates of the Brown Thrasher's movements in and out of an area are difficult to determine. In general it is reported more often in fall from mid-September to the end of October and in spring around the first part of April. As a general rule only one or two birds are found, but on 20 October 1974 one observer estimated 150 thrashers in about 100 square yards near Pottsboro, Grayson County; and on 30 September 1984 more than 100 birds were seen in groups of six to 20 in a morning's outing near Lewisville, Denton County. It is usually reported on all of the annual CBCs and is more abundant in the southern counts — Dallas–Fort Worth — than in the northern and western counts — Hagerman NWR, Palo Pinto, and Wichita.

Nesting: There are fewer reports during the nesting season, and in some areas they are seldom reported during the summer. Oberholser (1974) listed nesting records for only Dallas and Wilbarger counties, though no doubt some of his summer records represent nesting. Besides these counties there are nesting records for Collin, Denton, Grayson, Hunt, Tarrant, and Wichita counties, and the species has been assumed to nest in Bosque, Cooke, Ellis, Fannin, Hill, Kaufman, Navarro, Palo Pinto, Rains, and Van Zandt counties. Nesting dates for Dallas ranged from 15 April to 5 June with fledglings out of the nest from 17 May to 20 July, while in Tarrant County nesting was recorded from 6 April to 19 May with fledglings out of the nest on 9 July. These nesting dates are typical for north central Texas as a whole.

Specimens: Specimens have been located for Cooke (TNHC, USNM), Dallas (DMNH, FWMSH, WMP), Denton (DMNH), Ellis (DMNH), Fannin (WMP), Kaufman (DMNH), and Tarrant (DMNH, FWMSH, UTA) counties, as well as nearby Anderson (KU) and Henderson (DMNH) counties. Those indicated for Hunt County (Oberholser, 1974) could not be located.

The specimens examined for Dallas and Tarrant counties represent the nominate race *rufum*. Oberholser (1974) indicated that *longicauda* was the nesting race in Wilbarger County, but no specimens have been taken of this race. It is interesting, however, that Sutton (1967) identified all of the Oklahoma specimens as *T. r. longicauda*.

CURVE-BILLED THRASHER   *Toxostoma curvirostre* (Swainson)
Status: Casual to rare in the northwestern part of the study area, indicating movement into the area in the mid-1970s.
Occurrence: Oberholser (1974) gave no records of the Curve-billed Thrasher for north central Texas; however, he indicated that it occurred uncommonly toward the west in the middle Panhandle and gave several fall and winter sightings for the Amarillo area in the upper Panhandle. Ault (1984) presented an excellent summary of this species in southwestern Oklahoma counties ranging above the northwestern counties of the north central Texas study area. He gave the first nesting record from Oklahoma, near Eldorado, Jackson County, on 17 June 1975, and the second on 5 May 1979. These locations are about 15 miles north of the Texas border, above Hardeman County, and about 20 miles northwest of Wilbarger County. Interestingly, the dates of records for the project area coincide with the spread of the species into Oklahoma.

The records for the study area and adjacent counties are as follows: *Dallas*—one was observed bathing in the city limits of Dallas on 9 May 1985, but unfortunately the observation was made by a lone observer. It was carefully described in the report sent to me. *Palo Pinto*—one carefully observed northwest of Graford by three competent observers on 13 June 1983. *Tarrant* — reported in Fort Worth on 23 February 1964 and on 1 April 1964 (Pulich, 1979). *Throckmorton* — at least three observed in the southwestern part of the county, one of which was collected (WMP 2872) on 28 October 1983. *Young* — one was tallied on BBS on 8 June 1986. *Haskell* — first noted attending young out of the nest on 5 September 1976, and adults were seen again on 8 and 9 September 1979. *Shackelford* — first reported on BBS conducted in the Albany area on 21 June 1980 and each year afterward. The observer conducting this survey route has found an increase in numbers each year. He reported seven seen or heard on 17 June 1984 and 31 on 14 June 1986.

Family Motacillidae (Pipits)

WATER PIPIT   *Anthus spinoletta* (Linnaeus)
Status: Fairly common to common winter resident.
Occurrence: Water Pipits have been reported in 26 counties of the study area: Archer, Baylor, Bosque, Clay, Collin, Cooke, Dallas, Denton, Ellis, Fannin, Grayson, Hill, Hunt, Johnson, Kaufman, Navarro, Palo Pinto, Parker, Rains, Rockwall, Somervell, Tarrant, Van Zandt, Wichita, Wilbarger, and Wise. They would probably be found in the remaining counties during the winter if there were more bird-watchers in the outlying areas.

This species seeks open country, short grass, overgrazed areas, plowed fields, and the mud flats of lakes and ponds. It is much more common than the Sprague's Pipit and is often found in good-sized flocks, into the hundreds. Occasionally there is an estimate of thousands; however, these may be mixed with Horned Larks and longspurs. Although it normally spends its time on the ground, I have several times observed members of this species perched in trees.

Water Pipits come early to north central Texas, being found from late September through early May. Extreme dates for selected counties are: *Dallas* — 20 September 1980 to 11 May 1983; *Grayson* — 14 September to 16 May; *Tarrant* — 22 September 1956 to 22 May 1953; *Wichita* — a 31 August 1978 date, given without details, was discounted; 20 September 1975 to 6 May 1976 (10 May 1983 in nearby Wilbarger County).
Specimens: Specimens are available from the following counties: Collin (UTA), Cooke (TNHC), Dallas (DMNH), Denton (DMNH), Ellis (WMP), Hunt (DMNH), Kaufman (DMNH), Navarro (USNM), Tarrant (FWMSH, UTA), and nearby Henderson (DMNH). A spring bird said to have been collected in Wise County (Oberholser, 1974) could not be located.

The AOU *Checklist* (1957) recognizes three subspecies of Water Pipits in Texas: *A. s. rubescens*, *A. s. pacificus*, and *A. s. alticola*.

Only a few recent local specimens of this species have been examined

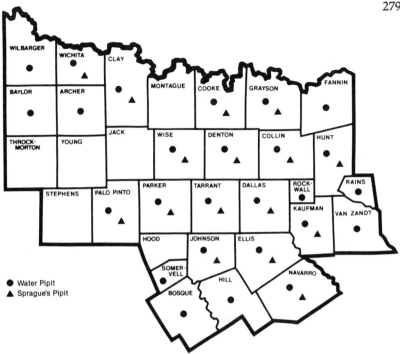

Map 80. Distribution of the Water Pipit, *Anthus spinoletta,* and Sprague's Pipit, *A. spragueii*

for race. Two specimens (FWMSH) from Tarrant County were examined by Allan R. Phillips: one was taken on 2 April 1956 and identified as *rubescens;* the second was collected on 12 December 1954 and tentatively assigned to the race *pacificus* or an intermediate of this subspecies (Pulich, 1979).

Oberholser (1974) indicated that the race *alticola* occurred in Collin County (22 March) and Dallas County (10 April, DMNH 1293), but the first specimen could not be located, and the second is so faded that it is difficult to ascertain its race. Undoubtedly, the first two races, *rubescens* and *pacificus,* occur in north central Texas, but, to be certain, a large series of fresh-plumaged specimens should be taken. Most of the existing specimens are so old and faded that their race cannot be determined properly.

SPRAGUE'S PIPIT *Anthus spragueii* (Audubon)
Status: Rare to uncommon winter resident.
Occurrence: Sprague's Pipits have been reported in 16 north central Texas counties: Clay, Collin, Cooke, Dallas, Denton, Ellis, Grayson, Hunt, Johnson, Kaufman, Navarro, Palo Pinto, Parker, Tarrant, Wichita, and Wise.

This pipit inhabits shortgrass prairies and may be more common than most observers realize. No more than a few are seen at a time, and occasionally in the dead of winter when observers are looking for longspurs, Sprague's Pipits are seen along with Horned Larks and Savannah Sparrows in grassy areas. The pipit's single call note often gives it away.

Sprague's Pipits are usually seen from late November through March; the overall dates for the study area range from 25 September 1878 (Wise County) to 20 May 1955 (Tarrant County). Because of their solitary nature there are few winter records: they have been recorded on only three CBCs. Extreme dates for selected counties are: *Cooke* — before the turn of the century Ragsdale gave dates of 26 October 1877 (specimen) to 10 May 1880. No observations since, but the habitat is still present. *Dallas* — 27 October 1982 to 18 April 1969. *Grayson* — very few records, 6 October and 5 November 1974, 20 October 1983, 20 November 1983, 1 and 8 December 1983, and 17 October and 14 November 1985. *Tarrant* — 31 October 1984 to 20 May 1955, next-latest 7 May 1955. Surprisingly, there are no January or February observations. *Wichita* — mid-November 1981 to 3 May 1975.

Specimens: Specimens were located for Cooke (TNHC, USNM), Ellis (DMNH), Navarro (USNM), Parker (FWMSH), and Tarrant (WMP) counties. A fall specimen indicated for Palo Pinto County (Oberholser, 1974) was not located.

Family Bombycillidae (Waxwings)

BOHEMIAN WAXWING   *Bombycilla garrulus* (Linnaeus)
Status: Irregular vagrant in north central Texas. Seldom reported.
Occurrence: There are very few reports of the Bohemian Waxwing in north central Texas. It rarely reaches the state, and then mainly the Panhandle of Texas, where it invades the southern limits from the boreal regions far to the north. The very irregular wanderings of this species are influenced by food supply. Although they are said usually to travel in flocks of their own kind, Bohemian Waxwings should be looked for in the company of Cedar Waxwings.

The county observations are: *Dallas* — 4 May 1956 and 20 January 1966; *Tarrant* — 2 February 1955 and 17 January 1966, both reports accompanied by careful details; *Wilbarger* — sight records for winter 1974–75; listed as hypothetical (Zinn and Moore, 1976).

Specimens: There are no specimens for north central Texas. Observers are urged to watch for this waxwing, and anyone finding a dead Bohemian Waxwing should get in touch with me or one of the local museums. It is larger than a Cedar Waxwing, having a distinctive grayish cast to its feathers and rich chestnut-colored undertail coverts. It also has conspicuous white wing patches and primaries edged in yellow.

CEDAR WAXWING *Bombycilla cedrorum* Vieillot
Status: Common to abundant transient and winter visitor.
Occurrence: This nomadic bird has been reported in all of the counties of the study area except Jack and Throckmorton, but it likely has occurred in these counties as well, since it has been observed in adjacent counties. It has also been observed in Eastland and Shackelford counties, where it had not been reported previously.

It is said that the first northers in October bring the Cedar Waxwings to Texas. Many bird-watchers do not realize this and seldom report them before the end of December or mid-January, when flocks invade cities and towns to feed on fruit-bearing plants such as hollies, ligustrums, and mulberries. When the first waxwings come to Texas, they usually visit cedar brakes to feed on juniper berries or search out the countryside for trees infested with mistletoe. The presence or absence of fruit, particularly mulberries, may govern Cedar Waxwing populations in late May or even early June.

Extreme arrival and departure dates for selected counties are: *Dallas* — 8 September 1983 to 28 May 1958; *Grayson* — 8 September 1968 to 28 May 1981; *Tarrant* — 7 October 1972 to 2 June 1957; *Van Zandt* — 1 November 1984 (none earlier, according to a local observer) to 7 June 1986; *Wichita* — 7 September 1975 to 28 May 1974, and nearby Wilbarger County an isolated date of 18 June 1974.

Waxwings have been reported on all of the CBCs and usually every year. They frequently number in the hundreds and occasionally in the thousands, although the large numbers do not peak until February and early March. The largest numbers, at least 100,000, were reported from Palo Pinto County on 15 March 1980, with a noticeable drop by 28 March.

Cedar Waxwings come readily not only to fruit-bearing plants but also to water and birdbaths, ponds, and even rain puddles. In one instance their social behavior of watering and bathing led to their being eaten by bull-frogs (Gollob and Pulich, 1978). Several birds crowding to drink at stock tanks in Palo Pinto County fell or were pushed into the water and were captured by bullfrogs. Nearly every author has written about waxwings gorging themselves on ripe fruit that has begun to ferment and becoming "drunk." A few years ago an occurrence of this behavior in Dallas County was reported in the *Wall Street Journal* (Morgenthaler, 1970).

Specimens: Specimens of Cedar Waxwings have been collected in the following counties: Bosque (DMNH), Cooke (TNHC), Dallas (DMNH, UTA, WMP), Denton (DMNH), Ellis (TCWC), Hood (FWMSH), Johnson (SUC), Navarro (USNM), Parker (FWMSH), and Tarrant (DMNH, FWMSH, UTA).

Family Laniidae (Shrikes)

NORTHERN SHRIKE   *Lanius excubitor* Linnaeus
Status: Casual in north central Texas; very few acceptable records.
Occurrence: Reports of the Northern Shrike are few and far between, and, unfortunately, some are in error. The species rarely reaches north central Texas, and extreme care should be exercised in attempting to identify it even in the hand. This is certainly true of the records for Denton County: two alleged specimens in the Dallas Museum of Natural History cited as Northern Shrikes by Oberholser (1974) proved upon reexamination to be Loggerhead Shrikes.

The following comments summarize the records for north central Texas counties: *Denton* — no valid records (see paragraph above). Sight records have been discounted, since they were made by the same person who mis-identified specimens listed by Peterson (1960). *Hunt* — all sight records were made in the fall, and the dates are too early for the species. Records are likely Loggerhead Shrikes with traces of fine barring, which young birds often show in early fall. *Palo Pinto* — one was carefully observed and de-scribed on CBC of 27 December 1978. Several competent observers viewed this bird. *Wichita* — oddly, a member of this species appeared in two dif-ferent winter periods and was viewed by numerous local and out-of-town bird-watchers, 28 November 1974 until 16 March 1975, and again 1 De-cember 1975 until 5 January 1976, when it was found dead. It is said that the bird also appeared during the winter of 1973, but the dates and details are vague. *Wise* — Oberholser (1974) gives two specimen records, one on 22 January 1889 and the other on 5 January 1890, but he does not give the whereabouts of the specimens, and the records cannot be evaluated.

Specimens: The only specimen (DMNH 6554) examined for north central Texas is one from Wichita County, now in the synoptic bird display in the Dallas Museum of Natural History.

LOGGERHEAD SHRIKE   *Lanius ludovicianus* Linnaeus
Status: Fairly common to common winter resident. Locally uncommon
to fairly common in summer.
Occurrence: Loggerhead Shrikes have been reported in all of the counties
of the study area as well as the adjacent counties. Although they are said
to be declining in numbers in some parts of the United States, this does
not appear to be true in north central Texas, where they are holding their
own and may even be increasing. They are probably more common in
winter because of the influx of transient birds into the area. They can readily be found from early September to March. A comparison of CBCs for
Fort Worth (Tarrant County) with Spring Counts from 1965 to 1978 averaged 50 shrikes in winter compared to 34 in spring.

Shrikes perch conspicuously on exposed branches or on the tops of trees
in rather open country or on telephone wires along highways. From these
vantage points they search for food. The old name of this species, "butcher
bird," was derived from its habit of impaling prey on thorns and barbed-
wire fences. Its food consists of scorpions and insects, small snakes, horned
lizards, small birds the size of bluebirds, mice, and even gophers. Its bill
is hooked for tearing food apart, yet its feet are rather weak and are not
raptorial. However, it has been observed using both its bill and its feet
to carry its food. By impaling the prey, the shrike can tear the animal apart
despite weak feet; impaling is not a method of food storage, as many persons believe.

Not many persons realize that the Loggerhead Shrike has a song, not
altogether unmusical, consisting of a slow, pleasing note that reminds some
observers of the call of the catbird, a name sometimes applied to shrikes.
Nesting: This species has been found nesting in 22 north central Texas counties: Archer, Clay, Collin, Cooke, Dallas, Denton, Ellis, Hill, Hood, Hunt,
Johnson, Kaufman, Navarro, Palo Pinto, Parker, Rockwall, Somervell,
Stephens, Tarrant, Wichita, Wilbarger, and Young.

Shrikes have been found nesting in Dallas County as early as 27 March
1980 (six eggs) through 26 July 1971 (young banded), and in Tarrant County
on 2 April 1955 (five eggs) through 18 July 1953 (three young). These are
typical dates that are applicable to the rest of north central Texas. Shrikes
are two-brooded, and in 1975 a pair was noted in Tarrant County still
tending young out of the nest as late as 11 October.
Specimens: Loggerhead Shrikes have been collected from the following
counties: Archer (MWU), Baylor (MWU), Clay (MWU), Collin (DMNH),
Cooke (DMNH, TNHC), Dallas (DMNH, OU, WMP), Denton (DMNH,
TCWC), Ellis (DMNH), Hill (WMP), Hood (FWMSH), Johnson (SUC),
Kaufman (DMNH), Navarro (WMP), Parker (FWMSH), Tarrant (DMNH,
FWMSH, UTA), Wichita (WMP), and nearby Henderson (DMNH).

Three subspecies of Loggerhead Shrike occur in north central Texas. In my collection a specimen taken on 19 December 1971 in Wichita County was identified as *gambeli*. A specimen of *migrans* was collected on 30 January 1976, and another nearest *migrans* tending toward *excubitorides* on 15 January 1976, both from Dallas County, while four May specimens, three from Dallas County and one from Hill County, were identified as *excubitorides*. H. C. Oberholser identified all three races (DMNH) from Tarrant County (Pulich, 1979).

Family Sturnidae (Starlings)

EUROPEAN STARLING   *Sturnus vulgaris* Linnaeus
Status: Abundant the year round. May be more common in winter than in summer.
Occurrence: European Starlings are widespread in north central Texas, especially around cities and towns, although they are found in the country as well. They have been recorded in all of the counties in north central Texas as well as in the adjacent counties.

This introduced species was apparently not present in most counties of the area until the 1930s. Stillwell (1939) indicated the presence of these starlings in Corsicana, Navarro County, in 1927. He also pointed out that they were first observed in Dallas County in the winter of 1930–31. Saunders (1933) reported "many flocks" in the area between Temple, Waco, and Fort Worth in the spring of 1933. In a footnote for Tarrant County Stillwell (1939) listed an observation on 18 October 1937, and a local Fort Worth birder recorded an observation on 21 December 1938. They were considered winter visitors in Hunt County by the winter of 1939–40, arriving by 31 October and departing on 8 March, according to Tarter (1940). More and Strecker (1929) did not list them as summer birds in Wilbarger County, although a few could have been present in the winter; that is unlikely, however.

Starlings are probably more numerous in the winter, when hordes of the "blackbirds" move south from the north. There seem to be more in recent years, but few studies have been made of their movements in north central Texas and thus their numbers are difficult to assess. During the winters of 1955 and 1956 an estimated 100,000 starlings roosted in the upper Lake Worth area of Tarrant County. This occurred before the species was known to nest in the county. At that time I gave the mean arrival and departure dates as 17 October and 11 March (Pulich, 1961). The largest winter concentrations of starlings recorded on the 1966 and 1970 Dallas CBCs were more than 401,000 and 313,000, respectively.
Nesting: Starlings were first reported nesting in north central Texas in 1956, when they were observed in Denton County. Oberholser (1974) indicated that they had probably been nesting before that time, though he gave no

details. The first record for Tarrant County was 12 May 1959 (young out of nest; Pulich, 1961), while the first nesting record for Dallas County was 23 April 1961. Today they nest in all the counties, wherever they can find woodpecker holes, bluebird boxes, and even houses and other buildings that afford nesting sites. They are two-brooded and lay five to six pale, blue eggs. Starlings search for nest sites early. The earliest nesting date was 19 February 1977, when one was observed carrying nesting material. By mid-March they are extremely busy, with earliest eggs (five) on 15 April 1968, small young four or five days old on 31 March 1985, and large young out of the nest on 14 May 1968 (all Dallas County records). They are aggressive, extremely competitive, and responsible for reducing populations of woodpeckers, martins, bluebirds, and other hole-nesting birds.

Specimens: Examples of this species are available from Dallas (DMNH, FWMSH, UTA, WMP), Denton (DMNH), Hood (FWMSH), Johnson (SUC), Tarrant (DMNH, FWMSH, UTA), and Wichita (MWU) counties. A specimen indicated by Oberholser (1974) for Archer County could not be located.

Family Vireonidae (Vireos)

WHITE-EYED VIREO   *Vireo griseus* (Boddaert)
Status: Fairly common to uncommon transient. Rare summer resident.
Occurrence: White-eyed Vireos have been recorded in all but four north central Texas study area counties — Archer, Baylor, Jack, and Stephens.

This vireo is normally found from late March to October in north central Texas. Extreme county dates are *Dallas* — 2 March 1963 (specimen), next-earliest 9 March 1974 to 28 October 1934 (Stillwell, 1939), next-latest 12 October 1958; *Grayson* — 25 March to 15 October; *Tarrant* — 12 March 1983, next-earliest 17 March 1955 to 20 November 1940 (exceptionally late), next-latest 9 October 1986; *Van Zandt* — 10 March 1986 to 9 October 1983. In most counties the records are few and scattered, making the period of stay difficult to determine for specific counties, but data given for the counties above are applicable to the other counties in the study area. The species may not be as abundant today as it was formerly. It is seldom encountered in large numbers. It is frequently heard before it is seen and is often missed in typical woodland habitats.

Nesting: Oberholser (1974) indicated that the species bred in Cooke, Dallas, Tarrant, and Wilbarger counties and gave summer records for Clay, Denton, and Grayson counties. Hood and Van Zandt counties should be added to counties having nesting White-eyed Vireos: in the first county a nest was found on 18 April 1977, and in the second five young were seen following their parents on 16 June 1985. Counties having recent summer sightings (June and July) are Bosque, Cooke, Dallas, Denton, Grayson (no nests since 1976), Hill, Hood, Somervell, and Tarrant.

Specimens: White-eyed Vireo specimens have been taken in the following counties: Bosque (WMP), Cooke (TNHC), Dallas (DMNH, OU, WMP), Denton (DMNH), Ellis (DMNH), Hood (DMNH), Kaufman (DMNH, WMP), Palo Pinto (DMNH), Parker (FWMSH), Tarrant (DMNH), and Henderson (DMNH). Specimens said to have been collected in Clay, Fannin, and Wise counties (Oberholser, 1974) were not located. Although not all of the specimens have been examined for race, all those that have been checked proved to be *V. g. noveboracensis*. It is not likely that any other race will be found in north central Texas.

BELL'S VIREO   *Vireo bellii* Audubon

Status: Formerly fairly common summer resident. Becoming increasingly scarce; rare in some areas where it formerly bred.

Occurrence: Bell's Vireos have been recorded in all but four north central Texas counties — Jack, Montague, Rains, and Throckmorton. They could probably be found in these counties as well.

The species should be looked for from early April through September. Extreme arrival and departure dates for selected counties are: *Dallas* — 4 April 1935 to 11 October 1939 (Stillwell, 1939), 7 April 1981 to 4 October 1971 (current data); *Denton* — 16 April 1941 to 7 September 1958; *Grayson* — 8 April 1972 to 26 September; *Tarrant* — 9 April 1983 to 24 October 1938, next-latest 6 October 1986; *Wichita* — 6 April 1973 to 12 September 1973.

Nesting: Oberholser (1974) lists Bell's Vireos nesting in Cooke, Dallas, Rockwall, Tarrant, Wilbarger, and Wise counties, with questionable records for Fannin and Young. They were also reported as summering in Baylor, Denton, Grayson, Hill, Navarro, and Palo Pinto counties. Brown-headed Cowbird parasitism and environmental changes have made inroads into the breeding population of the Bell's Vireo in north central Texas. This species may be becoming endangered; many persons remark on its absence from areas where it was formerly fairly common. The last nesting dates that I have on some county populations are: Cooke — none since before 1900; Dallas — last nest in 1971; Grayson — last actual nest in 1978, on 8 June 1969, 20 singing males in four places at Hagerman NWR, numerous in mid-1970s, since 1980 about two each summer; Tarrant — last nest, feeding young on 23 May 1942, probably nesting as late as mid-1970s, but no actual nests found; Wichita — two nests in 1977.

Specimens: Specimens of Bell's Vireo were located for Cooke (USNM), Dallas (DMNH, WMP), Denton (DMNH), Tarrant (DMNH, FWMSH), and Wichita (MWU) counties. Those said to have been taken from Clay, Collin, Kaufman, and Wise counties (Oberholser, 1974) were not located. All specimens that were examined represent the nominate race *bellii*.

BLACK-CAPPED VIREO   *Vireo atricapillus* Woodhouse
Status: Casual to rare summer resident.
Occurrence: Oberholser (1974) gave records for the Black-capped Vireo in four counties of the study area — Cooke, Dallas, Ellis, and Tarrant — and nearby Comanche, Eastland, Erath, and McLennan counties. I have added records for Bosque, Grayson, Palo Pinto, Parker, and Somervell counties.

The Black-capped Vireo is found in low, dense scrub thickets. When the brush grows to heights of ten to 12 feet, this species tends to disappear. Burning, which is no longer practiced, formerly retarded the growth of many of these thickets and helped limit the height of scrub cover for this vireo's requirements. Around cities this habitat has suffered from man's intrusion and urban sprawl. This is true in the Duncanville–Cedar Hill area, in southwestern Dallas County, where the Black-capped Vireo has almost disappeared. Goat grazing of underbrush also reduced nesting. Another factor in reducing the Black-capped Vireo populations has been the social parasitism of the Brown-headed Cowbird on the species. In 1984 the U.S. Fish and Wildlife Service initiated a study to determine the status of the Black-capped Vireo and thereby decide whether or not it should be placed on the endangered list. The surveys continued in 1985 and 1986 with emphasis on breeding sites to determine whether or not the cowbird was a serious threat to Black-capped Vireo populations. At this writing the survey data suggest that it will be placed on the U.S. Fish and Wildlife Service endangered species list. Present data show that the Black-capped Vireo has not spread. More recent sightings have led to further concern that this species may be losing habitat.

Records for the nine counties in the study area and four adjacent counties are: *Bosque* — a few found at Meridian SP ranging from 2 April 1977 to 11 September 1970, last reported in 1983; formerly more numerous. *Cooke* — no recent records; nested in the county before the turn of the century (G. H. Ragsdale). *Dallas* — known to inhabit the escarpment from the Cedar Hill–Duncanville area to the Mountain Creek area from the early 1930s. Present population has been dwindling since the mid-1970s, overall dates 2 April 1967 to 10 September 1961; nests 10 to 15 May (eggs), latest 7 July 1984 (three eggs hatched successfully). The only areas where any were known to exist in 1987 were the Green Hills Environmental Center and the adjacent undeveloped cedar brake. *Ellis* — said to have nested (Oberholser, 1974); no details of record. The county still has habitat, but no recent records. *Grayson* — 18 June 1954, nested south of Tom Bean, nest and one egg preserved at Austin College; no other records. *Palo Pinto* — 17 April 1958, 15 April 1960. *Parker* — 19 May 1974. *Somervell* — 5 May 1974, Dinosaur Valley SP, 13 March to 3 June 1984, and 31 March to 8 September 1985. *Tarrant* — three sightings, 1 April 1958, 7 April 1964, and 4 May 1974; no evidence of nesting. *Comanche* — Oberholser (1974) indi-

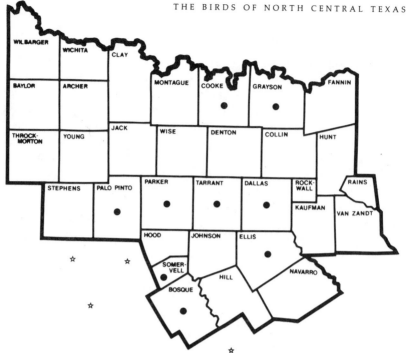

Map 81. Distribution of the Black-capped Vireo, *Vireo atricapillus*

cates a spring specimen (2 May 1878, taken by G. H. Ragsdale), but its whereabouts are unknown. *Eastland* — Oberholser (1974) indicates a spring sighting; no other details given. No recent sightings, though the county still has available habitat. *Erath* — Oberholser (1974) indicates a spring specimen (3 May 1878, G. H. Ragsdale), but the whereabouts of the specimen are unknown. *McLennan* — Strecker (1927) reported that he saw only six in 33 years. Oberholser (1974) lists a summer specimen, but it could not be located. There are no recent records for this county that I am aware of. *Specimens:* Specimens were taken in Cooke County on 25 June 1884 (USNM 99611) and 29 May 1888 (TNHC 1443). There are other specimens for this county, probably in USNM, but they were not located. Black-capped Vireos were also taken for Dallas County on 30 August 1958 (WMP 586 and 587) and 10 August 1959 (WMP 783), and for Palo Pinto County on 17 April 1958 (DMNH 5152).

SOLITARY VIREO *Vireo solitarius* (Wilson)
Status: Uncommon to fairly common transient. Rare to casual winter resident locally.
Occurrence: Solitary Vireos have been seen in 21 counties of north central Texas — Bosque, Collin, Cooke, Dallas, Denton, Ellis, Grayson, Hill, Hood,

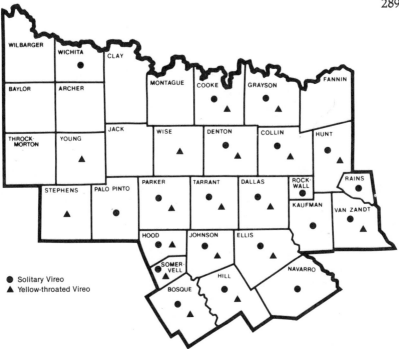

Map 82. Distribution of the Solitary Vireo, *Vireo solitarius,* and the Yellow-throated Vireo, *V. flavifrons*

Hunt, Johnson, Kaufman, Navarro, Palo Pinto, Parker, Rains, Rockwall, Somervell, Tarrant, Van Zandt, and Wichita – and nearby Henderson County.

The species seems to be more widespread in its distribution in north central Texas along the eastern side of the study area, especially in forested areas with big timber and along streams and rivers. It is usually observed alone or in small numbers, but on 5 May 1979 65 were counted in Tarrant County in spring passage. Sixty-nine Solitary Vireos were killed at a TV tower in southwest Dallas County on the night of 28–29 September 1959. Overall within the area it has been reported every month except July. It is primarily a migrant, but an occasional Solitary Vireo winters in the southern part of the study area, mainly in the Dallas–Denton–Fort Worth area.

Selected county dates are: *Bosque* – 17 February 1979. *Collin* – 23 April 1983 to 17 May 1980, and 15 September 1981 to 3 November 1984. *Dallas* – an isolated date of 4 March 1930, next-earliest 5 April 1967 to 21 May 1958, one unexplained isolated date of 30 June 1973, and 10 September 1976 to 18 November 1982. Winter sightings – eight times in December, twice in January, and one on 10 February 1935. *Denton* – 28 April 1974 to 13 May 1947 (specimen), and 7 September 1958 to 17 November 1984, and winter dates of 26 December 1984 and 26 February 1986. *Grayson* — 13 April 1975 to 18 May 1975, and 8 September 1979 to 8 November 1974. *Tarrant* — 3 April 1987 to 19 May 1957, and 12 August 1939 to 12 November 1982; winter, 9 December 1983, 15 December 1973, 3 and 4 February 1980, 6 February 1982, and 26 February 1986. *Wichita* — 6 April 1973 to 15 May 1976, and 7 September 1976 to 30 September 1976.

Specimens: Specimens belonging to the nominate race *solitarius* have been collected in the following counties: Cooke (TNHC); Dallas (DMNH, WMP); Denton (DMNH); Ellis (DMNH); Hunt, 28 November 1937 (FWMSH); Kaufman, 27 May 1941 (DMNH); and Tarrant (DMNH, FWMSH, WMP). Specimens indicated for Collin and Navarro counties (Oberholser, 1974) were not located.

YELLOW-THROATED VIREO   *Vireo flavifrons* Vieillot

Status: Uncommon to rare transient. Extremely rare summer resident.

Occurrence: Yellow-throated Vireos have been recorded in 18 counties of the study area: Bosque, Collin, Cooke, Dallas, Denton, Ellis, Grayson, Hill, Hood, Hunt, Johnson, Parker, Somervell, Stephens, Tarrant, Van Zandt, Wise, and Young.

In recent years nearly all the observations are from the southern and southeastern parts of the study area. Those from Cooke, Wise, and Young counties were made before the turn of the century or about 50 years ago. Most of the recent records are of transients; in many of the counties there are only one or two sightings.

Overall transient and summer dates range from 11 March 1979 (Johnson County) to 6 October 1962 (Tarrant County). Reported dates are: *Bosque* — twice, 2 and 3 June 1974, and 11 September 1970. *Dallas* — 21 April 1962 and 26 May 1935, 21 July and 26 August 1935, and 22 July 1939 (Stillwell, 1939). Recent records: seven times in spring, 28 March 1976 to 5 May 1979, and seven times in fall, 18 August 1964 to 9 October 1986 (twice in August and three times in September and October). *Denton* — once, 10 April 1987. *Grayson* — 9 May 1976 and 11 May 1982. *Hill* — only once, though given as rare summer resident and uncommon migrant in *Check-list of Lake Whitney* (Texas Parks and Wildlife Department, 1976), 8 September 1980. *Hood* — 26 April 1976. *Hunt* — 5 August 1986. *Johnson* — once, extremely early, 11 March (no details given). *Parker* — 14 August 1963 (specimen). *Somervell* — March and May (Guthery, 1974). *Stephens* — 22 May 1985. *Tarrant* — 19 March 1975 to 22 May 1951, and 8 August 1937 (Stillwell, 1939) to 6 October 1962. *Van Zandt* — 14 May 1983, 15 April 1985, and 27 April 1987.

Nesting: Oberholser (1974) indicates that this species nested in Ellis and

Wise counties (questionable) with summer records for Cooke, Dallas, and Somervell counties. It appears that this vireo seldom nests in north central Texas today. The only actual nesting records are from Tarrant County, where birds were noted weaving a nest on 10 April 1963. Since then it has been noted once, from 26 July to 2 August 1984.

Specimens: A few Yellow-throated Vireo specimens have been taken from the following counties: Cooke, 24 March 1879 (TNHC 1438); Dallas, 21 April 1962 (OU 15822); and Parker, 14 August 1963 (FWMSH 595). Oberholser (1974) indicated that a specimen was collected in Tarrant County, but it was not located.

WARBLING VIREO   *Vireo gilvus* (Vieillot)
Status: Uncommon to fairly common transient. Rare to fairly common summer resident in recent years.
Occurrence: Warbling Vireos have been reported in 18 counties of the study area — Bosque, Clay, Collin, Cooke, Dallas, Denton, Ellis, Grayson, Hill, Hunt, Kaufman, Palo Pinto, Parker, Somervell, Stephens, Tarrant, Van Zandt, and Wichita — and nearby Henderson County.

The Warbling Vireo is found in migration from mid-April to mid-May and again from early September to early October. It is observed more often in spring than in fall, possibly because it is often first heard and then looked for by bird-watchers. During the Spring Count in Tarrant County on 5 May 1979, 46 were tallied, while a TV-tower kill on 29 September 1959 in Dallas County produced 28 casualties.

Extreme spring and fall migration dates for selected counties are: *Dallas* — 8 April 1981 to 28 May 1971 and 24 August 1985, and 4 September 1974 to 28 October 1978, next-latest 22 October 1966; *Grayson* — 14 April to 18 May 1975, and 16 September to an extremely late date, 24 November 1985; *Tarrant* — 5 April to 19 May 1963, and 6 September 1986 to 9 October 1976; *Wichita* — 13 April 1974 to 15 May 1976, and 19 September 1976 to 19 October 1974.

Nesting: Earlier accounts of this species for north central Texas did not give much information on nesting. It may have moved into the area only recently. The first years that I know of its nesting in Dallas, Tarrant, and Wichita counties are 1964, 1972, and 1973, respectively. Nesting dates range from a nest on 30 May 1972 (Tarrant County) to young being fed on 7 June 1977 (Dallas County). With the exception of one nest in a green ash, all nests were in cottonwoods 18 to 50 feet above the ground. Summer data suggest that this vireo also nests in Collin, Clay, Denton, Grayson, Hill, Hunt, and Stephens counties, but no nests have been found.
Specimens: Specimens of Warbling Vireos have been taken from Dallas (DMNH, WMP), Ellis (DMNH), Kaufman (SFASU), Parker (FWMSH),

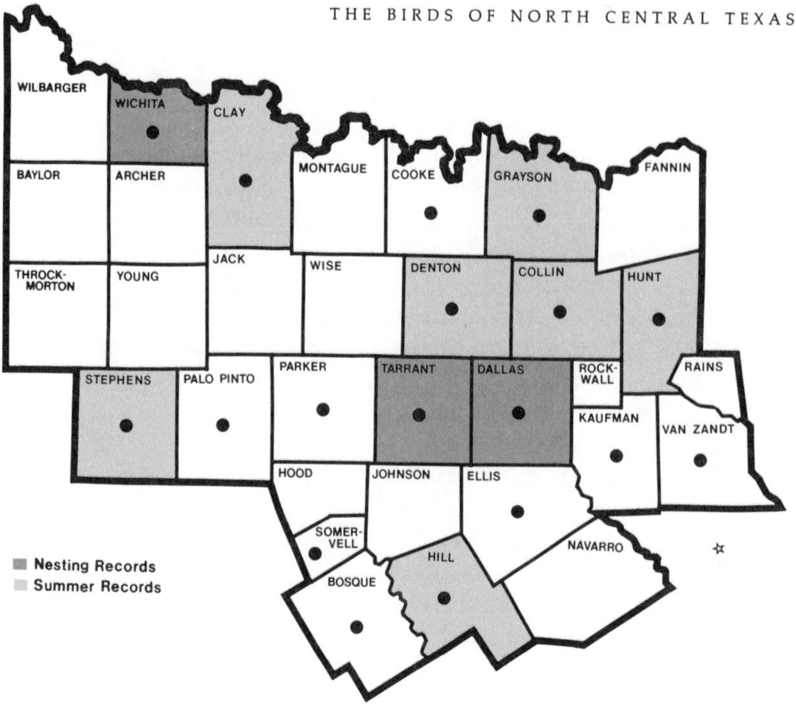

Map 83. Distribution of the Warbling Vireo, *Vireo gilvus*, with summer and nesting records

and Tarrant (FWMSH) counties, all representing the race *V. g. gilvus.* Examples from Cooke County indicated by Oberholser (1974) could not be located.

PHILADELPHIA VIREO   *Vireo philadelphicus* (Cassin)

Status: Uncommon to rare transient in spring. No fall specimens. Probably casual to irregular in fall.

Occurrence: Philadelphia Vireos have been reported in 16 counties of the study area: Archer, Bosque, Collin, Dallas, Denton, Ellis, Grayson, Hill, Hood, Kaufman, Palo Pinto, Rains, Somervell, Tarrant, Van Zandt, and Wichita.

The status of this species for north central Texas has been difficult to evaluate. I strongly believe that a number of reported observations of Philadelphia Vireos, especially in the fall, have been misidentifications. I have searched for the species and have examined numerous TV-tower kills but have found no fall examples. Interestingly, at times in the fall no Warbling Vireos, a rather common migrant, are reported, though Philadelphia Vireos are. Extreme care should be exercised in distinguishing these two species; both are yellow and white below, but on different parts of their undersides.

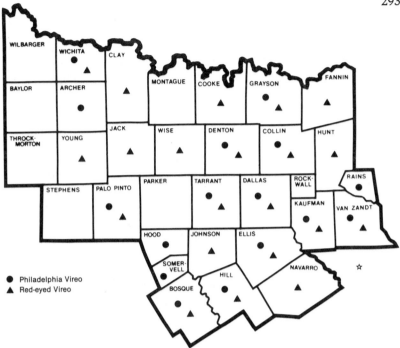

Map 84. Distribution of the Philadelphia Vireo, *Vireo philadelphicus*, and the Red-eyed Vireo, *V. olivaceus*

Over a five-year fall period (1974 through 1978, none in 1977) 24 Philadelphia Vireos were recovered at a TV tower near Coweta, Wagoner County, in northeastern Oklahoma (Norman, 1982). Dates of specimen collections range from 13 September to 15 October, with peak numbers (six) found on 9 October. None have been found in the southern part of the state. There also are few valid fall records on the Texas coast. It appears that Philadelphia Vireos take an eastern path toward the Mississippi River drainage after entering northeastern Oklahoma.

Overall dates for north central Texas range from 1 April 1982 to 22 May 1974 (both Grayson County), and 27 August 1978 (Denton County) to 31 October 1979 (Tarrant County), next-latest 26 October 1957 (Dallas County). Most of the dates are for spring; alleged fall dates total fewer than 25.

County dates are: *Archer* — 4 and 5 May 1974. *Bosque* — scarce migrant, no details given in field checklist (Pulich, 1980b). *Collin* — 6 October 1981, one banded; no other valid records. *Dallas* — early records by Stillwell (1939) give only spring dates. More recent records: 3 April 1976, next-earliest 11 April 1959 to 19 May 1959, and five times in fall, 28 August 1974, 14 September 1974, 16 September 1971, 12 October 1968, and 26 October 1957, some of which are probably misidentifications. *Denton* — Oberholser (1974) shows both spring and fall records, but only one has been reported in fall in recent years, 27 August 1978, questionable. *Ellis* — specimen, see below. *Grayson* — 1 April 1982 to 22 May 1974, and three fall sightings, 16 September 1973 and 22 September 1974 and 1979. *Hill* — 19 April 1978. *Hood* — 3 May 1981. *Kaufman* — specimen, see below. *Palo Pinto* — 9 October 1977. *Rains* — 10 April 1983. *Somervell* — spring (April) and fall (September and October) sightings, details not given (Guthery, 1974). *Tarrant* — 24 April 1983 to 18 May 1975; 21 counted on annual Spring Bird Count of 13 May 1972. Five fall sightings, some questionable, 5 September 1982, 20 and 28 September 1980, 9 October 1983, 14 October 1981, and 31 October 1979 (extremely late). *Van Zandt* — 14 April 1985. *Wichita* — 22 April 1974 to 15 May 1976, and 17 October 1977, 19 October 1974 and 22 October 1975; fall sightings questionable.

Specimens: Only spring specimens have been taken from the following counties: Dallas — 2 May 1964 (DMNH 5232), 8 May 1939 (DMNH 723), 10 May 1948 (DMNH 3769), 12 May 1948 (DMNH 3820), and 12 May 1968 (WMP 1649); Ellis — 15 May 1941 (DMNH 1634); Kaufman — 9 May 1950 (DMNH 4686).

RED-EYED VIREO *Vireo olivaceus* (Linnaeus)

Status: Fairly common transient. Rare summer resident.

Occurrence: Red-eyed Vireos have been recorded in 21 counties of the study area — Bosque, Clay, Collin, Cooke, Dallas, Denton, Ellis, Fannin, Grayson, Hill, Hunt, Jack, Johnson, Kaufman, Navarro, Palo Pinto, Tarrant, Van Zandt, Wichita, Wise, and Young — and adjacent Henderson County.

Red-eyed Vireos have been reported from 29 March 1978 (Grayson County), next-earliest 1 April 1985 (Van Zandt County) to 25 October 1984 (Grayson County). Extreme dates for counties where sufficient data are available are: *Collin* — 17 April 1982 to 23 May 1981, and 21 August 1982 to 30 September 1980; *Dallas* — 7 April 1935 (Stillwell, 1939) to 26 May 1957, and 12 August 1974 to 16 October 1960; *Grayson* — 29 March 1978 to 25 May 1984, and 10 September 1981 to 25 October 1984; *Tarrant* — 15 April 1976 to 19 May 1977, and 4 September 1942 to 15 October 1960; *Van Zandt* — 1 April 1985 to 18 May 1984, and 6 September 1984 to 23 September 1984; *Wichita* — 23 May 1977 and 19 October 1980 (specimen). Usually only one or two Red-eyed Vireos are seen, but as many as 28 were tallied on the 5 May 1975 Spring Count in Fort Worth.

Although this species is considered a summer resident throughout north central Texas, only a few counties have nesting records (nests or eggs): Cooke, Dallas, Tarrant, and Wise. The only two nesting dates that I am aware of are one from Tarrant County, a nest on 28 May 1960; and an adult feeding a fledgling in Dallas County on 30 June 1985. There are, however, a few summer sightings of the species for Bosque, Clay, Denton, Fannin, Grayson, Hill, Hunt, and Van Zandt counties. It is likely that this vireo could be found nesting in some of these counties.

Specimens: Specimens of Red-eyed Vireos have been recorded for the following counties: Clay (Oberholser, 1974; not located), Cooke (TNHC), Dallas (DMNH, OU, UTA, WMP), Denton (DMNH), Ellis (DMNH), Hunt (FWMSH), Kaufman (DMNH, WMP), Palo Pinto (DMNH), and Wichita (WMP) counties.

Family Emberizidae (Wood Warblers, Tanagers, Cardinals, Grosbeaks, Buntings, and Sparrows)

BLUE-WINGED WARBLER *Vermivora pinus* (Linnaeus)
Status: Rare in spring. Casual in fall locally.
Occurrence: Blue-winged Warblers have been reported in nine counties of the study area: Collin, Dallas, Denton, Grayson, Hill, Hunt, Palo Pinto, Tarrant, and Wichita. Sightings may reflect areas in which there is much bird-watching, for this warbler is not often seen. The overall records are more frequent for spring (23 March to 23 May) than for fall (10 August to 21 October), and in some areas it is observed only in the spring.

County records are: *Collin* — one banded 21 August 1982; *Dallas* — 13 times in spring, 6 April 1975 to 12 May 1983, and six times in fall, 16 and 23 August 1986, 29 August 1962, 4 September 1971, 16 September 1967 and 1984, and 21 October 1963; *Denton* — spring (Oberholser, 1974), and 27 August 1978; *Grayson* — 5 April 1980; *Hill* — 17 May 1980; *Hunt* — 23 March 1980, 8 April 1951, 29 April 1979, and 11 May 1947; *Palo Pinto* — 27 March 1976; *Tarrant* — five times in spring, 17 April 1976 to 23 May 1965, and six times in fall, 10 August 1958 to 16 September 1984; *Wichita* — twice, 21 April 1976 and 6 May 1974.

Nesting: Sutton (1938) discussed the possibility that this species nests in Tarrant County, but there are no specific dates to substantiate nesting. Four observations of a possible nesting bird were made between 1 June and 2 July 1958 in that county.
Specimens: There is only one specimen from north central Texas, a bird found dead on 19 April 1952 in Dallas County (DMNH 4857).

GOLDEN-WINGED WARBLER *Vermivora chrysoptera* (Linnaeus)
Status: Rare to casual transient.
Occurrence: Golden-winged Warblers have been recorded 29 times in five north central Texas counties. Dates for the counties are: *Collin* — 2 May 1986, a bird photographed and banded at Heard Refuge and another banded on 7 October 1986; *Dallas* (1959–82) — ten times in spring, 30 April 1974 to 13 May 1982, and twice in fall, 15 September 1976 and 18 September

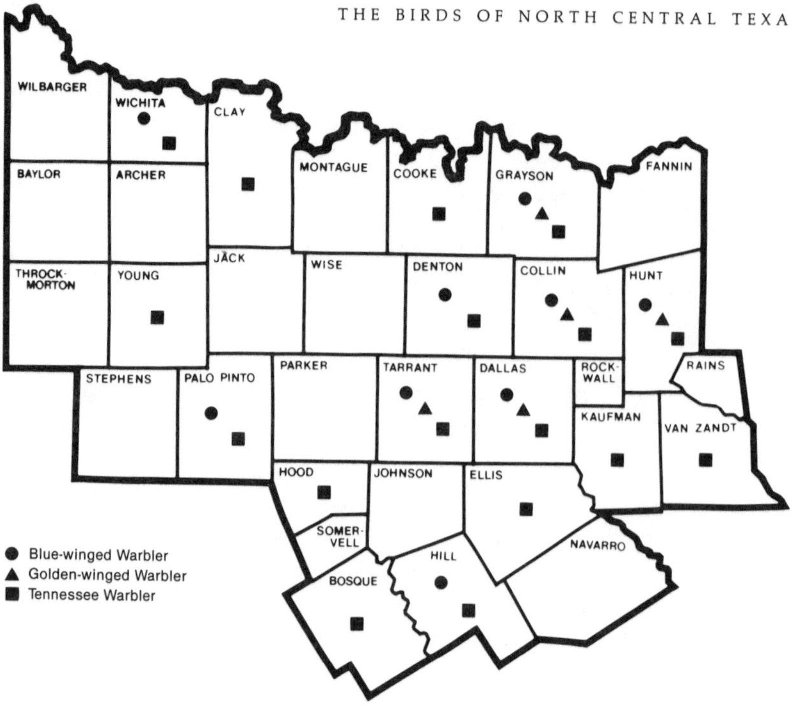

Map 85. Distribution of the Blue-winged Warbler, *Vermivora pinus;* the Golden-winged Warbler, *V. chrysoptera;* and the Tennessee Warbler, *V. peregrina*

1974; *Grayson* — 5 May 1979, 10 May 1972, and 23 September 1984; *Hunt* — 25 April (no year given); *Tarrant* (1955–84) — 11 times in spring, 16 April 1955 to 19 May 1972, and once in fall, 19 September 1974.
Specimens: There are no specimens of this species for north central Texas.

TENNESSEE WARBLER   *Vermivora peregrina* (Wilson)
Status: Uncommon to rare transient.
Occurrence: Tennessee Warblers have been recorded in 17 counties of the study area: Bosque, Clay, Collin, Cooke, Dallas, Denton, Ellis, Grayson, Hill, Hood, Hunt, Kaufman, Palo Pinto, Tarrant, Van Zandt, Wichita, and Young. Records are more numerous in spring than in fall and in counties where there is much bird-watching. There also are more sightings in counties with more woodland areas. In fall extreme care should be exercised in identifying this species, for it is easily confused with the Orange-crowned Warbler. The latter species is the more common migrant in north central Texas.

Extreme spring and fall overall county dates are 25 March (Tarrant County) to 29 May (Grayson County), and 3 September to 30 November (both Dallas County). Dates for selected counties for which sufficient observations are available are: *Collin*—26 April 1978 to 15 May 1981, and 8 October 1984 to 16 November 1985 (all banded birds); *Dallas*—4 April 1976 (mean arrival, 25 April, 14 years, 1966–82) to 27 May 1941, and 3 September 1980 to 30 November 1980, next-latest 16 October 1960 (specimen); *Grayson*—20 April to 29 May 1975, and 8 September to 24 October; *Tarrant*—25 March 1944, next-earliest 9 April 1958 to 23 May 1971, and 19 September 1943 to 11 October 1986.

Specimens: Tennessee Warblers have been collected only from Dallas (DMNH, WMP) and Ellis (DMNH) counties.

ORANGE-CROWNED WARBLER   *Vermivora celata* (Say)

Status: Common to fairly common transient. Uncommon winter resident.

Occurrence: Orange-crowned Warblers have been reported in 27 counties of the north central Texas study area: Archer, Bosque, Clay, Collin, Cooke, Dallas, Denton, Ellis, Fannin, Grayson, Hill, Hood, Hunt, Kaufman, Montague, Palo Pinto, Parker, Rains, Rockwall, Somervell, Stephens, Tarrant, Van Zandt, Wichita, Wilbarger, Wise, and Young. This common transient through north central Texas would also be found in the remaining counties if there were sufficient bird-watching. It is frequently found in dense, low thickets and brushlands.

Overall dates of extreme occurrence of this species in the study area range from 20 August 1980 (Hill County) to 28 May 1977 (Dallas County). It is more common in migration than during the winter: 52 birds hit the Cedar Hill TV tower in Dallas County on the night of 16 October 1960. It has been recorded on all the CBCs, though in some years it was absent from one or two counts. The numbers are fewer in winter along the Red River than in the southern part of the range. It occasionally visits feeding stations for suet; however, one was noted taking sunflower seeds in Tarrant County on 15 December 1980.

Dates for selected counties are: *Collin*—25 September 1980 to 14 May 1983 (all banded birds); *Dallas*—29 August 1981, next-earliest 4 September 1976 to 28 May 1977; *Grayson*—24 September to 18 May; *Tarrant*—1 September 1956 to 18 May 1986; *Wichita*—19 September 1978 (18 September 1981, Wilbarger County) to 21 May 1973.

Specimens: Specimens are available from the following counties: Cooke (TNHC), Dallas (DMNH, USNM, WMP), Denton (DMNH, UTA, WMP), Henderson (DMNH), Kaufman (WMP), Palo Pinto (DMNH, WMP), Parker (DMNH), Tarrant (DMNH, FWMSH, USNM, WMP), and Wichita (WMP). Both the nominate race, *V. c. celata,* and the race *V. c. orestera* have been collected in north central Texas.

NASHVILLE WARBLER   *Vermivora ruficapilla* (Wilson)

Status: Common to abundant transient, more in fall than in spring.

Occurrence: Nashville Warblers have been seen in 26 counties of the study area—Archer, Bosque, Clay, Collin, Cooke, Dallas, Denton, Ellis, Fannin, Grayson, Hill, Hood, Hunt, Johnson, Kaufman, Navarro, Palo Pinto, Parker, Rains, Rockwall, Somervell, Stephens, Tarrant, Van Zandt, Wichita, and Young—and nearby Eastland County.

This species is very common and is often observed foraging in low shrubbery as well as in trees. It seems to be more common in fall than in spring. Banders in Collin County often capture and band a dozen or so a day in late September and early October. The largest numbers banded were 46 on 9 October 1982 and 36 on 6 October 1984. Some examples of large TV-tower kills are 94 on the night of 10 October 1958, 49 on 28 September 1959, and more than 170 on 16 October 1960, all at a Dallas County TV tower. On the last date 34 hit another TV tower about 30 miles away, in Tarrant County.

Extreme overall dates from north central Texas for spring are 13 March 1971 (Ellis County) to 26 May 1979 (Dallas County), while in fall the extreme dates range from 20 August 1956, next-earliest 23 August 1954 (specimens, both for Tarrant County) to 1 December 1982 (Wichita County), next-latest 28 November 1981 (Dallas County).

Although the Nashville Warbler usually winters in extreme south Texas and Mexico, there are several winter reports for December and early January which suggest that very late birds may occasionally be expected. These probably represent very late stragglers. They have been found in Denton County on 18 December 1983, in Rockwall County on 20 December 1984, and in Tarrant County 1 through 3 January 1955 and on 1 January 1965. A specimen misdated 3 January 1981 (FWMSH) was actually taken earlier in the fall. Two references (Stillwell, 1939) to July dates for Dallas and Tarrant counties were not accepted.

Extreme dates for selected counties are: *Collin*—4 April 1982 to 16 May 1979, and 1 September 1983 to 6 November 1982 (all banded birds); *Dallas*—14 March 1978 to 26 May 1979, and 25 August 1980 to 28 November 1981; *Grayson*—30 March to 19 May, and 10 September to 5 November; *Tarrant*—14 March 1963 to 26 May 1968 and 20 August 1956, next-earliest 23 August 1954 (specimen) to 15 November 1973; *Wichita*—4 April 1978 to 25 May 1978, and 29 August 1974 to 1 December 1982, next-latest 25 October 1982.

Specimens: Specimens have been taken in the following counties: Cooke (TNHC), Dallas (DMNH, UTA, WMP), Denton (DMNH, WMP), Ellis (DMNH), Kaufman (DMNH), Navarro (USNM), Parker (FWMSH), Tarrant (DMNH, FWMSH, WMP), and Wichita (WMP). Oberholser (1974) indicated a specimen from Collin County, but it could not be located. Except for a specimen (DMNH 4907) taken on 29 March 1955 from Tarrant

County, which was identified by Oberholser as *V. r. ridgwayi*, all represent the eastern race *ruficapilla*; however, the *ridgwayi* specimen has not been reexamined.

LUCY'S WARBLER   *Vermivora luciae* (Cooper)
Status: Accidental, not to be expected again.
Occurrence: Lucy's Warblers are normally found in the El Paso area, in extreme west Texas. However, the late Connie Hagar, dean of Texas bird-watchers, is credited with carefully observing this little western warbler many times in "plain sight" from a window in her home in Corsicana, Navarro County, on 21 and 22 May 1928. This observation occurred before she moved to Rockport and made it a mecca where bird-watchers gathered in the spring. There have been no reports of this species for north central Texas since Connie's time.

NORTHERN PARULA   *Parula americana* (Linnaeus)
Status: Uncommon to rare transient during migration. Casual summer resident locally, but no recent nesting records.
Occurrence: The Northern Parula has been recorded in 13 north central Texas counties: Collin, Cooke, Dallas, Denton, Ellis, Grayson, Hunt, Kaufman, Navarro, Somervell, Tarrant, Van Zandt, and Wichita.

Extreme overall dates are 19 March 1964 (Dallas County) to 20 November 1982 (Grayson County) with more records during spring migration than in the fall. One report of 25 December 1953 (Tarrant County) lacked details and was dismissed.

Dates for selected counties are: *Dallas*—19 March 1964, next-earliest 31 March 1975 through 16 October 1960 (specimen); *Grayson*—eight records, 1969–83, 5 April to 30 May, and 1 September to 20 November; *Tarrant*—24 March 1973 to 15 October 1982; *Wichita*—13 April 1974 to 19 October 1980 (specimen).

Nesting: A report that this species has nested in Cooke County (Oberholser, 1974) probably represents a record by G. H. Ragsdale before the turn of the century. It probably still nests there; a bird was observed on 29 July 1982 in typical willow habitat on the Oklahoma side of the Red River at the head of Lake Texoma. Except for a report more than forty years ago, on 2 July 1943, there are no recent nesting reports for Tarrant County, although nesting is still suspected at the Fort Worth Nature Center —23 July to 19 September 1972, 26 July (three) to 2 August 1984, and 20 April to 27 June 1985 (no nests or young birds discovered). Two fledglings were observed on 14 June 1986 below White Rock Dam, Dallas County. Summer dates are available for earlier years, but no young or nests were found.

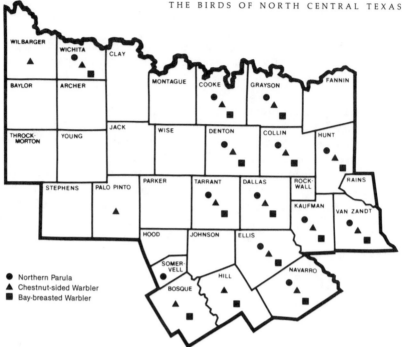

Map 86. Distribution of the Northern Parula, *Parula americana;* the Chestnut-sided Warbler, *Dendroica pensylvanica;* and the Bay-breasted Warbler, *D. castanea*

Specimens: Northern Parula Warblers have been collected from the following counties: Cooke (TNHC); Dallas (WMP); Ellis (DMNH), not located; Kaufman (DMNH); and Wichita (WMP).

Yellow Warbler *Dendroica petechia* (Linnaeus)
Status: Common spring and fall transient.
Occurrence: Yellow Warblers have been reported in 30 counties of the study area—Archer, Bosque, Clay, Collin, Cooke, Dallas, Denton, Ellis, Fannin, Grayson, Hill, Hood, Hunt, Jack, Johnson, Kaufman, Navarro, Palo Pinto, Parker, Rains, Rockwall, Somervell, Stephens, Tarrant, Throckmorton, Van Zandt, Wichita, Wilbarger, Wise and Young—and nearby Shackelford County.

This species has been found from 23 March 1970 (Grayson and Tarrant counties) to 2 June 1967 (Dallas County), and again from 24 July 1983 (Tarrant County) to 21 October 1978 (Denton County). Extreme spring and fall arrival and departure dates for selected counties are: *Dallas*—8 April 1968 to 2 June 1967, next-latest 27 May 1966, and 9 August 1939 (specimen) and 1972 to 17 October 1969; *Grayson*—23 April to 31 May, and 2 August to 19 October; *Tarrant*—23 March 1970, next-earliest 6 April 1986 to 31 May 1975 and 24 July 1983, next-earliest 31 July 1974 and 1982, to 21 October 1981; *Van Zandt* — 6 April 1986 to 27 May 1983, and 19 August 1985 (12 August, Rains County) to 3 October 1984; *Wichita* — 22 April 1977 to 24 May 1973, and 19 August 1978 to 10 October 1977; *Wise* — 17 May 1984, and 24 August 1983.

In passage the species is quite numerous; it is not uncommon to see 50 or more during the peak of migration in early May and September. More than 130 birds were seen on the annual May 1976 Spring Count in Tarrant County, and 20 or more were tallied, along with warblers of 13 other species on 13 May 1983 in Dallas County. On 28–29 September 1959, 76 birds struck the Cedar Hill TV tower in Dallas County, and on 5 September 1962 63 birds hit the same tower.

There is an unexplainable observation of an adult male Yellow Warbler by seven persons at a small stock tank in Wichita County on 15 December 1973. This may have been a sick or injured bird, for this species does not normally winter in north central Texas.

Formerly this species bred sparingly in north central Texas, mainly in the southeastern part of the study area, in Kaufman and Navarro counties (Oberholser, 1974). Oberholser also indicated that it summered in Cooke, Dallas, Grayson, and Hunt counties. There is an isolated date, 20 June 1954, for Tarrant County, but no other recent summer record.

Specimens: Specimens have been taken in Dallas (DMNH, USNM, UTA, WMP), Denton (DMNH, WMP), Ellis (DMNH), Parker (FWMSH), Stephens (WMP), and Tarrant (DMNH, FWMSH, WMP) counties. Those indicated by Oberholser (1974) from Cooke, Kaufman, and Wilbarger counties could not be located.

The races of many of the Yellow Warblers listed in the paragraph above are undetermined. Racial studies (*fide* Mario A. Ramos) indicate that there are several undescribed races of Yellow Warblers. Specimens (DMNH) taken from Denton County in 1939 were identified by Oberholser as *aestiva*, *amnicola*, *morcomi*, and *rubiginosa*. More recent examples in my collection (WMP) from Dallas and Tarrant counties were identified as *aestiva*, with examples of *amnicola* and *rubiginosa* and several undescribed races from Dallas County. The racial identifications of all the Yellow Warblers of north central Texas await further study.

CHESTNUT-SIDED WARBLER   *Dendroica pensylvanica* (Linnaeus)
Status: Uncommon to rare transient in spring. Extremely rare in fall.
Occurrence: Chestnut-sided Warblers have been reported in 16 north central Texas counties: Bosque, Collin, Cooke, Dallas, Denton, Ellis, Grayson, Hill, Hunt, Kaufman, Navarro, Palo Pinto, Tarrant, Van Zandt, Wichita, and Wilbarger. In some years they can be seen in fair numbers in mid-May, especially if weather conditions are favorable; however, in other

years only one or two are observed. On 13 May 1983, 12 were counted in Garland, Dallas County, along with warblers of 13 other species. They are seldom observed in the fall, there being fewer than 15 records.

Extreme dates of passage in spring and fall for selected counties are: *Dallas* — 21 April 1935 to 26 May 1963, and three fall sightings, 10 September 1960, 3 October 1959, and 6 October 1984; *Grayson* — 19 April 1975 to 23 May 1981, and 16 September 1979; *Tarrant* — 26 April 1968 to 30 May 1971, and fewer than eight reports in fall and an unexplainable early date of 16 August 1964, next-earliest 6 September 1972 to 31 October 1979. A record for Wilbarger County noted by Oberholser (1974) for summer but with no details is probably an error and should be deleted.

Specimens: Chestnut-sided Warblers have been collected from Dallas (DMNH) and Kaufman (DMNH) counties, all in May.

MAGNOLIA WARBLER *Dendroica magnolia* (Wilson)

Status: Fairly common to uncommon spring transient. Rare fall transient.

Occurrence: Magnolia Warblers have been recorded in 16 counties of the study area — Bosque, Collin, Dallas, Denton, Ellis, Grayson, Hill, Hunt, Jack, Johnson, Kaufman, Navarro, Somervell, Tarrant, Van Zandt, and Wichita — and adjacent Shackelford County.

Overall, this species has been recorded from 11 April 1954 (Tarrant County) to 10 June 1975 (Grayson County), and 24 August 1980 (Dallas County) to 20 October 1972 (Dallas County, WMP specimen). It is far more common in spring than in fall. It is one of the last warblers to pass through the area in the spring, and during exceptional spring movements 15 or so a day are not unusual. It may not be seen anywhere in north central Texas in the fall for several years at a time.

Extreme dates for selected counties are: *Dallas* — 22 April 1974 to 31 May 1971, and 24 August 1980 to 20 October 1972; *Grayson* — 20 April 1975 to 28 May; isolated dates, 9 and 10 June 1975; and twice in fall, 9 through 11 September 1976 and 10 September 1977; *Tarrant* — 11 April 1954 to 26 May 1974, and six fall records from 7 September 1954 to 13 October 1956.

Kelley (1935) listed an "unexplainable" record for the Magnolia Warbler on 26 December 1932 for Dallas County. Since a number of Kelley's other reports are so vague and questionable, this observation was deleted, as he gave no details.

However, there is a recent carefully documented record of 7 and 8 December 1986 for the Fort Worth Nature Center, Tarrant County. The weather prior to and during this period was extremely mild, which may help to explain this and several unusually late or winter sightings for the Dallas–Fort Worth area.

Specimens: Magnolia Warbler specimens have been collected in Dallas

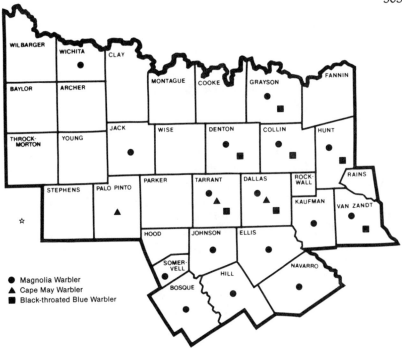

Map 87. Distribution of the Magnolia Warbler, *Dendroica magnolia;* the Cape May Warbler, *D. tigrina;* and the Black-throated Blue Warbler, *D. caerulescens*

(DMNH, WMP), Denton (DMNH), Ellis (DMNH), Kaufman (DMNH), Navarro (Oberholser, 1974, not located), and Tarrant (FWMSH) counties.

CAPE MAY WARBLER *Dendroica tigrina* (Gmelin)
Status: Very rare to accidental visitor.
Occurrence: The Cape May Warbler has been reported in three counties of the study area: Dallas, Palo Pinto, and Tarrant. Oberholser (1974) gives no records of this beautiful warbler for north central Texas. Indeed, the *Checklist of the Birds of Texas* (TOS, 1984) indicates only five documented records for the state.

The county records of the Cape May Warbler for north central Texas are: *Dallas* — 28 April 1935 (Stillwell, 1939), 6 to 26 January 1981, and 9 October 1986; *Palo Pinto* — 17 January 1975, a lone Cape May Warbler with Yellow-rumped Warblers (photograph confirmed by USNM personnel); *Tarrant* — 28 April 1972, and 13 May 1972 (an unusual spring bird count when 20 species of warblers totaling more than 300 warblers were recorded), and 24 January 1981 (the same year as the count in Dallas County).
Specimens: No specimens exist for north central Texas. An example of a

Cape May Warbler should be collected to document the occurrence of the species, especially if it should appear again in winter.

BLACK-THROATED BLUE WARBLER *Dendroica caerulescens* (Gmelin)
Status: Rare transient.
Occurrence: The Black-throated Blue Warbler has been reported in seven north central Texas counties: Collin, Dallas, Denton, Grayson, Hunt, Tarrant, and Van Zandt. There are a few more records for fall than for spring. Adult males are distinctive, but fall immatures and females can be confused with Tennessee Warblers and possibly with Philadelphia Vireos, and observations should be made carefully when birds of this species other than adult males are being identified.

Data on hand for the above counties are: *Collin*—13 April 1981. *Dallas*—two spring records, 13 May 1933, at height of warbler migration (Stillwell, 1939), and 3 through 9 May 1970, and five fall records—11 September 1974, 16 October 1960, 17 October 1964, 27 October 1963, and 31 October 1968. *Denton*—7 September 1958. *Grayson*—two spring records, 23 April 1971 and 28 May 1977, and one fall record, 13 October 1974. *Hunt*—17 May 1949. Oberholser (1974) also indicates a fall sighting, but details are lacking. *Tarrant*—some reports are discounted for lack of details. Fifteen spring reports, six given as males, 4 April 1955 to 6 May 1967 and 1984, and six fall reports, 2 October 1956 and 26 October 1954. *Van Zandt*—two reports, 5 May 1975 and 27 September 1978.
Specimens: There are two specimens for north central Texas, one from Dallas County on 16 October 1960 (WMP 1028) and the other from Tarrant County on 22 October 1966 (FWMSH 899).

YELLOW-RUMPED WARBLER *Dendroica coronata* (Linnaeus)
Status: Very common to common transient and winter resident.
Occurrence: Yellow-rumped Warblers have been recorded in all counties of the study area except Montague and Throckmorton. Lack of observers in these two counties no doubt explains why they have not been reported there. In addition, they have been seen in nearby Shackelford County, where they were not previously recorded. This species is the most common winter warbler found on all CBCs. Its numbers vary from year to year, and there may be a slight shift south from the Red River during extremely cold weather, especially in January and February. It is usually found by mid-October and remains until late April.

Extreme dates for selected counties are: *Dallas*—4 October 1984 to 20 May 1979; *Denton*—19 October 1972 to 9 May 1978; *Grayson*—24 September to 11 May 1972; *Hood*—11 September 1964 (specimen) to 28 April 1973; *Tarrant*—13 September 1957 to 30 May 1943; *Wichita*—6 September 1978 to 30 April 1977.

The Yellow-rumped Warbler was formerly considered two separate species, Audubon's Warbler and the Myrtle Warbler. These species are now considered subspecies of the Yellow-rumped Warbler (AOU, 1973), though they can be distinguished by their yellow throats and white throats, respectively. Audubon's Warblers have been recorded in Clay, Dallas (specimen), Denton, Grayson (specimen), Johnson, Navarro, Palo Pinto, Stephens, Tarrant, and Wichita counties and nearby Shackelford County. Extreme dates for Audubon's Warblers range from 30 September 1956 to 30 April 1941, both for Tarrant County; however, these dates are typical for the overall area.

A Yellow-rumped (Myrtle) Warbler banded on 2 October 1981 near Hudson, Wisconsin, was found dead in Dallas County on 6 January 1982. *Specimens:* Yellow-rumped Warblers have been collected in the following counties: Collin (DMNH), Cooke (TNHC), Dallas (DMNH, WMP), Denton (DMNH, WMP), Ellis (DMNH, TCWC), Grayson (WMP), Hood (DMNH), Hunt (FWMSH), Johnson (DMNH), Kaufman (DMNH), Navarro (WMP), Palo Pinto (DMNH), Parker (FWMSH), Somervell (FWMSH), Tarrant (DMNH, FWMSH, UTA, WMP), Wichita (MWU, WMP), and Henderson (DMNH). The specimens indicated by Oberholser (1974) for Clay and Wilbarger counties were not located. Among the specimens that have been examined, three subspecies have been found: *auduboni, coronata,* and *hooveri.*

BLACK-THROATED GRAY WARBLER   *Dendroica nigrescens* (Townsend)
Status: Casual visitor.
Occurrence: The Black-throated Gray Warbler has been reported in three north central Texas counties — Dallas, Tarrant, and Young — and nearby McLennan County.

The county records are: *Dallas* — a female was collected in Irving on 4 January 1959, as it fed in an evergreen, *Juniperus* sp. A second female was spotted on 29 January 1974 in Irving. *Tarrant* — Pulich (1979) discusses the occurrence of the species and points out that the Black-throated Gray Warbler resembles the Black-and-white Warbler, a common species in this area. I accept only two of the three sightings for this county, those of 9 October 1978 and 19 October 1963. *Young* — there is a sight record without details of a bird observed at Graham on 29 March 1964.

A bird was observed three miles southwest of Waco, in nearby McLennan County, on 12 November 1964. *Specimens:* The only specimen (WMP 732) for north central Texas is the Dallas County bird described above.

TOWNSEND'S WARBLER   *Dendroica townsendi* (Townsend)
Status: Accidental.
Occurrence: This western warbler has been observed once in north cen-

Map 88. Distribution of the Black-throated Green Warbler, *Dendroica virens,* and the Blackburnian Warbler, *D. fusca*

tral Texas. An adult male was observed and leisurely studied at close range by eight persons, including myself, in Irving, Dallas County, on 14 October 1976. The bird was in the company of several fall vireos and warblers.

BLACK-THROATED GREEN WARBLER   *Dendroica virens* (Gmelin)
Status: Common to fairly common transient.
Occurrence: Black-throated Green Warblers have been reported in 19 north central Texas counties: Archer, Bosque, Collin, Cooke, Dallas, Denton, Ellis, Grayson, Hill, Hood, Hunt, Johnson, Kaufman, Navarro, Palo Pinto, Parker, Tarrant, Van Zandt, and Wichita.

This species is much more common and widespread than many of the other warblers that pass through the study area. At the peak of spring migration in mid-May it is not unusual to see several dozen pass through the area. Overall dates within the area have been reported in spring from 13 March 1939 to 10 June 1973 (both Tarrant County), and from 6 August 1981 (Grayson County) to 11 November 1979 (Dallas County).

Typical overall dates for selected counties are: *Dallas*—29 March 1949 (specimen), 1959, and 1976 to 26 May 1958, and 25 August 1980 to 11

November 1979; *Grayson*—1 April 1975 to 26 May and 6 August 1981 (exceptionally early), next-earliest 26 August to 28 October 1969; *Tarrant* —13 March 1939 (Stillwell, 1939), next-earliest 21 Mach 1959 to 10 June 1973, next-latest 8 June 1975, and 10 August 1985 to 7 November 1959; *Van Zandt*—19 April 1984 to 25 May 1983, and 11 September 1983 to 19 October 1983.

Specimens: A number of Black-throated Green Warblers have been taken from north central Texas counties: Dallas (DMNH, UTA, WMP), Denton (DMNH), Ellis (DMNH, WMP), Kaufman (DMNH), Parker (FWMSH), Tarrant (DMNH, UTA), and Wichita (WMP). Specimens indicated for Cooke County (Oberholser, 1974) could not be located.

GOLDEN-CHEEKED WARBLER   *Dendroica chrysoparia* Sclater and Salvin
Status: Rare summer resident restricted to Texas.
Occurrence: Originally the Golden-cheeked Warbler ranged through 41 Texas counties (Pulich, 1976). Today it occurs in fewer than 30 counties and in only seven north central Texas counties, where mature cedar brakes —Ashe Juniper (*Juniperus ashei*)—exist.

The county records for the study area are: *Bosque*—Meridian SP is a favorite place of bird-watchers who wish to observe this unique species; however, the species can also be found elsewhere. Recorded every year to 1987, mainly in April and May. Extreme dates, 13 March 1977 to 1 August 1974. *Dallas*—formerly occurred in the Cedar Hills area, but habitat no longer exists. First seen in 1957 and last seen on 29 March 1964. *Hood* —few records, no recent ones. Extreme dates, 2 April 1964 to 27 June 1964. *Johnson*—records mainly above Lake Whitney Reservoir along the Brazos River. Extreme dates, 22 March 1972 to 23 June 1982. *Palo Pinto*—scattered records throughout the county. Extreme dates for Possum Kingdom SP, 24 March 1962 to 7 July 1960; latest years seen, 22 June 1984 and 14 April 1985. *Somervell*—limited habitat in county; small population can be found at the Dinosaur Valley SP, where 12 were sighted on 2 June 1985. Extreme dates, 23 March 1957 to 23 June 1984. *Stephens*—limited habitat in this county. There is one observation of two birds on 25 May 1974 at the Eastland county line.

The occurrence of this species in Hill and Tarrant counties given by Oberholser (1974) should be dismissed. There are no authentic records of Golden-cheeked Warblers for either county. I know of no specific records for the former county, and today what little habitat that may have existed along the Brazos River is gone. A very late record of 28 August 1954 (Baumgartner, 1955) for Tarrant County is very likely that of a misidentified Black-throated Green Warbler, which commonly passes through the area in the fall.

Specimens: Specimens of Golden-cheeked Warblers have been collected

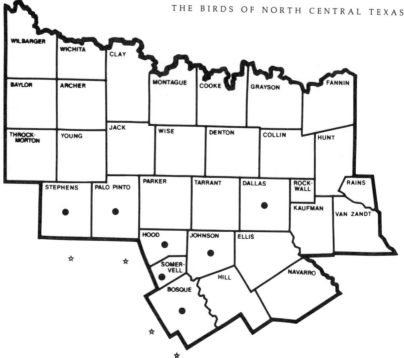

Map 89. Distribution of the Golden-cheeked Warbler, *Dendroica chrysoparia*

from the following counties: Bosque (USNM, WMP), Dallas (DMNH), Hood (WMP), Johnson (DMNH), Palo Pinto (NTSU, specimen missing 1983; WMP), and Somervell (WMP).

BLACKBURNIAN WARBLER   *Dendroica fusca* (Müller)
Status: Uncommon to rare transient.
Occurrence: Blackburnian Warblers have been reported in 15 north central Texas counties: Bosque, Collin, Cooke, Dallas, Denton, Ellis, Fannin, Grayson, Hill, Hunt, Kaufman, Navarro, Rains, Tarrant, and Van Zandt.

This species is usually observed high in trees and may be missed when the foliage leafs out in the spring. Extreme overall dates for counties in the study area range from 2 April 1982 (Dallas County) to 4 June 1984 (Tarrant County), and from 8 August 1964 (Tarrant County) to 21 November 1982 (Grayson County), next-latest 13 October 1936 (Dallas County). Numbers peak in early May and early September. It is far more numerous in spring than in fall: there are fewer than 20 fall reports.

Extreme dates for selected counties are: *Dallas*—2 April 1982, next-earliest 19 April 1984 to 26 May 1963, and 3 September 1974 to 13 October 1936 (Stillwell, 1939); *Denton*—Oberholser (1974) gives a spring record; two records since, 22 May 1984 and 28 August 1985; *Grayson*—

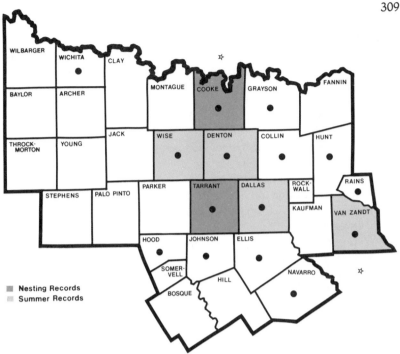

Map 90. Distribution of the Yellow-throated Warbler, *Dendroica dominica*, with summer and nesting records

4 May to 30 May and three fall dates, 3 September 1976, 6 October 1973, and an extremely late 21 November 1982; *Tarrant* — 10 April 1984 to 4 June 1984, next-latest 3 June 1980, and four fall dates, 8 August 1964, 5 September 1974, 18 September 1974, and 6 October 1972; *Van Zandt* — 29 April 1985 to 28 May 1986 (Hunt County), and 9 October 1983.
Specimens: Specimens have been collected in Dallas (DMNH, WMP), Ellis (DMNH), and Kaufman (DMNH, WMP) counties.

YELLOW-THROATED WARBLER   *Dendroica dominica* (Linnaeus)
Status: Uncommon to rare summer resident.
Occurrence: Yellow-throated Warblers have been reported in 15 counties in the study area — Collin, Cooke, Dallas, Denton, Ellis, Grayson, Hood, Hunt, Johnson, Navarro, Rains, Tarrant, Van Zandt, Wichita, and Wise — and in adjacent Henderson County and on the Cooke-Love county line, in Oklahoma.

It is difficult to distinguish the migrant Yellow-throated Warbler from summer visitors, especially in the spring, when there are more observations and some birds may already be nesting. Overall dates for counties for which there are sufficient data are: *Dallas* — 8 March 1975 to 21 October 1982; *Denton* — 22 March 1940 to 23 August 1939 (specimens); *Grayson* — 19 April 1975 to 22 May, and one record for fall, 6 October 1973; *Tarrant* — 19 March 1976 to 17 October 1964. If the reports for Tarrant County are valid, this species accidentally occurred in winter on a CBC on 12 December 1958 and again on 10 January 1959. There have been no other winter sightings for north central Texas since that time.

Nesting: Nesting Yellow-throated Warblers have been recorded in Cooke County (Oberholser, 1974), and in Tarrant County (feeding young, 23 May 1980). It is suspected of nesting in Love County, Oklahoma, on the Cooke county line, in addition to Dallas, Denton, Van Zandt, and Wise counties and nearby Henderson County, but evidence is lacking. The Wise County record was given by Oberholser (1974) as questionable and probably dates from before the turn of the century. Today there remain few, if any, nesting areas (swampy woods) in Wise County suitable for this species. Most of the riparian habitat has been cleared for farming.

Specimens: Yellow-throated Warbler specimens have been collected in the following counties: Cooke (TNHC), Dallas (DMNH), Denton and Ellis (DMNH; some specimens missing, but may be on exhibit and not indicated as such). Specimens have also been taken from nearby Henderson County (DMNH) and from Love County, Oklahoma (WMP). Oberholser (1974) indicated that specimens were collected in Collin and Navarro counties, but these have not been located. Specimens that have been examined represent the race *D. d. albilora.*

PINE WARBLER   *Dendroica pinus* (Wilson)
Status: Rare winter visitor.
Occurrence: Pine Warblers have been reported in 10 counties of the study area: Dallas, Denton, Fannin, Grayson, Hunt, Johnson, Tarrant, Van Zandt, Wichita, and Young.

Pine Warblers nest in east Texas and are found there regularly in winter. Their occurrence in winter in north central Texas, however, is rare, though in the 1980s there has been a rash of valid winter records, some with photographs, particularly in the winter of 1980–81.

Some of the reports below may be in error, since this species can be confused with immature Blackpoll and Bay-breasted Warblers. Extreme care should be exercised in identifying Pine Warblers, and details should be presented with reports. When there was a question about the record or if no details were given, I freely edited the reports of this species.

The records for the ten north central Texas counties are: *Dallas* — early dates given by Stillwell (1939) are questionable and have not been used. Recent records since 1956 range from 18 November 1972 to 14 February 1981. *Denton* — winter (Oberholser, 1974); one recent record, 31 Decem-

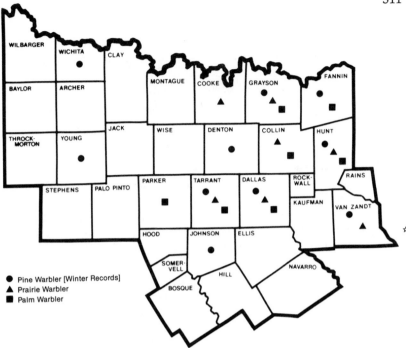

Map 91. Distribution of the Pine Warbler, *Dendroica pinus;* the Prairie Warbler, *D. discolor;* and the Palm Warbler, *D. palmarum*

ber 1985. *Fannin* —18 December 1984. *Grayson* — winter (Oberholser, 1974), four other records, 11 January 1975, 5 April 1975, and 1 May 1976 (spring sightings may be questionable, but the observer felt comfortable with the identifications), and 20 November 1982. *Hunt* — spring and fall (Oberholser, 1974), 25 November 1954. *Johnson* —26 November 1983. *Tarrant* — the dates 27 August 1940 and 19 May 1942 given by Pulich (1979) have been deleted. Other dates: 8 January 1955, 22 March 1955, 2 January 1960, 28 December 1963, 11 through 17 December 1980, 1 and 18 February 1981, 16 January to 23 February 1981 (two at two different locations; photograph of latter sighting); 22 January 1983, 1 February 1983, and 19 November 1983 and 31 January to 9 February 1985, confirmed 2 February 1985 by specimen (WMP 2930); the 1985 dates represent two different warblers at two locations. *Van Zandt* —9, 16 and 23 December 1984, 28 December 1984 (different location from that of earlier date), and the winters of 1985–86 and 1986–87. *Wichita* —2 February 1975. *Young* —21 December 1980.

Specimens: The November date for Hunt County given above represents a specimen (DMNH 4888). In addition, there is a specimen of a juvenile male (OU 393) taken near Willis, Marshall County, Oklahoma (across from Grayson County), on 3 August 1950. This suggests that the spring reports from Grayson County may represent a local population in the pinelands that extend into the northeast corner of the county along the Red River. Elsewhere in the area the only extreme dates now considered valid are 18 November to 22 March.

PRAIRIE WARBLER *Dendroica discolor* (Vieillot)

Status: Casual visitor.

Occurrence: This species has been recorded in seven counties of the study area: Collin, Cooke, Dallas, Grayson, Hunt, Tarrant, and Van Zandt.

Prairie Warblers nest to the east, in the vicinity of Tyler, Smith County, in old farmlands or burned-out areas reverting to brush with scattered secondary growth of pine and deciduous trees. Since the study area is on the edge of the east Texas ecosystem, the presence of this beautiful warbler is not unexpected; however, there are but ten records for all of the area.

County records are: *Collin* — 14 August 1983, one banded; *Cooke* — 21 May 1885 (Oberholser, 1974); *Dallas* — 16 May 1959; *Grayson* — 3 August 1978; *Hunt* — 20 September 1978 and 2 October 1978, one singing; *Tarrant* — immature on 19 April 1953, 3 September 1973, female or immature from 18 to 23 August 1974, and 24 September 1983; *Van Zandt* — 3 May 1978.

Specimens: A specimen said to have been taken by G. H. Ragsdale at Gainesville, Cooke County, in 1885 (Oberholser, 1974) could not be located.

PALM WARBLER *Dendroica palmarum* (Gmelin)

Status: Rare to casual transient.

Occurrence: Palm Warblers have been reported from seven counties of the study area: Collin, Dallas, Fannin, Grayson, Hunt, Parker, and Tarrant.

This warbler passes through north central Texas irregularly in spring and very seldom in fall. Overall county dates are: *Collin* — 19 April 1986 and 26 April 1981; *Dallas* — seven times in spring, 8 April 1981 to 17 May 1982, and twice in fall, 26 September 1939 and 16 October 1960; *Fannin* — fall (Oberholser, 1974); *Grayson* — seven times in spring, 23 April 1971 to 7 May 1972, and twice in fall, 8 October 1975 and 14 October 1979; *Hunt* — spring (Oberholser, 1974); *Parker* — 19 and 20 April 1975; *Tarrant* — seven times in spring, 13 April 1959 to 16 May 1951, and three times in fall, 8 October 1977, 12 October 1956, and 16 November 1966, plus a winter record of a bird photographed on 5 January 1985 that lingered until 27 January.

Specimens: The only specimen (WMP 1027) for north central Texas was a casualty at the Cedar Hill TV tower, Dallas County, on 15–16 October 1960. It represents the nominate race, *D. p. palmarum.*

BAY-BREASTED WARBLER   *Dendroica castanea* (Wilson)
Status: Uncommon to rare transient in spring. Casual in fall.
Occurrence: Bay-breasted Warblers have been reported in 14 counties of north central Texas: Bosque, Collin, Cooke, Dallas, Denton, Ellis, Grayson, Hill, Hunt, Kaufman, Navarro, Tarrant, Van Zandt, and Wichita.

This species is usually found every year in spring migration in wooded areas all along the eastern portion of the study area. It is usually seen from late April through mid-May. It is a different story in the fall: there are fewer than ten records for all of the counties.

Extreme dates for selected counties are: *Collin* – 29 April 1982 to 20 May 1983; *Dallas* – 25 April 1963 to 26 May 1963, and 7 September 1974; *Grayson* – 27 April 1974 to 24 May 1975; *Tarrant* – 24 April 1956 to 24 May 1952, and 5 September 1980 to 29 October 1966, next-latest 19 October 1980.

Specimens: Bay-breasted Warblers have been collected from the following counties: Dallas, 6 May 1944 (DMNH 2214) and 2 May 1963 (DMNH 5232); Kaufman, 9 May 1950 (DMNH 6484); Tarrant, 29 September 1959 (WMP 832); and Wichita, 19 October 1980 (WMP 2596). A spring specimen (Oberholser, 1974) from Denton County was not located.

BLACKPOLL WARBLER   *Dendroica striata* (Forster)
Status: Rare to casual transient.
Occurrence: Blackpoll Warblers have been recorded in nine counties in the study area: Archer, Bosque, Collin, Dallas, Denton, Grayson, Hunt, Tarrant, and Wichita. Oberholser (1974) gave records for only Dallas, Hunt, and Tarrant counties.

Except for two fall reports for Dallas and Hunt counties, this species has been observed only in the spring and not every year for more than a county or two. Only one or two birds are usually reported, usually in late April or early May.

All the known recent records for all the counties are: *Archer* – 4 and 5 May 1974; *Bosque* – 26 April 1984; *Collin* – 23 April 1974 and 4 May 1985; *Dallas* – about 15 times in the spring, 18 April 1966 to 20 May 1974, and once in the fall, 13 September 1969; *Denton* – 30 April 1983; *Grayson* – seven times, 16 April 1975, 6 May 1986, 10 May 1983, 11 May 1983, 13 May 1972, 14 May 1975, and 19 May 1983; *Hunt* – spring and fall (Oberholser, 1974); *Tarrant* – fewer than 12 spring sightings, 25 April 1964 to 20 May 1973; *Wichita* – 29 April 1977.

Specimens: No specimens have been taken for north central Texas.

CERULEAN WARBLER   *Dendroica cerulea* (Wilson)
Status: Casual transient.
Occurrence: The Cerulean Warbler has been reported in six counties in

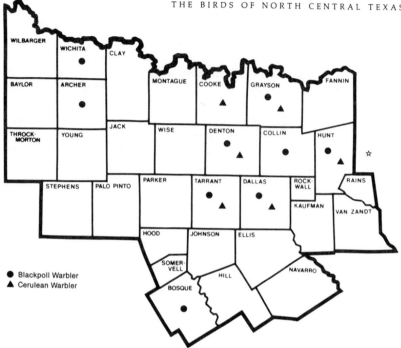

Map 92. Distribution of the Blackpoll Warbler, *Dendroica striata*, and the Cerulean Warbler, *D. cerulea*

the study area—Cooke, Dallas, Denton, Grayson, Hunt, and Tarrant—and adjacent Hopkins County. It is one of the rarest of the warblers that pass through north central Texas, and it visits only casually. There are fewer than 25 records.

There is an old nesting record for Dallas County, a nest and eggs discovered extremely early, on 17 April 1932 (Kelley, 1935). Oberholser (1974) also gives a nesting record for Cooke County on 26 April 1887. Today the environmental conditions of north central Texas have changed so markedly that it is not to be expected as a nesting species.

The county records are: *Cooke*—all records are before the 1900s; *Dallas*—seven spring sightings besides the nesting report above, 13 April 1970 to 3 May 1955, and once in fall, 16 September 1934 (Stillwell, 1939); *Denton*—spring (Oberholser, 1974); *Grayson*—twice, 27 May 1972 and 1 May 1976; *Hunt*—two spring reports, and one fall report (Oberholser, 1974); *Tarrant*—nine spring reports, 13 April 1972 to 25 May 1954; *Hopkins*—24 April 1975.

Specimens: The only known specimen from the project area is one collected in Cooke County on 10 April 1882 (TNHC 1425).

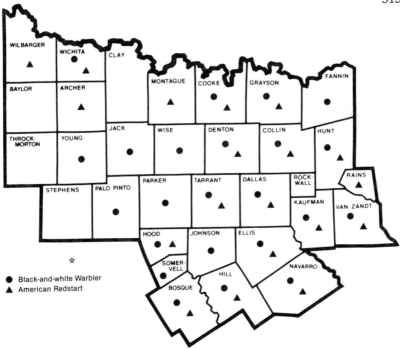

Map 93. Distribution of the Black-and-white Warbler, *Mniotilta varia,* and the American Redstart, *Setophaga ruticilla*

BLACK-AND-WHITE WARBLER *Mniotilta varia* (Linnaeus)

Status: Common to fairly common transient. Rare to casual summer visitor; nests in a few counties.

Occurrence: This "tree-climbing" warbler has been found in 23 counties of the study area — Bosque, Collin, Cooke, Dallas, Denton, Ellis, Fannin, Grayson, Hill, Hood, Hunt, Jack, Johnson, Kaufman, Navarro, Palo Pinto, Parker, Somervell, Tarrant, Van Zandt, Wichita, Wise, and Young — and adjacent Eastland County.

Although this beautiful warbler has been reported in every month of the year in some counties of north central Texas, it is observed mainly during migration. It is the first warbler species to arrive, and stragglers linger into winter if the weather is mild. The species is not usually found as late in the fall in the northern part of the study area (along the Red River) as in the southern part (the Dallas–Fort Worth area). There is only one January record, a bird observed on 7 January 1984 (Dallas County), and there are two records for February, one on 16 and 23 February 1974 (Wichita County) and another on 22 February 1939 (Tarrant County). Fall migration starts early, and July records probably represent birds passing south.

Records in late November — 22 November 1961 (Parker County) — and December — 12 December 1942, 1982, 16 December 1972, and 27 December 1970 (all Tarrant County) — represent stragglers, not winter residents.

Extreme dates for selected counties are: *Collin* — 23 March 1968 to 9 October 1972 (no dates for June or July); *Dallas* — 3 March 1970, next-earliest 14 March 1975 to 15 November 1980, next-latest 12 October 1958; *Denton* — 2 March 1974 to 8 May 1982, 28 June through 15 August 1951, and 7 through 30 September 1958; *Grayson* — 6 March to 30 May, and 16 August to 14 October; *Tarrant* — 9 March 1986 to 18 November 1978, and a few are reported during the summer nearly every year; *Van Zandt* — 13 March 1985 to 5 October 1986.

Nesting: Counties in which nesting has been reported are: Bosque — young out of the nest banded 22 April 1961; Cooke — (Oberholser, 1974) old records before the turn of the century; recent record, 29 July 1982, head of Lake Texoma, Oklahoma border; Dallas — two young just out of the nest, 26 May 1963; Denton — Oberholser (1974) gives one sight record; Fannin — questionable record (Oberholser, 1974); Van Zandt — 15 July 1984, two adults and an immature, and 15 May 1985, two young being fed, fourth summer observed. There is no evidence of actual nesting in Grayson, Hill, Hood, Somervell, Tarrant, and Wichita counties, but meager data at hand indicate that they may have nested or nest in those counties.

Specimens: Specimens have been located for Dallas (DMNH, WMP), Ellis (DMNH), Kaufman (DMNH, WMP), Palo Pinto (WMP), Parker (DMNH), and Tarrant (FWMSH) counties. Those indicated by Oberholser (1974) for Cooke, Navarro, and Wise counties were not located.

AMERICAN REDSTART   *Setophaga ruticilla* (Linnaeus)
Status: Fairly common transient.
Occurrence: This beautiful warbler has been recorded in the following north central Texas counties: Archer, Bosque, Collin, Cooke, Dallas, Denton, Ellis, Grayson, Hill, Hood, Hunt, Kaufman, Montague, Navarro, Rains, Tarrant, Van Zandt, Wichita, and Wilbarger.

Redstarts, among the latest spring migrants, pass through the area from late April to mid-May, while in fall their passage is of longer duration but mainly in September.

Typical county dates are: *Dallas* — 25 April 1963 to 30 May 1971 (mean departure date, 18 years, 16 May), and 5 August 1978 to 23 October 1971; *Grayson* — 19 April to 29 May, and 6 September to 13 October; *Tarrant* — 25 April 1957 to 28 May 1972, and 14 August 1957 to 15 October 1983; *Wichita* — 3 May 1976 to 27 May 1979, and 7 September 1976 to 9 October 1976.

There is little evidence that this species has ever nested in north central Texas. Except for the unexplainable date 14 July 1977 (Dallas County), there are no recent summer sightings. Oberholser (1974) indicated summer sight records for Denton and Tarrant counties but gave no specific dates. They may have been August sightings that were actually fall birds in passage.
Specimens: American Redstarts have been collected from Cooke (TNHC), Dallas (DMNH, WMP), Denton (DMNH), Ellis (WMP), Kaufman (DMNH), and Tarrant (DMNH) counties. A specimen from Collin County (Oberholser, 1974) was not located. Both the nominate race, *S. r. ruticilla*, and the race *S. r. tricolora* were identified among 11 specimens of American Redstarts from Dallas County in my collection (WMP).

PROTHONOTARY WARBLER   *Protonotaria citrea* (Boddaert)
Status: Fairly common to uncommon summer resident locally; uncommon to rare transient elsewhere.
Occurrence: Prothonotary Warblers have been reported in 15 counties in the study area — Archer, Clay, Cooke, Dallas, Denton, Fannin, Grayson, Hunt, Navarro, Palo Pinto, Parker, Rains, Somervell, Tarrant, and Van Zandt counties — and adjacent Henderson and Wood counties.

Overall dates for the study area range from 27 March 1985 (Van Zandt County) and 4 April 1950 (Henderson County, specimen) to 19 October 1986 (Dallas County). There are fewer records for fall than for spring. Many of the dates probably represent breeding birds, though they have not been

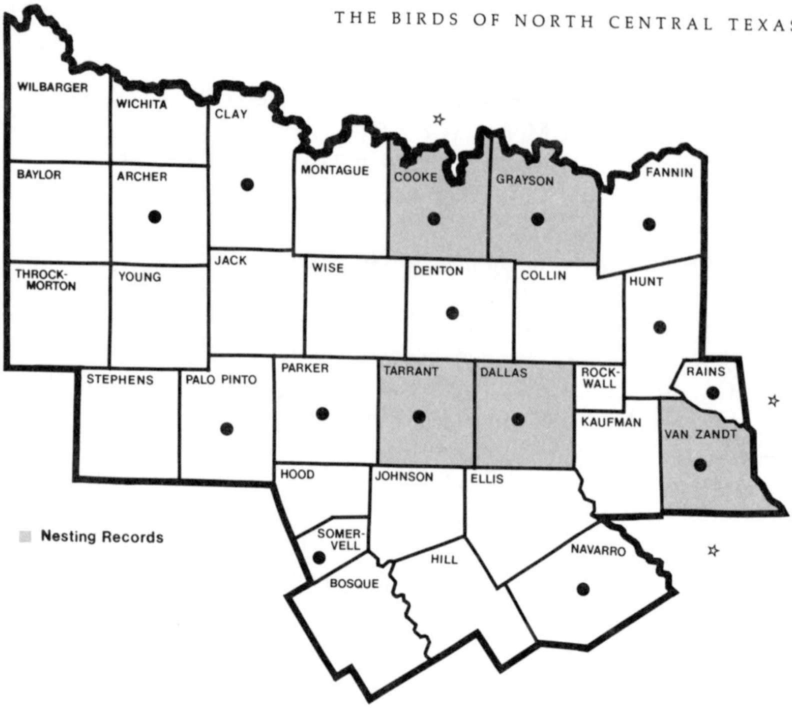

Map 94. Distribution of the Prothonotary Warbler, *Protonotaria citrea*, with nesting records

found nesting in all of the counties listed above. August, September and October dates for Archer, Clay, Palo Pinto, Parker, and Somervell counties are probably not nesting records but transient birds en route to their winter home. More study is necessary for an accurate evaluation of the status of this species in most counties.

This species seems to be well established where suitable nesting conditions exist, especially swampy areas with dead trees. Nesting has been reported in the following counties: Cooke — probably an old record of G. H. Ragsdale's (Oberholser, 1974); Cooke county line (Love County, Oklahoma), headwaters of Lake Texoma — a pair with a juvenile on 29 July 1982. Dallas — courtship and female gathering nesting material on 16 May 1970, and nest on 8 June 1985, fledgling seen on 4 July 1985. Grayson — 5 June 1980, nest with three eggs, on 28 April 1981, carrying nesting material (same nest hole as 1980), and June and July 1985, carrying nesting material. Tarrant — young birds being fed from 19 June 1978 to 23 July 1974. During the 1978 breeding season it was estimated that at least 20 pairs of this colorful warbler nested in the upper Lake Worth area. Van Zandt — nesting 13 June 1982, and 1 July 1984, four young, also reported nesting in 1985, young in and out of hole in a tree on 27 March 1985.

Specimens: Specimens have been collected in Cooke (ACG), Dallas (WMP), Denton (DMNH, WMP), and Henderson (DMNH) counties. The 29 July 1982 date for the Cooke county line given above also represents a specimen (WMP). A spring bird said to have been collected in Palo Pinto County (Oberholser, 1974) was not located.

WORM-EATING WARBLER *Helmitheros vermivorus* (Gmelin)
Status: Casual transient, mainly in spring.
Occurrence: The Worm-eating Warbler has been reported in only six counties in the study area—Cooke, Dallas, Grayson, Hunt, Tarrant, and Wichita—and nearby Henderson County.

This species is extremely rare and is reported only casually even in the counties listed. County records are: *Cooke*—no observation since a specimen was said to have been taken on 11 June 1879 at Gainesville by G. H. Ragsdale; however, the specimen could not be located. *Dallas*—two reports (Stillwell, 1939), 19 March 1932 and 21 April 1934; only four reports since, 13 May 1958, 5 and 6 October 1978, 12 May 1983, and 30 April 1984. The March date is unbelievably early and should not be accepted. Oberholser (1974) indicated that there was a spring specimen, but it could not be found. *Grayson*—two sightings at Denison, 15 May 1980 and 4 April 1983. *Hunt*—11 September 1950 and 15 April 1976. *Tarrant*—five times in spring, 13 May 1954, 6 May 1967, 4 and 5 May 1972, 14 May 1977, and 21 May 1978, and one extremely early fall record, 8 August 1942. *Wichita*—an undated sighting in May 1976 (Williams, 1976). *Henderson*—18 February 1932 (Stillwell, 1939), another very questionable record that should be discounted.

Some of the records above are questionable; however, it is possible that the species was formerly more abundant in some areas than it is today. Because it is a bird of the undergrowth and has solitary habits, it is not easy to observe. Photographs or specimens should be taken to document this species in north central Texas.

SWAINSON'S WARBLER *Limnothlypis swainsonii* (Audubon)
Status: Casual transient.
Occurrence: Swainson's Warbler is extremely rare in north central Texas. It has been reported in seven of the study-area counties—Collin, Dallas, Denton, Hill, Hunt, Navarro, and Tarrant—and adjacent Anderson and Wood counties. The last two counties may represent areas where the species would be found nesting. In these two counties there are typical canebrakes that provide dense undergrowth for nesting. There is a total of 12 records.

Available county data are: *Collin*—5 May 1987, one banded; *Dallas*—13 May 1959, 17 April 1967, 16 April 1968, and 24 April 1974; *Denton*—

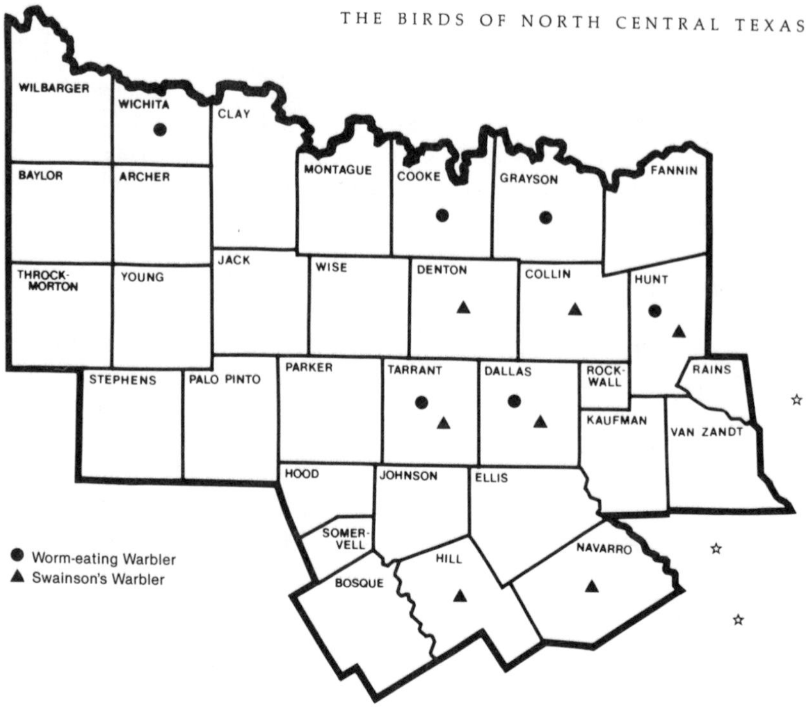

Map 95. Distribution of the Worm-eating Warbler, *Helmitheros vermivorus*, and the Swainson's Warbler, *Limnothlypis swainsonii*

9 May 1978; *Hill*—19 April 1980; *Hunt*—24 September 1950; *Navarro*—24 August 1880 (none since); *Tarrant*—3 May 1986; *Anderson*—29 June 1982, one banded; *Wood*—7 April 1977.
Specimens: A Swainson's Warbler was collected in Dallas County on 16 April 1968 (WMP 1643). A summer specimen indicated by Oberholser (1974) for Navarro County was not located.

OVENBIRD   *Seiurus aurocapillus* (Linnaeus)
Status: Fairly common to uncommon transient.
Occurrence: Ovenbirds pass through north central Texas in about equal numbers during spring and fall migration, though they may be somewhat more evident in spring. They have been recorded in 15 counties of the study area: Bosque, Collin, Cooke, Dallas, Denton, Ellis, Fannin, Grayson, Hunt, Kaufman, Navarro, Tarrant, Van Zandt, Wichita, and Young.

Extreme dates for spring and fall for the counties of the study area range from an isolated date, 7 March 1974 (Denton County), next-earliest 8 April 1976 to 1 June 1985, and 27 August 1957 to 28 October 1957 (all Dallas County). They peak from late April to early May and in mid-September.

Dates for selected counties are: *Collin*—1 May 1982 to 21 May 1980,

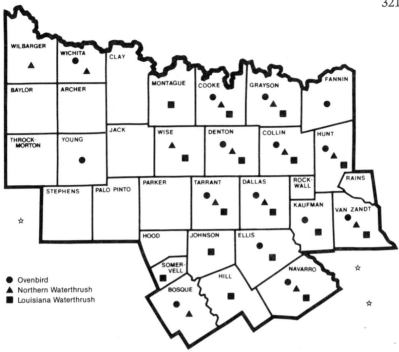

Map 96. Distribution of the Ovenbird, *Seiurus aurocapillus;* the Northern Water-thrush, *S. noveboracensis;* and the Louisiana Waterthrush, *S. motacilla*

and 11 September 1980 to 16 October 1982 (all banded birds); *Dallas —* 8 April 1976, next-earliest 22 April 1984 to 1 June 1985, and 27 August 1957 to 28 October 1957 (specimen); *Grayson —* 18 April 1977 to 29 May 1975, and 18 September to 7 October; *Tarrant —* 20 April 1976 to 20 May 1973, and 8 September 1956 to 15 October 1977.

Specimens: Specimens are available from Cooke (TNHC), Dallas (DMNH, WMP), Ellis (TCWC), Fannin (WMP), Hunt (WMP), and Tarrant (FWMSH, UTA, WMP) counties. All have been identified as the nominate race, *S. a. aurocapillus.*

NORTHERN WATERTHRUSH   *Seiurus noveboracensis* (Gmelin)
Status: Uncommon to rare migrant.
Occurrence: The Northern Waterthrush has been recorded in 13 north central Texas counties — Bosque, Collin, Cooke, Dallas, Denton, Grayson, Hunt, Navarro, Tarrant, Van Zandt, Wichita, Wilbarger, and Wise — and adjacent Henderson and Shackelford counties.

Extreme dates for selected counties are: *Collin —* 28 April 1982 to 17 May 1980, and 23 September 1980 (all banded birds); *Dallas —* an isolated date, 31 March 1983, next-earliest 19 April 1972 to 21 May 1960, and 9 August

1972 to 16 October 1960 (specimen), 1979; *Grayson* — 19 April to 27 May, no records for fall; *Tarrant* — 27 March 1964, next-earliest 31 March 1983 to 20 May 1973, and 22 August 1984 to 26 September 1985. The species tends to peak in early May and the first part of September. The March dates are questionable since the Northern Waterthrush can easily be confused with the Louisiana Waterthrush. There is an unexplainable late record of the Northern Waterthrush, carefully documented for the Lewisville CBC on 29 December 1986. The two species have similar behavioral characteristics as well as similar markings. The Northern Waterthrush has yellowish underparts with streaking that does not extend into the throat. The Northern Waterthrush also has a conspicuous creamy to yellowish eye stripe. Although more uniform in width, the stripe is not as long as the eyeline of the Louisiana Waterthrush, which ends farther back on the head. Also, the bill of the Louisiana Waterthrush is heavier than that of the Northern Waterthrush.

Specimens: Oberholser (1974) indicates specimens for Cooke and Navarro counties that represent the races *S. n. notabilis* and *S. n. noveboracensis*, respectively, but neither specimen was located. Northern Waterthrushes have been collected from Dallas (DMNH, UTA, WMP) and Denton (DMNH, WMP) counties, some of which represent *S. n. limnaeus* and *S. n. notabilis*. Unfortunately, the small group of specimens (eight) have been racially identified by several different authorities, and all the specimens from north central Texas should be reexamined.

LOUISIANA WATERTHRUSH   *Seiurus motacilla* (Vieillot)

Status: Uncommon to rare transient. Formerly nested in the study area and may still do so, but no nests or young have been found in recent times.

Occurrence: Louisiana Waterthrushes have been recorded in 16 counties of the study area — Collin, Cooke, Dallas, Denton, Ellis, Grayson, Hill, Hunt, Johnson, Kaufman, Montague, Navarro, Somervell, Tarrant, Van Zandt, and Wise — and adjacent Anderson County.

While both the Louisiana Waterthrush and the Northern Waterthrush occur in north central Texas, and there may occasionally be misidentifications of the two species, the Louisiana usually arrives earlier than the Northern Waterthrush in the spring and departs earlier in the fall.

Extreme spring arrival and departure dates for selected north central Texas counties are: *Collin* — 11 May 1985; *Dallas* — 19 March 1978 and 15 May 1957, and an isolated date, 5 June 1982; *Grayson* — 26 March and 29 May; *Hunt* — 23 March 1980 and 14 May 1983 (nearby Van Zandt County); *Tarrant* — 18 March 1972 and 19 May 1942.

Fall dates are not as numerous. This species is often absent for a period of years or is recorded on only one or two dates. Fall dates for selected counties are: *Collin* — one banded on 25 July 1979; *Cooke* — two specimens on 15 August 1881; *Dallas*—four times, 15 July 1977 to 17 September 1956 and isolated dates of 23 and 27 November 1986; *Grayson*—23 July 1983 and 31 August; *Johnson*—10 September 1970; *Somervell*—8 August 1984 and 21 July 1985; *Tarrant*—fewer than a dozen times, 7 July 1956 to 24 September 1985; *Van Zandt*—30 June through 5 August 1985 to 18 September 1983.

Nesting: Oberholser (1974) gives nesting records for Cooke and Montague counties before the turn of the century. He also shows summer dates for Denton, Navarro, and Tarrant counties. Some sightings probably represent early fall migrants, not nesting birds. Since that time Louisiana Waterthrushes have been suspected of nesting in Dallas, Grayson, and Van Zandt counties, but to date no nests, eggs, or young have been found. Birds have been seen repeatedly, however, at the same locations in July. Habitat changes in most counties of the study area have no doubt reduced the available nesting range.

Specimens: Specimens of the Louisiana Waterthrush have been located for Cooke County, 15 August 1881 (TNHC 1518, 1949), and Tarrant County, 23 August 1954 (DMNH 4862). Specimens referred to by Oberholser (1974) for Dallas and Wise counties were not located. The Dallas Museum specimen catalog indicates that one taken on 25 April 1944 in Kaufman County (DMNH 2204) was missing when the collection was inventoried in 1971 —apparently misplaced or lost.

KENTUCKY WARBLER *Oporornis formosus* (Wilson)
Status: Fairly common to rare transient and summer resident.
Occurrence: Kentucky Warblers have been recorded in 17 counties in the study area—Bosque, Clay, Collin, Cooke, Dallas, Denton, Ellis, Fannin, Grayson, Hill, Hunt, Kaufman, Navarro, Tarrant, Van Zandt, Wichita, and Wise—and adjacent Anderson and Henderson counties.

This species is found mainly along the east side of the study area and westward along the Red River to about Grayson County. It puts in an appearance fairly regularly, seeking shady, moist woods. There are fewer than 15 fall records.

Extreme dates of spring arrival and fall departure for which county data are available are: *Collin*—26 May 1981, and 24 September 1983 (both banded); *Dallas*—19 April 1972 to 29 May 1963, and 24 August 1986, next 15 September 1935 (Stillwell, 1939) to 8 October 1960; *Grayson*—22 April 1982 to 24 May 1975, and two fall dates, 1 August 1979 and 30 September 1973; *Tarrant*—26 April 1975 to 13 May 1967, and 31 August 1980 to 6 October 1971; *Wichita*—6 May 1976.

Oberholser (1974) lists a questionable winter record of this species for Decatur, Wise County (J. A. Donald), on 29 January 1890. Since no details of this sighting are given, and no other winter record exists for north

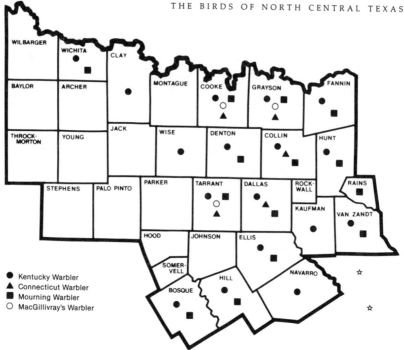

Map 97. Distribution of the Kentucky Warbler, *Oporornis formosus;* the Connecticut Warbler, *O. agilis;* the Mourning Warbler, *O. philadelphia;* and MacGillivray's Warbler, *O. tolmiei*

central Texas, this record has been discounted. This species normally winters from Mexico south into northern South America. It is possible that a wintering yellow-throat could have been misidentified as this species. *Nesting:* Oberholser (1974) indicated that Kentucky Warblers nested in Cooke County in the 1880s and in Wise County in the 1930s and gave a questionable record for Fannin County. However, there are no recent nesting records in any of these counties. Since 1979 it had been suspected that this species nests at the Hagerman NWR in Grayson County, but nesting was not confirmed until a fledgling was observed on 21 July 1983. A stub-tailed young was observed on 22 July 1984, and two out of the nest were seen with parents on 6 July 1986 in Van Zandt County. It is also likely that nesting takes place in adjacent Anderson and Henderson counties, since there are June records and suitable habitat for this species in those counties.

Specimens: Specimens of Kentucky Warblers from the following counties have been examined: Cooke (TNHC 1448, 1451), 12 June 1879, 23 June 1884; Dallas (DMNH 303, 715, 729), 24 April 1938, 6 and 8 May 1939

(WMP 1409, 1517, 2098), 29 May 1963, 15–16 September 1966, and 20 April 1975; Kaufman (DMNH 347, 6797), 25 April 1938 and 12 July 1983; and Tarrant (SM, mount, no date); Henderson (DMNH 4623, 4628), both 25 April 1950. Spring specimens from Clay County (Oberholser, 1974) were not located.

CONNECTICUT WARBLER *Oporornis agilis* (Wilson)
Status: Casual in spring. Accidental in fall; only one record accepted.
Occurrence: Evaluation of this species is difficult since it can be easily mistaken for its near relative, the Mourning Warbler, a relatively common bird of north central Texas. Extreme care should be exercised in identifying these two members of the *Oporornis* genus. Reports, especially fall reports, from Collin, Cooke, Dallas, Denton, Grayson, and Tarrant counties are questionable. Even though Oberholser (1974) shows fall occurrences, I have discounted most of them as erroneous. Only recently was a valid fall record added to the state of Texas, on the upper coast from High Island, Galveston County, where one was photographed on 16 September 1978 (TP-RF). Of the hundreds of fall bird casualties that I examined from local TV towers in the Dallas–Fort Worth area, none proved to be this species. Fall records are not to be expected and must be questioned until a photograph or a specimen is produced for north central Texas.
     County data are as follows: *Collin* — a bird that was probably a Connecticut Warbler was netted and banded on 17 September 1983. The bander, who was formerly a resident of Michigan and was thus familiar with the species, carefully examined and measured the bird in question. *Cooke* — the only specimen (adult female) said to have been taken for north central Texas by G. H. Ragsdale in 1878 was not located by Oberholser (1974), nor have I been able to find it. *Dallas* — Stillwell (1939) gives dates for 29 April 1938 to 11 May 1938. I have dates (about 12 from 1950 to 1978) from 19 April 1958 to 18 May 1975, some probably valid. One observer in the 1950s repeatedly reported this bird in spring and fall, but no details were given for these sightings, and most if not all of the reports were surely in error. Dates since the 1950s that appear to be valid are 25 April 1940 to 18 May 1975. Descriptions of the birds were given with these dates. *Denton* — a fall report only (Oberholser, 1974), two without details, and a very questionable record, 7 September 1958. This date is common for Mourning Warblers, but none were reported on this date. *Grayson* — 26 May 1981, reported by two competent observers. *Tarrant* — spring dates from 26 April 1956 to 24 May 1952 (Pulich, 1979).
Specimens: There are no known specimens for north central Texas or for the state of Texas.

MOURNING WARBLER *Oporornis philadelphia* (Wilson)
Status: Fairly common to summer transient.
Occurrence: Mourning Warblers have been recorded in 14 counties in the study area: Bosque, Collin, Cooke, Dallas, Denton, Ellis, Fannin, Grayson, Hill, Hunt, Rains, Tarrant, Van Zandt, and Wichita.

This species regularly passes through north central Texas in both spring and fall. It peaks in late April and May, and again from late August until early October. It is the most common member of the genus *Oporornis* that passes through the area.

Extreme spring and fall dates for counties for which sufficient data are available are: *Collin* — 27 April 1978 to 26 May 1981, and 20 August 1983 to 12 October 1982 (all banded birds); *Dallas* — 24 April 1983 to 3 June 1984, and 25 August 1972 to 12 November 1946 (specimen), next-latest 4 November 1983; *Denton* — 24 April 1984 to 2 June 1976 (specimen), and 11 September 1979; *Grayson* — 2 May 1975 to 2 June 1974, and 25 August to 20 October; *Tarrant* — 2 May 1982 to 1 June 1977, and 4 August 1951, next-earliest 20 August 1967 (specimen), to 18 October 1947; *Wichita* — 23 May 1977, and 30 August 1977 to 19 October 1980 (specimen).

Mourning Warblers seek dense ground cover of weeds and thickets, and not many are observed. However, ten were netted and banded on 17 May 1980 at the Heard refuge, Collin County, and 22 were found dead at a TV tower on 18 September 1958, and 20 on 28 September 1959 (both in Dallas County).
Specimens: Specimens have been collected from Cooke (TNHC), Dallas (DMNH, WMP), Denton (DMNH, UTA, WMP), Ellis (TCWC), Hunt (FWMSH), Tarrant (FWMSH, WMP), and Wichita (WMP) counties. A fall specimen said to have been taken from Collin County (Oberholser, 1974) was not located.

MACGILLIVRAY'S WARBLER *Oporornis tolmiei* (Townsend)
Status: Casual transient in spring only.
Occurrence: The north central Texas records of this western species are not numerous. It is easily confused with the Mourning Warbler, above, and the many birds identified as MacGillivray's Warblers should be carefully studied. To date I know of no valid fall records of this species for north central Texas even though Oberholser (1974) indicated fall sightings and specimens. The species was, however, taken in Oklahoma on 18 September 1959 (Sutton, 1967). I have examined hundreds of fall *Oporornis* casualties from TV towers in Dallas, Fort Worth, and Wichita Falls but have never found MacGillivray's Warblers — only Mourning Warblers.

County records are as follows: *Collin* — two said to have been banded, an extremely early bird on 11 April 1978 and a second on 15 May 1981, by the same bander at the Heard refuge, on the outskirts of McKinney. No Mourning Warblers were banded on either occasion. These records are questionable, for less than 25 miles south, in Plano, in the same type of habitat, another bander has never banded a MacGillivray's Warbler. It is very likely that Mourning Warblers were misidentified as MacGillivray's. *Cooke* — Oberholser (1974) lists spring and fall specimens. Both represent records before the turn of the century. The spring bird was taken on 16 May 1884 (TNHC 1446) and identified as *"austinsmithi"* (by A. R. Phillips), an unrecognized race. The whereabouts of the alleged fall specimen are unknown. *Dallas* — I consider all spring records for this county questionable and the one fall record in error since it was made by an inexperienced person, and no details were given. *Grayson* — one record at Hagerman NWR on 26 May 1967 was made by two competent observers. On the Hagerman checklist (U.S. Fish and Wildlife Service, 1984) the species is considered accidental. *Tarrant* — three sight records, 18 May 1977, 22 May 1965, and 5 June 1967.

Since the status of this species in north central Texas is so poorly known, any example of *Oporornis* suspected of being MacGillivray's Warbler should be saved and sent to me for identification.

COMMON YELLOWTHROAT   *Geothlypis trichas* (Linnaeus)
Status: Common to fairly common transient. Uncommon to rare in winter. Few birds summer in the study area.
Occurrence: Common Yellowthroats have been recorded in all north central Texas counties except Baylor, Jack, Montague, Throckmorton, and Wise. No doubt they also occur in those counties at times but have not been reported owing to lack of observers. They have also been reported in adjacent Shackelford County.

It is difficult to ascertain the present status of the Common Yellowthroat in a few counties of north central Texas since there is only a scattering of year-round dates. Very likely there is an overlap of transient birds with winter visitors and perhaps occasionally summer birds.

This species is common in moist areas, especially marshes; otherwise it will frequently be found in tall, grassy areas. On the basis of data for about 25 years where sufficient sightings exist, dates for transient birds for selected counties are: *Collin* — 3 April 1980 to 22 May 1981, and 6 September 1980 to 22 October 1982 (five years' banding in one study area); *Dallas* — 26 March 1971, next-earliest 15 April 1970 to 26 May 1963, and 22 August 1981 (specimen) to 21 October 1967; *Grayson* — 6 April to 31 May, and 3 September to 26 November; *Tarrant* — an isolated date, 28 March 1976, next-earliest 24 April 1949 to 23 May 1950, and 31 August 1974 to 31 October 1976, next-latest 25 October 1973; *Van Zandt* — 31 March 1984 to 18 May 1984, and 5 October 1986 to 13 November 1983 (Rains

County); *Wichita*—14 April 1976 to 25 May 1974, and 13 September to 24 October 1978.

Yellowthroats have been recorded in the winter in the following counties: Collin — 22 November 1981 and 15 December 1983; Cooke (Oberholser, 1974); Dallas—19 November 1938, 12 December 1935, 2 and 29 January 1961, 1 January 1964 and 1966, 4 December through 13 March 1982, including a number of CBCs; Denton—16 November 1974 to 14 February 1983, including a number of CBCs; Grayson—16 December 1972 to 2 January 1961, including several CBCs; Kaufman, 12 December 1938 (specimen); Palo Pinto (Oberholser, 1974); Rockwall—6 November 1970 to 26 January 1980; Stephens—1 February 1983; Tarrant—ten of 20 CBCs (1965–84); Wichita—17 November 1978 to 4 January 1975, 27 February 1976, and 5 March 1974, including several CBCs. Winter records seem to be more prevalent in the southern part of the range than in the northern part.

Nesting: Although this species is considered a breeding bird in many counties, there are few recent records of even summer visitors. Today few persons hunt for nests or young in the remaining breeding areas. Oberholser (1974) lists breeding for Cooke, Grayson, and Dallas counties and reports summer sightings for Denton, Navarro, and Wilbarger counties. Present dates (June, July, or early August, though yellowthroats nest before June) indicate that they may still nest in the following counties: Cooke—13 August 1980; Collin—5 July 1982; Dallas—12 June 1972, 16 June through 30 June 1984, and 2 August 1969, (no recent records for July); Denton—4 July 1955; Grayson—two to five singing males at Hagerman NWR during June, July, and August, at least ten of 16 summers, 25 July 1983; Hunt—25 June 1980 and 1983; Rockwall—6 June 1982; Tarrant—20 July to 3 August 1974, 17 June 1978, and 1 August 1978 (all upper Lake Worth); Van Zandt—18 July 1982 and 31 July 1983 (eight heard); Wichita—4 June 1976, 7 June 1979 (specimen), and late June 1984. Oberholser (1974), Garrett and Dunn (1981), and Phillips, Marshall, and Monson (1964) urge careful study and continued monitoring of the yellowthroat breeding population in their respective states because of habitat reduction.

Specimens: Specimens are available for the following counties: Cooke (TNHC), Dallas (DMNH, OU, USNM, UTA, WMP), Denton (DMNH, WMP), Ellis (DMNH), Fannin (WMP), Kaufman (DMNH), Navarro (USNM), Tarrant (DMNH, USNM, WMP), and Wichita (MWU). Specimens indicated by Oberholser (1974) for Clay and Collin counties could not be located.

The racial identifications of the Common Yellowthroat in north central Texas are poorly understood. It was earlier pointed out (Pulich, 1961) that a serious study is needed to clarify the status of the species in Tarrant County, and at that time some specimens were assigned to *brachidactylus* and *trichas*. In the second edition of The Birds of Tarrant County (Pulich, 1979) new material was assigned to *campicola, coloradonicola, minnesoticola, roscoe,* and *trichas*. While most of the material from north central Texas was not examined, material in my collection (WMP) from Dallas County was comparable to that of Tarrant County, and the same subspecies were also identified for Dallas County. It should also be pointed out that some of the assigned races are not recognized by the AOU (1957).

HOODED WARBLER   *Wilsonia citrina* (Boddaert)
Status: Rare transient in spring. Casual in fall.
Occurrence: This beautiful warbler has been recorded in seven north central Texas counties: Dallas, Grayson, Hunt, Johnson, Navarro, Tarrant, and Wichita.

County records are: *Dallas*—1 April 1967 to 20 May 1972, one unexplainable record (Williams, 1973) for summer, 22 July 1973 (said to be an adult male), and four times from 23 September 1979 to 18 October 1982; *Grayson*—five times in spring, 12 April 1975 to 18 May 1971, and once in fall, 13 October 1981; *Hunt*—3 October 1948; *Johnson*—18 April 1976; *Navarro*—latter part of August (1880s? Ogilby, 1882); *Tarrant*—22 March 1969, next-earliest 28 March 1975 to 14 May 1966, and five times in fall, 9 September 1972, 16 September 1956, 27 September 1982, 29 September through 4 October 1982, and 6 October 1969; *Wichita*—once, 30 April through 20 May 1977.
Specimens: As far as I can determine, the only Hooded Warbler specimens from north central Texas study area were two said to have been taken from Navarro County (Ogilby, 1882). These were not located, however.

WILSON'S WARBLER   *Wilsonia pusilla* (Wilson)
Status: Common to fairly common transient in both spring and fall.
Occurrence: Wilson's Warbler has occurred in 24 counties in north central Texas—Archer, Bosque, Collin, Cooke, Dallas, Denton, Ellis, Fannin, Grayson, Hill, Hood, Hunt, Johnson, Kaufman, Navarro, Palo Pinto, Rains, Rockwall, Somervell, Tarrant, Throckmorton, Van Zandt, Wichita, and Young—and nearby Eastland and Shackelford counties.

This species frequents a variety of habitats, including thickets and grassy edges with trees nearby; however, it prefers the lower levels. It is one of the more common migrants passing through the area and is probably more numerous in fall than in spring. It is not uncommon to see 20 or more in mid-May—48 were seen in the spring of 1978 (Tarrant County). On 18 September 1958, 38 birds of the species hit the Cedar Hill TV tower (Dallas County), and on 28 September 1959, 79 hit the same tower, and 75 to 100 were counted in seven hours on 15 September 1974 (Tarrant County).

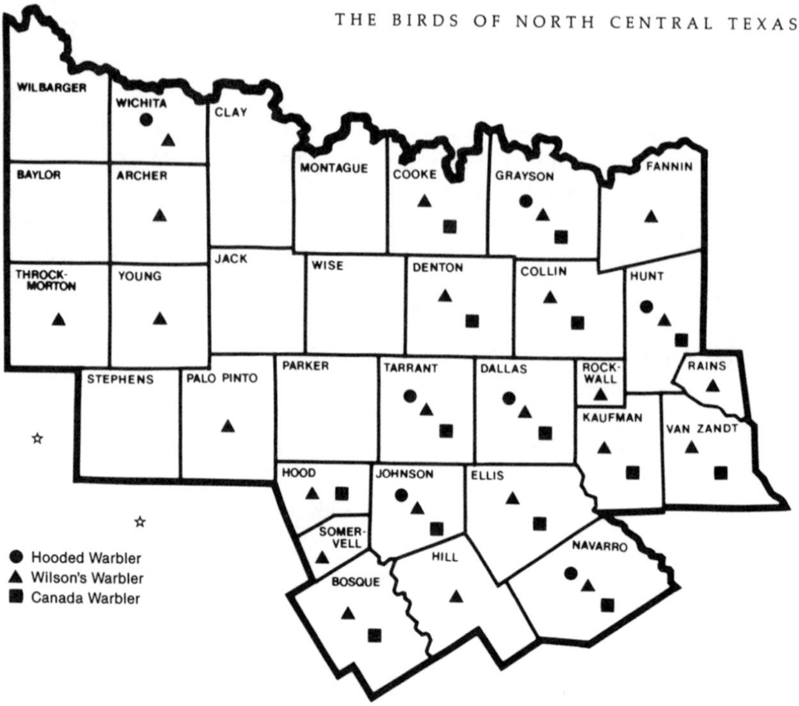

Map 98. Distribution of the Hooded Warbler, *Wilsonia citrina;* Wilson's Warbler, *W. pusilla;* and the Canada Warbler, *W. canadensis*

Extreme dates for selected counties are: *Collin* — 22 April 1982 to 25 May 1985, and 25 August 1985 to 17 October 1984 (the last banded); *Dallas* — 16 April 1980 to 27 May 1958 (mean departure, 17 May, nine years) and 2 August 1977, next-earliest 9 August 1978 to 5 November 1974, next-latest 23 October 1978; *Ellis* — 22 May 1983, and 30 August 1939 (specimen) to 8 October 1978; *Grayson* — 27 April to 4 June, and 16 August to 16 October 1986; *Tarrant* — 30 March 1975, next-earliest 3 April 1987 to 1 June 1971, and 23 August 1954 (specimen) to 13 November 1980, next-latest 4 November 1981; *Van Zandt* — 5 April 1985 to 19 May 1985, and 2 September 1985 (Rains County) to 15 October 1986; *Wichita* — 15 April 1973 to 13 May 1973, and 29 August 1978 to 19 October 1980 (specimen). *Specimens:* Specimens are available for the following counties: Dallas (DMNH, UTA, WMP), Denton (DMNH), Ellis (DMNH, WMP), Hunt (WMP), Palo Pinto (DMNH), Tarrant (DMNH, UTA, WMP), and Wichita (WMP). Specimens said to have been collected for Cooke and Eastland counties (Oberholser, 1974) could not be located.

Both the eastern race *W. p. pusilla* and the Alaska race *W. p. pileolata* have been collected in north central Texas. The former has been taken in

Tarrant County, and there are specimens of the latter race for Dallas, Hunt, and Wichita counties.

CANADA WARBLER *Wilsonia canadensis* (Linnaeus)
Status: Fairly common to uncommon spring transient. Rare fall transient.
Occurrence: Canada Warblers have been recorded in 14 counties in north central Texas: Bosque, Collin, Cooke, Dallas, Denton, Ellis, Grayson, Hood, Hunt, Johnson, Kaufman, Navarro, Tarrant, and Van Zandt.

This "necklace"-bedecked warbler is usually found in thickets in the eastern portion of the study area, west to about Cooke County, and south through Hood and Bosque counties. It is found more often in the spring than in the fall. Its passage in spring is relatively short, tending to peak in mid-May. Fall passage is of longer duration.

Extreme migration dates in counties for which sufficient data are available are: *Dallas* — 20 April 1971 to 4 June 1929 (Stillwell, 1939), next-latest 1 June 1975, and 25 August 1977 to 23 October 1978, next-latest 17 October 1926 (Stillwell, 1939). Late-October dates can be viewed with skepticism and may be dismissed, since fall Canada Warblers usually pass through the area in mid-September. The sightings may have been Wilson's Warblers, more common fall transients in north central Texas. *Grayson* — 29 April to 26 May 1986, and 25 August to 15 September. *Hood* — earliest record for north central Texas, 18 April 1971. *Tarrant* — 28 April 1972 to 29 May 1971, and 24 August 1980 to 30 September 1984.
Specimens: Specimens of Canada Warblers have been reported from the following counties: Cooke — one for spring and one for summer (Oberholser, 1974); the latter is in error; it probably represents an August migrant; neither specimen was located. Dallas (DMNH, WMP). Denton (DMNH). Kaufman (DMNH). Navarro (Ogilby, 1882) — "Last week in Aug" represents a fall migrant in passage through north central Texas, not summer as given by Oberholser (1974); not located.

YELLOW-BREASTED CHAT *Icteria virens* (Linnaeus)
Status: Fairly common transient. Formerly nested; no evidence that it does so today.
Occurrence: The Yellow-breasted Chat has been reported in 20 counties of north central Texas — Bosque, Clay, Collin, Cooke, Dallas, Denton, Ellis, Fannin, Grayson, Hill, Hood, Hunt, Kaufman, Navarro, Palo Pinto, Parker, Tarrant, Van Zandt, Wichita, and Wilbarger — and adjacent Eastland and Shackelford counties.

Extreme spring and fall dates for counties for which sufficient data are available are: *Collin* — 28 April 1982 to 21 May 1981, and 22 August 1982 to 6 October 1982 (all banded birds); *Dallas* — 8 April 1978 to 28 May 1955,

Map 99. Distribution of the Yellow-breasted Chat, *Icteria virens*

and 24 August 1985 to 9 October 1958, and an isolated date, 30 October 1984; *Denton*—21 April 1956, and 20 September 1949 to 4 October 1949 (specimen); *Ellis*—21 April 1983 to 10 May 1981; *Grayson*—14 April to 31 June, and 4 through 29 September and 3 through 25 August, which may have been a local (nesting) bird; *Tarrant*—15 April 1976 to 28 May 1955, and 15 August 1977 to 9 October 1962, and an isolated date, 5 November 1966.

Nesting: This species formerly nested in north central Texas. Oberholser (1974) gave breeding (eggs or nests) records for Cooke, Dallas, Fannin, Kaufman, and Tarrant counties. The last nests were discovered in Tarrant County in the late 1920s and in Dallas County in the mid-1930s. The records for the other three counties were in the late 1800s. Present-day sightings for June and July are few. More recent county records for these months are: *Dallas*—19 June 1970 and 2 June 1975 and 1984; none in July since the 1930s; *Denton*—4 July 1955; *Grayson*—at Hagerman NWR during June and July from 1969 through 1979 and only one record since, 5 June 1980; *Tarrant*—2 June through 14 July 1956 and 4 July 1974; *Van Zandt*—27 June through 24 July 1982, 24 July 1983, and 28 July 1985.

Specimens: Specimens are available from Dallas (DMNH, WMP), Denton (DMNH), Ellis (DMNH), Tarrant (DMNH, FWMSH), and Wilbarger

(WMP) counties. Earlier specimens mentioned by Oberholser (1974) for Clay, Cooke, and Wilbarger counties were not located. The status of the two races in north central Texas is not clear. All specimens in my collection (WMP) represent the nominate race, *I. v. virens*. Oberholser identified *longicauda*, which is now recognized as *auricollis*, from Kaufman, Tarrant, and Wilbarger counties, none of which could be located.

SUMMER TANAGER   *Piranga rubra* (Linnaeus)
Status: Fairly common summer resident.
Occurrence: Summer Tanagers have been observed in all but two counties in north central Texas: Baylor and Throckmorton. They have also been observed in nearby Henderson and Shackelford counties, where they had not been reported previously.

Some members of this species are found in north central Texas from early April to September, though as the summer advances they become difficult to find. Some observers may miss this species altogether if they are not familiar with its call or alarm notes. The Summer Tanager usually stays high in the leafy canopy of trees.

Extreme spring and fall dates for selected counties for which sufficient data are available are: *Dallas*—4 April 1973 to 10 October 1979; *Grayson* —8 April 1972 to 30 September; *Hood*—13 April 1986 (nearby Somervell County) to 7 September 1979; *Hunt*—6 April 1979 to 14 September 1980; *Tarrant*—15 March 1970 and 1984 to 13 November 1978, next-latest 19 October 1969; *Wichita*—23 April 1975 to 9 September 1976.

There are several observations for winter. A female was reported in Tarrant County on 31 January and again on 7 February 1972, and another was carefully described from Dallas County on 3 February 1963.
Nesting: Nesting (Oberholser, 1974) has been recorded in Cooke, Dallas, Fannin, Tarrant, Wise, and Young counties. The only recent records known to me are for Dallas, Hood, and Tarrant counties. Nesting dates range from adults at the nest site on 25 April (Hood County) to young out of the nest on 21 June 1956 (Tarrant County).
Specimens: Summer Tanager specimens have been located for the following counties: Dallas (DMNH, WMP), Denton (DMNH, WMP), Ellis (DMNH), Hunt (FWMSH), Parker (FWMSH), Tarrant (DMNH, FWMSH, SM, mount), and Henderson (DMNH). Specimens indicated by Oberholser (1974) for Clay, Collin, Kaufman, and Wise counties were not located.

The eastern race *P. r. rubra* is the only subspecies recorded in north central Texas.

SCARLET TANAGER   *Piranga olivacea* (Gmelin)
Status: Rare to casual spring transient.
Occurrence: The Scarlet Tanager has been recorded in spring and early

Map 100. Distribution of the Scarlet Tanager, *Piranga olivacea*

summer in 15 counties in the study area: Bosque, Collin, Cooke, Dallas, Denton, Ellis, Grayson, Hunt, Palo Pinto, Parker, Somervell, Tarrant, Van Zandt, Wichita, and Wilbarger. No more than one bird at a time is reported, usually the striking male. In some years there are no reports. There are no acceptable fall reports, and the few early summer observations are unexplainable and therefore unacceptable. June birds may represent stragglers, while July dates may be misidentified as Summer Tanagers.

Records for the counties in which they have been reported are: *Bosque* — one report, 8 June 1974, without details. *Collin* — one banded, 4 May 1987. *Cooke* — 30 April and 13 May 1969. *Dallas* — probably fewer than 25 records since 1935, 14 April 1980 to 21 May 1935, next-latest 19 May 1962, and an unexplainable isolated date, 2 July 1959, which has been discounted. *Denton* — Oberholser (1974) gives a summer record without details. There is one other record, 9 May 1978. *Ellis* — 4 May 1981. *Grayson* — four records, 20 April 1974, 3 May 1972, 10 and 13 May 1979, and 28 May 1970. *Hunt* and *Palo Pinto* — Oberholser (1974) gives sight records for spring and summer, without details. The source of the summer sighting is unknown and has been dismissed. No other records. *Parker* — Oberholser (1974) shows a questionable record on the species' range map, with no details. *Somervell* — a questionable date, 26 June 1971, that has not been accepted. *Tarrant*—fewer than 20 reports, 18 April 1982 to 14 June 1981 (the latter carefully documented). *Van Zandt*—one record, 28 April 1970. *Wichita*—three reports, a published date of 4 July 1973, not accepted, another in May of the same year, and 4 May 1976. A fall report was also discounted. *Wilbarger*—Oberholser (1974) indicates that a specimen of this species was collected in this county on 4 June; however, this is likely in error, since More and Strecker (1929) gave the reference as an observation. They wrote that "Mr. George E. Maxon saw a male specimen of this tanager in the Pease River valley on June 4, 1929." There are no other records or references for this county.

Specimens: No Scarlet Tanager specimens are known from north central Texas (see Wilbarger County, above).

Western Tanager   *Piranga ludoviciana* (Wilson)

Status: Casual visitor.

Occurrence: The Western Tanager has been recorded in four counties of the study area and one nearby county. This bird is usually associated with the conifer areas of west Texas, and the occurrence of any species out of its range is exciting. Oberholser (1974) lists sight records of this species for Dallas, Hunt, and Tarrant counties. There are not many observations, and some may be questionable. A casual observer may misidentify female Western Tanagers with female orioles. It may also be possible for some observers to confuse immature Summer Tanagers (with plumage changing to adult) with Western Tanagers.

All the data for the Western Tanager known to me for four counties of the study area and one adjacent county are: *Dallas*—except for mention, without details, of a summer record for this species by Oberholser (1974), there is only a fall sighting on 8 September 1984, a female observed by a lone observer. Since neither source is very convincing, more proof (photograph or specimen) is needed to establish the occurrence of this species in this county. *Hunt*—summer and fall records (Oberholser, 1974), with data probably taken from the *Check-List of East Texas Birds* (Tarter, 1940), are extremely doubtful. Two isolated dates, 29 August and 2 September, by the same observer, who gave no details, are very likely in error. The checklist has a number of errors regarding unusual species in Hunt County, to which these two dates should probably be added. *Navarro*—two observers reported studying this species within 25 feet on 2 May 1979. *Tarrant*—six reports. Except for an unusual sighting by a lone observer on 18 June and again on 8 July 1983, all of the records are for May. The bird in question visited the home of the observer a number of times and remained long enough to permit accurate identification. The May dates are 4 May 1974, 5 May 1973, 9 May 1970 and 1981, and 12 May 1957. This county has many more sightings than the other counties, perhaps because it is the only county in which a local bird group sponsors a Spring Bird Count, in which a number of observers participate. *Comanche* – a sight record of a male was carefully documented on 12 August 1970. *Specimens:* There are no Western Tanager specimens for north central Texas.

NORTHERN CARDINAL   *Cardinalis cardinalis* (Linnaeus)
Status: Common to abundant resident throughout the area.
Occurrence: The Northern Cardinal is found throughout north central Texas in a variety of habitats. It is not as abundant along the western side of the study area as in the middle and eastern portions, but it is usually found along creeks and rivers. It frequents not only edges, thickets, and bottomland shrubs but also shrubbery in cities and towns, especially in older, well-established yards.

Few persons need any introduction to the "red bird," as it is often called locally. It visits feeders regularly and becomes quite tame. Many persons feed wild birds just to have this species in their yards. This species and the Purple Martin are probably the most popular birds in the study area.

In the winter cardinals become numerous and tend to concentrate. At that time it is not uncommon to find 50 or more in a single area. In late January and early February they begin to sing, especially during mild weather, while most of the other birds of the area are still quiet.

Nesting: Northern Cardinals nest at least twice a year and occasionally even three times a year in north central Texas. They frequently desert their nests after even a slight disturbance by human beings or animals. They are commonly parasitized by the Brown-headed Cowbird, and it is not unusual to see cardinals feeding young cowbirds. In Tarrant County as late as 18 September 1959 a cowbird was observed being fed by a female cardinal. Although no special effort has been made to find nests, they have been recorded in 24 of the 32 counties of the north central Texas study area and can be found in the other counties as well. Nesting ranges from 16 March (building nest) to 6 August (young in nest), 9 August (three eggs), and 20 August (young just out of the nest) in Dallas County and from 16 April (nest) to 29 August (young in nest) in Tarrant County. These dates would apply to all the other counties in north central Texas. A full clutch of eggs is usually three, although it is not uncommon to find four eggs and, occasionally, a nest with three cowbird eggs in addition to the cardinal eggs. In no instance were more than six eggs in combination found.

Specimens: Specimens indicated by Oberholser (1974) for Baylor and Collin counties were not located. Other specimens included material from the following counties: Bosque (DMNH), Clay (MWU), Cooke (USNM), Dallas (DMNH, UTA, WMP), Denton (DMNH, TCWC, WMP), Ellis (DMNH), Grayson (UTA), Hood (FWMSH), Hunt (WMP), Kaufman (DMNH), Parker (FWMSH), Tarrant (DMNH, FWMSH, UTA, WMP),

Wichita (MWU), and Wilbarger (DMNH), and adjacent Henderson County (DMNH).

According to the *Checklist of the Birds of Texas* (TOS, 1984) three races of Northern Cardinals occur in north central Texas. Both *cardinalis* and *magnirostris* have been identified from Tarrant County, while *C. c. canicaudus* was identified along the Red River in Grayson, Clay, Wichita, and Wilbarger counties; however, not all the specimens were examined. The nominate race has also been identified from Denton, Grayson, and Hunt counties. A thorough study of all the material listed above, together with additional selective collecting, is needed.

PYRRHULOXIA *Cardinalis sinuatus* Bonaparte
Status: Accidental.
Occurrence: There are reports of Pyrrhuloxias from four north central Texas counties and one adjacent county: *Denton* – a Pyrrhuloxia visited a feeder in Denton from mid-December 1972 until 12 April 1973 (photographs in my file). *Tarrant* – two reports, one in Fort Worth on 22 January 1976 and the other in Arlington on 13 and 17 February 1984. Both are considered questionable since details of observations are not convincing. *Throckmorton* – two birds were carefully studied by two competent observers on 22 May 1984. *Wilbarger* – brief sighting by one person at Vernon on 8 June 1975. *Shackelford* – three times on the Albany BBS – 28 June 1981, 4 June 1983 (four counted), and 15 June 1985.

There is little doubt that this species is moving northward from southwestern Texas because of the spread of mesquite and the existing arid conditions. There is sufficient habitat in the western part of the study area to maintain it. Birders along the western part of the study area are urged to study carefully any cardinal-like birds they suspect may be Pyrrhuloxias. Photographs or specimens should be taken to confirm their presence, since they can easily be confused with Northern Cardinals.

ROSE-BREASTED GROSBEAK *Pheucticus ludovicianus* (Linnaeus)
Status: Uncommon to fairly common transient, especially in spring.
Occurrence: Rose-breasted Grosbeaks have been recorded in 18 north central Texas counties: Archer, Bosque, Collin, Cooke, Dallas, Denton, Ellis, Fannin, Grayson, Hill, Hunt, Johnson, Navarro, Rains, Somervell, Tarrant, Van Zandt, and Wichita.

This transient species is reported in both spring and fall, though the records for spring far outnumber those for fall. In spring they range from late April to mid-May, while in fall there are scattered records from late September to early November, most reports being for October. There are several alleged winter reports of this species, but they have been recorded simply as grosbeak sightings, since the reports are vague or lacking details

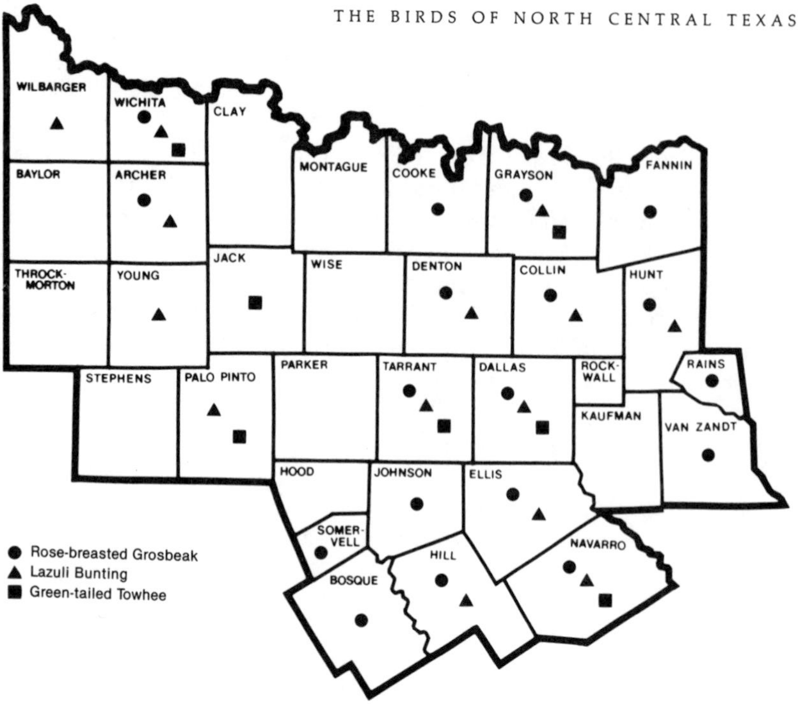

Map 101. Distribution of the Rose-breasted Grosbeak, *Pheucticus ludovicianus;* the Lazuli Bunting, *Passerina amoena;* and the Green-tailed Towhee, *Pipilo chlorurus*

about species. Observers are urged to take care in distinguishing this species from the Black-headed Grosbeak, with which it can be easily confused, especially the immatures and females.

Some extreme transient county dates are: *Collin* — 27 April 1985 to 14 May 1983, and two fall records, 29 September 1984 and 8 October 1981 (both banded); *Dallas* — 21 April 1973 to 20 May 1972, and five fall records, 1 October 1978 to 20 October 1972 (specimen) and 1974; *Grayson* — 21 April to 25 May, and 30 September 1969 to 23 October; *Hill* — 29 May 1980; *Tarrant* — 19 April 1976 to 19 May 1965, and six fall records, 22 September 1978 (specimen) to 4 November 1978, one alleged to be this species on 14 December 1986; *Wichita* — 30 April 1976 to 23 May 1977, and 7 November 1978 (specimen).

Specimens: Specimens have been taken from the following counties: Cooke (TNHC), Dallas (DMNH, WMP), Denton (WMP), Tarrant (UTA), and Wichita (MWU).

BLACK-HEADED GROSBEAK   *Pheucticus melanocephalus* (Swainson)
Status: Casual, irregularly reported.
Occurrence: Oberholser (1974) listed only three counties for this species:

Dallas (spring), Hunt (fall and winter), and Tarrant (spring). Recent data indicate records for Collin, Cooke, Dallas, Ellis, Grayson, Hunt, Tarrant, and Wichita counties.

There are more records of this species for spring than for fall. The species of grosbeaks of several winter records could not be determined. Thus the status and occurrence of the Black-headed Grosbeak have been difficult to assess. It is suspected that older reports, and perhaps some of the present reports, may represent Rose-breasted Grosbeaks, rather than Black-headed Grosbeaks. Unfortunately, many observers failed to give details of their observations or the sexes of the grosbeaks. Females and immatures of the two species, particularly in the fall, closely resemble each other and usually cannot be distinguished without careful study. Furthermore, the two species hybridize freely north of north central Texas.

County records known to me are: *Collin* — one record, 30 April 1967. *Cooke* — 15 May 1983. *Dallas* — an old record, 13 May 1938 (Stillwell, 1939), nine recent records — several questionable — an isolated record, 4 March 1974, next-earliest 19 April 1974 (male) to 15 May 1976, and one record for fall, 5 September 1964. A 28 December 1973 record of an immature grosbeak has been discounted because the species is uncertain. *Ellis* — 4 May 1981 (male). *Grayson* — two spring records, 19 and 20 April 1975 and 22 May 1980, and one fall record, 8 September 1979 (male). *Hunt* — no records except those reported by Oberholser (1974). *Tarrant* — this county has the most records, but some are misidentifications or very doubtful. Ten spring reports range from 28 March 1974 to 21 May 1981, and two fall reports are 8 October 1965 and 11 October 1980. *Wichita* — two spring reports, 2 May 1982 (female) — no details given — 5 May 1979, and one for fall, 21 September 1976 (female), but with vague details of the observation. A report of a bird allegedly seen on 25 January 1977 was not accepted. *Specimens:* No Black-headed Grosbeak specimens have been taken for north central Texas. Most Texas specimens have been taken west of 100th meridian.

BLUE GROSBEAK   *Guiraca caerulea* (Linnaeus)
Status: Fairly common summer resident.
Occurrence: Blue Grosbeaks have been recorded in all counties of the study area except Baylor, Montague, and Throckmorton and very likely would be recorded in those counties if more birding occurred there. They have also been recorded in nearby Eastland and Henderson counties.

Although it is not numerous, this species is found in tall grass and brushy edges near wooded areas, and in migration it may frequent a wide variety of habitats. It is found from late April through early October. Extreme dates for selected counties are: *Collin* — 16 April 1983 to 1 November 1986, next-latest 30 October 1983 (both banded). *Dallas* — 16 April 1965 to 19

October 1974. Two sightings recorded on the Dallas CBC on 20 December 1975 have been dismissed as misidentifications, even though the editor indicated "details sufficient." *Grayson*—24 April 1971 to 5 October 1975. *Tarrant*—15 April 1939 to 2 October 1956. *Van Zandt*—13 April 1986 to 15 October 1983. *Wichita*—21 April 1976 to 15 September 1975.

Nesting: Nesting has been recorded in Bosque, Cooke, Dallas, Grayson, Navarro, Stephens, Tarrant, Van Zandt, Wichita, and Wise counties.

Specimens: Specimens have been located for Cooke (CMNH, TNHC, USNM), Dallas (DMNH), Denton (DMNH), Ellis (DMNH), Kaufman (DMNH), and Tarrant (DMNH) counties. A spring specimen indicated for Hood County (Oberholser, 1974) was not located. Most of the specimens examined represent the nominate race, *G. c. caerulea*, although a Tarrant County (DMNH 4194) specimen taken on 9 May 1949 was identified by Oberholser as *G. c. interfusa*. This specimen has not been reexamined. Sutton (1967) pointed out that Oklahoma specimens represent intergrades.

LAZULI BUNTING *Passerina amoena* (Say)

Status: Rare transient in spring.

Occurrence: Lazuli Buntings have been recorded in 14 counties of the study area: Archer, Collin, Dallas, Denton, Ellis, Grayson, Hill, Hunt, Navarro, Palo Pinto, Tarrant, Wichita, Wilbarger, and Young. With the exception of an extremely old report for fall, all sightings of this western species are for spring. The county records are: *Archer*—4 May 1974; *Collin*—30 April 1987 (banded), possible female on 9 May 1981 and 7 May 1986; *Dallas*— at least 17 sightings from 1950 to 1985, the number owing to the extensive bird-watching that occurs there, 15 April 1985 through 29 May 1957; *Denton*—11 May 1957; *Ellis*—24 May 1971; *Grayson*—five records, 5 May 1968, 7 and 11 May 1986, 14 May 1982, and 23 May 1971; *Hill*—16 May 1980; *Hunt*—30 April 1950 and 7 May 1984 (slide); *Navarro*—8 May 1934 and 1935 (Stillwell, 1939), and 17 September 1883; *Palo Pinto*—a female studied carefully on 7 May 1977; *Tarrant*—six records, 21 April 1986, 27 April 1984, 30 April 1950, 5 May 1978, 10 May 1977, and spring 1973 (exact date unknown); *Wichita*—30 April 1983; *Wilbarger*—10 May 1983; *Young*—(Oberholser, 1974).

Nearly all of the records above represent observations of males. Females and young can be distinguished from Indigo Buntings by their broad, whitish wing bars (young Indigo Buntings have narrower wing bars), and unless one makes very careful note of this, misidentifications are very possible. Hybrids of this species with Indigo Buntings are known, and it is possible that some range through north central Texas. However, none have been noted among the TV-tower casualties examined from Dallas County.

Specimens: The only specimen from north central Texas known to me is the Hill County record (TCWC 10923) above. Ogilby (1882) said that he obtained a specimen from Navarro County on 17 September, but its whereabouts are unknown. He indicates that "it was a young male – a wretched specimen – with feathers abraded and dirty."

INDIGO BUNTING *Passerina cyanea* (Linnaeus)
Status: Fairly common to common migrant. Fairly common summer resident locally.
Occurrence: The Indigo Bunting has been recorded in all counties of the study area but Baylor, Jack, Palo Pinto, Stephens and Throckmorton. There is little doubt that a careful search for this species in those counties would produce records. It has also been recorded in nearby Eastland and Shackelford counties, where it was not previously reported.

In summer this species is restricted to riparian areas where heavy cover is broken by brushy clearings, but in migration it is found in a variety of habitats.

Although usually only one or two birds are seen, the peak number recorded during migration was 66 in 1976, and the average for 14 Tarrant County Spring Bird Counts (1965–78) was 27. In the fall the peak number was 48 casualties at a TV tower in Cedar Hill, Dallas County, on 10 October 1958.

Indigo Buntings are found from early April to early October throughout the study area. Extreme dates for selected counties are: *Collin* – 20 April 1984 to 3 November 1984 (banded bird); *Dallas* – 17 April 1976 to 23 October 1984; *Denton* – extremely early date, 22 March 1983, next-earliest 16 April 1972 to 11 October 1974; *Grayson* – 21 April 1971 to 18 October 1980; *Tarrant* – 4 April 1974 to 30 October 1954; *Van Zandt* – 8 April 1987 to 19 October 1986; *Wichita* – 21 April 1976 to 15 September 1973.
Nesting: Indigo Buntings have been recorded breeding in Cooke, Dallas, Denton, Grayson, Tarrant, Van Zandt, Wichita, Wilbarger, Wise, and Young counties. One can frequently observe it in June and July in the eastern portion of the study area, especially along river bottoms. Actual nesting records in recent years are meager, however; one of the few records was a nest of three young on 24 July 1983 in Van Zandt County. There is little doubt that it would still be found nesting in nearly all counties of the study area if one were to search for nests.
Nesting: Specimens of this species have been located for seven counties – Dallas (DMNH, UTA, WMP), Denton (DMNH), Ellis (DMNH), Hunt (WMP), Kaufman (SFASU, TNHC), Tarrant (FWMSH, WMP), and Wichita (WMP) – and nearby Henderson (DMNH). Oberholser (1974) indicated that there were examples for Cooke and Navarro counties, but these were not located.

PAINTED BUNTING   *Passerina ciris* (Linnaeus)
Status: Fairly common to common summer resident.
Occurrence: Members of this beautiful species have been recorded in all the counties in the study area. They inhabit edges, thickets, and dense undergrowth, particularly the drier habitats, though they are seldom observed in towns and cities. Few visit feeders even during migration. Although brightly colored males are frequently heard, they are difficult to observe. After the end of August males are seldom seen, since most of them depart as soon as nesting is completed, after which only females and immatures are usually recorded.

Painted Buntings can usually be found in north central Texas from late April to early September. Extreme arrival and departure dates for selected counties are: *Collin*—adult male banded on 1 October 1983; *Cooke*— 3 April 1884 through 4 September 1940 (both specimens); *Dallas*—16 April 1965 through 11 October 1958 (specimen), next-latest 29 September 1959; *Ellis*—13 April 1972 through 17 September 1982; *Grayson*—18 April to 30 September; *Tarrant*—15 April 1964 through 23 September 1985 and an isolated date, 1 November 1978, next-latest 12 October 1956.

The only two possible winter records were one specimen said to have been taken in Cooke County on 7 February 1884 (Oberholser, 1974; not located) and a sight record for Dallas County on 21 February 1970.
Specimens: Specimens are available from the following counties: Archer (MWU), Cooke (CC, TCWC, TNHC), Dallas (DMNH, WMP), Denton (DMNH), Ellis (DMNH), Hill (WMP), Hood (FWMSH), Johnson (SUC), Kaufman (DMNH), Navarro (TCWC, USNM, WMP), Parker (FWMSH), Tarrant (DMNH, FWMSH, SM, mount, UTA, WMP), and Wichita (MWU). Those said to have been taken for Clay, Rockwall, and Wilbarger counties (Oberholser, 1974) could not be located.
Nesting: Nests or young have been observed in Bosque, Cooke, Dallas, Fannin, Grayson, Hill, Hunt, Kaufman, Navarro, Rockwall, Tarrant, Wichita, Wilbarger, and Wise counties. One of the latest nesting dates was of a female feeding three full-grown young on 30 October 1970 (Grayson County). Most nesting is finished by early August.

Although not all of the specimens have been racially examined, most are *P. c. pallidor*. Oberholser (1974) indicated that *P. c. ciris* was taken from Wilbarger County, and one was taken from Tarrant County (UTA) during the spring of 1975, but this specimen was not typical.

DICKCISSEL   *Spiza americana* (Gmelin)
Status: Fairly common to common summer resident. Sometimes abundant as transient. Accidental in winter.
Occurrence: Dickcissels have been recorded in all of the counties of the study area and a number of adjacent counties. They are commonly found

from mid-April until mid-June in monotonous, repetitious song that seems more incessant as the day's temperature rises. After early July they cease to sing and become difficult to find. However, they normally pass through the area in fall until early October and may be common. They give characteristic calls in flight, a distinct *br-r-r-r-rt* note. To one familiar with this call, the birds can be readily identified as they pass over both day and night.

The numbers of Dickcissels vary from year to year. On 14 (1965–78) Spring Bird Counts in Tarrant County they averaged 237, with a minimum of 33 (1977) and a maximum of 720 (1969).

Dickcissels are found wherever grass abounds, especially if it has not been cut for several years, with small bushes beginning to invade the area. They prefer prairies but are found in vetch fields, and in the western part of the study area they frequent wheat fields, sometimes to the detriment of the nesting birds since the grain fields are often cut after nests have been built.

More Dickcissels will be found when north central Texas has good rainfall and adequate growing season for grass cover. This was true in 1971, when a University of Kansas graduate student found more than 32 nests in a plot of fewer than 90 acres near Lake Ray Hubbard, in Rockwall County. Populations tend to fluctuate, probably depending on weather conditions, though in recent years some authorities have expressed concern about a possible decrease in the species because of adverse environmental conditions.

Extreme arrival and departure dates for selected counties are: *Dallas* — 12 April 1975 (mean 21 April, 18 years, 1957–75) to 16 October 1960 (mean 25 September, 16 years, 1959–75). Bent (1968) gives a later date of 22 October. *Denton* — 12 April 1978 to 10 October 1974. *Grayson* — 23 April 1976 to 28 October 1972 and an isolated date, 13 November 1969. *Tarrant* — 5 April 1984 (mean 23 April, 18 years, 1959–77) to 3 November 1986, next-latest 27 October 1973. *Wichita* — 23 April 1976 to 6 August 1969. *Van Zandt* — 18 April 1984 to 8 November 1985.

Although Dickcissels usually winter in Central America, there are several winter records for Dallas County, including one on 25 December 1965. Another appeared at a feeder on 24 January 1969 and remained until 5 March 1969, and one was observed at Coppell from 7 through 9 January 1986. One was also reported at Sherman, Grayson County, on 17 January 1977. During the winter they can be confused with House Sparrows if they are not studied carefully.

Nesting: Nesting has very likely taken place throughout north central Texas, depending on the availability of weedy vegetation, even though they have been recorded in Cooke, Dallas, Denton, Ellis, Fannin, Grayson, Kaufman, Montague, Navarro, Palo Pinto, Rockwall, Tarrant, Van Zandt, Wichita, Wilbarger, and Wise counties. Observations have been recorded in all of the study area counties during the nesting season.

Typical nesting dates for selected counties are: Dallas – 8 May to 21 June, small young just out of the nest. Ellis – 8 May 1985, two nests, each with four eggs. Kaufman – 14 May, five eggs. Navarro – Ogilby (1882) indicated that they are two-brooded and gave dates from the middle of May on, although I have no data to support more than one brood; female feeding young out of the nest near Rice on 20 August 1986. Tarrant – 9 May, eggs, to 5 June, young out of the nest (Sutton, 1938). Wilbarger – 16 May to 30 July, nests (More and Strecker, 1929).

Specimens: The Dickcissel has been a frequent TV-tower casualty in the Dallas–Fort Worth area, especially in the fall. On 5–6 September 1962, 63 birds were killed at Cedar Hill, Dallas County. Large kills of this species have occurred in other years, and a number of examples have been preserved.

Specimens have been collected from the following counties: Bosque (SM), Cooke (TNHC), Dallas (DMNH, UTA, WMP), Denton (DMNH, FWMSH), Ellis (DMNH, WMP), Johnson (SUC), Kaufman (DMNH), Tarrant (DMNH, FWMSH, UTA, WMP), and Van Zandt (WMP). Specimens indicated for Hunt and Wilbarger counties (Oberholser, 1974) were not located.

GREEN-TAILED TOWHEE   *Pipilo chlorurus* (Audubon)
Status: Rare transient and winter visitor.
Occurrence: This distinctive western species rarely reaches north central Texas. Although one may expect it in typical brushy habitats, it may occasionally visit feeding stations and become rather tame, permitting birders to observe and become well acquainted with this towhee.

The Green-tailed Towhee has been recorded from early October to late May in seven counties in the study area: *Dallas* – 15 March 1938, specimen (DMNH 287, which Oberholser [Stillwell, 1939] identified as *P. c. zapolia*, a race not recognized by AOU [1957]), 24 April 1938, 21 December 1972 through 23 March 1973, 8 May 1973, 6 April 1974, and 23 January through 10 March 1983; *Grayson* – 29 March 1980; *Jack* – Fort Richardson, 8 May 1974; *Navarro* – 5 October 1983, specimen (WMP 2868); *Palo Pinto* – 31 December 1965, 17 November and 21 December 1968, and 23 December 1972; *Tarrant* – 29 March 1953, 28 November 1978, and 8 December 1970; *Wichita* – 17 April through 27 May 1974 and 3 May 1975.

RUFOUS-SIDED TOWHEE   *Pipilo erythrophthalmus* (Linnaeus)
Status: Fairly common to common winter resident.
Occurrence: Rufous-sided Towhees have been recorded in all north central Texas counties except Baylor County, where there are few observers.

This striking large sparrow is common in brushy areas, overgrown fields, and secondary growth providing thickets and tangles. Its noisy habits when

A.P.

it is excited and its colorful plumage make it easy to identify. Although it may come to some residential areas, particularly along drainages with much brush, it does not frequent all yards. It ranges in north central Texas from 18 September to 19 May. Extreme dates for selected counties are: *Dallas* — 21 September 1936 (Stillwell, 1939), next-earliest 4 October 1980 to 19 May 1979; *Denton* — 18 September 1976 to 7 May 1978; *Grayson* — 15 October to 29 April; *Hood* — 16 October 1977 to 1 May 1976; *Palo Pinto* — 10 October 1976 to 1 May 1977; *Tarrant* — 23 September 1956, next-earliest 5 October 1980 to 14 May 1977; *Wichita* — 5 October 1973 to 6 May 1976.

Like a number of other winter sparrows, Rufous-sided Towhees have been recorded on all the CBCs in north central Texas. Their numbers on the counts do not seem to vary throughout the area if one searches the proper habitats.

Specimens: Rufous-sided Towhee specimens have been taken in the following counties: Clay (Oberholser, 1974, not located), Cooke (TNHC, USNM), Dallas (DMNH, OU, WMP), Denton (DMNH, WMP), Ellis (DMNH), Hill (KU), Hood (FWMSH), Kaufman (DMNH), Montague (MWU), Navarro (USNM), Parker (FWMSH), Somervell (FWMSH), Tarrant (DMNH), and Wise (DMNH).

Three races of Rufous-sided Towhees occur in north central Texas. The nominate race, *P. e. erythrophthalmus,* has been taken in Cooke (USNM), Dallas, and Denton (both DMNH) counties, while *arcticus* and *montanus* have been collected in Dallas and Tarrant counties.

BROWN TOWHEE *Pipilo fuscus* Swainson
Status: Casual. Extremely rare outside the southwestern part of the study area.
Occurrence: The Brown Towhee has been reported in three counties of north central Texas — Johnson, Palo Pinto, and Tarrant — and three adjacent counties. The few reports, all sight records, are: *Johnson* — a singing male noted at Lake Pat Cleburne on 2 May 1981; *Palo Pinto* — Oberholser

(1974) indicates a summer record for this county, but I could not locate the basis for this record; *Tarrant* — a bird was observed for several minutes near Eagle Mountain Lake on 6 July 1981. It was carefully studied and documented by two persons. *Young* — two members of this species were tallied on the BBS on 31 May 1987. Other recent records known to me are from adjacent counties: *Erath* — adult feeding two young out of the nest, southeast of Thurber, on 16 August 1981; *Mills* — a bird seen on 4 and 5 September 1980 on the Colorado River, west of Goldthwaite; the observers indicated that they had seen this species three or four years before; *Taylor* — Abilene CBCs on 2 January 1982 and 31 December 1983.

In recent years Brown Towhees appear to be more often reported from the Edwards Plateau and in the western part of the lower Panhandle region. This species should be photographed or collected to substantiate its occurrence in the study area.

BACHMAN'S SPARROW   *Aimophila aestivalis* (Lichtenstein)
Status: Formerly occurred along the east side of the study area to Cooke County and south in Navarro County. No records since 1965 in north central Texas, where its present status is uncertain.
Occurrence: This species is said to prefer pine woods with a grassy understory. This habitat is extremely limited in the study area, and many of the counties are not typical, since they have no conifers. All the county records are given to help clarify the status of this bird: *Cooke* — all records are before the 1900s; specimens, 11 August 1892 (USNM, number not available), 10 April 1879 (USNM 78385), 11 August 1879 (USNM 78386), and 29 April 1879 (USNM 78387). *Dallas* — May and February dates given by Stillwell (1939) without details (observer reported "flocks") may be in error; none since 1931–32. *Denton* — fall record given by Oberholser (1974) without detail is questionable and should be deleted. *Navarro* — specimen, September 1880 (USNM 80831), only record. *Van Zandt* — the only county in which I have observed Bachman's Sparrow in north central Texas. A nest with two eggs was discovered on 5 July 1965 southwest of Ben Wheeler, in the southeastern part of the county. This is the only recent sighting of Bachman's Sparrow for all of north central Texas. A search of this same area on 18 May 1984 failed to reveal this species. The habitat has been greatly disturbed since the 1960s. *Young* — Oberholser (1974) gave a questionable summer sighting in the 1880s. Since none of the records above are summer records and the sighting was far to the west, it may represent a misidentification and should be deleted.

In recent years the only records of this species are from nearby counties: *Anderson* — on the Gus Engeling Wildlife Management area, one netted on 8 July 1984 (TCWC); *Henderson* — one heard on the BBS of 11 June 1984, and a specimen from Wood (WMP 2315) on 23 October 1976.

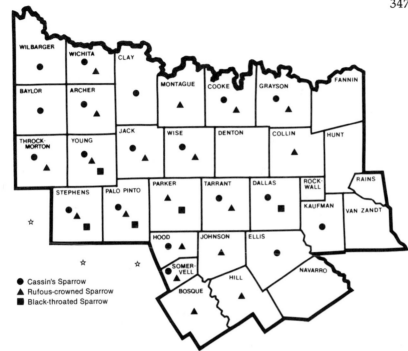

Map 102. Distribution of Cassin's Sparrow, *Aimophila cassinii;* the Rufous-crowned Sparrow, *A. ruficeps;* and the Black-throated Sparrow, *Amphispiza bilineata*

CASSIN'S SPARROW *Aimophila cassinii* (Woodhouse)
Status: Fairly common to common summer resident in the western counties of the study area.
Occurrence: Cassin's Sparrows have been recorded in 19 north central Texas counties—Archer, Baylor, Clay, Cooke, Dallas, Ellis, Grayson, Hood, Jack, Kaufman, Palo Pinto, Somervell, Stephens, Tarrant, Throckmorton, Wichita, Wilbarger, Wise, and Young—and adjacent Knox County.

This species is confined to areas of short grass but only in old fields containing native grasses with few forbs and weeds, although scattered low mesquites and small bushes may furnish flight perches. It is from these that males skylark, courting females hidden in the grass. Cassin's Sparrow is predominantly a bird of the western portion and the southern parts of the study area.

Most of the records are for spring and early summer; there are few sightings after early July. Extreme overall dates range from 2 April 1977 (Palo Pinto County) to 31 August 1948 (Dallas County). Extreme dates for counties for which data are available are: *Dallas*—very few recent records; very little, if any, habitat left, 26 April 1978 to 31 August 1948 (specimen); *Grayson*—very local, recorded only four times since 1974, 1 May to 10 July 1980; has not been recorded at Hagerman NWR; *Palo Pinto* — 2 April 1977 to 15 August 1976; *Tarrant* — found regularly each year, primarily in the Benbrook Lake area, 8 April 1956 to 21 July 1956; *Wichita* — 8 April 1978 to 10 August 1975.

Nesting: Late-spring and early-summer records along the western edge of the project area no doubt represent nesting birds even though no nests have been found. Oberholser (1974) indicated actual nesting only in Baylor, Wichita, and Wilbarger counties, while other nesting records toward the eastern edge of the range are from Dallas, but not since 8 July 1937 (four young; Stillwell, 1939). In Grayson County there was a record of three young on 5 June 1980. Sutton (1938) gave four nesting records for Tarrant County from 12 April to 20 May 1915. The April nest, an extremely early one, was discovered by a local egg collector named Graham. He mentioned that the eggs were white but "about the size of a Catbird's." On 15 June 1978 I found a well-concealed nest on a branch of a prickly pear west of Benbrook, in Tarrant County. The female flushed from the nest, which contained five white eggs. The recent records for Dallas, Ellis, and Kaufman counties probably represent transients.

Specimens: Cassin's Sparrow specimens have been taken in Cooke (Oberholser, 1974, not located), Dallas (DMNH), Knox (KU), and Tarrant (DMNH) counties.

RUFOUS-CROWNED SPARROW   *Aimophila ruficeps* (Cassin)
Status: Rare to uncommon permanent resident locally.
Occurrence: The Rufous-crowned Sparrow has been observed in 19 north central Texas counties: Archer, Bosque, Collin, Cooke, Grayson, Hill, Hood, Jack, Johnson, Montague, Palo Pinto, Parker, Somervell, Stephens, Tarrant, Throckmorton, Wichita, Wise, and Young.

This species seems to be mainly restricted to the Brazos River drainage, especially dry, rocky outcrops, though similar habitats along the Red River have small populations. It is quite wary and often heard but not seen. It will respond to squeaking or owl calls. Small numbers formerly could be found regularly in the eastern counties of its range, but it has recently disappeared from those counties or become infrequent. For example, it has not been reported in Grayson County since the fall of 1979, and the sightings in Tarrant County are not as frequent. It is likely that habitat disturbances and urban development are eliminating it in the latter county.

Rufous-crowned Sparrows are permanent residents in small pockets of habitat, where they can be found regularly, yet there may be some local movement, for one was found dead near the courthouse in downtown Fort Worth in the fall of 1964. Records are scattered and not year round except in several western counties where considerable bird-watching is conducted. The largest numbers of observations seem to be for the spring and winter periods, when the birds are most active.

Nesting: Nesting has been recorded in the following counties: Cooke (Oberholser, 1974); Grayson — young begging for food on 28 July 1970, and family group seen on 11 September 1971; Johnson — juvenile collected on 22 May 1959 (DMNH 5170); Hood — immature birds observed in the summer of 1969; Palo Pinto — two juveniles being fed on 24 July 1976; Somervell — two adults with one young on 9 June 1984; Tarrant — adults with immature birds in July 1964 and 1965.

Specimens: Specimens have been located from the following counties: Bosque (UTA), Hood (FWMSH), Johnson (DMNH), Palo Pinto (DMNH, WMP), Somervell (DMNH, TCWC, WMP), Stephens (DMNH), and Tarrant (FWMSH). Those examples said to have been taken in Cooke and Wise counties (Oberholser, 1974) were not located. The specimens belong to the subspecies *A. r. eremoeca.*

AMERICAN TREE SPARROW   *Spizella arborea* (Wilson)
Status: Irregular to rare winter resident. Not reported every year.
Occurrence: American Tree Sparrows have been recorded in 19 counties in the study area — Archer, Clay, Collin, Cooke, Dallas, Denton, Fannin, Grayson, Hunt, Kaufman, Montague, Navarro, Palo Pinto, Somervell, Stephens, Tarrant, Wichita, Wilbarger, and Wise — and nearby Hardeman County.

In recent years this species seems to be recorded more often (possibly because there are more competent bird-watchers), though in some years it is missed. It has been recorded on all but one of the CBCs, but not as frequently on the southern counts. It was observed on all but one of the ten years (1973–82) of the Wichita Falls (Wichita County) CBCs and most of the Hagerman NWR (Grayson County) counts. Only in years of severe winter weather does it seem to reach the Dallas–Fort Worth area, and then one can expect it in many localities, especially north of the metroplex area.

Overall winter dates range from 14 November (several different years in several counties) to 4 April 1973 (Dallas County). Dates of American Tree Sparrows seem to be more prevalent from late December through February. Extreme arrival and departure dates for selected counties are: *Dallas* — 14 November 1980 to 28 February 1956 and an isolated date, 4 April 1973; *Grayson* — 14 November 1976 to 12 March 1977; *Tarrant* — 14 November 1964 to 7 March 1979; *Wichita* — 16 November 1974 to 30 March 1976, next-latest 5 March 1974.

Specimens: American Tree Sparrow specimens have been taken in Dallas (DMNH, WMP), Denton (DMNH, WMP), Grayson (WMP), Palo Pinto (WMP), and Tarrant (WMP) counties. In the first two counties the races *ochracea* and *arborea* have been taken, while in Grayson and Palo Pinto

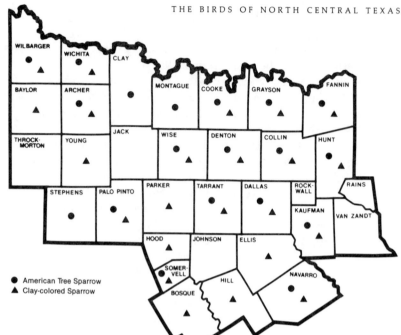

Map 103. Distribution of the American Tree Sparrow, *Spizella arborea,* and the Clay-colored Sparrow, *S. pallida*

counties only *ochracea* was collected. In Tarrant County the only example represents *arborea* tending toward *ochracea*. Oberholser (1974) indicated that a specimen of the race *ochracea* was taken in Cooke County, but I have been unable to locate it.

CHIPPING SPARROW *Spizella passerina* (Bechstein)
Status: Fairly common to common transient, rare to irregular in winter.
Occurrence: Chipping Sparrows have been reported in all of the north central Texas counties except Jack and Montague. It is likely that they would be found in these counties, too, if more bird-watching took place there. In addition, they have been reported from nearby Shackelford and Wood counties. The records are more abundant in the eastern part of the study area than in the western part.

This species is usually observed as a transient, though it has been reported on all of the CBCs of the area. However, the winter sightings are scattered, and it is frequently missed. It is not to be expected every winter. There are few sightings for January and February, and some of the December observations could be considered late-fall stragglers.

Extreme dates of migration for selected counties are: *Dallas* – 12 October 1982 to 27 November 1982, scattered December records to 31 December 1954, no records for January, and an isolated date of 21 February 1970, next-earliest 19 March 1959 to 24 May 1960; *Grayson*—19 September to 20 December, four scattered December records until 28 December 1959, several mid-January dates, and 11 March to 29 May; *Tarrant*—29 August 1973 to 18 November 1954, six CBCs (1956–86), several January records, and 21 February 1986 to 26 May 1966; a 15 June 1973 date is unexplainable and could be in error; *Van Zandt*—8 to 30 October 1983, several December sightings, and 4 February to 18 May 1984; *Wichita*—19 October 1980 to 29 October 1973, none for November, several December observations, and one observation in early January 1973. Most spring records are from 28 March 1975 to 24 May 1973.

Nesting: Chipping Sparrow nesting (eggs or young) for the north central Texas study area has not been documented. There is a questionable record for Wise County (probably before the turn of the century), and it is said to summer in Bosque and Clay counties, but all these reports need confirmation.

Specimens: Specimens, all representing the nominate race *passerina*, were collected in Cooke (TNHC), Dallas (DMNH, WMP), Denton (DMNH), Ellis (DMNH), Navarro (USNM), Palo Pinto (DMNH), Tarrant (DMNH, FWMSH), and Wichita (WMP) counties in the study area and in adjacent Wood County (DMNH). A bird found dead (WMP 2952) in Dallas County on 5 October 1984 was identified as *arizonae*.

CLAY-COLORED SPARROW *Spizella pallida* (Swainson)

Status: Uncommon to fairly common transient in spring and fall.

Occurrence: Clay-colored Sparrows have been recorded in 23 north central Texas counties: Archer, Baylor, Bosque, Collin, Cooke, Dallas, Denton, Ellis, Fannin, Grayson, Hill, Hood, Hunt, Kaufman, Navarro, Palo Pinto, Parker, Somervell, Tarrant, Wichita, Wilbarger, Wise, and Young.

This species is usually found in passage from mid-April to mid-May and from late September through October. November records are considered to be observations of stragglers, not of winter birds. Clay-colors are much more abundant in spring than in fall, probably because their song makes them easier to find and to identify.

Extreme overall dates for selected north central Texas counties in spring and fall are: *Collin*—12 April 1969 to 3 May 1980, and 31 August 1985 (banded) to 22 October 1982; *Dallas*—4 April 1948 (specimen) to 30 May 1982, next-latest 15 May 1959, and 10 September 1976 to 10 November 1963, next-latest 2 November 1982; *Denton*—30 March 1982, next-earliest 1 April 1986 to 16 May 1976, and 25 September 1959 to 2 November 1982, next-latest 19 October 1984; *Grayson*—17 April 1980 to 12 May 1972, and 24 September 1983 to 1 November 1984; *Tarrant*—21 March 1956, next-earliest 11 April 1984 to 21 May 1955, and 14 September 1983 to 18 November 1952, next-latest 29 October 1979; *Wichita*—1 April 1976 to 1 June 1956 (specimen), and 25 September 1976 to 17 October 1978.

Because this species is easily confused with immature Chipping Sparrows, a number of dates have been discounted. The Chipping Sparrow is more common and occasionally winters in the study area. The only sure way to distinguish immatures of the two species is to note the colors of their rumps. The Chipping Sparrow has a gray rump, and the Clay-colored Sparrow has a buffy-brown rump. Several CBC reports for Collin, Dallas, and Hunt counties are probably examples of this identification problem and have been dismissed. Oberholser (1974) also gave a winter sight record for Navarro County. Whether this sighting represented a lingering November bird or was a misidentification could not be determined, and because no details were available to evaluate the report, I have dismissed it as a winter record. There appears to be no valid winter record for north central Texas.

Specimens: Specimens have been located from the following counties: Cooke (TNHC), Dallas (DMNH, WMP), Denton (DMNH), Ellis (DMNH), Tarrant (DMNH), and Wichita (MWU).

FIELD SPARROW   *Spizella pusilla* (Wilson)

Status: Fairly common to common transient and winter resident. Nesting was formerly more widespread than it is today, though there are still summer records of its occurrence in a number of counties.

Occurrence: Field Sparrows have been reported in all counties in the study area except Baylor County, where they would no doubt be found if more bird-watching occurred there.

Most of the migration records range from mid-October to early April. Extreme arrival and departure dates for counties for which sufficient data are available are: *Collin*—13 October 1982 to 16 April 1980 (all banded birds); *Dallas*—8 September 1957 (recent record, 8 October 1977) to 17 May 1970; *Grayson*—an early date, 6 August 1981, next 14 August 1986 to 4 April 1981; *Tarrant*—8 September 1957 (recent record, 9 October 1977) to 26 May 1946 (recent record, 21 May 1978); *Wichita*—19 October 1980 (specimen) to 6 May 1976 and an isolated date, 17 June 1982.

Field Sparrows are usually recorded on all of the CBCs conducted in the study area. Their numbers throughout seem to be fairly constant, varying with environmental conditions and weather.

Nesting: Although Oberholser (1974) gave nesting records for Dallas, Grayson, Stephens, Tarrant, Wilbarger, and Wise counties (probably all at the turn of the century or in the 1920s), there is only one recent record. Apparently there have been changes in the nesting status of this species in north central Texas.

More and Strecker (1929) mentioned that the Field Sparrow was a "somewhat common summer resident, breeding in May and June" in Wilbarger County; however, I have no data indicating that it does so today. Sutton (1938) also reported Field Sparrows nesting in Tarrant County, but I have no recent nesting records for that county. Three or four adults have been always present on the Hagerman NWR, Grayson County—as late as June and July in 1983—but nesting has not been confirmed in recent years. Sutton (1967) found them nesting across the Red River from Grayson County, in Marshall County, Oklahoma, in the mid-1950s.

The only recent nesting record was a streaked-breast young out of the nest with adults on 9 June 1984 at Dinosaur Valley SP, Somervell County. It is possible that the population (summer residents) of the Field Sparrow from the Edwards Plateau, south of the project area, extends this far north, since it has been recorded on 15 of sixteen BBSs conducted in early June in nearby Hood County. Other summer records since the 1960s include Bosque, Denton, Hill, Hunt, Palo Pinto, Parker, Van Zandt, Wichita, Wise, and Young counties.

Specimens: Specimens are available from the study area—for Bosque (DMNH, UTA), Cooke (TNHC), Dallas (DMNH, USNM, WMP), Denton (DMNH), Ellis (DMNH), Fannin (WMP), Hill (UTA), Johnson (DMNH), Kaufman (DMNH), Palo Pinto (WMP), Parker (FWMSH), Tarrant (DMNH, FWMSH), Wichita (MWU, WMP), and Wise (DMNH) counties and adjacent Henderson (DMNH) and Wood (WMP) counties. Specimens indicated by Oberholser (1974) for Collin and Navarro counties could not be located.

Although not all of the specimens have been examined, those examined from Dallas, Palo Pinto, Wichita, and Wood counties, all in my collection (WMP), represent the western race *arenacea*. Field Sparrows (DMNH, FWMSH) from Tarrant County represent the nominate race, *pusilla*, and *arenacea*.

Vesper Sparrow   *Pooecetes gramineus* (Gmelin)
Status: Fairly common to rare winter resident. More abundant as a transient.
Occurrence: Vesper Sparrows have been observed in all of the counties of the study area and in nearby Shackelford County. This species is usually found from early October to early May, with the peak of migration from mid-October to early November and late March to late April. In spring loose flocks of 40 or 50 Vesper Sparrows are not uncommon. They frequent open pastures, dirt roadsides, and plowed fields in small flocks, often accompanying Savannah Sparrows. Although they have been recorded on all of the CBCs, they seem to be more prevalent in the Dallas–Fort Worth area (possibly because more bird-watching takes place here), but the num-

bers counted along the Red River in the north are never as high, and they are frequently absent from some of those counts.

Extreme fall and spring arrival and departure dates for selected counties are: *Dallas* — 8 October 1976 (mean, 21 October) to 2 May 1964 (mean, 22 April), the date 23 August 1934 given by Stillwell (1939) is unacceptable; *Grayson* — 24 September to 31 December, and 1 March to 28 April 1972, and 8 January, 24 February, and 28 February; *Palo Pinto* — 9 October 1977 to 9 April 1977; *Tarrant* — 30 September 1956 to 17 May 1974; *Wichita* — 29 September 1976, next-earliest 12 October 1974 to 26 May 1974.

Specimens: Vesper Sparrows have been collected in the following counties: Cooke (TNHC), Dallas (DMNH, WMP), Denton (DMNH, WMP), Ellis (DMNH), Navarro (USNM), Palo Pinto (FWMSH), Parker (WMP), Stephens (WMP), Tarrant (DMNH), Wichita (DMNH, WMP), and Wise (DMNH). Oberholser (1974) indicated that a specimen was taken in Clay County, but it was not located.

Both subspecies of the Vesper Sparrow, *gramineus* and the western race, *confinis*, have been taken in Dallas and Tarrant counties.

Lark Sparrow   *Chondestes grammacus* (Say)
Status: Common to abundant summer resident. A few birds winter in secluded areas of many counties.
Occurrence: The Lark Sparrow has been observed in every county of the study area. It has been seen in many counties the year round, but more often during migration periods and in summer. Most birds occur from mid-March to late October, when good-sized flocks may be seen. Lark Sparrows range over a wide variety of habitats where hedgerows, brush, or secondary growth is interspersed with grass and forbs. It is not unusual to find them along secondary highways and local county roads. Their characteristic gait (walking and sometimes hopping) makes these "quail-headed" birds with noticeable white tail-edge markings easy to identify.

The Lark Sparrow is seen on all of the CBCs of the study area, though it may be missed some years on CBCs in the northern part of the study area. It appears to be influenced by weather and the availability of food, which may account for fewer sightings in January and February. Then it can be found only in more localized areas.
Nesting: Counties in which nests or young have been discovered are: Archer, Bosque, Clay, Collin, Cooke, Dallas, Denton, Grayson, Hill, Hood, Hunt, Johnson, Kaufman, Navarro, Palo Pinto, Parker, Rockwall, Somervell, Tarrant, Van Zandt, Wichita, Wilbarger, Wise, and Young. The species would be found nesting in all of the north central Texas study-area counties if one were to look for nests there. Nesting ranges from late April to

early July—2 April 1973 (nest being built) to 28 July 1971 (young in nest), both for Tarrant County; these dates would be typical for other counties. Peak of nesting dates is late May and June. The species is frequently parasitized by the Brown-headed Cowbird; a Lark Sparrow was noted feeding a young cowbird as late as 2 August 1979. A nest found in Young County on 21 May 1985 contained three cowbirds, a Lark Sparrow, and two unhatched eggs, one of each species.

Specimens: Specimens were located for the following counties: Bosque (WMP), Cooke (KU, TNHC), Dallas (DMNH, OU), Denton (DMNH), Ellis (DMNH), Hood (FWMSH), Johnson (SUC), Kaufman (DMNH), Navarro (WMP), Parker (FWMSH, WMP), Somervell (TCWC), Tarrant (DMNH, FWMSH), and Wise (DMNH).

Both the eastern race *C. g. grammacus* and the western race *C. g. strigatus* have been taken in north central Texas. Not all of the specimens have been examined for racial identification, but many of those examined belong to *strigatus*, which seems to represent the nesting race of the study area.

BLACK-THROATED SPARROW *Amphispiza bilineata* (Cassin)
Status: On rare occasions found irregularly in the southwestern part of the study area.
Occurrence: Black-throated Sparrows have been recorded in five north central Texas counties: Dallas, Palo Pinto, Parker, Stephens, and Young. All but Dallas County were cited by Oberholser (1974), who also gave records for nearby Eastland, Erath, Hardeman, Knox, and Shackelford counties. The species tends to be restricted to brushy areas interspersed with cacti, a habitat that is limited to the southwestern part of the study area. Today range improvement has removed much of this vegetation from the area. This sparrow is extremely rare and is no longer observed in some counties. It is shy and can be missed unless one searches for it or knows its song.

County records in the study area are: *Dallas*—one bird seen on 16 April 1960 in the cedar brakes near Cedar Hill; *Palo Pinto*—seen off and on through the 1960s at various times of the year until 25 December 1975, once since, on 12 June 1985; three young and a cowbird banded on 20 June 1970; *Parker*—Weatherford, 26 May 1935 (Stillwell, 1939); *Stephens*—summer (Oberholser, 1974); *Young*—recorded on five BBSs, 1 June 1979 (one), 5 June 1983 (three), 23 June 1984 (one), 16 June 1985 (one), and 8 June 1986 (three). Oberholser (1974) cited a questionable nesting record for which I can find no details. It was probably before the 1900s.
Specimens: The only specimen for the area was one that I collected in Palo Pinto County on 15 April 1960 (WMP 991) and identified as the nominate race, *bilineata*.

Map 104. Distribution of the Lark Bunting, *Calamospiza melanocorys*

LARK BUNTING *Calamospiza melanocorys* Stejneger
Status: Some years fairly common, especially in migration along the western side of the study area; irregular winter visitor.
Occurrence: The Lark Bunting has been recorded in 21 counties of the study area: Archer, Baylor, Bosque, Clay, Collin, Cooke, Dallas, Denton, Hood, Jack, Johnson, Montague, Navarro, Palo Pinto, Stephens, Tarrant, Throckmorton, Wichita, Wilbarger, Wise, and Young. It has also been observed in nearby Eastland and Shackelford counties, where it apparently had not been previously recorded.

Although the Lark Bunting is an extremely common bird of west Texas, this species reaches the study area in any numbers only along the western edge, especially in spring migration. It is somewhat erratic and is not recorded every year. It is a bird of the grasslands, quite conspicuous, and seldom observed alone. In north central Texas it has not been recorded east of Cooke, Collin, Dallas, and Navarro counties.

Extreme overall arrival and departure dates are 11 August 1979 (Dallas County), next-earliest 13 September 1978 (Denton County) to 16 May 1983 (Throckmorton County). Selected county dates are: *Dallas* — 11 August 1979 to 6 May 1958; *Denton* — 13 September 1978 to 6 May 1977; *Tarrant* — 29 September 1956 to 14 May 1966; *Wichita* — 9 November 1977 to 3 May 1974.

Lark Buntings have been recorded during the winter period in Cooke, Dallas, Denton, Johnson, Palo Pinto, Stephens, Tarrant, Throckmorton, Wilbarger, Wise, and Young counties. Unfortunately, the records, especially for the western parts of the study area, are insufficient to give a clear picture of its winter status, which is due to lack of regular observers. However, in Tarrant County, where considerable bird-watching was carried on for a number of years (1940–83), it occurred during the winter of 1940–41, the winter of 1953, and the winter of 1956–57; 12 December 1979 through 15 March 1980, widespread over the study area as far east as Dallas County, and 31 December 1982 and 9 January 1983.

Nesting: The only nesting record for north central Texas was one found by R. L. More (Oberholser, 1974) on 8 June 1935 in Wilbarger County. He collected a set of eggs on that date.

Specimens: Specimens of the Lark Bunting in various plumages have been taken in Tarrant (WMP), Wichita (MWU, WMP), and Wilbarger (MWU) counties. Those said to have been collected in Dallas County (Stillwell, 1939) were probably taken before the turn of the century by W. A. Mayer and lost, for their whereabouts are unknown. Oberholser (1974) also indicates specimens for Cooke and Wise counties, but these too could not be located.

SAVANNAH SPARROW   *Passerculus sandwichensis* (Gmelin)
Status: Common to abundant transient and winter resident.
Occurrence: The Savannah Sparrow has been recorded in all of the counties of north central Texas. This small, nondescript grass sparrow is commonly found as a transient and is locally abundant in winter.

Typical extreme arrival and departure dates for selected counties are: *Dallas*—15 September 1984 to 15 May 1969; *Denton*—24 September 1982 to 25 April 1982; *Grayson*—16 September 1978 to 20 May; *Kaufman*—16 September 1980 to 6 May 1979; *Tarrant*—1 September 1956, next-earliest 14 September 1978 (mean, 12 October, ten years) to 15 May 1973 (mean, 5 May, 13 years); *Wichita*—13 September 1975 to 11 May 1974.

This species has been recorded on all of the CBCs of the area, usually every year, and always on counts away from the Dallas–Fort Worth area. In winter it is not uncommon to find 50 to 100 or more if the observer walks some favorite field of short grasses, especially native grasses. At least 450 birds were seen on 9 March 1972 in Grayson County. Savannah Sparrows are often found with Vesper Sparrows.

Specimens: Savannah Sparrow specimens are available from the following counties: Bosque (DMNH), Clay (Oberholser, 1974; not located), Collin (DMNH), Cooke (TNHC), Dallas (DMNH, WMP), Denton (DMNH), Ellis (DMNH, WMP), Fannin (DMNH), Hunt (DMNH, WMP), Johnson (DMNH, SUC), Kaufman (DMNH), Navarro (USNM), Parker (FWMSH),

Tarrant (DMNH, UTA, WMP), Wichita (MWU, WMP), Wilbarger (USNM), and Wise (DMNH).

Not all of the specimens have been examined, but among those studied were six recognized races (AOU, 1957) — *anthinus, labradorius, nevadensis, oblitus, rufofuscus,* and *savanna* — and an unrecognized race — *mediogriseus.* All but *labradorius* and *rufofuscus* are widespread. The races *oblitus, anthinus, nevadensis, savanna,* and *mediogriseus* were found in Dallas and Tarrant counties, while examples of only the first three subspecies were identified from Wichita County. *Labradorius* was found only in Dallas County (16 October 1960, WMP 1064), and a specimen of *rufofuscus* listed by Oberholser (1974) for Navarro County (11 January 1880) was not located. The race *savanna* has been taken as far west as Parker County (20 January 1967, FWMSH 353).

BAIRD'S SPARROW *Ammodramus bairdii* (Audubon)
Status: Not to be expected, casual if it does occur. Formerly ranged throughout north central Texas, probably irregularly.
Occurrence: Although Baird's Sparrows have been reported in nine north central Texas counties — Cooke, Dallas, Denton, Grayson, Hunt, Rockwall, Somervell, Tarrant, and Wise — many of the records are questionable. Some are very likely misidentified Savannah Sparrows, common migrants throughout the area. The records thus provide a very unsatisfactory picture of the status of Baird's Sparrow.

County records are: *Cooke* — a specimen cited by Oberholser (1974) of 19 March, which probably represents an old record of G. H. Ragsdale taken in the 1880s; example not located. *Dallas* — Stillwell (1939) gave questionable sightings in the late 1930s. Recent reports — one on the 1960 CBC and several others for January and February — are discounted. An observation east of Dallas by two competent observers on 28 March 1974 is plausible. *Denton* — the local checklist (Rylander, 1959) presented far too many sightings, which were dismissed. *Grayson* — two reports, both possible sightings, 23 and 29 April 1973, neither observed by more than one person. *Hunt* — fall, spring, and winter, according to Oberholser (1974), not acceptable. *Rockwall* — near Lake Ray Hubbard, one briefly seen by several persons for about ten seconds on 20 December 1984; the written report not convincing because of the brevity of the sighting. The area harbors Le Conte's Sparrows and Savannah Sparrows. *Somervell* — January sighting (Guthery, 1974); no details given; not accepted. *Tarrant* — 17 March 1970, rare migrant; for details of status see Pulich (1979). *Wise* — specimen indicated for spring (Oberholser, 1974) could not be located; no details given.

Most authorities agree that drastic environmental changes in the prairies, especially in the provinces where the species nests, have affected the overall population of Baird's Sparrow. From the records at hand this species probably never was very abundant in north central Texas and today is even less so. Observers who visit the prairies are urged to study carefully the species inhabiting grasslands in an effort to document them. Baird's Sparrows are said to prefer dense shortgrass prairies. Sparrows thought to be Baird's Sparrows should be photographed if possible, or observers should take extensive notes of their sightings while they are in the field to help clarify the status of this species. Because there are no known specimens for north central Texas, one should be collected to document its occurrence.

GRASSHOPPER SPARROW *Ammodramus savannarum* (Gmelin)
Status: Fairly common summer resident. Uncommon to rare winter resident.
Occurrence: Grasshopper Sparrows have been reported in 27 counties of the study area—Bosque, Clay, Collin, Cooke, Dallas, Denton, Ellis, Fannin, Grayson, Hill, Hood, Hunt, Johnson, Kaufman, Navarro, Palo Pinto, Parker, Rains, Somervell, Stephens, Tarrant, Throckmorton, Van Zandt, Wichita, Wilbarger, Wise, and Young—and adjacent Eastland and Shackelford counties.

Extreme arrival and departure dates (late November and December dates are considered to be wintering birds) for counties for which there are sufficient data are: *Collin*—7 April 1984 to 3 November 1984; *Dallas*—13 April 1982 through 7 November 1978, next-latest 4 November 1979; *Grayson*—28 March to 20 October; *Palo Pinto*—12 March 1966 through mid-June; *Tarrant*—18 March 1955 (mean, 11 April) through 9 November 1981; *Wichita*—1 April 1976 through 19 October 1980.

This species is widespread over shortgrass pastures, having been reported throughout the year. It is more common in migration, and many are killed at TV towers in the Dallas–Fort Worth area and in Wichita Falls. In winter it does not seem to be abundant, at present being found on only six of the ten CBCs of the north central Texas study area: McKinney (Collin County), Lewisville (Denton County), Caddo National Grasslands (Fannin County), Palo Pinto (Palo Pinto County), Fort Worth (Tarrant County), and Lake Tawakoni (Van Zandt County). Except for the Fort Worth CBC, where the species was reported on four counts, and Lake Tawakoni CBC, where it was seen on three counts, the others represent single counts. This may be due to the bird's secretive nature, which makes it more difficult to find at this time of the year. There are few reports anywhere for January, February, or November.
Nesting: The Grasshopper Sparrow nests in north central Texas in fair numbers. There are records (nests or young) for Cooke, Dallas, Ellis, Grayson, Johnson, Kaufman, Navarro, Tarrant, Wichita, and Wilbarger

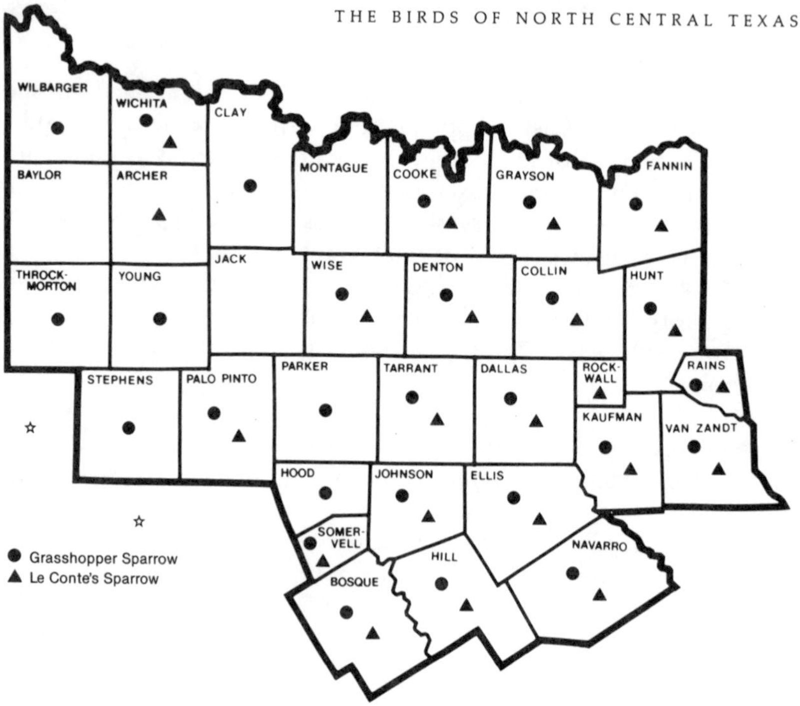

Map 105. Distribution of the Grasshopper Sparrow, *Ammodramus savannarum*, and Le Conte's Sparrow, *A. leconteii*

counties, while it has been found summering in Collin, Denton, Palo Pinto, Rains, Throckmorton, Wise, and Young counties. Many authors indicate that it is two-brooded, and dates on hand tend to support this claim. Nesting ranges from May to early July.

Specimens: Specimens have been collected in the following counties: Clay (Oberholser, 1974, not located), Cooke (TNHC 1631, 9 March 1885; TNHC 1626, 9 November 1885), Dallas (DMNH, UTA, WMP), Denton (DMNH, WMP), Ellis (DMNH, WMP), Kaufman (WMP), Parker (FWMSH), Tarrant (DMNH, FWMSH, WMP), Wichita (MWU, WMP), and Wise (DMNH).

Although not all specimens of Grasshopper Sparrows were identified by subspecies, both *A. s. pratensis* and *A. s. perpallidus* were identified in my collection (WMP) from Dallas and Denton counties, while the latter race was found in Kaufman, Tarrant, and Wichita counties.

HENSLOW'S SPARROW *Ammodramus henslowii* (Audubon)
Status: Uncertain; at best casual to accidental.
Occurrence: Despite a concentrated effort to locate the Henslow's Sparrow in north central Texas, it has eluded me. For that matter I have never

seen this shy little grassland species anywhere in Texas. It represents one of the rarest sparrows in north central Texas and possibly in Texas as a whole. There is, however, a small nesting population southwest of Houston in Harris County that has been described as a separate subspecies (Arnold, 1983).

The distribution map for Henslow's Sparrow in *The Bird Life of Texas* (Oberholser, 1974) shows records for the species in Clay, Cooke, Dallas, Hunt, Navarro, and Tarrant counties, with specimen records given for Cooke and Dallas counties. It is possible that in earlier times, especially before the turn of the century, this elusive sparrow was more abundant; however, many of the sightings, especially the more recent ones, are undoubtedly in error. For example, an attempt to question older observers about their records for Dallas and Tarrant counties was unsatisfactory. In most instances no details were given about alleged sightings, and I had difficulty evaluating most of the records.

In addition to the counties listed above for Henslow's Sparrow there are records for Archer, Hill, Rockwall, and Wichita counties. To help readers who may bird in various parts of north central Texas, comments are offered for the ten counties in which this species is said to have been recorded: *Archer* — one brief sighting near Scotland in an overgrown field on 26 May 1974 (Zinn, 1975). Since no other details were given and the observer seems to have been influenced by probably erroneous summer records from nearby counties, I have dismissed this sighting. *Clay* — a summer record given by Oberholser (1974) is highly improbable; details of this record, as well as its source, are lacking. As far as I know, Henslow's Sparrow never summered in this part of Texas. *Cooke* — Oberholser (1974) indicated specimen records for fall and winter, but I have been unable to locate the specimens. These records very likely represent references to specimens allegedly taken by G. H. Ragsdale before the turn of the century. A sight record on 22 April 1969, without details, has not been accepted. *Dallas* — although the Dallas Museum of Natural History specimen card catalog cites six specimens, only one (DMNH 752) is at the museum, a mounted bird on display. The specimen is listed as having been collected ten miles east of Dallas on 10 May 1939. Incidentally, this represents the only known example of Henslow's Sparrow for all of north central Texas. On each of the other museum catalog cards of the missing Henslow's Sparrows there is a notation that the specimens were sent to Oberholser, but there is no record of their being returned. To date I have been unable to locate these specimens. Inquiries about possible deposition in a number of leading museums have proved futile. It is also rather odd that these alleged specimens were not mentioned in Oberholser's *The Bird Life of Texas* (1974). All other records (none since the mid-1960s) for Dallas are highly improbable and have been dismissed as errors. *Hill* — a sighting by a lone observer in the Aquilla Creek watershed on 27 April 1980 was not accepted. The observer was vague about details and unfamiliar with this species. *Hunt* — spring and summer records (Oberholser, 1974) are questionable. From what information I can find, there is only a listing of species in the county checklist, without information on the rarity of the birds in question. *Navarro* — listed as a fall record probably on the basis of Ogilby's (1882) account of the species as "an autumn visitor in small numbers." There have been no observations since that time. *Rockwall* — a sparrow fitting the description of Henslow's Sparrow was reported by several observers at the same location on the shoreline of Lake Ray Hubbard on 17 February 1983 and in the following year on 12 and 24 February. In all instances the birds were observed by more than one observer, most of whom were experienced birders. From detailed descriptions of the birds sent to me for evaluation, they were probably Henslow's Sparrows. *Tarrant* — in *Birds of Tarrant County* (Pulich, 1979) this species was placed in the list of species of uncertain occurrence, which does not agree with the *Checklist of the Birds of Texas* (TOS, 1984) that it will be found in Tarrant County. I prefer to question the records for this county. *Wichita* — Peterson (1960) indicated that a bird summered at Wichita Falls; the report is probably based on a Clay County record that is questionable and has been dismissed. Oberholser (1974) gave no reference to Wichita County.

Because of the vague details and discrepancies in records given by various authors, the status of the Henslow's Sparrow in north central Texas is not clear. Future sightings should be carefully documented with all the characteristic field marks. Observers are urged to obtain photographs and even specimens to help clarify the occurrence of this species in the study area.

LE CONTE'S SPARROW   *Ammodramus leconteii* (Audubon)
Status: Fairly common to rare winter resident locally.
Occurrence: Le Conte's Sparrows have been recorded in 22 north central Texas counties — Archer, Bosque, Collin, Cooke, Dallas, Denton, Ellis, Fannin, Grayson, Hill, Hunt, Johnson, Kaufman, Navarro, Palo Pinto, Rains, Rockwall, Somervell, Tarrant, Van Zandt, Wichita, and Wise — and nearby Eastland County.

Le Conte's Sparrows prefer thick, damp, grassy areas containing broom sedge and even cattails. They have been recorded on all of the CBCs in north central Texas except the Wichita Falls count, though they have been recorded in the latter area in winter as well. They are missed some years but can be found in localized areas that have enough moisture to provide the proper habitat. This species can usually be found in winter at the Lewisville Fish Hatchery (Denton County) and the Hagerman NWR (Grayson

County); otherwise, the records are scattered. The birds' habit of remaining hidden in grassy cover makes them difficult to find.

Most Le Conte's Sparrows are found in the area from November through February. Extreme dates for selected counties are: *Dallas* — 8 October 1982 to 3 May 1958; *Grayson* — 5 October 1980 to 10 April 1981; *Johnson* — 27 October 1980 to 19 April 1980; *Rains* — 5 November 1983 to 27 April 1985; *Tarrant* — 18 October 1985 to 3 May 1980. An alleged report of 3 September 1942 has been discounted.

Specimens: Specimens are available from five counties — Cooke (UCM, USNM), Dallas (DMNH, WMP), Navarro (USNM), Palo Pinto (WMP), and Tarrant (DMNH, mounted specimen, FWMSH) counties and nearby Eastland County. A specimen said to have been collected in Denton County (Oberholser, 1974) could not be located.

Fox Sparrow   *Passerella iliaca* (Merrem)
Status: Fairly common to uncommon winter resident.
Occurrence: Fox Sparrows have been reported in all counties in the study area except Baylor, Throckmorton, and Wilbarger. The only reason they have not been observed in these counties is a lack of observers during the winter period. They have also been seen in adjacent Shackelford County.

This species is one of the winter sparrows that tend to arrive late and depart rather early. Most of the population is usually found from late November into early March. Some extreme arrival and departure county dates are: *Collin* — 15 October 1983 to 25 March 1984 (banded birds); *Dallas* — 16 October 1974 to 3 May 1937 (Stillwell, 1939), next-latest 13 April 1938 (Stillwell, 1939); *Grayson* — 23 October to 8 April 1972; *Tarrant* — 19 October 1951 to 12 April 1982, and an isolated date, 5 May 1973; *Wichita* — 18 October 1975, next-earliest 3 November 1980 to 29 April 1978, next-latest 22 March 1975.

Fox Sparrows have been reported on all the CBCs in north central Texas and usually every year, although they are occasionally missed on one or two counts. They are not found in great numbers, and they seldom come to feeders except during extremely severe weather. They tend to be local and are found in river-bottom thickets in flocks of up to a dozen or so birds. Although most counts had fewer than 150 Fox Sparrows, on 14 February 1974 an unbelievable 1,500 were reported, along with hundreds of other sparrows, along a three-mile stretch of road at Hagerman NWR, Grayson County (Williams, 1974).

Specimens: Specimens have been taken in the following counties: Cooke (TNHC), Dallas (DMNH, WMP), Denton (DMNH), Ellis (DMNH), Hunt (FWMSH), Kaufman (DMNH), Navarro (USNM), Parker (WMP), Tarrant (DMNH, FWMSH, UTA, WMP), and Wise (DMNH) and nearby

Henderson (DMNH) County. A winter Fox Sparrow specimen said to have been collected from Collin County (Oberholser, 1974) was not located.

All of the Fox Sparrows in my collection (WMP) from Dallas, Parker, and Tarrant counties belong to the race *zaboria*. Oberholser (1974) also pointed out that *iliaca* was taken from Cooke and Dallas counties, and he indicates that *zaboria* was taken from Cooke County. However, the specimens in the Dallas Museum from Dallas, Denton, Kaufman, Tarrant, and Wise counties were reexamined by George Lowery, Jr., and labeled *zaboria*.

SONG SPARROW   *Melospiza melodia* (Wilson)
Status: Fairly common to common winter resident.
Occurrence: The Song Sparrow has been seen in all of the counties of the study area except Baylor and Throckmorton. It usually arrives in north central Texas in early October and departs in early May. Extreme dates for the overall study area counties range from an unbelievably early 21 August 1977 (Palo Pinto County), next-earliest 3 September 1956 (Tarrant County), to 26 May 1930 (Dallas County; Stillwell, 1939). Extreme arrival and departure dates for selected counties are: *Collin* — 23 September 1980 to 17 April 1983 (all banded birds), 15 May 1982, (sight record); *Dallas* — 20 September 1980 to 26 May 1930; *Grayson* — 25 September to 28 April, and a late date, 14 May; *Palo Pinto* — 21 August 1977, next 23 September 1978 to 17 April 1976; *Tarrant* — 3 September 1956 to 16 May 1953; *Wichita* — 20 September 1975 to 26 April 1975.

This species is always observed on CBCs throughout the area. One should look for it along streams, in thickets, and in marshes. It tends to be wary, and one gets only a fleeting glimpse of it diving or flying into some rank vegetation. Its characteristic "tail-pumping" action gives it away. It does not seem to be any more abundant during migration, a conclusion supported by banding.
Specimens: Specimens have been located for the following counties: Dallas (DMNH, WMP), Denton (DMNH, WMP), Ellis (DMNH), Grayson (WMP), Hood (FWMSH), Kaufman (DMNH), Navarro (USNM), Palo Pinto (WMP), Tarrant (DMNH, UTA), and Wise (DMNH). Examples indicated by Oberholser (1974) for Clay, Collin, Cooke, and Wichita counties could not be located.

All the specimens (recent) in my collection (WMP) from Dallas (four), Denton (one), Grayson (one), and Palo Pinto (one) counties represent *M. m. juddi*. Other specimens taken in 1938 and 1939 from Dallas, Denton, and Tarrant, all in DMNH collection, were labeled *euphonia* by George Lowery, Jr. Oberholser (1974) lists *montana* for Cooke County (specimen not found). A reexamination of the specimens from north central Texas is needed to verify races; however, foxing (fading) of old specimens will present some problems in identification.

LINCOLN'S SPARROW *Melospiza lincolnii* (Audubon)
Status: Common to abundant migrant. Rare to fairly common winter resident.
Occurrence: This little sparrow has been reported in all counties of the study area except Baylor and Jack. It is widespread and is found as a transient in a number of habitats, all, however, having much cover. It is usually found in north central Texas from late September to early May. Extreme overall dates are 15 September (Grayson County) to 31 May 1982 (Palo Pinto County), next-latest 26 May 1977 (Tarrant County). Extreme arrival and departure dates for counties for which sufficient data are available are: *Collin* — 23 September 1980 to 8 May 1981 (banding record), 15 May 1983 (sight record); *Dallas* — 20 September 1980 to 21 May 1960; *Grayson* — 15 September to 18 May; *Tarrant* — 22 September 1972 to 26 May 1977; *Van Zandt* — 26 September 1984 to 9 May 1984, and 13 May 1984 (Hunt County); *Wichita* — 27 September 1973 to 4 May 1975.

The Lincoln's Sparrow has been observed on nearly all of the CBCs. On some cold winters it frequently moves farther south, and it will not be found at all on CBCs along the Red River, probably owing to adverse weather. It is much more abundant in migration. Hundreds pass through the Dallas–Fort Worth area in both fall and spring. It is easy to see during migration, when it does not seem as secretive. In October banders may band hundreds of birds; 45 were captured and banded in one day at a banding station in Collin County on 22 October 1982.

An unconfirmed report (Oberholser, 1974) of a nesting Lincoln's Sparrow for Dallas County on 3 May 1964 was dismissed as a misidentification since no details were presented and since this species nests far north of Texas.
Specimens: Lincoln's Sparrow specimens have been collected from the following counties: Bosque (SM), Collin (DMNH), Dallas (DMNH, OU, UTA, WMP), Denton (DMNH, WMP), Ellis (DMNH), Fannin (WMP), Hill (SM), Hunt (FWMSH, WMP), Kaufman (DMNH), Parker (FWMSH), Tarrant (DMNH, FWMSH, UTA, WMP), Wichita (WMP), and Wise (DMNH). There also are specimens from nearby Henderson County (DMNH). Specimens indicated by Oberholser (1974) for Clay and Cooke counties were not located.

Both the nominate race, *lincolnii*, and the western race, *alticola*, are represented in specimens in my collection (WMP) from Dallas and Tarrant counties.

SWAMP SPARROW *Melospiza georgiana* (Latham)
Status: Rare to uncommon transient; more found in winter than during migration.
Occurrence: Swamp Sparrows have been reported in 18 counties of the

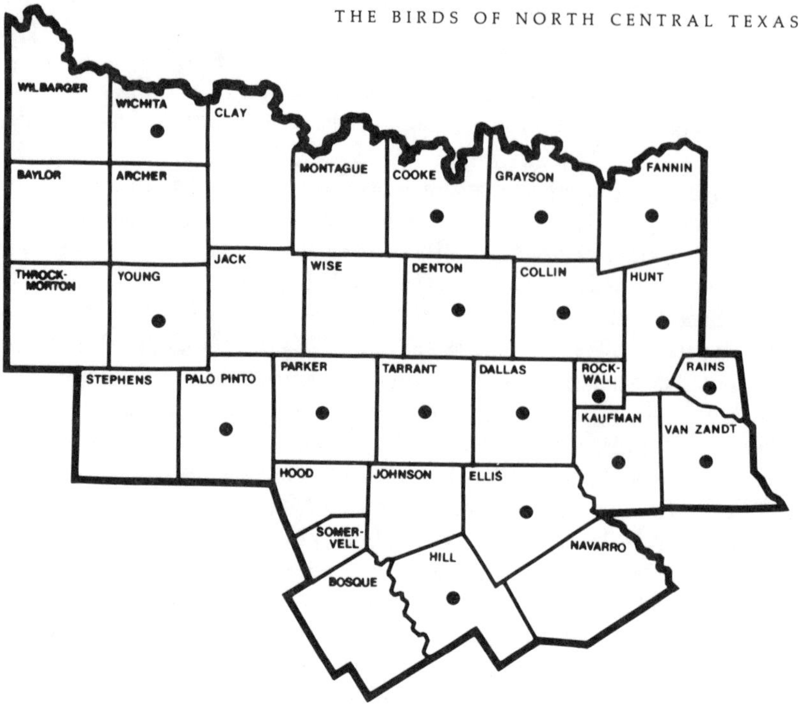

Map 106. Distribution of the Swamp Sparrow, *Melospiza georgiana*

north central Texas study area: Collin, Cooke, Dallas, Denton, Ellis, Fannin, Grayson, Hill, Hunt, Kaufman, Palo Pinto, Parker, Rains, Rockwall, Tarrant, Van Zandt, Wichita, and Young.

Swamp Sparrows are usually found from mid-October through early April. Overall extreme dates range from 20 September 1980 (Dallas County) to 16 May 1883 (Cooke County). Extreme dates for selected counties are: *Collin* — 3 October to 17 April, both 1981 (banded birds); *Dallas* — 20 September 1980 (extremely early), next-earliest 6 October 1976 to 27 April 1929 (Stillwell, 1939); *Grayson* — 2 October to 3 May 1975; *Palo Pinto* — 20 October 1960 to 5 March 1977; *Tarrant* — 10 October 1980 to 10 May 1969; *Van Zandt* — 14 October 1983 to 12 April 1977; *Wichita* — 17 October 1976 to 16 April 1973.

This species is more common along the east side of the study area than in the western portion. It has been observed on all CBCs, although not every year, and it seems to be more prevalent on the Dallas and Denton county counts, possibly because of better coverage. There are few records from counties along the Red River and to the west in winter. Its distribution is limited to swamps and marshes, which are lacking toward the west. *Specimens:* Specimens were located for Cooke County, 16 May 1883 (TNHC 1601); Dallas County, 12 February 1938 (DMNH 260), 9 March

1940 (DMNH 1206), and 16 October 1960 (WMP 1031); Denton County, 7 January 1978 (WMP 2385, 2386); Ellis County, 14 March 1940 (DMNH 1239, 1241, 1243). All the specimens from the last three counties proved to be *M. g. ericrypta*.

WHITE-THROATED SPARROW   *Zonotrichia albicollis* (Gmelin)
Status: Common to abundant winter resident.
Occurrence: White-throated Sparrows have been reported in all counties of the study area except Baylor and Throckmorton. The absence of reports in these two counties is probably due to oversight or lack of observers.

Like a number of other winter sparrows, White-throated Sparrows are commonly found in a wide variety of brushy habitats, particularly forested areas and at many residences where birds are fed. They have been reported on all the CBCs, being more numerous in the southeastern part of the study area than along the western and northwestern parts. On the Dallas and Fort Worth CBCs it is not uncommon to tally several hundred birds in some years.

This species is usually found from mid-October to early May. Extreme dates for the study area are 7 September (Denton County) to 24 May (Grayson and Hill counties). Extreme dates for counties for which sufficient data are available are: *Collin* — 7 October 1982 to 2 May 1982 (banded birds); *Dallas* — 4 October 1978 and 1980 to 12 May 1960; *Grayson* — 14 October to 24 May; *Tarrant* — an isolated date, 16 September 1970, next-earliest 7 October 1948 to 23 May 1978; *Van Zandt* — 6 October 1986 (Hunt County) to 5 May 1983; *Wichita* — 30 September 1973 to 2 May 1982.
Specimens: White-throated Sparrow specimens are available for the following counties: Collin (DMNH), Cooke (TNHC), Dallas (DMNH, UTA, WMP), Denton (DMNH), Ellis (DMNH), Grayson (UTA), Hunt (FWMSH), Kaufman (DMNH), Parker (FWMSH), Somervell (DMNH), Tarrant (DMNH, FWMSH, UTA, WMP), Wise (DMNH), and nearby Henderson (DMNH). Specimens said to have been taken from Navarro County (Oberholser, 1974) were not located.

WHITE-CROWNED SPARROW   *Zonotrichia leucophrys* (Forster)
Status: Common to abundant transient. Fairly common to common winter resident.
Occurrence: White-crowned Sparrows have been recorded in all the counties of the north central Texas study area. They are found in drier habitats wherever brush and thickets exist. They are seldom found in deep woods along river drainages. Although they have been found on all of the CBCs of the study area, they are much more abundant in migration. On the CBCs they outnumber White-throated Sparrows on the Palo Pinto and Wichita counts. Some years, especially during spring migration, it is not uncom-

mon to find hundreds in a day, particularly in the western counties of the study area.

It is usually found from mid-October to early May. Extremes for selected counties are: *Collin* — 30 September 1984, next 15 October 1983 to 7 May 1980 (all banded birds), 9 May 1981 (sight record); *Dallas* — 9 October 1976 to 17 May 1975, mean departure 2 May (16 years); *Denton* — 7 October 1983 to 6 May 1980; *Grayson* — 27 September to 18 May; *Palo Pinto* — 16 October 1976 to 17 April 1976; *Tarrant* — 29 September 1974, mean arrival, 17 October (nine years), to 22 May 1977; *Wichita* — 5 October 1976 to 16 May 1975.

White-crowned Sparrows are among the more abundant winter sparrows that visit my yard every year in Irving, Dallas County. They usually arrive around the first of the year and remain in my yard until May. The return of banded White-crowned Sparrows from my banding station the following year is about 10 percent. Occasionally a bird is retrapped that is five years old, and one was at least eight years old upon recapture, for it was an adult when it was first trapped and banded.

Specimens: White-crowned Sparrows have been collected from the following counties: Bosque (UTA, WMP), Cooke (TNHC), Dallas (DMNH, UTA, WMP), Denton (DMNH), Ellis (DMNH), Hill (UTA), Johnson (DMNH, SUC), Navarro (USNM), Somervell (FWMSH), Tarrant (DMNH, UTA, WMP), Wichita (MWU, WMP), and Wise (DMNH). Specimens indicated for Wilbarger County (Oberholser, 1974) could not be located.

Although not all of the specimens listed above were examined, those examined from Dallas, Tarrant, and Wichita counties were identified as the nominate race, *leucophrys*. Oberholser (1974) lists the western race *Z. l. gambelii* for Cooke (specimens not located), Dallas, Navarro, and Tarrant counties. The only specimen of this race that was located was one from Denton County (DMNH 4895) taken on 10 February 1955. Birders are urged to observe adults carefully. If the bird has black lores, it is *leucophrys*; if it does not, it is *gambelii*.

HARRIS' SPARROW *Zonotrichia querula* (Nuttall)
Status: Fairly common to common winter resident.
Occurrence: Harris' Sparrow has been observed in all counties of the study area except Throckmorton, where no doubt it occurs but has probably been overlooked.

This species always visits north central Texas in winter, although in some years it is more numerous than in others. It has been recorded on all CBCs and is commonly found along forest edges, in shrubbery, and in weedy areas (especially ragweed). It seems to be more common in the western portion of the study area, where counts of more than 1,000 Harris' Sparrows are often tallied. The highest number was 1,038 on 31 December 1965 on the Palo Pinto count.

Harris' Sparrow usually arrives in the latter part of November and stays until early May. Extreme dates for the study area are 20 October (Grayson and Tarrant counties) to 16 May (Wichita County). Extreme dates for selected counties are: *Collin* — 12 November 1983 to 3 May 1978 (all banded birds); *Dallas* — 27 October 1936 (Stillwell, 1939), next-earliest 30 October 1982 to 10 May 1978, mean dates 24 November (18 years) and 26 April (23 years); *Denton* — 7 October 1985, next-earliest 28 October 1979 to 7 May 1984; *Grayson* — 20 October to 6 May; *Tarrant* — 20 October 1956, next-earliest 5 November 1982 to 13 May 1987; *Van Zandt* — 7 November 1984 to 7 May 1983 (Hunt County); *Wichita* — 1 November 1976 to 16 May 1976.

Like the White-crowned Sparrow Harris' Sparrow also winters in my yard in Irving, Dallas County. Banding records show that birds return, and several Harris' Sparrows at least four years old have been recaptured. *Specimens:* Harris' Sparrow specimens were found for the following counties: Baylor (MWU), Bosque (SM, UTA), Cooke (TNHC, UCM, USNM), Dallas (DMNH, UTA, WMP), Denton (DMNH, WMP), Ellis (DMNH), Hill (UTA), Hood (FWMSH), Hunt (FWMSH), Johnson (DMNH), Kaufman (DMNH, WMP), Navarro (USNM), Parker (DMNH, FWMSH), Somervell (FWMSH), Tarrant (DMNH, FWMSH, UTA, WMP), Wichita (MWU), and Wise (DMNH). Specimens indicated for Clay and Montague counties (Oberholser, 1974) were not located.

DARK-EYED JUNCO *Junco hyemalis* (Linnaeus)
Status: Common to abundant transient and winter resident.
Occurrence: Dark-eyed Juncos have been reported as transients wintering in all counties of the study area except Baylor and Throckmorton; however, they would probably be found in those counties too, if more persons birded there.

Juncos arrive in mid-October but do not become abundant until winter, when they are sometimes pushed south by the cold weather. Most of them leave before May, although a straggler or two may be spotted in early May. A Slate-colored Junco was collected in Hood County on 11 June 1984, according to the label attached to the specimen (FWMSH 1461). When I questioned the museum personnel, they clearly recalled collecting the bird. The next-latest date represents a sight record for Cooke County on 18 May 1976. They are widely distributed and are found in an array of habitats, preferring thickets and tangles. Flocks vary in size from a dozen or so to hundreds, but seldom if ever are they found alone. They readily come to feeders placed on the ground. They are relatively unsuspicious yet timid birds, easily frightened when alarmed, but they never fly great distances and return to feed rather quickly if not disturbed again. Although they usually feed on the ground, in spring they may seek budding trees that attract small insects; however, one wonders how successful they are at capturing insects.

Extreme arrival and departure dates for selected counties are: *Collin* — 16 October 1976 to 1 April 1982; *Dallas* — 5 October 1934 to 5 May 1935 (Stillwell, 1939), later dates 11 October 1979 to 22 April 1959, and 27 October 1959 to 12 March 1960 (Oregon complex); *Grayson* — 2 October to 1 May, and 21 October to 9 March (Oregon complex); *Tarrant* — 10 October 1977 to 14 May 1966, next-latest 1 May 1966, and 23 October 1945 to 4 April 1953 (Oregon complex); *Wichita* — 13 October 1978 to 12 April 1975.

Interestingly, some Dark-eyed Juncos from the study area travel 2,000 miles or more to their nesting grounds. A bird banded at Plano, Collin County, on 16 December 1982 was found dead at Manning, in northwestern Alberta, Canada, on 6 May 1983.

Formerly four species of juncos — Slate-colored (*J. hyemalis*), Gray-headed (*J. caniceps*), Oregon (*J. oreganus*), and White-winged (*J. aikeni*) — occurred in Texas (AOU, 1957). Present classification includes all of these as subspecies under Dark-eyed Junco (*J. hyemalis*). The current *Checklist of the Birds of Texas* (TOS, 1984) recognizes eight subspecies occurring in the state, five of which are found in north central Texas.

Not all examples of specimens taken in north central Texas have been examined, but those checked (mainly in my collection) show that the nominate race, *J. h. hyemalis*, is common throughout the area. Numerous examples have been taken, and there are specimens from the following counties: Bosque (SM, WMP), Cooke (TNHC, USNM), Collin (WMP), Dallas (DMNH, UTA, WMP), Denton (DMNH, WMP), Ellis (DMNH), Hood (FWMSH), Hunt (FWMSH), Johnson (DMNH), Kaufman (DMNH), Navarro (USNM), Palo Pinto (FWMSH, WMP), Parker (FWMSH), Tarrant (DMNH, FWMSH, UTA). A specimen reported for Wichita County (Oberholser, 1974) was not located.

Specimens examined from Dallas (WMP 1706, 2178) and Denton (WMP 2703) counties were identified by A. R. Phillips as *henshawi,* a race not recognized by the AOU *Check-list* (AOU, 1957) or the *Checklist of the Birds of Texas* (TOS, 1984). These would be *cismontanus* in the current system of classification.

Examples of *J. h. shufeldti* were also identified from the area — Collin County (WMP 2852) tending toward *henshawi,* and Dallas County (WMP 551, 1387) and (WMP 977) with a tendency toward *cismontanus* or *montanus.* Under the present classification system, *shufeldti* would be called *montanus* by some.

One example of *J. h. mearnsi* (WMP 2591) was taken as a TV-tower casualty on 19 October 1980 in Wichita County.

There are recognizable photographs, as well as carefully documented sight records, of *J. h. caniceps* for the Dallas–Fort Worth area. However, they rarely reach north central Texas, and no specimens have yet been taken from the area. Dates for Dallas County are 22 January to 13 March 1974, while one remained in Tarrant County from 18 December 1979 to 14 March 1980 (photograph). Another *caniceps* was briefly glimpsed in Denton County on 18 October 1984.

A sight record of *J. h. aikeni* was allegedly observed in Fort Worth, Tarrant County, on 19 February 1959, but evidence of its occurrence in north central Texas must await a photograph or specimen. The presence of wing bars is not conclusive, for some *aikeni* lack them, and they occasionally occur in other races. In *aikeni* the amount of white in the tail is more extensive, and the back is blue-gray.

McCOWN'S LONGSPUR *Calcarius mccownii* (Lawrence)
Status: Rare to fairly common winter resident, irregularly.
Occurrence: McCown's Longspurs have been recorded in 16 north central Texas counties: Cooke, Dallas, Denton, Ellis, Fannin, Grayson, Hill, Hunt, Johnson, Montague, Navarro, Palo Pinto, Tarrant, Wichita, Wise, and Young.

This species seems to be very localized and is not found every year. It has been reported on only five of the CBCs, once on the Dallas count, twice on the Fort Worth count (Tarrant County), once on the Hagerman count (Grayson County), three times on the Caddo National Grasslands count (Fannin County) and once on the Palo Pinto count. In many of the counties the records are old ones or are the only sightings. The species is not as common today as it was formerly, probably before the turn of the century. Loss of habitat, on both the wintering and the nesting grounds, has decreased the McCown's Longspur population, and in many years one has to work hard to find this species anywhere in north central Texas.

Extreme overall dates of arrival and departure for north central Texas

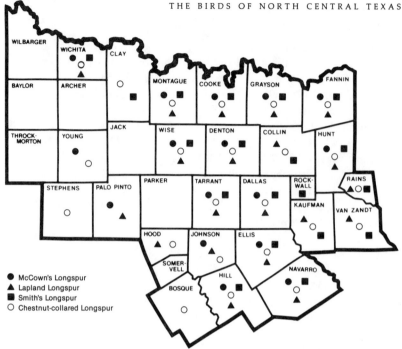

Map 107. Distribution of McCown's Longspur, *Calcarius mccownii;* the Lapland Longspur, *C. lapponicus;* Smith's Longspur, *C. pictus;* and the Chestnut-collared Longspur, *C. ornatus*

counties are 26 October 1956 (Tarrant County) to 9 April 1889 (Wise County). Other county dates are: *Dallas* — sightings decreasing owing to destruction of habitat, 30 December 1961 to 28 February 1960; *Grayson* — seven records, 5 December 1982 to 13 March 1976; *Tarrant* — 26 October 1956 to 30 March 1977; *Wichita* — 24 March 1974, and 24 December 1974.

McCown's Longspurs have been collected in the following counties: Cooke — 5 December 1883 (TNHC 1623); Dallas — 8 January 1940 (DMNH 1102, 1103); Ellis — all January specimens, 12 study skins (DMNH 1111–17, 3256, 4009, 4013, 4017, and 4019) and two mounted birds on display (DMNH 1104 and 1106); Navarro — 8 November 1880 (USNM 81084); Tarrant — 30 December 1953 (WMP 393) and 3 February 1973 (WMP 1974). The specimen indicated for 9 April 1889 for Wise County was not located.

LAPLAND LONGSPUR *Calcarius lapponicus* (Linnaeus)
Status: Fairly common to common winter resident. Likely to be seen more often than any of the other species of longspurs.
Occurrence: Lapland Longspurs have been reported in 20 counties in the study area: Collin, Cooke, Dallas, Denton, Ellis, Fannin, Grayson, Hill,

Hood, Hunt, Johnson, Kaufman, Montague, Navarro, Palo Pinto, Rains, Tarrant, Van Zandt, Wichita, and Wise.

Extreme dates for the overall north central Texas study area range from 25 October 1967 (Van Zandt County) to 27 March 1974 (Grayson and Tarrant counties). Extreme dates for several counties having sufficient data are: *Dallas* – 29 November 1970 to 20 March 1971; *Denton* – 6 November 1976 to 20 February; *Grayson* – 6 November 1976 to 27 March 1977 and 1980; *Tarrant* – 11 November 1983 to 27 March 1974.

Lapland Longspurs often appear in large flocks and are usually observed every year. However, most of the records are for December through early February. At that time the severe winter weather (snowstorms to the north) may drive many longspurs into north central Texas in search of food. They have been reported on all of the CBCs except Palo Pinto and Lake Tawakoni, in Rains and Van Zandt counties, respectively although they are often found wintering in these counties but happen to be missed on count day. There was a phenomenal kill of more than 10,000 Lapland Longspurs in Ellis County and nearby Dallas County on 20 and 21 February 1978 (Gollob and Pulich, 1978).

Specimens: Lapland Longspurs have been collected from the following counties: Cooke (TNHC), Dallas (DMNH, WMP), Denton (DMNH, WMP), Ellis (DMNH, UTA, WMP) Navarro (USNM), and Palo Pinto (FWMSH). Until the large sample was collected in Ellis County on 21 February 1978, all specimens had been identified as the nominate race, *C. l. lapponicus*. All longspurs of this particular kill were classified as the Alaskan race *C. l. alascensis* by Allan R. Phillips.

SMITH'S LONGSPUR   *Calcarius pictus* (Swainson)
Status: Irregular to rare winter resident, not to be expected every year.
Occurrence: Smith's Longspurs have been recorded in 19 counties of the study area: Clay, Collin, Cooke, Dallas, Denton, Ellis, Fannin, Grayson, Hill, Hunt, Kaufman, Montague, Navarro, Rains, Rockwall, Tarrant, Van Zandt, Wichita, and Wise.

This longspur is the rarest of the four species that occur in north central Texas, as well as the most difficult to find because of its habit of confining itself to shortgrass fields. In some of the counties it has been reported only once or twice, and it has become scarcer since the mid-1970s. It should be looked for around rural airports having rather unkempt grass borders. It is seldom observed on bare ground. Its buffy appearance and distinctive clicking and ticking notes set it apart from other longspurs. It is the only longspur that I have seen that alights on fences near fields. Smith's Longspurs are seldom seen with other members of the family.

Smith's Longspurs stay in north central Texas rather briefly, usually from late November through February. Most observations are in late December and early January. Local birders regularly find this species in grassy fields just north of Terrell, Kaufman County, and along the grassy shoreline of Lake Tawakoni, in Rains County, in flocks numbering 100 or more. Extreme arrival and departure dates before the turn of the century ranged from 10 November 1885 (Fannin County) to 27 April 1889 (Wise County). Current extreme dates for selected counties are: *Dallas* — no records since 1978 — habitat nearly gone owing to urbanization — earlier records 29 December 1970 to 31 March 1957, next-latest 20 February 1965 (Denton County, 30 December 1983); *Grayson* — 24 November 1968 to 25 February 1969; *Kaufman* — 20 November 1983 to 27 February 1984; *Rains* — 17 November 1984 to 17 February 1985; *Wichita* — 23 March through 9 April 1974.

Specimens: Specimens have been located from Collin (WMP), Cooke (ACG, CMNH, TNHC), Dallas (DMNH, WMP), and Navarro (USNM) counties.

Chestnut-collared Longspur   *Calcarius ornatus* (Townsend)
Status: Fairly common to rare winter resident locally.
Occurrence: Chestnut-collared Longspurs have been reported in 23 counties in north central Texas: Bosque, Clay, Collin, Cooke, Dallas, Denton, Ellis, Fannin, Grayson, Hill, Hood, Hunt, Johnson, Kaufman, Montague, Navarro, Rains, Stephens, Tarrant, Van Zandt, Wichita, Wise, and Young.

Although Chestnut-collared Longspurs have been reported in more counties than any of the other longspurs, they are not as abundant as Lapland Longspurs and seem to be more localized. In the Fort Worth area they are often seen with McCown's Longspurs. It may be that this species is not as numerous as it was in the early days owing to human activities which have adversely affected both its wintering grounds and its nesting prairies to the north.

Like other members of the longspur family it does not spend much of its time in north central Texas, and some years it is missed. Overall it has been observed from 19 October 1980 (Wichita County) to 28 April 1968 (Dallas County). Extreme dates for selected counties are: *Dallas* — 28 October 1973 to 28 April 1968, next-latest 11 April 1937 (Stillwell, 1939), only one sighting (9 February 1980) since 1976; *Grayson* — 30 October 1976 to 20 March 1976; *Tarrant* — 11 November 1956 to 3 April 1954 (specimen); *Wichita* — only one fall date, 19 October 1980 (specimen), and 13 January 1975 to 2 April 1974.

Surprisingly, Chestnut-collared Longspurs have been seen on more CBCs than any other longspur species, but usually not in large numbers, though the Fort Worth count produced as many as 200 birds. More birds are tallied when the birds start back north in February and early March. The largest

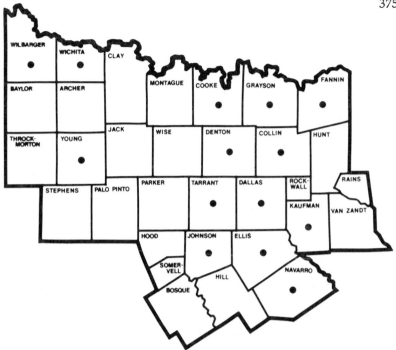

Map 108. Distribution of the Bobolink, *Dolichonyx oryzivorus*

number was about 1,000 on 3 March 1974, at an airfield in Grayson County. *Specimens:* Specimens of Chestnut-collared Longspurs have been found for the following counties: Cooke (TNHC), Dallas (WMP), Denton (WMP), Ellis (DMNH, mount), Tarrant (FWMSH, WMP), and Wichita (WMP). Those specimens indicated by Oberholser (1974) for Clay, Navarro, and Wise counties were not located.

BOBOLINK *Dolichonyx oryzivorus* (Linnaeus)
Status: Rare to casual transient.
Occurrence: The Bobolink is rare in north central Texas and is found mainly in the eastern part of the study area. In a few counties it may be a regular transient, for it is reported nearly every year.

This gregarious species is not as numerous today as it was earlier. Seldom are more than a dozen or so noted, usually in grain fields. Spring Bobolinks are usually seen in early May and frequently stay a few days. Spring observations outnumber fall sightings. Most fall reports are old and total only ten sightings.

Bobolinks have been reported from 14 counties in the north central Texas study area: *Collin* — 20 April 1980, 4 May 1986, and 8 May 1980 (60 birds), sightings from different locations. *Cooke* —18 May 1980. *Dallas*

—four old reports, 14 May 1939 to 8 June 1929 (Stillwell, 1939; it is possible that the latter date is in error, for male Lark Buntings can easily be misidentified as Bobolinks); eight recent spring reports from 5 May 1973 to 18 May 1969, last reported 1974, only one or two birds; and one fall report, 19 August 1968. *Denton*—3, 18, and 19 May 1977. *Ellis* and *Fannin* —spring records (Oberholser, 1974). *Grayson*—12 records, 25 April 1974 to 19 May 1972 and 1983, and 100 counted on 11 May 1986, and one fall sighting on 2 October 1969. *Johnson*—6 October 1984 (Williams, 1985), and 2 and 4 May 1986. *Kaufman*—recent spring records from 1 May 1979 to 13 May 1982. *Navarro*—three May records for the 1930s from Corsicana (Stillwell, 1939). *Tarrant*—seven spring records, 5 May 1956 to 30 May 1947, five fall records from 15 August 1954 to 7 September 1951 (three of which are flocks of more than 200 birds); the latter dates may be misidentified Lark Buntings that occasionally pass through the area in large flocks. *Wichita*—7 May 1973. *Wilbarger* and *Young*—spring and fall, respectively, both records by Oberholser (1974); these probably represent records from the turn of the century, for there are no recent records for these two counties.

Specimens: The only Bobolink specimens known to me are from Dallas County (WMP) and Kaufman County (SFASU). Oberholser (1974) records "300 shot, spring 1884, H. F. Peters" (Fannin County), and three were said to have been taken on 8 May 1898 (W. A. Mayer, Dallas County); however, none could be located. The latter specimens may no longer exist, for many of Mayer's specimens have been lost.

RED-WINGED BLACKBIRD *Agelaius phoeniceus* (Linnaeus)
Status: Fairly common to common summer resident. Abundant winter resident.
Occurrence: This familiar blackbird has been recorded the year round in all of the north central Texas counties of the study area as well as the adjacent counties. It is fairly common to common around freshwater habitats in the breeding season and is also widespread over croplands and pasturelands in the winter.

At the end of the breeding season redwings segregate into flocks, males usually apart from the females. The winter period finds an increase in numbers, and estimates of a half million Red-winged Blackbirds by various observers is not uncommon. They are reported every year on all of the CBCs, with large roosts in various parts of the study area. Some of the largest roosts are found in Dallas, Denton, Palo Pinto, Tarrant, and Wichita counties. In Wichita County 2 million redwings were reported in 1979, 1981, and 1982, which may be in error since there were no details of the manner in which the estimates were made, but the large numbers cannot be completely dismissed. Roosts are found in cedar thickets, deciduous trees, and cattail marshes. The winter roosts shift from year to year and on occasion have been "nuisance" problems, causing the birds to be poisoned and killed.

Very little about the migration movements of Red-winged Blackbirds in north central Texas is known to me. A redwing banded on 18 February 1967 in Fort Worth, Tarrant County, was recovered more than a year later, on 18 May 1968, in Dallas County, while color-marked (leg streamers) blackbirds of fall from South Dakota were recovered the following March in Dallas County. On 21 January 1967 I trapped a blackbird in Irving that had been banded on Sand Lake NWR, South Dakota, between 10 and 16 September 1966. Only further banding studies will show precisely the exact movements of this species in and out of north central Texas.

Nesting: During the nesting season redwings gather in rather loose colonies to breed in wetland areas, marshes, willow thickets, and flooded fields, each male having several females on his territory. Nesting starts in late April and continues through early July; nests have been found in almost every county. Nesting dates for Dallas and Tarrant counties are typical and applicable to other counties in north central Texas: Dallas — 24 April 1970 (nest ready for eggs), 4 May (one egg) to 28 July 1971 (young still in the nest); Tarrant — 12 May to 9 August, with peak of nesting in late May. Many local redwings are two-brooded.

Although it is indicated that this species is seldom, if ever, parasitized by the Brown-headed Cowbird, it has been noted that in the Dallas area some colonies are free of this social parasite, while others may serve an occasional cowbird and actually produce foster young.

Specimens: Red-winged Blackbirds have been collected for the following counties: Bosque (SM), Clay (MWU), Collin (UTA), Cooke (TNHC), Dallas (DMNH, UTA, WMP), Denton (DMNH, WMP), Ellis (TCWC, UTA), Grayson (UTA), Hunt (DMNH, FWMSH), Kaufman (DMNH, USNM, WMP), Tarrant (DMNH, FWMSH, UTA, WMP), Wichita (DMNH, MWU), and Wise (DMNH). Specimens indicated for Navarro County (Oberholser, 1974) were not located.

There was no racial examination of all of the specimens. In Tarrant County representative samples show the breeding Red-winged Blackbird to be the nominate race *phoeniceus* in size, and the female to be closest to this race in color, except for the ventral streaking, with a tendency toward reduced spotting on the throat. Kenneth C. Parkes interprets this as approaching the Rio Grande redwing race *megapotamus*. Most races taken in Tarrant County during the winter and migration periods are *fortis* and *phoeniceus.* H. C. Oberholser identified a bird collected in Tarrant County on 15 June 1950 (DMNH 4742) as *littoralis* and another taken on 18 January 1964 as *arctolegus*. He indicated that the latter race was to be found in Dallas County. Occurrence of *arctolegus* is not unlikely, but that of *littoralis* requires substantiation.

EASTERN MEADOWLARK   *Sturnella magna* (Linnaeus)
Status: Fairly common to common summer resident. Abundant winter resident.
Occurrence: Eastern Meadowlarks have been reported in all of the counties of north central Texas and in many counties the year round. Numbers tend to be largest in winter, probably representing winter transients augmenting the local populations. However, like many other common birds, we know less about the populations of Eastern and Western Meadowlarks, than about many of the rarer species. Much could be learned through a systematic study of the two species.

Since few persons can tell the difference between Eastern and Western Meadowlarks by plumage, or only under favorable conditions (e.g., song), many reports of meadowlarks are merely given as meadowlark species, and rightly so.
Nesting: Breeding records given by Oberholser (1974) are for 14 counties — Clay, Collin, Cooke, Ellis, Fannin, Grayson, Hunt, Kaufman, Navarro, Tarrant, Wichita, Wilbarger, Wise, and Young. Several of the local checklists imply nesting, but the source of the data has not been determined. A case in point is Dallas County, for which I could find no nesting records before this study, yet my studies show nesting from 26 April 1959 (young just out of the nest) to 12 July 1969 (eggs). Data indicate that Eastern Meadowlarks are two-brooded in the area.

As far as can be determined, only Eastern Meadowlarks nest over all of the north central Texas area. However, More and Strecker (1929) gave only the Western Meadowlark as the nesting species, while Oberholser (1974) indicated that Eastern Meadowlarks bred in Wilbarger County. In my brief visits to that area both species were noted during spring and early summer months as far east as Clay County. It is very likely that the six or seven counties in the northwestern part of the study area may serve both species as nesting areas. This is just one study that should be undertaken in future investigations of *Sturnella*.
Specimens: Eastern Meadowlark specimens have been located for the following counties: Archer (MWU), Baylor (MWU), Bosque (UTA), Collin (DMNH, WMP), Cooke (DMNH, TNHC, USNM), Dallas (CMNH, DMNH, UTA, WMP), Denton (DMNH, SM, WMP), Ellis (DMNH, WMP), Grayson (KH, UTA), Hill (SM), Hood (FWMSH), Hunt (FWMSH), Kaufman (WMP), Navarro (USNM), Rains (AMNH), Rockwall (WMP), Tarrant (DMNH, FWMSH, UTA, WMP), Van Zandt (WMP), and Wichita (MWU).

While few of the above specimens have been examined racially, the specimens from Tarrant County represent the nominate race, *S. m. magna*, and Oberholser (1974) indicates that *argutula* occurs in Cooke County. A specimen in my collection (WMP 2941) taken from Van Zandt County has been identified as *S. m. hoopesi* × *magna* or *argutula*. Most authorities agree that the ranges of Eastern Meadowlark races are poorly understood. Readers are urged to read Sutton's (1967) discussion of the complex problem of Eastern Meadowlark races occurring in Oklahoma.

WESTERN MEADOWLARK   *Sturnella neglecta* Audubon
Status: Fairly common to common winter resident. A few are found in seven counties along the west side of the study area in late spring and summer.
Occurrence: Western Meadowlarks have been reported in all counties in the study area except Jack, Montague, and Throckmorton, and they would be found in these counties as well as in adjacent counties if more birding took place there. They have also been observed in nearby Shackelford County (previously not recorded). They usually occur in most counties in winter, from October to late April.

Extreme dates for several counties for which data are available are: *Dallas* — 14 October 1973 to 26 May 1970; *Grayson* — 7 October to 24 April (singing birds) and one date, 26 July 1979; *Tarrant* — 25 September 1954 to 13 May 1972.
Nesting: Oberholser (1974) indicated that this western species nested in Tarrant County, but this statement is misleading. If he based his data on a breeding-bird study of Tarrant County by Sutton (1938), the latter author states only that possible environmental changes have taken place that may have brought a change in the status of Eastern and Western Meadowlarks. There is no proof that Western Meadowlarks ever nested in Tarrant County or, for that matter, anywhere else in north central Texas. Stillwell (1939) found this species only in the winter in Dallas County. Present data show that the species is found in Archer, Baylor, Clay, Wichita, Wilbarger, Wise, and Young counties, and nearby Shackelford County, in late spring and summer; however, no nests have been found. The Western Meadowlark is not as abundant here as the Eastern Meadowlark. A careful study is urged to delineate the actual nesting ranges of the two species of meadowlarks in north central Texas.
Specimens: Western Meadowlark specimens were located from the following counties: Archer (MWU), Clay (MWU), Cooke (TCWC, TNHC, USNM), Dallas (DMNH, WMP), Denton (DMNH, WMP), Ellis (DMNH), Hill (SM), Hood (FWMSH), Somervell (SM), Tarrant (DMNH, FWMSH, UTA), and Wichita (MWU). Specimens indicated by Oberholser (1974) for Wilbarger County were not located.

YELLOW-HEADED BLACKBIRD   *Xanthocephalus xanthocephalus* (Bonaparte)
Status: Fairly common to common transient in spring. Fairly common to uncommon in fall. A few birds may winter.

Occurrence: This beautiful blackbird has been recorded in all of the counties of north central Texas except Montague. It may be more common along the western side of the study area than on the eastern side. It passes through the area in both spring and fall, with more sightings in the spring. It can usually be found in spring from mid-April to mid-May, and in fall from mid-July through early October. In Dallas County it has been found every month except June.

Spring dates for selected counties are: *Dallas* — 5 March 1978 and 1980 to 23 May 1967; *Denton* — 8 April 1976 to 7 May 1984; *Grayson* — 30 March to 23 May; *Palo Pinto* — 14 April 1971 to 16 May 1976; *Tarrant* — 7 April 1964 to 20 May 1955; *Wichita* — 4 April 1977 to 30 May 1975. Fall dates for some counties are: *Dallas* — 24 July 1975 to 14 October 1978; *Denton* — 15 September 1953 to 28 September 1984; *Grayson* — 4 July 1977 to 15 November; *Palo Pinto* — 8 July 1978 to 22 September 1978; *Tarrant* — 15 July 1956 to 1 November 1953, next-latest 14 October 1978; *Wichita area* — 7 July (Wichita County), 20 July 1974 (Clay County) to 13 October 1974 (Archer County) and 28 October 1983 (Throckmorton County).

If one carefully searches the winter hordes of blackbirds, immature Yellow-headed Blackbirds can occasionally be spotted. This is particularly true in the Dallas–Fort Worth area, where much birding takes place. Lone birds may come regularly to feeders. They have been recorded in Dallas County on 30 December 1961, 16 December 1976, 2 February 1977, 4 January 1979, and 20 through 25 December 1979, and in Tarrant County on 31 December 1975, 2 January 1981, and 1 December 1984.

At times flocks of up to 100 birds are seen, a sight to behold, especially the attractively colored males. More often, however, flocks of 20 to 50, or even fewer, are the rule. One of the largest flocks recently reported was about 1,000 at Hagerman NWR, Grayson County, on 8 May 1983, a year that seems to have been exceptionally good for sightings of this species over north central Texas. On 21 April 1984, 1,000 were observed in Dallas County.

Nesting: There is no evidence that the species has nested in north central Texas. In recent years the nearest nesting (eggs or young) known to me has been in the Panhandle — the Dimmitt area, Castro County — in the spring of 1978.

Specimens: Specimens have been collected from Clay (MWU), Cooke (TNHC), Dallas (DMNH, WMP), Denton (DMNH), Kaufman (SFASU), Parker (FWMSH), Tarrant (FWMSH, UTA), and Wichita (DMNH) counties. An example from Wilbarger County (Oberholser, 1974) could not be located.

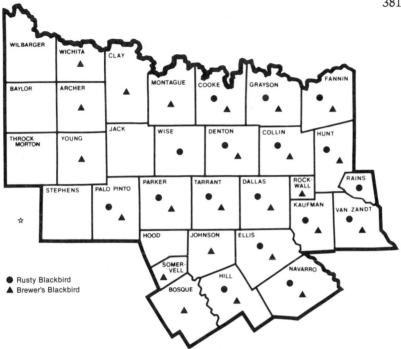

Map 109. Distribution of the Rusty Blackbird, *Euphagus carolinus,* and Brewer's Blackbird, *E. cyanocephalus*

RUSTY BLACKBIRD   *Euphagus carolinus* (Müller)
Status: Rare to uncommon winter visitor.
Occurrence: Rusty Blackbirds have been recorded in 17 north central Texas counties: Collin, Cooke, Dallas, Denton, Ellis, Fannin, Grayson, Hill, Hunt, Kaufman, Navarro, Palo Pinto, Parker, Rains, Tarrant, Van Zandt, and Wise. There are no records for the western part of the study area. They have ranged only as far west as Cooke, Wise, and Palo Pinto counties.

This species favors wet wooded areas and usually is not found in the same habitat as the more common Brewer's Blackbird which is often misidentified as the Rusty Blackbird. Observers are urged to exercise caution in identifying this rare species.

Rusty Blackbirds are usually observed from November to March. Extreme dates for several counties for which sufficient dates are available are: *Dallas* — 23 October 1971 to 22 April 1935 and an isolated late date, 19 May 1966. An extremely early date, 15 September 1935, as well as a 14 July 1935 date (Stillwell, 1939), should be dismissed since all the valid dates occur into mid-October. *Grayson* — 17 October to 21 April 1979. *Tarrant* — 1 November 1951 to 23 April 1951 and an isolated date, 1 May 1965.

This species has been reported on all of the CBCs except the Palo Pinto and Wichita counts. The reports for the various counts are scattered, and numbers are seldom large and are missed on some counts year after year. However, during the winters of 1954, 1955, and 1956, I estimated that about 5,000 Rusty Blackbirds were part of a large blackbird roost in the upper Lake Worth area, in Tarrant County (Pulich, 1961).

Specimens: Rusty Blackbird specimens have been located for the following counties: Cooke (TNHC, USNM), Dallas (DMNH), Ellis (DMNH, mounted), Hunt (FWMSH), Navarro (WMP), and Tarrant (FWMSH).

BREWER'S BLACKBIRD   *Euphagus cyanocephalus* (Wagler)
Status: Fairly common to uncommon winter visitor.
Occurrence: Brewer's Blackbirds have been reported in 24 counties of the study area—Archer, Bosque, Clay, Collin, Cooke, Dallas, Denton, Ellis, Fannin, Grayson, Hill, Hunt, Johnson, Kaufman, Montague, Navarro, Palo Pinto, Parker, Rockwall, Somervell, Tarrant, Van Zandt, Wichita, and Young—and nearby Shackelford County. Their numbers are greater along the eastern side of the study area than on the western side.

Although occasionally this species may be found with Rusty Blackbirds, Brewer's Blackbirds are much more widespread and are much easier to find in open fields, cattle pastures, and feedlots. In fall Brewer's Blackbirds are often confused with Common Grackles, and for this reason all August and most September records were eliminated as misidentifications.

Brewer's Blackbirds can usually be found from mid-November to December and March. Extreme dates for counties for which sufficient data are available are: *Dallas*—8 November 1969 to 28 April 1973; *Grayson*—29 October to 12 April, and a single bird (possibly injured) on 1 June 1978 with a flock of Common Grackles; *Tarrant*—4 October 1951, next-earliest 21 October 1957 to 13 May 1972; *Wichita*—11 November 1975 to 18 April 1973; a 24 September 1978 date is possible but was not accepted.

Many Brewer's Blackbirds were killed by a tornado that swept across a farm near Terrell, Kaufman County, on 6 April 1979.

This species has been reported on all of the CBCs in the study area, occasionally in large flocks, more than 5,700 (1966) in Grayson County and about 2,300 (1966) and more than 2,000 (1977) in Fort Worth, Tarrant County, but they are usually found in smaller numbers and sometimes not at all.

Nesting: More and Strecker (1929) reported nesting (13 May 1928, eggs) near a lake at Harrold, Wilbarger County. There are no other nesting records for north central Texas.

Specimens: Brewer's Blackbird specimens were located from Cooke (CMNH, TNHC), Dallas (UTA, WMP), Denton (DMNH), and Wichita (KU) counties. Specimens indicated by Oberholser (1974) for Clay County were not found.

GREAT-TAILED GRACKLE *Quiscalus mexicanus* (Gmelin)

Status: Common to fairly common permanent resident over much of the area. More numerous on the eastern side of the study area than on the western side.

Occurrence: Great-tailed Grackles have been reported in all counties of the study area except Jack and Montague. There is little doubt that they would be found in those counties too, if they were searched for in the proper habitat.

As many readers know, Great-tailed Grackles invaded inland Texas from the south in the 1940s. Various sources indicate that the species arrived in north central Texas after World War II. County dates of arrival known to me are: *Dallas* — first bird recorded in 1947, nesting reported in 1952, and commonly reported by 1956. *Denton* — 13 June 1946, three juvenile specimens (DMNH). *Grayson* — grackles collected near Willis, Oklahoma, above Lake Texoma, just north of this county on 14 July 1957. Thus it would be reasonable to assume that they were already present in this county in the 1950s. They were well established at Sherman by the spring of 1963. *Hunt* — grackle feeding young on 4 July 1949 in the vicinity of Commerce. *Tarrant* — first seen on 26 April 1944 (first date for north central Texas), nesting by 1952. *Van Zandt* — nesting in 1956.

These grackles are widespread near cities and many towns, and they can be found the year round, especially in pastures, feedlots, and garbage dumps, and they often come to bird feeders. In recent years they do not seem to be as abundant as Common Grackles. It may be that the novelty of reporting them no longer exists and that careful recording of their numbers is seldom taken seriously. There are also indications that Common Grackle populations may be increasing, especially in outlying areas, at the expense of the Great-tailed Grackles. Unfortunately, the average bird-watcher may find it difficult to estimate actual numbers of "blackbirds" that invade north central Texas, particularly in winter, and many of the population figures are questionable.

CBC figures for the Great-tailed Grackle averaged 10,650 (Dallas County, 17 years), 244 (Denton County, 17 years), 11 (Grayson County, 12 years), 8,977 (Tarrant County, 18 years), and 2,716 (Wichita County, nine years).

The movement of various populations is poorly understood. A grackle of this species that was at least a year old when it was banded at Poteau, Le Flore County, Oklahoma, on 9 May 1976 was recovered at Denison, Grayson County, on 22 May 1980. Another grackle, however, recovered in Garland, Dallas County, on 13 March 1981 was originally banded in east Texas at College Station, Brazos County, on 3 December 1974. Another Great-tailed Grackle banded on 23 May 1970 was retrapped at the same banding station five years later in the spring of 1975, indicating no movement.

Nesting: No concentrated effort was made to determine whether or not the Great-tailed Grackle nests in all of the counties of north central Texas, but it has been reported nesting (nests or young) in all the areas where much bird-watching takes place (especially cities and large towns). It is always found in colonies and often nests in heronries. It commonly nests in the Dallas–Fort Worth heronries from early April to early July. Actual dates for nesting birds in Irving, Dallas County, in 1968 were from 19 April (two eggs and small young) to 25 July (young out of nest banded, still being cared for by parents). It is not found in heavily wooded forests or in the drier habitats of the west. Thus, as mentioned above, it is found in cities and towns and farming areas where sufficient food to feed its young is available.

Specimens: Great-tailed Grackles have been collected in Dallas (DMNH, TCWC, WMP), Denton (DMNH, WMP), and Tarrant (DMNH, FWMSH, UTA, WMP) counties. The specimens found in north central Texas represent *Q. m. prosopidicola.*

COMMON GRACKLE   *Quiscalus quiscula* (Linnaeus)

Status: Uncommon to common summer resident throughout the study area. Common to abundant transient and winter resident.

Occurrence: Common Grackles have been recorded the year round throughout north central Texas.

CBC figures for Common Grackles average 5,835 (Dallas County, 17 years), 414 (Denton County, 15 years), 2,272 (Grayson County, 14 years), 1,817 (Tarrant County, 18 years), and 1,307 (Wichita County, ten years). This destructive grackle is widespread in both rural and urban areas, and since the late 1970s it has become more numerous than the Great-tailed Grackle. It is well adapted to human environments.

The movement of the Common Grackle in and out of the area is poorly understood. On 7 August 1965 this species was collected in Tarrant County; it had been banded three years before in Nacogdoches, in east Texas. Two others banded on 30 and 31 March 1977 at the same location in Dallas County also showed interesting recoveries. The first was encountered on 26 May 1979 in almost the same location, while the second was recovered less than two months later on 9 May 1977 at New Effington, South Dakota. Extensive banding in the area would very likely give us a better understanding of the movement of this grackle in north central Texas.

Both this species and the Great-tailed Grackle are omnivorous, feeding on almost anything available. A Common Grackle was reported feeding on a snake (probably dead beforehand). Both species of grackles have been known to feed on eggs and young birds in the nest, and I have observed both species dunking dry dog food in my birdbath in Irving, Dallas County.

Nesting: Like its relative, the Great-tailed Grackle, it nests in colonies and is often a nuisance, destroying the eggs and young of other birds. Nesting starts in mid-April and continues through June. Although Common and Great-tailed Grackles may sometimes roost together in winter, they nest separately.

Specimens: Common Grackle specimens were located for the following counties: Cooke (TNHC, USNM), Dallas (DMNH, FWMSH, UTA, WMP), Denton (DMNH), Grayson (OU, UTA, WMP), Tarrant (FWMSH, UTA, WMP), and Henderson (DMNH). Those mentioned by Oberholser (1974) for Navarro and Wilbarger counties were not located. Specimens represent the race *versicolor.*

BROWN-HEADED COWBIRD   *Molothrus ater* (Boddaert)

Status: Common transient and summer resident. Abundant winter resident locally.

Occurrence: The Brown-headed Cowbird has been reported in all the counties in north central Texas in a variety of habitats, including backyard feeders, feedlots, and pastures. It is more common in agricultural areas than in woodlands, but it will be found even there during the breeding season.

Brown-headed Cowbirds are more numerous in winter. The numbers of this species may vary, but few if any scientific studies have been made locally to determine their exact numbers. They are found on all of the CBCs, but the numbers do not reflect their actual population. Often a particular roost may influence the count number. Winter roosts may consist of more than 1 million icterids, of which this species is one, but not the main, species. For example, in the mid-1950s I estimated 17 percent of a roost (of a total of more than 1 million blackbirds) to be Brown-headed Cowbirds, while the CBC figures were actually far lower. In spring many cowbirds migrate north, and others scatter to nest and are inconspicuous because of their breeding habits. It is not until late summer or early fall, when small groups begin to assemble into large flocks for the winter, that they again become noticeably common.

In the cities of Dallas and Denton counties, where "blackbirds" place their roosts near human habitations, the roosts may create considerable nuisance, and many birds may be killed by various means. There is no easy solution to these problems, and unless all vegetation is removed from such areas the problems will continue.

Partly albino Brown-headed Cowbirds are not uncommon. They may be more evident since they stand out among large flocks of blackbirds.

The movement of Brown-headed Cowbirds in and out of north central Texas is poorly known. What little information there is from the Dallas–Fort Worth area shows out-of-state recoveries from Arkansas, Illinois, Mis-

souri, and Oklahoma. Among those banded it is not uncommon to find cowbirds at least three years old.

Nesting: The Brown-headed Cowbirds' breeding habit of social parasitism — depositing their eggs in the nests of other birds and shifting the nesting responsibilities to foster parents — has caused them to be despised by many persons. Friedmann, Kiff, and Rothstein (1977) list more than 215 species of birds parasitized by Brown-headed Cowbirds. Favorite hosts in cities and small towns are Northern Cardinals and Lark Sparrows. In Tarrant County an unusual host was the Scissor-tailed Flycatcher, which is seldom parasitized. A female Painted Bunting was observed feeding a fledgling cowbird at Hagerman NWR on 6 August 1976. Two hosts whose nesting populations in north central Texas have declined considerably owing to cowbird parasitism are Bell's Vireo and the Orchard Oriole, and other species may decline in the future. The Black-capped Vireo populations are also said to be affected by cowbird parasitism.

Specimens: Brown-headed Cowbird specimens are known from the following counties: Bosque (USNM), Cooke (TNHC), Dallas (DMNH, TCWC, UTA, WMP), Denton (DMNH, WMP), Hood (FWMSH), Hunt (DMNH, WMP), Johnson (SUC), Parker (FWMSH), Somervell (TCWC), Tarrant (FWMSH, UTA, WMP), Wichita (DMNH, MWU), and Wise (DMNH). Specimens reported for Wilbarger County (Oberholser, 1974) were not located.

Although not all of the above specimens were examined for race, the nominate form, *M. a. ater,* occurred in Dallas and Tarrant counties, and *M. a. artemisiae* was found among examples for Dallas, according to Oberholser (1974). He identified specimens taken on 11 December 1935 (DMNH 101), 6 September 1936 (DMNH 120), and 28 November 1938 (DMNH 446) as the western race *M. a. artemisiae.* However, *M. a. ater* is the more common of the two races.

ORCHARD ORIOLE   *Icterus spurius* (Linnaeus)
Status: Formerly fairly common summer resident, becoming increasingly scarce in recent years. Still fairly common transient.
Occurrence: Orchard Orioles have been recorded in all but three counties of north central Texas—Jack, Stephens, and Young—though all the surrounding counties provide records.

This species is usually found in north central Texas from mid-April to early September. Extreme dates for selected counties are: *Dallas*—17 April 1938 (Stillwell, 1939), more recent, 20 April 1981 to 1 October 1984, next-latest 28 September 1977; *Grayson*—4 April to 24 September; *Tarrant*—31 March 1946 (mean 19 April) to 29 September 1959; *Wichita*—16 April 1975 to 13 October 1974, the latter an isolated date in nearby Archer County.

There is one unexplainable winter sighting, a female bathing in a birdbath in Fort Worth, Tarrant County, on 26 December 1975. This species does not usually occur in winter in north central Texas.
Nesting: This species was formerly considered fairly common and even a common nesting bird of the area, but since the mid-1970s few nests have been reported. Oberholser (1974) gave a number of nesting records, as well as many summer sightings, for north central Texas. The last nesting records known to me are from Dallas County—27 June to 17 July 1975 (successfully reared two young of its own and a Brown-headed Cowbird), and 8 June 1985, a female gathering nesting material and carrying food to the nest on 4 July; Tarrant County—23 June 1975 and 19 June 1985. In addition to these nesting records, I have late May, June, and early July records for this species in Bosque, Clay, Denton, Ellis, Grayson, Hill, Hood, Montague, Palo Pinto, Somervell, Throckmorton, and Van Zandt counties.

No doubt Brown-headed Cowbirds are partly responsible for the decline of the species nesting in the study area. In one instance seven cowbird eggs were found in the small nest of an Orchard Oriole along with three oriole eggs. The net result of this large deposit of eggs was the rearing of one cowbird.
Specimens: Specimens of Orchard Oriole were located for the following counties: Collin (DMNH), Cooke (TNHC), Dallas (DMNH, WMP), Denton (DMNH), Ellis (DMNH), Kaufman (DMNH), Somervell (TCWC), Tarrant (DMNH, FWMSH, UTA), Van Zandt (WMP), and Wichita (DMNH). Oberholser (1974) listed specimens for Clay and Wilbarger counties, but they were not found.

NORTHERN ORIOLE   *Icterus galbula* (Linnaeus)
Status: Fairly common to common transient. Uncommon to fairly common summer resident. Occasionally overwinters.
Occurrence: Northern Orioles have been reported in all of the north cen-

tral Texas counties except Montague, where it probably also occurs, since there are many records for the species in the surrounding counties.

Both Baltimore Orioles and Bullock's Orioles occur in north central Texas. Formerly they were considered two species, but today they are considered subspecies of the Northern Oriole. Examples of hybrids nesting are known from Dallas, Parker, and Tarrant counties, from which there are limited numbers of specimens (WMP). Oberholser (1974) reported Baltimore nesting as far west as Wilbarger County; however, he also showed Bullock's Oriole nesting in that county. The Baltimore has been found in Wichita County along with Bullock's. Bullock's Oriole ranges as far east as Grayson and Dallas counties, where it has been found nesting with the Baltimore Oriole. The presence of mesquite favors the distribution of Bullock's Oriole, while the Baltimore Oriole is commonly associated with cottonwoods. More thorough study and collecting may show many orioles to be intermediate in one or more characteristics.

Northern Orioles (the race dependent upon the locale) are more often reported during migration than during the nesting season, but in several counties they have been seen every month of the year except November.

Arrival and departure dates for selected counties are: *Dallas* — Baltimore, two isolated dates, 20 March 1965 and 27 March 1974, and 17 April 1982 to 31 May 1960, and 27 August 1957 to 6 October 1966; Bullock's, 21 April 1970 to 5 September 1960 and an isolated date, 28 October 1979. Baltimores tend to nest in cottonwoods on the eastern side of the county, while Bullock's Orioles nest in mesquite in the northwestern part. Some hybridization occurs. *Grayson* — 14 April (Northern) to 6 October (Baltimore) and two isolated dates, 26 October and 13 November. *Tarrant* — Baltimore, 21 April 1957 to 29 May 1977, and 14 August 1956 to 4 October 1975; Bullock's, 13 April 1970 to 20 September 1975. Both races nest in this county, and some hybridize. *Van Zandt* — 27 April 1984 to 5 October 1986. *Wichita* — Northern, 9 April 1977 to 27 September 1978. Bullock's Oriole occurs commonly, but both races have been recorded in migration and nesting. Since I had no specific arrival and departure dates for the southwestern part of the study area, dates for Shackelford County are applicable: Bullock's, 13 April 1974 to 17 September 1966.

During the winter they have been reported from four counties: Dallas — seven times, 4 January 1971 (Northern), 14 January 1972 (Northern female), 17 January to 22 February 1978 (Northern), 4 December 1983 to 18 February 1984 (adult male, photograph), and again 21 January to 6 February 1985 at the same location as in the winter of 1983-84, and again in 1986-87; Grayson — 21 and 22 December 1974; Palo Pinto — 5 February 1979; Tarrant — five times, 16 January 1965 (Baltimore), 11 February and again 19 March 1969 (Bullock's), 9 December 1969 (Northern female or immature), 14 January 1980 (Northern female), and 14 December 1986 (Baltimore).

Specimens: Specimens of both races of Northern Oriole have been collected from north central Texas. The Baltimore race, *I. g. galbula*, has been collected from the following counties: Clay (TTU, not examined), Cooke (TNHC), Dallas (DMNH, UTA, WMP), Denton (DMNH, FWMSH, WMP), Ellis (DMNH), Kaufman (SFASU), Somervell (FWMSH), and Tarrant (FWMSH, UTA, WMP). Specimens listed by Oberholser (1974) for Navarro and Wise counties were not located. The Bullock's Oriole, *I. g. bullockii*, has been collected from the following counties: Baylor (MWU), Dallas (WMP), Parker (WMP), Tarrant (WMP), Wichita (DMNH, both mounted and study skins), Wilbarger (DMNH, WMP), and Young (UTA).

Family Fringillidae (Finches)

PINE GROSBEAK   *Pinicola enucleator* (Linnaeus)
Status: Casual visitor.
Occurrence: There is only one record of this fringillid for north central Texas. A beautiful male Pine Grosbeak, identified as *P. e. montana*, was found dead in downtown Dallas, Dallas County, on 24 November 1969. This is the only specimen (WMP 1753) known to me for the state. A bird was reportedly found in the Panhandle (Pampa, Gray County) and died two weeks later, but the whereabouts of this specimen are unknown. My efforts to find it were futile. It may not have been saved, for its preservation is questioned in *The Bird Life of Texas* (Oberholser, 1974).

PURPLE FINCH   *Carpodacus purpureus* (Gmelin)
Status: Uncommon to fairly common winter resident.
Occurrence: Purple Finches have been reported in 26 counties of the study area: Archer, Bosque, Clay, Collin, Cooke, Dallas, Denton, Ellis, Fannin, Grayson, Hill, Hood, Hunt, Johnson, Kaufman, Navarro, Palo Pinto, Parker, Rockwall, Somervell, Tarrant, Van Zandt, Wichita, Wilbarger, Wise, and Young.

This species is widespread and is recorded from mid-November to April or early May, though most of the reports are from late December to the end of February. It has been reported on all of the CBCs in north central Texas except the Lake Tawakoni count. It is sporadic in its visits, fairly common some years and seen only once or twice other years, and occasionally it is even missed. It is easily attracted to backyard feeders provided with sunflower seeds, and it may put away great quantities of seed, so much that a woman purchased an outdoor vacuum cleaner to pick up

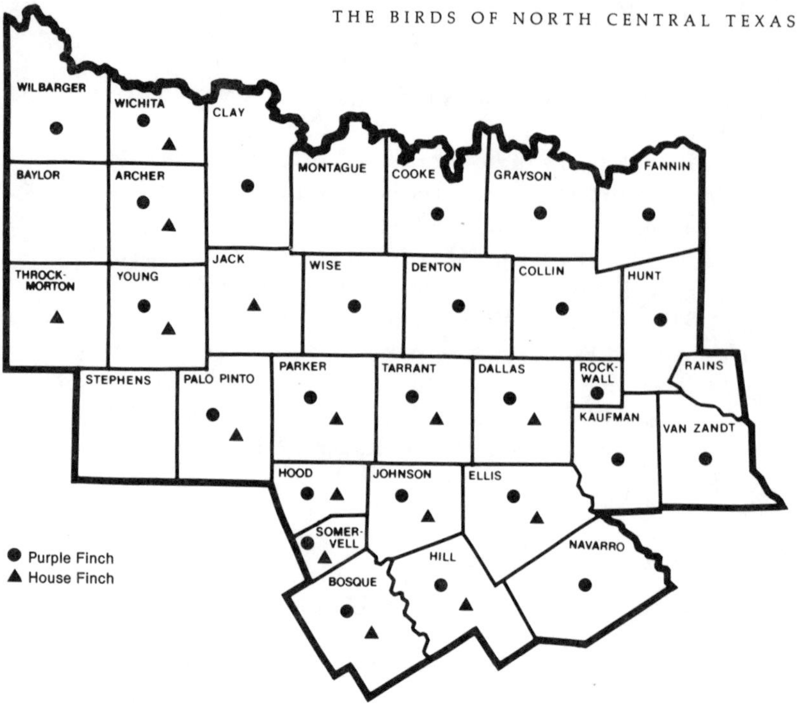

Map 110. Distribution of the Purple Finch, *Carpodacus purpureus,* and the House Finch *C. mexicanus*

the hulls shelled by Purple Finches. It is also found wherever weed patches provide seeds, and in spring it may frequent elms for the succulent buds before the trees leaf out.

Some extreme dates that would also apply to nearby counties not mentioned are: *Collin* — 27 November 1980 to 4 April 1980; *Dallas* — 5 November 1976 to 8 May 1976; *Grayson* — 27 October to 28 April; *Palo Pinto* — 23 November 1968 to 7 May 1966; *Tarrant* — 4 November 1976 to 11 April 1972; *Van Zandt* — 13 November 1983 to 15 April 1984; *Wichita* — 2 November 1976 to 23 April 1974. There is a very questionable record for 1 June 1975 for Wichita Falls; it may have been a House Finch, which is fairly common in that area.

Specimens: Specimens have been located for the following counties: Cooke (TNHC), Dallas (DMNH, WMP), Denton (DMNH), Ellis (DMNH, TCWC), Kaufman (DMNH), Parker (FWMSH), Tarrant (DMNH, FWMSH, UTA), and Wise (DMNH). Another specimen said to have been collected in Cooke County (Oberholser, 1974) was not located. An example of a Purple Finch has also been located for nearby Henderson County (DMNH).

CASSIN'S FINCH *Carpodacus cassinii* Baird
Status: Casual visitor.
Specimens: This western finch has been recorded only once in north central Texas: a lone female was discovered and collected in Bosque County on 8 April 1961 (WMP 1218). It was the typical nominate race, *C. c. cassinii.* A specimen (TNHC 1638) labeled this species from Cooke County on 9 January 1879 was reidentified by Allan R. Phillips as *C. p. purpureus.*

HOUSE FINCH *Carpodacus mexicanus* (Müller)
Status: Fairly common to casual locally in isolated populations in the western parts of the study area.
Occurrence: House Finches have been reported in 15 counties of north central Texas: Archer, Bosque, Dallas, Ellis, Hill, Hood, Jack, Johnson, Palo Pinto, Parker, Somervell, Tarrant, Throckmorton, Wichita, and Young.

Although House Finches have not been recorded regularly throughout the study area, they are now fairly well established in pockets or small groups on the western side of the study area. Zinn and Moore (1976) list them as moderately common to uncommon residents in and around Wichita County. Observers in Hood, Palo Pinto, and Somervell counties frequently report them in spring or during winter at feeders, while the records for the remaining counties are not numerous, probably for lack of observers. In two counties they have been frequently reported on the annual CBCs: seven times in Palo Pinto in 13 years (1965–77) and five times in Wichita Falls in ten years (1973–82).

Sightings of House Finches, probably representing wandering birds from the Edwards Plateau (Brazos River drainage), have been recorded in the following counties: Dallas — twice, 9 January 1960, and 3 January to 12 March 1981; Ellis — reported by Oberholser (1974); Tarrant — four times, 21 March 1941, 16 April 1938, 10 August 1956, and 26 October 1982.

Readers, especially those in the western parts of the study area, are urged to observe reddish finches carefully. Adult male House Finches have bright-red heads, bibs, backs, and rumps, while Purple Finches have dull rosy-red heads, backs, and rumps. Females and immatures are streaked brown and lack the ear patch of the Purple Finch. The tails of House Finches are square, while those of Purple Finches are notched.
Nesting: The only nesting records (nests or young) for the study area are for Hood, Palo Pinto, and Wichita counties.
Specimens: Specimens representing *C. m. frontalis* have been collected from Dallas (WMP), Jack (DMNH), Johnson (DMNH), and Wichita (WMP) counties. A specimen allegedly taken by E. A. Mearns in Tarrant County on 2 February 1892 was not located (Pulich, 1979).

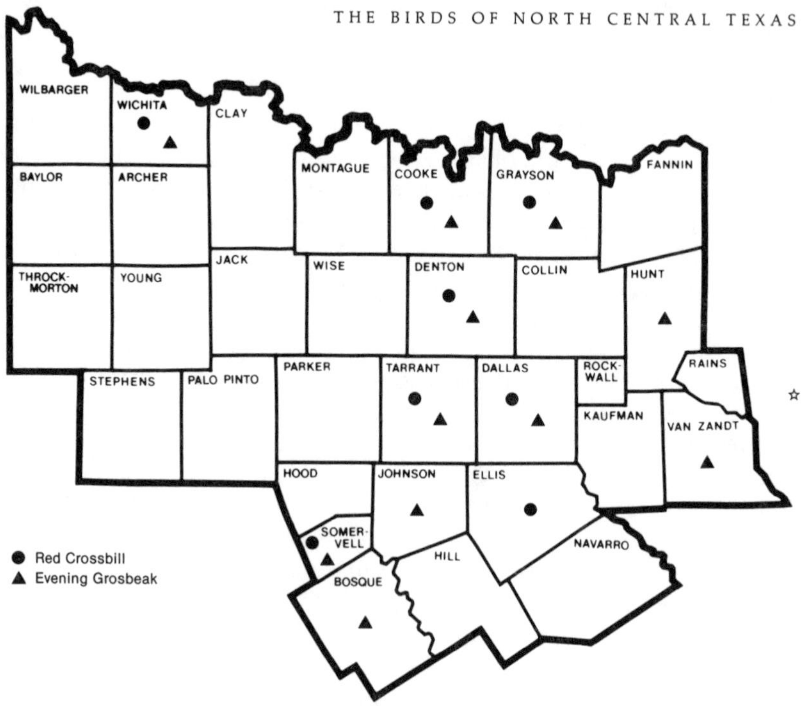

Map 111. Distribution of the Red Crossbill, *Loxia curvirostra,* and the Evening Grosbeak, *Coccothraustes vespertinus*

RED CROSSBILL   *Loxia curvirostra* Linnaeus
Status: Casual winter visitor, often lingering into spring.
Occurrence: Red Crossbills have been reported at eight north central Texas counties. They are not usually abundant; the largest number was reported during the winter of 1972–73, when groups of 20 or so appeared in Tarrant County.

All county records are presented here: *Cooke* – 8 May 1970; *Dallas* – six times, 2 May 1898 (specimen, not located), 21 through 26 March 1954, 9 March 1961, 29 October 1972, 15 November 1972, 11 February 1978, and 5 April 1978; *Denton* – 5 April 1978 and 29 December 1986; *Ellis* – 18 November 1972; *Grayson* – five times, 2 November 1969, 20 to 28 December 1969 and 31 December 1969 (the last two observations at different locations), 20 February 1970, 11 November 1972, and 21 January through 24 February 1985; *Somervell* – reported for January (Guthery, 1974); *Tarrant* – 17 May 1954, 23 to 30 October 1972, and again 2 to 7 April 1973, and 26 April 1973 (the last two records in different cities); *Wichita* – 8 February 1973, 22 February 1973, and 1 and 2 December 1979.
Specimens: Although a Red Crossbill was said to have been taken in Dal-

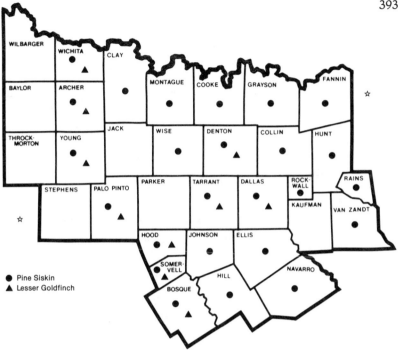

Map 112. Distribution of the Pine Siskin, *Carduelis pinus,* and the Lesser Goldfinch, *C. psaltria*

las County (see above), only two specimens are available from the study
area. Both of these are for Tarrant County—*L. c. stricklandi,* 17 May 1954
(USNM 458021), and *L. c. benti,* 23 October 1972 (WMP 1955). This record so far northeast is apparently exceptional for *stricklandi,* which is
mainly a Mexican race. Specimens should be saved from future flights so
that their origin can be determined.

PINE SISKIN   *Carduelis pinus* (Wilson)
Status: Uncommon to fairly common winter resident. Sporadically invades
north central Texas, becoming very common at that time.
Occurrence: Pine Siskins have been recorded in 25 counties in the study
area—Archer, Bosque, Clay, Collin, Cooke, Dallas, Denton, Ellis, Fannin,
Grayson, Hill, Hood, Hunt, Johnson, Montague, Navarro, Palo Pinto,
Rains, Rockwall, Somervell, Tarrant, Van Zandt, Wichita, Wise, and Young
counties—and adjacent Lamar County.
　　Pine Siskins can be considered erratic in their winter occurrences, scarce
to absent in some years, to very common in other winters. During the winter
of 1981–82 they invaded north central Texas by the thousands, and more

than 500 were banded at a banding station in Hunt County. Sometimes they do not put in an appearance until the end of the year, especially at feeding stations.

This species is usually found from late October to early May, with extreme dates 18 October 1976 (Hood County) to 4 June (Grayson County), next-latest 30 May 1888 (Cooke County, specimen). Dates for selected counties are: *Dallas* — 27 October 1983 to 29 May 1970; *Grayson* — 28 October 1984 to 13 May, and an isolated date, 4 June; *Palo Pinto* —16 November 1983 to 10 April 1983; *Tarrant* —19 October 1976 to 14 May 1978; *Van Zandt* —15 October 1986 to 24 May 1982 (Hunt County); *Wichita* — 29 October 1978 to 11 May 1974.

Specimens: Pine Siskin specimens were collected in the following counties: Cooke (TNHC), Dallas (DMNH, WMP), Denton (DMNH, WMP), Ellis (DMNH), Hunt (WMP), Montague (WMP), Tarrant (FWMSH, WMP), and Young (DMNH).

LESSER GOLDFINCH   *Carduelis psaltria* (Say)
Status: Rare to casual visitor, though fairly regular in several counties.
Occurrence: This southwestern goldfinch has been recorded in ten counties of the study area — Archer, Bosque, Dallas, Denton, Hood, Palo Pinto, Somervell, Tarrant, Wichita, and Young — and nearby Shackelford County.

Lesser Goldfinches have been reported as far east as Dallas and Denton counties, the remainder of the records being to the west, and many rather old ones. Some of the observations may be misidentifications of American Goldfinches. They have been reported on nine of 13 Palo Pinto CBCs (1965–77). Most sightings represent one or two birds.

All the data at hand for the ten study-area counties and Shackelford County are: *Archer* — one unconfirmed record of 15 December 1973 (Zinn, 1975). *Bosque* —18 March 1974 and 4 April 1976 (photograph). *Dallas* — an alleged specimen taken by W. A. Mayer on 2 May 1898 (Stillwell, 1939) was not located. I carefully studied a Lesser Goldfinch at my bird feeder in Irving on 17 April 1985. *Denton* — ten reported on 7 September 1978 by two observers, but such a large number is questionable. *Hood* —15 August 1964 and 13 June 1980. *Palo Pinto* — 8 May 1976, 5 June 1978, 23 November 1968, six times in December (mainly on CBCs), 11 December 1977 through 31 December 1965, and three times in January, 1 January 1970 and 1971 and 30 January 1971. Some of these records are questionable, particularly those of the CBCs. *Somervell* — six times, 3 May 1974, 11 May 1986, 12 May 1961, 1 July 1970, 23 June 1984, and 8 September 1985. *Tarrant* — four times, 30 April 1938, 19 September 1956, 18 November 1952, and 18 December 1971. *Wichita* — hypothetical, 29 September 1973 (Zinn, 1975). *Young* — summer record (Oberholser, 1974) and 2 September 1961. *Shackelford* — recorded on BBS on 17 June 1984.

Specimens: There are no known Lesser Goldfinch specimens for north central Texas (see Dallas County above).

AMERICAN GOLDFINCH   *Carduelis tristis* (Linnaeus)
Status: Common to abundant winter visitor. Widespread in passage, particularly in the spring. In a few counties they are found the year round. Nesting, if it occurs, is extremely rare.
Occurrence: American Goldfinches have been recorded in all the counties of the study area except Parker and Throckmorton counties, although there is no doubt that they would also be found in those counties too, if they were searched for at the proper times. They have also been found in nearby Shackelford County.

Usually they do not appear until November or December, reported when they come to feeding stations supplying black-thistle seed. They are inconspicuous in their fall plumage. They frequent giant ragweed, wild sunflowers, and other seed-bearing plants, particularly after the first of the year, in some years lingering until late May.

In good years hundreds of goldfinches are banded, and at times they become extremely abundant at feeding stations. It was estimated that 1,500 utilized a banding station in Hunt County on 12 March 1984. They have been recorded on all of the CBCs of the area every year, although in some years they are difficult to find. For example, Fort Worth CBCs (1958–77) averaged 435 goldfinches with a minimum of 135 (1960) and a maximum of 1,290 (1968), and in Dallas (1965–82) counts averaged 960 goldfinches with a minimum of 256 (1967) and a maximum of 1,922 (1982).

Arrival and departure dates for selected counties for which sufficient data are available are: *Dallas*—12 September 1985 to 23 May 1958, next-latest 19 May 1962; *Grayson*—7 August 1986, next-earliest 1 September 1978 to 2 May 1981; *Tarrant*—11 September 1954 to 26 May 1956; *Wichita* —16 October 1975 to 11 May 1973.

Nesting: Summer birds have been reported from Denton, Grayson, Hunt, Rains, Wilbarger, and Young counties. There is a reference to "a nest noted" but no specimen for the latter county between 1884 and 1890 (Oberholser, 1974). At Hagerman NWR, Grayson County, in some years they are seen the year round, and there is an observation on 6 October 1971, an extremely late date, of an adult feeding a stub-tailed young. To my knowledge no nests, eggs, or young have been collected from the north central Texas study area, though the above records imply nesting on rare occasions. A bird was reported to be "breeding" at Paris, in nearby Lamar County, from 1 through 15 June 1915 (Oberholser, 1974).

Specimens: American Goldfinches have been collected from the following counties: Collin (Oberholser, 1974; not located), Cooke (TNHC), Dallas (DMNH, WMP), Denton (DMNH, WMP), Ellis (DMNH), Hunt (FWMSH), Kaufman (DMNH), Tarrant (DMNH, UTA, WMP), Wise (DMNH), and nearby Henderson (DMNH) and Wood (DMNH). Although not all specimens have been examined for race, both *tristis* and *pallidus* have been taken from Dallas and Tarrant counties.

EVENING GROSBEAK *Coccothraustes vespertinus* (Cooper)
Status: Rare irregular visitor.
Occurrence: This beautiful grosbeak has been reported in 11 study-area counties and one nearby county, starting in 1962. County dates are: *Bosque* —14 April 1962; *Cooke*—18 February 1973; *Dallas*—13 through 15 January 1969, 27 December 1972, 28 January 1978, 26 March 1978, 12 September 1979, 4 January 1986, and 5 December 1986. *Denton*—25 January 1969, 23 November 1972, 28 January 1978, and 21 February through 16 March 1986; *Grayson*—22 and 23 January 1978, 20 March 1982, and 1 December 1985 to 3 April 1986; *Hunt*—26 March 1978 and 29 March through 5 May 1986; *Johnson*—1 March through 6 April 1986; *Somervell* —winter periods, 1968–69 and 1972–73; *Tarrant*—1 December 1962, April 1963, 13 September 1964, 20 January 1973 (two different locations), 30 January 1973, 17 and 20 November 1985, 13 January through 23 February 1986, and 2 February 1987; *Van Zandt*—from February until mid-March 1986; *Wichita*—7 January 1972, 18 April 1973 (MWU, photographs), and late winter 1973; *Wood*—2 December 1975.

Specimens: The only Evening Grosbeak specimen (FWMSH 442) known to me from the study area is one found dead in April 1963 at Fort Worth, Tarrant County. It has been identified as an intermediate between *vespertinus* and *brooksi* (Pulich, 1971).

Family Passeridae (Weaver Finches)

HOUSE SPARROW   *Passer domesticus* (Linnaeus)

Status: Common to abundant resident.

Occurrence: This imported sparrow is well known to nearly everyone, and many call it English Sparrow, or weaver finch, since it belongs to an Old World family of weavers. It has been recorded all year round in all of the counties of north central Texas.

Weaver finches, as I prefer to call them, reside abundantly in cities and towns but venture into the countryside in some areas. Usually one finds them near man-made structures, but they often show their gregarious habits by nesting in large trees at roadside parks or under bridges with swallows, away from cities and towns, and especially on large farms and at ranch headquarters. As all Purple Martin fanciers know, these sparrows occupy martin houses, as well as bluebird houses. They have also been observed nesting on the undersides of hawk nests, and they redo swallow, oriole, and other bird nests, covering the tops to build the bulky messy nests that are characteristic of House Sparrows.

This species has been recorded on all of the annual CBCs; however, their numbers seldom reflect true population, since many observers make little effort to count them accurately. Around silos and other grain-storage structures their numbers swell along with those of blackbirds and starlings, especially in fall and winter if much grain has been spilled on the ground. House Sparrows also frequent feeding stations and may become extremely numerous, to the dismay of persons feeding native species.

Although owls and hawks — especially accipiters — may take House Sparrows, neighborhood boys may shoot them, and rat snakes may seek their nests for eggs and young, their population numbers tend to remain static. Trapping them at feeding stations may reduce their numbers or keep them away, but once the action stops, other sparrows arrive to fill any gaps that may have occurred from eradication.

Nesting: House Sparrows lay large clutches of four to seven eggs and many times nest two or three times in a season. By late February they are busily engaged in starting nests, continuing until late July. There is one record of a House Sparrow about four days old found below a billboard structure in Dallas County on 12 December 1979. Another interesting observation, also in Dallas County, was a bird that took it upon itself to feed a young Cardinal out of the nest on 25 July 1981, although there were young House Sparrows out of the nest foraging at a feeding station nearby.

Specimens: House Sparrow specimens have been located for the following counties: Cooke (TCWC), Dallas (DMNH, UTA, WMP), Denton (DMNH), Grayson (OU), Parker (FWMSH), Tarrant (FWMSH, UTA, WMP), Wichita (MWU), and Van Zandt (WMP).

Mutant white feathers are often reported on members of this species, and pure — "white" (albinistic) sparrows have been reported from the Dallas–Fort Worth area. Oberholser (1974) actually described a new race from Idaho because of the paleness developing in populations from the western United States.

Species of Uncertain Occurrence

This section covers those species needing more conclusive evidence of their occurrence in north central Texas before they can be accepted without question. In addition, this section contains accounts of two extinct species, several species extirpated from the study area but not the state, and some introduced species, particularly game birds. These game birds do not represent part of the present-day avifauna of Texas; most have been stocked by the Texas Parks and Wildlife Department.

Some readers may feel that if a particular species may occur elsewhere in Texas, either validated with a specimen or published in *The Bird Life of Texas* (Oberholser, 1974), it should be accepted as a valid record for north central Texas. The decision to include various species in this section has been solely mine. In this study I have attempted to determine with extreme care the current status of the birds of north central Texas. A number of records need more conclusive proof of occurrence before the species are added to the main list. In a few instances the species may indeed occur in the area, but photographs or specimens are needed to substantiate their presence. Some species are so difficult to identify even in the hand that they must be referred to authorities familiar with the species, and birds in photographs that are not of first quality are not always identifiable. In instances where some ducks, gulls, and shorebirds are known to have strayed far from their normal range and since they seldom return to their site of origin, it is suggested that discriminate collecting would conclusively identify them. They are often found dead and decaying and are difficult to identify; however, readers who find unusual dead birds are urged to save them and to get in touch with a nearby museum or university that has bird collections. Even if the person has identified the bird to his own satisfaction, he should not dispose of the specimen but should let the museum curator or scientist decide whether or not the specimen is important. Birds have feather characteristics with which many observers are unfamiliar. The salvaging of dead birds is another way of conserving our avifauna.

There are several specimens in my collection that have resulted in state records, while others serve as important comparative material.

Bird banders can help too by making careful notes and measurements, and even plucking tail or wing feathers as evidence of certain features. Photographing birds in the hand in a number of poses or positions is often helpful. On rare occasions a bird can be captured and taken to a local authority for identification. Unfortunately, banders unfamiliar with rarer species have made mistakes (see the account of the Virginia Rail or of the Acadian Flycatcher) that have been entered into the banding records and even into published records.

In recent years the practice of rehabilitating injured birds has become an important conservation measure. Persons working in rehabilitation facilities can assist, first, by trying to obtain careful documentation of the exact date and place where the bird was taken. A record of only the name and address of the person who brings in the bird complies with the law but does not reveal where the bird was found. I vividly remember spotting a Saw-whet Owl at one such facility and wondering where it came from. The records of the local rehabilitator told me only that it came from an address in Texas. Upon checking further with the local game warden, I learned that the bird had been taken in Colorado and transported to Texas. Acceptance of this record as a Texas occurrence would certainly have clouded the issue. Careful record keeping is a must.

Another common error made by persons salvaging dead birds for a scientific collection is the failure to record the *exact* date on which the bird was found. I remember discovering in a local museum a specimen of a warbler that is not found in north central Texas in the winter period; it was dated 10 January. Upon checking again with the person who brought the specimen to the museum, I determined that the bird had been found in the fall, when it is normally expected, and had not been taken to the museum until January, when several other casualties, all marked with the same date were brought in. If the exact date is unknown, the record should so indicate. It is better not to date a specimen than to mark it with an incorrect date.

This list will indicate to readers what species they should look for so that they may be able to help obtain the evidence needed to transfer the species to the regular list. In a few instances I completely excluded a species from this list because it is so unusual in north central Texas that it should be confirmed by authentic specimens or some other unquestionable proof of occurrence.

Fieldwork by careful observers in years to come will no doubt add some species to those currently recorded as occurring in north central Texas, even though they are not now listed even among the following species of uncertain occurrence.

LEAST GREBE   *Tachybaptus dominicus* (Linnaeus)
The TOS Texas Bird Records Committee has not accepted records of this species farther north than the upper Coastal Prairies where it is an occasional winter visitor, and one accidental occurrence in Waller County, in east Texas, where it attempted to breed.

I chose to follow the TOS *Checklist* (1984) and discounted two Dallas County records, one an unconfirmed sighting reported on 6 September 1969 (Oberholser, 1974) and the other an alleged Least Grebe specimen that was brought to me on 4 November 1979, which proved to be an extremely small, immature Pied-billed Grebe. Extreme caution should be exercised in identifying this species. Small-sized (immature) or winter-plumaged pied-bills may mislead inexperienced birders.

Until an acceptable photograph or specimen of a Least Grebe is produced for north central Texas, its presence must continue to be questioned.

REDDISH EGRET   *Egretta rufescens* (Gmelin)
Records of this egret for north central Texas given for Denton (1952), Hunt (1947), and Tarrant (1959) counties, all sight records (Oberholser, 1974), are unacceptable. The Reddish Egret is a coastal species and is seldom reported away from the Texas Gulf Coast. It is possible to confuse this species with the mature Little Blue Heron, a common species of north central Texas. The occurrence of the Reddish Egret should be documented by a photograph or specimen.

GLOSSY IBIS   *Plegadis falcinellus* (Linnaeus)
The Glossy Ibis is listed as hypothetical in *The Bird Life of Texas* (Oberholser, 1974). The current *Checklist of the Birds of Texas* (TOS, 1984) does not list this species as occurring in the state.

There are eight specimens labeled *Plegadis falcinellus* in the Dallas Museum of Natural History (DMNH 24, 25, 26, 27, 1819, 1820, 3929, and 4828). I sent two of the specimens in winter plumage (DMNH 24 and 27), together with a specimen from Archer County (MWU 10) and two from Tarrant County, to Richard C. Banks, at the National Museum of Natural History, in Washington, D.C. The two specimens from Tarrant County were collected on 17 September 1983 (FWMSH 1444) and on 22 December 1984 (WMP 2924). With the exception of the one I collected, they appeared to be White-faced Ibis (*P. chihi*). Banks spent considerable time studying the five specimens and on the basis of measurements named all five White-faced Ibis.

The details of the bird from Fort Worth (WMP 2924) are as follows: On 3 November 1983 two birders observed an ibis, which they identified as a Glossy Ibis, feeding with seven other dark ibises. Several days later the bird was photographed; when the slide was finally developed in August 1984, it caused much debate over the identity of the bird. The slide was sent to me, and in turn I sent it to the U.S. National Museum, whose personnel concurred with me that the bird was *P. chihi.* Soon afterward one of the slides was enlarged by a Fort Worth birder and sent to H. Douglas Pratt, of Louisiana. He agreed with the Fort Worth birders that the bird was a Glossy Ibis.

The next fall, on 20 October 1984, another ibis (or perhaps the same one) appeared at the same location where the bird was discovered in 1983, and it, too, was identified as *P. falcinellus.* The ibis remained until 22 December 1984, when I collected it, and it proved to be a male. I sent the specimen to the U.S. National Museum in Washington, D.C., where it was identified as a White-faced Ibis. The measurements were: right wing, 275 mm; tail, 95 mm.

Because authorities are not in agreement on the identification of these birds and there is no specimen to document the species, I continue to question its occurrence in north central Texas, and in Texas as a whole, until a Glossy Ibis is collected in full nuptial plumage. Because both species are so similar in their winter plumage, it is nearly impossible to distinguish them unless they are in spring (alternate) plumage.

Sutton (1955) presented the details of the only Glossy Ibis taken for Oklahoma (near Reagan, Johnson County), and Lowery (1974) indicated that it breeds in the Mississippi River delta. For this reason it may be only a matter of time until the Glossy Ibis is properly validated for Texas. It should also be pointed out that some authorities (Palmer, 1962) consider the two species to be nothing more than subspecies or that they represent only color phases of one species.

TRUMPETER SWAN   *Cygnus buccinator* Richardson
Oberholser (1974) placed this species on the list of extirpated species— species that no longer occur in Texas. He lists the last record for Texas as a bird shot at High Island, Galveston County, on 15 February 1927. Most of the few records are before the turn of the century, and they may have been misidentifications of Tundra Swans, *C. columbianus.*

The Trumpeter Swan was apparently never abundant, and it probably visited Texas only rarely. Two records for north central Texas were given: Clay County—Red River on approximately 21 February and 18 January 1880 (A. Hall, specimens preserved?), and Navarro County, given only as "*Olor* (sp.)? . . . shot near Corsicana during the winter of 1879–80," but not examined by Ogilby (1882), who believed it to be "*buccinator*" from the description given by a friend who collected it.

The *Checklist of the Birds of Texas* (TOS, 1984) makes no mention of this swan. Since the records for it are so vague, and the whereabouts of the specimen said to have been collected could not be located, one may question whether this species ever reached Texas.

BARNACLE GOOSE *Branta leucopsis* (Bechstein)

The *Check-list of North American Birds* (AOU, 1983) states that the Barnacle Goose is casual in North America and on rare occasions can be expected inland through some of the prairie states — Colorado, Nebraska, and Oklahoma — south to the Gulf Coast of Texas. It also implies that some records may be escapees, since this goose is commonly kept in captivity and sometimes escapes. Oberholser (1974) included this species as hypothetical, based on coastal sight records. The *Checklist of the Birds of Texas* (TOS, 1984) has not accepted the species for Texas.

In north central Texas the only record of a Barnacle Goose is one that was observed in a small flock of Canada Geese by a knowledgeable hunter scouting waterfowl before the opening of the hunting season, about a mile west of Hagerman NWR on 2 and 6 November 1981. On the latter date it was said to have been seen briefly on the refuge. However, since only one person saw the bird, and there is no way of knowing its origin, the status of the Barnacle Goose in north central Texas must remain uncertain. The refuge checklist (U.S. Fish and Wildlife Service, 1984) considers this species accidental.

There are three records of Barnacle Geese from the Tishomingo NWR, Oklahoma, from 16 December 1971 through 1 March 1972, on 7 November 1974, and from 21 November 1979 until at least 16 January 1980 (Williams, 1972, 1975, 1980). Since the Oklahoma refuge is across Lake Texoma from Hagerman NWR, it is possible that this species has occurred in north central Texas, but its acceptance must await a photograph or specimen.

WHITE-TAILED HAWK *Buteo albicaudatus* Vieillot

Oberholser (1974) gave sight records for summer and winter in Dallas County and indicated that it was casual in Dallas. However, the White-tailed Hawk was excluded from the main list of species in the Dallas County checklist (Pulich, 1977b) and was listed as hypothetical.

Since this species is a local resident from the Rio Grande valley to the Houston area along the coast of Texas, its occurrence in north central Texas must be questioned. Unfortunately, buteos are found in many color phases in this area and are frequently misidentified. In summer certain color phases of Swainson's Hawks can easily be confused with this south Texas hawk, and in winter light-colored Red-tailed Hawks can be misidentified as White-tailed Hawks.

The acceptance of this species must await a photograph or specimen to verify its presence in north central Texas.

ZONE-TAILED HAWK   *Buteo albonotatus* Kaup

The occurrence of the Zone-tailed Hawk in north central Texas is at best accidental and always questionable, though it formerly ranged to the Edwards Plateau, and today a few are still found along the western edge of the plateau. This black buteo resembles a vulture and frequently associates with them. It can easily be confused with the Turkey Vulture.

There are three reports of this species for the north central Texas study area. One is given for Hill County by Oberholser in *The Bird Life of Texas* (1974), whose editor lists the species as casual but presents no details to support the sighting. The second report is a lone individual seen on 2 and 3 April 1984 near Terrell, Kaufman County, first by one observer and on the second date separately by two other competent observers. All agreed on the identification of the bird in question, although one observer mentioned the possibility that it was a released bird. This is questionable, since the species is seldom if ever captured, and, as far as I can determine, it has not been acquired by any of the falconers in north central Texas.

The third record is a hawk observed north of the Dallas–Fort Worth airport, in Tarrant County near the Dallas county line on 26 December 1985. A lone observer spotted the dark hawk flying with a Red-tailed Hawk. At first he thought that the bird was a Turkey Vulture but upon checking further identified it as a buteo. Although the observer thought the hawk was a Zone-tailed Hawk and took photographs, the details are not conclusive, and I do not concur with his identification. To reinforce my contention, on 17 February 1986 another observer identified a similarly marked (dark-phase) buteo as a Rough-legged Hawk flying over his home in Lewisville, Denton County, less than ten miles from the first sighting. Roughlegs often reach the north central Texas area and come in many color phases, making identifications difficult. Since there are similarities between the two species, they may be misidentified.

Until a satisfactory photograph or a valid specimen of a Zone-tailed Hawk is obtained, its status must remain in doubt in north central Texas.

CHUKAR   *Alectoris chukar* (Gray)

This introduced partridge is only rarely reported, and then mainly in or around the Dallas–Fort Worth area. It is usually an escapee from a game farm or a local hunting club.

Chukars have not established themselves anywhere in Texas, but there are some wild populations in the western United States, primarily in the mountainous areas of California, Nevada, and Oregon as well as parts of the Dakotas, Idaho, and Washington. They prefer barren, rocky areas.

RING-NECKED PHEASANT   *Phasianus colchicus* Linnaeus

The Ring-necked Pheasant has occasionally been reported in north central

Texas, but it has not established itself and probably will not do so. This Asian species represents hatching stock released by the Texas Parks and Wildlife Department or escapees from a game farm or hunting club. Ring-necked Pheasants require extensive irrigated farmlands, which are lacking in most of the north central Texas counties. In addition, the temperatures in late spring and early summer may be too high for successful hatching of eggs. This species does not do well around urban areas, and north central Texas is generally unsuited to this majestic game bird. Only in parts of the Panhandle, or near El Paso, or in portions of the Upper and Central Coastal Prairies of the state does the species seem to have maintained itself.

GREATER PRAIRIE-CHICKEN *Tympanuchus cupido* (Linnaeus)
Like the Lesser Prairie-Chicken the Greater Prairie-Chicken has disappeared from north central Texas. Both species were common in the 1880s. Apparently they disappeared soon after the turn of the century, though there may be some confusion about the distribution records of the two species. This species had a wider occurrence in the area than the Lesser Prairie-Chicken. Oberholser (1974) indicated that it ranged along the Red River and south through several counties to Navarro County. In that county it was considered "very common and resident" by Ogilby (1882). Oberholser (1974) reported that the last 12 birds were shot near Corsicana, in Navarro County, on 14 November 1900. More and Strecker (1929) stated that this species had not been recorded in Wilbarger County since 1907. Sutton (1938) surmised that the species occurred in Tarrant County, and in Pulich (1979) I indicated that they disappeared from this area between 1890 and 1895.

Today the only remnants of this population left in Texas are the southern race—the Attwater's Prairie-Chicken of the coastal prairie along the Gulf Coast.

Although Oberholser (1974) indicated specimen records for six counties —Clay, Cooke, Dallas, Denton, Navarro, and Wichita (specimens shot by hunters)—only three specimens were located for Cooke County. Two specimens taken at Gainesville on 1 January and 24 December 1878 (USNM 79085, 79086) by G. H. Ragsdale are identified as *T. c. pinnatus*, while a third specimen taken by Ragsdale on 21 December 1878 (TNHC 1694) at the same location was assumed to be the same race but was not examined.

LESSER PRAIRIE-CHICKEN *Tympanuchus pallidicinctus* (Ridgway)
The Lesser Prairie-Chicken was said to inhabit north central Texas in earlier times, though they were never as widespread as their near relative, the Greater Prairie-Chicken. Lessers differ from Greater Prairie-Chickens in their rather slight size, paleness of color, and reddish rather than orange air sacs of the males, all rather distinct features, though some authorities consider the two species conspecific. It is often suggested that the two spe-

cies frequented distinct ecological habitats: the Lesser Prairie-Chicken in-habited sandy "sage and shinnery country" in shortgrass prairies, while the Greater Prairie-Chicken was found in oak savannas bordering tallgrass prairies. Neither niche, however, is distinct to the untrained eye.

Oberholser (1974) listed records for Lesser Prairie-Chickens for Cooke and Young counties in north central Texas and a questionable record for Dallas County. The *Checklist of the Birds of Texas* (TOS, 1984) says that they "formerly ranged eastward to Clay and Tarrant Counties." The basis for most of these records is vague and could not be located. It is possible that there was some confusion of the Clay and Cooke county records. An alleged specimen for Cooke County said to have been taken by G. H. Rags-dale on 3 January 1878, in the same year he took a Greater Prairie-Chicken, is rather unbelievable. However, the occasional occurrence in the area can-not be completely dismissed, since the type specimen location is given in the *Check-list* (AOU, 1983) as "prairie of Texas (near latitude 32°N)." Bailey (1928) placed the type location "not far from the Clear Fork of Brazos River near the present town of Abilene, Taylor County, Texas," only a few coun-ties west of the study area.

Eskimo Curlew *Numenius borealis* (Forster)

Eskimo Curlews formerly occurred in spring migration in several north central Texas counties; however, there are no records of this species in the study area in the twentieth century.

This species is on the verge of extinction. Eskimo Curlews must have been fairly abundant in Texas before the turn of the century. There are records from Cooke, Navarro, Wise, and Young counties, according to Oberholser (1974); see that publication for further details. The last sight record (photograph) for Texas was from the Gulf Coast at Padre Island in 1972 (AOU, 1983).

From G. H. Ragsdale's notes (Oberholser, 1974), the Eskimo Curlew was numerous in Cooke County, ranging from 7 March to 8 April, the last sighting from north central Texas apparently occurring on 27 March 1889.

There is only one fall record for the area—that of 15 October 1877, an observation made by Ragsdale near Gainesville, Cooke County. The rec-ords show that the Eskimo Curlew was primarily a spring transient, oc-curring in all of the counties mentioned above.

Oberholser (1974) indicated that five Eskimo Curlews were collected by Ragsdale in Cooke County on 8 April 1876, 7 March 1879 (three), and 17 March 1880, but unfortunately the whereabouts of these specimens are unknown to me.

Purple Sandpiper *Calidris maritima* (Brünnich)

This rather small sandpiper usually ranges from the arctic regions of Greenland and Iceland to the Middle Atlantic coastal areas of the United States. In Texas it is considered to be an occasional rare winter visitor (I believe that casual or accidental would be more appropriate) along the upper coast of Texas from Galveston County as far south as Freeport, Brazoria County (TOS, 1984). Although it has never been collected in the state, it was included on the state list on the basis of photographs. Most records are from the Galveston area along rock jetties. It is said to associate with Ruddy Turnstones and Sanderlings.

There is only one (unsubstantiated) observation for north central Texas. A Purple Sandpiper was supposedly sighted by a lone observer at Lake Dallas, Denton County, on 29 March 1955 (Oberholser, 1974). However, until a photograph or specimen is taken for the area, the occurrence of the Purple Sandpiper must remain questionable.

RUFF *Philomachus pugnax* (Linnaeus)
I observed and carefully studied a female Ruff (or Reeve) for more than half an hour at a water-treatment plant in Dallas, Dallas County, on 18 September 1977. Although I noted all of the distinguishing characteristics of the species, no one else saw the Ruff when others later tried to find it. The bird was slightly smaller than a Greater Yellowlegs and larger than a Pectoral Sandpiper, and it stood erect. Its legs were orange, and its tail showed two oval patches as given by Peterson (1980), not the U-shaped white band shown in *Birds of North America* (National Geographic Society, 1983).

There are no other records for the north central Texas area, and until a photograph or a specimen is taken from the study area, I prefer to list the species here, following the confirmation rules that at least two persons should identify a species before it can be accepted. Ruffs, however, have been documented in Texas; the one nearest the north central Texas study area is a specimen (SFASU 2551) taken in Nacogdoches County, in east Texas, on 28 August 1978.

THAYER'S GULL *Larus thayeri* Brooks
Although the Thayer's Gull has been reported in Dallas and Grayson counties, its occurrence is very questionable. The reports are so vague that I prefer to list this species as one of uncertain occurrence until there is more conclusive evidence. This gull seldom passes inland. Because it is extremely rare everywhere in Texas, its status must be questionable until it has been substantiated by either a photograph or a specimen. Herring Gulls passing through the area, especially immature birds, could easily be mistaken for this species. It should also be pointed out that the evidence of photographs is far from foolproof (Pulich, 1980a).

GULL-BILLED TERN   *Sterna nilotica* Gmelin

There are no valid records of Gull-billed Terns for north central Texas, though this species, which inhabits coastal salt marshes, is said to have reached the study area (Dallas and Denton counties) (see Stillwell, 1939), particularly in the 1930s and again in the late 1950s. The records are extremely vague and without details and should have been dismissed at the time as misidentifications. It is possible that the Forster's Tern, the common tern of north central Texas, was mistaken for this species; however, if it had been carefully examined, it would not have been misidentified. A valid photograph or specimen must be obtained before this tern can be added to the list of birds for north central Texas.

SOOTY TERN   *Sterna fuscata* Linneaus

Oberholser (1974) listed a sight record for Dallas County. However, I have dismissed the occurrence of this species because the record is doubtful and unconfirmed, and apparently was made by only one person. Kelley (1935) allegedly saw one on 29 August 1932 which "was exhausted and barely able to fly," and "when approached it flew weakly over some reeds and dropped into them." Unfortunately, the bird in question was not recovered, nor was it described. In the *Check List of Birds of Dallas County, Texas* (Stillwell, 1939) Kelley reported another Sooty Tern at the same site on 26 August 1934, without giving any details. However, it is rather strange that this observer did not list this second record in his original publication but passed it on to Stillwell. Many of Kelley's records are highly suspicious and typical of an inexperienced bird-watcher. Black Terns, sometimes common during migration in north central Texas, could easily be mistaken for Sooty Terns. Until a photograph or a specimen is produced for north central Texas, I prefer to question the inland occurrence of the Sooty Tern.

RINGED TURTLE-DOVE   *Streptopelia risoria* (Linnaeus)

This popular cage bird is frequently reported around large cities, as the result of an intentional release or escape from captivity. It has not established itself in the north central Texas study area. For example, ten Ringed Turtle-Doves released in Irving, Dallas County, a few years ago remained for a time in the immediate area but gradually disappeared after a two-month period. Some of the birds were extremely tame, and they probably were taken by predators such as cats and owls. If they were to establish themselves as a nesting population, I hope readers will notify me of the nesting locale.

A casual observation might mistake this dove for a Mourning Dove or even a Rock Dove. Some Ringed Turtle-Doves are very light, almost white; however, they can usually be identified by their narrow black collar.

PASSENGER PIGEON *Ectopistes migratorius* (Linnaeus)
Oberholser (1974) gives an excellent account of the Passenger Pigeon's occurrence in Texas, and readers are urged to read this interesting account for details. This now extinct species was once an abundant wintering bird, arriving in late October or early November and returning to favorable feeding grounds of oaks, feeding on mast and fruits, berries, weed seeds, and even grain. They roosted in huge flocks and were said to break the limbs of trees often by the weight of their great numbers. Apparently, after the food supply was exhausted in a particular area they wandered to find new sources of food until they left Texas in January.

Many of Oberholser's research data for Texas were gathered from information of old-timers who hunted or were interested in the species and obtained data from their friends, especially in Henderson and Anderson counties, adjoining the southeastern counties of the north central Texas study area. Many of the data were obtained from interviews with Judge Royall R. Watkins, of Dallas.

Passenger Pigeons, or "wild pigeons," as they were called by early settlers, were recorded from the following north central Texas counties — Collin, Cooke, Fannin, Hood, Jack, Johnson, Palo Pinto, Parker, Tarrant, Van Zandt, Wise, and Young — and adjacent Anderson, Henderson, and Wood counties.

Except for those of Cooke and Henderson counties, the records were apparently winter birds migrating through respective counties or roosting and feeding in favorable food areas. Although no nests or eggs were collected, the nesting accounts for the state occurred about 1856 near Gainesville, in Cooke County, and near Goshen, in Henderson County, where "considerable numbers remained through summer and nested in large trees, ca. 1883–1892."

It is always amazing to me, when I read accounts stressing the vast numbers of Passenger Pigeons of about 100 years ago, that they became extinct so rapidly. Oberholser (1974) gave 1896 as the last date for north central Texas, in Van Zandt County, and, for Texas, March 1900, when two birds were said to have been taken in upper Galveston Bay, Galveston County. This species passed from the face of the earth when its last member died in the Cincinnati Zoo on 1 September 1914.

LESSER NIGHTHAWK *Chordeiles acutipennis* (Hermann)
There are no authentic records of the Lesser Nighthawk for north central Texas. Although this tropical nighthawk has been reported several times in three counties, there are no photographs or specimens to document its occurrence in north central Texas. Each of the reports represents a sighting that was made by only one observer or under unfavorable light condi-

tions. The one alleged specimen (DMNH), said to be from Dallas County, proved to be a Common Nighthawk, *C. minor;* therefore, the record must be discounted. Because it is possible to confuse this species with the Common Nighthawk, the inclusion of Lesser Nighthawk in the list for north central Texas must await more positive proof.

RED-COCKADED WOODPECKER   *Picoides borealis* (Vieillot)
Sutton (1938) reported that he took a specimen of this species on 30 January 1914 "in a dense patch of woods about three miles south" of Fort Worth along the Clear Fork of the Trinity River, Tarrant County. Unfortunately, he did not give the location of the alleged specimen.

Since Sutton's time this species has never been recorded in any of the north central Texas counties. In Texas it is limited to local longleaf pine areas in the east, a habitat nonexistent in the study area. Any occurrence of the Red-cockaded Woodpecker in the study area is unlikely, and it is questionable whether the Red-cockaded Woodpecker ever occurred in north central Texas.

IVORY-BILLED WOODPECKER   *Campephilus principalis* (Linnaeus)
This huge woodpecker once ranged into north central Texas, although it was probably never common in the study area. Ivory-billed Woodpeckers were listed by Oberholser (1974) for Cooke, Dallas, Fannin, and Kaufman counties. It inhabited the heavy, virgin-timbered bottomlands along the Trinity River through small portions of Kaufman County to about Dallas County. According to Oberholser (1974), there were sightings as late as 1927 in Kaufman County, although none appear to have been confirmed by competent observers. Since the Pileated Woodpecker also inhabited the Trinity River drainage and can still be found there, it is possible that some sightings were not ivory-bills. Reports — all false alarms — from the area in recent years proved to be Pileated Woodpeckers. Elsewhere, in Cooke and Fannin counties, the sightings of ivory-bills were before the turn of the century.

A male Ivory-billed Woodpecker mounted specimen on display (DMNH 6216) was reportedly taken on Bois d'Arc Island, which was said to be in Kaufman County, by W. A. Mayer about 1900, according to Oberholser (1974). However, Bois d'Arc Island is in Dallas County, and the museum personnel informed me that Mayer did most of his collecting in Dallas County. Thus it is very likely that this fine specimen was taken in Dallas County, not Kaufman County. At the turn of the century the bottomlands of the Trinity River were a vast wilderness, and it must have been very difficult for Mayer to know exactly where he was when he went collecting in the area of Bois d'Arc Island. He claimed to have seen this majestic woodpecker as late as 1910, while another source (R. E. Huck) claimed to have examined an ivory-bill in the winter of 1927, but apparently this one was not saved. A footnote in the *Check List of Birds of Dallas County, Texas* (Stillwell, 1939) relates a conversation with a farmer on Bois d'Arc Island in 1928 in which the farmer said that another bird had been killed "some ten years before." This date was given by Oberholser (1974) as "about 1920."

There is little evidence to support the occurrence of the Ivory-billed Woodpecker anywhere in Texas or the United States. However, in early April 1986 at least one male and one female have been rediscovered and confirmed by a party from the American Museum of Natural History in a remote area of Cuba.

VIOLET-GREEN SWALLOW *Tachycineta thalassina* (Swainson)
Although there are scattered fall sight records of Violet-green Swallows for three north central Texas counties—Dallas, Grayson, and Wichita—none is acceptable. In fact, there are no valid records of Violet-green Swallows for any counties of north central Texas. Unfortunately, the records mentioned above were published as valid in *The Bird Life of Texas* (Oberholser, 1974) and *American Birds* (Williams, 1974, 1976) though this species is normally found only in the Trans-Pecos regions of Texas. The records above probably represent misidentified Tree Swallows. These erroneous records may have even found their way into the AOU *Check-list* (1983), which states that violet-greens are found (casual or accidental) in "central Texas." Until a specimen or a photograph has been taken for proper verification, these records are not acceptable.

BLACK-CAPPED CHICKADEE *Parus atricapillus* Linnaeus
There are no valid records of this northern species for Texas, and occurrence of the Black-capped Chickadee anywhere in the state is extremely doubtful. Oberholser (1974) lists this species for Dallas, Navarro, and Tarrant counties and claims that there are specimens from Navarro County and, in west Texas, from Concho County. I have no indication of where the alleged specimens are deposited, or whether they were correctly identified. Sight records are not acceptable since this species and the Carolina Chickadee cannot be identified in the field on the basis of song or even on the amount of white on the secondaries. Even ornithologists have difficulty distinguishing the two species in the hand. The occurrence of the Black-capped Chickadee in Texas or north central Texas must await validation by a specimen. Readers are urged to send any chickadees found dead to the proper authorities if they suspect that they are Black-capped Chickadees.

PLAIN TITMOUSE *Parus inornatus* Gambel
There are no valid records of the Plain Titmouse for north central Texas.

Oberholser (1974) shows a questionable record for Dallas County in the range map for the state of Texas but gives no details in the text of his book. A specimen (MWU 576) from Montague County said to be *P. inornatus* upon examination proved to be a Tufted Titmouse (*P. bicolor*). Several other sight records of the Plain Titmouse for Wichita County have been deleted as misidentifications. This species has been found only in extreme west Texas and constitutes a superspecies with *P. bicolor*, according to the AOU *Check-list* (1983).

AMERICAN DIPPER   *Cinclus mexicanus* Swainson
There are eight observations of the American Dipper for Texas, all sight records of single birds. No specimens of this species have been taken for the state, and its occurrence in the state is based on a photograph (TP-RF, TCWC no. 37) from Crosby County, in west Texas.

This western species has been reported from three counties in north central Texas. Oddly, this aquatic passerine was said to have been seen at a stock tank south of Vernon, in Wilbarger County, on 14 May 1939 and, by coincidence on the same day by the same observers, at the west end of Lake Kemp, in Baylor County. It was assumed to have been two different birds, since the two observations were some distance apart. Oberholser (1974) gave no other details of these dubious sightings. An American Dipper was said to have been seen on 21 April 1975 by two observers along a tree-lined creek in north Dallas, Dallas County. This species is excluded from the main list of species in the Dallas County checklist (Pulich, 1977b). It is considered hypothetical there.

Since the circumstances of the two north central Texas sightings are vague and the details are not convincing, I prefer to await a photograph or specimen of the American Dipper to substantiate its occurrence in north central Texas.

BACHMAN'S WARBLER   *Vermivora bachmanii* (Audubon)
Authors of several popular field guides (e.g., Peterson, 1980; Robbins, Brunn, and Zim, 1983) point out that this species is the rarest of the United States warblers. It is said that if it still exists it is local in moist deciduous woods of South Carolina. However, many authorities now believe that it is extinct.

Bachman's Warbler was considered hypothetical for Texas in *The Bird Life of Texas* (Oberholser, 1974) on the basis of sight records for Fort Worth, in Tarrant County; Texarkana, in Bowie County; and the Big Thicket. The last two locations are in the Piney Woods, outside the north central Texas study area.

I discuss (Pulich, 1979) the Tarrant County records and exclude Bachman's Warbler from that county. Thus there are no valid records of this species in Texas, and I doubt that it ever occurred in the state. The alleged sightings could have been of Hooded or Wilson's Warblers.

BREWER'S SPARROW   *Spizella breweri* Cassin

Although Oberholser (1974) indicates that Brewer's Sparrow occurred in three north central Texas counties — Cooke, Dallas, and Tarrant — there appears to be little evidence to support these contentions. Data on hand for this western sparrow in the three counties are: *Cooke* — an alleged specimen collected by G. H. Ragsdale on 5 May 1884 (TNHC 1597) at Gainesville has been reidentified as *S. pallida* by Allan R. Phillips. *Dallas* — a record based on an alleged spring specimen that was said to have been taken on 5 May 1898 (Stillwell, 1939). This specimen could not be located, though it is said that Oberholser identified it. (On the other hand, Oberholser also misidentified the Cooke County specimen as *breweri*.) The specimen was taken before the Dallas Museum of Natural History was established, and museum personnel could shed no light on its whereabouts. Two other sight records, one in fall on 30 October 1971 and one in spring on 6 May 1978, have been discounted. *Tarrant* — reported once in the fall on 22 September 1946. The record is not acceptable because details are lacking.

Fall records of this species are difficult to identify since fall plumage of Brewer's Sparrow closely resembles that of the Clay-colored Sparrow and the immature Chipping Sparrow, both of which occur regularly in north central Texas.

Until a valid specimen or photograph is produced to verify the occurrence of Brewer's Sparrow for north central Texas, its presence must be questioned.

SHARP-TAILED SPARROW   *Ammodramus caudacutus* (Gmelin)

The Sharp-tailed Sparrow account in *The Bird Life of Texas* (Oberholser, 1974) listed Dallas, Hunt, and Tarrant county sight records. The records for all but Dallas County are questioned. The records for Dallas County were probably established on the basis of one observation at a grassy shoreline at North Lake by a number of persons on 25 October 1969. Two later records for that county have been dismissed, since the details are vague.

There are also three reports from Hagerman NWR, in Grayson County, on 15 and 16 October 1977, 9 October 1979, and 19 and 26 October 1986. These were made by several observers and are said to have been carefully studied. The local refuge checklist (U.S. Fish and Wildlife Service, 1984) lists this species as accidental.

Because of its rarity and the lack of verification for north central Texas, the Sharp-tailed Sparrow's occurrence should remain hypothetical, awaiting either an identifiable photograph or a specimen.

BRONZED COWBIRD   *Molothrus aeneus* (Wagler)
Records indicate that this species may have made its way to two north central Texas counties. In the early 1970s an alleged Bronzed Cowbird was found dead at a feeder in Forth Worth, Tarrant County, but unfortunately the bird was not saved so that its identification could be substantiated. Another bird was observed around 1 April 1983 at a bird feeder. There are also two sightings for Palo Pinto County—one on 29 April 1978 near Possum Kingdom Lake and the other on 27 October 1979 on the Brazos River.

For the time being this species should be considered hypothetical even though all the records in question are by competent bird-watchers. Proof of the occurrence of the Bronzed Cowbird in north central Texas must await a specimen or a photograph.

HOODED ORIOLE   *Icterus cucullatus* Swainson
Oberholser (1974) gave one fall sighting, 3 October 1956, and a questionable winter sighting of this oriole for Dallas County. Since there are so many variations in plumage among Northern Orioles, which are common migrants throughout north central Texas, and since the account in Oberholser is not consistent in a number of sightings, it is very likely that these reports were misidentifications. The *Checklist of the Birds of Texas* (TOS, 1984) ignored this reference and has not accepted the occurrence of the Hooded Oriole in north central Texas.

SCOTT'S ORIOLE   *Icterus parisorum* Bonaparte
An adult male was identified as a Scott's Oriole as it bathed in a birdbath in Flower Mound, Denton County, on 26 May 1987. Before this date north central Texas had been subjected to storms originating in Mexico and the southwestern part of the state. Unfortunately, this sighting, which represents the only report of it for north central Texas, was made by only one birder, although two members of the observer's family concurred with the identification.

This species is normally found in Texas in the Trans-Pecos region and the southern part of the Edwards Plateau. The only other nearby report of this species in north Texas was a sighting west of the study area near Abilene at Camp Barkeley, Taylor County (Oberholser, 1974).

Even though the above sighting may have some credibility, more conclusive proof is needed before I can accept the occurrence of Scott's Oriole in north central Texas. Until a photograph or a specimen of this species is taken in the study area its status must remain in doubt.

COMMON REDPOLL   *Carduelis flammea* (Linnaeus)
Oberholser (1974) listed a report by H. F. Peters of the Common Redpoll

from Fannin County in the winter of 1885–86. The only other sight record was a bird seen by two observers for two days at a feeder during snowstorms on 18 and 19 February 1978 in Commerce, Hunt County.

The occurrence of the Common Redpoll in north central Texas should be considered hypothetical. A photograph or specimen should be taken to establish its occurrence in the study area, though the Texas Ornithological Society Bird Records Committee (TOS, 1984) has based its acceptance of the species occurrence in the state on two sight records from the Texas Panhandle.

Checklist of Species in the Counties

Checklist of Species in the Counties

Species	Archer	Baylor	Bosque	Clay	Collin	Cooke	Dallas	Denton	Ellis	Fannin	Grayson	Hill	Hood	Hunt	Jack	Johnson	Kaufman	Montague	Navarro	Palo Pinto	Parker	Rains	Rockwall	Somervell	Stephens	Tarrant	Throckmorton	Van Zandt	Wichita	Wilbarger	Wise	Young
Red-throated Loon						*																										
Common Loon	*	*	*	*		*	*	*		*		*	*		*			*	*			*			*	*		*	*	*	*	*
Pied-billed Grebe	*	*	*	*	*	*	*	*	*	*		*	*	*	*	*	*	*	*	*	*		*		*	*	*	*	*	*	*	*
Horned Grebe	*	*		*	*		*	*		*		*	*		*	*	*			*	*	*				*	*		*	*	*	*
Red-necked Grebe						*				*			*							*						*						*
Eared Grebe	*			*	*	*	*	*	*	*		*	*			*	*			*	*	*				*		*	*	*		*
Western Grebe		*				*	*		*		*		*	*						*	*					*		*	*	*	*	
American White Pelican	*		*	*	*		*	*	*	*	*	*	*	*	*	*	*	*	*	*	*	*	*		*	*		*	*	*	*	*
Brown Pelican					*	*		*																								
Double-crested Cormorant	*	*	*	*		*	*	*		*	*	*	*	*	*	*	*	*	*	*	*	*		*	*	*	*	*	*	*	*	*
Olivaceous Cormorant	*			*	*		*	*	*							*			*		*					*		*	*			
Anhinga		*			*	*	*	*				*				*	*		*		*					*		*			*	
American Bittern	*	*	*	*	*		*	*					*			*			*							*		*			*	*
Least Bittern		*			*	*		*								*				*									*			
Great Blue Heron	*	*	*	*		*	*	*		*	*	*	*	*	*	*	*	*	*	*	*	*		*	*	*	*	*	*	*	*	*
Great Egret	*	*		*	*	*	*	*	*		*		*	*		*	*		*	*	*					*		*	*		*	*
Snowy Egret	*	*		*	*	*	*	*	*	*		*		*		*	*		*	*	*	*				*		*	*		*	*
Little Blue Heron	*	*	*		*	*	*	*	*	*		*		*	*	*	*		*	*	*					*		*	*	*	*	*
Tricolored Heron			*		*	*	*	*	*	*		*				*	*		*	*						*		*	*		*	
Cattle Egret	*	*		*	*	*	*	*	*	*		*	*	*		*	*		*	*	*	*				*		*			*	*
Green-backed Heron	*	*	*	*	*	*		*		*		*		*	*	*	*		*	*	*				*	*		*	*	*	*	*
Black-crowned Night-Heron		*		*	*	*	*	*	*		*		*	*		*	*			*						*		*	*		*	*
Yellow-crowned Night-Heron	*		*	*	*	*	*	*	*		*		*			*	*	*	*	*					*	*		*	*		*	*
White Ibis					*	*	*	*				*				*	*									*		*			*	
White-faced Ibis	*		*	*	*		*	*	*		*		*			*	*	*		*	*					*		*			*	*
Roseate Spoonbill			*	*			*	*		*		*	*		*			*	*							*						
Wood Stork						*	*	*	*	*	*						*		*							*		*				
Fulvous Whistling-Duck						*																				*						
Black-bellied Whistling-Duck			*	*			*									*										*						
Tundra Swan	*					*	*	*	*	*						*										*		*			*	*
Greater White-fronted Goose	*		*	*	*		*	*	*	*	*	*		*		*	*	*			*					*		*		*	*	*
Snow Goose	*		*	*	*		*	*	*	*	*			*		*	*	*	*	*			*			*		*		*	*	*
Ross' Goose					*		*		*																	*						
Brant						*				*																*						
Canada Goose	*	*	*		*		*	*				*			*			*			*	*			*	*		*		*	*	*
Wood Duck	*	*	*	*	*	*		*		*	*	*		*	*	*	*		*	*	*	*	*		*	*		*	*	*	*	*
Green-winged Teal	*	*	*	*	*	*		*		*	*	*	*	*	*	*	*		*	*	*	*	*		*	*		*	*	*	*	*
American Black Duck	*				*	*		*	*		*			*						*						*						
Mottled Duck			*						*				*			*			*		*					*						
Mallard	*	*	*	*	*		*	*		*	*	*		*		*	*	*			*	*			*	*	*	*	*	*	*	*
Northern Pintail	*	*	*		*		*	*	*	*		*	*			*	*			*	*				*	*	*	*	*	*	*	*
Blue-winged Teal	*	*	*	*		*	*	*	*	*	*	*	*	*	*	*	*	*	*	*	*	*			*	*	*	*	*	*	*	*
Cinnamon Teal	*	*	*		*		*	*	*	*		*		*		*	*			*	*				*	*		*			*	*
Northern Shoveler	*	*	*	*		*	*	*		*		*	*			*	*		*	*	*				*	*	*	*	*	*	*	*
Gadwall	*	*	*	*	*	*	*	*	*	*		*	*			*	*		*	*	*	*			*	*	*	*	*	*	*	*
Eurasian Wigeon					*											*																
American Wigeon	*	*	*	*		*	*	*		*		*	*			*	*		*	*	*				*	*	*	*	*	*	*	*
Canvasback	*	*	*	*	*	*	*	*	*	*		*	*	*		*	*		*	*	*				*	*	*	*	*	*	*	*
Redhead	*	*	*		*	*	*	*		*		*				*	*			*	*				*	*		*	*	*	*	*
Ring-necked Duck	*	*	*		*	*	*	*		*		*	*			*	*	*	*	*	*				*	*	*	*	*	*	*	*
Greater Scaup	*	*	*	*		*	*		*			*					*			*						*		*				
Lesser Scaup	*	*	*	*	*		*	*	*	*		*	*	*	*		*		*	*		*	*	*		*		*	*		*	*
Oldsquaw	*			*			*	*												*						*						
Black Scoter							*																			*						
Surf Scoter	*						*									*			*							*		*				

Checklist of Species in the Counties (cont.)

	Archer	Baylor	Bosque	Clay	Collin	Cooke	Dallas	Denton	Ellis	Fannin	Grayson	Hill	Hood	Hunt	Jack	Johnson	Kaufman	Montague	Navarro	Palo Pinto	Parker	Rains	Rockwall	Somervell	Stephens	Tarrant	Throckmorton	Van Zandt	Wichita	Wilbarger	Wise	Young
White-winged Scoter	*			*		*	*	*	*		*					*				*						*		*	*			*
Common Goldeneye	*	*	*		*		*	*		*			*	*		*		*	*	*	*	*	*			*		*	*			*
Barrow's Goldeneye														*																		
Bufflehead	*	*	*	*		*	*	*		*		*		*	*		*	*	*	*	*		*	*		*		*	*	*	*	*
Hooded Merganser	*	*		*	*	*	*	*	*	*		*			*		*	*		*		*		*		*		*	*	*	*	*
Common Merganser	*	*	*				*	*	*		*		*	*	*		*	*								*		*	*		*	*
Red-breasted Merganser	*	*		*	*	*	*	*				*	*					*		*		*				*		*	*			
Ruddy Duck	*	*	*	*	*		*	*	*		*		*	*		*		*	*		*		*			*		*	*	*	*	*
Masked Duck				*																												
Black Vulture		*		*		*	*	*	*	*	*	*	*	*	*	*	*	*	*	*	*	*	*			*			*		*	*
Turkey Vulture	*	*	*	*		*	*	*	*	*	*	*	*	*	*	*	*	*	*	*	*	*	*	*	*	*	*	*	*	*	*	*
Osprey	*	*	*	*	*	*	*	*	*	*	*	*	*	*	*	*	*	*	*	*	*	*	*	*	*	*	*	*	*	*	*	*
American Swallow-tailed Kite						*	*	*	*			*				*					*					*					*	*
Black-shouldered Kite			*	*		*	*	*	*			*								*		*				*						*
Mississippi Kite	*	*	*	*	*		*	*	*	*	*	*	*	*	*	*	*	*	*	*		*				*		*	*	*	*	*
Bald Eagle		*	*	*	*	*	*	*	*	*	*			*		*	*		*	*		*				*			*		*	*
Northern Harrier	*	*	*	*	*	*	*	*	*	*	*		*	*	*	*	*	*	*	*	*	*			*	*		*	*	*	*	*
Sharp-shinned Hawk		*		*	*	*	*	*	*	*	*	*	*	*	*		*	*		*	*	*			*	*		*	*	*	*	*
Cooper's Hawk	*	*	*	*		*	*	*	*	*	*	*	*	*	*		*	*	*	*	*	*			*	*		*	*	*	*	*
Northern Goshawk					*	*						*					*															
Harris' Hawk					*		*		*						*											*				*		
Red-shouldered Hawk	*		*	*		*	*	*	*	*	*	*		*		*	*		*	*		*	*			*		*	*		*	*
Broad-winged Hawk		*		*	*	*	*	*			*	*	*	*		*	*		*	*		*	*			*		*				
Swainson's Hawk	*	*	*	*		*	*	*	*	*	*	*	*	*	*		*	*	*	*	*	*	*	*	*	*		*	*	*	*	*
Red-tailed Hawk	*	*	*	*		*	*	*	*	*	*	*	*	*	*		*	*	*	*	*	*	*	*	*	*		*	*	*	*	*
Ferruginous Hawk		*				*	*	*			*										*					*			*	*	*	
Rough-legged Hawk		*	*	*		*	*	*	*		*		*		*	*		*		*	*	*		*			*		*	*	*	*
Golden Eagle		*		*		*		*	*		*		*		*									*		*			*	*	*	*
Crested Caracara	*	*				*		*		*	*	*	*		*	*								*	*	*						
American Kestrel	*	*	*	*		*	*	*	*	*	*	*	*	*	*		*	*	*	*	*	*	*	*	*	*		*	*	*	*	*
Merlin		*		*		*	*	*	*	*	*		*		*			*		*	*	*			*	*		*	*	*	*	*
Peregrine Falcon						*		*	*	*								*		*		*				*		*			*	
Prairie Falcon		*	*				*				*															*			*		*	
Wild Turkey	*	*	*	*	*		*			*	*	*	*	*	*	*	*	*		*	*				*	*		*	*	*	*	*
Northern Bobwhite	*	*	*	*	*		*	*	*	*	*	*	*	*	*	*	*	*	*	*	*	*	*	*	*	*		*	*	*	*	*
Scaled Quail	*	*				*			*		*	*								*								*		*	*	
Yellow Rail						*																										
Black Rail																																
King Rail					*	*	*					*			*				*	*		*				*				*	*	
Virginia Rail	*				*	*	*	*											*			*				*		*			*	
Sora	*		*		*	*	*	*			*			*			*	*		*	*	*	*			*		*		*	*	*
Purple Gallinule						*	*	*		*		*						*		*	*					*					*	*
Common Moorhen						*	*	*		*		*						*		*	*					*					*	
American Coot	*	*	*	*	*	*	*	*	*	*	*		*	*	*		*	*		*	*	*	*	*	*	*		*	*	*	*	*
Sandhill Crane	*	*	*	*		*	*	*	*	*		*	*		*			*		*	*					*	*		*	*	*	*
Whooping Crane		*		*		*		*		*	*						*		*	*		*				*						*
Black-bellied Plover	*		*	*	*	*	*	*		*		*		*	*		*		*	*		*	*			*		*	*	*	*	*
Lesser Golden-Plover	*		*		*	*	*		*		*	*	*				*		*			*				*		*	*	*	*	
Snowy Plover			*			*	*															*				*					*	
Semipalmated Plover			*		*	*	*	*			*	*					*				*				*			*		*	*	
Piping Plover		*			*	*	*	*			*										*					*						
Killdeer	*	*	*	*	*		*	*	*	*	*		*	*	*	*	*	*	*	*	*	*	*	*	*	*		*	*	*	*	*
Mountain Plover			*	*							*	*		*												*						
Black-necked Stilt			*	*			*	*	*		*			*			*									*					*	*
American Avocet	*		*	*	*		*	*	*	*		*	*		*						*		*	*	*		*		*	*	*	*

Checklist of Species in the Counties (cont.)

	Archer	Baylor	Bosque	Clay	Collin	Cooke	Dallas	Denton	Ellis	Fannin	Grayson	Hill	Hood	Hunt	Jack	Johnson	Kaufman	Montague	Navarro	Palo Pinto	Parker	Rains	Rockwall	Somervell	Stephens	Tarrant	Throckmorton	Van Zandt	Wichita	Wilbarger	Wise	Young
Greater Yellowlegs	*		*	*	*	*	*	*	*	*	*	*	*	*		*	*	*	*		*	*	*	*		*		*	*		*	
Lesser Yellowlegs	*	*	*	*	*	*	*	*	*	*	*	*	*	*	*	*	*		*	*	*	*	*	*		*	*	*	*		*	*
Solitary Sandpiper	*	*	*	*	*	*	*	*	*	*		*	*	*		*	*		*		*	*	*	*		*	*	*	*	*	*	*
Willet			*	*		*	*	*			*	*	*	*			*		*		*	*	*	*		*						
Spotted Sandpiper	*		*	*	*	*	*	*	*	*	*	*	*	*		*	*	*	*		*	*	*	*		*		*	*		*	*
Upland Sandpiper	*	*	*	*	*	*	*	*	*	*	*	*	*	*		*	*	*	*		*		*	*		*	*	*	*	*	*	*
Whimbrel					*	*					*	*														*						
Long-billed Curlew	*		*		*	*	*	*			*	*				*	*		*	*			*	*		*	*		*	*	*	
Hudsonian Godwit	*				*	*					*	*				*	*									*						
Marbled Godwit					*	*								*			*									*						
Ruddy Turnstone					*	*	*						*			*					*		*	*		*		*				
Red Knot					*	*																										
Sanderling			*	*	*											*							*			*						
Semipalmated Sandpiper		*	*	*	*	*	*		*	*	*	*		*		*	*				*					*		*				*
Western Sandpiper					*	*	*	*		*	*	*		*			*			*	*	*				*		*	*	*	*	
Least Sandpiper	*	*	*	*	*	*	*	*		*	*	*		*	*	*	*		*	*	*	*		*		*	*	*	*	*	*	*
White-rumped Sandpiper	*	*	*		*	*	*	*			*	*		*		*	*		*		*			*		*	*	*	*	*	*	*
Baird's Sandpiper	*		*	*	*	*	*	*			*	*		*		*	*		*		*	*		*		*	*	*	*	*	*	*
Pectoral Sandpiper	*		*	*	*	*	*	*			*	*		*		*	*		*	*	*			*	*	*	*	*	*	*	*	*
Dunlin			*	*	*	*	*							*		*	*		*		*			*		*		*				
Stilt Sandpiper	*				*	*	*	*			*	*		*		*	*		*		*	*		*		*	*		*			*
Buff-breasted Sandpiper			*		*	*	*	*			*	*		*		*	*		*		*	*		*		*						
Short-billed Dowitcher					*	*	*				*															*						
Long-billed Dowitcher	*	*	*	*	*	*	*	*			*	*	*	*	*		*		*		*	*		*	*	*		*			*	
Common Snipe	*		*	*	*	*	*	*	*		*	*	*	*		*	*		*		*	*	*	*		*		*	*		*	*
American Woodcock			*		*	*	*	*					*		*	*	*	*			*					*		*	*	*	*	*
Wilson's Phalarope	*			*		*	*	*				*	*	*	*	*	*				*		*	*		*	*	*	*	*	*	*
Red-necked Phalarope					*	*						*														*		*	*	*		
Red Phalarope						*						*														*						
Pomarine Jaeger	*																															
Laughing Gull						*						*																				
Franklin's Gull	*	*	*	*	*							*														*		*	*	*	*	*
Little Gull						*											*															
Bonaparte's Gull	*			*	*	*	*	*		*	*	*				*	*				*		*			*		*	*		*	*
Ring-billed Gull	*	*	*	*	*	*	*	*	*	*	*	*		*		*	*		*		*	*		*		*	*	*	*	*	*	*
Herring Gull			*	*	*	*	*	*			*	*				*	*					*				*		*				
Lesser Black-backed Gull																										*						
Glaucous Gull			*				*																									
Black-legged Kittiwake														*												*		*				
Sabine's Gull					*					*						*										*		*				
Caspian Tern				*	*	*	*									*	*		*	*		*				*		*				
Common Tern	*				*	*	*	*																		*		*				
Forster's Tern			*	*	*	*	*	*		*	*	*		*		*	*				*			*		*		*			*	*
Least Tern			*	*	*	*	*	*	*	*	*	*		*			*				*			*		*		*			*	*
Black Tern	*	*	*	*	*	*	*	*	*	*	*	*		*			*				*			*		*		*	*	*	*	*
Black Skimmer					*						*															*						
Rock Dove	*	*	*	*	*	*	*	*	*	*	*	*		*		*	*				*	*	*	*		*	*	*	*	*	*	*
Band-tailed Pigeon																										*						
White-winged Dove	*				*	*	*	*		*	*	*				*	*		*			*		*		*						
Mourning Dove	*	*	*	*	*	*	*	*	*	*	*	*		*	*	*	*		*		*	*	*	*		*	*	*	*	*	*	*
Inca Dove		*			*	*	*	*		*	*	*				*	*		*		*	*		*		*	*		*	*		
Common Ground-Dove					*	*	*	*		*	*		*				*				*			*		*	*		*	*		
Monk Parakeet				*		*								*																		
Black-billed Cuckoo			*	*		*	*			*			*													*		*				
Yellow-billed Cuckoo	*	*	*	*		*	*	*	*	*	*	*		*	*		*	*	*	*	*		*	*	*	*		*	*	*	*	*

Checklist of Species in the Counties (cont.)

	Archer	Baylor	Bosque	Clay	Collin	Cooke	Dallas	Denton	Ellis	Fannin	Grayson	Hill	Hood	Hunt	Jack	Johnson	Kaufman	Montague	Navarro	Palo Pinto	Parker	Rains	Rockwall	Somervell	Stephens	Tarrant	Throckmorton	Van Zandt	Wichita	Wilbarger	Wise	Young
Greater Roadrunner	*	*	*	*	*		*	*	*	*		*	*	*	*			*	*	*	*			*	*		*	*	*	*	*	*
Groove-billed Ani						*												*										*		*		
Common Barn-Owl	*		*		*	*	*	*	*	*		*	*			*		*	*		*					*		*	*	*	*	*
Eastern Screech-Owl	*		*		*	*	*	*	*	*		*	*	*		*		*	*		*				*	*		*	*	*	*	*
Great Horned Owl	*	*	*	*		*	*	*	*	*		*	*	*	*		*	*	*	*		*	*	*	*		*	*	*	*	*	*
Snowy Owl	*				*					*																						
Burrowing Owl	*	*		*	*		*	*	*			*	*			*		*			*					*		*	*	*	*	*
Barred Owl	*		*	*	*	*	*	*	*	*	*	*	*			*			*		*			*		*		*		*	*	*
Long-eared Owl			*	*	*	*	*	*									*		*		*							*		*	*	*
Short-eared Owl	*				*	*	*	*	*			*	*	*				*								*		*			*	
Northern Saw-whet Owl						*																		*								
Common Nighthawk	*	*	*	*	*	*	*	*	*			*	*			*		*	*		*		*		*	*		*	*	*	*	*
Common Poorwill	*	*	*	*	*													*							*			*	*	*	*	*
Chuck-will's-widow			*	*	*	*	*	*			*	*	*	*				*			*					*		*		*	*	*
Whip-poor-will			*	*	*	*	*	*	*	*								*					*			*				*	*	*
Chimney Swift	*	*	*	*	*	*	*	*	*		*	*	*			*	*	*	*		*		*		*	*		*	*	*	*	*
Ruby-throated Hummingbird		*	*	*		*	*	*	*	*	*	*	*	*		*		*	*		*		*	*		*			*		*	*
Black-chinned Hummingbird		*			*	*	*	*	*	*	*	*	*	*		*		*			*					*					*	*
Anna's Hummingbird																								*								
Calliope Hummingbird																								*								
Rufous Hummingbird		*					*	*				*			*	*					*								*		*	
Belted Kingfisher	*	*	*	*	*	*	*	*	*	*	*	*	*	*		*	*	*	*		*		*		*	*		*	*	*	*	*
Green Kingfisher																																*
Lewis' Woodpecker			*		*			*				*																				*
Red-headed Woodpecker	*		*	*	*	*	*	*	*	*	*			*	*		*	*			*		*	*		*		*	*	*	*	*
Golden-fronted Woodpecker	*	*	*	*							*							*		*			*			*	*	*	*	*	*	*
Red-bellied Woodpecker	*	*	*	*	*	*	*	*	*	*	*	*	*	*	*	*	*	*	*		*		*	*		*	*	*	*	*	*	*
Yellow-bellied Sapsucker	*	*	*	*	*	*	*	*	*	*	*	*	*	*	*	*	*	*	*		*		*	*		*	*	*	*	*	*	*
Ladder-backed Woodpecker	*	*	*	*							*				*	*		*		*			*			*	*	*	*	*	*	*
Downy Woodpecker	*		*	*	*	*	*	*	*	*	*	*	*	*	*	*	*	*	*		*		*	*		*		*	*	*	*	*
Hairy Woodpecker				*	*	*	*	*	*	*	*	*		*	*		*	*			*					*		*		*	*	
Northern Flicker	*	*	*	*	*	*	*	*	*	*	*	*	*	*	*	*	*	*	*		*		*	*		*	*	*	*	*	*	*
Pileated Woodpecker				*	*	*	*	*	*	*							*				*					*		*				
Olive-sided Flycatcher	*		*	*	*	*	*	*	*		*	*		*	*		*	*			*		*			*		*		*	*	*
Western Wood-Pewee																										*						
Eastern Wood-Pewee	*	*	*	*		*	*	*	*	*						*		*	*		*					*			*		*	*
Yellow-bellied Flycatcher			*		*	*	*	*	*	*		*	*	*							*		*			*		*			*	
Acadian Flycatcher					*	*	*	*				*	*	*							*					*		*				
Alder Flycatcher				*		*	*			*	*		*	*												*						
Willow Flycatcher						*					*		*													*						
Least Flycatcher	*		*		*	*	*	*	*	*	*		*		*	*		*	*		*		*	*	*	*		*		*	*	*
Black Phoebe			*																													
Eastern Phoebe	*		*	*	*	*	*	*	*	*		*	*	*		*	*	*	*		*		*		*	*		*	*	*	*	*
Say's Phoebe			*				*	*			*		*			*		*			*					*			*	*	*	*
Vermilion Flycatcher		*					*	*			*		*			*		*	*		*					*		*			*	
Ash-throated Flycatcher	*		*	*									*						*								*	*	*	*	*	*
Great Crested Flycatcher	*		*	*	*	*	*	*	*	*	*	*	*	*	*		*	*	*		*		*	*		*	*	*	*	*	*	*
Western Kingbird	*	*	*	*	*	*	*	*	*	*	*	*	*	*	*	*	*	*	*		*		*	*		*	*	*	*	*	*	*
Eastern Kingbird	*	*	*	*	*	*	*	*	*	*	*	*	*	*	*	*	*	*	*		*		*	*		*	*	*	*	*	*	*
Scissor-tailed Flycatcher	*	*	*	*	*	*	*	*	*	*	*	*	*	*	*	*	*	*	*		*		*	*		*	*	*	*	*	*	*
Horned Lark	*	*	*	*	*	*	*	*	*	*	*	*	*		*	*	*	*	*		*		*	*		*	*	*	*	*	*	
Purple Martin	*	*	*	*	*	*	*	*	*	*	*	*	*	*	*	*	*	*	*		*		*	*		*	*	*	*	*	*	*
Tree Swallow	*		*	*	*	*	*	*	*	*	*		*	*	*		*		*		*					*		*	*	*	*	*
Northern Rough-winged Swallow	*		*	*	*	*	*	*	*		*	*	*	*			*	*			*		*	*		*		*	*	*	*	*
Bank Swallow			*		*	*	*		*		*		*	*			*	*			*							*	*	*	*	

Checklist of Species in the Counties (cont.)

	Archer	Baylor	Bosque	Clay	Collin	Cooke	Dallas	Denton	Ellis	Fannin	Grayson	Hill	Hood	Hunt	Jack	Johnson	Kaufman	Montague	Navarro	Palo Pinto	Parker	Rains	Rockwall	Somervell	Stephens	Tarrant	Throckmorton	Van Zandt	Wichita	Wilbarger	Wise	Young
Cliff Swallow	*	*	*	*	*		*	*	*	*	*	*	*	*	*		*	*	*	*	*		*	*	*	*		*	*	*	*	*
Barn Swallow	*	*	*	*	*	*	*	*	*	*	*	*	*	*	*		*	*	*	*	*		*	*	*	*		*	*	*	*	*
Blue Jay	*			*	*	*	*	*	*	*	*	*	*	*			*		*		*		*	*	*	*		*	*	*	*	*
Green Jay																*																
Clark's Nutcracker																										*						
Black-billed Magpie																											*					
American Crow	*	*	*	*	*		*	*	*	*	*	*	*	*	*		*	*	*	*	*		*		*	*	*	*	*	*	*	*
Chihuahuan Raven	*	*																										*		*		
Carolina Chickadee	*	*	*	*	*		*	*	*	*	*	*	*	*	*		*	*	*	*	*		*	*	*	*		*	*	*	*	*
Tufted Titmouse	*	*	*	*	*		*	*	*	*	*	*	*	*	*		*	*	*	*	*		*	*	*	*		*		*	*	*
Verdin	*			*																	*					*		*		*		*
Bushtit		*																														
Red-breasted Nuthatch	*			*		*		*													*							*			*	
White-breasted Nuthatch		*		*	*			*									*			*			*			*			*		*	*
Pygmy Nuthatch					*																											
Brown Creeper	*			*		*	*	*			*										*				*	*		*		*	*	*
Cactus Wren					*																					*		*			*	
Rock Wren		*	*	*		*	*		*					*	*					*				*		*			*		*	
Canyon Wren		*	*	*		*								*	*					*				*		*			*		*	
Carolina Wren	*		*	*	*								*				*			*				*		*	*					
Bewick's Wren	*	*	*	*		*								*						*				*		*	*		*		*	*
House Wren			*	*	*	*	*	*			*		*	*						*						*						
Winter Wren			*		*	*	*	*												*						*						
Sedge Wren			*		*	*	*				*									*			*			*						
Marsh Wren	*			*	*		*	*											*	*				*		*			*			
Golden-crowned Kinglet	*		*		*		*	*	*	*	*						*		*		*		*	*		*		*		*	*	*
Ruby-crowned Kinglet	*		*	*	*		*	*	*	*	*		*	*			*		*	*	*		*			*		*		*	*	*
Blue-gray Gnatcatcher	*	*	*	*	*		*	*	*	*	*		*	*			*		*	*	*		*			*		*	*	*	*	*
Eastern Bluebird	*	*	*	*	*		*	*	*	*	*		*	*			*		*	*	*		*			*		*	*	*	*	*
Western Bluebird						*																			*			*				
Mountain Bluebird		*	*			*	*	*			*		*			*				*						*		*		*		
Townsend's Solitaire			*			*		*								*							*			*						
Veery			*		*	*	*	*			*																					
Gray-cheeked Thrush			*		*	*	*	*			*					*							*			*				*		
Swainson's Thrush			*		*	*	*	*			*	*	*	*						*						*		*				*	*
Hermit Thrush	*		*	*		*	*	*			*			*						*						*		*	*	*	*	
Wood Thrush			*		*	*	*				*															*		*				
American Robin	*	*	*	*	*		*	*	*	*	*		*				*		*	*	*		*	*		*	*	*	*	*	*	*
Gray Catbird			*		*	*	*	*			*						*									*		*		*	*	
Northern Mockingbird	*	*	*	*	*		*	*	*	*	*		*	*			*		*	*	*		*			*	*	*	*	*	*	*
Sage Thrasher		*		*	*	*					*		*	*						*						*		*			*	
Brown Thrasher	*		*	*		*		*			*						*		*	*						*		*		*	*	
Curve-billed Thrasher			*		*						*		*	*			*		*	*				*		*		*				*
Water Pipit	*	*	*	*	*		*	*			*		*	*			*		*	*			*			*		*	*	*	*	*
Sprague's Pipit		*	*		*	*	*	*					*				*		*	*						*		*				
Bohemian Waxwing					*																					*						
Cedar Waxwing	*	*	*	*	*		*	*	*	*	*		*	*			*		*	*	*		*			*		*	*	*	*	*
Northern Shrike																	*														*	
Loggerhead Shrike	*	*	*	*	*		*	*	*	*	*		*	*			*		*	*	*		*			*	*	*	*	*	*	*
European Starling	*	*	*	*	*		*	*	*	*	*		*	*			*		*	*	*		*			*	*	*	*	*	*	*
White-eyed Vireo		*	*		*	*	*	*	*		*		*			*	*		*	*	*		*			*		*	*	*	*	*
Bell's Vireo	*	*	*	*	*		*	*	*	*	*		*				*		*	*	*		*			*		*	*	*	*	*
Black-capped Vireo		*				*			*	*			*			*									*			*		*		
Solitary Vireo		*			*	*		*			*									*	*					*		*		*		
Yellow-throated Vireo		*		*	*	*	*		*	*	*					*								*		*		*		*	*	*

Checklist of Species in the Counties (cont.)

Species	Archer	Baylor	Bosque	Clay	Collin	Cooke	Dallas	Denton	Ellis	Fannin	Grayson	Hill	Hood	Hunt	Jack	Johnson	Kaufman	Montague	Navarro	Palo Pinto	Parker	Rains	Rockwall	Somervell	Stephens	Tarrant	Throckmorton	Van Zandt	Wichita	Wilbarger	Wise	Young
Warbling Vireo			*	*	*	*	*	*			*	*		*		*			*		*					*	*	*	*			
Philadelphia Vireo	*		*	*	*	*	*	*			*	*	*			*			*		*	*	*	*		*		*	*			
Red-eyed Vireo			*	*	*	*	*	*	*	*	*	*	*		*	*	*		*		*					*		*	*		*	*
Blue-winged Warbler					*		*	*			*		*						*							*		*				
Golden-winged Warbler					*		*				*															*						
Tennessee Warbler			*	*	*	*	*	*	*		*	*	*	*		*			*		*					*		*	*		*	*
Orange-crowned Warbler	*		*	*	*	*	*	*	*	*	*	*	*	*			*	*	*		*	*	*	*	*	*		*	*	*	*	
Nashville Warbler	*		*	*	*	*	*	*	*	*	*	*	*	*		*	*	*	*	*	*	*	*	*	*	*		*	*		*	
Lucy's Warbler																	*															
Northern Parula					*	*	*	*	*	*	*		*			*			*							*		*	*		*	
Yellow Warbler	*		*	*	*	*	*	*	*	*	*	*	*	*		*	*	*	*		*	*	*	*	*	*		*	*		*	*
Chestnut-sided Warbler			*		*		*	*			*	*	*	*												*		*	*			
Magnolia Warbler			*	*	*		*	*			*	*												*		*		*	*			
Cape May Warbler					*														*													
Black-throated Blue Warbler					*		*	*			*			*												*						
Yellow-rumped Warbler	*	*	*	*	*	*	*	*	*	*	*	*	*	*	*	*	*	*	*		*		*	*	*	*		*	*	*	*	*
Black-throated Gray Warbler					*																					*						
Townsend's Warbler					*																											
Black-throated Green Warbler	*		*		*		*	*			*	*		*		*			*		*					*		*	*			
Golden-cheeked Warbler			*		*									*										*	*							
Blackburnian Warbler			*		*		*	*	*		*	*	*			*			*		*					*		*				
Yellow-throated Warbler					*		*	*	*		*	*	*	*		*			*		*			*		*		*	*			*
Pine Warbler					*		*	*	*	*	*		*	*		*										*		*	*			
Prairie Warbler			*		*		*				*															*						
Palm Warbler					*		*		*		*			*							*					*						
Bay-breasted Warbler			*		*		*	*	*		*	*				*			*							*		*	*			
Blackpoll Warbler	*		*		*		*	*			*	*	*													*		*				
Cerulean Warbler					*		*	*			*	*														*						
Black-and-white Warbler			*		*		*	*	*	*	*	*	*	*		*		*	*		*			*		*		*	*		*	*
American Redstart	*		*		*		*	*	*		*	*	*			*	*	*						*		*		*	*			
Prothonotary Warbler	*			*	*		*	*			*			*					*	*	*		*			*		*				
Worm-eating Warbler					*		*	*			*	*														*						
Swainson's Warbler					*		*												*							*						
Ovenbird			*		*		*	*	*	*	*					*			*							*		*	*		*	*
Northern Waterthrush			*		*		*	*	*		*								*							*		*	*		*	*
Louisiana Waterthrush			*		*		*	*	*	*	*	*				*	*	*	*					*		*		*	*			*
Kentucky Waterthrush			*	*	*		*	*	*	*	*	*				*		*								*		*	*			
Connecticut Warbler					*		*	*			*	*														*						
Mourning Warbler			*		*		*	*	*	*	*											*				*		*	*			
MacGillivray's Warbler								*				*																				
Common Yellowthroat	*		*	*	*	*	*	*	*	*	*	*	*	*		*	*		*		*	*	*	*	*	*		*	*		*	*
Hooded Warbler							*	*			*	*	*			*										*						
Wilson's Warbler	*		*	*	*		*	*	*	*	*	*	*	*		*			*		*		*	*		*		*	*	*	*	*
Canada Warbler			*		*		*	*	*		*	*	*			*										*		*	*			
Yellow-breasted Chat			*	*	*		*	*	*	*	*	*	*			*			*		*					*		*	*		*	
Summer Tanager	*		*	*	*		*	*	*	*	*	*	*			*			*		*			*		*		*	*		*	*
Scarlet Tanager			*		*		*	*	*		*								*							*		*				
Western Tanager																			*													
Northern Cardinal	*	*	*	*	*	*	*	*	*	*	*	*	*	*	*	*	*	*	*	*	*	*	*	*	*	*	*	*	*	*	*	*
Pyrrhuloxia					*																						*	*				
Rose-breasted Grosbeak	*		*		*		*	*	*		*	*	*			*					*			*		*		*	*			
Black-headed Grosbeak			*		*		*	*	*		*	*	*			*			*							*		*	*		*	*
Blue Grosbeak	*		*	*	*		*	*	*	*	*	*	*			*			*		*		*	*	*	*		*	*		*	*
Lazuli Bunting	*				*		*	*	*	*	*	*	*							*	*					*			*		*	*
Indigo Bunting	*		*	*	*	*	*	*	*	*	*	*	*	*		*	*	*	*		*	*	*	*		*		*	*		*	*

Checklist of Species in the Counties (cont.)

Species	Archer	Baylor	Bosque	Clay	Collin	Cooke	Dallas	Denton	Ellis	Fannin	Grayson	Hill	Hood	Hunt	Jack	Johnson	Kaufman	Montague	Navarro	Palo Pinto	Parker	Rains	Rockwall	Somervell	Stephens	Tarrant	Throckmorton	Van Zandt	Wichita	Wilbarger	Wise	Young
Painted Bunting	*	*	*	*	*	*	*	*	*	*	*	*	*	*	*	*	*	*	*	*	*	*	*	*	*	*	*	*	*	*	*	*
Dickcissel	*	*	*	*	*	*	*	*	*	*	*	*	*	*	*	*	*	*	*	*	*	*	*	*	*	*	*	*	*	*	*	*
Green-tailed Towhee					*						*							*	*							*						
Rufous-sided Towhee	*		*	*	*	*	*	*	*	*	*	*	*	*	*	*	*	*	*	*	*		*	*	*	*					*	
Brown Towhee														*				*								*						*
Bachman's Sparrow					*											*										*						
Cassin's Sparrow	*	*		*		*		*										*			*	*	*		*		*	*		*	*	
Rufous-crowned Sparrow	*		*		*						*	*	*		*	*		*		*	*			*	*		*		*	*	*	*
American Tree Sparrow	*	*		*	*	*	*	*		*	*		*		*		*	*			*	*			*		*	*	*	*	*	*
Chipping Sparrow	*	*	*	*	*	*	*	*	*	*	*	*	*	*		*	*	*	*	*	*	*	*	*	*	*	*	*	*	*	*	*
Clay-colored Sparrow	*	*	*		*	*	*	*	*	*	*	*	*	*		*	*		*		*				*	*		*	*	*	*	*
Field Sparrow	*	*	*	*	*	*	*	*	*	*	*	*	*	*	*	*	*	*	*	*	*	*	*	*	*	*	*	*	*	*	*	*
Vesper Sparrow	*	*	*	*	*	*	*	*	*	*	*	*	*	*	*	*	*	*	*	*	*	*	*	*	*	*	*	*	*	*	*	*
Lark Sparrow	*	*	*	*	*	*	*	*	*	*	*	*	*	*	*	*	*	*	*	*	*	*	*	*	*	*	*	*	*	*	*	*
Black-throated Sparrow							*									*				*					*		*					*
Lark Bunting	*	*	*	*	*		*	*	*							*				*					*		*	*	*	*		*
Savannah Sparrow	*	*	*	*	*	*	*	*	*	*	*	*	*	*	*	*	*	*	*	*	*	*	*	*	*	*	*	*	*	*	*	*
Baird's Sparrow			*	*		*		*						*						*								*				
Grasshopper Sparrow			*	*	*	*		*	*	*	*	*	*	*		*				*			*	*	*	*	*	*	*	*	*	*
Henslow's Sparrow				*	*	*										*			*		*											
Le Conte's Sparrow	*			*		*	*	*	*	*	*	*	*			*				*			*	*	*		*	*		*		*
Fox Sparrow	*		*		*	*	*	*	*	*	*	*	*			*				*			*	*	*		*	*		*	*	*
Song Sparrow	*	*	*	*	*	*	*	*	*	*	*	*	*		*	*	*		*	*	*		*	*	*		*	*	*	*	*	*
Lincoln's Sparrow	*	*	*	*	*	*	*	*	*	*	*	*	*		*	*	*		*	*	*		*	*	*		*	*	*	*	*	*
Swamp Sparrow			*	*	*	*	*	*	*	*	*	*	*			*			*	*	*		*	*	*		*	*			*	*
White-throated Sparrow		*		*	*	*	*	*	*	*	*	*	*	*	*	*	*		*	*	*	*	*	*	*	*		*		*	*	*
White-crowned Sparrow	*	*	*	*	*	*	*	*	*	*	*	*	*	*	*	*	*	*	*	*	*	*	*	*	*	*	*	*	*	*	*	*
Harris' Sparrow	*	*	*	*	*	*	*	*	*	*	*	*	*	*	*	*	*	*	*	*	*	*	*	*	*	*	*	*	*	*	*	*
Dark-eyed Junco	*		*	*	*	*	*	*	*	*	*	*	*	*	*	*	*	*	*	*	*	*	*	*	*	*		*		*	*	*
McCown's Longspur				*	*	*	*	*		*	*		*			*				*	*	*				*			*		*	*
Lapland Longspur				*	*	*	*	*	*		*	*	*			*	*		*		*				*	*		*		*	*	*
Smith's Longspur					*	*	*	*		*	*			*		*	*				*		*			*		*			*	*
Chestnut-collared Longspur			*	*	*		*	*								*				*	*					*			*		*	*
Bobolink					*	*	*	*	*		*	*		*		*										*			*		*	*
Red-winged Blackbird	*	*	*	*	*	*	*	*	*	*	*	*	*	*	*	*	*	*	*	*	*	*	*	*	*	*	*	*	*	*	*	*
Eastern Meadowlark	*	*	*	*	*	*	*	*	*	*	*	*	*	*	*	*	*	*	*	*	*	*	*	*	*	*	*	*	*	*	*	*
Western Meadowlark	*	*	*	*	*	*	*	*	*	*	*	*	*	*	*	*	*	*	*	*	*	*	*	*	*	*	*	*	*	*	*	*
Yellow-headed Blackbird	*	*	*	*	*	*	*	*	*	*	*	*	*	*		*	*		*	*	*		*	*	*	*	*	*	*	*	*	*
Rusty Blackbird				*	*	*	*	*	*	*	*		*	*		*			*		*				*	*		*			*	*
Brewer's Blackbird	*		*	*	*	*	*	*	*	*	*	*	*	*	*	*	*		*	*	*		*	*	*	*		*			*	*
Great-tailed Grackle	*	*	*	*	*	*	*	*	*	*	*	*	*	*	*	*	*	*	*	*	*	*	*	*	*	*	*	*	*	*	*	*
Common Grackle	*	*	*	*	*	*	*	*	*	*	*	*	*	*	*	*	*	*	*	*	*	*	*	*	*	*	*	*	*	*	*	*
Brown-headed Cowbird	*	*	*	*	*	*	*	*	*	*	*	*	*	*	*	*	*	*	*	*	*	*	*	*	*	*	*	*	*	*	*	*
Orchard Oriole	*	*	*	*	*	*	*	*	*	*	*	*	*	*	*	*	*	*	*	*	*	*	*	*	*	*	*	*	*	*	*	*
Northern Oriole	*	*	*	*	*	*	*	*	*	*	*	*	*	*	*	*	*	*	*	*	*	*	*	*	*	*	*	*	*	*	*	*
Pine Grosbeak					*																											
Purple Finch	*		*	*	*	*	*	*	*	*	*	*	*	*		*	*		*		*				*		*	*		*	*	*
Cassin's Finch		*																														
House Finch	*					*	*					*	*							*	*				*			*	*			*
Red Crossbill							*																	*		*						
Pine Siskin	*		*	*	*	*	*	*	*	*	*	*	*		*		*		*	*	*	*			*		*	*		*	*	*
Lesser Goldfinch	*		*			*	*				*																					*
American Goldfinch	*	*	*	*	*	*	*	*	*	*	*	*	*	*	*	*	*		*	*	*	*			*		*	*	*	*	*	*
Evening Grosbeak			*	*	*		*	*			*		*		*											*		*		*	*	
House Sparrow	*	*	*	*	*	*	*	*	*	*	*	*	*	*	*	*	*	*	*	*	*	*	*	*	*	*	*	*	*	*	*	*

Literature Cited

Aldrich, J. W., and A. J. Duvall. 1958. Distribution and migration of races of the Mourning Dove. *Condor* 60:108–28.

American Ornithologists' Union [AOU]. 1957. *Check-list of North American Birds.* 5th ed. Baltimore, Md.: American Ornithologists' Union.

———. 1973. Thirty-second Supplement to American Ornithologists' Union *Check-list of North American Birds. Auk* 93:875–79.

———. 1983. *Check-list of North American Birds.* 6th ed. Baltimore, Md.: American Ornithologists' Union.

Arnold, K. A. 1983. New subspecies of Henslow's Sparrow (*Ammodramus henslowii*). *Auk* 100:504–505.

Ault, J. W., III. 1984. The Curve-billed Thrasher in southwestern Oklahoma. *Bull. Oklahoma Ornith. Soc.* 17(2):12–14.

Bailey, F. M. 1928. *Birds of New Mexico.* Santa Fe, N. Mex.: New Mexico Department of Game and Fish.

Baumgartner, F. M. 1951. Southern Great Plains region. *Audubon Field Notes* 5(3):213.

———. 1952. Southern Great Plains region. *Audubon Field Notes* 6(1):25.

———. 1955. Southern Great Plains region. *Audubon Field Notes* 9(1):38; 9(3):267.

———. 1957. Southern Great Plains region. *Audubon Field Notes* 11(3):276–77.

———. 1959. Southern Great Plains region. *Audubon Field Notes* 13(5):439.

———. 1960. Southern Great Plains region. *Audubon Field Notes* 14(5):460.

———. 1961. Southern Great Plains region. *Audubon Field Notes* 15(1):56.

———. 1963. Southern Great Plains region. *Audubon Field Notes* 17(4):414.

Bellrose, F. C. 1976. *Ducks, Geese, and Swans of North America.* Harrisburg, Pa.: Stackpole Books.

Bent, A. C. 1968. Life histories of North American cardinals, grosbeaks, buntings, towhees, finches, sparrows, and allies. *U.S. Natl. Mus. Bull.* 237. Washington, D.C.

Blair, W. F. 1950. The biotic provinces of Texas. *Texas Jour. Sci.* 2:93–117.

Brown, C. R. 1973. A second brood attempt by the Purple Martin. *Auk* 90:442.

———. 1977. Nocturnal Lesser Yellowlegs migration in North Central Texas. *Bull. Texas Ornith. Soc.* 10(2):47.

———. 1978. Clutch size and reproductive success of adult and subadult Purple Martins. *Southwestern Nat.* 23(4):597–604.

———. 1980. Implications of juvenile harassment in Purple Martins. *Wilson Bull.* 92:452–57.

———. 1981. The impact of starlings on Purple Martin populations in unmanaged colonies. *Amer. Birds.* 35(3):266–68.

Brown, I. S. 1985. Successful nesting of the House Wren in western Oklahoma. *Bull. Oklahoma Ornith. Soc.* 18(3):17–20.

Cain, B. W., and K. A. Arnold. 1974. Black-bellied Tree Duck (*Dendrocyana autumnalis*) nesting in the central Brazos Valley of Texas. *Southwestern Nat.* 18(4):474–75.

Carter, W. A., and C. L. Fowler. 1983. Black-shouldered Kite in Oklahoma: 1860 and 1982. *Bull. Oklahoma Ornith. Soc.* 16(2):9–11.

Dallas Morning News. 1982–83. *Texas Almanac.* Dallas, Tex.

Dalquest, W. W. 1958. Pomarine Jaeger from the interior of Texas. *Condor* 60:258.

Dobie, J. F. 1941. Bob More: Man and bird man. *Southwest Review* (Dallas) 27(1).

Donald, J. A., and R. L. More. 1894. A list of the birds of Wise County, Texas. *Naturalist* 1(5):56–57.

Fenneman, N. M. 1931. *Physiography of Western United States.* New York: McGraw-Hill Book Co.

Friedmann, H., L. F. Kiff, and S. I. Rothstein. 1977. A further contribution to knowledge of the host relations of the parasitic cowbirds. *Smithsonian Contrib. to Zool.* no. 235, Washington, D.C.

Garrett, K., and J. Dunn. 1981. *Birds of Southern California: Status and Distribution.* Los Angeles: Los Angeles Audubon Society.

Godfrey, C. L., G. S. McKee, and H. Oakes. 1973. General soils map of Texas. College Station: Texas Agricultural Experiment Station, Texas A&M University.

Gollob, T., and W. Pulich, Sr. 1978a. Bullfrogs preying on Cedar Waxwings. *Herp Review* 9:2.

———. 1978b. Lapland Longspur casualties in Texas. *Bull. Texas Ornith. Soc.* 11(2):44–46.

Gould, F. W. 1969. Texas plants—a checklist and ecological summary. College Station: Texas A&M University.

Guthery, F. S. 1974. Ecology of the Squaw Creek Reservoir area: A report submitted to Texas Utilities Services Inc., Dallas, Texas, on the results of a biological inventory and ecological survey of the proposed site of the Comanche Peak Steam Electric Station, Hood and Somervell counties, Texas. College Station: Texas A&M University.

Haller, K. W. 1972. Late nesting of Yellow-billed Cuckoos in southeast Oklahoma. *Bull. Oklahoma Ornith. Soc.* 5(3):19–20.

———. 1976. Red Knot in northern central Texas. *Bull. Oklahoma Ornith. Soc.* 9(3):22–23.

———. 1978. Ross' Goose in Grayson Co., north central Texas. *Bull. Oklahoma Ornith. Soc.* 11(4):29–30.

Haller, K. W., and J. H. Beach, III. 1984. A Glaucous Gull in Bryan County, Oklahoma, and Grayson County, Texas. *Bull. Oklahoma Ornith. Soc.* 17(4):27–28.

Henderson, J. C. 1960. A Texas record of the Black Brant. *Auk* 77:227.

Iseley, F. B., H. N. Iseley, R. N. Iseley, and F. B. Iseley, Jr. 1926. Fort Worth, Texas (Christmas Count). *Bird-Lore* 28:50.

Johnston, R. F. 1964. *The Breeding Birds of Kansas.* University of Kansas Publication 12(14):575–655.

Keating, P. 1975. Caracara sighted in north Texas. *Bull. Oklahoma Ornith. Soc.* 8(3):27–28.

Kelley, C. 1935. Birds of Dallas County. *Amer. Midland Nat.* 16:936–948.

Lowery, G. H., Jr. 1974. *Louisiana Birds.* 3d ed. Baton Rouge, La.: Louisiana State University Press.

Miller, F. W. 1955. Black Skimmer in north central Texas. *Condor* 57:240.

More, R. L. 1927. Mississippi Kite in Texas. *Oologist* 44:24.

More, R. L., and J. K. Strecker. 1929. *The Summer Birds of Wilbarger County, Texas.* Contr. Baylor Univ. Mus. no. 20.

Morgenthaler, E. 1970. Tweet, tweet, hic! Fermented berries lead to blotto birds. *Wall Street Journal,* September 8, 1970, p. 1.

Nanney, K. 1983. Goshawk in southern Oklahoma. *Bull. Oklahoma Ornith. Soc.* 16(4):31.

National Geographic Society. 1983. *Birds of North America.* Washington, D.C.: National Geographic Society.

Newell, J. G., and G. M. Sutton. 1982. The Olivaceous Cormorant in Oklahoma. *Bull. Oklahoma Ornith. Soc.* 15(1):1–5.

Nice, M. M. 1931. *The Birds of Oklahoma.* Publ. Univ. Oklahoma Biol. Survey 3(1).

Norman, J. L. 1982. The Coweta TV tower kill. *Bull. Oklahoma Ornith. Soc.* 15(3):19–22.

Oberholser, H. C. 1974. *The Bird Life of Texas.* Austin: University of Texas Press.

Ogilby, J. D. 1882. A catalogue of birds obtained in Navarro County, Texas. *Sci. Proc. Royal Dublin Soc.* 3:169–249.

O'Neil, Mrs. M. 1957. A check list of the birds of the Commerce area, Hunt County, Texas. Mimeographed.

Palmer, R. S. 1962. *Handbook of North American Birds.* Vol. 1, *Loons through Flamingos.* New Haven, Conn.: Yale University Press.

Peterson, R. T. 1960. *A Field Guide to the Birds of Texas.* Boston: Houghton Mifflin.

———. 1980. *A Field Guide to the Birds.* 4th ed. Boston: Houghton Mifflin.

Phillips, A. R. 1975. Semipalmated Sandpiper: Identification, migrations, summer and winter ranges. *Amer. Birds* 29(4):799–806.

Phillips, A. R., J. Marshall, and G. Monson. 1964. *The Birds of Arizona.* Tucson: University of Arizona Press.

Pulich, W. M. 1961. *Birds of Tarrant County.* Fort Worth, Tex.: Allen & Co.

———. 1966. A specimen of the Little Gull, *Larus minutus,* from Dallas County, Texas. *Auk* 83:482.

———. 1971. Some Fringillid records for Texas. *Condor* 73:111.

———. 1976. *The Golden-cheeked Warbler.* Austin: Texas Parks and Wildlife Department.

———. 1977a. American Woodcock nesting in Smith County. *Bull. Texas Ornith. Soc.* 10(2):44–45.

———. 1977b. *Field Check List of Birds, Dallas County, Texas.* Dallas: Dallas County Audubon Society.

———. 1979. *Birds of Tarrant County.* 2d ed. Fort Worth: Branch-Smith.

———. 1980a. A Thayer's Gull specimen from Texas: A problem in identification. *Southwestern Nat.* 25(2):257–82.

———. 1980b. *Birds of Meridian State Park: A Field Checklist.* 2d ed. Austin: Texas Parks and Wildlife Department, Resource Management Section.

Ragsdale, G. H. 1881. *Larus glaucous* in Texas. *Bull. Nutt. Ornith. Club.* 5:239.

Ramos, M. A., and D. W. Warner. 1980. Analysis of North American subspecies in migrant birds wintering in Los Tuxtlas southern Veracruz Mexico. Pp. 173–80 in A. Keast and E. S. Morton, eds. *Migrant Birds in the Neotropics.* Washington, D.C.: Smithsonian Institution Press.

Robbins, C. S., B. Brown, and H. S. Zim. 1983. *Birds of North America: A Guide to Field Identification.* New York: Western Publishing.

Runnels, S. 1980. Louisiana Heron (*Hydranassa tricolor*) breeding in north central Texas. *Bull. Texas Ornith. Soc.* 13(1):23.

Rylander, R. A. 1959. *A Checklist of the Birds of Denton County, Texas.* Denton, Tex.: Published by author.

Saunders, G. B. 1933. Starling wintering in central and western Texas. *Auk* 50:440.

Seyffert, K. 1971. The Verdin in northwestern Texas. *Bull. Oklahoma Ornith. Soc.* 4(1):1–3.

Simmons, G. F. 1925. *Birds of the Austin Region.* Austin: University of Texas.

Smith, J. C. 1974. A survey of the Bald Eagle and Osprey in Texas, 1971–1973. 9th Conference of the Wildlife Society Texas Chapter, Laredo, Tex., March, pp. 1–27.

Stillwell, J. E. 1939. *Check List of Birds of Dallas County, Texas.* 3d ed. Dallas: Dallas Ornithological Society.

Strecker, J. K., Jr. 1927. *Notes on the Ornithology of McLennan County, Texas.* Spec. Bull. Baylor Univ. Mus., no. 1.

Sutton, G. M. 1938. The breeding birds of Tarrant County, Texas. *Ann. Carnegie Mus.* 27:171–206.

———. 1955. Glossy Ibis in Oklahoma. *Condor.* 57(2):119–20.

———. 1963. Interbreeding in the wild of Bobwhite (*Colinus virginianus*) and Scaled Quail (*Calipepla squamata*) in Stonewall County, Northwestern Texas. *Southwestern Nat.* 8:(2)108–11.

———. 1967. *Oklahoma Birds.* Norman: University of Oklahoma Press.

Tarter, D. G. 1940. *Check-List of East Texas Birds.* 2d ed. Commerce: East Texas Ornithology Club Training School, East Texas State Teachers' College.

Telfair, R. C., II. 1980. Additional inland nesting records of Texas of 4 species of colonial water birds. *Bull. Texas Ornith. Soc.* 13(1):11.

Texas Ornithological Society [TOS]. 1984. *Checklist of the Birds of Texas.* 2d ed. Austin.

Texas Parks and Wildlife Department. 1976. *Birds of Lake Whitney State Recreation Area.* Austin: Texas Parks and Wildlife Resource Management Section.

Tyler, J. D. 1979. *Birds of Southwestern Oklahoma.* Contrib. Stovall Mus., University of Oklahoma, no. 2. Norman.

U.S. Fish and Wildlife Service. 1984. *Birds of Hagerman National Wildlife Refuge.* [Checklist.]

Williams, D. 1975. *The Cardinal: Newsletter of the North Texas Bird and Wildlife Club* 3(3).

Williams, F. C. 1966. Southern Great Plains region. *Audubon Field Notes* 20(4):523.

———. 1967. Southern Great Plains region. *Audubon Field Notes* 21(5):584.

———. 1968. Southern Great Plains region. *Audubon Field Notes* 22(4):548.

———. 1970. Southern Great Plains region. *Amer. Birds* 24(1):64.

———. 1971. Southern Great Plains region. *Amer. Birds* 25(1):75.

———. 1972. Southern Great Plains region. *Amer. Birds* 26(3):624; 26(5):874.

———. 1973. Southern Great Plains region. *Amer. Birds* 27(3):634; 27(4):789; 27(5):889.

———. 1974. Southern Great Plains region. *Amer. Birds* 28(1):74; 28(3):660; 28(5):920.

———. 1975. Southern Great Plains region. *Amer. Birds* 29(1):79; 29(3):709; 29(4):873.

———. 1976. Southern Great Plains region. *Amer. Birds* 30(1):93; 30(3):735; 30(4):860–61; 30(5):973–74.

———. 1977. Southern Great Plains region. *Amer. Birds* 31(3):346; 31(6):1155.

———. 1980. Southern Great Plains region. *Amer. Birds* 34(3):286.

———. 1982. Southern Great Plains region. *Amer. Birds* 36(3):308.

———. 1983. Southern Great Plains region. *Amer. Birds* 37(6):1002.

———. 1984. Southern Great Plains region. *Amer. Birds* 38(2):230.

———. 1985. Southern Great Plains region. *Amer. Birds* 39(1):74.

Wilson, P. W. 1981. Successful nesting of the Bank Swallow in Oklahoma. *Bull. Oklahoma Ornith. Soc.* 14(2):9–11.

Wolfe, L. R. 1967. The Mississippi Kite in Texas. *Bull. Texas Ornith. Soc.* 1(5):23; 1(6):12–13.

Wolfe, L. R., W. M. Pulich, and J. A. Tucker. 1974. *Check-List of the Birds of Texas.* Edited by K. A. Arnold and E. A. Kutac. Waco: Texas Ornithological Society.

Zinn, K. S. 1975. *The Birds of Wichita County, Texas.* Master's thesis, Midwestern University, Wichita Falls, Tex.

———. 1977. Olivaceous Cormorants nesting in north central Texas. *Southwestern Nat.* 21(4):556–57.

Zinn, K. S., and N. Moore. 1976. *The Birds of North Central Texas.* 2d ed. Wichita Falls: North Texas Bird and Wildlife Club. [Checklist.]

Index

The Birds of North Central Texas has been composed into type on a Compu-graphic digital phototypesetter in ten point Palatino with two points of spacing between the lines. Palatino was also selected for display. The book was designed by Jim Billingsley, typeset by Metricomp, Inc., printed offset by Thomson-Shore, Inc., and bound by John H. Dekker & Sons. The paper on which the book was printed bears acid-free characteristics for an effective life of at least three hundred years.

TEXAS A&M UNIVERSITY PRESS : COLLEGE STATION